John Reeves

History of the English Law

Vol. 1

John Reeves

History of the English Law
Vol. 1

ISBN/EAN: 9783744774697

Printed in Europe, USA, Canada, Australia, Japan

Cover: Foto ©Suzi / pixelio.de

More available books at **www.hansebooks.com**

REEVES'

History of the English Law,

FROM THE

TIME OF THE ROMANS

TO THE

END OF THE REIGN OF ELIZABETH.

WITH NUMEROUS NOTES, AND AN INTRODUCTORY DISSERTATION ON THE NATURE AND USE OF LEGAL HISTORY, THE RISE AND PROGRESS OF OUR LAWS, AND THE INFLUENCE OF THE ROMAN LAW IN THE FORMATION OF OUR OWN.

BY

W. F. FINLASON, Esq.,

BARRISTER-AT-LAW.

A New American Edition,

COMPLETE IN FIVE VOLUMES.

VOL. I.

FROM THE TIME OF THE ROMANS TO THE END OF THE REIGN OF JOHN.

PHILADELPHIA:

M. MURPHY,

LAW BOOKSELLER, PUBLISHER, AND IMPORTER,

No. 715 SANSOM STREET.

1880.

PHILADELPHIA:
COLLINS, PRINTER.

TO

THE RIGHT HON. SIR JOHN TAYLOR COLERIDGE,

SOMETIME

ONE OF THE JUDGES OF THE COURT OF QUEEN'S BENCH,

WHO, BEFORE HIS ELEVATION TO THE OFFICE OF JUDGE, HAD
ACQUIRED REPUTATION AS A JURIST, BY HIS
VALUABLE EDITION OF

THE COMMENTARIES ON THE LAWS OF ENGLAND,

THIS EDITION

OF

THE HISTORY OF THE LAWS OF ENGLAND

(WITH HIS KIND PERMISSION)

IN TESTIMONY OF PROFOUND VENERATION FOR THOSE GREAT GIFTS, AND
EMINENT ACQUIREMENTS BY WHICH, DURING HIS DISTINGUISHED
CAREER, HE ADORNED THE JUDICIAL BENCH, AND
ADDED NEW LUSTRE TO A NAME AND
FAMILY ALREADY ILLUSTRIOUS.

CONTENTS
OF THE FIRST VOLUME.

	PAGE
ADVERTISEMENT, ...	vii
AUTHOR'S PREFACE TO THE FIRST EDITION, ...	ix
PREFACE TO THE PRESENT (LAST ENGLISH) EDITION, . . .	xvii
✔ INTRODUCTION TO THE PRESENT EDITION, ...	xx

CHAPTER I.
THE SAXONS.

The Laws of the Saxons — Thainland and Roveland — Freemen — Slaves — The Tourn — County Court — Other Inferior Courts — The Wittenagemote — Nature of Landed Property — Method of Conveyance — Decennaries — Criminal Law — Were — Murder — Larceny — Deadly Feuds — Sanctuary — Ordeal — Trials in Civil Suits — Alfred's Dom-boc — Compilation made by Edward the Confessor — Saxon Laws . 159-224

CHAPTER II.
WILLIAM THE CONQUEROR TO HENRY II.

The Conquest — Saxon Laws Confirmed — The Laws of William the Conqueror — Trial by Duel in Criminal Questions — Establishment of Tenures — Nature of Tenures — Different Kinds of Tenures — Villenage — Of Escuage — Consequences of Tenure — Of Primogeniture — Of Alienation — Of Judicature —✔The Curia Regis — Justices Itinerant — The Bench — The Chancery — Judicature of the Council — Of the Spiritual Court — Of the Civil and Canon Law — Doctrines of the Canon Law — Probate of Wills —✔Constitutions of Clarendon — Of Trial by Duel in Civil Questions — Of Trial by Jury — By the Assize — Of Deeds —✔A Feoffment — A Fine — Of Writs — Of Records 225-346

CHAPTER III.

HENRY II.

Of Villeins — Dower — Alienation — "Nemo potest esse Hæres et Dominus"— Of Descent — Of Testaments — Of Wardship — Marriage — Of Bastardy — Usurers — Of Escheat — Maritagium — Homage — Relief — Aids — Administration of Justice — A Writ of Right — Essoins — Of Summons — Of Attachment — Counting upon the Writ — The Duel — The Assize — Vouching to Warranty — Writ of Right of Advowson — Of Prohibition to the Ecclesiastical Court — The Writ de Nativis — Writ of Right of Dower — Dower unde Nihil   347–414

CHAPTER IV.

HENRY II. TO JOHN.

Of Fines — Of Records — Writ de Homagio Recipiendo — Purpresture — De Debitis Laicorum — Of Sureties — Mortgages — Debts ex empto et vendito — Of Attorneys — Writ of Right in the Lord's Court — Of Writs of Justices — Writs of Replevin — and of Prohibition — Of Recognitions — Assisa Mortis Antecessoris — Exceptions to the Assize — Assisa Ultimæ Præsentations — Assisa Novæ Disseisinæ — Of Terms and Vacations — The Criminal Law — Of Abjuration — Mode of Prosecution — Forfeiture — Homicide — Rape — Proceeding before Justices Itinerant — The King and Government — The Charters — The Characters of these Kings as Legislators — Laws of William the Conqueror — Of the Statutes — Domesday-Book — Glanville — Miscellaneous Facts   415–489

ADVERTISEMENT.*

NO elaborate explanation is required to justify the printing of an American edition of Reeves' History of the English Law. It seems remarkable that its publication in this country has been so long delayed. A work that is necessary to the historical student, valuable to the legislator, and the source from which the philosopher abstracts the facts upon which he bases theories of government, it has provoked little adverse criticism, but has been often eloquently commended. It has no rival in English legal literature. It furnishes an accurate view of the progress of the law from the time of the Saxons to the reign of Elizabeth; and the scholar who desires a comprehensive knowledge of the relation of law to modern civilization, and wishes to trace the rise and growth of our present system of jurisprudence, will find it indispensable in his researches.

---

*The first edition, published in 1784–85, consisted of two volumes. In these the author did not advance beyond the reign of Henry VII. The second edition, 1787, four volumes, brought the History to the end of the reign of Philip and Mary. In 1829, another volume was added, including the reign of Elizabeth. In 1869 the edition by Mr. Finlason appeared.

The historical symmetry of the work has been carefully considered in the division into five volumes, and the convenience of the reader been assured. The English division into three volumes was an artificial one, and the volumes were large and unwieldy.

The last edition, with the learned notes of W. F. Finlason, Esq., has been literally followed, except that numerous errors in the cross-references have been corrected.

PHILADELPHIA, Jan. 1, 1880.

AUTHOR'S PREFACE

TO THE

FIRST EDITION.

THE History which I now presume to offer to the profession of the law, is an attempt to investigate and discover the first principles of that complicated system which we are daily discussing (*a*).

It has happened to the law, as to other productions of human invention, particularly those which are closely connected with the transactions of mankind, that a series of years has gradually wrought such changes as to render many parts of it obsolete; so that the jurisprudence of one age has become the object of mere historic remembrance in another. Of the numerous volumes that compose a lawyer's library, how many are consigned to oblivion by the revolutions in opinions and practice!—and what a small part of those which are still considered as in use, is necessary for the purposes of common business! Notwithstanding, therefore, the multitude of books, the researches of a lawyer are confined to writers of a certain period. According to the present course of study, very few indeed look further than Coke and Plowden. Upon the same scale of inquiry, the Year-Books are considered rather in the light of antiquities; and Glanville, Bracton, and Fleta as no longer a part of our law.

(*a*) The author, no doubt, meant the origin of those principles, his being a work, not on law, but legal history. It may be doubted, however, whether he was sufficiently alive to this distinction, and whether he did, to his mind it did not appear that the statement of the law, as it stood at successive periods in our history—was not all that was involved in a history of our law. But it is conceived that, to satisfy the requirements of legal history, it is necessary to trace the whole course and progress of our laws, so as to show their gradual development, and the causes which led to the changes to be observed in them. And further, that the history must be traced back to the earliest period at which civilized law can have had its origin.

It is in such a state of our jurisprudence that a history of the causes and steps by which these revolutions in legal learning have been effected, becomes curious and useful. But, notwithstanding the inquisitive spirit of the present age has given birth to histories of various sciences, we have nothing of this kind upon our law, except Sir Matthew Hale's *History of the Common Law*, published from a posthumous manuscript at the beginning of the present century. There have not, however, been wanting historical discourses, which have incidentally, and in a popular way, examined the progress of certain branches of the law, and during certain periods; such as those of Bacon, Sullivan, Dalrymple, Henry, and others.

Sir Matthew Hale, as a writer upon English law, possesses a reputation which can neither be increased nor diminished by anything that may be said of his History. We may therefore freely observe, that it is only an imperfect sketch, containing nothing very important nor very new. What seemed most to be expected, namely, an account of the changes made in the rules and maxims of the law, is very lightly touched (a). In short, the early period to which this work is confined, and the cursory way in which that period is treated, scarcely serve to give a taste of what a history of the law might be.

Sir William Blackstone, though in a smaller compass, has given a plan of a much better history than the former; and if the one excited a wish for something more complete, the other seems to have traced out a scheme upon which it might be executed. It was the chapter at the end of the *Commentaries* which persuaded me of the utility of such a work, if filled up with some minuteness upon

---

(a) It is conceived that the author very much undervalued Lord Hale's history, and that, so far as it went, it far more resembled a real history of law than his own. It exhibits far more of the cause and progress of our laws, and gives a more just and comprehensive view of the materials whence our laws were derived. Hale's account, for instance, of the true measure and nature of the effect of the Conquest upon our laws and institutions, is infinitely more complete and more correct than our author's, and therefore is embodied in the notes to the text. So Hale distinguishes the reigns between the Conquest and the Great Charter, especially the important reigns of Henry I. and Henry II., each of which makes an era in the history of our law; whereas the author treats the whole of that period together, and hence fails to give a clear idea of the course of our legal history during that important period. The present Editor has made Lord Hale his model of what a legal history should be.

the outline there drawn. It seemed, that after a perusal of that excellent performance, the student's curiosity is naturally led to inquire further into the origin of the law, with its progress to the state at which it is now arrived.

The plan on which I have pursued this attempt at a History of our Law is wholly new. I found that modern writers, in discoursing of the ancient law, were too apt to speak in modern terms, and generally with a reference to some modern usage. Hence it followed, that what they adduced was too often distorted and misrepresented, with a view of displaying, and accounting for, certain coincidences in the law at different periods. As this had a tendency to produce very great mistakes, it appeared to me that, in order to have a right conception of our old jurisprudence, it would be necessary to forget, for a while, every alteration which had been made since, to enter upon it with a mind wholly unprejudiced, and to peruse it with the same attention that is bestowed on a system of modern law. The law of the time would then be learned in the language of the time, untinctured with new opinions; and when that was clearly understood, the alterations made therein in subsequent periods might be deduced, and exhibited to the mind of a modern jurist in the true colors in which they appeared to persons who lived in those respective periods. Upon the same reasoning, it appeared to me, that if our statutes, and the interpretation of them, with the variations that have happened in the maxims, rules, and doctrines of the law, were presented to the reader in the order in which they successively originated; such a history, from the beginning of our earliest memorials down to the present time, would not only convey a just and complete account of our whole law as it stands at this day, but place many parts of it in a new and more advantageous light than could be derived from any institutional system; in proportion as an arrangement conformable with the nature of the subject surpasses one that is merely artificial.

The following volumes are written upon this idea; and being, in that view, an introductory work, they will, I trust, be as intelligible to a person unacquainted with law books as to those of the profession. It was partly with this design that I have contented myself with a simple narrative, making few allusions to what the law became in later times, but leaving that to be mentioned in its proper place. Many inferences and discussions which seem to be suggested by our ancient laws have not entirely escaped me; but are reserved for a place to which, agreeably with the plan of this history, I thought them better adapted. Every one who looks into our old law feels a strong propensity for remarking on the changes it has since undergone; but when the several steps which led to those changes are traced in a continued narrative down to the present time, such observations would be premature, unnecessary, and irksome.

My object being jurisprudence, and not antiquities, I have confined my researches to certain printed books of established reputation and authority, where alone I could hope to find the juridical history of the times in which they were written (*a*). It may not, perhaps, be unsatisfactory to the reader, who knows what respect is due to the venerable remains of our ancient law, to be told that the whole of GLANVILLE, and what seemed to be the most interesting part of BRACTON, is incorporated into this work.

A few observations may be necessary to prevent the reader being disappointed in that part of the following work which treats of the statutes. The old statutes have long been considered in a remote point of view, being rarely taken into the course of a student's reading, but referred to as occasion requires, and are then understood by the help of notes and commentaries. It might be expected that a History of the Law should furnish more notes and more commentaries upon this subject, as the only known means of illustration; on the contrary, the laws of Henry III. and Edward I. are here very little

---

(*a*) The author no doubt meant the *materials* for the History; but, as already observed, there is great reason to believe that he supposed the mere statement of the law, as it stood at successive periods, was legal history. For the authors whom he names did no more than state the law at the times at which they wrote, and the author simply copies them into his pages. That, it is manifest, is not of itself history, however valuable may be the *materials* they afforded for history. The author unhappily failed to appreciate a work more illustrative of our whole legal history for the period from the Saxon monarchy to the Great Charter, than any other work extant, and that is the *Mirror of Justice*— a work of which large portions were, it is manifest, written in the time of Alfred, and which was recomposed in the time of Edward I. Lord Coke thought very highly of it; but our author failed to draw much information from it as to the course of our legal history. So of the *Leges Henrici Primi* and Britton. In the present edition these deficiencies are supplied as far as possible in notes.

more than clearly stated, in a language somewhat more *readable*, if I may use the expression, than that of the Statute-book.

What was before said upon the general design of the work will, I hope, satisfy the reader that nothing further was requisite on this subject. As an account of the revolutions in our law antecedent to the making of those statutes must, altogether, contain an account of the law as it stood when they were made, it follows that the reader enters upon them with a previous information, which will enable him to comprehend their import, on the bare statement of their contents. As to the opinions and principles that were founded on those statutes in after ages, to take any notice of them would not only exceed the plan of the work, but very often anticipate the materials which are to contribute towards the subsequent parts of the History.

The text of our old statutes was translated in the time of Henry VIII. The ear of a lawyer, by long use and frequent quotation, has been so familiarized to the language of this translation, that it has obtained in some measure the credit of an original. Conformably with the general deference paid to this translation, I have mostly followed the words of it, except where I found it deviated from the text, or the matter required to be treated more closely or more paraphrastically.

There is one point of juridical history which has been greatly misconceived by many. It has been apprehended that much light might be thrown on our statutes by the civil history of the times in which they were made; but it will be found on inquiry that these expectations are rarely satisfied (a). The *lay* historians, like the body of

---

(a) Here, it is obvious, the author can hardly have fully appreciated the bearing of history upon law. No doubt it rarely happens that we have any account of the actual debates or discussions upon a law, and it is surprising, for instance, what little attention the contemporary chroniclers seem to have given to the Great Charter. But it was not the less clear that the only true exposition of that or any other ancient law is to be found in the history of the times immediately preceding it. As to *modern* law, indeed, what the author says may be true, that the only proper exposition is to be sought in the previous laws on the same subject; but that is because there *is* always a body of previous law which affords the most apt exposition of the new law. It is otherwise with ancient laws, which are enacted *de novo*, and are very *general*, and of which the only possible exposition is to be found in the facts of contemporary history. Had the author read the chronicles of the times previous to the Great Charter, he would have observed this; and not failed to apply the maxim of Montesquieu, "*Il faut éclairer les lois par l'histoire, et*

the people, were as unconcerned in the great revolutions of legal learning in those days as in ours; and we now see a statute for enclosing a common, or erecting a workhouse, make no small figure in the debates of parliament; while an act for the *amendment of the law*, in the most material instances, slides through in silence. Yet the latter would become an important fact to the juridical historian, while the former was passed by unnoticed. I believe little is to be acquired by travelling out of the record—I mean out of the statutes and Year-Books, the parliament-rolls, and law-tracts.

The following History, to the end of Edward I., was published in one volume in quarto, in March, 1783; the remainder, as far as the end of Henry VII., in March, 1784. These two volumes have undergone a revision, and have received some considerable additions. I have also subjoined the reigns of Henry VIII., Edward VI., and Queen Mary, or, as it is more properly styled by lawyers, Philip and Mary (*a*). This brings us to the close of that period, which appears to be almost wholly abandoned to the researches of the juridical historian. We have passed the times of the Year-Books and of their appendages, Fitzherbert and Brooke, the manuals of practisers in former times; we have even touched on those materials, to which the practisers of the present day do not disdain to owe obligations. Dyer and Plowden stand among the earliest of those authorities that are vouched in Bacon, in Viner, and in Comyns, who rarely refer to any antecedent to the reign of Elizabeth (*b*).

---

l'histoire par les lois." To fail to appreciate the bearing of history upon law, is to fail to realize the true idea of *history*, as applied to law.

(*a*) The author's first work stopped there; but he subsequently, after a long interval, added a fifth volume on the reign of Elizabeth, and he never went farther. He died, indeed, soon afterwards.

(*b*) And, therefore, as a history of our older law, the work, as far as it went, was a complete one; for undoubtedly, at the end of the reign of Elizabeth our laws had reached a point of development at which they assumed an entirely new character, and started, so to speak, in a course of improvement, interrupted no doubt by the troubles of the Rebellion and the Revolution, but resumed and continued from the Revolution to the present period, from the reign of Anne to the reign of Victoria. The present work displays the origin of the laws thus developed, and their progress up to that period when their character was about to alter altogether, and assume the modern aspect. The work, therefore, is, in that sense, a complete work, as a history of the law to the end of the reign of Elizabeth; that is to say, a history of our older law.

PREFACE TO THE FIRST EDITION.

At this juncture in our legal annals, between the law of former days and that of the present, we may be permitted to pause for a while. A new order of things seems to commence with the reign of Elizabeth, which strikes the imagination as a favorable point of time for resuming this historical inquiry afresh.

In pursuing the changes in our laws thus far, it is hoped, that if nothing is added to the stock of professional information, something is done towards giving it such illustration and novelty as may assist the early inquiries of the student. The investigation here made into the origin of English tenures, the law of real property, the nature of writs, and the ancient and more simple practice of real actions, may perhaps facilitate the student's passage from *Blackstone's Commentaries* to *Coke upon Littleton*, and better qualify him to consider the many points of ancient law which are discussed in that learned work.   J. R.

January 25, 1787 (a).

(a) In 1814 a fifth volume was published, without any further preface, bringing the law down to the *end* of the reign of Elizabeth; and that completes the present work. As originally published, it was to the reign of Elizabeth,—that is, to its commencement. The additional volume carried it to the *end* of that long reign, and so completed the history of our older law. At the end of that reign came the rise or dawn of *modern* law. At that era, the feudal system had become obsolete; villenage had disappeared (the last case of it occurred in that reign); the trial by battle was disused (the last actual instance of it also occurred in that reign); the old real actions were becoming superseded by the action of ejectment; for the ancient cumbrous remedies, actions on the case were substituted; our judicature and procedure began to assume something of their modern form; and altogether, a new era in our legal history commenced, which may be called the era of our *modern* law. A work or legal history, therefore, ending with the close of that reign, might well be deemed complete as a history of our older law. "With some exceptions," says our author, "it may be pronounced that the general cast of learning, in the days of Queen Elizabeth, comes within the help of that kind of law which is now in use. The long period of this reign gave sufficient opportunity for the discussion of almost every legal question; and the learning of former times being laid open to the world by the late publications, the whole of the law seems to have undergone a reconsideration, as it were, and those parts which were then mostly in use were settled upon principle, and so delivered down to succeeding times. To us, who view things in the retrospect, there seems to arise a new order of things about this time, when the law took almost a new face. When we consider Queen Elizabeth's reign in this light, it becomes a very interesting period in the history of our jurisprudence. From hence the commencement of modern law may be dated" (*Hist. Eng. Law*, c. xxxv., *post*, vol. v.). That reign, therefore, fitly terminates the history of the "old law," and thus the author's work was complete. The reign of Elizabeth presents a junction between the old law and the modern. There is hardly any subject of the old law which did not either become obsolete in that reign, or was not superseded or modified by some statute of that reign — the basis of more modern legislation. Thus, the act 27 Eliz., as to the liability of the hundred for riots or robberies, founded on the ancient statute of hue and cry, became the basis of the modern act 8 Geo. II., c. xvi. The acts of Elizabeth remedy faults or defects not *substantial*, as pleading or process became the basis of the act of Anne for the amendment of the law; which, in its turn, afforded a foundation for our more recent reforms in common law procedure. There is, indeed, no part of our law, however ancient or obsolete, which has not some connection, however remote, with the present. Thus, the ancient law as to the essoin *de ultra mare* shows that, at common law, a subject, although out of the realm, was liable to be sued in our courts — a principle affirmed also by the old statutes as to outlawry, and lately revived by the Common Law Procedure Act. Again, the statute 17 Edw. *de prærogativa Regis*, is deemed the basis of the jurisdiction exercised in Chancery over idiots or lunatics (2 *Inst.* 14; Hume *v.* Burton, 1 *Ridgway P. C.* 224; Lord Ely's case, *ib.* 519). The ancient writ of *ad quod damnum* formed the basis of the procedure in the Highway Act, 13 Geo. III., and the substance of it is preserved (Davison *v.* Gill, 1 *East*, 76). These are only a few illustrations whence may be seen the advantage of the study of the legal history even of that older age of our law which may be deemed to have concluded with the reign of Elizabeth. The history of that age, therefore, appears to form in itself a complete work; and with the history of the subsequent reigns, the history of modern law may be said to commence. It is the ambition and intention of the editor to continue the history to the present period. In the meantime, he has done his best in his notes to the last volume of the present work to bring the history of the law down to our own times.

PREFACE

TO THE

PRESENT EDITION,

[Being the Preface to the Last English Edition,] with a Single Elimination.

IN presenting a new edition of "Reeves' History of the English Law," the Editor desires briefly to explain the plan upon which it has been executed. In the first place, as the work was written the greater part of a century ago, since which time our ideas of legal history have much advanced, and our sources of information have been greatly enlarged, while the law has been so largely altered as to render the period covered by the history more remote and the law less applicable to the present than when the author wrote, the question arose whether it would not be necessary to rewrite or remodel the work. On the whole, however, it has been thought better, for many reasons, to adhere to the author's text, and therefore it is preserved intact. But it has been necessary to insert a great number of notes, some of considerable length, in order to secure the advantages of later information and enlarged views of legal history. The principles which have governed the Editor have been, as far as possible, to exhibit the rise, the growth, and gradual progress of our laws and institutions; and especially to trace them from their earliest origin. This appeared to render necessary an Introductory Essay on the prevalence of the Roman law in this country, and on its influence in the formation of our own; the more so since our author himself, who had not entered into that subject, had in one of his notes[1] indicated some sense of its importance; and the great historian, Hallam, had distinctly suggested it.[2] Our author had entirely passed over the long period of the Roman occupation, during which the Roman laws and institutions were firmly rooted and established here; and he passed so cursorily over the Saxon period as not to have shown how little our laws had derived from the barbarians, and how much they must have owed to the Romans. It appeared, therefore, proper to introduce the present edition by an essay on that subject; and, on the other hand, to supplement, in the notes, the account given by the author of the laws and institutions of the Saxon age.

. . . .

Although the author's text has been preserved, his arrangement required to be altered. He had blended different and important reigns. Thus he had dealt with the whole of the long period from the Conquest to the reign of John under the same head, so as not to mark the reigns of Henry I. and Henry II.; and he had blended the two very distinct reigns of Henry VI. and Edward IV., and those still more distinct, of Edward VI. and Mary. The Editor, therefore, without having altered the text, has entitled some chapters differently, and, sometimes, transposed matter to the proper reign, so as to mark the distinctions between the more important eras; and he has done his best to keep up in the notes the continuity of the progress of our laws, and to fill up any deficiencies in the history. With regard to the notes, the object has

---

[1] *Vide* vol. i., c. ii., p. 225.

[2] "Our common law may have indirectly received greater modification from the influence of Roman jurisprudence than its professors were ready to acknowledge, or even than they knew. A full view of this subject is still a desideratum in the history of English law, which it would illustrate in a very interesting manner" (*Middle Ages*, c. viii.).

been to afford as much as possible of *contemporary* illustration or explanation (a); the cardinal principle kept in view being that laid down by the author, to endeavor to look at the laws and institutions of any age by the light of the *ideas of that age*, and not to fall into the error of considering ancient institutions by the light of modern ideas.

(a) A distinguished jurist (Sir Roundell Palmer) has lately observed, in an address to law students, that our author was "valuable, though sometimes tedious," and it has been attempted, while illustrating the text, to render it more interesting and readable.

INTRODUCTION

TO THE

PRESENT EDITION.

IN presenting a new Edition of this work, upon "the History of the English Law, from the time of the Saxons to the end of the Reign of Elizabeth;"—a work first published the better part of a century ago;—it may be proper to explain the ideas and principles upon which it has been undertaken, and the views of legal history upon which it has been supplemented or corrected; and upon which it has also been thought necessary to introduce it by some observations upon the Roman laws and institutions, and their influence upon the formation of our own.

It seems obvious that, in any work on legal history, as it is important, as far as possible, to trace laws and institutions to their real origin, however remote, it is necessary to go back to the period when regular laws and civilized institutions first existed in the country, because, however much its laws may have been (as in ours was certainly to a great extent the case) the growth of custom and usage, subject to change in course of time, yet it must be that the rise and growth of *civilized* customs and laws must have been mainly influenced and determined by the earliest civilized institutions existing in the country; the primitive source whence they were in all probability originally derived.

This must be more especially the case in a country which, as was the case with our own, was still in a state of barbarism,[1] conquered by a nation, like the Romans, in

---

[1] That the Britons were in a state of barbarism on the arrival of the Romans is clear from the pages of Cæsar, de Bell. Gall., lib. iv., and Tacitus, in Vit. Agric., and it is idle and absurd to talk of their "laws." Montesquieu truly says: "Du temps des Romains, les peuples du nord de l'Europe vivai-

possession of a most complete and comprehensive system of government, and was for centuries subject to their rule — a portion of the Roman empire,[1] living under the Roman laws and institutions, and becoming first civilized under their influence.

It was the peculiar boast of the Roman emperors who first consolidated and codified the Roman laws[2] that they governed the various provinces of their vast empire not

---

ent sans arts, sans education, presque sans lois (*De l' Esprit des Lois*, liv. xiv., c. 3); and he observes, "C'est le partage des terres qui grossit principalement le code civil; chez les nations ou l'on n'aura pas fait ce partage, il y aura, tres peu de lois civiles. On peut appeler les institutions de ces peuples des mœurs plutôt que des lois" (l. xviii., c. 13). Sir J. Mackintosh, in his history, describes the inhabitants of the country at the time of the arrival of the Romans as in a state of barbarism. He points out that they grew no corn, and says: "It is vain to inquire into forms of government prevalent among a people in so low a state of culture. The application of the terms which denote civilized institutions to the confused jumble of usages and traditions, which gradually acquires some ascendancy over savages, is a practice full of fal... It is an abuse of terms to bestow the name of government on such ... of society" (*Hist. Eng.*, c. i.).

[1] The empire was divided into dioceses, under vicars (representing the Prætorian prefect), and these into provinces, under presidents or proconsuls. One of the dioceses was Britain, and it was divided into five provinces. "Vicarius pro præfecto prætorio mittebatur in tractum vel diœcesim aliquam aliqnot in se provincias continentem. Diœcesis Thraciæ, etc. Fuit etiam Romæ, Italiæ, Britanniæ, (singulis suberant quinque provinciæ)" (*Cod. Just.*, lib. i., tit. xxxviii. et xl. *in notis.*) As early as the reign of Caracalla, all the free subjects of the empire had the rights of Roman citizens. There were "comites," or military commanders, but the vicars were supreme in civil matters. "In civilibus, causis vicarios comitibus militum convenit anteferre" (*Cod. Just.*, lib. i., tit. xxxviii., s. 1, *De Officio Vicarii*). The proconsuls had legates, who could decide civil or criminal matters, subject, however, to revision by the proconsuls. "Legati non solum civiles sed etiam criminales causas audiant, ita ut si sententiam in reos ferendam providerint, ad proconsules eos transmittere non morentur" (*Cod. Just.*, lib. i., tit. xxxv., *De Officio Proconsulis*). The greater part of the first book is taken up with edicts as to the functions and duties of the officers of the empire or the provinces, which show a most elaborate and comprehensive system of government, which must have spread its ramifications into every corner of the empire. From the *Notitia Imperii*, and from the old chronicle of Richard of Cirencester, it will be seen that the Roman rule extended over the whole country; that there were two "municipia," nine "colonies," and upwards of one hundred and twenty stations, comprising nearly all the chief towns and cities now existing.

[2] "Barbaricæ gentes, subjugata nostra, omnes vero populi legibus tam a nobis promulgatis, quam compositis, reguntur" (*Præm. Inst. Just.*). The Roman law was first codified under Theodosius, during the Roman rule in Britain, and the subsequent code of Justinian is of course mainly made up of edicts previous to the termination of that rule. The very object of the code was to gather up the imperial edicts, and render them available for all the numerous provinces of the empire, so far as they might be applicable, as almost all of them were, in point of principle.

merely by force, but by the influence of their rule, and that they not only subdued the barbarians by their power, but civilized them by their law.

It was a law, in its nature so comprehensive, and based upon right reason and general principle, that it was not the law of one state only, it was the law of nature and of nations,[1] fitted by its character for universal dominion, for which reason, no sooner after the barbarian conquests did the barbarian races become civilized enough to be capable of law, than this great system of law had everywhere a resurrection and an ascendancy.

Such was so clearly the character of the Roman law, that it was recognized in the earliest ages of Christian history, and by none so clearly, none more emphatically, than by the first fathers of the Christian church,[2] and by natives of other races and distant countries subject to its rule. And it was the boast not only of the Romans, but the testimony of the most impartial writers, that the excellence of the Roman laws rendered them worthy of the admiration and adoption of other nations. Nor is it to be doubted that this opinion would be shared and followed by the prelates of the Christian church, who had so powerful an influence in the conversion and civilization of the barbarian races.

The general character of the Roman law,[3] as expounded

---

[1] Thus it was said by a writer in the middle ages: "Jus Justiniani præscriptum libris, non civitatis tantum est, sed et Gentium et naturæ; et aptatum sic est ad naturam universam, ut imperio extincto, ipsum jus diu sepultum surrexerit tamen, et in omnes se effuderit gentes humanas. Ergo et principibus stat, etsi est privatis conditum a Justiniano" (*Albericus Gentilis*, lib. i., *de Ju. Bell.*, cap. iii.).

[2] Thus St. Augustine says: "Iis omnibus artibus tanquam vera via nisi sunt ad honores, imperium, gloriam; honorati sunt in omnibus ferè gentibus; imperii sui leges imposuerunt multis gentibus; hodieque literis et historia gloriosi sunt penè in omnibus gentibus" (*De Civit. Dei*, lib. v., c. xii.). Insomuch that he goes on to say: "Per populum Romanum placuit Deo terrarum orbem debellare, ut in unam societatem reipublicæ, legumque perductum longè latéque pacaret" (lib. xviii., *De Civit. Dei*, c. xxii.). St. Augustine was a prelate of the African Church, and a perfectly impartial judge of the merits of the Roman law; and that opinion which he had of it would no doubt be followed by other prelates of the church, in this or any other country.

[3] "Justitiam colimus, et boni et æqui notitiam profitemur, æquum de iniquo separantes, licitum ab illicito discernentes, bonos non solùm metu pœnarum, verùm etiam præmiorum quoque exhortatione efficere cupientes; veram, nisi fallor, philosophiam non simulatam affectantes" (lib. i., *Dig. de Just. et Jur.*). This was the description justly given of it by one of its greatest professors, Ulpian, and another, even still greater — the illustrious Papinian,

by its most distinguished professors, after the spread of
the Christian religion, was largely in accordance with
those great principles of justice and morality which are
recognized by Christianity, and are, indeed, common to
all men; and its character, as it would be seen administered in this country, under the auspices of some of its
ablest professors, would be calculated, it may be conceived,
to commend it to the reason and consciences of all, and to
attract the respect, the confidence, and admiration of the
barbarians among whom it was administered.[1]

The fundamental principles of the Roman law, as to
the bases, or sources of law,[2] being broad, enlightened,

who was raised to the prefecture by the Emperor Severus in this country.
It was Papinian who laid it down: "Quæ facta lædunt pretatem, existima-
tionem, verecundiam nostram, et contra bonos mores fiunt, nec facere nos
posse credendum est" (L. xv., *Co. de Condit. Inst.*) There is reason to believe that the later of the Roman jurists had felt the influence of the Christian morality. Tertullian says of the Romans: "Eorum leges ad innocentiam
pergere, et de divina lege ut antiquiore, ferme mutuatus" (*Apol. Tert.*).

[1] Thus it was a principle of the Roman law that that which long use sanctioned became law without being written, for long-prevailing customs become
of the same nature as law by the consent of those who follow them (*Just.*,
lib. i., tit. ii., s. 59). And hence it was supposed in the Roman law that the
authority of custom sprang from consent; for what (it was asked) was the
difference between the consent of the people, given by their votes, and their
will, signified by their acts? (*Pand.*, lib. i., tit. iii., *De Legibus*, lib. xxxii., tit.
xxxiii.)

[2] "Omne jus aut consensus fecit, aut necessitas constituit, aut firmavit consuetudo" (*Modestinus*, l. xl., *Dig. de Legib.*). And as the authority of custom
was based upon consent, the foundation of all law, apart from actual necessity, would, upon the Roman principle, be consent. This head of law is appealed to in the Digest, lib. i., tit. iii., c. xcii., and it is thus that Ulpian expounds it: "De quibus causis scriptis legibus non utimur id custodire oportet,
quod moribus et consuetudine inductum est. Inveterata consuetudo pro lege
non immerito custoditur, et hoc est jus, quod dicitur moribus constitutum;
nam eum ipso leges nulla alia ex causa nos teneant, quam quod judicio populi receptæ sunt: merito et ea quæ sine ullo scripto populus probavit tene-
bunt omnes; nam quod interest suffragis populus voluntatem suam declaret,
an rebis ipsis et factis?" (*Ulpian*, lib. ii.) But, as St. Augustine observes,
who had well studied the Roman law: "Rei non bonæ consuetudo pessima
est. Nemo consuetudinem rationi et veritati præponat" (lib. iii., *De Bap-
tismo*, cited in the canon law, dist. viii., c. iv.). This consent, however, was
presumed to be based upon reason and experience; the very argument assigned for not changing a custom without sufficient cause implied that there
might be such cause. "In rebus novis constituendis evidens esse utilitas debet, ut recedatur ab eo jure quod diu æquum visum est" (*Ulpian;* lib. ii., *dig.
de constit. princ.*). According to the wise teaching of the imperial law, precedent was not to be blindly adhered to contrary to principles. "Non enim
si quid non bene derimatur, hoc et in aliorum judicium vitium extendi oportet, cum non exemplis sed legibus judicandum sit" (lib. xiii., *co. de sent. et
inter leg. omn jud.*), though it was recognized: "Rerum perpetuo similiter
judicatarum autoritas vim legis obtinet" (*Call.*, lib. xxxviii., *dig. de leg.*).

and elastic, eminently adapted it for universal empire. It acknowledged a general law based upon principles common to all mankind, and yet leaving ample scope for national or municipal law; admitting the authority of custom as resting on consent, yet making custom subject to reason, and the local or private law subordinate to the general or public law; it was equally adapted to maintain imperial sway, and influence, and incorporate local usages.

It was well understood, by the oracles and expositors of the Roman law, that any good system of laws must contain in them some elements common to all nations,[1] though it was equally understood that the municipal law or custom of a state must, in some respects, add to or depart from that natural law, and this, indeed, was what formed the scope of civil or municipal law.[2]

In their development of law upon these fundamental principles, the Romans were eminently *progressive*, and open to the influence of new ideas and altered circumstances, so that, as observed by a very learned writer,[3] "the notion of a body of customary law, mainly unwritten, which was not abrogated, but was *evaded* or *amplified* by persons *acting under the ideas of later times*, is the notion which, above all others, must be embraced clearly by any one who wishes to understand the Roman law." It is manifest that a system of law so comprehensive and so expansive, so enlightened, so elastic, and so progressive, must have been eminently adapted to universal rule, and calculated for the government of subject races.

In accordance with these principles and these characteristics of the Roman law, the Roman policy towards subject or subjugated races, though at first exclusive, had become, during the Roman dominion in this country,

---

[1] "Omnes populi, qui legibus et moribus reguntur, partim suo proprio, partim communi omnium hominum jure utuntur" (*Gaius*, lib. ix., *dig. de Just. et Jur., et vide Inst. de ju. nat. gen. et civ. Parag.* 1).

[2] "Lex municipalis, sive consuetudo, juri communi derogat; lex cujusque loci inspicienda est, sive scripta sit, sive non" (*Ga. Obs.*, lib. ii., obs. 124). "Jus civile est quod neque in totum à naturali jure, vel gentium, recedit, neque per omnia ei servit: itaque cum aliquid addimius vel detrahimus juri communi, jus proprium id est, civile, intelligimus" (*Ulpian*, lib. vi., *Dig. de Just. et Jur.*).

[3] Sandar's Introduction, p. 9. It is impossible adequately to express the obligations which the profession are under to the author of that most interesting and valuable work, which forms the best possible introduction to the study of our own law.

extremely liberal and enlarged. The ideas of the Romans on this subject, as on all others,[1] advanced and expanded with the growth of their mighty empire, and at the very time when their dominion here had become firmly settled, their law had attained its highest development of excellence, and their policy towards their provincial subjects had reached the highest point of enlightenment.

That policy is thus described by the able and learned writer already quoted: "The conquest of Italy, and the gradual spread of the Roman conquest, materially altered the character of the legal system. A branch of law almost entirely new sprang up, which determined the different relations in which the conquered cities and nations were to stand with reference to Rome. As a general rule, and as compared with other nations of antiquity, Rome governed those whom she had vanquished with wisdom and moderation. Particular governors, indeed, abused their powers; but the policy of the state was not severe, and Rome connected herself with her subject allies by conceding them privileges proportionate to their importance or their services."

"The *jus Latinum*[2] and the *jus Italicum* are terms familiar

---

[1] The Theodosian code had been compiled. Ulpian and Papinian, the greatest of Roman jurists, had written upon it (and Papinian was appointed to the Præfecture by the Emperor Severus in this country), and it was in the same state in which it was when St. Augustine, the greatest father of the Christian church, wrote upon it in the terms of eulogy already quoted.

[2] The *jus Latinum* is not to be confounded with the *jus Italicum*. The latter was the privilege of towns, the former of individuals, and it was that which was extended by Caracalla to all the free inhabitants of the empire. What it was, and what it involved, may be seen expounded in an edict addressed by the Emperor Justinian to the Prætorian prefect (*Cod. Justin.*, lib. vii., tit. 6, " De Latina Libertate tollenda, et per certos modos in civitatem Romanam transfusa"), in which may be seen that the *jus Latinum* did not carry with it full Roman citizenship. It may be premised that it was the *Lex Julia*, A. U. c. 404, which gave the right of Latinity—*jus Latii*, as it was called — to all free inhabitants, and the *Lex Junia* conferred it upon freed men. It was a question, it should seem, what precise privileges the *jus Latinum* conferred, and to this question the edict refers. The *Latini colonarii* mentioned by Ulpian were the provincial communities which had acquired the right of Latinity. The edict of Justinian, above quoted, relates to the *liberti*, the freed men, who, by the *lex Junia*, had the *jus Latinum* or *jus Latii* conferred upon them, and as to which difficulties had arisen — whence the edict recites: "Cum deditii liberti jam sublati sint, ea propter imperfecta Latinorum libertas incertis vestigiis titubat. . . . quod autem ex re ipsa rationabile est, hoc in jus perfectum deducitur. Cum enim Latini liberti ad similitudinem antiquæ Latinitatis quæ in coloniis missa est, videntur esse introducti, ex qua nihil aliud reipublicæ nisi bellum accessit civile; satis absurdum est,

to all readers of Roman history. The first expressed that, with various degrees of completeness, the rights of Roman citizens were accorded to the inhabitants of different towns, some having the *commercium* only, and some also the *connubium*. Towards the end of the Republic (A. U. C. 663), the *Lex Jurica* gave the full rights of citizenship to almost the whole of Italy. The *jus Italicum* expressed a certain amount of municipal independence, and exemption from taxation attached to different places on which the right was bestowed."[1]

During the Roman occupation of the country, while on the one hand the Roman law in the provinces was consolidated and improved under the auspices of the ablest of jurists,[2] on the other hand, all free subjects in the prov-

ipsa origine res sublata, ejus imaginem derelinqui. Cum igitur multis modis et innumerabilibus Latinorum introducta est conditio, et leges diversæ introducta sunt, et hexis difficultates maximæ emergebant ex lege Junia," etc. And then it proceeds to prescribe modes by which the freed man "libertatem et civitatem Romanam habeat," which distinguishes the two rights, though not strongly. The great jurist, Ulpian, divided the inhabitants of the Roman empire into three classes, *cives*, *Latini*, *peregrini*, or foreigners. The *civis* was entitled to every privilege of a Roman citizen; the *peregrinus* was excluded from all the rights arising from the peculiar character of the Roman law. He had not the *connubium* nor the *commercium*, but he had all that was recognized by the *jus gentium*. The *Latinus* stood between the *civis* and *peregrinus;* he had the *commercium*, and could hold property as Roman citizens could do, and could make testaments, but he had not the *connubium*. This is the inference Mr. Phillimore draws from various passages in Ulpian, "Connubium habent cives Romani, cum civibus Romanis, cum Latinis autem, et peregrinis, ita si concessum sit" (tit. v., s. 4). "Mancipatio locum habet inter cives Romanos et Latinos colonarios, Latinosque Junianos, eos que peregrinos quibus commercium datum est" (tit. xix., s. 4).

[1] "The citizens of some particular places in the provinces possessed the *jus Latinum*, and the *jus Italicum* was attached to certain privileged cities, but the provinces generally had no participation in either right. They were subject to a proconsul or proprætor, paid taxes to the treasury of Rome, and had as much of the law of Rome imposed upon them, and were made to conform as nearly to Roman political notions as their conquerors deemed expedient" (*a*). Caracalla, in A. D. 212, made all persons citizens who were subjects of the empire (*b*). And then all the free inhabitants of the civilized world were *cives*, and beyond were nothing but *barbari* and *hosti* (*c*).

[2] As early as the reign of Adrian, a great jurist, by order of the emperor, composed an edict (as it was called), drawn from the edicts of the *prætor peregrinus:* of the *ædiles* and the *edictum provinciale*. The edict thus composed became the rule of law in the provinces, and was a code of Roman law (*Phillimore's Study of the Roman Law*, p. 222). By the *Lex Julia*, "De civitate sociis et Latinis danda" (A. 663), the freedom of the city was given to Latins and Italian allies who would accept it, "*qui ei legi fundi fieri vellent*" (*Cic. pro Balb.* 8); and this was afterwards extended to all the provincial subjects of the empire. And under Caracalla, in the early part of the

(*a*) Sandar's Introduction to the Institutes, p. 10. (*b*) *Ibid.*, p. 21. (*c*) *Ibid.*, p. 30.

inces were admitted to the rights of Roman citizens; and this came fully under the protection and under the influence of that law.

There was nothing to which the Roman law attached more importance than to *status* and citizenship. The first great element of *status* was freedom; the next was citizenship; and the exposition of its privileges embraced all the most important relations and transactions of life. "The second great element of the *status* was *citizenship*. In the early times of Rome, the *cives* were members of the state: all beyond were *hostes* or *barbari*. But as civilization progressed, the number of foreigners who resorted to Rome for trade, or were otherwise brought into friendly relations with the citizens, was so great, that they were looked upon as a distinct class—that of *peregrini*. A *peregrinus* was subject only to the *jus gentium;* citizens alone could claim the privileges of the *jus quiritium*. But when her conquests placed Rome in new and varying relations with the nations, an intermediate position between the citizen and the *peregrinus* was accorded to the more privileged of the vanquished. Some of the rights of the citizen were given to them, and some were withheld. These peculiar rights of the citizens were summed up in the familiar term *suffragium et honores*—the right of voting and the capacity of holding magisterial offices,

---

third century, all the free subjects of the empire were admitted to the rights of free citizenship. At this time, too, be it observed, all free citizens had equal rights of citizenship. Long before the Roman conquest of Britain, the distinction between the two great ranks or orders of freemen had been done away with. In 309 A.U.C., the Cornelian law gave the connubium to the plebs, and the marriage of a patrician with a plebeian was no longer forbidden by law. And by the *lex Hortensia*, A.U.C. 467, the distinction between the two orders was really done away with, and the plebeian, by their law, acquired a full share in the *jus publicum*. The equality between the two orders was so complete, that the plebeian could be consul or prætor, and could administer justice. The effect of this all over the empire, especially when *provincials* were admitted to the privileges of citizenship, must have been to produce a great tendency to the amalgamation of all classes of society, and of Romans with natives. Previously to the above alteration of the law, no Roman citizen was permitted to marry a serf, a barbarian, or a foreigner, without special permission (lib. xxxviii., 36). "Connubium et matrimonium inter cives; inter civem et peregrinæ conditiones hominum aut serviles non est connubium" (*Bœth. in Cic.* 4). It may be observed, that the *jus Latii* or *Latinitas* was inferior to *jus civitatis* and superior to the *jus Italicum;* but the precise difference is a matter of dispute, and became immaterial after the law of Caracalla. Even plebeians might, after the above alteration, possess municipal privileges in the provinces (*Nieb.*, i., p. 275).

and in the terms *connubium* and *commercium*. *Connubium* is a term which explains itself. The foundation of the Roman family was a marriage according to the *jus quiritium*, and not to have the *connubium* was to be incapable of entering into the Roman family system. In the word *commercium* were included the power of holding property, and of making contracts according to the Roman law; and also the *testamenti facti*, or power to make a will, and to accept property under one. By the *jus Latinum* and *jus Italicum*, various modifications of the rights implied in citizenship were granted: the one granted private rights to individuals, the latter gave public rights to towns. In course of time other shades between the *cives* and the *peregrinus* were introduced, but all distinction between them was gradually swept away by the recklessness with which the rights of citizenship were bestowed, until at last Caracalla made all the free subjects of the empire citizens, and thenceforth the days of *peregrini*, properly speaking, ceased to exist. All the inhabitants of the civilized world were *cives*, and beyond were only *barbari* and *hostes*" (*Sandar's Introduction to Justinian*, p. 30).

Such was the character of the Roman rule as it prevailed in this country for centuries[1] after the inhabitants had become subjugated to its power, and subject to its influence. And as they were undoubtedly mere barbarians when the Roman invasion took place, they would natu-

[1] Even in the course of the first century, this policy was civilizing and influencing the barbarian Britons; and there could not be a better picture of it than is presented in a passage from Tacitus, in his Life of Agricola. "Quibus rebus multæ civitates quæ in illum diem ex æquo egerant, datis obsidibus, iram posuere: saluberrimus consiliis absumta, namque et homines dispersi ac rudes, eoque bello faciles, quieti et otio per voluptates assuescerent; hortari privatim, adjuvari publice, ut templa, fora, domus exstruerant, laudando promtos, et castigando segnes, ita honoris emulatio, pro necessitate erat. Jam vero principum filios liberalibus artibus erudire, et ingenia Britannorum studiis Gallorum anteferre; ut qui modo linguam Romanam abnuebant, eloquentiam concupiscerent, inde etiam habitus nostri honor et frequens toga," etc. It is obvious that the barbarian race were already eagerly adopting the usages of Rome, and would readily adopt her laws. It may be imagined what progress they had made by the time of the edict of Caracalla, and what rapid progress in the amalgamation of the races and the adoption of the Roman institutions would be made after that edict. Municipia and colonia are alluded to by Tacitus in his Life of Agricola (v. 32), and they rapidly overspread the whole country, from York to Colchester, from Colchester to Exeter; as the *Itinerary* shows, coupled with the chronicle of Richard of Cirencester. That the Britons were barbarians when the Romans came, is clear from Cæsar and Tacitus, as already has been shown.

rally, as they became civilized, adopt the laws and usages of those to whom they owed their civilization.

That the Roman institutions were established and existed in this country for centuries is an historical fact, and those institutions necessarily embodied much of their laws. The Roman system, it is well known, was originally and essentially municipal;[1] and it need hardly be said that the municipal organization was eminently complete; and when the provincial subjects of the empire were admitted, more or less, to the privileges of Roman citizens, and municipal colonies, or even *municipia*, with privileges like those of Rome, were established in the provinces, the municipal system in the provinces became the subject of constant and careful legislation.

And the whole system of Roman rule, which, on the one hand, by its general spirit of equity, justice, and wisdom, was likely to impress the mind of the barbarian nations subject to its sway, was, on the other hand, by its complete organization,[2] its municipal institutions, and its rural colonization, admirably fitted for the settlement and civilization of a country in a state of barbarism; and calculated to fix itself very deeply and firmly in its social soil.

---

[1] The Roman law is full of provisions upon this subject. The parent city was, of course, the model of all other Roman municipalities (*vide Cod. Just.*, lib. xii., tit. 13, "De decurialibus urbis Romanæ"); and under the municipal institutions there were other corporate bodies (*vide ibid.*, tit. 14, "De privilegiis corporatorum urbis Romanæ"). When the provincials, under Caracalla, were made Roman citizens, the municipal offices were opened to them; and there is a large part of Roman law relating to the "curia" and the elections, and the functions of the "curiales" (*Cod. Just.*, lib. x., tit. xxxi., "De decurionibus"). For instance, sec. 46, "De curialibus eligendis," "ad subeunda patriæ munera, dignissimi meritis et facultatibus curiales eligantur; ne tales forte nominentur qui functiones publicas implere non possint."

[2] The Roman organization was extremely elaborate. It has already been mentioned that Britain, like every other part of the empire, was divided into provinces, of which there were five, under presidents or proconsuls; but there is every reason to believe that these were divided into smaller districts under the comities or counts; and thus the word comitatus, or county. Further, the Roman system of rural organization included subdivisions into centuries and decennaries; and as these were found to exist among the Romanized Britons, it is reasonable to suppose they were derived from the Romans, especially as there is no trace of any Saxon law establishing them. As regards the municipal system of the Romans, it is hardly necessary to state how complete it was. But of the whole system of court government in the provinces, Guizot observes emphatically that it comprehended all things and all classes, that it had to do with all society, and all society with it. (*Lect. sur la Civiliz. en France*, lect. ii.)

But the Roman system was not only municipal, it was also colonial;[1] and as the municipal system organized the inhabitants of towns, not only in civic but in other corporations, so the colonial system under which the municipalities themselves were established, extended itself from the towns into the country, and there established another organization — rural in its nature.

The Roman system allowed grants of land by the state either to cities or colonies, or to individuals, and the latter in its development proved the parent of the manorial system. The Roman law in particular made special provision for the appropriation of waste or vacant lands by the " curia," or corporations of the cities or colonies to which they appertained or belonged ; the principle of the law being that, until such appropriation, the land remained the common property of all free citizens, but the exclusive property of none. And this, it is manifest, was a part of the law especially important in conquered countries such as Britain, where there would be vast tracts of territory vacant.[2]

With regard to allotments of land to individuals, the Roman system was primarily military in the provinces, and carefully defensive in its character. Hence, in all the conquered provinces, lands were assigned to soldiers, " milites " on military tenure, or on condition of military

---

[1] The Roman system became colonial for the very reason that it was originally municipal. The Roman went forth from his city to conquer and cultivate the country, and hence the very term "colony" was derived from that which signified to cultivate, and the very definition of coloni was a body of people sent forth as planters with an allotment of land for their support. They had great privileges, and the Romans had a passion for the country. " Existimamus meliore conditione esse coloniæ quam municipia," (*Gell.*, xv. 13.) This system of course applied peculiarly to the provinces. (*Vide* Sigonius, "de jure provinciarum.") The grants of land were either to the municipal bodies, or the colonies as corporate bodies ; or afterwards by allotment to individuals; the principle was the same — it was a colonization of the country with a view to its cultivation. The Roman provincial got a grant of land in the country, and built his villa, and had his "coloni" to cultivate the land.

[2] See, for instance, the heading of the *Code Just.*: " De omni agro deserta " (lib. xi., tit. lviii.), and especially the first section. " Prædia deserta decurionibus loci cui subsunt, assignari debent." So s. 5. " Possidens prædia sterilia et fertilia, non potest retuntiare sterilibus, et fertilia retinere ; " and, "Qui utilia reipublicæ loca possident, permixtione facta etiam deserta, suscipiant est ut si carum partium graventur accessu, quas antea per fastidium reliquerunt, cedant aliis curialibus qui utraque hac conditione retineant, ut prestatione salva cum desertis et culta possideant, sublata a paucis, quos iniquum est electa retinere cum municipes gravatura sit pars relicta."

service: and this was especially so in the latter period of the Roman empire, during which the constant incursions of barbarians took place.¹

When grants of public land were made to individuals —usually upon this military tenure, the holders had to allot a portion of it out to those who were the actual occupiers and cultivators, and who, although by the Roman law attached to the soil, and, in a sense, serfs, were not slaves, and soon acquired rights by custom.²

Although, therefore, originally the Roman system was municipal, yet as the empire was enlarged, and the system of colonization was extended to the provinces, the Roman law, or legislation, extended its care to the condition of the rustic population; and the Roman legislation contained many provisions on the subject,³ the general result of which is, that the *coloni* or actual cultivators of the soil were a species of free serfs attached to the soil, but not slaves.

---

¹ "Agros etiam limitaneos universos cum paludibus . . . quos limitanei *milites* . . . ipsi curare . . . atque arare, consueverant ab his . . . detineri . . . volumus" (*Nov. Theod.*, tit. 32, vol. vi., p. 14). So Lampidius says, speaking of Alexander Severus, "Sola quæ de hostibus capta sunt limitaneis ducibus et *militibus donavit* ita ut eorum ita essent si hæredes eorum militarent" (p. 58). It is impossible not to see that though this may not have been the direct origin of the feudal system, still it contained the germ or principle of it, as it undoubtedly was military tenure, and this principle may have been imperfectly adopted by the Saxons; so as to occasion the controversy as to whether the feudal system was known among them as it afterwards was established by the Normans.

² The Roman would have his "villa," and around it the farm or land in his own personal occupation; but then, to secure the cultivation of the rest of the land for his support he would have to allot it out in portions to free laborers, called "coloni," attached to the soil, but not slaves. Hence villicus —a husbandman or farmer; the bailiff of a manor, or steward, even in the city. "Villicus agri colendi causa constitutus et appellatus à villa" (*Varr. R.*, i. 2). "Villaris; of, or belonging to a village, farm, or country-house. Villanus, a farmer or villager, conditione colonariæ addictus" (*Bud.*). Hence the Anglo-Norman phrase "villein." Hence also the old English word, still remaining, "vill," or village. All these terms, be it noted, and the state of things they indicate, were well established when the Romans were here.

³ *Cod. Theod.*, lib. v., tit. 9, "De fugitivis colonis, inquilinis et servis;" tit. 10, "De inquilinis et colonis;" tit. 11, "Ne colonus inscio domino suum alienat," etc. *Cod. Just.*, lib. xi., tit. 47, "De agricolis et censitis et colonis;" tit. 49, "In quibus causis coloni censiti dominos accusare possint;" tit. 50, 51, 52, "De colonis;" tit. 61, "De fugitivis colonis," etc.; tit. 67, "De agricolis et mancipiis dominicis," etc. So under the title of "Defensores," there is a special head, "De rusticis." The coloni, rustici, adscriptitii, etc., were serfs, not slaves. *Cod. Just.*, lib. xi., tit. 51, "Licet conditione videantur ingenui, servi tamen terræ ipsius cui nati sunt, existimentur. Sed possessores eorum jure utantur, et patroni solicitudine et domini potestate."

The general principle pervading these laws was, that these "coloni," the actual tenants or occupiers of the lands belonging to an estate, were bound to render certain services to the lord connected with the cultivation of the soil, according to the custom of the estate;[1] and that, on the other hand, their services could not be increased or rendered more burdensome than they were by that custom—a principle which contained the germ of that customary tenure which was the essence of a manor.[2]

Numerous imperial edicts refer to these relations of lord and tenant to the manorial system. The fundamental principle of copyhold tenure—that is, of holding according to custom—will be found laid down in the Roman edicts as to the coloni of the provinces; who, on the one hand, were not allowed to usurp the land against the cus-

---

[1] "We must carefully distinguish between the domestic slaves and the prædial or rural slaves" (or serfs). "As to the former, their condition was nearly everywhere the same; but as to those who cultivated the soil, we find them designated by a variety of different names—coloni, rustici, agricolæ, tributarii, aratores, adscriptii, each name well-nigh indicating a difference of condition. Some were domestic slaves sent to a man's country estate to labor, while he lived there, instead of working indoors at his own home; some were regular serfs of the soil, who could not be sold except with the domain itself; others were farmers, who cultivated the ground in consideration of receiving half the produce; others farmers of a higher class, who paid a regular rent; others free laborers, who worked for wages. Sometimes these different denominations were mixed up under the general denomination of coloni" (Guizot, *Lect. sur la Civiliz. France*). Elsewhere the same learned author identifies a class of those coloni as the originals of the villeins of a later age.

[2] Thus, as to the subject of the rights of rural settlers, and the coloni, or actual cultivators of the soil (*Cod. Just.*, lib. xi., tit. 47, "De agricolis et colonis"). Thus, for instance, s. 5, "Quid dominus prædiorum præstatur:"—"Domini prædiorum id quod terra præstat, accipiant pecuniam, non requirant, quam rustici optare non audent; nisi *consuetudo prædii* non exigat." So s. 2, "Si quis prædium vendere voluerit, retinere sibi transferendos ad alia loco colonos privata pactione non possit. Qui enim colonos utiles credunt; aut cum prædiis eos tenere debent, aut profuturos aliis derelinquere, si ipsi prædium sibi prodesse desperant." So the coloni were attached to the estate. But then, on the other hand, "Agricolarum alii quidem sunt adscriptitii, et eorum peculia dominus competunt; alii vero tempore annorum triginta coloni fiunt, liberi manentes cum rebus suis; et ii etiam coguntur terram colere, et canonem præstare. Hoc et dominis et agricolis utilius est" (*Ibid.*, s. 18). And again, "Omnes fugitivos adscriptios, vel colonos, ad antiquos penates, ubi censiti adque educati natique sunt, provinciis præsidentes redere compellant" (*Ibid.*, s. 6). But the Roman law allowed them the benefit of custom (*vide* s. 23), and by the force of custom the coloni afterwards, under the name of villani, acquired full personal freedom, and a certain tenure of their land, and were converted into the modern copyholders.

tom,[1] nor, on the other hand, were they allowed to be ousted, contrary to custom.

There can be no doubt that this important relation was established in the conquered provinces. Many of the imperial edicts issued into the provinces mention its existence, and show a strong desire to protect the interests of the provincials from the rapacity of the military,[2] and especially to protect the agriculturists; whether the owners, or the coloni, the actual cultivators of the soil.

It was entirely in accordance with the spirit of the Roman law that these lords of manors should on their estates exercise a sort of domestic jurisdiction, and hence the origin of "courts barons," immemorial incidents to manors.[3]

These, however, were rather municipal or domestic institutions of the Romans, which, it is manifest, were established here by the Romans. There were political

---

[1] Thus an edict of Constantine: "Si villa locata in emphyteusim conceditur non possunt coloni usurpare totum territorium ejusdem:" — "Emphyteuticarios gravant coloni, agros præter consuetudinem usurpantes, quos nullis culturis erudierunt," etc. (*Cod. Just.*, lib. xi., tit. lxi.). So, again, "Cognovimus à nonullis qui patromoniales fundos meruerunt, colonos antiquissimos perturbari, atque in eorum locum vel servos proprios, vel alios colonos surrogari" (*Ibid.*).

[2] For instance, there is this edict of Theodosius and Honorius, addressed, "Comitibus et magistris militum:" "Prata provincialium nostrorum, et precipue rei privatæ nostræ, perniciosum est militum molestia fatigari, ideoque lege ad amplissimam præfecturam promulgata, censemus, ne hoc deinceps usurpetur, super qua re universos quorum interest, convenire tua magnificentia non moretur neque permittat possessores vel colonos pratorum gratia qualibet importunitate vexari" (*Cod. Just.*, lib. xi., tit. lx., s. 3).

[3] Lords had at first a domestic jurisdiction, in order to compel their tenants' services, and maintain peace and order amongst them. Afterwards, in imitation of the sovereigns' court, lords caused records to be made before their own officers of the transactions which had taken place in their courts (*Traités sur les Coutumes Anglo-Normandes*, par *M. Houard*, p. 507, tom. 1). This necessity of a domestic jurisdiction, recognized among the Normans, would no doubt have been equally recognized among the Romans, especially in the provinces. And this, no doubt, led to the establishment of local courts, not only in our great cities, such as London, and York, and Bath, and Bristol, and Cambridge, and Oxford, and Chester, and Exeter, but in places which now are, and always have been, so far as is known, mere villages, such as Dunster in Somersetshire, or Stratton in Cornwall (*Cro. C.* 259), and numerous other similar places to be found mentioned in the old reports. A court-baron is incident to a manor (*Bro. Abr.*, "*Court-Baron*," pl. 1), and cannot be separated from it (*Bro. Abr.*, "*Incidents*," pl. 34). So that if the manors are of Roman origin, the courts must be, and so of the court-leet, the court of the hundred or manor, "the most ancient court in the realm" (*Y.-B., Hen.* 6). The ancient style of the court-baron was: "Curia de milite, secundum consuetudinem villæ" (2 *Inst.*).

institutions or divisions of a country, which, in all probability would be established or originated by them in any country subjugated by them, as it was a characteristic of their system of government to establish an organization as complete as possible. As they had the large territorial divisions under greater rulers,[1] so they had smaller divisions, under lesser rulers; and thus they had a division into centuries and decennaries.

The various officers or functionaries at the head of these different divisions of a county were expected and directed to govern according to the Roman law.[2] And even the governors of provinces were strictly directed not to be satisfied to make the decisions in Rome their guides, but to determine always according to justice and right. On the other hand, the law was firmly upheld and enforced among all classes of subjects. The great characteristic of the Roman system of rule was the one eminently fitted for the subjugation and civilization of a barbarous race. Its fundamental principle was the supremacy of the sovereign power, and this was equally exemplified with ref-

---

[1] It has already been mentioned that the empire was divided into dioceses, and præfectures, and provinces, under vicars, and præfects, and presidents; and it appears also that there were "duces" and "comites" (*Cod. Just.*, lib. xii., tit. 12, "De Comitibus qui provincias regunt"). The organization was rendered as elaborate as possible for political and fiscal purposes. For political purposes, there was the division into centuries and decennaries. The division by centuries and decennaries was universally adopted in the Roman system, and it was not merely numerical or military, but it was also territorial or local, for it was applied to the land as well as to the people; and this is to be observed in distinguishing it from the numerical division into hundreds, which existed among some of the barbarians, as the Germans. That was purely military, and therefore only numerical. The Romans divided land by hundreds, "centenarius ager," and therefore, though at first a century contained a hundred citizens, it did not afterwards. This also is to be observed, that, as it would be only the free citizens who could be included in the centuries, and the head of each household would be numbered, it would virtually be an enumeration of households or residences, and, in the country, of estates or manors.

[2] Thus, the governors of provinces were directed to govern according to law and right, not regarding even decisions at Rome which appeared contrary thereto. "Licet is qui provinciæ præest, omnium Romæ magistratuum vice et officio fungi debeat, nec tamen spectandum est quod Romæ factum est, quam quid fieri debet" (lib. xii., *Dig. De off. Præsid.*). Justinian gave the reason: "Non enim si quid non bene derimatur, hoc et in aliorum judicium vitium extendi oportet, cum non exemplis, sed legibus judicandum sit" (lib. xiii., *Co. de Sent.*). Again: "Universi omnino ex comitibus, vel ex præsidibus, qui suffragio perceperint, dignitates civilibus oneribus muneribusque teneantur, adstricti, ne commoda publica cum umbratili suffragiorum pactione lacerentur" (*Cod. Just.*, lib. x., tit. 63, *De Legationibus.*).

erence to dominion over the land, or upholding the supremacy of law. So great was the care of the Roman law to discourage all violence, even for the vindication of right, as unbecoming a well-governed and civilized state, that there was a special law against it;[1] and if any one was turned out of possession of land or immovable property, he might obtain immediate restitution by a summary process of law, even though he had not the strict legal right of property, as against him who expelled him. It was a first principle of the Roman law to uphold the supremacy of law as a means of redress for injury or wrong,[2] and to treat as a serious offence against the state any recourse to force or arms for that purpose. But while, in accordance with this principle, the Roman law deemed it the first duty of the state to repress violence, it deemed it its next and not less sacred duty to administer justice.

Upon all matters which could be the subject of civil rights or claims in a civilized country, the Roman law made ample provision. Thus, all matters relating to the origin, the succession, or the transfer of property in lands, were the subject of careful and copious regulations. As to the creation of property in land,[3] its provisions were,

---

[1] The *Lex Julia, de vi*. It was provided by an imperial edict that any one placing himself forcibly in possession of that which is his, shall forfeit the property; and that, if it be not his, he shall pay the value, and restore the land to the person wronged. And persons so offending are also liable to the *Lex Julia, de vi*, and are held guilty of *vis privata*, if unarmed, and *vis publica*, if they use any other means or weapons of offence beside their own bodies (*Cod.*, lib. viii., tit. iv., lib. v., 7).

[2] "Recuperandæ possessiones causa solet interdici si quis expossessione fundi vel ædium vi dejectus fuerit; nam ei proponitur interdictum unde vi per quod is qui dejecit, cogitur ei restituere possessionem, licet is ab eo qui vi dejecit, vi clam precario possideat. Sed ex constitutionibus sacris (ut supra diximus), si quis rem per vim occupaverit. Si quidem in bonis ejus est domino ejus privatur; si aliena, post ejus restitutionem rei dare vim passo compellitur. Qui autem aliquem de possessione per vim dejecit tenetur lege Julia de vi privata aut de si publica. Sed de vi privata si sine armis vim facerit. Sin autem armis enim de possessione vi expulerit de vi publica tenetur. Armorum autem appellatione non solum scuta et gladios, sed et fustes et lapides" (*Inst. Just.*, lib. iv., tit. 15, which is copied into the *Mirror*).

[3] It was a first principle of the Roman law that the property in land must emanate from the state, and as the Romans acquired land by conquest, the Roman people were the lords of the soil. In foreign countries, however, the former owners were usually left, to a large extent, in occupation, but there were extensive tracts of land which were taken into the hands of the state, and called *ager publicus*. These were deemed the joint property of all Roman citizens, but until a division or appropriation under the authority of the state,

from the position of the parent city, peculiarly applicable to the condition of a conquered country, as it admitted of the original inhabitants retaining possession as tributaries to the conquerors.

The descent of land was regulated upon the principles of equality or equity which pervaded the Roman law, and in the absence of a will, the land was divided among the children or other heirs;[1] while, on the other hand, the owner was not permitted to leave away from his family the whole of his property, but was obliged to leave them a reasonable part. The rules of descent were all carefully fixed and defined.

The right of testament was one of the privileges of Roman citizenship, and all that related to it was carefully regulated. With regard to the important subject of the authentication of testaments or wills, ample provision was made, in a system of public registry, which other nations, and ourselves among them, have doubtless derived from the Romans.[2]

So with respect to the various kinds of donation, and, among others, *donatio mortis causa;* and as to all matters of contract, whether as to realty or personalty, and, among others, the contracts of lease of real property, or loan of

---

no one had an exclusive right of property therein. Colonies were sent out to foreign countries to found or occupy cities, and to these a proportion of the land was allotted (*Nieb.*, i., p. 256; ii., p. 42). Public lands were also let out to persons who paid a tenth part of the produce as rent, whence they were called *decennarii*, and these lands *agri decennarii* (*Cic. Verr.*, 52).

[1] By the law of the Twelve Tables, the succession of one who died intestate was vested in the "hæredes" *i. e.*, "liberi, aut qui in liberorum loco sunt." In later times, the sons seem to have divided the estate. And by the Falcidian law, the owner could not make a will unless he left to near relatives, "liberis et parentibus," a portion —"pars legitima," or reasonable part — which the law fixed at a fourth.

[2] There were two constitutions of Arcadius, and Honorius, and Theodosius, which show that, among the Romans, there was an authentication of testaments by means of registration in the office of a civil functionary, or among the records of the court of justice, or of a municipium (*Cod.*, lib. vi., tit. 23, *De Test.*, l. 17). It also appears from a later law that the registration of wills was transferred to the præsides in the provinces (*Ibid.*), and thus the magistrate not only registered the instrument, but authenticated it with his seal, upon the faith of the depositions of the subscribing witnesses. From this, no doubt, the probate of wills was derived, and it is not difficult to divine how it came into the ecclesiastical courts, or, in some instances of special custom, into courts of lords of manors. Under the Roman law, as the magistrates were educated, the registry could be entrusted to them, and therefore the claims of the clergy to the registry were rejected (*Cod.*, lib. vi., tit. xxiii., l. 23).

personalty ; so as to prescription, and the rights acquired thereby, whether of property, or of "servitudes" over property.[1] In short, upon all the multitudinous affairs and transactions of life there were copious provisions in the Roman law, sufficient for the regulation of any civilized community, and which, so soon as a community became civilized, must necessarily have become insensibly introduced and incorporated in their every-day usages, and thus at last converted into law, more especially when constantly illustrated and enforced under an admirable administration of justice.

Thus, therefore, there was an admirable system of law, and there was an equally admirable system for the administration of justice.

In nothing was the Roman law more certain to commend itself to the admiration and adoption of barbarians than in what related to the general administration of justice, whether civil or criminal. Every one knows that the most barbarian nations have the sense or feeling of justice, but with them it is only a sense or feeling, and the modes they adopt to secure justice are always rude and ignorant. Justice, to be certain, must have a fixed procedure,[2] founded upon rules and principles, and be raised from a mere impulse into a science; and in the Roman law it was raised into a science, and developed into a system.

In civil or criminal cases the Roman law, above all, had a rational system of trial by sworn judges; while, in criminal cases, it required clear proof,[3] and its maxims

---

[1] The titles of law above mentioned, and indeed almost every head of law that could be mentioned, were of Roman origin, and will be found copiously expounded in the codes and digests, and *nowhere else*, in that age. Nothing is more clear than that in Europe there were only barbarous usages beyond the limits of Roman law.

[2] In nothing was the Roman law more remarkable than in the importance it attached to procedure, the practical part of law, the actual means and processes by which justice is obtained and administered. The Roman law provided a remedy for every injury, and a proper procedure for every remedy. It gave civil actions by way of obtaining compensation; it had a rational system of procedure, under which the questions in dispute were first ascertained, and then, if there was any fact in dispute, they were remitted to a rational trial by sworn judges, upon sworn evidence, and the parties could examine each other as witnesses.

[3] There was an imperial edict to the effect that prosecutors must be prepared with proper proof. "Sciant cuncti accusatores eam se rem deferre in publicam notionem debere, quæ munita sit idoneis, testibus: vel instructa

were marked by great mildness, mercy, and humanity, strongly contrasting with the rude and savage character of criminal justice among the barbarians, and likely to arrest their attention and attract their imitation.

Upon this subject, and especially with reference to foreigners, or foreign subjects, a learned writer already quoted, says:—" The changes wrought by intercourse with foreign nations, and the new duties of extended dominion, produced a corresponding change in the mode in which justice was administered. At home, the prætors, and in the provinces, the præsides, or præfects, who held *conventus* or assizes in the principal towns at stated intervals, sat as magistrates. As *judices*,[1] there were in certain cases the *recuperatores*, in others the *centumviri*, but principally those citizens whose names appeared in the yearly list drawn up by the prætor"[2] (*Sandar's Introduc. to Institutes*, p. 23). The same learned author thus explains the Roman system of administration of justice, which deserves attention, from its having been the foundation of our own:—" In enforcing rights, two very different functions have to be exercised by those to whom the powers of the state are delegated. First, there must be some one invested with magisterial authority, giving the sanction and solemnity of his position to the whole proceeding, and who shall represent the law, and say what the law is, and who shall have power to employ the force which the state places at the disposal of those whom it selects to administer justice. Secondly, an inquiry has to be made into particular facts, evidence has to be received and weighed, and an opinion formed and pronounced as to the real merits of the case. The person who exercised the one function was spoken of by the Romans as *magistratus*: the person who exercised the other, as *judex*. To the law, represented, pronounced, and vindicated by the magistrate, they applied the term

---

apertissimis documentis vel indiciis, ad probationem indubitatis, et luce clarioribus expedita" (l. xxv., *de probat.*). And the Roman criminal law was full of humane maxims, some of which have passed into our own, as those well known ones, that it is proper to give the accused the benefit of a doubt, and that it is better that the guilty should escape than the innocent be condemned. "Semper in dubiis benigniora præferenda sunt:" "Satius est impunitum manere facinus nocentis quam innocentem condemnare" (*Dig. de Reg. Ju.*, l. lvi., l. clviii.).

[1] That is, *judices facti*, as Bracton calls the jury.
[2] The resemblance between this and the jury-lists will be apparent.

THE ROMAN SYSTEM OF JUSTICE.

jus: to the examination of contested facts by the judge, the term *judicium*. Among the Romans, the *magistratus* was a different person from the *judex* until the introduction of the system of *extraordinaria judicia*. The two functions were kept almost entirely apart, and from a comparatively early period of Roman history the notion of a judge distinct from the magistrate was familiar to the national mind. First the consuls, then the *prætor*, and in some cases the *ædiles*, acted as magistrates. As *judex*, any member of the senatorial body could act when chosen by mutual consent of the parties, or, if they could not agree, by lot. There was also a standing body of judges — the *centumviri*, elected annually by the *comitia*. Lastly, in cases where the interests of *peregrini* were involved, the *recuperatores* furnished the body who were to act as *judices*."[1] There therefore was trial by jury, and regular jury-lists — that is, lists of those qualified to act as "*judices facti*," as jurors are called in our law. It is true that in the course of the Roman occupation this system of trial was departed from in consequence of the spread of that system of despotism[2] which probably more than anything else undermined the strength of the Roman empire,[3] but it was never altogether destroyed.

---

[1] That is, *judices facti*, as the jurors were called in Bracton.

[2] The same learned writer says: "In the later period of the Roman system of civil process, the summary jurisdiction was the only jurisdiction the magistrate exercised; the magistrate and the judge were the same person. By a constitution, published in A. D. 294, Diocletian directed all magistrates in the provinces to decide causes themselves, and the practice was in course of time extended throughout the whole of the empire" (*Sandar's Introd.*, p. 71). This extraordinary jurisdiction, which at first was only exercised either for restitution, or for the execution of judgments or sentences of judges, was, the learned writer thinks, extended by that edict to all cases. This the writer ventures to doubt. See, on this subject, the next note.

[3] The edict by which this was done was this: "Placet nobis, præsides de his causis in quibus, quod ipsi non possent cognoscere, ante hac pedaneos judices dabant, notionis suæ examen adhibere, ita, tamen, ut, si vel propter occupationes publicas, vel propter causarum multitudinem omnia hujus modi negotia non potuerint cognoscere, judices dandi habeant potestatem. Quod non ita accipi convenit, ut in his etiam causis, in quibus solebant ex officio suo cognoscere, dandi judices licentia eis permissa credatur: quod usque adeo in præsidum cognitione retinendum est, ut eorum judicia non deminuta videantur; dum tamen de ingenuitate super qua poterant etiam ante cognoscere, et de libertinitate præsides ipsi dejudicent — A. D. 305" (*Cod. Just.*, lib. iii., tit. iii., s. 2). The comment is: "Pedanei judices quasi plano pede aut stantes judicabant, non pro tribunali aut sedentes, imo collatitio aut fortuito scamno vel cespite. Pedaneis singulæ causæ cognoscendæ a magistratibus de-

The administration of the Roman government in the provinces was, as Montesquieu says, absolute, but there were, as Guizot points out, some great exceptions and some great qualifications. The præfects, prætors, or governors, had the whole civil and criminal jurisdiction in their hands, with this exception, that in the towns which possessed the municipal privileges of Roman citizens, the right of administering justice to the citizens, at least in civil matters, appertained to municipal magistrates, elected by the citizens themselves. And, next, there was, as regarded those who had the privileges of Roman citizens in the provinces, the benefit of a regular system of judicature, and a settled administration of justice, by skilled judges and sworn jurors. It is this which is the essence of our own system of judicature, and it is of Roman origin.

Nor was this all. There was an intelligent and effective system of procedure. It was a first principle of the Roman law in the administration of justice that it was in vain to proceed to a trial until the question in dispute was ascertained and defined,[1] a principle the result of reason, instructed by experience, which would not suggest itself to the untutored and unlettered minds of barbarians.

Guizot thus describes the system: "He to whom the jurisdiction appertained, prætor, provincial governor, or municipal magistrate, on a case being submitted to him,

---

legabantur, cognitionem habuerunt, non jurisdictionem." After the above edict, however, another issued: "In quibus causas præsides possunt judices dare." "Quædam sunt negotia in quibus superficium est moderatorem expectare provinciæ: ideoque pedaneos judices (hoc est qui negotia humiliora disceptant) constituendi damus præsidibus potestatum: datum A. D. 362" (*Ibid.*, s. 5). The decree seems limited to the *judices pedanei*, a species of inferior judges, or rather delegated arbitrators, so called, "vel quod non vehantur curru, sed pedibus proficiscantur in forum, vel quod judicantes in uno loco considerent, ubi magistratus subsellia pedum habebant, vel quia pede plano judicarent, non pro tribunali" (*Cujaccius*). The edict abolishing reference to these judices can hardly be deemed an abolition of the office of judex, nor does it appear to have been so considered by other eminent writers on the subject. Moreover, the reader must observe the *date* of the edict, which was not until the system had been established in this country above two centuries.

[1] "Res in judicium deducta non videtur, si tantum postulatio simplex celebrata sit, vel actionis species ante judicium reo cognita. Inter litem enim contestatam et editam actionem permultum interest. Lis enim tunc contestata videtur, cum judex per narrationem negotii, causam audire cæperit" (*Cod. Just.*, lib. iii., tit. ix., *de litis contestatione*). The *litis contestatio* marked the time when the suit was deemed to have really commenced.

merely determined the rule of law, the legal principle according to which it ought to be adjudged. He decided, that is to say, the question of law involved in the case, and then appointed a private citizen, called the *judex*, the veritable juror, to examine and decide the question of fact. The legal principle laid down by the magistrate was applied to the fact found by the judex, and so the case was determined " (*Lect. sur la Civiliz. en France*, Lect. ii.). Thus the principle of the Roman system was the separation of the law from the fact, which is essential to anything like a science of law, or any regular procedure.

The system of trial under the Roman law[1] was the original of trial by jury, with which, in all essential respects, it was identical. The essence of it was trial by sworn judges taken from the people, and open to objection by either party. And in criminal cases which were capital, there could be no sentence without an appeal to the people.

Another eminent writer on the subject says, "And the distinction between the *magistratus*, the person under whose jurisdiction a particular cause arose, and particular parties contended—and the judge or judges to whom the investigation of the facts in dispute was referred, is to be traced throughout the changes of Roman jurisprudence. The duty of the magistrate in matters of contentious jurisdictions, was to conduct the preliminary proceedings, to ascertain the points really in dispute between the parties, to instruct the judges, and sanction their appointment" (*Phillimore's Introduc. to Roman Law*, 19). When the question was ascertained, then it would be remitted

---

[1] Montesquieu thus describes it: "Chaque année le préteur formait une liste, ou tableau de ceux qu'il choisissait pour faire la fonction de jugés pendant l'année de sa magistrature. On en prenait le nombre suffisant pour chaque affaire. Ce se pratique à peu près de meme en Angleterre. Et ce qui était très favorable à la liberté c'est que le preteur prenait les juges du consentement des parties. Le grand nombre des recusations qui l'on peut faire aujourd'hui en Angleterre revient à peu près à cet usage. Ces juges ne decidaient que des questions de fait, par example si une somme avait été payée ou non, si une action avait été commise ou non, mais pour les questions de droit, commes elles demandaient une certaine capacité, elles étaient portées au tribunal des centumviri. Les rois se réserverent le jugement des affaires criminelles, et les consuls leur succedèrent en cela. Cela fit faire la loi Valerienne, qui permit d'appeler au peuple de toutes les ordonnances des consuls qui mettraient en peril la vie d'un citoyen. Les consuls ne purent plus prononcer une peine capitale contre un citoyen romain que par la volonté du peuple" (*De l'Esprit des Lois*, l. xi., c. 18).

for trial (a). In short, under the Roman system, there were the *judices legis* and *judices facti*, who answered to our jurors. And in criminal matters, it was a fundamental principle of Roman law that a free citizen could not be condemned without the judgment of his fellow-citizens.

At all events, trial by jury, so often supposed to be essentially of English origin, was part of the Roman system. It has been well said by a learned and talented writer, whose untimely loss in this country all lovers of learning and genius deeply deplore, " It is hardly possible to conceive a stronger proof of that ignorance of the most ordinary topics connected with general jurisprudence which has been so long the characteristic of the most eminent lawyers in this country, than the notion so vehemently entertained and so popularly received, that the jury is of peculiarly English origin. The principle and essence of a jury — which involves the selection of judges unknown beforehand from a particular body, and gives to those judges the power of deciding, with certain restrictions, and under the direction of certain rules, on the question in dispute — is to be found in the institutions of many other countries. The trial of a citizen by other citizens and a judicial authority, in causes civil as well as criminal, inherent in every freeman, was the corner-stone of the Athenian constitution, and was thence restored to the Roman " (*Phillimore's Intro. to Roman Law*, p. 17).

The Roman law treated very carefully the functions and duties of the magistrates or officers to whom were entrusted the exercise of criminal jurisdiction in the provinces of the empire,[1] which was subject to supreme

---

(a) " Quas actiones, ne populus prout vellet, institueret, certas solemnesque esse voluerunt" (*Dig. de orig. Jur. leg.*, ii., sec. 6). The object was, to fix the question. "Les Romains introduisirent des formules d'actions, et établirent la necessité de diriger chaque affaire par l'action qui lui était propre. Cela était necessaire dans leur manière de juger; il fallait fixer l'état de la question, pour que le peuple l'eut toujours devant les yeux. Autrement, dans le cours d'une grande affaire, cet état de la question changerait continuellement, et on ne le reconnaitrait plus" (*Montesquieu, de l'Esprit des Lois*, l. vi., c. 4).

[1] The pro-consuls had legates who could decide civil or criminal causes subject as to criminal sentences to the revision of the pro-consul. " Legati non solum civiles sed etiam criminales causas audiant, ita ut si sententiam in reos ferendam providerint ad pro-consules eos transmittere non morentur"

control; and, when allowed to be exercised by delegates, was in cases of conviction submitted to the revision of the superior ruler. And, more particularly, in the Roman law are to be found all the principles of a just and intelligent system of criminal procedure; a fair opportunity for defence, and a just examination into the truth.[1]

It cannot but be observed that a just and rational system such as this was well calculated to attract the respect and confidence of provincial subjects among whom it was established; and all who were Roman citizens were entitled to the benefit of it. But, further, so well fitted for imperial sway was the Roman law, that it made careful provision for the administration of justice, not only as between Roman citizens, or foreign subjects entitled to the rights and privileges of Roman citizens, but also as between them and foreigners, or foreign subjects, not entitled to those privileges. And this jurisdiction was found so excellent, that it was afterwards adopted for the whole body of the Roman citizens. "As there was intercourse, without community of law, between the Roman *civis* and the *peregrinus*, particular magistrates were required to adjust litigation that arose between them, and these were the *recuperatores*. It was usual for the Romans, in their treaties, to stipulate expressly that a tribunal should be constituted to determine the differences of individuals belonging to the foreign nation and to their own. The judges, therefore, were not to proceed according to the strict rules of Roman law, but according to substantial equity. The *recuperatores* were not at first included in the list of judges between Roman citizens (*de curiæ judices*). The term was confined to those here mentioned, and to *the judges in the provinces*, who were called *peregrini recuperatores*, in the same sense as one of the prætors was called *peregrinus*. The proceeding before *recuperatores* was after-

---

(*Cod. Just.*, *lib.* i., *tit.* xxxv., *de officio pro-consulis et legati*). This is an instance of the careful regulation of these offices.

[1] "Defensionis facultas danda est his quibus aliquam inquietudinem fiscus infert" (*Lib.* 7, *co. de Jur. fisc.*). So Paulus: "Ne hi qui defendendi sunt subitis accusatorum criminibus opprimantur; quam vis defensionem quocunque tempore, postulante reo, negare non oportet; adeo ut propterea et differantur et proferantur custodiæ" (*L.* 18, sec. 19, *Dig. de Quest.*). "Sciant cuncti accusatores eam se rem deferre in publicam notionem debere, quæ munita sit idoneis testibus, vel instructa apertissimis documentis vel indiciis ad probationem indubitatis, et luce clarioribus expedita" (*L.* 25, *co. de probat*).

wards extended to the deputies of Roman citizens, and the matter was thus brought to a more speedy conclusion" (*Phillimore's Study of the Roman Law*, p. 30). Thus, therefore, the jurisdiction provided for *foreign* subjects was so good that it was afterwards adopted for *citizens*.

In order to provide every possible security against injustice, appeals[1] were allowed from the provinces to the supreme tribunal of the empire, and the appellate jurisdiction was protected by numerous edicts.

Nor was this all. For in every city there was special provision made, by means of a particular public officer,[2] for the protection of the provincial subjects from oppressive abuse, and it was his peculiar duty and function to interpose for their protection; and repeated edicts were issued to enforce the observance of this duty, especially in

[1] Thus, as to judicial functionaries in the provinces, and appeals allowed from them to the imperial city, there is an edict, "Ad Universos Provinciales:" "A proconsulibus, et comitibus, et his qui vice praefectorum cognoscunt, sive ex appellatione, sive ex delegatione, sive ex ordine judicaverint, provocari permittemus, etc. A praefectis autem praetorio, provocare non sinimus" (*Cod. Just.*, lib. vii., tit. 62, s. 19). And again, "De provinciis ex quibus appellatur ad praefectum urbi." "Cum appellatio interposita fuerit per Europam, etc., praefecturae hujus urbis judicium sacrum appellator observet" (*Ibid.*, s. 23). The judicial and equitable functions of the governor of a province were recognized: "Si residuum debiti paratus es solvere, praeses provinciae dabit tibi arbitrum, apud quem quantum sit, quod superest ex debito, examinabitur," etc. (*Cod. Just.*, lib. viii., tit. 27, s. 5).

[2] The "defensor," a functionary whose office was peculiar to the Roman system, and, if its duties were in any degree carried out, it must have been of infinite service. In the *Cod. Just.*, lib. i., tit. lv., there is a distinct head, "De Defensoribus Civitatum," and under this head an edict, s. 4, "De Officio Defensorum," applying to all the provinces. "In defensoribus universarum provinciarum erit administrationis haec forma; scilicet, ut *in primis parentis vicem plebi exhibeas;* descriptionibus rusticos urbanosque non patiaris adflige; officialium insolentiae, et judicum procacitate occuras, ingrediendi, cum voles, ad judicem liberam habeas facultatem," etc. (*Ibid.*) And there is a special edict in favor of the husbandmen, s. 3, "De Rusticis:" "Utili ratione perspectum est, ut innocens et quieta rusticitas, peculiaris patrocinii, id est defensoris locorum beneficio, perfruatur." Another edict is remarkable: it runs thus — "Si qui eorum provinciarum rectoribus obsequuntur, quique in diversis agunt officiis principatus, et qui sub quocunque praetextu publici muneris possunt esse terribiles, rusticano cupiam necessitatem obsequii quasi mancipio sui juris imponant, aut servum ejus vel forte bovem in usus proprios necessitatesque converterint; ablatis omnibus facultatibus perpetuò subjugentur exilio" (*Cod. Just.*, lib. xi., tit. 53, s. 2). This shows that the coloni were capable of property, though, as they themselves were attached to the estates of their lords, so was their property, and hence it could not legally be employed for the advantage of others, off the estates. The language of the edict, it will be observed, is extremely expressive as to the possibility of oppression on the part of the officers of the provincial governors, and shows a sincere desire to prevent it.

THE ROMAN SYSTEM OF RULE. xlv

regard to the weaker and humbler classes of the community.

Nor was this all. For the Roman system, as established under the emperors,[1] made provision for obtaining, by means of provincial councils or assemblies, the general sense of the community, and thus ascertaining their wants and wishes, as a means of assisting the judgment, either of the provincial ruler or of the emperor, as to the measures to be adopted for their welfare.

And although it is true that, under the Roman rule, the provincial subjects of the empire were embraced in a comprehensive and elaborate system of taxation, it was administered by regular officers, carefully regulated and controlled by law. And as the revenue was mainly levied by contributions in kind,[2] analogous to those derived by private owners of estates from the coloni or cultivators, the combined effect of both systems was rather, by enforcing industry, and encouraging energy, to promote the cultivation of the soil, and to develop the resources of the country.

An elaborate organization for the purpose of collection

[1] Thus there was an edict of Theodosius: "Si quid extraordinarium consilium postulatur, cum vel ad nos est mittenda legatis, vel nostræ sedi aliquid intimandum; id quod inter omnes communi consilio tractatuque convenerit, minime in examen cognitoris ordinarii referatur, provincialium enim desideria, quibus necessaria sæpe fortuitis casibus remedia deposcuntur, vobis a cognoscere atque explorare permittimus; ut sint examinis tui, quæ ex his, auxilio tuo protinus implenda sint, et quæ clementiæ nostræ auribus intimanda videantur. In loco autem publico, de commune utilitate provincialium sententia proferatur; atque id quod majoris partis probaverit ad sensus, solennis firmet auctoritas." This was in the year 395, some time before the abandonment of Britain by the Romans, and it contains the whole principle of popular councils, not as mere turbulent assemblies, but for the intelligent purpose of ascertaining the wishes and views of the people. Montesquieu therefore did injustice to the Roman rule in the provinces when he described it as a Turkish despotism, " La liberté était dans le centre, et la tyrannie aux extrémités" (De l'Esprit des Lois, liv. xi., c. 19). He forgot that the provincial subjects, in a large proportion, had the rights of Roman citizens.

[2] The tenth book of the Code is most copious upon these subjects. The revenue was collected by the "procurator." It was in a great degree from impositions of a certain proportion of the produce of the earth — corn, hay, etc. — which was paid in kind or in money, according to arrangement. In some provinces a tenth was exacted (frumentum decimarum); in others — those which were conquered — an arbitrary quantity (frumentum stipendiarum). Besides this, the natives supplied the corn wanted for the army at a fixed price (frumentum emptum), and a certain quantity for the use of the governor, for which a compensation was usually paid in money (frumentum æstimatum). This was on a principle similar to that on which the coloni were bound to supply their lords a certain proportion of the produce of their farms. Allusions to these services or impositions are frequent in the Code.

of a revenue by regular officers of the state[1] under the control of law, that revenue in the main derived from the cultivation of the soil, aided by a social rural organization directed to the same object, as it had such an obvious effect in developing the resources of the country, would be likely to be perpetuated under any subsequent rule. And so, it will be found, it was under the Saxons.

So much for the civil laws and institutions of the Romans. It remains to notice their *ecclesiastical* laws and institutions, which, after the conversion of the empire to Christianity, and the establishment of the Christian church, became adapted to the relation of union between the church and the state.

The ecclesiastical divisions and organization of the Romans, after this period, appear to have been based upon the civil; and thus, as there were civil "dioceses" or provinces, there were ecclesiastical; and as there were "manors," so there were parishes, which appear originally to have been derived out of, or founded upon them, by endowments of lands, and glebes, and tithes,[2] emanating from the lords of manors.

---

[1] Thus, an edict of Theodosius relating to the order in which dignities should be conferred, has this under the second head, "Secundo veniant vacantes, qui præsentes in comitatu illustris dignitatis cingulum meruerunt. Sed administratores quidem etiam, comites rei privatæ vacantibus, omnibus honorarii, anteponi censemus. . . . . ut præfectorius questorio præponatur; non vacans *comes thesaurorum*, vel comes rei privatæ, honorario questorio, vel magistri officiorum præferatur" (*Cod. Just.*, lib. xii., tit. 8, s. 2). The "comes thesaurorum" is by the commentator explained as "præpositus regulium thesaurorum" (which answers well to the original functions of the sheriff, who was, and is still, the collector of the royal dues) or "Præfectus ærarii." Now, in the most ancient of our chronicles, it is mentioned that there were "consuls," or "counts," and vice-consuls, or viscounts, and the Latin title of the sheriff is vicecomes.

[2] By a Roman council A.D. 380, it was decreed, "Ut decennæ atque primitias a fidelibus darentur" (*Baron. Annal.*, tom. iv., an. 382, p. 375). There can be no doubt that tithes, or endowments out of the produce, as well as glebes, or endowments out of the land itself, were of Roman origin, as also all church dues or oblations. The Romans, when pagans, often devoted a tenth of the produce to the support of temples. Thus, for instance, in Cicero, "Decimam Hercule devovere" (*Cic. Nat. Deor.* 3, 36). "Neque Herculi quisquam decimam vovit, unquam si sæpius factus fuisset." The dedication was recognized by the Roman law, as in the law received from Ulpian by Justinian: "Si decimam quis bonorum vovit, decima non prius esse in bonis definit quam fuerit separata, et si forti qui decimam vovit, de cesserit ante se positionem, hæres ipsius, hæreditario nomini decimæ obstrictus est, voti enim obligationem ad hæredem transire constat" (*Tit. de poll. cit.*, b. ii., c. 2). The idea of a compulsory obligation to pay tithes arose at a later period, and was founded upon the dedication. But the dedication was originally customary.

Upon this subject, however, of ecclesiastical law, it is very necessary, before coming to the consideration of the history of English law, to consider what had been the imperial law of the Christian empire of Rome, as to the province of the church and the power of the bishops, and the privileges of the clergy, not merely in matters spiritual or ecclesiastical, but even in matters temporal.[1] Because, as the Roman law in general was the foundation of the laws of Christian Europe, so, especially upon this matter of the power of the church and the privileges of the clergy, it naturally formed the model for the laws of the various monarchies which arose out of the ruins of the empire, and, in particular, for those of our own, and it would be, it is evident, impossible to form a fair judgment upon the controversies which arose, on the settlement of our laws and constitutions, upon this subject, without having some regard to the laws which formed the source and origin of the pretensions out of which these controversies arose.

An enlightened and philosophical historian,[2] who has been cited more than once, has described the extent and the causes of the influence acquired by the church on the decline of the empire: "From the commencement of the fifth century, the Christian clergy had a powerful means of influence. The bishops and clergy had become the first municipal magistrates. Of the Roman empire there remained, strictly speaking, nothing but its municipal government. By the ruin of the cities, and the oppression of despotism, the curiales, or municipal bodies, had fallen into apathy and disarrangement. The bishops, on the contrary, and the body of the clergy, full of life and zeal, naturally came forward to superintend and to direct all. It would be injustice to reproach them with it, to accuse them of usurpation; it was the natural course of things. The clergy alone had moral strength and energy; they became powerful everywhere. Such is the law of the world."

"This resolution is manifest in all the legislation of the emperors of that age. Open the Theodosian or Jus-

---

[1] *Vide Cod. Theod.*, lib. xvi., tit. 11; *Cod. Justin.*, lib. i., tit. 4; *Bingham, Origines sive Antiq. Eccles.*, tom. i., lib. ii., cap. 7.
[2] Guizot's *Hist. Gen. de la Civiliz. en Europe*, 2me Lecon., p. 55-58.

xlviii   INTRODUCTION TO THE PRESENT EDITION.

tinian Code, and you find an immense number of laws referring municipal affairs to the bishops and the clergy."[1]

The Christian emperors commenced with the *protection* of the Christian church, and then lent to its laws all the sanction of the state.[2] The canons of the councils were made part of the laws of the empire, and the powers of the state were exerted to enforce them, so that in the course of time there was no portion of ecclesiastical discipline which was not confirmed by imperial decrees. As, for example, the observation of Sundays,[3] and other festivals of the church, the canonical penalties decreed by the church against the transgression of her laws, among her members;[4] the canons relating to the election of bishops, to residence, or to simony.[5]

The fundamental principle laid down by the imperial

[1] For this M. Guizot cites *Cod. Just.*, lib. i., tit. 4, "De episcopali audientia, et diversis capitulis quæ ad jus curamque pertinent Pontificalem," which amply bears out his testimony. One section is "De his qui ex consensu litigant apud episcopum" s. 7 (Honorius, A. D. 398). So s. 8, "Episcopali judicium ratum sit omnibus, qui se audiri a sacerdotibus elegerint, eamque illorum judicationi adhibendam esse reverentiam jubemus, quam vestris deferri necesse est potestatibus, quibus non licet provocare. Per judicium quoque officia, ne sit cassa episcopalis cognitio, definitioni executio tribuatur" (*Arcad. and Hon.*, A. D. 408). So s. 13, "De clericis lite pulsantibus;" so s. 19, "De defensoribus civitatum;" "ita enim eos præcipimus ordinari, ut reverendissimorum episcoporum nec non clericorum ac possessorum, et curialium, decreto constituantur" (A. D. 505). So *Just.*, lib. i., tit. 4, "de episcopali audientia;" lib. i., tit. 55, "De defensoribus." And so in numerous other titles.

[2] The canons of the four general councils which had sat before the time of Justinian, and which had been successively confirmed by the emperors under whom they were convened, were placed by him among the laws of the empire: "Sancimus igitur vicem legum obtinere sanctas ecclesiasticas regulas, quæ à sanctis quatuor conciliis ex positæ sunt aut formatæ. Prædictarum enim quatuor synodorum dogmata sicut sanctas Scripturas accipimus, et regulas sicut leges observamus" (*Just. Novella*, 131, c. 1; *et vide Cod. Just.*, lib. i., tit. 1, s. 7). This was after the Roman occupation of this country ceased, but before the foundation of the Christian Saxon kingdom, and, upon its foundation, the princes and prelates naturally took these Roman laws as their guides, as is manifest from the preambles of their written laws.

[3] Thus, as to the observation of Sunday, there was this edict, "Omnes judices, urbanæque plebes, et cuncturum artium officia, venerabili die Solis (*i. e.*, Dominico die) quiescant. Ruri tamen positi, agrorum culturæ liberè inserviant, quoniam frequenter evenit ut non aptus alio die frumenta sulcis, aut vinæ scrobibus mandentur, ne occasione momenti pereat commoditas cælesti provisione concessa" (*Cod. Just.*, lib. iii., tit. 12, s. 3).

[4] (*Cod. Theod.*, lib. xvi., tit. 2; *Just. Nov.*, c. i., s. 10.)

[5] (*Cod. Just.*, lib. i., tit. 3, n. 31). All this may have been wrong in principle, but that is a question which does not belong to a work on legal history, which deals with the facts, as to the origin, the causes, and the development of laws.

law of Christian Rome was, that to the church belonged the direction of spiritual matters, to the state the regulation of matters temporal; so that, as the state recognized the church, it was the duty of the state to protect, to sanction, or to enforce the laws of the church; a principle, it will be observed, based entirely upon the *voluntary* adoption by the state of the laws of the church, in consequence of the state's acknowledgment of her divine authority, and, therefore, not at all involving any impeachment or disparagement of the independence of the state.[1]

The policy of these laws is a question which belongs rather to the philosophy than the history of laws. The points important to be observed in a work on legal history are, that these laws were laws of the state; that they were based upon the will of the state, founded, rightly or wrongly, upon certain views of the state, as to their tendency to promote the welfare of the empire; that they belong, therefore, to the domain of secular law; and that, as they formed the basis of the policy of the empire as to the church, they naturally and unavoidably influenced the laws and legislation of the Christian states derived out of the ruins of the empire, and, in particular, of our own.[2]

Upon this fundamental principle, all the former privileges or immunities conferred by the state upon the church or the clergy were granted as voluntary concessions by the state; the very granting of which implied and involved that they emanated from the state, so that no extent to which they were carried could affect its indepen-

---

[1] "Maxima quidem in hominibus sunt dona Dei á superná collata clementiá sacerdotium, et imperium, et illud quidem divinis ministrans, hoc autem humanis præsidens ac diligentiam exhibens. Ex uno eodemque principio utraque procedentia humanam exornant vitam. Bene autem omnia geruntur, et competenter, si rei principium fiat decens et amabile Deo. Hoc autem futurum esse credimus, si sacrarum regularum observatio custodiatur, quam justi et laudandi et adorandi inspectores et ministri Dei verbi tradiderunt apostoli, et sancti patres custodierunt et explanaverunt" (*Just. Nov.*, vi., Pref.). This was putting it on the ground of the will of the state, with a view to its own benefit, and the good of the empire. And so it was always put.

[2] It will be observed all through the voluminous imperial edicts on the subject, that this legislation is based upon the imperial mind, and will as to what would be the proper policy to pursue, and as to the advantages to be derived from the establishment of the church; and all the rest is deduced from that establishment. It is not put upon any inherent or precedent right of the church to control the civil power; and so as to the laws founded afterwards upon this view.

dence. Thus it was with the immunities of the clergy from taxation or services;[1] and thus it was with the still more important question of their exemption from secular jurisdiction, which afterwards, in the middle ages, occasioned such controversies, in our own and in other countries.

Upon that principle, above all, was this privilege of the clergy based; and upon that principle, indeed, it was carried much further by the imperial edicts — even to the extent of allowing laymen to decline the jurisdiction of the lay tribunals, and refer their disputes to the bishops.[2] And the governors of provinces were directed to enforce the episcopal decrees.

This, be it observed, was clearly only a delegation of the power of the state to the bishops; it was open to the state to select, or allow the people to select, ecclesiastical judges as well as secular; it was a matter entirely of state policy, of state regulation, and therefore, to whatever extent it was carried, it could not possibly involve any disparagement of the independence of the state.[3]

---

[1] The principle of such exemption, at all events, from all services or burdens detrimental to the independence, or derogatory to the dignity, of ecclesiastics, is abundantly established in the imperial edicts (*Cod. Theod.*, lib. xvi., cit. 2.). The Emperor Honorius restored or confirmed the real immunities of the clergy from mean taxes and duties, or extraordinary burdens (*Cod. Theod.*, lib. xvi., tit. 2), " nihil extraordinarium ab hâc (jugatione) superi inducti tum ve flagitetur, nulla positium instauratio, nullo translationum solicitudo gignantur" (*Ibid.*). The principle was followed by our law in exempting the benefices of the church from feudal burdens.

[2] This the ecclesiastical historians tell us was done by Constantine; whose father died at York, and in whose time there was the closest connection between Rome and Britain. " Fuit hoc etiam argumentum vel maximum reverentiæ quam pius princeps erga religionem gerebat. Nam et omnes ubique clericos immunitate donavit, lege hac de re specialiter datâ; et litigantibus permisit ut ad episcoporum judicium provocarent, si magistratus civiles rejicere vellent eorum autem sententia rata esset, aliorumque judicum sententiis prævaleret perinde oc si ab imperatore ipso data fuisset; utque res ab episcopis judicatas, rectores provinciarum eorumque officiales executione mandarent" (*Sozomen Eccl. Hist.*, lib. i., c. ix.; *Annales du Moyen Age*, v. i., c. ii.; *et vide Theod. Cod. Extrav.*, i., p. 260).

[3] The imperial policy in fact varied upon it; thus we find a decree of Honorius rather restrictive of the episcopal jurisdiction to spiritual causes. "Quoties de religione agitur, episcopos convenit judicare; cæteras vero causas quæ ad ordinarios cognitores (seu judices), vel ad usum publici juris (*i.e.*, juris communis) pertinent legibus oportet audiri" (*Cod. Theod.*, lib. xvi., tit. xi., c. i.). On the other hand, in the Justinian code, we find two constitutions of the same emperor giving to the bishops generally, the power of judging definitely even in temporal matters, like the prætorium prefect, but with two qualifications: that the jurisdiction could only be exercised by consent of the parties, and only in civil, not criminal matters. "Si quis ex consensu

In an age when the policy of the state actually allowed its own tribunals to be displaced, and the episcopal authority substituted even as between laymen, and as regarded temporal matters, it is not surprising that it should have allowed the episcopal authority an extensive jurisdiction over the ecclesiastics, either in civil or criminal matters, and whether as regarded their persons or their property.[1]

The imperial law upon this principle laid it down that in civil matters clerics must be brought before the episcopal jurisdiction in the first instance, and in criminal matters, before the episcopal or the lay tribunal; but that the guardians of churches could not be cited except before the bishops, and that the bishops could not be prosecuted before the secular judge, for any cause: on which it will be observed that the very laws by which the state endeavored to secure the independence of the church attested its own independence, and showed that it was not a claim of inherent right in the church, but of voluntary concession by the state. Nor can it be surprising that the law of the church should have supported in this matter the law of the state, and that canonists should have followed jurists and legists.[2]

Indeed, the laws of the empire upon this subject went to the full extent of the most extreme pretensions of canonists in later times; and it is impossible to study them at this day without surprise. The judicial powers of the bishops either over ecclesiastics or laics, were by no means the greatest of their powers. The imperial laws

---

apud sacræ legis antistitem litigare voluerint, non vetabuntur; sed experientur illius in civili duntaxat negotio; more arbitri sponte residentes judicum" (*Cod. Just.*, lib. i., tit. iv., s. 7). "Episcopale judicium ratum sit omnibus, qui se audiri a sacerdotibus elegerint, eamque illorum judicationi adhibendam esse reverentiam jubemus, quam vestris deferri necesse est potestatibus (*i. e.*, potestatibus præfecti prætorio) a quibus non licet provocare" (*Ibid.*, s. 8). These fluctuations and variations of imperial legislation on the subject clearly show that it was a matter entirely of state policy, and could not compromise state independence.

[1] Thus we find a law of the Emperor Honorius: "Clericos non nisi apud episcopos accusare convenit. Igitur si episcopus vel presbyter apud episcopum (siquidem alibi non oportet) a qua libet persona fuerint accusati, noverit docenda probationibus, monstanda documentis crimina se debere inferre" (*Cod. Theod.*, lib. xvi., tit. ii., c. 61). It is true that another emperor rather varied this; but then Justinian, it will be seen, restored it; and again it may be observed that these variations and fluctuations of imperial policy only prove its entire independence of ecclesiastical power.

[2] *Cod. Just.*, lib. i., tit. 4. Episcopali audientia (*Just. Nov.*, 131, c. 1).

conferred upon them the most important powers, and confided to them the most important functions of secular administration, or the affairs of government.[1] The imperial laws charged the bishops in the provinces of the empire with the protection of orphans, slaves, prisoners, and generally of all wretched or defenceless persons, whose age or condition rendered them more liable to oppression. By virtue of these laws, the bishops were bound, in conjunction with the civil magistrate, to interfere in the nomination of tutors and trustees, to watch over the liberty of children abandoned by their parents, to visit prisoners and ascertain the causes of their detention, and watch over the police; to admonish the civil magistrates of any disorders, and to report to the emperor any neglect of the magistrate to repress such disorders.[2]

---

[1] Thus an imperial edict (A. D. 368) charged the bishops to watch over merchants, in order to prevent or correct injustice, especially to the poor. "Negotiatores, si qui ad domum nostram pertinent, neamodum mercandi videantur excedere, Christiani (quibus verus cultus est, adjuvare pauperes, et positos in necessitate), provideant episcopi" (*Cod. Just.*, lib. i., tit. iv., s. i.). So a law of the Emperor Honorius and Theodorus the younger (A. D. 409) ordered that the defensors of cities should be chosen by the bishops at a meeting of the clergy and chief citizens. It has already been mentioned that, as a part of the policy of the Christian empire, there was in every city a public functionary charged with the protection of citizens against all oppressions, either of magistrates or private citizens (*Cod. Theod.*, lib. i., tit. xi.; *Cod. Just.*, lib. i., tit. iv.). Another edict of the emperor was this: "Defensores ita præcipimus ordinari, ut sacris orthodoxæ religionis imbuti mysteriis, revendissimorum episcoporum nec non clericorum, et honoratorum, ac possessorum, et curialium decreto constituantur; de quorum ordinatione referendum est ad illustrissimam prætorianam potestatem; ut literis ejusdem magnificæ sedis eorum solidetur auctoritas" (*Cod. Just.*, lib. i., tit. lv., s. 8, tit. iv., s. 19). Other edicts allowed young people, free or slave, to have recourse to the protection of the bishop against their parents or owners, when these were vicious; as the court of Chancery in this country is resorted to to remove improper guardians. "Si lenones patres, et domini suis filiabus vel ancillis peccandi necessitatem imposuerint, liceat filiabus et ancillis, episcoporum imploratio suffragio, omni miseriarum necessitate absolvi" (*Cod. Just.*, lib. i., tit. iv., s. 12, c. 14). So under many similar titles.

[2] Most of these imperial constitutions are collected in the first book, *Justinian Code*, tit. 4, s. 22-24, 30, 33. One instance may suffice as a specimen. "Neminem volumus in custodiam conjici, absque jussu magistratuum provinciarum, aut defensorum civitatum. De his autem quicunque conjecti aut conjiciendi sunt, Deo amabiles locorum episcopos jubemus per unam cujusque hebdomadæ diem, eos qui in custodiâ habentur visitare, et diligenter inquirere causam ob quam detinentur, et sive servi sint, sive liberi, sive pro pecuniis, sive pro aliis criminationibus, sive pro homicidiis conjecti, magistratus admonere, quam eos qui sunt in provinciis, ut ea exequantur circa ipsos, quæ divalis nostra constitutio, ad illustres præfectos, ea de re emissa præcipit, licentiâ datâ Deo pro tempore episcopis, si quam negligentiam admissam cognoverint, ab magistratibus vel iis quæ illis parent officiis, talem ipsorum negligentiam in-

These laws themselves no doubt abundantly indicate the independence and supremacy of the state in secular matters, and show that all these concessions of power to the ecclesiastical authorities were emanations of state policy; but for that very reason it is not surprising that they should have been made, in after ages, in all countries which had been parts of the Roman empire, and where these laws had been enforced, and among others, in our own, the basis of a system of policy similar in character.[1]

Such was the system of rule — civil and ecclesiastical — established in this country for some centuries. It seems a probable and reasonable opinion that under such circumstances the laws and constitutions of the Romans should, as the Britons grew more and more civilized, be adopted by them, and become in a great degree blended with their customs and institutions, even if the two races were not in a great degree blended, as they undoubtedly were to a very considerable extent.[2]

It will have been seen how calculated such a wise, complete, and salutary system of rule must have been, on the one hand, to implant itself firmly in a country, and, on the other hand, to attract the respect and confidence of

---

dicandi, ut conveniens adversus negligentes animi nostri motus insurgat" (*Justinian Code*, s. 22).

[1] Imperial laws were sometimes even addressed to prelates. Thus, for instance, the eighth novella of Justinian, which regards elections and duties of magistrates, was addressed to metropolitans: "Traditæ nobis à Deo reipublicæ curam habentes, et in omni justitia vivere nostros subjectos studentes, subjectam legem scripsimus; quam tuæ sanctitati, et per eam omnibus qui tuæ provinciæ sunt, facere manifestam bene habere putavimus. Tuæ igitur sit reverentiæ et cæterorum (episcoporum) hæc custodire, et si quid transcendatur à judicibus, ad nos referre" (*Just. Edict. Archiepiscopis, Nov.* viii.).

[2] Thus Sir M. Hale, writing upon this subject in his *History of the Common Law*, c. 5, though clinging, as all our common law writers do, to the notion of British laws, says, that "though a change of the laws of a conquered country was rarely universally made, especially by the Romans, yet that they in their own particular colonies, planted in conquered countries, observed the Roman law, which might by degrees, without any rigorous imposition, gain and insinuate themselves into the conquered people, and so gradually obtain and insensibly conform them — at least so many of them as were conterminous to the colonies and garrisons — to the Roman law;" and that the Romans rarely made a rigorous and universal change of the laws of the conquered country, "unless they were such as were foreign or barbarous, or altogether inconsistent with the victor's government;" which those of the Britons on the arrival of the Romans undoubtedly were. As regards nations which have settled laws and civilized institutions, what Hale says is undoubtedly true, and it applies to the invasion of the *Saxons* upon the *Romanized* Britons — civilized and settled by four centuries of Roman occupation.

the inhabitants, and blend its laws and institutions with their customs. And it is to be borne in mind that not only would the Britons naturally adopt the laws and institutions of the Romans, but a large portion of the population, in that, as in all the other European provinces of the empire, was, from various causes, and especially from the constant influx either of military or civilian colonists,[1] actually Roman, or composed of Roman citizens.

The influence of Roman laws and institutions upon the barbarian nations they subdued has not escaped the attention of historians. Several passages in the earlier chapters of Gibbon abundantly attest it.[2] And then other two causes would co-operate largely to extend the influence of the Roman law in its subject states, even when that law was not actually imposed. The one was the ad-

---

[1] Montesquieu, citing Tacit. Ann., lib. xiii., c. 27, "date fusum in corpus," etc., notices this constant flow of citizens or enfranchised slaves, as colonists, into the provinces: "Le nombre du petit peuple, presque tout composé d'affranchis ou de fils d'affranchis, devenant incommode, on en fit des colonies, par le moyen des quelles on s'assura de la fidélité des provinces. C'était une circulation des hommes de tout l'univers. Rome les recevait esclaves, et les renvoyait Romains" (*Grand et Decad. des Rom.*, c. 13). Montesquieu also alludes to the important influence of intermarriage, "Les lois favorisèrent les marriages, et mêmes les rendirent nécessaires" (*Ibid.*).

[2] "The same salutary maxims of government which had secured the peace and obedience of Italy were extended to the most distant conquests. A nation of Romans was gradually formed in the provinces, by the double expedient of introducing colonies, and of admitting the most faithful and deserving of the provincials to the freedom of Rome. That wheresoever the Roman conquers he inhabits, was a very just observation of Seneca, confirmed by history and experience. The natives of Italy hastened to enjoy the advantages of victory. These voluntary exiles were engaged in the occupations of agriculture, etc. But after the legions were rendered permanent, the provinces were peopled by a race of soldiers, and the veterans usually settled in the country where they spent their youth. Throughout the empire, but more particularly in the western parts, the most fertile districts and the most convenient situations were reserved for the establishment of colonies, some of which were of a civil and some of a military nature. In their manners and internal policy the colonies formed a perfect representation of their great parent; and they were soon endeared to the natives by the ties of friendship and alliance, and a desire of sharing in due time its honors and advantages. The municipal cities insensibly equalled the rank and splendor of the colonies. The right of Latium, as it was called, conferred on the cities to which it had been granted a more partial favor. The magistrates, at the expiration of their offices, assumed the quality of Roman citizens, and as these offices were annual, they in a few years circulated round the principal families. Thus the bulk of the people acquired, with the title of citizens, the benefit of the Roman laws, especially as to marriage testaments and inheritances" (*Dec. and Fall.*, c. 2). It would be impossible to give a more lucid account.

vantage derived from becoming a Roman citizen, which could only be by adopting the Roman laws, and the other was the policy of the Romans in settling colonies in conquered states. These results are thus clearly described by a late lamented writer, who admirably united the gifts of genius and of erudition, and whose untimely death has been so deeply deplored, not only by the profession but by the nation: "It was a principle of Roman law that no Roman citizen could be the citizen of any other community distinct from that of Rome, and governed by different institutions. The towns which the Romans admitted to a share of their rights were termed *municipia*. The adoption of the Roman laws was a necessary condition" (*Study of the Roman Laws*, p. 190).

Again,—"It was the profound policy of the Romans to confiscate a portion of the conquered territory and to occupy it with their own citizens, thereby at once increasing ultimately their own population, providing for the more indigent citizens, and riveting the chain around the vanquished. Originally the colonies were not on a level with the municipal towns; they were not admitted to a participation in the rights of Roman citizens. If one of the states became a *municipium* of Rome, it at first retained its internal administration, but latterly magistrates were sent from Rome for the purpose of administering justice, *præfecti juri dicendo*. The *Lex Julia* gave the rights of Roman citizens. There were magistrates who held an office analogous to that of the Roman prætor or consuls, and who were chosen by the people, and whose chief duty was the administration of justice" (*Study of the Roman Law*, p. 15).

The Roman system of government in the provinces[1]

---

[1] The learned Lingard gives a short but clear sketch of it: "The governor was denominated the præfect, or proprætor. He united in his own person every species of authority which was exercised by the different magistrates in Rome. He commanded the army; he was invested with the administration of justice. The power of the præfects, however, was confined by the Emperor Hadrian, who, in his 'perpetual edict,' laid down a system of rules for the regulation of their conduct, and established a uniform administration of justice throughout all the provinces. Subordinate to the præfect was the procurator, whose duty it was to collect the revenue of the provinces. When the Roman conquests in Britain had reached their utmost extent, they were divided into six provinces, under prætors appointed by the præfect. Throughout the provinces were scattered a great number of towns and military posts, the names of which are preserved in the 'Itineraries' of Richard of Ciren-

was one so complete and perfect in all its parts, with such an elaborate organization, not only extending over every part of the country, but entering into all the relations of life and all classes of society, that it could hardly fail to implant its laws and institutions very deeply even among the native population; and when to this is added the establishment of colonies, the erection of municipal corporations, the operation of the manorial system, and the effect of intermarriages in blending the Roman and the British races, it is impossible not to see that Roman laws, institutions, and ideas must have taken firm root, especially as there was a uniform administration of justice.

Those who had been so long accustomed to the Roman rule would probably, even while asserting their independence of it, desire to preserve the laws and institutions, the advantage of which they had so long enjoyed:[1] and

---

cester, and of Antoninus. (There were in all not less than one hundred and sixty-six stations, besides smaller forts.) They were partly of British and partly of Roman origin, and were divided into four classes, gradually descending in the scale of privilege and importance. The colonies, of which there were nine, included among them London, Colchester, Bath, Gloucester, Chester, and Lincoln. It was the policy of Rome to reward her veterans with a portion of the lands of the conquered nations. Each colony was a miniature representation of the parent city. It adopted the same customs, was governed by the same laws, and, with similar titles, conferred on its magistrates a similar authority. In Britain there were nine of them, two civil and two military. In the constitution of the latter we discover a striking similitude to the feudal tenures of later ages. Secondly, there were the municipal cities, the inhabitants of which were exempted from the operation of the imperial statutes, and, with the title of Roman citizens, possessed the right of choosing their own *decuriones* or magistrates, and of enacting their own laws. Privileges so valuable were reserved for few, and Britain could boast of only two *municipia*, Verulam (St. Albans) and York. But the *jus latii*, or Latian right, was bestowed more liberally. Ten of the British towns had obtained it from the favor of different emperors, and were indulged with the choice of their own magistrates, who, at the expiration of the year, resigned their offices, and claimed the freedom of Rome. That freedom was the great object of provincial ambition, and, by the expedient of annual elections, it was successively conferred on almost all the members of each Latin corporation. The remaining towns were stipendiary, compelled to pay tribute, and governed by Roman officers appointed by the prætor. These distinctions, however, were gradually abolished. Antoninus granted to every provincial the freedom of the city; Caracalla extended the indulgence to the whole body of the natives" (*Hist. Eng.*, vol. i., ch. 1); so that the edicts prohibiting natives from holding offices of trust, or holders of such offices from marrying natives, would not apply (*Cod. Theod.*, viii.; *Pand.*, xxii., tit. ii., tit. xv., leg. 1).

[1] Thus the learned Lingard, citing Zosimus, tells us that when the Emperor Honorius wrote to the British authorities to provide for their own safety, and the Roman magistrates were deposed, "the British states themselves re-estab-

the voice of history assures us that this was so in point of fact. From these causes, it was impossible but that, in the course of the centuries during which the whole fabric of Roman society and of Roman civilization,[1] with all its

---

lished civil government on a similar foundation." And the historian adds: "As the colonies, 'municipia,' and Latin towns had always formed so many separate commonwealths, under the superintendence of the provincial presidents, they would probably wish to retain the forms of government to which they had so long been accustomed" (*Hist. of Eng.*, vol. i., c. 1). The learned historian, indeed, seems to have supposed that a state of anarchy ensued, in which all laws and institutions perished; but this is opposed to the views of Savigny and of Guizot, and is not sufficiently supported by authority. And even if it were, the tradition of such laws and institutions would remain long after the institutions were destroyed.

[1] One of the most learned and acute writers on our earlier history, Sir Francis Palgrave, has ably enforced this view. "The Romans," he says, "fortified many strong cities in different parts of the island, and these colonies, or 'municipia,' were peopled with Roman inhabitants, who came hither from Italy accompanied by their wives and children. The Britons, or at least those tribes who inhabited the vicinity of the Roman colonies, soon adopted and emulated the customs of their masters. They learned to speak the Latin language, adopted Latin names and Roman manners. British princes were allowed to retain their dominions beneath the Roman supremacy. In other districts the land was allotted out to the Roman colonists, under whose power the British cultivators of the soil passed into a state of prædial slavery or villenage. The colonial policy of Rome sustained some alterations in form between the age of Agricola and the fifth century, but the main principles remained unchanged. Taking the reign of Constantine as the middle point of development, the whole Roman empire was divided into four great 'prefectures' or governments, Britain being included in the jurisdiction of the prefect of Gaul. The prefectures were divided into dioceses, and Britain was a diocese. The dioceses were divided into 'provinces,' subjected to presidents or consulars, and vicars or vice-consulars, each order in their degree invested with the various powers of judicial government and civil policy. The military command of the provinces was intrusted to the 'comites,' each having his own district or territory" (in which we see the origin of the *comitatus*, or county). "From the reign of Constantine these functionaries held a conspicuous rank in the state, and were gradually invested with civil as well as military rank. The cities enjoyed considerable privileges, and possessed a distinct political existence. The ruling body, termed the *curia*, was composed of senators or *decuriones;* and, moreover, besides the municipal corporations, each city had its 'colleges,' or guilds, of tradesmen and artificers. The prefects and other governors were practically in their own departments despotic; yet a species of controlling power existed in the provincial councils or assemblies, the constitution of which cannot be precisely defined, though deputies from the cities and great landed proprietors, and probably the bishops, had seats" (*Rise and Progress of the English Commonwealth*, c. x. and xi.). "The councils assembled in course, and at stated times of the year, unless any emergency arose, in which case they were summoned by the rescript of the emperor. If local regulations only were required, the councils were authorized to enact ordinances; but in matters of importance, and especially if the provincials needed the redress of any grievances, they could only address their petitions to the em-

laws and institutions, was firmly established here, those laws and institutions must have taken deep root, the institutions through their being everywhere planted, and the laws through their becoming incorporated with the customs of the people.

It is the opinion of those whose researches into our early history give their opinions highest authority, that, after the decline of the Roman empire and the withdrawal of the Roman legionaries,[1] the Romanized Britons (the two races having been so long together that they must, to a great extent, have become blended) retained, as might be expected, the Roman ideas of government, and the Roman laws and institutions, and that these were likewise, in a similar way, transmitted to subsequent races of barbarian invaders, who, before their conquests were complete, became blended with the Romanized inhabitants of the island.

---

peror. In many parts of the empire, such as Narbonensian Gaul, these councils appear to have been engrafted upon the institutions existing among the conquered nations. Was this the case in Britain? The question is interesting, but difficult. It is sufficient to observe, however, that these local legislatures, however qualified their powers might be, continued to keep alive a feeling of national or independent existence, and prevented the provinces from being merged in the vast orb of the empire. And transmitted through the middle ages, they became one of the elements at least out of which the parliaments, states-general, and other legislative assemblies of modern Europe were gradually formed" (*Ibid.*). The exact conformity of all this with the tenor of the imperil edicts, on the one hand, and the language of the Roman or Saxon historians, on the other, will be apparent; and there is also an entire accordance between the views of Palgrave on the subject and those of Savigny, Mackintosh, and Guizot. Elsewhere Sir F. Palgrave says: "These provincial assemblies participated in all the feelings and opinions of their countrymen, and virtually represented the wealth and respectability of the land" (*Hist. of the Anglo-Saxons*, ch. i.). What strong tendency all this must have had to deepen the hold of Roman laws and institutions on the country, and how contrary it is to the common notion that these assemblies were of Saxon origin, need not be pointed out. The Saxon assemblies were mere turbulent assemblies of the people, without representation.

[1] This was only a withdrawal, be it observed, of the legions who had remained embodied, or had newly arrived. There was no wholesale withdrawal of the Roman population, or of the settled Roman colonists; and indeed it is obvious that the British must have become Romanized, and the two races blended, in the course of centuries. Sir F. Palgrave says: "The Bretwaldas (or British or Saxon rulers) must be considered as the successors of the Roman emperors or rulers," and we may affirm that, so soon as the royal authority became developed among any of the barbarians who settled on Roman ground, all their kings took upon themselves, as far as they could, to govern according to the spirit of the Roman policy, and agreeably to the maxims prevailing in the decline of the empire, and declared in the imperial law (*Ibid.*).

GRADUAL ADOPTION OF THE ROMAN LAW. lix

Nothing is more remarkable in the history of this country than the gradual blending of the successive races and their laws and institutions, and one of the most remarkable, though perhaps least recognized illustrations of this, is afforded by the manner in which the Roman occupation[1] paved the way for the Saxon invasion, and, on the other hand, prepared the way for the adoption by the Saxons of the Roman institutions.

There would, therefore, it is manifest, be every reasonable probability that the Roman laws and institutions would be adopted in this country, and would continue to exist here even after the Roman rule was at an end. Nor is it left to probability; it is converted to the positive certainty of historic truth by the actual existence of the laws of the Romanized Britons,[2] compiled at a period pos-

[1] It has already been mentioned that it was the habit of the Romans to form military colonies in conquered countries, settling their legions in the districts in which they were posted, by grants of land, on military tenure. Thus Sir F. Palgrave says: "The general system of defence was founded upon the principle of paying the soldier by giving him land. Thus the march or border countries were granted almost entirely to the Limitanean soldiery, upon conditions which have been well described as containing the germ of the feudal tenures. Such land could not be alienated to a non-military owner. The Limitanean soldiery, as their name imports, continued settled on the frontiers; but in the same manner, or nearly so, were all the other Roman legions rooted and fixed in the interior of Britain. They were permanently established in the island, and military service was an imperative condition." In process of time the same system was applied to barbarian troops in the service of the empire, and thus, as Sir F. Palgrave states, two German tribes became established in Britain, and of course Romanized. The result of this in promoting the invitation, or invasion of others and their adoption of the Roman institutions, will be apparent. And this system, on the one hand, greatly conduced to the rise of barbarian rule, and, on the other hand, tended to subject it to the influence of Roman institutions. For, as Sir F. Palgrave points out, the power of the local legionaries, combined with the influence of provincial assemblies, would combine to support provincial rulers who assumed an independent position. That there were such rulers in Britain after the decline of the Roman emperor, is a fact of which there is no doubt. These rulers aped Roman power, and called themselves emperors. And, as Sir F. Palgrave says, "Unconscious of the ends which they were destined to accomplish, the provincial emperors may be considered as the precursors of the barbarian dynasties. The political ancestry of the ancient monarchs of Anglo-Saxon Britain must therefore be sought amongst these sovereign Britons" (*Hist. of the Anglo-Saxons*, c. i.). "Princes reigned in Britain long after the extinction of the Roman power who traced their descent from Maximus" (*Ibid.*). "And when the connection between Rome and Britain was entirely severed, Britain broke into various independent states; but there remained a Roman party, headed by men of Roman name" (*Ibid.*).

[2] The body of laws compiled by Howell Dhu in Wales in the tenth century, — A. D. 940, — about the time of the laws of Edgar. It has already been

terior to the termination of the Roman rule in the island, and anterior to the later Saxon laws.

The Roman Britons are found, according to these laws, to have had, in the first place, a clear, definite, and decided view of the superior powers and prerogatives of the sovereign ruler, as representing the state,[1] especially as to the ultimate ownership of land unappropriated, or on failure of legal owners, or the like.

In these laws, of which there was a Latin version, will be found clear traces of the Roman system of organization,[2] of Roman division, and of Roman laws and institutions, which could never have been derived from the Saxons, seeing that they are vastly superior to the latest Saxon laws, and there is no mention in the Saxon laws of their establishment, and such of them as are mentioned at all, are only in the earliest laws as already in existence.

The Roman system of the occupation of the land belonging to an estate, by tenants bound to the cultivation of the soil, or to servile labor upon the estate, appears

---

seen that the Britons, before the Romans came, were mere barbarians, and had no laws at all; so that any laws they had afterwards, especially as they corresponded closely with the Roman, can only be ascribed to a Roman source. It need hardly be stated that, at the close of the Saxon Conquest, the independent Britons had been forced mainly into Wales, and Lord Hale admits, in commenting on the "Statutum Walliæ" (*temp.*, Edward I.), which recites a certain law or custom in Wales, differing from our own, that it is evidence of what was the British law. But then he forgot that this must have been a British law derived from the Romans.

[1] Thus all lands were deemed to be held of the sovereign as paramount lord, and reverted to him if the conditions on which they were held were not fulfilled, or on failure of the heirs of the possessor: "Si clericus fundum sub rege tenuerit, cujus nomine servitium regi præbere obligatur, is in curia pro fundo isto et rebus ad eandem pertinentibus respondere tenebitur; terra enim totius regni ad regem pertinet. Et nisi promte responderit ad regem, fundus iste redebit" (*Leg. Wall.*, lib. 4, c. cxxvi., s. 5). So the prerogative of the sovereign was held to confer on him, besides the ultimate property of all the lands within his territories, the ownership of the sea-coast, and of all unoccupied or waste places, as among the Romans the *vacua regia* pertained to the state (*Ibid.*, lib. i., c. 47). He was also entitled to the property of persons dying without issue (*Ibid.*).

[2] Thus it appears that the country was divided into counties, and into "cantreds" or "hundreds," and also into tithings or tens. So it appears that there were "tons" or "towns," which were farms or vills — no doubt the Roman manors. Beyond all doubt there were the Roman "coloni" or serfs, for they are mentioned by the name of "villani," and these belonged to manors. The counties and hundreds could not have been of Saxon origin, for the "shire" is mentioned in the earliest Saxon laws — those of Ina — as already existing; and, on the other hand, hundreds are not mentioned until the laws of Edgar — later than these British laws.

clearly to have continued, and with it all the incidents of such a tenure at the will of the owner, or lord, without any permanent estate or any property in the lands occupied, as in which, however, customs or rights existed, or were afterwards acquired.[1]

These Romanized Britons had, like the Romans, evidently derived from them regular rules of inheritance, and as to the devolution of land by descent, dividing the lands as the Romans did,[2] among the children of the former owner. And, at the same time, they had cherished a clear and definite idea of property in land in the sense of dominion.[3]

These Romanized Britons, too, had a regular administration of justice, both local [4] and supreme,[5] in which latter the rules and forms of procedure, plainly borrowed from the Roman law, are laid down fully and correctly, embodying all the substantial features of the Roman civil procedure.

It would of course be idle to suppose that these laws and institutions could have emanated from the barbarian Britons, and equally idle to suppose that, though

---

[1] "Villanorum filii in fundos paternos non succedent, communes enim erunt illis cum cæteris villanis. Filius tamen natu minimus cujuslibet eorum patre mortuo domicilium ejus jure hereditario habebit" (*Leg. Wall.*, lib. ii., c. 12, s. 11). "Nulla pars terræ quem villani incolunt, regi decidet. Nec ulli villani licebit alterius partem emere, singulorum enim partes æquales erunt: nec regi ulla pars decidet eo quod æqualiter inter omnes villanos dividenda sit" (*Ibid.*, lib. i., c. xliii., s. 2). The Roman "coloni" are clearly here meant, for they are mentioned under that name in the Latin version of the Laws of Ina, where also they might have been derived from the Romans.

[2] There was a fluctuation in the Roman law upon the subject. The Twelve Tables divided the land among the sons only; the later law among all the children. The general principle was a division of the property. The Roman Britons appear, by these laws of Wales, to have retained the laws of the Twelve Tables, and divided the land among all the sons. This is recited in the *Statutum Walliæ*, temp. Edward I., and Lord Hale says this is good evidence of what the law was among the Romans, *i.e.*, the Roman Britons (*Hist. of Com. Law*).

[3] Dominus. Is qui rei dominium et proprietam habet (*Gloss. a Leg. Wall.*).

[4] Controversia etiam de fundis hereditariis inter aliquos inferiore cognationis gradu quam qui partitionem peculiarem petere possunt, in curia principali terminare debent; sed tales lites inter propinquos intra tertiam generationem, terminandæ sunt in curia cui fundus litigatus subjacet (*Triads*, cclviii., 4).

[5] There is a regular system of procedure described in the superior courts, with all the forms in real actions afterwards described in Glanville or Bracton.

lxii   INTRODUCTION TO THE PRESENT EDITION.

compiled in Saxon times, they could have been derived from the Saxons, who at that time had them not themselves.[1] And as by a kind of exhaustive process it has been shown that the laws and institutions existing here at the time of the decline of the Roman empire must have been derived from the Romans, because the British were mere barbarians before the Romans came, so a similar process leads to the same conclusion as to the Saxons, who had not, when they came over, the very rudiments of law, nor even the idea of sovereign power which lies at its basis, but were mere wandering predatory warriors.[2] The habits and character of the Saxons,[3] when they in-

[1] Sir F. Palgrave shows that the Saxons had not even the idea of supreme sovereignty: having only numerous popular chiefs called eldermen (*Hist. of Anglo-Saxons*, c. iv.). And, of course, such a people had not any notion of settled property, of regular judicature, or of regular law. They were mere wandering predatory tribes, each having its own chieftain. This is the account which Guizot gives of the German invaders generally, and it was eminently true of the Saxons (*Lect. sur la Civiliz. en l' Europe*). So our own Hume calls them "those generous barbarians," though it would be more correct to call them savage barbarians. Taking the most favorable view of them given by Tacitus, it is evident that they were barbarians.

[2] This can be seen by a comparison of their laws with the contemporary Saxon laws, which were utterly barbarous. Added to this, the Britons in Wales were those who had upheld their independence, and were in constant hostility with the Saxons.

[3] As they are described by Tacitus, they appear to have been very much in the same state as the Britons on the arrival of the Romans, a rude, wandering, warlike race, who had many barbarous usages, but nothing that could be called laws or civilized institutions. This indeed was impossible, as they did not cultivate the ground, and had no idea of that fixed property on land which lies at the basis of all civilization and law. "Honoratissimum assensus genus est armis laudare. Eliguntur in iisdem conciliis et principes, qui jura per pagos vicosque reddunt. Centeni singulis ex plebe comites consilium simul et auctoritas adsunt." Those sentences, detached from the context, are often cited to show that they had the division into counties and hundreds; but the context shows that this was merely a numerical division for military purposes, not a civil institution. "Nihil autem neque publicæ neque privatæ rei, nisi armati agunt . . . Principes pro victoria pugnant, comites pro principe . . . Nec arare terram, aut expectare annum, tam facile persuaseris, quam vocare hostes et vulnera mereri . . . Nullas Germanorum populis urbes habitari, satis notum est, ne pati quidem inter se junctas sedes. Colunt discreti ac diversi, ut fons, ut campus, ut nemus placuit. Vicos locant, non in nostrum morem, connexis et cohærentibus edificiis; suam quisque domum spatio circumdat, etc. Agri pro numero cultorum ab universis per vices occupantur. . . . Arva per annos mutant, et super est ager, nec enim cum ubertate et amplitudine sole labore contendunt, ut prata sepiant; sola terra seges imperatur" (*De Mor. Germ.*). It is obvious that the usages of these people were as unlike the institutions of the Romans or the Romanized Britons as possible; so that if afterwards we find them with those institutions, it could only be from the latter they were derived.

vaded this country, were such as to preclude the possibility of their having brought hither any of those civil laws or institutions which were afterwards found among them, and which therefore they must have derived from the Romanized inhabitants and institutions they found established here. All the original habits and usages of the Saxons were rude and truly barbarian, and such as suited unsettled, wandering, and uncivilized tribes, and not such as were fitted for civilized life.

Naturally, and indeed necessarily, these barbarians, when once settled in the country, and finding very admirable and convenient institutions already implanted in it,[1] would adopt them; and having adopted the institutions, would as naturally, although gradually, adopt a good deal of the laws which had become blended with them, and mixed up with the customs of the country, the more so, since, having no settled institutions of their own, there was nothing to oppose to them. And the history of our laws and institutions, from the time of the Saxon invasion, is a history of this gradual progress, and of a struggle between the principle of reason, represented by the Roman law, and the principle of custom, represented by the rude usages of the barbarians.

[1] Thus Sir F. Palgrave says, "So soon as the royal authority became developed among any of the barbarians who settled upon the Roman ground, all their kings took upon themselves, as far as they could, to govern according to the spirit of the Roman policy, and agreeable to the maxims prevailing in the decline of the empire and declared as the imperial law. This copy of the Roman majesty was very rude and inartificial. The 'witan' of the Anglo-Saxon and other of the barbarian kingdoms used the codes and rescripts of the emperors as their church architects attempted to imitate the models afforded by the sacred structures of imperial Rome." "This assumption of power, however," he goes on to say, "was not unchecked or uncontrolled. While the kings of the barbarian nations were striving to clothe themselves with an imperial authority, the people, or the communities or bodies of people which they governed, strove equally to maintain their own Germanic freedom; and the nobles in particular were fully able to resist all the coercion from the royal power. The infusion of Roman or Romanized doctrines into the administration did not derogate from the full exercise of all the laws and legal customs of the barbarians, which they considered as their birthright and best privilege. Taking these things together, we must consider the practical government of the state as resulting from two opposite principles, often discordant, and sometimes entirely hostile to each other: Roman law, which the king tried to introduce into the administration, and a Germanic law or usage upon which that Roman law was imposed" (*Hist. of the Anglo-Saxons*, c. iv.). The philosophical Guizot gives a very similar representation of the contest between Roman law and barbarian usages, a contest not terminated until long after the Norman conquest.

Tribes which live a wild, wandering, warlike life, as the Saxons did, and have no idea of settled property nor cultivation of the soil, have no idea of regular law, nor of that supreme and sovereign power which is its foundation,[1] and hence they have only some rude usages rather than laws, popular assemblies instead of regular judicature, a rough kind of arbitration instead of regular law.

A barbarous tribe, who had neither cities nor cultivation nor civilization, could not have originated civil institutions,[2] which it would be absurd to attribute to them, when it is an undoubted fact that the Romans had been at pains to implant their laws and institutions, and had left them here on their departure, along with their language and their laws.

[1] Thus Montesquieu says: "C'est le partage de terres qui grossit principalement le code civil. Chez les nations où l'on n'aura pas fait ce partage, il y aura très peu de lois civiles. On peut appeler les institutions de ces peuples des mœurs plutôt que des lois" (*De l' Esprit des Lois*, l. xviii., c. 13). He adds: "Ces peuples jouissent d'une grande liberté, car comme ils ne cultivent point les terres, ils n'y sont point attachés ils sont errants, vagabonds," etc. (*Ibid.*, c. 14). And then he applies this to the Germans, and cites Tacitus and Cæsar: "Nec regibus libera, aut infinita, potestas: cæterum neque animadverte," etc. (*De Moribus Ger.*). " In pace nullus est communis magistratus, sed principes regionum atque pagorum inter suos jus dicunt" (*De Bell. Gall.*, lib. vi.). So Guizot. "How can it be maintained that German society was well-nigh fixed, and that the agricultural life dominated there, in the presence of the very fact of migration, of invasion, of the incessant movement which drove the Germanic nations beyond their territory? How can we give credit to the empire of manorial property, and of the ideas and institutions which are connected with it, over men who continually abandoned the soil in order to seek fortunes elsewhere" (*Hist. de Civiliz. en France*). There was but the beginning of agricultural life, and that only by the means of slaves: "Servis non in nostrum morem descriptis per familiam ministeriis, utuntur. Suam quisque sedem, suos penates regit. Frumenti modum dominus, aut pecoris, ut colono, injungit, et servus hactenus paret" (*De Morib. Germ.*).

[2] What could such a race know of either civic institutions, or of such a system as that which the Romans had for the cultivation of the rural districts, and which they always established in their colonies? There were as many as nine of their civic colonies established in this country, and they were centres of civilization, not only by their civic institutions, but by those rural institutions by the means of which they cultivated the surrounding country. Thus of one, the most ancient and important of these colonies — Colchester — the historian says, in narrating the rebellion, "Quippe in coloniam Camalodunum recens deducti, pellebant domibus, exturbabant agris, captivos, servos appellando" (*Tac. An.*, lib. 14). So the historian, speaking generally of the enlightened rule of Agricola, says, "Jam vero principum filios liberalibus artibus erudire, et ingenia Britannorum studiis Gallorum anteferre, ut qui modo linguam Romanum abnuebant, iloquentiam concupiscerent, inde etiam habitus nostri honor et frequens toga," etc. (*Tac. Agric. Vita*).

EFFECTS OF THE SAXON INVASION.

The Saxons, therefore, did not bring any institutions or laws worthy of the name with them. They brought only rude barbarian usages, as will be seen in their written laws, which express for the most part their own usages: such, for instance, as the ordeal. It is manifest that they created nothing civilized.

On the other hand, it is equally clear that they destroyed nothing civilized; that is, they destroyed no existing institutions; they eradicated none of the existing laws or usages, in which lay so much of Roman law. They neither created nor destroyed; they adopted and appropriated, trying, no doubt, to mix up their own barbarous usages, which, however, it was found, as will be seen, would not coalesce or unite with civilized institutions, so that this baser matter soon fell off, and left the entire fabric of Romanized laws and institutions, save that the Saxons infused into the Roman institutions their own rough spirit of freedom, which gave them fresh life and vigor. But they did not destroy the Roman laws and institutions. The notion that they did so arose from an erroneous idea as to the nature of their invasion. It is imagined that there was a sudden and sweeping Saxon conquest, and hence it is supposed that institutions entirely perished and disappeared. The conquest of the country by the Saxons was a slow and gradual process, extending over five centuries, and scarcely completed when the Danish invasion occurred. And during that long period, there was of course, to a great extent, an amalgamation between the races and a mixture of usages and laws. Guizot points out how fallacious it is to suppose that these barbaric conquests of a country are ever so rapid and so complete as to effect any general and sweeping revolution; and he also points out that in those early times, when, of necessity, the country, being thinly inhabited, contained large tracts of unoccupied land, it would naturally be here that the successive tribes of invaders would settle down, leaving the cities and towns, which would be stronger and more thickly populated, to subsequent acquisitions; and the Saxon chronicle shows that this was so in this country, and that the conquest took centuries, by which time the two races and their usages were greatly merged.[1]

---
[1] Lect. sur la Civilization.

Thus it was, as the great historian of European civilization pointed out, with the barbarian invasions generally. They were gradual and progressive. "Hence it happened, Roman society," says Guizot, "had not so completely perished (in the south of Gaul) as elsewhere; a little more order and life remained in the cities. There civilization attempted to lift its head. Roman society had acted upon the Goths, and had, to a certain degree, impressed them with its likeness" (*Lectures on Civilization*, Lect. iii., p. 57). "There remained in the towns many wrecks of Roman institutions. There is mention made of public assemblies and municipal magistrates. The affairs of the civil order, wills, grants, and a multitude of acts of civil life, were legalized in the curia by its magistrates, as was the case with the Roman municipality" (Lect. vii., p. 131). "The spirit of legality, of regular association, came to us from the Roman world, from the Roman municipalities and laws" (Lect. vii., p. 432). "The towns, the primitive elements of the Roman world, survived almost alone amidst its ruin. The rural districts became the prey of the barbarians. It was there that they established themselves with their men; it was there that they were about to introduce by degrees totally new institutions, and a new organization" (p. 440).

Thus it followed, that through the long period occupied by the Saxon invasions, there was ample time for amalgamations of races and of usages, of laws and of institutions; and there was not any sudden and general wreck of Roman institutions, as is often supposed, but, on the contrary, a gradual and progressive adoption of them; the more so, as the Saxons, being little better than savages, had no civilized institutions of their own.

Since the time when Reeves wrote, the most learned works have been written which have shown the influence of Roman laws and institutions upon those of a later age. Thus, for instance, the *History of the Roman Law in the Middle Ages*, by Savigny, a work the purpose of which was to show that the Roman law never perished in Europe, but is to be met with throughout the period extending from the fifth to the thirteenth centuries in a multitude of institutions, laws, and customs. This great work was followed up by the great work of Guizot, on the *Civilization of Europe*, in which it is thus spoken of: —

"The work of Savigny, on the history of the Roman law after the fall of the empire, has changed the face of the science; it has proved that the Roman law had not perished; and that, notwithstanding great modifications, without doubt, it was transmitted from the fifth to the fifteenth century, and has always continued to form a considerable part of the legislation of the west" (*Lectures sur la Civiliz. en France*, Lect. xxx.). And the illustrious Guizot himself attests the truth of this: "It follows evidently from the facts laid before you, that not only in municipal institutions and civil laws, as Savigny has proved, but in political order — in all departments of social and intellectual life, the Roman civilization was transmitted far beyond the date of the empire; that we may everywhere discern a trace of it; that the thread is nowhere broken; that we may recognize everywhere the translation of Roman society into our own; in a word, that the part played by the ancients in modern civilization is greater and more continuous than is commonly thought" (*Ibid.*).

And the great writer confirms this conclusion by drawing our attention to the gradual character of the conquests by the barbarians, which is peculiarly true of the successive Saxon invasions in this country, occupying as they did a period of not less than five centuries; and the subjugation of the country not being entirely completed, even at the time of the conquest, during the whole of which period an amalgamation of races and institutions was going on. The natural result of all this would be, that, so soon as the barbarians were civilized enough to aspire after regular law, they would soon begin, by degrees, to resort to the Roman. "After the conquests of the barbarians," says Guizot, "there remained considerable wrecks of the Roman civilization. The name of the empire, and the recollections of that great and glorious society, disturbed the memories of men, particularly of the senators of towns, of bishops, and of all those who had had their origin in the Roman world. Among the barbarians themselves, or their barbaric ancestors, many had been witnesses of the grandeur of the empire: they had served in its armies; they had conquered it. The image and name of Roman civilization had an imposing influence upon them, and they experienced the desire of imitating, of reproducing, of preserving something out of it" (*Lectures sur la Civilization*, Lect. iii.).

This, certainly, was not less likely to be true in this country than in Europe generally. Accordingly, as the same great writer remarks, the earliest efforts at legislation among the barbarians were soon felt to be rude and inadequate to the state of things they found existing. "One is surprised," says M. Guizot, "that the permanence of the Roman law, after the fall of the empire, should ever have been doubted. Not only do the barbaric laws everywhere make mention of the Roman laws, but there is scarcely a single document or act of that epoch which does not, directly or indirectly, attest their daily application. It was the Pandects which reappeared in the twelfth century; and when people have celebrated the resurrection of the Roman law, it is of the legislation of Justinian they have spoken, not the perpetuity of other portions of the Roman law in the west; the Theodosian code, for instance, and all the collections of which it was the basis" (*Lect. sur la Civilization*).

This would be the natural result, and was the actual result, of the manner in which the Saxon Conquest was ultimately, after ages, effected, viz., that the conquered race simply became their tributaries.[1] There could be nothing in this to disturb or destroy the existing institutions, rural or municipal. The Saxons established themselves in the manors, and adopted the manorial system. By degrees they conquered the towns, and preserved the municipal system. There is no trace either of their creation or destruction of either system. They, indeed, established a system of frankpledge, which led to the formation of "boroughs;" but they did not destroy the privileges of the cities. On the contrary, the first

---

[1] Thus Lingard says, after the Saxons had formed fixed and permanent settlements, they gradually suffered the natives to retain their national institutions, and their own chiefs as subordinate and tributary. Bede gives an instance of both in Edelfred, in the year 600: "Qui terras eorum subjugatis indigenis, aut tributarias genti anglorum, aut habitabiles fecit" (*Hist. Eng.*, vol. i., c. 2). What these institutions were has been seen; they were—whether urban or rural, municipal or manorial—of Roman origin; and thus the chain of descent from the Roman time to the Saxon is distinctly kept up in legal history. It is to be observed that it was only a portion of the Britons who preserved their independence, and were driven into Wales. The greater part of Britain was subjugated and subdued by the Saxons, and the races amalgamated. (See Sir E. Creasy's "*English Constitution*.")

Saxon monarch (Athelstane) who professed to reign over the whole Saxon portion of England — and it was but a portion — recognized the customs of the cities,[1] and established privileges of coinage there.

All the civil or political divisions of the country into hundreds[2] and counties were, there is every reason to believe, continued substantially as they before existed. The common notion that Alfred divided the country into hundreds and counties, is a vulgar error. There is no trace in the Saxon laws of their formation, and they are mentioned in the earliest of them as already existing, although it is probable that the Saxon institution of frankpledge was applied to tithings.

So as to the officers of these civil divisions of the country, especially the sheriff, whose functions were from the first fiscal, and connected with the system of revenue, not of barbarian origin. It is probable, and it appears, from express statements in these laws;[3] that the institu-

---

[1] See the *Laws of Athelstane I.*, s. 14; *Anglo-Saxon Laws*, vol. i., p. 207.

[2] The Saxon "hynd⬛⬛⬛⬛⬛d, consisted of ten persons, and appears to have been formed fr⬛⬛⬛⬛⬛' of which the original meaning was ten. The "hynden," therefo⬛ ⬛rrespond to the *turba* of the civil law, "quia turba decem dicuntur," ⬛⬛ tourbe of the French coutumes, "continue si doit verifier par deux tourbes et chacun d'i celles par dix temoins" (*Louel*, liv. v., tit. 5, c. 13). And "hyndens" and "shires" are mentioned in the earliest Saxon laws (*Laws of Ina*) ; and, as already known, there is no mention of the establishment of either in any of the Saxon laws. Clearly, then, they were known before the Saxons, and that was the opinion of Lord Coke (1 *Inst.*, 248). Again, "shires" are mentioned as already known in the earliest Saxon laws (in those of Ina, s. 39 and 361). The notion that Alfred instituted shires and hundreds and tithings is a vulgar error. It seems probable, therefore, that the real origin of the hundreds and tithings is to be found in the Roman usages introduced among the Britons. This seems to have been supposed in the Saxon times: see the *Mirror of Justice*, for instance. So the Saxon laws, *vide post*.

[3] Thus, in the laws of the Confessor, compiled soon after the Conquest, is a passage: "Et similiter olim apud Britones temporibus Romanorum, in regno isto Britanniæ, vocabuntur senatores, qui postea temporibus Saxonum, vocabuntur aldermanni . . . Debent enim et leges, et libertates, et jura, et justas consuetudines regni et antiquas a bonis prædecessoribus approbatas, inviolabilitur modis omnibus, pro posse suo servare." Lord Coke was of opinion that the country was divided into counties in the Roman times, and that in those times also are to be found the origin of our towns, cities, and boroughs, of which there can be no doubt. He also was of opinion that there were præfects or consuls, and sub-præfects or vice-consuls, to the counties; and that the sheriff (Saxon shire-reeve), by the Normans called viscount, and in Latin vice-comes, would, under the Romans, have been subpræfect. That there were such officers in Roman times no one can question. That they would remain during the long period in which the Saxons were

tions which prevailed in this country during the period of the Roman occupation, were, in a great degree, revived and restored, and were embodied in the Saxon law.

In the earliest of the Saxon laws are to be seen constant traces of the old institutions derived directly from the Romans, and the earliest of the Saxon historians[1] speak of them as framed more or less in accordance with the ideas and examples of the Romans; or of those who had been subject to them, and who had imbibed their spirit, and adopted their institutions.

It is a matter of historical fact that, no sooner was the Saxon Conquest accomplished, than, under wise monarchs, the work of consolidation and civilization was commenced, the Roman institutions and divisions of government were adopted, and the terms they had used were employed.[2]

As might naturally be expected, so soon as the Saxons became civilized enough for anything like law, they resorted to the laws of the Romans. As an ~~eloquent~~ *great* writer has justly and truly remarked: "The inheritance of Roman wisdom was transmitted to t●●●●ce barbarians of

---

gradually and slowly acquiring dominion ●●●●● ●●●●untry, there can be as little doubt; and that the Saxons, as they th●● ●●quired dominion and became civilized, would retain them, giving them the Saxon names, is most probable. It is thus, Lord Coke conjectures, the consul became the earl, and the vice-consul the sheriff; and probably the modern lord-lieutenant is the nearest approach to the ancient Saxon earl or Roman præfect of a province, or county, or shire. And Alfred only revived these divisions and institutions (1 *Inst.*, sec. 248).

[1] Thus Bede speaks of Ethelbert, whose laws are among the earliest: "Qui inter cætera bona, quæ genti suæ consulendo conferebat, etiam decreta illi judiciorum, juxta exempla Romanorum, cum consilio sapientium constituit; quæ conscripta anglorum sermone hactenus habentur, et observantur ab ea; in quibus primitus posuit, qualiter id emendare deberet, qui aliquid rerum vel ecclesiæ vel episcopi, vel reliquorum ordinum facto auferret; volens scilicet tuitionem eis, quos et quorum doctrinam susceperat, præstare" (*Hist. Eccles.*, ii. 5).

[2] Thus in the laws of Ina we find mention of the "aldermanni, quam Latine comitem vel seniorem dicunt" (s. 40). And in the laws of Edward, the king commands "omnibus prefectis," and he declares that he who shall have deforced any one should do right, "coram preposito suo;" and again, "de prepositis audito testimoni rectum facere volentibus" (s. 5); and again, "ut omnis prepositus habeat gemotium ad quatuor ebodomadus;" whence it is plain that the "præfectus" or "prepositus" answered to the Saxon sheriff, and that the Saxon sheriff was the Roman prefect. So the "comes" is spoken of as equivalent to the Saxon alderman or earl (*Anglo-Saxon Laws*, vol. ii., p. 485). It is impossible not to see that Roman words were used as describing the certain officers or functionaries, which could only have been from their already existing at the time of the Saxon invasion.

the west, and, as they wrought the materials of the temple and amphitheatre into their own rude fortresses and dwellings, so did they occasionally incorporate the precious fragments of Roman law into their own unformed and scanty jurisprudence. This, however, they sometimes did unconsciously, and, at most, against their will. But when society improved, men looked on the Roman law with increasing veneration, as the surest basis of civil order"[1] (*Phillimore's Introd. to Roman Law*, p. 11).

That our *municipal institutions* had a Roman origin is not to be doubted, and is acknowledged by the most eminent historians.[2] Nor was it only *municipal* corporations which we owe to the Romans, although these, as Guizot points out, were the nurseries of freedom, of commerce,

---

[1] The epoch of barbarian legislation, the learned author adds in a note, reaches from the fifth to the tenth century, including the laws of the Anglo-Saxons (*Ibid.*), which implies that the law prevailing here before was not barbarian. A similar account is given by Guizot (*Hist. de la Civilization en France*, vol. i., p. 30), a work of which it has been well said, "France may be proud." "Should we open," says Guizot, "a barbarian code, we shall everywhere find the traces of the Roman society, of its institutions and magistrates, as well as of ●●● civil legislation. The municipal system occupies an important plac●●●● curia and its magistrates meet us at every step, and attest that th●●●●● unicipality still subsisted and acted. And not only did it exist, b●●●● uired more importance and independence. At the fall of the emp●●●● governors of the Roman provinces — the præsides, the consulares — disappeared. In their place we find the barbarian counts. But all the attributes of the Roman governors did not pass to the counts; they made a partition of them. Some belonged to the counts, and these in general were those in whom the central power was interested, such as the levying of taxes, etc.; the others, which only concerned the private life of the citizens, passed to the curiæ and the municipal magistrates" (*Lectures sur la Civiliz. en France*, Lect. ii.). This was written of Gaul, but it was as true of Britain, which formed part of the same prefecture; and we find the vice-comes, or sheriff in this country, exercising a portion of the functions here described as having belonged to the Roman officers of the empire, especially in relation to the taxes, etc., while the "comes" succeeded to the "consul or prætor."

[2] Thus Sir James Mackintosh says, "One part of the Roman institutions had permanent consequences, of which we trace the fruits at this day. This was their care in providing for the government and privileges of towns. Thirty-three towns were established in this country, with various constitutions. The choice of the decurions, or senators, out of whom the magistrates were taken, was left to the inhabitants. To these magistrates belonged the care of the public worship, the municipal property, and the local police, together with some judicial powers. Whatever may have been some of the consequences which are attributed to the condition of these subordinate republics, it cannot be doubted that the remembrance and the remains of them contributed to the formation or preservation of their elective governments, customs which were the foundation of liberty among modern nations" (*Mack. Hist. Eng.*, vol. i., p. 25).

and of civilization (*Lectures sur la Civiliz. de l'Europe*, Lect. vii.). There were other corporations, such as guilds or trading confraternities, which are usually ascribed to the Saxons, but which, as that great author shows, we really owe to the Romans. And the way in which they arose well illustrates the silent, unobserved growth of laws and constitutions. He says, "By one of those revolutions which work on slowly and unseen, until they become accomplished and manifest at a particular epoch, whose course we have not followed, and whose origin we never trace back, it happened that industry threw off the domestic menial character it had so long borne, and that, instead of slave artisans, the world saw free artisans. This was an immense change in the state of society, a change pregnant with incalculable results. When and how it was operated in the Roman world, I know not; but at the commencement of the fifth century it was in full action. There were already in all the large towns of Gaul (the prefecture which included Britain) a numerous class of free artisans, already created into corporations, into bodies formerly represented by some of their own members. The majority of these trade corporations, the origin of which is usually assigned to the Middle Ages, may readily be traced back to the Roman world" (*Lect. sur la Civiliz. France*, Lect. ii.). And it is beyond a doubt, though not so generally understood, that the Roman system was the origin of our manorial institutions.[1]

That the system existed here when the Saxons came has been already shown; that they would adopt it, would, *à priori*, be probable; and as a certain fact, that they did so, the great author already quoted observed. "The Saxon invaders would, as they seized upon the villas or man-

---

[1] What Guizot says of the Gaulo-Romans is just as applicable to the Britano-Romans. "They first established themselves in the habitations, whether in the cities or in the *villæ*, amidst the country districts, and the agricultural population; and rather in the latter dwellings, whose situation was most conformable to their national habits. Accordingly, the *villæ*, of which constant mention was made under the first race, were the same, or almost the same, as they had been before the invasion, that is to say, they were the centre of improvement, and habitation of great domains and buildings, scattered throughout the country districts, where barbarians and Romans, conquerors and conquered, masters, freemen, laborers, slaves, lived together" (*Lect. sur la Civiliz. en France*, Lect. 4). It is manifest that thus the manors would become centres of civilization in the country, as much as the municipal in the cities; and both were of Roman origin.

sions, and the manors or estates, adopt that system of cultivation and tenure which they found existing, and would soon find to be the most convenient, and thus the manorial institutions would become as much the centres of civilization in the country as the municipal in the cities."

The same great author shows how gradually the Roman institutions grew upon the barbarians, and by degrees got rooted beside their own. "Since we have studied the barbarian laws, we advance more and more to the same result; the fusion of the two societies (*i. e.*, the Roman and the barbarian) becomes more and more general and profound; the Roman element, whether civil or religious, dominates more and more. . . . It exercises a prodigious influence over the institutions and manners which associate themselves with it; it gradually impresses on them its character; it dominates over and transforms its conquerors. . . . In fixing themselves and becoming proprietors, the barbarians contracted among themselves relations much more varied and more durable than any they had hitherto known. Their civil existence became much more extensive and permanent. The Roman law alone could regulate it; that alone was prepared to provide for so many relations. The barbarians, even in preserving their customs, even while remaining masters of the country, found themselves taken, so to speak, in the nets of this learned civilization, and found themselves obliged to submit in a great measure, doubtless not in a political point of view, but in civil matters, to the new social order" (*Lect. sur la Civiliz. en Europe*).[1]

In the early Saxon laws and institutions there is no trace of the establishment of a *manorial system*; and it is beyond a doubt that they found it here and adopted it. The earliest of the Anglo-Saxon laws make allusions to a state of things and a class of tenants necessarily involving the existence of the system. It is manifest that the villeins, or villani, who are admitted to have been the originals of the modern copyholders, were identical with

---

[1] Les barbares, tout en conservant leurs coutûmes, tout en demeurant les maitres de pays — se trouvèrent pris, pour ainsi dire, dans les filets de cette legislation savante et obligés de lui soumettre en grande partie, non sans doute, le point de vue politique, mais en matière civile, le nouvel ordre social (*Lect. sur la Civ.*, vol. iii., 386).

the Saxon ceorls and the Roman "coloni;" and thus it is shown that manors were of Roman origin, since copyholds were held of manors by immemorial usage and the custom of the manor.[1]

Thus, then, all the more important and influential institutions of the country, civil or ecclesiastical — the municipal, the manorial, the parochial, and the episcopal — none of which, except the *obligation* of tithes and other ecclesiastical dues,[2] were established by the Saxons, but were found existing here, and simply adopted by them, were derived from the Romans. So as to the law, written or unwritten, all of it which can be deemed worthy of the name of law, was derived from the same source.

It would be a great mistake — but it is one into which our author and most other writers on our legal history have fallen — to imagine that all the law of this country in Saxon times was contained in the Saxon laws. These were the *leges scriptæ;*[3] but beyond and above these there was a great body of law, far more valuable and influential, which was unwritten, and derived by tradition from the

---

[1] Thus, for instance, in the laws of Ina there is a section "de colono regis" (s. 19), and another "*de colono vel villano.*" *Si tuus colonus vel villanus furetur;* so that the "colonus" and the "villanus" were spoken of as identical (s. 22). And in another, headed "De villani mansione claudenda," the villani are called "ceorls" (s. 40); and so, in another, "De villanorum pascius claudendis:" it commences, "Si ceorli habeant herbagum," etc.; so that here, again, the "ceorls" and the "villani" are spoken of as identical, and the ceorls, villani, and coloni are clearly identified with each other. Thus it is demonstrated that manors were of Roman origin, and the whole system of copyholds (*Anglo-Saxon Laws*, vol. ii., p. 461). At the time of the Conquest, it was well understood that the "villani," as they were then called, were those who held land upon servile tenure, such as tilling the soil, taking care of cattle, etc. (*Anglo-Saxon Laws*, vol. ii., p. 433); and after the Conquest, they were well understood to be the "coloni" of the Roman times. "Coloni" are then spoken of as "terrarum exercitores;" non vexentur ultra debitum et statutum; nec licet dominis removere colonos a terris, dummodo debita servitia persolvant (*Laws of William the Conqueror*, s. 29). It is well understood, and is stated by Guizot, that the "coloni" of the Romans were identical with the "villeins" of the later times; and in the Latin versions of the Saxon laws they are called "villani," while, in the Saxon version, they are "ceorls" (pronounced "churls"), or husbandmen.

[2] As, the payment of church-scot (*Laws of Ina*); and Peter's pence (*Laws of Edgar*).

[3] This distinction between the *lex scripta* and the *lex non scripta* was itself derived from the Roman law, and is laid down in Justinian's Institutes at the outset. The Roman ecclesiastics were well aware of this, and of the value of tradition.

Romans. Much of it was embodied in the institutions they had established, political or social, as the municipal and the manorial. And there was much more, derived by tradition from the Romans.
It would be a great error to suppose that the Saxon laws contained all the law the Saxons had. They derived a whole system of laws and institutions from the Romans; their written laws were only *additions* thereto, and for the most part rude and barbarous. When the Saxons, like the other barbarian nations which had conquered portions of the Roman empire,[1] became desirous of forming a regular law, they could do no more at first than put into writing their own barbarous usages. But by degrees they became sensible of their barbarism; they learnt a better law, and there grew up among them an unwritten law, derived from the traditions of the Roman law, which remained when their own rude written laws had become obsolete. And hence a constant struggle after something better — a continual tendency towards the laws and institutions of Rome. In treating of the various attempts at extricating European society from barbarism, the same great writer says: "The first attempt made, though but slightly effective, must not be overlooked, since it emanated from the barbarians themselves, was the drawing up of the barbaric laws. Between the sixth and eighth centuries the laws of almost all the barbarous people were written. Before this they had not been written; the barbarians had been governed simply by customs, until they had established themselves upon the ruins of the Roman empire. We may reckon the laws of the Saxons. There was manifestly a *beginning* of civilization — an endeavor to bring society under regular and general principles. The success of this attempt could not be great; it was writing the laws of a society which no longer ex-

---

[1] "Lorsque les nations germaines conquirent l'empire romain, elles y trouvèrent l'usage de l'écriture; et, à l'imitation des Romains, elles rédigèrent leurs usages par écrit; et en firent des codes. Les invasions, les guerres intestines, replongèrent les nations victorieuses dans les ténèbres dont elles étaient sorties, on ne sut plus lire ni écrire. Cela fit oublier les lois barbares écrites, le droit romain. Et par la chute de tant di lois, il se forma partout des coutumes. Ainsi, comme dans l'etablissement de la monarchie on avait passé des usages des Germaines à des lois écrites, on revint, quelques siecles après, des lois écrites à des usages non écrits" (*Mont. Esprit des Lois*, lib. ii., 8, c. 11).

isted — the laws of the social state of barbarians before their establishment upon the Roman territory, before they had exchanged the wandering for the sedentary life; the condition of nomade warriors for that of proprietors. We find indeed here and there some articles concerning the lands which the barbarians had conquered, and concerning their relations with the ancient inhabitants of the country; but the foundation of the greater part of these laws is the ancient mode of life — the ancient German condition; they *were inapplicable to the new condition,* and occupied only a trifling place in its development" (*Ibid.*).

All this was eminently true of the Saxons in this country, and their earlier laws, which bear the traces of their rude and savage state, and are obviously only the first attempts at anything like settled law. And though they allude to institutions as already existing, such as the "hundred" and the court of the hundred, there is no trace of their having themselves introduced or established any but the most barbarous usages, as the ordeal, compurgation, etc. And if Alfred's institution of frankpledge be an exception, it appears to have been founded upon an organization already existing.

As regards all *secular* institutions, indeed, beyond the mere adoption of the municipal or manorial institutions, which the Saxons found here, there is nothing in their laws except rude and barbarous usages, save so far as they had derived some first principles and elementary ideas of law from Roman sources. Thus as to the general principles of jurisprudence, and the administration of justice, there can be no question that they were derived by the Saxons from the Roman system, although doubtless in a very rudimentary form. Thus, for instance, as to the fundamental principle, which lies at the basis of all law, the supremacy of public justice over private revenge,[1] a prin-

---

[1] As Guizot observes, the German notions of law, as exemplified in the earlier Saxon laws, did not rise so high as the prohibition of private revenge; it only sought to mitigate it by levying it off, so to speak, under a system of pecuniary fines or compensation. But in the laws of Ina we find the great principle laid down which lies at the basis of all law; that a man must demand justice before he takes revenge, even when that revenge is allowed by law, as in the instance of a distress damage peasant, a relic of the old national law still remaining in our law (*Laws of Ina,* s. 9). If any one commit the offence of forcible seizure of land, and ouster of another, he should give up what he had seized, and pay a fine to the king (*Laws of Ina,* c. 10). So if any one take revenge, *i. e.,* a distress, before he demand justice, let him

ciple so utterly antagonistic to the usages and ideas of barbarians like the Saxons,[1] it will be found laid down for the first time as Saxon law, enacted after the Roman influence had revived. Enacted no doubt in simple cases, and in an elementary form; but still there was the germ which afterwards grew, the principle ultimately developed.

So as to the next great principle, that the duty of securing that justice should be administered rested with the sovereign, and that in case of failure or defeat of justice in the local and popular tribunals, the sovereign power must provide for and enforce it. This principle also, plainly derived from the Roman system, as it rather ran counter to the original Saxon institutions, is scarcely to be found in the earliest Saxon laws, though it by degrees was recognized and developed.

So as to the important principle of the origin of right and property in land, as derived from the sovereign, and

give up what he has taken and pay damage. Here was the principle. It was afterwards developed. The best comment upon this is afforded by a reference to the statute of Marlbridge (*temp.* Henry III.), in which the same principle is laid down and enforced. "Et nullus de cætero ultiones aut districtiones faciat per voluntatem suam;" and upon which Lord Coke's comment is, "Ultiones; that therefore they (refusing the course of the king's laws) took upon them to be their own judges in their own causes, and to take such revenges as they thought fit until they had ransom at their pleasure." That is taking distresses not according to law, as for services, rents, or damage feasant, but for revenge, without lawful cause. Here we see how the ancient law illustrates the later.

[1] The Saxon tribunals, those of the county or hundred, were merely rude and noisy assemblies. They could not all at once be got rid of, since the barbarians clung to their native usages; but in the Saxon laws which show the first signs of reviving civilization, there is a provision which indicates rather a jealousy of the royal prerogative to enforce justice; though perhaps, on the other hand, it may be deemed to contain the germ of a better system. It was provided that if any one demand justice before a shire man, or other judge, *i. e.*, the ealderman or hundredor, and cannot obtain it, and the other will not give him security, let him pay a fine, and within so many days do justice; the breach of which would be an offence against the general law, which the king could visit (*Laws of Ina*, s. 8). And the same provision is to be found in subsequent laws (*Canute*, s. 17). In the laws of Edgar, provision is made for the regulation of fine or forfeiture to the king, in case of disregard of the courts of the hundred (*Laws of Edgar II.*, 7); and there is also mention made of outlawry, the effect of which was to put a man out of the protection of the law, and his property in the power of the king (*Ibid.*). So a law of Athelstane: if the lord denies justice, and the king be appealed to on that account (*Athelstane*, s. 3). So a law of Ethelred, that no man made a fine for any accusation, except it be with the witness of the king's reeve (*Ethel.*, s. 1). It is obvious that the principle was gaining ground, that justice was the king's prerogative.

7*

reverting to him, by way of forfeiture, on breach of allegiance. This, like the other great principle, that justice was the prerogative of the crown, was of Roman not of Saxon origin; and is to be found at first obscurely implied, and then gradually arising in the Saxon laws, and implied, though imperfectly and obscurely, in various ways.[1] So as to the transfer of land by donations or deeds,[2] which are alluded to in the Saxon laws; and the use of charters, or deeds, by way of grant or conveyance, all which must have been of Roman origin, seeing that such

[1] These two principles are closely connected, and lie at the basis of any settled system of government. Thus in the laws of Ethelred, it is laid down that the king is entitled to the penalties that those incur who have "bocland," *i. e.*, freehold land held of no one, but thus regarded as held really under the crown; a plan and system of the Roman principle, that property in land could only be derived from the sovereign power of the state, and held under its sanction (*Ethel.*, s. 1). So if a man fled from his lord, he was to forfeit all he had, and the lord might seize his possessions, but if he had bocland, that was to go to the crown (*Can.*, s. 78.). So in another law the bocland was to be forfeited to the king (*vide ibid.*). The very distinction between bocland or land conferred or conveyed by deed or written instrument, and as distinct from land simply held in common folkland, must have arisen among the Saxons subsequent to their arrival in this country, when they certainly could have no deeds, and writing was unknown even to their kings. Moreover, the very idea of a deed granting and delivering an estate or land implies an idea of different estates or kinds of property in land, far too complex for barbarians, and which it is natural to suppose came from the Romans; the distinction in question being known to the Romans.

[2] The whole subject of donation, it need hardly be stated, is treated of profusely in the Roman law, entire tables of which have been transferred to our own, as, for instance, *donatio mortis causa*. The idea of donation, however, involves property, and settled property in land could scarcely have existed among the Saxons in their native country, still less could donations by deeds or instruments in writing have been known among the people, whose kings, it is clear, could not write, since their charters, mentioned in the Saxon laws, were always signed by them as marksmen. Instances, however, of such deeds are to be met with in the Saxon chronicles as early as the seventh century, always associated with ecclesiastics, who, doubtless, drew them up, and derived them from the Roman law. It is mentioned as a most remarkable thing of Alfred that he could read; and in his time there is a Saxon law which shows that deeds of grant were used. "The man who has bocland, and which his kindred left him, must not give it from his kindred, if there be writing or witnesses that it was forbidden by those men who at first acquired it, and by those who gave it to him, that he should not do so; and then let it be declared in the presence of the king and the bishop before his kinsmen." This was the Saxon mode of transfer by public declaration or delivery, and the instruments or deeds were obviously of Roman origin. "Si scriptam intersit testamenti, et testi, quid eorum prohibuerit qui hunc adquiserit," etc. The idea of conditional donations was far too artificial to have been invented by a rude race like the Saxons, and was plainly derived from the Roman law (*Pand.*, lib. xxviii.) through the traditions of the Romanized Britons.

WRITTEN INSTRUMENTS DERIVED FROM THE ROMANS.   lxxix

transfers could not have existed among the Saxons in their native state, in which the very idea of settled property itself could hardly have arisen; nor could deeds or written instruments have been used among a people whose very king could neither read nor write.

So as to the whole subject of the dominion over land, or the possession or occupation of land, and the rights which long use or possession might confer, or contracts for the use and occupation of land, all heads of law which could never arise in a country which had not reached a certain stage of civilization and ideas of settled property, to which the Saxons certainly had not attained when they originally invaded Britain, and all treated of fully on the Roman law; there can be no reasonable doubt that the provisions on such subjects contained in the Saxon laws were derived from that source, though, no doubt, at first in an elementary form, and in the simplest possible cases.[1]

Thus, therefore, on these different subjects, so important as lying at the basis of any system of law — the only traces of law the written laws of the Saxons had — were derived from the Roman law; and these are the only portions of their laws not barbarous. These portions of the Saxon written laws, however, are but few and fragmentary; and the bulk of the laws will be found to have been either mere barbarous usages, or moral and religious precepts, inserted by the ecclesiastics who framed them, and which belong rather to the moral law than to the municipal. The little that is in them that deserves the name of law, is clearly of Roman origin, and that portion

---

[1] Thus, as to the law of possession and dominion, the Roman law held that a man might be in possession of land occupied by his farmers or tenants as much as if he himself occupied personally (*Inst.*, lib. iv., tit. xv., s. 3; *Cod. Just.*, lib. vii., tit. xxxii.). The bearing of this principle upon the manorial system, under which lands, portions of the lord's demesnes, were held at his will, according to custom, will be obvious, and no one will suppose it had ever occurred to the Saxons; and the Roman law had always recognized as to landed property, the effect of *usucapio*, to which the Christian emperors had added the effect of prescription for a certain number of years, which Justinian made applicable to the provinces, fixing the period of prescription as to land at about twenty years — the very period which, from time immemorial, raised a possessory right, according to our common law. This, again, is far too artificial to have arisen among the Saxons. So as to the whole law of servitudes to which land may be subjected, it is essentially of Roman derivation. So as to leases of land at a rent, as to which there is a provision in the laws of Ina with reference to emblements, where the landlord had terminated a tenancy after a crop was sown (*Laws of Ina*, c. 67).

is but small. The rest of their law — that is, the great bulk and body of civilized law among the Saxons — must have been derived from the Romans by tradition.[1]

There was, indeed (as already hinted), one great benefit derived from the Saxons, and that was the infusion into our institutions of that spirit of freedom and equality which gave them fresh life and vigor, and enabled them to endure. Thus the philosophical historian, Hume, observes of them: "At the Teutonic invasion, Europe, as from a new epoch, rekindled her ancient spirit; and if that part of the globe maintains sentiments of liberty, honor, equity and valor superior to the rest of the world, it owes these advantages chiefly to the seeds implanted by these generous barbarians" (*Hume's Hist.*, vol. i., Appendix).

The great French writer, Guizot, has expressed similar opinions: that the benefit we derived from the barbarians was the spirit of freedom. This spirit was embodied in this country in the popular tribunals introduced by the Saxons in their county courts. Guizot described how, at the decline of the Roman empire,[2] the spirit of despotism had prevailed, and destroyed the energy of nations. And our own acute historian, Sir J. Mackintosh, has described

---

[1] These laws are divided for the most part into provisions as to pecuniary compensation for bodily injuries, the ordeal and other barbarous usages, and pious precepts as to the observance of moral and religious duties. It is not too much to say that there is not any piece of municipal law except either such few fragments of Roman law as have happened to get in, or such provisions as relate to the assemblies of the hundred and the county, which were really mere turbulent popular meetings, utterly unfitted for any judicial duty.

[2] Guizot thus describes the state of things towards the close of the empire: — "The governors — the emperor's immediate representatives, charged throughout the empire with the interests of the central government, with the collection of taxes, and the whole executive power — by degrees absorbed the judicial, not only as between the sovereign and the subject, but as between the subjects themselves. The whole civil and criminal jurisdiction was in their hands. With two exceptions, they adjudicated all suits; in the first ages, the governor deciding only the law, and appointing a private citizen called the *judex*, or juror, to decide on the question of fact; but by degrees a despotism established itself, and the ancient liberties of the people disappeared, the intervention of the judex became less regular, and the institution fell into disuse. The entire jurisdiction, then, in all cases, appertained to the governors, agents and representatives of the emperor in all things, and masters of the lives and fortunes of the people, with no appeal from their judgment but to the emperor in person. Thus the jurisdiction of the governors comprehended all things, all classes of society" (*Guizot, Lect. sur la Civ.*, v. i.; *Gibbon*, c. ii.).

the Saxon spirit of freedom[1] infused into their popular tribunals, breathing life, and vigor, and energy into all their institutions. It was out of these popular tribunals was afterwards derived the system of trial by jury, which had, no doubt, originally belonged to the Roman system, but had declined and died away in the provinces under the stipendiary influence of despotism, and was destined to be revived by degrees in a far more vigorous form through the medium of the popular tribunals of the Saxons. It was, however, by a long, a slow, and a laborious process that this was effected, and the rough popular assemblies as established by the Saxons were far more remote from anything like judicial tribunals. There was, however, an element in them which ultimately led to the restoration of legal tribunals and judicial trials, and that was the presence of the bishops in these assemblies. It was indirectly through their influence that these popular assemblies were by degrees transformed, and that an intelligent

[1] "The meetings of the people at the courts of shires, hundreds, and tithings, at which the humbler classes were necessarily more important than in the ordinary assemblies, contributed still more to cultivate the generous principles of equal law and popular government; and though trial by jury was then unknown, it cannot be doubted that the share of the people in these courts, where all ordinary justice was administered, must have led the way to that most democratical of juridical institutions. It is an ingenious and probable conjecture that the smaller of these courts produced the assembly immediately above it in regular order. In their original seats, indeed, we learn from Tacitus that there were hundredors in the district, as well as in the supreme assemblies of the whole people" (*Hist. Eng.*, by Mackintosh, v. i., p. 81). "The spirit of equity and freedom breathed into our government by the Saxons has never entirely departed from it, and we follow their example still, employing legal and aristocratic temperaments to render the ascendancy of the people more safe for public order, and therefore more insured against dangerous attack" (Sir J. Mackintosh's *Hist. Eng.*, v. i., p. 83; Lardner's ed., Cab. Cyc.). There is a passage in Guizot's lectures upon the civilization of France, in which that thoughtful and philosophical writer finely describes the distinguishing elements or agencies in that European civilization; and it applies equally to this country. He says: "The spirit of legality, of regular associations, came to us from the Roman world, from the Roman municipalities and laws. It is to Christianity, to the religious society, that we owe the spirit of morality; the sentiment and empire of rule; of a moral law, of the mutual duties of man. The Germans" (including of course the Saxons) "conferred upon us the spirit of liberty — of liberty such as we conceive of and are acquainted with it — in the present day; as the right and property of each individual: master of himself, of his actions, and of his fate, so long as he does not injure others" (*Lectures sur la Civilisation*, Lect. vii.).

administration of justice restored by infusing the Saxon spirit into Roman institutions.

To understand this it is necessary to attend to the state of ecclesiastical institutions among the Saxons. The country had already been divided into ecclesiastical dioceses,[1] during the latter portion of the Roman occupation, when the empire had become Christian. And the division of dioceses into smaller districts, afterwards called parishes, was founded upon the manorial system, already shown to have been derived from the Romans, and was in existence here when the Saxons arrived, and were adopted by their conversion to Christianity, with the whole ecclesiastical system to which they belonged.

---

[1] The Roman empire in its later ages had a civil system of division, which included provinces and dioceses, and when the empire became Christian, that division was adopted for ecclesiastical purposes; and no one who has read Bede's Ecclesiastical History or other early chronicles, needs to be told that the Christian religion was established here under the Romans, and that this ecclesiastical division was established in Britain during the Roman occupation. When the Saxons were converted by the Roman ecclesiastics, this same ecclesiastical organization was re-established, and, though in some instances the dioceses may have altered, the system was the same. So as to parishes, they would appear to have been of Roman origin, and to have existed here before the Saxon times. There can be no doubt that when the Romans became Christian, they made a regular provision for the support of the clergy; the owners of the "villas" or country estates, afterwards called lords of manors, made such provision by means of grants of lands; and at the same time the Roman institutions of tithes and oblations were adapted to the same object, the lords being patrons of the "livings" thus created; and thus in an ancient legend of the time of St. Augustine, to be found in the *Historia aurea* of Johannes Anglicus MS., part 2, lib. xvii., c. 72, mention is made of the *patronus villæ*, or lord of the manor, as being patron of the church, and entitled to the tithes. This was just at the end of the sixth century, and indicates at that early period such an identity with the Roman institutions as to afford the strongest evidence of an adaptation of them by the Romanized inhabitants of this country during the Roman occupation. In the laws of Ina, mention is made of church-scot; a species of oblation, which was probably the origin of church-rates; and which even then was compulsory, for the law was, that church-scot shall be paid (s. 61); and though it does not say to whom, it should seem that it must have been to the priest of the parish, that is, of the "vill" or manor. Mention is made in the same laws of churches as sanctuaries (c. 57). This was in the eighth century. In the laws of Ethelbert, at the close of the sixth century, mention is made of the property of the church and of bishops and priests: and in the laws of Edgar, mention is made of tithes, which, however, existed much earlier. That tithes existed prior to the middle of the eighth century appears from one of the canons of Archbishop Egbert, A. D. 750; that tithes ought to be paid, and they are alluded to as having been declared by Augustine, "ut Augustinus dicit; decimæ igitur tributæ sunt ecclesiarum et egentum animarum" (s. 102, *Anglo-Saxon Laws*, vol. ii., p. 112). At the end of the eighth century, Offa, king of Mercia, made a grant to the church of all the

It will be seen by reference to the Saxon laws, that not only were the endowments of the church protected, but all its privileges and immunities as established in the imperial laws were recognized and re-established — as the right of sanctuary,[1] and the immunity of the clergy from secular jurisdiction.[2]

And not only were the immunities and privileges of the church fully recognized, but her powers: that is, her powers as derived either from her pastoral office and mission, or from her function of spiritual direction *in foro conscientiæ*. As regards the first, her freedom from secular corruption or state control was distinctly asserted.[3]

---

tithes of his kingdom, and Ethelwulph half a century afterwards extended it to the whole realm. In the laws of Edward and Guthrum, towards the end of the ninth century, the payment of tithes and other oblations is enforced (c. 61). And so by the laws of Athelstane, about the year 930. Thus in a law of Edgar it was ordained that every tithe be rendered to the old minster to which the district belonged (the Saxon word "hyrnes" being in the Latin version rendered *parochia*); and it is then added, that any thane who on his bocland had a church with a burial-place, might give the third part of his tithes to that church (*Anglo-Saxon Laws*, vol. ii., p. 263). So in the laws of Ethelred, s. 17, it was ordained that tithes should be paid at specific periods; that is, to the church to which they of right belonged, *i. e.*, the church of the ecclesiastical district or parish. And so in a subsequent law of Ethelred, it was provided that a third part of the tithes should go to the reparation of the church, *i. e.*, the church to which it was payable — the church of the district or parish (*Anglo-Saxon Laws*, vol. i., p. 343). About the same period, mention is made in the Ecclesiastical Institutes of parishioners; that is a word used which is so translated in the Latin (*Anglo-Saxon Laws*, vol. ii., p. 423). Thus, therefore, it appears that parishes in the sense of ecclesiastical districts, with endowments of lands or houses set apart for the support of the clergy, had become adopted by the Saxons, and was protected by their laws. And not only so, but payment was enforced: of tithes, church-scot, and Rome-feoh,—Rome-fee, that is, Peter's pence (*Laws of Ethelred and Canute*).

[1] The right of sanctuary is recognized in the Saxon laws from those of Alfred to the time of the Confessor. *Vide Anglo-Saxon Laws*, vol. i.

[2] This also it appeared was recognized in the time of Alfred, for the *Mirror* states that he caused a judge to be hanged who had condemned a clerk to death, when he had no jurisdiction to try (*Mirror of Justice*, c. v., s. 1). So in the laws of Ethelred. If a priest become a homicide, or otherwise flagrantly commit crime, let him forfeit his order and country, and be an exile as far as the pope may prescribe to him, and do penance. If a priest commit perjury or theft, let him be cast out of his order, and unless he make amends as the bishop may direct; and if he desire to clear himself, let it be, etc. (c. 26). These laws are re-enacted by Canute (c. 4). If a man in holy orders commit a crime worthy of death, let him be seized and held to the bishop's doom as the deed may be.

[3] Thus in the laws of Ethelred, "Let no man henceforth reduce a church to servitude, nor unlawfully make church-mongering; nor turn out a church minister without the bishop's counsel" (*Ethelred*, vi., c. 15). That is, the privilege of patronage was not to be pressed so as to assert in effect a power

And as to the power of spiritual direction or correction, *in foro conscientiæ*, in the declaration of spiritual sentences for spiritual offences — in other words, the administration of canon or ecclesiastical law — the Saxon law abundantly and emphatically recognized it; and not only so, but to a great extent enforced it by temporal penalties, as a secular correction for spiritual purposes.[1]

Thus it will be seen that the position, the privileges, and the powers of the church were fully secured and protected by the Saxon laws; and that, therefore, her prelates were possessed of the most powerful influence. And when it is borne in mind that they were in close connection with Rome, and that the great fathers of the church had written in terms of the highest eulogy of the Roman law, it would be likely that the influence should be exerted in favor of a recurrence to Roman laws and institutions.

This, indeed, is what, according to the opinion of the most eminent historians, actually took place. Guizot repeatedly refers to the influence of the prelates upon the barbarians as an important agent in civilization. The same view was taken by our own philosophical historian, Mackintosh. He says: "The only institution of the civilized Romans which was transmitted almost entire into the hands of the barbarians, was the Christian church. The bishops succeeded to much of the local power of the Roman magistrates; the inferior clergy became the teachers of their conquerors, and were the only men of knowledge diffused throughout Europe; the episcopal authority afforded a model of legal power and regular jurisdiction, which must have seemed a prodigy of wisdom to the disorderly victors. The synods and councils formed by the clergy afforded the first pattern of elective

---

of control over the pastorship, nor was a cleric to be either appointed or ejected without the bishop's consent.

[1] As already mentioned, the laws enforced the payment of church dues and tithes, and Peter's pence; they also enforced the observance of fee Sundays and festivals or fasts (*Laws of Canute*, 45). So the bishop was invited to attend the county court, for the express purpose of declaring the law of God — by which was meant the law of the church, the canon or ecclesiastical law. The laws of Ethelred speak of pecuniary penalties for spiritual offences, to be applied according to the direction of the bishops, as a secular correction for divine purposes (c. 51). So the laws of Edward the Confessor collected by the Conqueror speak of enforcement by the law of episcopal sentences in case of ecclesiastical offences. The laws of the Conqueror declared that the bishops should administer ecclesiastical law.

and representative assemblies, which were adopted by the independent genius of the Germanic race. The ecclesiastics alone had any acquaintance with business; they only could conduct affairs with regularity and quiet. They were the sole interpreters and ministers of whatever laws were suffered to act, or felt to exist. To these powerful means of influence must be added the inexhaustible credulity of the superstitious barbarians, disposed to yield a far more blind deference than the conquering Romans had ever paid to their priests. . . . All the other institutions of the empire were worn out. Christianity, however, attired in its doctrines, was still a youthful and vigorous establishment, and the power which it speedily exercised in blending the two races, by gradually softening the ferocious courage of the Germans so as to make it capable of union with the reviving spirit of the Roman provincials, afforded an early instance of its efficacy in promoting civilization" (*Hist. Eng.*, vol. i., p. 44).

The Saxon chronicles and Saxon laws afford ample authority for the view conveyed in the above passages. The chronicles show that the kings could not read or write, and had to attest their charters by their marks; and the preambles to all the laws show that the bishops were consulted in framing them: and, as our historian goes on to add, "this influence, on the whole, was exerted for the benefit of civilization, and had a natural tendency to the institutions and laws of Rome." Hence all through the Saxon laws may be observed traces of this influence, and proofs of a gradual approximation to the laws and institutions of Rome, although these were no doubt influenced by the spirit of the barbarians, which was one of popular liberty and equality, having its manifestation in popular assemblies. Thus it was in the union of this influence of the Saxon spirit with the principles of the Roman system, that we derived our whole system of judicature and jurisprudence, and especially trial by jury.

The Saxon laws not only allowed, but invited the attendance of the bishops in the courts of the county, to assist in the administration of justice;[1] and it need hardly

---

[1] Thus in the laws of Canute: "Let there be twice a year a shire-mote, and let there be present the bishop of the shire and the alderman, and there let them expound the law of God and the secular law;" the "law of God" mean-

be said that in those times the bishops were the only persons who had any notion of law. The canon law, or ecclesiastical law, founded upon the civil law, and, indeed, being the application of that law to ecclesiastical purposes, provided them with a system of law, and instructed them in the administration of justice; and they would naturally use their influence to the utmost in favor of an intelligent system of trial, and against barbarous usages.

The canon law required a trial by witnesses, and the civil law was, as we have seen, singularly strict in its requisites of proof in criminal cases. It may be imagined how intelligent ecclesiastics would revolt from the trial of men for their lives by clamorous assemblies, without the sanction of an oath, the testimony of sworn witnesses, or any of the safeguards of a judicial trial; and how still more they must have shrunk from the barbarous absurdity of the ordeal. Hence by degrees the practice was introduced of *swearing* those of the freeholders who were of the neighborhood, and would be most likely to know the truth, to testify of it to the rest; and the ordeal was only resorted to when trial by witnesses failed, or was not possible. And thus it is that trial by jury, in the sense of trial by witnesses, became, in criminal cases, established, whenever it was possible, *i. e.*, whenever there were witnesses; which explains why, even up to the time of the Conquest, and afterwards, the ordeal was still at times resorted to.[1]

Thus, also, there were endeavors made to introduce trial by witnesses, whenever it was possible, in civil cases, and with that view there are a series of provisions in the Saxon laws to secure witnesses of transactions who might

---

ing the law of the church, the canon or ecclesiastical law. So in the laws of Henry I., it is said that the bishops ought to attend the county courts. The canon law was adverse to such barbarous usages as the ordeal; and there is a passage in the *Mirror* which shows that the church had used all her influence against it; but it is astonishing how tenacious barbarian races are of their ancient usages, and the Saxons clung to the ordeal until the reign of John. The canon law required trial by witnesses.

[1] In Alfred's reign, as stated in the *Mirror of Justice* (a work based upon an earlier one written in his time), several judges were executed for causing prisoners to be hanged, either without a trial by twelve *sworn* men, or where the jury were not unanimous, or where they were in doubt (*Mirror of Justice*, c. 5). The germ of the system is to be seen in the Laws of Ethelbert; but there is no trace of it earlier, and all writers are agreed that at all events the Saxons had not trial by jury when they first came to this country, so that they must have adopted it here.

afterwards give testimony as jurors. For jurors, it will be observed, in that age, and until long afterwards, were sworn witnesses, upon whose testimony, of their own knowledge, the body of men who acted as judges determined. Trial by jury in the modern sense of the phrase, as a trial by jurors upon evidence, was yet far distant, and was only to be the result of gradual development.[1]

The administration of criminal law had undoubtedly become more advanced and developed among the Saxons than the civil law, and this for the obvious reasons that criminal justice is of earlier necessity, and is more simple in its nature, than civil justice; and in criminal justice the Saxons had so far learned from the Roman system as to have an intelligent mode of trial by king's judges, and "jurors," or sworn judges, of the facts; and, as we find, from the only relics of this system,[2] they had so far advanced as to have acquired the advantage of judicial decisions and settled precedents.

But these judicial decisions, although of the greatest

---

[1] Thus, in the laws of Edgar it is provided, that in every borh (*i. e.*, borough) and hundred a certain number of men, in each hundred twelve, were to be appointed as witnesses, who were to be sworn to give true testimony, and some of whom were to witness every transaction, that they might be afterwards called to give testimony in any civil or criminal proceeding arising out of the transaction (*Edgar*, iv., 5, 6). There are similar provisions in later Saxon laws.

[2] In the *Mirror of Justice*, which, though in its present form as recent as the reign of Edward I., incorporates an earlier work of the age of Alfred, and gives several judicial decisions of that time which are unmistakably Saxon, all the names being Saxon, and all the names of the judges after the Conquest being known through the learned labors of Mr. Foss. Thus, under the head of Mayhem (a copious head of law under the Saxons, as we see from their laws), we read, "And Turgis *saith*, that the loss of the fore-teeth is Mayhem. And Sennall *said*, that the loss of the eyes is Mayhem;" in which the difference of tense will be observed, and it is implied that Turgis was still living when this passage was written. "And Billing saith," etc., as to which the same remark applies; and it is to be added that Billing appears among the names of judges hanged by order of Alfred, as stated in a subsequent chapter (*Mirror of Justice*, c. i., s. 9). So again (s. 10), "And Burmond enacted that all goods of those who fled should be awarded to the king. And Iselgram said," etc. Here the names are clearly Saxon, and Burmond also appears among the names of judges hanged by order of Alfred. So again (c. ii., s. 26), it is said that "Hailif gave a notable judgment," which must have been in Saxon times, for the name is Saxon, and there is no mention of any such judge after the Conquest. So, in s. 12, it is expressly stated that there was such a course taken in a case mentioned, "in the time of king Edmund." There are also forms of indictments given, one of which is stated to have been used in the case just mentioned, and in all of which the names are pure Saxon.

interest, as the earliest extant, yet are, as might be expected, extremely rude and rudimentary; and the records yet remaining of contemporary history show[1] that, though there was trial by jury and judicial authority, both parts of the judicial system were in the rudest possible state, as might be supposed when a new system, borrowed from a highly civilized law like the Roman, was engrafted on the usages of a rude and barbarous race like the Saxon. And it must be manifest that, while the Saxon institutions remained in their primitive form, there could be no regular judicature, and therefore no regular law.

The Anglo-Saxon system, indeed, had advanced thus far, that judicial decisions were of value as precedents, and as having a kind of quasi-legislative authority, at all events as declaratory or explanatory of the law, and they seem even to have gone a step further, and to have given to such decisions the effect almost of legislative ordinances.[2]

---

[1] Thus, in the *Mirror of Justice* it is stated, that Alfred caused forty-four justices in one year to be hanged as murderers for their false judgments. The instances are all given, and some of them well illustrate the system, and confirm the above observations upon it. "He hanged Cordwine, because that he judged Hackwy to death without the consent of all the jurors. He hanged Markes, because he judged During to death by *twelve men who were not sworn*. He hanged Billing, because he judged Leston to death by fraud, in this manner: he said to the people, 'Sit ye all here but he who assisted to kill the man,' and because that Leston did not sit with the others, he commanded him to be hanged, and said that he did assist, whereas he knew that he did not. He hanged Thurston, because he judged Thuringer to death by a verdict of inquest without issue joined. He hanged Athelsan, because he judged Herbert to death for an offence not mortal. He hanged Rombold, because he judged Lischild to death in a case not notorious, and without indictment. He hanged Friburne, because he judged Harpen to die, whereas the jury were in doubt in their verdict, for in doubtful cases we ought to save rather than condemn. He hanged Wolmer, because he judged Graunt to death by color of a larceny of a thing he had received by bailment. He hanged Therberne, because he judged Oscot to death for a fault whereof he was acquitted before. He hanged Oskitell, because he judged Catlin to death by the record of the coroner, without trial of the truth." And it is stated that Alfred hanged all the judges who had falsely saved a man guilty of death, or had falsely hanged any man against law or any reasonable exception. The number of these justices shows that they might only have been sheriffs or local judges, and it is to be borne in mind that in criminal cases the trial must be local, and the sheriff was the criminal judge in the county.

[2] There is a remarkable passage in the *Mirror*, in which it is stated that Thurmond ordained that criminal actions should cease at the year's end if not brought before, and the same time he appointed in all actions for things lost, and in personal actions he appointed the term after the last eyre (*i. e.*, seven years), and in real actions forty years (c. ii., s. 23.). Now, Thurmond was clearly neither a Saxon nor a Norman king, neither was he a judge after the Conquest, for the names of the judges since then are known. He was

But this would be comparatively of little importance so long as there were only numerous inferior local judges, without the control of a regular superior judicature.

The study of those portions of the *Mirror*, which are plainly, from their internal evidence, Saxon, undoubtedly shows a far greater progress and development in law than could be gathered from the perusal of the written laws of the Saxons, and affords a remarkable illustration of the fallacy of looking to the written laws alone as evidence of the state of their law. The truth is, that the written laws only represented part of their law, and that part the worst. It represented most of what was of their own growth and introduction, and therefore was barbarian. It did not represent much that was infinitely more valuable, which was unwritten, and had been handed down by tradition, or was embodied in institutions. The written laws, for example, represent the usages of compurgators and the ordeal, but scarcely give a glimpse of trial by jurors or witnesses, and a whole system of criminal procedure, to be gathered from the *Mirror*.[1]

There are allusions to incidents of the manorial system, as the state of villenage, but only allusions, and not even allusions to the municipal system, with all its valuable privileges. It is from another source we must obtain information as to those portions of the law which were most valuable to the people, and were unwritten and embodied in customs or traditions or institutions; and this will explain much that is otherwise inexplicable in our history.

It can be shown from other sources, and has been partly shown already, that the most valuable rights of the people were embodied in *customs*, which were unwritten. It can be shown, for instance, that the bulk of the people held their lands entirely by custom.[2]

---

therefore some Saxon judge or sheriff, and, as a baronial judge, he must have been a judge of the county, either as sheriff or by special commission for the county. But he evidently assumed a power to ordain. There is a similar passage as to one Lenfred, who, it is said, ordained the "wager of law" as to contracts, but this may have been only a judicial application of the system of compurgators: out of which wager of law certainly arose.

[1] A system of presentment by grand jurors, of indictment upon their oaths, and of trial by juries.

[2] There is a passage in the *Mirror* which states that when the "first conquerors" distributed the lands, "they enfeoffed the earls of earldoms, the barons of baronies, the knights of knights-fees, villeins of villenages, and

It was difficult in that age to collect and embody unwritten law, insomuch that when after the Conquest it was attempted to put the Saxon laws into writing,[1] the first collection contained so little worthy of regard, that historians have been disposed either to dispute their authenticity, or to wonder at the importance which appears to have been attached to them by the body of the people. But afterwards, when, probably after further inquiry, another collection of laws was framed,[2] containing more of the *unwritten* customs of the country, it was easy to see their value and importance, seeing that they contained recognitions of the customs as to the villeins or cultivators of the soil, in entire accordance with the Roman law, and sometimes almost to the exact effect of imperial edicts on the subject, assuring the possession of their lands on condition of rendering their services; and also contained recognitions of those free popular tribunals or assemblies, on which perhaps the people most relied for the maintenance of these customs.[3] And it is to be ob-

burgesses of boroughs (no mention being made, it will be observed, of common freeholders), whereof, it is added, some received their lands to hold by villein customs, as to plough their lord's lands, to reap, cut, and carry his hay or corn; and although the people have no charters, deeds, or muniments of their lands, yet if they were ejected or put out of their possessions wrongfully, they might be restored, because they knew the certainty of their services." And then it is stated that St. Edward, in his time, caused inquiry to be made of all such who held and did to him such services; and after-. wards (*i. e.*, after the Conquest), many of these villeins, by wrongful distresses, were forced to do their lords services, to bring them into servitude again (*Mirror*, c. 2, s. 28), which is confirmed by a passage in Bracton, "Fuerunt etiam in conquestu liberi homines qui libere tenuerunt tenementa sua per libera servitia vel per liberas consuetudines, et cum per potentiores ejecti essent, postmodum reversi receperunt eadem tenementa sua tenenda in villenagio faciendum inde opera servitia sed certa," etc. (lib. i., c. 11, fol. 7).

[1] The collection of the laws of the Confessor, made by order of the Conqueror.

[2] The laws of the Conqueror — those first passed by him in affirmance of the Confessor's customs and laws.

[3] "Isti sunt leges et consuetudines quas Willielmus Rex post adquisionem Angliæ omni populo Anglorum concessit tenendas, eadem videlicet quas predecessor suus Edwardus rex, servavit in Anglorum regno." This was not entirely true, but to a great extent it was; at all events, as to the rights of the rural tenants, the villani, "Coloni et terrarum exercitores, non vexentur ultra debitum et statutum, nec liceat dominis removere colonos a terris dummodo debita servitia persolvant" (c. 29). This will be found in exact accordance, on the one hand, with the Rectitudines personarum of the Saxon times, "Villani rectum est varium, *secundum quod in terra statutum est;*" and, on the other hand, is also in exact accordance with the imperial edicts on the subject. So, again, "Nativi non recedant a terris suis, nec querant in-

SAXON LAW RECOGNIZED AT THE CONQUEST. xci

served that in the recognition by the Conqueror of the
Saxon's "laws," allusion is expressly made to others[1] not
recorded, and which were doubtless unwritten laws or
customs, relating to the customary rights of the people,
chiefly as to the tenure of lands and their popular assemblies or tribunals; in other words, relating to the municipal and manorial systems, and the popular tribunals, or
assemblies of the people.

And in the laws of the Conqueror[2] it is to be observed

---

genium unde dominum suum debito servitio sui defraudent" (c. xxx.). "Si
domini terrarum non procurent idoneos cultores ad terras suas colendas justiciarii hoc faciant" (c. xxxii.). These laws, again, are entirely in accordance with the Roman edicts on the subject.

[1] The report of the Royal Commission of Enquiry into the Anglo-Saxon
Laws already alluded to, has these statements added to it: "Quam cum ipse
Willielmus rex (i. e., the Conqueror) audivit, et alias leges de regno, maxime
appreciatus est eam, et voluit ut ipsa observaretur per totum regnum; quia
dicebat quod antecessores sui et omnium de Normanni de Norweia venerunt,
et legem eorum cum honesta erat, bene deferent sequi cum profundior et
honestior, sit omnibus aliis, sicut Britonum et Anglorum. Sed omnes compatrioti qui leges narraverunt summopere precati sunt eum ut permitteret eis
leges et consuetudines habere cum quibus vixerant antecessores eorum et
ipsi nati sunt, quia durum erat eis suscipere leges et judicare de eis quas nesciebant. Tandem concilio et precatu baronum adquievit et sic auctoritati
sunt leges Regis" (Anglo-Saxon Laws and Institutes, v. 1).

[2] In these laws many of the Saxon laws or institutions are recognized —
indeed, all that relate to the rural or civil system of the country as apart
from the military. The functions of the "hundredors," for instance (s. 5).
So the system of local trials, the original of trials by jury: "Si voluerit
quis convencionem terræ tenendæ adversus dominum suum disracione per
pares suos de eodem tenemento, quos in testimonium vocaverit, disracionabit,
quia per extraneos id facere non poterit" (s. 23). "Nemo querelam ad regem deferant nisi ei jus defecerit in hundredo vel comitatu" (s. 43). Then
in a charter—the original of Magna Charta: "Volumus etiam ac concedimus ut omnes liberi homines habeant et teneant terras suas et possessiones
suas bene et in pace libere ab omni exactione injusta, et ab omni tallagio,
ita quod nihil ab eis exigatur vel capiatur nisi servitium suum liberam, quod
de jure nobis facere debent et facere tenentur et prout statutum est eis, et illis
a nobis datum et concessum jure hereditario in perpetuum" (s. 5; Anglo-
Saxon Laws, vol. i., p. 491). The principle of this would extend even to the
villeins, and was, indeed, applied to them in one of the laws of the Conqueror, embodying the whole principle of the Roman law upon the subject:
"Coloni et terrarum exercitores non vexentur ultra debitum et statutum:
ne licet dominis removere colonos a terris dummodo debita servitia persolvant" (s. 29). And again: "Si domini terrarum non procurent idoneos
cultores ad terras suas colendas, justiciarii hoc faciant." So as to boroughs,
there was this important recognition of their privileges: "Si servi permanserunt sine calumnia per annum et diem in civitatibus nostris vel in
burgo a die illa liberi efficiantur et liberi a jugo servitutis suæ sunt in perpetuum" (s. 16; A.-S. L., p. 494). And there was a general re-enactment
of the laws of Edward, with the addition of those enacted by the Conqueror
(s. 13, p. 473).

that beyond the general recognition of former customs, there is an express mention made of the popular tenure of land, as villenage (which had then acquired the character of customary right), and also of the popular tribunals. And so, from the time of the Conquest to the time of Magna Charta,[1] there were repeated confirmations of the laws and *customs* which prevailed previous to the Conquest, except so far as altered by positive enactments; that is to say, the municipal and manorial systems, neither of them being inconsistent with the feudal, and both of which were, as has been seen, of Roman origin, were preserved, with the rights and customs appertaining thereto; and, on the other hand, as guarantees of popular rights and customs, the ancient popular tribunals, or rather assemblies, of the county and the hundred, were also preserved.

Beyond these, indeed, there was really little to preserve that was worthy of the name of laws, except such scraps and fragments of Roman law as had got into the *written* Saxon laws; and as to these, it is to be observed, the people showed no anxiety. It was their customary laws and rights for the preservation of which they were anxious, and of which the explanation has been given. But *customs*, although valuable as sources of grounds of rights, or the origin of institutions, afford of themselves no adequate source of a system of law or a source of jurisprudence. There is, indeed, often an antagonism between custom, and reason, which is the only true basis of *law;* for customs, having their origin in rude and primitive times, may by no means have been founded upon reason, and therefore can afford no sure basis for law. This was

---

[1] The charter of the Conqueror has already been cited in which it was declared, "Hoc quoque præcipimus ut omnes habeant et teneant, leges Edwardi regis in omnibus rebus adauctis, hiis quas constituimus ad utilitatem anglorum" (*Ang.-Sax. Laws*, v. 1, p. 493). So there was a charter of Henry I. in which are these words, "Lugam (legem) Edwardi regis vobis reddo cum illis emendationibus quibus eam emendavit pater meus consilio baronum suorum" (*Ibid.*, p. 51); and there are references to specific clauses in the collection of the laws of the Confessor, already alluded to, and hastily discarded, by Spelman, Hume, and Reeves, as "spurious." This charter formed the basis of the subsequent charters, which all contain confirmations of the ancient laws and customs of the country. There was also a charter of Henry I. to the city of London, in like manner the basis of all subsequent charters of the civic liberties of that and other ancient cities, whose privileges, it has been seen, were of Roman origin.

illustrated in the county courts, the popular tribunals of the Saxons, which, rude, turbulent, and tumultuous, were wholly unsuited for law or justice. These institutions might have sufficed for the rude times in which they were established, but as wealth increased, and interests became more complicated, there arose a necessity for a regular system of law and jurisprudence, which require to be developed from principles, and derived from some certain standard. Such a source of law and jurisprudence was to be found in the Roman law, and there alone; but a system of law could only be deduced therefrom by judicial decisions, which required a regular judicature, learned judges, and legal tribunals.

And the difficulty was to attain this object consistently with the maintenance of those great local popular tribunals to which the people clung so closely, as the guarantees of those customs on which their dearer rights depended. And it is most interesting and instructive — perhaps one of the most interesting points in the whole history of our law — to observe how the difficulty was surmounted, and the object attained; and, above all, to observe how easily it was done, with how little of apparent change, with what an utter absence of any violent or sudden change, and by what a happy adaptation of the existing institutions to the recognized exigency of the age.

The institutions of this country, as they arose by usage and prescription, were adapted to the wants and usages of the time in which they arose; on the other hand, became in course of time, as circumstances changed, obsolete; and other institutions grew up, in like manner, to meet the circumstances and exigencies of a subsequent age.[1] This was eminently the case with the popular tribunals of the Saxons.

[1] Thus, the court leet, which, as was said in the *Year-Book*, is the most ancient court of the realm (7 *Hen. V.*, 12), was restricted, by the very prescription which created it, to matters of common nuisance and the like, and had no cognizance of other offences (*Year-Book*, 4 Ed. IV., c. 31; 8 Ed. IV., 15, 27; assize 6, 22 Ed. IV., 22). And a particular or private wrong could not be inquired of there, as an assault (*Martin, J.*, 4 *Hen. VI.*, 10). It is governed by usage and prescription in all its proceedings (2 *Inst.*, 72–163). Hence, when new matters arose, as the tanning of leather, or the like, it was held to have no jurisdiction (*Brooke's Abr., tit. Jurisdiccion*). And even as to the sale of bread, as to which it had jurisdiction, it was held that it had not jurisdiction in cases arising under a modern statute fixing the weight of a

In those early times, the only notion the northern nations had of administration of justice, was a kind of rough arbitration, or rude determination by a popular assembly,[1] which bore no resemblance to a judicial tri-

loaf, without reference to price, because that was not strictly an assize of bread, and the jurisdiction of the leet was by prescription restricted to that; and Lord Mansfield said "These courts were very properly adapted to the customs and manners of a people upon their first settlement; but, like all other human jurisdictions, vary in the course and progress of time, as the government and manners of a people take a different turn, and fall under different circumstances. From the time of Magna Charta, the local jurisdictions had been gradually abridged, never enlarged. Experience shows the wisdom of widening, instead of contracting, the circle of civil and criminal jurisdiction" (*Colebrook* v. *Elliot*, 3 Burrow's Rep., 1859). "Justice, in this kingdom, of which it has always been tender, is singularly adapted to the frame of the English government, and the disposition of the English nation; and such, as by long experience and use, is, as it were, incorporated into their very temperament, and became, in a manner, the complexion and constitution of the English commonwealth" (*Hale's Hist. Com. Law*, c. 3). Hence it is that the Parliament have always been jealous of the reformation of what has been at any time found defective in it, and so to remove all such obstacles as might obstruct the free course of it, and support the use of it as the best and truest rule of justice in all matters civil and criminal (*Ibid.*). Thus also Sir M. Hale says: "From the nature of laws themselves in general, which, being to be accommodated to the condition, exigencies, and conveniences of the people, for or by whom they are appointed, the administration of those exigencies and conveniences do insensibly grow upon the people, so many times there grows insensibly a variation of laws; but though those particular variations and accessions have happened in the laws, yet they, being only partial and successive, are the same laws," etc. (*Ibid.*, c. 4).

[1] "The various expedients which were employed in order to introduce a more regular, equal, and vigorous administration of justice, contributed greatly towards the improvement of society. What were the particular modes of dispensing justice in their several countries, among the various barbarous nations which overran the Roman empire, and took possession of its different provinces, cannot now be determined with certainty. We may conclude from the form of government established among them, as well as from their ideas concerning the nature of society, that the authority of the magistrate was extremely limited, and the independence of individuals proportionately great. The magistrate could hardly be said to hold the sword of justice; it was left in the hands of private persons. Resentment was almost the sole motive for prosecuting crimes, and, to gratify that passion, was considered as the chief end of punishing them. He who suffered the wrong was the only person who had the right to pursue the aggressor, and to exact or to remit punishment. From a system of judicial procedure so crude and defective that it seems to be scarcely compatible with the subsistence of civil society, disorder and anarchy naturally flowed. To provide remedies for these evils so as to give a more regular course to justice, was during several centuries one great object of political wisdom" (*Robertson's Hist. Charles V., Prelim. Dissert. State of Europe*, s. 5). "The greater part of affairs in common life or business was carried on by verbal contracts or promises. This, in many civil questions, not only made it difficult to bring proof sufficient to establish any claim, but encouraged falsehood and fraud by render-

bunal; and which, conscious of its incapacity to get at the truth, took refuge in such wretched expedients as the ordeal.

Such an assembly was the Saxon county court; and, originally, the only court of general and ordinary jurisdiction was the county court.[1] Before the Conquest, it was the only such court: at the Conquest, the court continued to exist with its ancient jurisdiction, and was even called the court of the king, there being still for some time no other court of general and ordinary jurisdiction; though it was not long before its defects were discovered, and measures were taken to modify and improve it.

And, at that time, the only remedy which the suitor could require from the king,[2] was a writ to compel the

---

ing them extremely easy. Even in criminal cases where a particular fact must be ascertained, or an accusation must be disproved, the nature and effect of legal evidence were little understood by barbarous nations. To define with accuracy that species of evidence which a court had reason to expect, to determine when it ought to insist on positive proof, and when it should be satisfied with a proof from circumstances, to compare the testimony of discordant witnesses, and to fix the degree of credit due to each, were discussions too intricate and subtle for the jurisprudence of ignorant ages. In order to avoid encumbering themselves with these, a more simple form of procedure was introduced into courts, as well civil as criminal. In all cases where the notoriety of the fact did not furnish the clearest and most direct evidences, the person accused, or he against whom the action was brought, was called or offered to purge himself by oath. . . . This, however, proved a feeble remedy. . . . and the sentences of courts. . . . became so flagrantly iniquitous as to excite universal indignation against this method of procedure. Sensible of these defects, but strangers to the manner of correcting them, our ancestors appealed to heaven, and adopted the ordeal," etc. (*Robertson's Hist. Charles V., Prelim. Dissert.*, s. v.). This is very accurate, and applicable.

[1] All through the Saxon laws, it is so spoken of, and there is no trace of any court of superior jurisdiction. Even after the Conquest — though steps were taken to improve it by sending down the king's justiciary to preside over it — still it continued with its ancient jurisdiction; and in the laws of Henry I., it is called the *curia regis* (*Leges Hen. Prim.*, c. 31), in which the bishops and barons of the county sat, and which had jurisdiction, without any limitation, over all causes arising within the county, with power to cite or summon defendants, or parties sued, even though residing in other counties (*Leges Hen. Prim.*, c. 41).

[2] Thus in the laws of the Conqueror, c. 43: — "Nemo querelam ad regem deferat, nisi ei jus defecerit in hundredo vel in comitatu." This was one of the laws he passed at the instance of the people as one of their ancient laws: "Isti sunt leges et consuetudines quas Willielmus rex omni populo Anglorum concessit tenendas eidem, videlicet, quas predecessor suus observavit." The previous Saxon laws contained similar enactments; and there can be no doubt that the people were obstinately attached to their old popular tribunals until experience had shown their mischievous character.

xcvi INTRODUCTION TO THE PRESENT EDITION.

sheriff to hear and determine the cause in the county court.¹ Nor even to that extent, until an attempt had been made to get the cause so heard in that court. Indeed, the people were at that time obstinately attached to their ancient popular tribunals; and even the power of the Conqueror could not anticipate the effects of experience, or venture at once to alter or abolish them.

The county court, originally, was simply an assembly of the people of the county,² who, from necessity, formed a kind of natural tribunal, composed of neighbors, who, by a kind of mutual arbitration, settled disputes among themselves, rather by discussion, or perhaps acclamation, than with any forms of regular justice, or the rules of a legal tribunal.

There can be no doubt that the ancient county court jurisdiction, in so far as it was not one of mere rough arbitration by neighbors, mainly regulated by what came to very much the same thing — viz., the local customs of the counties,³ which, from various causes, varied greatly,

---

¹ Thus, in the *Mirror*, it is said, indeed, that a man might have a remedial writ to the sheriff in this form: "Questus est nobis, quod, etc. Et ideo tibi (vices nostras in hac parte committentes), præcipimus, quod causam illam audias et legitimo modo decidas" (c. 182).

² This, indeed, is the language used by the *Mirror* in one of the earlier and more ancient chapters, in which it treats of superior courts. It says, from the first assemblies came consistories, which we now call courts, and these courts are called county courts, where the judgment is by the suitors, if there be no writ, and it is by ordinary jurisdiction (c. i., s. 15). Hence in the Saxon laws the county court is called folcmote, or meeting of the people. Even in the reign of Henry I., it is called shire-mote (*Leg. Hen. Prim.*, s. 8). Hence the suitors, *i.e.*, the freeholders, were — so long as the ancient jurisdiction was exercised — the judges of the court. This, it is obvious, was practically an assembly of the people; and, naturally, in such a simple tribunal, the opinion and testimony of the near neighbors of the parties, the inhabitants of the same hundred or vill, would be sought, so that, virtually, the trial was by the neighbors.

³ The county in those days was put for the country. It was always well understood that it was the custom of the county, not any particular place in it, which could be called the custom of the country, though any mere local custom might be called in the particular locality where it existed. Thus in the report of an ancient case, *temp.* Edward II. it is said — "Nota, en cas usage defait commune ley, que usage usée permy le pais defait commune ley, mes usage de un vill'ou de deux, ne defait commune ley: que un feme porta son breve de dower de la mort, etc., des tenements que furent a son baron, le que tient les tenements en soccage, et ne fut pas respond a cet demande, avant quel allega usage de tout le counte que femes furentdowables de les tenements que lour barons tiendrent en soccage per tout le counte" (*Year-Book*, 17 *Edw. II.*, 212). So "le custome et usage de Oxenford" (*Year-Book*, 21 *Edw. III.*, 46). "Le custome de Northamptonshire par le delivery d'un

and the observance of which, of course, as the only rule of law (though under certain limits it may be useful) must be fatal to anything like that uniformity of law to obtain which is one of the great objects of an intelligent system of justice.

It will be manifest, on a moment's reflection, that where the laws are, with the exception of mere rude usages or rudimentary institutions, unwritten — a system of law can only be developed by judicial decisions of men learned in some system of law.[1] And as there was then no system of law extant, but the wondrous comprehensive system of the Roman law, in itself all-sufficient — and there was that — it would follow that the object could only be attained by placing the administration of justice virtually in the hands of judges learned in that law, and who might, by the light of its principles, applied and modified as need might be, work out a system of law suited to English customs and English institutions. There was no difficulty in finding such an order of men for judges.

These were, as Mackintosh and Guizot have pointed out, the Roman ecclesiastics; and these had acquaintance with the Roman law.[2] The difficulty was how to get the

---

distresse en l'absence de'l bailey del francpledge" (30 *Edw. III.*, 23). So in Bracton mention is made of "the custom of Epswic" (Ipswich). So in Glanville it is said that the customs of the county courts varied in different counties as to criminal law (lib. xiv.), which may have been one reason why Magna Charta took away the jurisdiction criminal from the sheriffs.

[1] Guizot points out the necessity, for the reason above mentioned, of a judicial order; of a class of persons especially devoted to the administration of justice; and shows how justice could not be duly administered under the feudal system from the want of such an order, and also from the want of an independent body of judges of the facts. "The vassals," he says, "it was very difficult to collect, that they might judge. They came not, or when they did come, it was the suzerain who arbitrarily selected them. That great and beautiful system, the intervention of the country, therefore, necessarily fell into decline, from the most powerful of causes, *inapplicability*" (vol. ii., lec. 151). He shows how, as from these causes, the feudal principle of judgment by peers became impracticable, another judicial principle was then introduced — a class of men devoted to the function of judges. "Thus," he says, "commenced the modern judicial order, of which the great characteristic is the having made of the administration of justice a distinct profession; the special and exclusive task of a certain class of citizens." And another characteristic he points out was its central character; the royal superseding all local jurisdictions by establishing one sovereign and supreme (lec. 14).

[2] There had been an absurd tradition among English lawyers and historians, from the time of Blackstone, to the effect that the Roman law had per-

administration of justice virtually under their control throughout the country.

They were members of a *curia regis*, the great court or council of the king; and as, in that age, they were the only persons who had any notion of law or jurisprudence, they were necessarily the chief members of that supreme tribunal, which, however, does not appear to have had any original or ordinary jurisdiction, and was rather a council than a court of justice: a council in which the sovereign sat to hear complaints of the administration of justice, in the exercise of his prerogative, the care of the justice of the realm.[1]

And by those, as already seen, under the Saxon law, which had been solemnly recognized and established, the general justice of the realm, civil and criminal, was administered in the local popular tribunals of the county or the hundred, in which—in civil cases, at all events—the "suitors," or freeholders, were the judges, although it had become recognized even in Saxon times that the sheriff was the king's judge in criminal cases, and that it was proper to swear a select body of the suitors, and constitute a tribunal of sworn judges or jurors.[2]

---

ished, and that it was suddenly brought to light by the discovery of a copy of the Pandects at Amalfi in the middle of the twelfth century. As already shown, the whole course of the Saxon laws and Saxon history shows that the Roman law had never been lost sight of, and, as Mr. Hallam observes, "That this body of laws was absolutely unknown in the West during any period, seems to have been too hastily supposed. Some of the more eminent ecclesiastics occasionally refer to it, and bear witness to the regard which the Roman Church had uniformly paid to its decisions" (*Europe in the Middle Ages*, c. viii.).

[1] Thus in the laws of the Conqueror there is mention made of the sheriff being convicted before the king's justiciary, which means the supreme judicial minister or officer of the kingdom, who exercised a supreme jurisdiction over the sheriffs. In the laws of the Confessor (c. xvii.), there is a provision that except in cases of special franchises, persons should do right before the justice of the king, in the hundred or the shire (s. 22). This was upon the principle that the sheriff was the justice of the king, as no doubt he was, although he sat in popular tribunals; and in the civil, if not the criminal sessions of the county court, the suitors or freeholders were the judges; yet he was the justice of the king in criminal cases, and, as already has been seen, even under the Saxon kings, it had become recognized that properly the freeholders ought to be made jurors—that is, be selected and sworn to decide justly. At all events, this was done in the time of Alfred.

[2] That juries were used in criminal cases in the time of Alfred is manifest from the *Mirror of Justice*, which states that he caused several justices to be hanged for false judgment, and one of them because he judged a man to death without the consent of all the jurors; and another "because he judged

From this an inference was drawn, which led to the
first step in the course of improvement: that the crown
could appoint a *special* justiciary to hold a county court.
Accordingly, when the unfitness of the county court to
determine matters of importance was observed, the course
at first adopted to remedy the evil was[1] by sending down
king's justices into the counties to convene the counties,
either being appointed sheriffs, or, under special commissions issued for the purpose, to preside at the trial of
particular cases, a course necessarily taken when the
sheriff was personally interested.

It would very soon occur to a judge, with any knowledge of what was due to the administration of justice, to
have a certain number of the freeholders sworn and empanelled to give their verdict. This made them jurors,
and converted a turbulent county court into a judicial
body of jurors, under the direction of a judge with some
notion of law. And this mode of proceeding was often
adopted, either by making skilled judges sheriffs,[2] or by

---

a man to death by twelve men who were not sworn;" and another "because
he hanged a man to die whereas the jury were in doubt of their verdict; for
in doubtful cases one ought rather to save than to condemn." And he
hanged the "suitors" of one place because they judged a man to death by
jurors for a felony he did out of their liberty. It is clear that the justices
and jurors in these cases are equally distinguished from the suitors, and that
the justices were the sheriffs, and the jurors sworn suitors or freeholders.

[1] This was done soon after the Conquest, in a great case in the Kent county
court between the Archbishop of Canterbury and Odo of Bayeux. A foreign
prelate — "qui in loco regis fuit vel justiciam habuit," and who was no
doubt chosen as skilled in law — was sent down under a special commission,
as king's justiciary, to hold the county court (1 *Mad. Ex.*, 32), and its turbulence was so obviously unsuited for justice, that he ordered twelve freeholders
to be sworn and empanelled — the first trial by jury (*Dugdale's Orig. Jurid.*,
21). Other similar instances occurred even in the reign of the Conqueror.
Sir J. Mackintosh took the view above suggested as to the origin of trial by
jury, and its arising out of the county court. "Perhaps," he says, "the first
conception of it may have been suggested by the very simple expedient of
referring a cause by the county court to a select body of their number, who
were required to be twelve, for no reason that has been discovered. . . . In
civil cases, the obvious analogy of arbitrators might have contributed to the
adoption of jurors. . . . A case is preserved in the reign of William I.
which has much the appearance of the dawn of trial by jury." He cites it,
and then observes, "Here we see a reference from the county court to twelve
men. The trial by twelve (*i. e.*, twelve sworn men-jurors) became so much
the usual course of proceeding, that it was now called the course and order
of the common law" (*Hist. Eng.*, vol. i.).

[2] In those times the sheriff was always himself a potent person — perhaps
a prelate or a peer — and he might have suits against others or against himself; and there might, for this and other reasons, be necessity for sending

sending them as justices into the counties, under special royal commissions, to try particular cases whenever there was found any excuse for so doing.

This, however, was only a remedy in particular cases, and under the Conqueror and his successors, until the middle of the reign of Henry I., the common justice of the realm was still administered in the county court and other local courts of an inferior order.[1] Indeed, at that time the county court was still called *curia regis*, and there is no trace of any other court — at all events, of primary or ordinary jurisdiction. And an attempt was made to improve the county court by compelling the barons to attend there.

The administration of the justice thus dispensed in numerous local courts[2] was in a state utterly unsatisfactory,

---

kings' justices, as in the case of the suit between the bishop of Rochester and the sheriff of Cambridgeshire, which was tried in the county court before the king's justiciary, who was a prelate, and who also, no doubt, had a sworn jury (*Dugdale's Orig. Jurid.*, 21). But the king's justices were often made sheriffs. Numerous instances of this are given in the learned work of Mr. Foss (*Lives of the Judges*, vol. i., p. 186, 189, 377). The same person was sometimes sheriff of several counties (*Ib.*, p. 292), and held the office for years (345), and the chief justiciary was often made sheriff of several counties (264). The most remarkable instance of this was the illustrious Glanville, who had been for many years a justice and a sheriff, and was ultimately made chief justiciary (p. 130).

[1] Thus in the *Leges Henrici Primi*, the barons of the county (c. xxix.) are said to be the king's judges: "Regis judices sunt barones comitatus qui liberas in eis terras habent," which (as Spelman says) clearly means the freeholders; and afterwards it is said that the bishops and counts, etc., ought to be in the county court, and that no one can dispute the record of the court of the king, which clearly means the county court mentioned just before. "Interesse comitatu debent episcopi comites, etc. Recordationem curiæ regis nulli negare potest. Unusquisque per pares suos judicandus est et ejusdem provinciæ" (c. xxxi.). That is, by the fellow-suitors, the fellow-freeholders of the county. Afterwards it is said: "Si quis in curia placitum habent convocet pares et vicinos suos; ut, inforciati judicio, gratuitam, et cui contradici non possit, justitiam exhibeat" (c. 33).

[2] "The administration of the common justice of the kingdom," says Hale, speaking of a period even later, "seems to have been wholly dispensed in the county courts, the hundred courts, and courts baron. This doubtless bred great inconvenience, uncertainty, and variety in the laws: First, by the ignorance of the judges who were the freeholders — and though the bishops, barons, and great men were, by the laws of Henry I., to attend the county courts — they seldom attended there, and if they did, in process of time they neglected the study of the English laws" (as if, at that time, there were any English laws to study!) "Secondly, another inconvenience was, that this bred great variety of laws, especially in the several counties; for, the decision being made by divers courts and several independent judicatories, who had no common interest among them in their several judicatories,

which led of necessity to great uncertainty, variety, and want of uniformity in the law.

thereby, in process of time, every several county would have several laws, customs, rules, and forms of proceeding, which is always the effect of several independent judicatories administered by separate judges. Thirdly, all the business of any moment was carried by parties and factions, for, the freeholders being generally the judges, and, as it were, the chief judges, not only of the fact but of the law, every man that had a suit there sped as he could make parties: and men of great power and interest in the county did easily overbear others in their own causes, or in such wherein they were interested, either by relation of kindred, tenure, service, dependence, or application" (*Hist. Com. Law*, c. 7). "The administration of justice in the county, and other inferior courts, notwithstanding some striking advantages, was certainly pregnant with great evils. The freeholders of the county, who were the judges, were seldom learned in the law. Again, the determinations of so many independent judges, presiding in the several inferior courts dispersed about the country, bred great variety in the laws, which in process of time would have habituated different counties to different rules and customs, and the nation would have been governed by a variety of provincial laws. Besides these inherent defects, it was found that matters were there carried by party and passion. The freeholders, often previously acquainted with the subjects of controversy, or with the parties, became heated and interested in causes, which, added to the influence of great men, rendered these courts unfit for cool deliberation and impartial judgment. Besides, a judicial authority, exercised by subjects in their own names, must weaken the power of the prince, one of whose most valuable royalties, and that which most conciliates the confidence and good inclination of the people, is the power of providing that justice should be duly administered to every individual. Though the appeal from the hundred to the court of the sheriff was kept in check, it was to be wished that justice should be administered in the first instance by judges having their commission from the crown" (*Litt. Hen. II.*, vol. v., 273; *Reeve*, p. 53). So another great author points out how the necessity for regular judges would be gradually recognized. "Men, as soon as they were *acquainted* with fixed and general laws, perceived the *advantage* of them, and became impatient to ascertain the principles and forms by which judges should regulate their decisions. . . . These various improvements in the system of jurisprudence and the administration of justice occasioned a change in manners of great importance, and of extensive effect. This gave rise to a distinction of professions. . . . Among uncivilized nations there is but one profession honorable — that of arms. . . . Nor did the judicial character demand any degree of knowledge beyond that which untutored soldiers possessed. . . . But when the forms of legal proceedings were fixed, when the rules of decision were committed to writing, and collected into a body, law became a *science*, the knowledge of which required a regular course of study, together with long attention to the practice of courts. . . . Not only the judicial determination of points which were the subject of controversy, but the conduct of all legal business and transactions were committed to persons trained by previous study and application to the knowledge of law. The functions of civil life were attended to, the talents requisite for discharging them were cultivated" (*Robertson's Hist. Charles V., Prel. Dissert.*). Thus this eminent author regarded a regular procedure, and the cultivation of justice as a science, and the law as a profession, as great advances in civilization, and a vast improvement in society. And this was so among our ancestors.

For such a state of things it was necessary to find a remedy,[1] and as the attempt to find it in the attendance of persons of eminence at the county courts either proved inadequate, or failed probably from their indisposition to take part in proceedings so turbulent, or perhaps from the want of due regularity in the discharge of a duty which necessarily, in such a state of things, was vague and indefinite: it was therefore necessary, in order to apply a remedy, to apply some new system, and it could only be devised by men who had derived some knowledge of the principles of rational and civilized procedure. There was no source at that time whence that knowledge could be derived except the Roman law, and happily, at that time, the study of that law had revived, and was established in this country.[2] Its results were at once made manifest in a great improvement in our law.

---

[1] The experience already had of a better mode of administering justice no doubt stimulated the desire for it, as Guizot observes. "Instead of a regular gradation of courts, all acknowledging the authority of the same general laws, and looking up to these as the guides of their decisions, there were in every feudal kingdom a number of independent tribunals, the proceedings of which were directed by local customs and contradictory forms. The collision of jurisdiction among these different courts often retarded the execution of justice. The variety and caprice of their various modes of procedure must have forever kept the administration of it from attaining any degree of uniformity or perfection. But the usurpations were so firmly established that kings were obliged to rest satisfied with attempts to undermine them. . . . The attempt, nevertheless, was productive of good consequences. . . . It turned the attention of men towards a sovereign jurisdiction. . . . This facilitated the introduction of appeals, by which princes brought the decisions of the local courts under the review of the royal judges. . . . The sovereigns appointed the royal courts, which were originally ambulatory and irregular with respect to their times of meeting, to be held in a fixed place and at stated seasons. They were solicitous to appoint judges of distinguished abilities. . . . They labored to render their forms regular and their decrees consistent. Such judicatories became, of course, the objects of public confidence. Thus kings became the dispensers of justice," etc. (*Robertson's Hist. Charles V., Introd. Diss.*, s. 5).

[2] It was in the reign of Stephen it was publicly taught at Oxford by Vacarius. From some cause, its study was prohibited by that king, but, says Selden, happily the prohibition failed. "Sed parum valuit Stephani prohibitio, nam eo magis invaluit virtus legis Deo favente qui eam amplius nitebatur impietas subvertere" (*Dissert. ad Flet.*, c. vii., par. 6). That, however, was only on the occasion of its being taught to students at the university, and there might have been reasons for prohibiting it there on the ground of its diverting the students from other studies. There can be no doubt, however, that it had for some time previously been studied by the ecclesiastics, who, in that age, were the only persons possessed of any learning, for the treatise or compilation, called the Laws of Henry I., which was evidently written at the close of his reign, is in a great degree made up of civil and canon law.

The study of that law taught[1] the necessity for a more regular judicature, derived from an order of men devoted

[1] That it had taught this to some eminent persons who were engaged in the administration of justice at that time, is manifest from the composition called "Laws of Henry I." Lord Hale observes of it, that it has a taste of the civil law, but that is far beneath the truth. It is composed, perhaps, in equal portions of Roman law and Saxon law, and is an obvious endeavor to engraft the former upon the latter, or rather to unite a Roman system with Saxon institutions. As to the influence exercised at this important period by the Roman laws upon the formation of our own there can be no doubt; and it is attested by the most eminent of modern historians, who have fully exposed the absurd idea which first gained credence in the pages of Blackstone—that the study of the Roman law was quite a novelty in the twelfth century, and was at once expelled. Thus, Sir James Mackintosh, writing of the reign of Henry I., says, "It is essential to observe, at this step of our progress, that the Roman law never lost its authority in the countries which formed the western empire, and it was adopted into the codes of the Germanic conquerors. All Europe obeyed a great part of the Roman law, which had been incorporated with their own usages, when these last were first reduced to writing, after the Conquest. The Roman provincials retained it altogether as their hereditary rule. The only historical question regards not the obligation of the Roman law, but the period of its being taught and studied as a science. It is not likely that such a study could have been entirely omitted in Roman cities; and where there were probably many who claimed the exercise of the Roman law." The historian here, in a note, cites references from Savigny i., 16, of instances, from 800 to 1160, where the Roman law had been referred to as binding; and he cites, from the same author, instances of prelates who studied the Roman law, among others a Saxon bishop, who studied Roman law at York in the 7th century. "But the Roman jurisprudence did not become a general branch of study till after the foundation of universities. It had made its way to England, and was taught with applause by Vacarius at Oxford about the middle of the 12th century. The late researches of Savigny and other German jurists on the subject have merited the gratitude of Europe. It was, indeed (he adds), a most improbable supposition that a manuscript found at the sack of Amalfi, not adopted by public authority, should suddenly prevail over all other laws in the greater part of Europe." The treatises called *Leges Henrice Primi*, was the first attempt at anything like an intelligent system of procedure, and it lays down all its essential principles. It is, therefore, in these points of view, one of the most interesting documents of our legal history, and has been strangely disregarded. Hale alludes to it, and quotes it several times, and so does our author; but they evidently did not appreciate it in the point of view in which it is now presented, as a step or stage, so to speak, in the history of our law. Lord Hale, however, had evidently given more attention to it than our author, and remarks how much of it is devoted to procedure. That of itself was an immense advance ; for, as Guizot observes, the study of procedure is the beginning of civilization. "If," he says, "you find, in place of the oath of compurgators, or the judicial duel, the proof by witnesses, and a rational investigation of the question, there is the beginning of civilization" (*Lectures on Civilization*). Now that is what we do find in the laws of Henry I. It is impossible not to perceive that the compilation contains the groundwork of a regular system of judicature and of jurisprudence. The laws bear internal evidence that they were composed by an ecclesiastic, and one who had been thoroughly acquainted with the laws in force; as there were few in that age who could have composed such an elab-

to the judicial duty, and qualified for its discharge by knowledge of legal principles; and it furnished ample stores of learning whence that knowledge could be acquired. And it suggested the attempt to mould the popular assemblies into something like regular tribunals, and to blend the Roman system with Saxon institutions. The result was the institution, in the reign of Henry I.,[1]

orate body of laws in Latin, and there was only one man of whom it can be deemed at all probable. That was the celebrated Roger, Bishop of Salisbury, described in the *Dialogus de Scaccario* as "vir prudens consiliis providus," and of whom it is added, "maximis in regno fungebatur honoribus, et de Scaccario plurimum habuit scientiam." This eminent man was in the highest judicial office during nearly the whole reign of Henry I., first as chancellor, and next as chief justiciary and chief baron of the exchequer; and it is remarkable that the provisions in the laws in question, as to the fiscal rights of the crown, were very acute, and show great knowledge of the subject. He died a few years after Henry, and had leisure during the close of his life to make such a compilation; and there was not a single man of his age but himself who could have done it. In the *Mirror of Justice*, a work in its present form written in the reign of Edward I., there are various laws mentioned as ordained by Henry I., and not to be found elsewhere than in this collection. Several chapters at the outset, evidently drawn from the civil and canon law, lay down the general principles on which administration of justice must rest; a judicial order of men; proper judicature and regular procedure, all directed to the due examination of the truth and justice of the case, " Judices in omni discussione probitatis idonei, nullaque exactione permixti." " Causarum qualitas sincera perscrutatione pensanda " (c. v.). "De causis singulorum justis examinationibus audiendis, de præpositi et meliorum hominum presentiæ" (c. vi.). It was laid down that it belonged to the king to look to failure of justice or unjust judgments, or perversion of the law. "Injustum judicium defectus justitiæ prevaricatio legis regiæ" (c. x.). "Defectus justitiæ et violenta recti eorum destitutio est qui causas protrahunt in jus regium " (c. xxxiii.). " Defectus justitiæ commune regis placitum est super omnes" (c. lix.); and that it is the duty of all to obey the summons of the king's justice, " Qui secundum legem submonitus a justitiæ regis ad comitatum venire supersederit reus sit," etc. (liii.). A great lawyer who was profoundly versed in the antiquities of the law of England, has well described the ascendancy which, at this era in the history of our law, the Roman law had gained; and showed how it was resorted to as a guide when there was neither special enactment nor local usage, or when it was desired to have recourse to that perfection of reason which is the solid basis of all law. " Ita jam, id est, sub annum 1145, receptus fuit juris Justinianæi usus, ut quoties interpretandi jura, sive vetera, sive nova, sive ratio, sive analogia desideraretur aut mos aut lex expressior non reperiretur, ad jus illud Justinianæum tum veluti rationis juridicæ promptuarium optimum ac ditissimum, tum ut quod legem in nondum definitus ex ratione seu analogia commode suppleret, esse recurrendum. Certe ita ferme Rhodiam recepere veteres Romani legem in rebus nauticis ut etiam apud nos, et gentes vicinas leges recepiuntur Oleronionæ; cum interim nec hæ nec illæ ex authoritate sui, quâ primo conditæ sunt, vim sic obtinuerint " (*Selden and Flet.*, c. vi., p. 4). So in his *History of Tithes*, c. vii., the same learned author puts its adoption on the ground of reason.

[1] From the 18 Henry I., the rolls in the exchequer show that the justices

of itinerant justices to proceed into the counties under the king's commission, and try such classes of cases, civil or criminal, as might be committed to them by their commissions. This was the first foundation of a regular judicature; of a judicial order of men devoted to the administration of justice. And in the result it worked a revolution in the law of the country.

It is beyond a doubt, whether the laws or the legal

---

went, how long before then is not known, but it is probable that they had gone — though perhaps less regularly, or on special occasions — before then. Indeed it is, as already mentioned, an historical fact that they had gone as early as the reign of the Conqueror in special cases, and instances of it have been adduced. Hence Sir J. Mackintosh observes of the more regular institution of justices itinerant, that it probably only gave permanence to a practice which already existed. In these attempts were the beginnings of regular law and justice. Thus Guizot (*Hist. Civiliz.*, Lect. iii.), pointing out the beginning of civilization among the people of Europe, says, " Look to the system of procedure, and you find in place of the oath of compurgators, or the judicial combat, the proof by witnesses, and a rational investigation of the matter in question. The law begins to bear a systematic and social character. There was a beginning of civilization — an endeavor to bring men under general and regular principles." So Mr. Mill (*Hist. Brit. India*), though rather an admirer of Hindoo and Mahometan systems as "simple and natural" (*i. e.*, rude), admits that they made no provision for uniformity (vol. i., p. 171), and that the Indian system of procedure is liable to the evil of arbitrary power (*Ibid.*, p. 641). He thinks that a regular system of procedure would not prevent this; but it is the object of the present treatise to show that it does. It is very observable that in the early laws of all countries there are few rules of procedure. The laws of Menu scarcely contain any; see Sir W. Jones' Works, vol. iii. So of the Saxon law. So of the Mahometan, as described by Mr. Mill. " The first considerable step towards establishing an equal administration of justice was the abolishment of the right which individuals claimed of waging war with each other. . . . Not only questions concerning uncertain or contested facts, but general and abstract points of law, were determined by the issue of a combat. . . . Thus the form of trial by combat, like other abuses, spread gradually, and extended to all persons and almost to all cases. . . . By this barbarous custom, the natural course of proceeding, both in civil and criminal questions, was entirely prevented. Force usurped the place of equity in courts of judicature, and justice was banished from her proper temple. . . . The clergy from the beginning remonstrated against it as repugnant to Christianity and subversive of justice and order. . . . The spirit of courts of justice became averse to it, and it went more and more into disuse, though instances of it occur as late as the 16th century, in the histories both of France and England. In proportion as it declined, the regular administration of justice was restored; the proceedings of courts were directed by known laws; the study of them became an object of attention to judges; and the people of Europe advanced towards civilization" (*Robertson's Hist. Charles V., Prel. Dissert.*, s. 4). So Hale says, that the "persuasions of the clergy," and the sense of its barbarousness, by degrees drove out the ordeal, so that, although it prevailed all through the reign of John, it was not to be met with in the reign of Henry III.; and, in like manner, the " duel," or trial by battle, gradually died out.

history of the age be looked at,[1] that as early as this reign — the first settled reign after the Conquest, and the first which afforded leisure for anything like a settlement of the judicature and administration of justice of the country — they were settled upon the basis of Saxon institutions, but on the principles of the Roman system; and so as to secure the advantages of a regular judicature with a local administration of justice; and unite trial by jury with settled law.

It is also beyond a doubt that, as necessary to trial by jury, which was thus, at this early period after the Conquest, established in civil cases, there was a procedure for the settlement of the issues to be tried.[2] This, which is essential to such trial in civil cases, where, from their nature, the questions in dispute, and issues to be deter-

---

[1] In the *Mirror of Justice*, it is stated, as it is also stated in the laws of Henry I., above alluded to, that no one had authority without the king's writ to "send for the people: but the king's officers could do so" (c. i., s. 13), whence it would follow that the king's justices could convene the men of the county, as they did in the "itineraries" or assizes, and the laws of Henry I. had a provision that men of the county who did not attend at their summons should be liable to a penalty. And it is also stated in the *Mirror of Justice* (c. xi., s. 4), that in the time of Henry I. it was ordained that *jurors sworn upon assizes* should not have fees. Hence it appears from this ancient law book that in this reign there were trials by jury at the assizes. The records of judicial history show the same thing. It is shown by Mr. Foss (*Lives of the Judges*, vol. i.), that the itineraries of the judges into the counties commenced in this reign, and as they had learned, even under the Conqueror, to turn a county court into a jury, there could be no doubt they continued to do so. But the records of the exchequer show the "itineraries" from the 18 Henry I. Sir J. Mackintosh also observes of this period, "Henry II. divided England into six circuits, not very unlike the present distribution, each of which was to be visited by three itinerant justices, to bring the dispensation of laws home to every man's door" (*Hoveden*, 314). "This statute, however, like others, appears only to have given authority and universality to practices occasionally adopted before" (*Hist. Eng.*, v. i.). Elsewhere also that acute historian observes upon the slow and gradual character of the changes in our laws (*Ibid.*).

[2] The above cited passage plainly proves that trial by jury in civil cases was established in the reign of Henry I., and a subsequent passage in the *Mirror*, coupled with passages in the "Laws of Henry I.," already noticed, as to "exceptions," answers, etc., shows that a system of pleading, in order to settle the issues, must have been established about the same time; and, indeed, without some such system, trial by jury in civil cases would be impossible. The effect of the passage here referred to in the *Mirror* (c. ii., s. 23), is that, as there were great delays in the examinations, and exceptions in an assize, Glanville had ordained an assize by a quicker process; to be tried by twelve jurors of the next neighbors. This shows what, indeed, would be manifest, *à priori* — that there had before his time been some system of pleading anterior to trial.

mined, cannot be known beforehand, as in criminal cases, was also established, substantially, upon the Roman model.

The justices itinerant were sent down by the king's court or council[1] into the counties, chiefly and primarily to hear pleas of the crown, but with commissions, also, to hear pleas in actions as to realty, up to a certain value or amount, sent down to them by the chief justice, or chief justiciary, of the kingdom, or the chief council of the king.

The result of this administration of justice by the justices itinerant on the one hand, and of the study of the civil law upon the other, was that in the reign of Henry II., there was a marked improvement in our system of laws, as indicated by the great treatise of Glanville,[2] which shows an immense advance, and a great superiority over

---

[1] It is stated by Hoveden, 337, that under Henry II., "magno concilio celebrato, rex divisit Angliam in quatuor partes, et unicuique partium præfecit viros sapientes ad faciendam justitiam in terra sua. Isti sunt justiciæ in curia regis constituti ad audiendam clamores populi" (foi. 37). Here it is evident that the phrase *in curia regis* means in the king's council, though it is often supposed that *curia regis* means a superior court of justice. The justices itinerant were not justices of any superior court; they were of an inferior order of judges, as is shown by the limitation of their jurisdiction, which was chiefly *capitula coronæ;* and "capitula de Judæis" (i. e., to rob and oppress the Jews), and "Placita per breve domini regis vel per breve capitalis justiciæ, vel a capitali curia regis, coram eis (justiciis) missa." The civil cases sent down were real actions; and the power of the justices itinerant in these cases was limited to a certain nature: "De magnis assisis quæ sunt de centum solidis et infra," or "De magnis assisis usque ad Decem Libratas Terræ, et infra," etc. Thus in the reign of Henry II., commissions were issued to the itinerant justices, which provided that suits as to real property not above a certain value, should be taken by them in the several counties; but that if questions of weight or doubt should arise, they should be reserved for the justices of the bench; "Quod justiciæ faciant omnes justicias et rectitudines spectantes ad dominium regis per breve domini regis vel illorum qui in ejus loco erunt de feodo dimidii militis et supra. Nisi tam grandis sit quærela quod non possit deduci, sine domino rege vel talis quam justiciæ ei reponunt pro dubitatione sua; vel ad illos qui in loco ejus erunt" (*Hale's Hist. Com. Law,* c. 7). And the justices of the bench, (i. e., of the bench of the exchequer, which appears to have been the only *curia regis* at that time,) were so called, to distinguish them from the justices itinerant, who were more numerous, and of less weight and authority.

[2] "Henry II.," says Hale, "raised the municipal laws of the kingdom to a greater perfection, and a more orderly and regular administration, than before. We need no other evidence of this than the treatise of Glanville, by comparing which with the laws of the Conqueror, or even the laws of Henry I., it will easily appear that the rule and order, as well as the administration of the law, was greatly improved beyond what it was formerly, and we have more proofs of their agreement and concord with the laws, as they were used from the time of Edward I. and downwards, than can be found in these obsolete laws of Henry I., which were indeed but disorderly, confusedly general things, if compared with Glanville's treatise of our laws"

the former state of the law. And this advance was still further aided by the establishment of a superior king's court of civil jurisdiction,[1] and by allowing the defendant in an action the alternative of trial by jury in preference to the brutal "battle," or duel. Thus, on the one hand, a regular judicature was established for determination of questions of law, and, on the other hand, an approach to an intelligent system of trial. There can be no doubt of the tendency of this to improve civil procedure, and to promote the development of law.

The distinguishing feature in the great work of Glanville, and that which more than anything else, perhaps, marks it as an era in our law, is the importance which it attaches to procedure,[2] and, above all, to an intelligent and rational system of trial, by selected and sworn judges, or jurors — precisely upon the principle of the Roman law — open to exception by either party, and so virtually agreed upon by both.

(*Hist. Com. Law*, c. 7, p. 120). Our author also observes of the work of Glanville: "The work of Glanville, compared with the Anglo-Saxon laws, is like the code of another nation; there is not the least feature of resemblance between them" (c. 4). But our author, through not having studied the *Legis Henrici Primi* and the *Mirror*, had missed the intermediate works in the chain of legal history, and lost the course of progression.

[1] The work of Glanville is confined to cases within the cognizance of the *curia regis*, which, it is plain, then meant a regular court of justice, which, there is reason to believe, was the exchequer. The defendant was allowed, in a writ of right, the option of trial by jury, but then the jurors were still witnesses, so that if they had no knowledge of the case, Glanville was in perplexity as to what course ought to be pursued. Nevertheless, as Sir J. Mackintosh observes, "an important attempt was made to banish the absurd usages of ordeal and battle, and *to pave the way for the more general adoption of juries*, by allowing the defendant to support his right by the assize" (*Hist. Eng.*, vol. i.). The assize was, in fact, a trial by twelve jurors, called "recognitors," because they "recognized" of their own knowledge.

[2] The work is largely occupied with procedure. Thus, in describing the trial of an assize, the author is careful to lay down that jurors may be excepted against on the same ground on which witnesses in the court Christian were rejected; (a reference to the canon law, by which witnesses interested on either side were rejected); and, therefore, in order to provide for such objections to jurors, he points out that a larger number than twelve should be summoned, so as to allow for exclusion of some of them by either party (c. 12). It is to be observed, that though unanimity was required to the verdict of a jury, yet there was a rational course resorted to for securing it; that is, by the addition of fresh jurors until twelve should be obtained to decide in favor of one side (c. 17). It is observable that there is the principle of this course still retained in our criminal law, in which grand juries are composed of twenty-three, in order to allow for difference of opinion, and enable a majority of twelve to find or reject the accusation.

So as to criminal procedure,[1] although the old barbarian Saxon or Norman usages were not at once abolished; it was virtually superseded by its being postponed to, and made dependent upon, a more rational examination of the case, on the model of the Roman system; and thus the result was, that they soon became obsolete, and an intelligent system of trial by jury was, by a series of wise judicial decisions, substituted for it. Thus all the great changes in procedure were effected simply by affording the suitors the alternative of a rational system, and putting obstacles in the way of the other.

In the time of Glanville, indeed, civil procedure, though regular, was still in its most simple stage of regular procedure: still, in substance, it was the Roman system. It was conducted under a regular judicature: the case came first before judges, whose province was to settle the question to be decided, and to determine it if it was one of law, or to remit it to the jury — *i. e.*, to sworn judges; to determine it by regular trial, if it was one of fact. And though the discussion was oral, and not formal, it had all the substantial requisites of a rational system of trial, which, though not enforced to the exclusion of the old Saxon institution, was allowed as an option to the party sued, and was therefore virtually substituted: the other becoming gradually superseded until it was obsolete.[2]

---

[1] Thus Glanville says, that on a criminal charge made by public fame, the truth of the matter should be inquired into by means of inquisitions and interrogations made in the presence of the justices, and by taking into consideration the probable circumstances of the facts, and weighing each conjecture that tends in favor of the accused, or makes against him; and it was only if the prosecutor made out his case by proofs that the accused had to purge himself by the ordeal (*per legem apparentem*, which Spelman considers means the ordeal), or entirely absolve himself of the crime imputed to him (B. xiv., c. 1). So that if the accused could, in the opinion of the judges, clear himself, or if there was not a sufficient case, he need not resort to the ordeal. It is not surprising to learn that the ordeal scarcely survived a single reign, and that a short one, after this; and that in the reign of Henry III., it is not heard of (*vide Hale's Com. Law*). So of the trial by battle, it was obsolete ages before it was abolished, though not abolished until our own age.

[2] Thus Glanville says, in describing the procedure in a suit as to real property: "Both parties being present in court, it is usual to inquire of the tenant whether he can show any reason why the assize should not proceed." Then he goes on to say that it should not proceed if the case for the claimant was entirely admitted; but if not entirely so, then the court proceeded to decide the disputed points, whatever they might appear to be (b. 13, c. 11); and the trial might be by a jury. If no exception be taken in court, on account of which the suit ought to cease, then it shall proceed; and in the pres-

The administration of justice, however, was still so unsatisfactory, that complaints were brought before the king in person, or his chief justiciary[1] sitting in the exchequer. But as the suits became more numerous, other justices were added, called justices of the bench, to distinguish them from justices itinerant; and thus a superior court, or *curia regis*, became by degrees established, in which common pleas between party and party could be brought and heard. As this last, however, followed the king, and this was most injurious to the suitor, Magna Charta provided that common pleas should not follow the king; and hence a separate court of "common pleas," established at Westminster.[2]

The Great Charter made two important provisions with reference to common law judicature; one, that common pleas should not follow the person of the king (which implied that they should be heard in some fixed court);

---

ence of both parties, the land shall be on the oath of twelve jurors, and according to their verdict be adjudged to the one or the other as described (*Ibid.*).

[1] Thus it appears, from a case in the *Abbreviatio Placitorum*, says John, that charters of exceptions were granted not to be sued except before the king or his chief justiciary; and in that case, in a suit against the Abbot of Leicester, he pleaded such a charter of king Richard: "quod idem abbas pro nullo respondent, nisi coram ipso rege, vel capitali justiciario suo;" but it was decided that pleas decided before justices of the bench, were in law heard before the king. "Quia omnia placita quæ coram justiciariis de banco tenentur, coram Domino Rege vel ejus capitali justiciario teneri intelliguntur." This shows that, by that time, in the reign of John, the justices of the banc, as they were called, sat in the place of the king, and with or without his chief justiciary; and that there was a court in which common pleas were heard. In the reign of Henry II., the court called *curia regis* was well established, for Glanville has a treatise of cases determined in that court. Thus Magna Charta said that "communia placita non sequantur curia nostra:" that common pleas shall not follow our court; where it will be observed that the term *curia nostra* is used, as it is in the *Leges Henrici Primi*, to signify, not a court of justice, but the royal court or residence; which shows how mistaken those are who suppose that from the mention made of *curia regis*, that there was necessarily a king's court of justice. And from that time, the court of common pleas became established.

[2] Communia placita non sequantur curiam nostram, sed teneantur in aliquo certo loco. Recognitiones de morte antecessoris, etc., non capiantur nisi in suis comitatibus, et hoc modo; nos, vel capitalis justiciarius noster, mittemus duos justiciarios per unumquemque comitatum per quatuor vices in anno: qui, cum quatuor militibus cujus libet comitatus electis per comitatum, capiant in comitatu, et in die et loco comitatus assisæ prædictas. Et si in die comitatus assisæ prædictæ capi non possint tot milites et liberi tenentes remaneant de illis qui interfuerint comitatui die illo, per quos possint sufficienter judicia fieri secundum quod negotium fuerit, majus vel minus (Art. xvii., xviii., xix.).

and the other, that an order of judges superior to the ✓
justices itinerant should be sent down regularly into the
counties to take all the "assizes" or actions relating to
real property, substantially in substitution for the county
court. The result of which, combined with the commissions of the justices itinerant to take the pleas of the
crown, was to virtually supersede the ancient turbulent
county court as a legal tribunal, in any but trivial matters.[1]
The institution of justices itinerant, the first approach
to anything like a regular judicature, had a powerful
effect on the gradual improvement of the law, by the development and embodiment of legal principles in judicial
decisions[2] by responsible judges, whose decisions were
recorded and preserved, and might be the subject of complaint to the king in council, even before there was any
regular appellate jurisdiction. It is an undoubted fact
that such decisions were recorded and preserved, and by
degrees insensibly moulded and altered the law of mere ✓
custom,[3] by reducing it to accordance with legal principle.

[1] Therefore in the reign of Henry III., as the *Mirror* states, the bishops and barons, whose attendance at the county court had been directed by Henry I., were excused from their attendance (*Mirror*, c. 1, s. 16). This is a fact of much significance in our legal history, and marks the era of the decline of the county court as a judicial tribunal. It was not, however, until the reign of Richard II., it was virtually deprived of that character. A statute of that reign directs that no lord, little or great, should sit upon the bench with the king's justices, when they came to take the assizes, under the general commissions first issued by Edward I.

[2] Such decisions are recorded as early as the reign of John, in the *Abbreviatio Placitorum*, and at a later period in the work of Bracton. One or two are mentioned under the name of judicial ordinances in the *Mirror*. Sometimes there are decisions of justices itinerant, sometimes of the chief justiciary or his associates of the "curia regis," the royal court or council. Thus it is mentioned that Ranulph de Glanville, who was chief justiciary under Henry II., and the author of the celebrated Treatise, "ordained," that is to say, either judicially decided in some case, or made, with the assent of the council or authority of the king, a general judicial rule or ordinance, probably upon some case brought before the council by way of appeal or complaint, as cases at that time undoubtedly were. The effect of such judicial decisions must have been immense.

[3] There is a remarkable instance of this, quoted from the *Abbreviatio Placitorum*, by Hale. In the time of John, be it observed, as he mentions, the descent of common freehold land to the eldest son, was established, unless there was a special custom that the lands were partible, inter masculos; and therefore he says, Mich. secundo Johannis, in a (writ of) Rationabili parte bonorum, by Gilbert Beville, against William Beville, his eldest brother, for lands in Ganthorpe, the defendant pleaded, quod nunquam partita vel partibilia fuere, and because he could not prove it, judgment was

The decisions of the justices itinerant, especially when pronounced by men of known learning and ability,[1] nat-

given for the demandant, the younger brother. But by degrees, says Hale, whereas at this time the averment came on the part of the heir, that the land was *not* partible, nunquam partita vel partibilis extebit; in course of time the averment was turned on the other side — viz., that unless the demandant averred and proved that it was partible land, he failed in his demand (*Hist. Com. Law*, c. vii.). Now this, it is obvious, was by judicial decisions, thus practically altering the law, for it shifted the burden of proof, and thus, by degrees, it becoming impossible to prove a special custom, the right of primogeniture was established. These decisions, it will be observed, are cited from the Rolls, by the year of the reign of the king, and the county in which the cases were decided, and the name of the judge or justice itinerant by whom they were determined. The point of the decision is given shortly but clearly, and with all the requisites of a legal report. The brief entries in the *Abbreviatio Placitorum*, which are of the reign of John, are of great interest, as being the earliest of our law reports, and as embodying the very first germs or elements of regular law, afterwards so largely developed and expanded by a long course of judicial decisions founded upon them, and extending through the Year-books, from the reign of Edward II. to the reign of Henry VIII. It is manifest that these earlier decisions, studied in the work of Bracton, or derived, as he had derived them, from the Rolls, formed the basis of the subsequent judicial decisions, as they in like manner were the foundation of later ones; and so the law went on progressing gradually from one stage of development to another, until it was established as it existed under Elizabeth. It is manifest also that as the Saxon laws were barbarous, and the Norman usages little better, save so far as they had derived any light from the Roman law, there existed no source whence the judges of that age could have derived instruction in legal principle except that law; and as it is a historical fact that it was studied at that time, it may fairly be inferred that it was studied by the judges. It is at all events a fact that a great part of Bracton is taken from the civil law.

[1] Thus they are cited all through Bracton's Treatise, *De Legibus;* no doubt, especially those of known value from the learning of the justices who pronounced them, as, for instance, the celebrated Martin de Pateshall, who was a man of ability, and whose decisions were evidently regarded as of authority, and are cited in the *Mirror* as well as in Bracton. Thus, for example, Bracton cites and adopts a decision of his upon an important point as to donations of land to ecclesiastical bodies, that if the heir knew of the grant, "Et quod hæredes tenentur warrantizare si chartam cognoverint, vel probata fuerunt, habetis de itinere M. de Pateshall, de loquela diversorum comitatuum quæ fuerint super judicium in itinere suo anno regni Henrici tertio de magistro militiæ Templi in Anglia" (*De Legibus*, lib. ii., c. 10). That is, he cites the case of the Knights Templar, which seems to have been an important case. So another decision of the same judge, to the effect that though a donation *in articulo mortis*, would not be valid, "Si autem tres dies vel quatuor ante mortem suam, dederit et seysinam domni religiosæ fecerit, non succurritur hæredi per assissam ad seysinam recuperandam; ut de ultimo itinere M. de Pateshall in comitatu Eborum" (*Ibid.*). Another point on the same subject is cited as decided — "De termino Hilarii anno regni regis Henrici in comitatu Norff, de Cecilia de Stradsete et Priore Hospitali Sancti Joannis de Jerusalem in Anglia" — the case of the Prior of the Hospital of St. John of Jerusalem (*Ibid.*), and the cases are cited as decided in the king's superior court at Westminster, before the justices of the bench, so called to distinguish them from the justices itinerant, who were not permanently on the

urally had some weight and authority, and were recorded and regarded as precedents. And these, and the civil law, whence the principles on which they were founded were necessarily derived, formed the staple of the great treatise of Bracton, which formed the basis of our common law.

Thus, under the influence of these great though gradual changes in our system of judicature, as contained in the Great Charter, the law was still further developed, until it had reached the more finished state in which it is presented in the elaborate treatise of Bracton,[1] which marks the next great era in the history of our law.

The great feature of the work of Bracton is the attention it evinces to procedure, and the greater degree of care shown to carry out the principle of the Roman system, the ascertainment of the question in dispute, and the separation of the fact from the law, before sending the case to trial, which might, indeed, be useless if the matter was one of law; and hence the care which by Bracton will appear to have been given to enforce precision of statement on the part of suitors.[2]

---

bench, but were sent on such itinera, and were not always judges (c. v., fol. 26). "Dictum est in curia regis coram justiciariis de banco apud West. per Joh. de Metingham et socios suos justiciarios" (*Ibid.*).

[1] In which, composed as it was by an ecclesiastic, and one who had studied the civil law, the influence of that law is, as might be supposed, plainly apparent. The charter of John was not observed, and the great charter of Henry III. was in 1225, containing the important enactments that assizes should be tried in the country by king's judges, and that matters of law should be determined in a fixed court at Westminster. Bracton, who was an ecclesiastic, and had studied the civil law, was a judge in 1245, and died about twenty years afterwards, and his great treatise was probably written in the course of that period. Lord Coke speaks of it in the highest terms, as one of the great sources of our law, though he was probably not aware that it was founded on the Roman law, and that a great part of it is taken, indeed, from the Institutes of Justinian.

[2] Thus, says Bracton, speaking of the writ of right, "it will not suffice simply to say, I demand such land as my right, unless the demandant (or claimant) make out his right, and show how and by what means it has descended to him" (*Bracton*, 374, b.). Neither will it suffice to allege that the ancestor was seized in fee, unless it is added that he was so seized by right, which composes the right of property. Nor will this suffice unless he took the property; and it will be seen how this tended to eliminate the real point in dispute, and also to see if it was fact or law. No one at all acquainted with the Roman system can fail to see that this was derived therefrom, and as Sir J. Mackintosh observes, "It is impossible not to admire the logical art with which fact is separated from law, and the whole subject of litigation reduced to one or a few points on which the decision must turn" (*Hist. Eng.*, vol. i.). The great feature of Bracton's work is the accurate and lucid manner in which this is followed out.

In the time of Bracton we find the supremacy of regular judicature established, and the last remains of the rude and barbarous Saxon system virtually obsolete or abolished. This was done, not, indeed, by any direct abolition or sudden change, but by gradual alteration and indirect means, not the less effectual because unobserved.[1]

As the treatise of Glanville shows a great advance in our laws had been made in the time of Henry II., so the treatise of Bracton shows a still greater advance had been made in the time of Henry III.,[2] and this either from the resources of the civil law, or from the gradual development, by judicial decisions of principles and doctrines deduced therefrom.

In the celebrated treatise of Bracton we have the first formal treatise upon our law as a *whole*[3] — the first at-

---

[1] The criminal jurisdiction of the sheriff was abolished by Magna Charta after it had probably become obsolete by the quiet substitution of itinerant justices, either by making them sheriffs or sending them into the counties by special commission to convene the courts. And so, as to civil cases, the sheriff was virtually made a king's judge by special writ in all but trivial cases, and from Bracton we learn that the sheriff exercised jurisdiction over matters which did not belong to him merely by his office of sheriff; but in such cases he acted not as sheriff, but by the king's precept, as *justiciarius regis* (*Bracton*, 154 b.). And as the suitor had to purchase this writ and pay for it, he would naturally consider that he might as well sue in the king's superior court, and have the advantage of a regular judge; and thus the *civil* judicature of the Saxons was superseded.

[2] Hale says, "We have two principal monuments of the great advance the English laws attained to under this king — viz., the tractate of Bracton, and the records of pleas, as well in the benches as before the justices itinerant, the records of which are still extant. Touching the former — Bracton's tractate — it yields us a great evidence of the growth of our laws between the times of Henry II. and Henry III. If we do but compare Glanville's book with that of Bracton, we shall see a very great advance of the law in the writings of the latter over what they are in Glanville. The proceedings are much more regular and settled, as they are in Bracton, above what they are in Glanville. The book itself, in the beginning, seems to borrow its method from the civil law; but the greater part of the substance is either of the course of procedure in the law known to the author, or of resolutions and decisions in the courts of the bench, and before justices itinerant" (*Hist. C. L.*, c. vii.). But Hale, in the first place, greatly underrates the proportion of Bracton derived from the civil law. According to Sir W. Jones, it is almost entirely derived from that source, and certainly the greater portion of it. And as to the decisions of judges, which it cites, though these no doubt form some considerable part of it, yet it is to be observed that these decisions, like the doctrines of Glanville, must in the main have been deduced from the principles and doctrines of the Roman law; from whence else could it be derived, seeing that there was no other source to which judges or lawyers could possibly have resorted for instruction in law?

[3] The work of Glanville having only dealt with part of it.

tempt made to reduce it to something like system, if not to science,—and it is impossible not to see that in a great degree[1] it is founded upon, if not almost copied from, the Roman law.

This is admitted by the historians of the Middle Ages. Thus Hallam wrote: "About the time of Edward I., the civil law acquired some credit in England, but a system entirely incompatible with it had established itself in our courts of justice, and the Roman jurisprudence was not only soon rejected, but became obnoxious" (*Europe in the Middle Ages*, c. ix.).

The only authority, however, cited for this is Selden, and Mr. Hallam adds in a note: " Yet, notwithstanding Selden's authority, I am not satisfied that he has not extenuated the effect of Bracton's predilection for the Roman jurisprudence. No early lawyer has contributed so much to form our own system as Bracton, and if his definitions and rules are sometimes borrowed from the civilians, as all admit, our common law may have indirectly received greater modifications from that influence than its professors were ready to acknowledge, or even than they knew. A full view of the subject is still, I think, a desideratum in the history of English law, which it would illustrate in a very interesting manner" (*Ibid.*, p. 828).

Our author himself amply recognizes at this era the influence of the Roman law in the formation of our own: " The study of the civil and canon law had contributed to further this improvement (of the law), and to furnish considerable accessions both of strength and ornament.

---

[1] Sir W. Jones, in his treatise on Bailments, citing Bracton, said: "I am aware he has copied Justinian almost word for word" (p. 75); yet Lord Coke speaks of him as one of the highest authorities on our law, evidently in entire unconsciousness that he took his law from the Roman. Edward I., as Mr. Hallam mentions, encouraged the study of the Roman law (*Hist. of Europe in the Middle Ages*, c. ix.), and in the reign of Edward II., when we have our earliest reports of the courts of law, it appears to have been cited, and on one occasion it was said by the chief justice of the Common Pleas, from the bench, *that our law was founded upon the civil law*—"la ley imperiel, donques sur quel ley de terre est fondu" (*Year-Book*, 5 Edward II., 148). So, Selden has preserved several instances in which it was cited, but it seems to have very much declined, and the celebrated treatise of Fortescue, *De Laudibus Legum Angliæ*, written in the time of Henry VI., is written in a tone of ignorant disparagement. Blackstone admits that Bracton, Fleta, and Britton contain frequent transcripts from the Roman law (*Comm.*, v. i., p. 22—Coleridge's edition).

Those two laws, besides exciting an emulation in the professors of the common law to cultivate their own municipal customs, afforded from their own treasures ample means of doing it. Much was borrowed from them, and engrafted on the original stock of the common law; but the manner in which this was done is very remarkable. Though our writs and records are in the language in which the Roman and pontifical jurisprudence are written and taught, there is not in either the least mark of imitation; the style of them is peculiarly their own. The use made of the civil and canon law was much nobler than that of borrowing their language. To enlarge the plan and scope of our municipal customs, to settle them upon principle, to improve the course of proceeding, to give consistency, uniformity, and elegance to the whole—these were the objects the lawyers of those days had in view, and to further them they scrupled not to make a free use of those more refined systems. Many of the maxims of the civil law were transplanted into ours; its rules were referred to as part of our own customs, and arguments founded upon the principles of that jurisprudence were attended to as a sort of authority. This was more particularly so in what related to personal property, while the laws of descent and purgation,[1] and other parts of our judicial procedure, seem borrowed from the canonical jurisprudence.[2] A considerable accession had been made to the original canon law by the publication of the decretals. This must have given new vogue and reputation to canonical studies, and no doubt encouraged the common lawyers of that age to pursue their inquiries in that way with more freedom. The application they made, whether of the canon or civil law, in treating subjects of discussion in the law of England, is visible from the account given of Bracton. To consider particularly how much of the latter is indebted to those two systems, either for its origin or improvement, would seem to be an object of separate consideration, and might, perhaps, make a proper appendage to a history of the English law."[3]

No doubt the law of England has always been entirely independent of the Roman law;[4] and it has only to any

---

[1] Upon the oath of the party.   [2] C. viii.   [3] C. viii.
[4] Thus as to dower, in the Roman or matrimonial endowment among the Romans, it was to the husband rather than to the wife, though in our law it

extent, become incorporated into our law by voluntary adoption and assent.[1]

The influence of the civil law upon the formation of our own, as it had no compulsory authority, could only arise from its voluntary adoption, on the ground of its own excellence. And on that ground it gained the influence on our own law which, at this era in its history, led to such marked hostility, and manifest improvement.[2]

Whence, then, came this improvement in our law? It could not be derived from the *Norman law;* for, as our author himself observes, "it was not until after the publication of Glanville, and even of Bracton and of Britton,

---

is to both. So though the principles of the law of inheritance, whether by testament or descent, were derived from the Romans, our law, except in some cities where by custom the Roman rules have prevailed, has departed from the Roman in various respects. So as to the effect of marriage, in legitimating previous issue, for the purposes of inheritance, though by Papal constitution that effect was given to it in the Roman canon law. Yet in the time of Glanville it was otherwise; and he says that, by the law and custom of the realm, the son born before marriage, "though by the canons and the Roman laws he is considered lawful heir, yet he is not so according to the law and custom of the realm, and cannot demand the inheritance by the law of the realm" (c. xv.). Upon which Lord Littleton remarks, that "it shows the entire independence of the law of England on the canon or civil law" (3 *Littlet. Hist. Hen. II.*, p. 125). But these instances are so few that they are exceptional, and the whole form and texture of our laws and institutions is plainly Roman.

[2] The parliament in the reign of Henry III., when an attempt was made to alter the law upon the subject noticed, declined to accede to it. "Et omnes comites et barones, una voce responderunt quod nolunt leges Angliæ mutare, quæ hucusque usitatæ sunt et approbatæ" (*Stat. of Merton*, c. ix.). But this refusal was based upon the ground of user, and on the same ground, as we have seen, a vast deal of Roman law has become embodied with ours, and for the very reason that the adoption was voluntary, the superior excellence of the Roman law is made manifest. The commons in the reign of Richard II. declared that this country had never been governed by the civil law, which was no doubt meant in the sense of compulsory obligation or authority. But they were very little aware of the extent to which the civil law had even then been adopted into ours, and as barbarous Saxon and Norman usages died out, the ascendancy of Roman law became more marked.

[3] Thus Selden said of it—"Valet pro ratione, non pro inducto jure, et pro ratione, quantum Reges et respublicæ intra potestates suæ fines valere patiuntur" (*Hist. Tithes*). It was always held, in our courts, that the civil or canon law had no force *proprio vigore* in suits on questions of temporal rights, etc. Therefore, Mic. 8 Hen. IV., pl. 72, *coram rege*, when the Chancellor of Oxford proceeded according to the rule of the civil law in a case of debt, the judgment was reversed in B. R. (King's Bench), the principal error assigned being that they proceeded "per legem civilem ubi quilibet ligeus Domini Regis Regni sui Angliæ in quibuscunque placitis et querelis infra hoc regnum factis et emergentibus de jure tractare debet per communem legem Angliæ" (*Hist. Com. Law*, p. 33).

that the Normans had any treatise upon their law " (c. 4); "a work," he adds, "so like an English performance that, should there remain any doubt of its being formed upon our model, there can be no doubt of the great similarity between the laws of the two nations at that time " (*Ibid.*). But here our author forgot a fact which, had it occurred to him, would have satisfied him that the *Grand Constumier of Normandy* was derived from the English treatises which preceded it; viz., that, as Glanville himself mentions, the great merit of our system of assize or trial was, that it provided a substitute for the trial by battle, which was essentially the brutal mode of trial the Normans had adopted — not one whit better than the savage Saxon usage of the ordeal. The new system, therefore, was not derived from the Normans, who were as barbarous as the Saxons. It was derived by development from the Roman.

Arrived at this great era in our legal history, and at the era of the great reign of Edward I., which marks a still greater, it is natural to take at such a standing-point a retrospective view of our progress. And it is impossible not to be struck at this era with the fact that the main and *distinctive* features of the Saxon and Norman systems had already died out, or were declining and becoming obsolete; while all that was of Roman character or origin survived and endured, Trial by ordeal was gone; the turbulent county court, as a tribunal, was superseded; and trial by battle was disappearing; but the Roman systems of law and of justice were established. The best and most practical test of the Roman origin of our institutions, or how much we owe comparatively to Roman as compared with Norman or Saxon laws, is this; to see what are the institutions, either undoubtedly Saxon or undoubtedly Roman, which remain to this day. The institutions undoubtedly Roman — municipal and other corporations, certainly manors, and probably hundreds and counties; a regular judicature; and regular judicial tribunals, with skilled judges for the law, and jurors or sworn judges — *judices facti* — for the matters of fact — all these, and more, were Roman institutions, and they remain. The institutions undoubtedly Saxon had gone, although the Saxon spirit which had been embodied in the old turbulent popular assemblies still survived, infused into Roman institutions, and inspiring them with fresh vigor. So of the Normans; all that was *distinctive* in their system, which seems reduced to trial by battle — since all the rest was derived from the Roman system — was already disappearing, and was doomed to vanish away, although it is true that the principle of the supremacy of royal authority was developed and applied by them, and formed a solid basis for all the improvements in our law which were afterwards attained. But this was a slow and gradual progression. So far as our law, however, in any material degree was altered after the Conquest, it was without a sudden change; and it was gradually and insensibly, and almost unobservedly,[1] and chiefly by means of legal decisions, developing the principles of law, which was indeed the custom of the nation.

The whole course and progress of our law, up to and after the age of Edward I., when it was substantially settled as it existed from that time to the age of Elizabeth, when our author's history closes, and when, as is observed in his Preface, a new era opened, resembled that of Rome, as one of gradual development; and, in the opinion of our most acute and philosophical historians, it exhibited, at this important period, the influence of the Roman law, which determined its whole character. Thus Sir J. Mackintosh observes: — "The progress of our common law, till the reign of Edward I., bears a strong resem-

[1] This may be well illustrated by a reference to the law of descent. Lands held on the feudal military tenure, introduced at the Conquest, naturally became descendible to the eldest son; but other land — ordinary freehold land — held in free socage, as it was called, remained partible among all the sons, until long after the Conquest; so that it is impossible to ascertain the precise period when the law was altered, or rather it was not altered at any particular period; for it was altered thus — by holding that the land was partible only by custom. Thus Spelman says that "the Normans by their feuds settled the whole inheritance on the eldest son on account of military tenure" (*Spel. Reliq.*, s. 3). But in land not held by military tenure it was otherwise, and thus Glanville says in such case "the inheritance should be equally divided among all the sons, however numerous — *provided the land had been anciently partible*" (*Ibid.*, c. 7, s. 3). "That is," as Lord Hale puts it, "the *commune jus*, or common right, was for the eldest son to be heir, no custom intervening to the contrary" (*Hist. Com. Law*, 216). So that, as one learned writer on the subject said very truly, "the right of primogeniture made every day greater progress, until, in the reign of John, it had fairly excluded partible descent — the presumption being held to be that the land (unless in Kent, where, by a local custom recognized by general law, all land is held in gavelkind) was descendible to the eldest son until the contrary was proved" (*Robinson on Gavelkind*, p. 26). Thus a great revolution was effected in the country, gradually and unobservedly, and by a mere legal artifice, without any legislative sanction.

blance to that of Rome. The primitive maxims and customs were applied to all new cases, which, appearing similar to them, it was natural and convenient to subject to like rules. Courts in England, private lawyers, judicial writers, as at Rome, in delivering opinions on specific cases, extended the analogy from age to age, until an immense fabric of jurisprudence was at length built on somewhat rude foundations. The legislature itself occasionally interposed to amend customs, to widen or narrow principles, but these occasional interpositions were no more than petty repairs on a vast building. From the reign of Edward I. we possess the Year-books, annual notes of the cases adjudged by our courts, who exclusively possessed the power of authoritative interpretation, scarcely to be distinguished from the legislation which the tribunals of Rome shared with its imperial ministers and with noted advocates. In a century after him, elementary treatises, methodical digests, and works on special subjects, were extracted from these materials by Littleton,[1] Fortescue,[2] and Brooke.[3] So conspicuous a station at the head of the authentic history of our uninterrupted jurisprudence, has contributed, more than his legislative acts, to procure for Edward the name of the English Justinian" (*Hist. Eng.*, v. i.).

Through all these successive changes, the great thing to be noticed is their slow and gradual character, and the careful manner in which they were each evolved, so to speak, out of actual experience and practical wisdom.[4]

[1] *Littleton's Tenures*, temp. Hen. VI., the subject of "Coke's Commentaries."
[2] *De Laudibus' Legum Angliæ*, temp. Hen. VII.
[3] *Brooke's Abridgment of the Year-books*, temp. James I. The historian perhaps meant Fitzherbert.
[4] Sir James Mackintosh more than once remarks upon this; and he observes even of the Great Charter, "It was a peculiar advantage, that the consequences of its principles were, if we may so speak, only discovered gradually and slowly. It gave out in civil occasions only so much of the spirit of liberty as the circumstances of succeeding generations required — as their character could safely bear" (*Hist. Eng.*, vol. i.). So as to the constitution of Henry II. sending the judges on circuits or itineraries, he observes that, "This, like others, appears only to have given authority and universality to practice occasionally adopted before" (*Ibid.*). Our law has always been customary, which implies gradual growth and formation. "The consuetudinary, or common law," remarks the eminent historian elsewhere, "consisted of certain maxims of simple justice, which we are taught by nature to observe and enforce, blended with certain ancient usages, often in themselves convenient and equitable, but chiefly recommended by the necessity of adhering to long and well-known rules of conduct" (*Ibid.*, p. 274).

This, indeed, is the great lesson to be learnt from the study of our legal history, as it was one of the chief advantages of our law, this facility of growth, of progress, and of happy adaptation to the wants of every age.

This, indeed, is the way in which, in a free country, institutions are developed, so to speak, gradually, by common agreement and tacit consent, from the results of practical experience.[1] The whole history of our law is a record of this process of development; the true merit of our free Saxon constitution is that it allowed of it, and left scope for it; and the great defect of our author is that he lost sight of it.

This has already been illustrated with reference to our judicial system, and may be remarkably illustrated with reference to the feudal system. The great feature of the era marked by the Conquest, is the commencement of the movement which was completed in the reign of Edward I., in the assertion of the civil supremacy of the sovereign power; and the most important aspect of this movement, and one in which it has produced consequences most permanent and most important, was its relation to the administration of justice; but it was also, and first, connected with the development of the feudal system,[2] and

---

[1] This is pointed out by Sir James Mackintosh in a passage well worth quoting. "Governments are not framed after a model, but all their parts and powers grow out of occasional acts, prompted by some urgent expediency, or some private interest, which in the course of time coalesce and harden into usage; and thus this bundle of usages is the object of respect, and the guide of conduct, long before it is embodied and defined, and enforced in written laws. Government may be in some degree reduced to system, but cannot flow from it. It is not like a machine or a building, which may be constructed entirely and according to a previous plan, by the art and labor of man. It is better illustrated by a comparison with vegetables, or even animals, which may be improved by skill or care, but cannot be produced by human contrivance. No government can, indeed, be more than a mere draught or scheme of will, when it is not composed of habits of obedience on the part of the people, and of an habitual exercise of certain portions of authority by the individuals or bodies who constitute the sovereign power. These habits, like all others, can only be formed of repeated acts; they cannot suddenly be imposed by the legislator" (*Hist. Eng.*, vol. i., p. 72). This fine passage is the best eulogy upon our constitution, — because pointing out its best feature.

[2] Guizot contests the view of most historians, that the feudal system was of sudden origin, the result of the special necessities of the age; and he contends that it was the progressive development of ancient facts" (*Lect. sur la Civiliz. en France*, Lect. vi.). He says the history of the word "miles," which designated "knight," is a proof of this, and he cites Du Cange, who thus traces its history to the Roman age, "Towards the end of the Roman

in both respects it was remarkable for its gradual character, and its Roman origin.

The common notion that the feudal system was of sudden growth, is shown to be erroneous; it was the result of gradual development from the grants of land by the sovereign power in the Roman times,[1] to those who served for the defence of the state, and was, therefore, really based upon the manorial system. Hence it was, that its development by no means interfered with that system, or with the rights and interests which had arisen out of it; and thus these interests continued to be developed under it.

The growth of the feudal system was one of slow and gradual development from simple elements; the substance of it, tenure on military service, having existed from the time of the Romans; and it was only elaborated by the Normans. It was the development of a system which became complex in its character[2] from its involving so

---

empire, *militare* expressed simply to *serve*, to acquit one's self of service towards a superior — not merely of a military service, but a civil service." And he elaborately traces the progress of the system.

[1] It has been seen that such grants of land were made in this country by the Romans usually on military tenure; and our best historians — such as Palgrave and Lingard — conceive this to have been the germ of the feudal system. These estates became, under the Roman system, manors; and Guizot represents the villa or estates thus held, as military tenure, and under which the villeins held by servile tenure, as the basis of the feudal system. Then the barbarians seized large portions of land comprising their estates, and granted them unto others their companions in arms as military tenure; and through the entire Saxon laws, there are to be found traces of an infant feudal system, forfeiture to the lord, relief, etc. This was developed at the Conquest. Every owner of a manor was its "lord," and had a court baron incident to it; and all the holders of manors were thanes or barons: those who held direct of the king being greater barons, others the lesser.

[2] Guizot points out that the system involved the nature of territorial property hereditary, and yet derived from a superior (as opposed to allodial property held of no one), the union of sovereignty with property, the lord having sovereign rights within the limits of his territory; and the present civil system of legislative, judicial, and military institutions which united the possessors of feuds among themselves. And he shows how, from the fifth to the tenth century, from causes he explains, freehold property became gradually less extensive, and land became converted into beneficies; and how, from the tenth to the twelfth centuries, beneficies became gradually converted into fiefs or feuds (*Lect. sur la Civ. en France*, lect. ii.). He insists, at the outset, upon its progressive formation. "No great social state," he says, "makes its appearance completé and at once. It is formed slowly and successively: it is the result of a multitude of different facts of different origin, which combine and modify themselves in a thousand ways before constituting a whole. There is this much of truth, no doubt, in the view

many incidents; and one of these connected it with the administration of justice.

In the legal history of this, or of any other country, nothing is so important as that which relates to the administration of justice; and in our own legal history, nothing is more remarkable than the gradual growth of a regular system of justice, derived from the principle of supreme sovereignty, and based upon a regular judicature, deriving its jurisdiction therefrom. At no time was there any sudden change, and yet the ultimate result was to render the justice of the state supreme in its character, even while local in its exercise.[1]

And one of the most remarkable features in the legal history of the period which intervened between the time of the Conquest and the age of Edward I., is, that along with the growth and development of the feudal system, founded on what may be called a military policy, there was a gradual growth and consolidation of the sovereign power,[2] by reason of a great social necessity; and thus a more regular judicature, and a more settled and satisfactory administration of justice.

The connection of the subject with the administration

---

of those who attribute the feudal system to a special exigency of the times, that its promotion was aided and urged by the exigencies of the time, as it was suited to a period of limitation and transition; and hence it gradually disappeared when that age was over."

[1] As already mentioned, long after the king's justices had been used to administer justice in the counties, either as sheriffs, or in the place of the sheriffs, by royal authority, Magna Charta enacted that assizes should be taken in the counties, and that such pleas should be determined by a fixed tribunal. The result was, that the civil justice of the state, at the assizes, superseded the county court, in all important matters. Then the custom arose of compelling suitors in the county courts to sue out a writ from the crown to the sheriff, to give him jurisdiction by making him a king's justice in the case, if it was of more than small value: and this was fixed by custom at forty shillings — a sum, however, equivalent probably at the least to £50 in our own day.

[2] Guizot traces this progress, and describes this necessity very skilfully in his lectures upon Civilization in France (lect. 10–15); and although he speaks particularly of France, all that he says is equally applicable to England, as our legal history will abundantly show. He traces the progress of the royal power as giving to royalty its character of a public protector, and as the fountain of the justice of the realm; and what he says of Philip Augustus, is eminently true of our Edward I. Under the royal power, he shows that the judicial system arose, and a regular administration of justice, under an order of persons — the judicial order — specially devoted to it, and having a general jurisdiction derived from the sovereign power. All this took place equally in this country.

of justice was this, that according to the strict principle of the feudal system, each lord exercised the judicial power in his own territory or domain,[1] as between his own tenants, or, in some cases, between them and their lord: a jurisdiction, however, it will be obvious, necessarily limited, and extremely rude and unsatisfactory, and only suited to domestic matters. The feudal system had nothing like a regular judicial system, or a regular administration of justice. It involved, however, this great principle, which was carried out by Magna Charta, that a man should be judged by his peers or equals.

So, with reference to our political system, the same principle of gradual progress and progressive growth may be illustrated.

Nothing could be compared in importance with the judicial system, except the political;[2] and that also, like the other, was of slow growth and gradual development: from first rude elements into an organized system; from rude popular assemblies into regular constituted bodies. The political system, like the judicial, arose out of experience of the evils of the feudal; and just as the practical

---

[1] The principle was, that men should judge each other, of the same rank. Thus the tenants in the lords' courts judged disputes arising among themselves, or even between their lords and themselves, if arising out of the feudal relation. Otherwise, the question must be determined in the court of the lord's superior. The judgment by peers was essential, as Guizot says, to the feudal system. But then, as he also pointed out, there was no regular judicial system, no order of judges, no class of men charged with judicial duty; while, on the other hand, the execution of judgments was a mere application of irregular force. There were, as he expresses it, no judicial guarantees by peaceful procedure (*Lect. sur la Civ. en France, lect.* 10). Hence arose, as he shows, a general sense of the necessity for some complete jurisdiction which should comprehend all classes of cases, and some regular system of justice, which should deal with them judicially; and this could only be derived from the sovereign power.

[2] Allusion is here made, of course, to the rise of a legislative assembly, founded upon popular election. There is a masterly sketch of it in the history of Sir J. Mackintosh (v. i., c. 5), who shows its gradual rise from the time of the great council of the Saxons and Normans, to the regular return of popular members in the age of Edward I. He cites from Bracton some words in which allusion is made to that council: "Legis habet vigorem, quicquid de consilio et consensu magnatum, et reipublicæ commune sponsione, authoritate regis, juste fuerit definitum" (lib. i., c. 1, fol. 1.). And he traces its rise partly from the feudal system itself, in this way, that the scutages and aids under that system were levied by the consent of the tenants; that the crown, by degrees, exacted talliages from those who were not military tenants; and that this led by degrees to grants of subsidies by representatives of the counties and the burghs, and thus to a House of Commons.

social necessity for regular judicature, and a comprehensive administration of justice, led to the establishment of the courts of sovereign jurisdiction, so the political necessity for a regularly constituted body of representatives to assess feudal impositions, and adjust feudal burdens, led to the constitution of popular elective assemblies. For electors, or for jurors, some great constituent body of freemen, it appears, was required; and the same constituency originally served for both.

The two systems had this in common, that they were both, necessarily, in the main, based upon the same great constituency: the freeholders in the counties, the burgesses in the towns and cities.

These bodies, from whom the juries came, were also the bodies upon whom the political franchise was ultimately conferred.[1] They formed, then, the great mass of the free

[1] Thus Sir J. Mackintosh points out that the suitors at the county court — from whom it has been shown the juries came — became afterwards the voters at county elections; and that, as the suitors acquired votes, the whole body of the freeholders became the constituencies in counties. And some part of the same process, he thinks, may be traced in the share of representation conferred on the towns. These communities had retained, he says, some vestiges of their elective forms, and of that local administration, which had been bestowed on them by the civilizing policy of the Roman conquerors; and in England, charters were early granted, which exempted towns from baronial tyranny, and recognized their local laws. The boroughs, however, were part of the ancient demesnes of the crown, and were subject to the feudal incidents. Talliages were levied, and subsidies demanded; and this led, as in the counties, to their sending representatives to parliament. When the consent of parliament was made necessary to the levy of talliage, of subsidies, and, in effect, of all taxes, as well as of the feudal dues, in the latter years of Edward I., the burgesses became integral and essential parts of the legislature (*Hist. Eng.*, vol. i.). The burgesses and freeholders formed the body of the electors, as they did of the jurors; and as, at the same time, freeholds had become divided, and many of them were small, qualifications were deemed necessary in order to secure men of substance. It is very observable that the earliest legislation on this subject had reference to jurors; and there was an act of Edward I., the first of a long series of similar acts, directed to secure substantial men for jurors. In the reign of Henry VI., the well-known act was passed which required a qualification for electors of knights of the shire, the qualification being an annual income from freehold of forty shillings, the same sum, as already shown, fixed for the exclusive jurisdiction of the county court, and equal to £50 at the present day (*vide* p. cxxxi.). In the reign of Edward IV., copyholders were held to have legal customary rights to their tenements; and about the same time, leaseholders, likewise, had their estates fully recognized and protected in law; and in later times, copyholders and leaseholders, to a certain amount, were admitted as jurors and electors. Here we see the alteration of laws in order to adapt them to the altered circumstances of society, and preserve the substantial identity of institutions: — all based on the same general principle,

subjects of the realm, at a time when to be a freeholder was to be a freeman, and when the only freemen were freeholders. In later times, when, on the one hand, freeholders — by reason of the division of estates, and the mode of emancipation — had multiplied, and many of them were holders of very small properties, qualifications became required; and, on the other hand, as the villeins acquired customary rights, and became merged in the modern copyholders; and, as leasehold estates became stable, they became virtually as much entitled to judicial or political franchises as freeholders, and became included among the constituencies of the jurors or electors. But the system remained, in substance, the same, through all these changes, and laws were only altered by reason of changes in the circumstances of society, and in order to preserve the substantial identity of our institutions. In a word, laws were altered, that institutions might be maintained.

As gradual progress and slow development marked the character of our legal history from the Conquest to the reign of Edward I., it was equally so from the age of Edward I. to the reign of Elizabeth, which closes our author's history. As the former period was marked by the gradual development of the feudal system, so the later period was marked by its slow and gradual decline;[1] and as the former period was marked also by the establishment of a general judicial system, based upon the supremacy of sovereign power and authority, so the latter period, long as it was, hardly had elapsed before its entire ascendancy was attained.[2] The progress of decay was as slow as that of growth. Old systems were rarely ever abolished, and were left to become obsolete, and died away as they had arisen up — by slow degrees.

---

that of founding our judicial and political systems on the broad and solid ground of a substantial interest in the property and liberty of the country.

[1] In the reign of Elizabeth, the feudal system had become in a great degree, if not entirely, obsolete; and the last instance of a claim of villenage occurs in the reports of that reign (Yelv. *Reports*, 2). So in this long reign the last instance occurred of "trial by battle," which was not abolished until our own day; and so as to "wager of law," (by the oath of the defendant), the remains of the Saxon system of compurgators. So also in this long reign the local criminal jurisdictions (save such as were derived from royal authority) died out (*vide Crispe* v. *Viroll*, Yelverton's *Reports*); never having been directly abolished.

[2] The state system of justice was left to assert its superiority over the other, only by *reason* of its superiority.

During this long period, the anomalous jurisdiction of those local courts, which had existed in most of our villages and towns from the time of the Romans, and many of which had criminal jurisdiction in capital cases, gradually died out, save as to the local jurisdiction, to which the county court had virtually been limited, and except as to the civil courts of some great cities, as London and Bristol.[1] This, however, it must again be observed, was by a slow and gradual progress; and to observe and trace this progress is the great object of legal history.

No institution — at all events none which *endured* — was all at once established; none was all at once abolished. Every change, either in the way of abolition of old institutions or the introduction of new, was gradual and progressive. Each alteration advanced by degrees from its first germinal element and imperfect form, on its original introduction, until it had reached its final stage of development into a perfect and settled institution. Thus it was, for instance, with trial by jury,[2] which, in its *present*

---

[1] The jurisdiction of these courts was in ancient times criminal as well as civil; and hence, in the reign of Edward IV., there was an instance of a capital execution by sentence of a court-baron. In the time of Richard III., we find it mentioned in the *Year-Book* that the steward of a liberty had executed a man under color of what the Saxons called "engfangenthief," or taking a thief in the act, within the manor or other liberty (*Year-Book*, 2 Richard III., f. 9, s. 10). So, as lately as the reign of Elizabeth, it was admitted that the local court of the cinque courts could try and execute a man for murder committed within the liberty, provided he could be taken there; for otherwise he could only be arrested and tried at common law (*Crispe* v. *Viroll*, Yelverton's *Reports*. 13).

[2] All through the Saxon laws, its first germ or element can be traced in the usage of selecting such of the suitors of the county court as had any knowledge of the matter, and making them sworn witnesses or jurors. Before the Conquest, it was the usage in criminal cases to swear, and even after the Conquest it was adopted in civil cases. From that step, however, to trial by jury in the latter sense of the phrase, there was a long interval; for these jurors were witnesses, and if there were no witnesses, there could be no jurors. The earliest mention of a trial by jury, says our author, that bears a near resemblance to that which it became in after times, is in the Constitutions of Clarendon, where it is directed that the sheriff "faciet jurare duodecim legales homines de *vicineto* seu de *villa* quod inde veritatem secundum conscientiam suam manifestabunt," (1 *Reeves' Hist. Eng. Law*, 335). The proceeding was "per recognitionem," or by recognition — of their own knowledge. Some, or all, might know the truth of the matter, or might be ignorant of it. If none of them knew anything of the matter, and they testified the same in court upon their oaths, the court resorted to others, *until they found those who did know the truth*. If some were acquainted with the facts, and some were not, the latter were rejected, and others called in. And all who were called in were sworn not to speak what was false; and the knowl-

form, was never established or set up, but grew by degrees, from its first form into its present, in the course of several centuries.

The two great difficulties in the way of an efficient and satisfactory administration of justice were as to the proper mode of trying questions of fact, and as to the method of securing certainty and uniformity in matters of law; it took centuries to settle and to solve. It may appear easy to hear witnesses; but the difficulty has always been great of deciding upon contradictory testimony, and discriminating the balance of credibility.[1] And it was not until

edge they were expected to have of the matter must have been from what they themselves had seen or heard, or from declarations of their fathers, such evidence as claimed equal credit with that of their own eyes or ears, "per proprium visum suum, et auditum, vel per verba patrum suorum, et per talia quibus fidem teneantur habere ut propriis" (*Glanville*, lib. ii., c. 17; *Reeves*,332,;*Bracton, De Legibus—De Assise*). That in the time of Henry II. the jurors were still witnesses, is clear from the *Treatise* of Glanville, who treats of trial by jury in the *curia regis*, the king's superior court, and calls the jurors "recognitors," because they "recognized" of their own knowledge; and when he has to deal with the case of their having no knowledge of the matter, betrays considerable perplexity (c. 14). So in the *Mirror*, where ordeal and trial by battle are mentioned as modes of proceeding resorted to from necessity, where there were no witnesses of the matter, so that there could be no trial by jury. So Bracton, *temp.* Henry III., long after Magna Charta, speaks of the jurors as deciding upon what they had seen or heard (lib. iv.). And it took probably at least another century, if not more, before juries were of sufficient intelligence to listen to and decide upon *evidence*. This stage in the history of trial by jury had, however, been reached in the reign of Henry VI., because we find Fortescue, his chancellor, describing trial by jury as a trial by *evidence*; and in the Year-Books of that reign there is a case about showing a man evidence in a lawsuit (*Year-Book, Hen. VI.*). But this development, it will be seen, took ages. From the time of Ethelred to Edward III. is a period of five centuries. That trial by jury arose out of the court of the hundred is manifest from this, that by the course of the common law the jury must always have been composed of hundredors, unless there could not be sufficient impartial jurors therefrom, in which case the writ of *decem tales* was awarded, to summon jurors from the adjoining hundred (*Year-Book*, 3 *Henry VI.*, 39). An essential quality of a juror being that he should come from a place as near as possible to the place where the matter arose; at all events, out of the hundred (*Co. Litt.*, 155). So that it came to this, that the common law jury were simply *twelve of the hundredors sworn*. Up to the time of Elizabeth it was a cause of challenge to a juror, that he was not a hundredor (*Waters* v. *Walsh, Bendl.*, 263). The jury, indeed, must have come *de vicineto*, from the vicinage of the place within the hundred where the matter arose, as from a vill or manor (*Co. Litt.*, 125); but it must have come from the *hundred*. It was not until the 4th and 5th Anne, c. xvi., s. 6, that it was enacted that the want of hundredors should not be a cause of challenge to a jury, and that they might come from the body of the country.

[1] It was for ages a firmly rooted rule of the law that the jury must come from the "vill," or vicinage, a rule plainly derived from the old system of

the people had acquired some experience in the administration of justice that this difficult duty could be exercised by them, which is of the essence of trial by jury. Then, and not until then, its advantages were fully attained, and this it took several centuries to attain.

All the advantages of a local tribunal were gained, it was considered, by sending a case down for trial, (where there was no special reason why it should not be so), into the county, to be tried, and having a jury from the vill or vicinage, (as it was called,) where the matter in dispute arose, in order that it might be tried by neighbors of the parties, with such knowledge of them and of the subject-matter as might either enable them to decide the case of their own knowledge, or serve to test the credibility of the witnesses brought before them to give evidence. On

the county courts, held in the hundred, from month to month, or in which the neighbors from the hundred where the matter arose would be called upon to testify. Hence a fixed rule that there must be hundredors upon a jury, which existed until Lord Somers' act for the amendment of the law. The rule originally arose no doubt from the principle that jurors were witnesses, and, of course, to be witnesses they must come from the neighborhood, and the nearer, it was thought, the better. And even at a later period, when jurors had evidence given, and no longer decided on their own mere knowledge, their knowledge of the parties, it was thought, would assist them in judging of the testimony. This is well put by Fortescue, c. xxvi., "Twelve good and lawful men being sworn, etc., then either party by himself or his counsel shall open to them all matters and evidences whereby he thinketh that he may best inform them of the truth, and then may either party bring before them all such witnesses on his behalf as he will produce . . . not unknown witnesses, but neighbors," etc. And then, in c. xxviii., "The witnesses make their depositions in the presence of twelve credible men, neighbors to the deed that is in question, and to the circumstances of the same, and who also know the manners and conditions of the witnesses, and know whether they be men worthy to be credited or not." At that time, it will be observed, the jury had ceased to determine merely upon their own knowledge, and had evidence given; for there are cases in the Year-Books at that time as to obtaining of evidence. Moreover, there is a case in the Year-Books that a man may enter another's park, to show him evidence in a lawsuit (*Year-Book*, 17 *Hen. VI.*). The theory of trial by jury is thus explained by Hale: "In this recess of the jury, they are to consider the evidence, to weigh the credibility of the witnesses, and the force and efficacy of their testimonies, whence they are not precisely bound by the rules of the civil law — viz., to have two witnesses to prove every fact, (unless it be in cases of treason), nor to reject one witness because he is single, or always to believe two witnesses, if the probability of the fact does, upon other circumstances, reasonably encounter them; for the trial is not here simply by witnesses, but by jury; nay, it may so fall out that a jury, *upon their own knowledge*, may know a thing to be false that a witness swore to be true, or may know a witness to be incompetent or incredible, though nothing be objected against him, and may give the verdict accordingly" (Hale, *Hist. Com. Law*, cited in *De Lolme* on the *Const.*, c. 13).

I

the other hand, if the suitors were desirous of resorting to the old system of arbitration by neighbors,[1] it was always open to them to do so, by referring their cases to such arbitration, on the principle of mutual selection and assent. This principle, indeed, has never been abandoned in our legal system; but the domestic jurisdiction of arbitration has always been maintained.

Thus, by slow degrees, and in the course of several centuries, the institution of trial by jury, as it now exists, was ultimately established. So as to the ascendancy acquired by the king's courts as courts of ordinary jurisdiction; it was only acquired by slow degrees and gradual progression. By degrees it became established as a rule or maxim, quite contrary to ancient usage,[2] that without

---

[1] Thus in the *Year-Book* it was said, speaking of challenges to jurors, "If the plaintiff and the defendant do both refer themselves to the arbitration of certain persons, to act for *both*, it would be good, that is, where one side chooses one and the other another; there, although they are to be on different arbitrations, yet as each is unknown to the other, it is good cause of challenge" (*Year-Book*, 23 *Henry VI.*, 39). Arbitrations have always been allowed in our law, although some attempts were made to confine their jurisdiction (14 *Hen. IV.*, 19). In Lord Coke's time it was not unusual for men to agree that differences between them should be referred to the arbitration of "neighbors" (*Co. Litt.*, lib. i., c. vii., s. 67, p. 53); and although questions were raised as to the power to refer *future* differences, no question was ever raised as to *present* differences.

[2] For before the Conquest there was no other court but the county court; and even after the Conquest suits relating to land to any extent came into that court, as was seen in the celebrated case relating to the Bishop of Rochester's lands, which is mentioned by all historians as tried in the county court; and so of other cases, although, if they concerned the sheriff, or for any cause could not be properly or fairly tried before him, a king's justiciary was sent down to *hold* the court, as in the first case mentioned, and in others recorded of the time. The jurisdiction between lord and *tenant* was in the court of the *lord;* but where different *lords* claimed, the suit could only come into the court of their superior lord, and of course the ultimate court was that of the lord paramount—the king. By degrees it became established that the sheriff could not hold plea of land without the king's writ, whence it is said by Bracton, *temp.* Henry III., that in such cases the sheriff sat, *not* as sheriff, but as king's justiciary (*Bracton*, fol. 176). Then, as we find from the *Mirror of Justice*, after justices itinerant had been sent (in the reign of Henry I.), suits of too high a nature for the sheriff, as suits relating to land, were deemed to be and were suspendable until the coming of the king's justices into the county (*Mirror*, c. ii., s. 28). Then, in the time of Henry II., when a *curia regis* (the exchequer) was established, chiefly for suits as to land, those suits were naturally brought there, the king's writ being required to bring them in the county court. Thus by slow degrees the maxim became established, as Fleta expresses it, that without a king's writ there was no warrant of jurisdiction in land. Now, a king's writ meant a *fee to the king*, for fees were charged for his writs (which the *Mirror* bitterly complains of); and a principle so valuable to revenue was not likely to be

the king's writ there could be no jurisdiction over suits
relating to land, a doctrine no doubt partly deduced from
the principles of the feudal system, which made the court
of the superior lord the tribunal for controversies between
inferior lords which could not be determined in the courts
of either.

Then as regards personal actions, the rule which limited
the jurisdiction of inferior local courts, courts baron, or
the like,[1] to cases not exceeding the amount of forty shillings was applied to the county court, which, at the time
the supposed rule must have originated, was the only
court of ordinary jurisdiction.

Even, however, if the jurisdiction were limited to forty
shillings,[2] it is certain (though it is difficult to form a

lost sight of by the Norman sovereigns. So, in the reign of Edward III.,
it was held that if upon writ the question of title arose, it should be determined in the county; but otherwise, if upon plaint, it should be removed
into the court of the king (*Year-Book*, 30 *Ed. III.*, f. 28).

[1] That the rule originally applied only to these courts appears plainly
from the *Mirror*, which, in describing the jurisdiction of inferior courts,
temp. Edward I., first mentions the county courts, saying nothing of any
limitation of jurisdiction. Then it proceeds — "The other inferior courts
are the courts of every lord, to the likeness of hundred courts, and also in
fairs and markets in which justice is administered without delay, in which
courts they have cognizance of debts and of such small things as pass not
forty shillings in value (c. i., s. 15). But it is obvious that the rule could
not have applied to the county court, the only court of ordinary jurisdiction,
and which, even in the reign of Henry I., was called "curia regis."

[2] In the time of Alfred or Athelstane a shilling was the penalty for stealing a foal or calf (*Laws of Alfred*, c. xvi.). An ox was worth only thirty
pence (Judicia Civitatis Londiniæ), and a cow twenty pence, and a sheep a
shilling (a shilling being fivepence in Anglo-Saxon currency). The whole
value of a citizen's property was often only thirty pence, or six shillings
(*Ibid.*). The pecuniary penalty for a man's life was only thirty shillings
(*Anglo-Saxon Laws*). These instances may suffice to give an idea of the
relative value of forty shillings, before the Conquest, and at the present day.
And although in the *Mirror* forty shillings is spoken of as comparatively a
small sum, that was in comparison with suits for property to any amount,
and the book was completed in the reign of Edward I. Even taking that
era, however, it would be difficult to give forty shillings a less comparative
value than fifty pounds at the present period. Forty shillings a year was
the amount of income fixed by the legislature in the reign of Henry VI., as
the qualification for knights of the shire. Twenty pounds a year was the
salary of a judge in those days (Foss's *Lives of the Judges*, vol. vi., pp. 3, 41,
54, 61), so that forty shillings was a tenth of it, which, as the salary of a judge
is now five thousand pounds, would make the present equivalent of forty
shillings not less than five hundred pounds. It is difficult to get an accurate
idea on the point, and the estimate may vary between fifty and five hundred
pounds; one is the *minimum*, the other the *maximum* amount of the present
equivalent. At the time of Magna Charta twenty shillings was the sum due
on every knight's fee, on the marriage of his daughter, and two shillings was

correct idea of the relative value of money, in an age so distant as that in which such a limitation must have arisen), that the amount could not have been less than fifty pounds of our present currency.

There were, however, many undoubted advantages to be gained by bringing suits in the king's superior courts, and it was often, indeed, a matter of necessity to do so. There was one very evident ground of necessity, upon which the prerogative of justice was vested in the sovereign — viz., that from the supreme power alone could emanate the authority to enforce justice. This was most apparent in that age of turbulence and violence, when it was constantly necessary to resort to force to execute the law,[1] and when men, on the other hand, were always ready

---

an ordinary subsidy on a "plough land," *i. e.*, in modern language, a farm, (Wade's *History of England*, temp. Henry III., p. 49). Madox says the king in that reign gave his poet one hundred shillings salary; the salary of the poet laureate is one hundred pounds, just twenty times as much in moneys numbered, but how much in point of real effective value, a few further data may help to show. In the reign of Edward III. the famine price of wheat was twenty shillings (Wade's *History of England*, p. 50), and forty shillings was the amount of the capitation tax of a baron (*Ibid.*, p. 58). A bailiff in husbandry received less than forty shillings a year as his salary in the reign of Henry VII. (*Ibid.*, p. 104). Now he would receive at least fifty pounds. In the same reign forty shillings a year was all that was allowed for the whole washing in the household of a great peer like the Duke of Northumberland (*Ibid.*, p. 109). In the reign of Edward IV., as we learn from the old ballad "King Edward IV. and the Tanner of Tamworth," a wealthy tradesman boasted of a horse for which he paid four shillings. Nowadays a rich tradesman would hardly boast of a horse for which he paid less than fifty pounds. In the reign of Henry VIII. the pound of beef was a halfpenny a pound, now it is one shilling, just twenty-four times as much, which again makes forty shillings equal to about the sum of fifty pounds. Lord Coke, in commenting upon the limitation of forty shillings, remarks that this was equal to six pounds in his time. But the effect of the discovery of America was vastly to decrease the value of money, insomuch that it sank two-thirds in value, and hence Hume observes that a crown in Henry VII.'s time served the same purpose as a pound in his own time (*Essay on Money*). But the comparison of data shows that the difference was far greater, and the lowest possible estimate makes the present equivalent of the ancient forty shillings at least fifty pounds. Lord Coke says that a day's "plough service," which, of course, comprised the use of the horses or oxen with the plough, and a man to hold the plough, and another to guide the horses, in his time, would be compensated for by eightpence (4 *Inst.*, p. 269). That was in the reign of James I., after the long reign of Elizabeth, when such a prodigious advance had been made in wealth. And the sum of eightpence at that time, was, no doubt, worth ten times what it was at the time of the Conquest, as it was probably worth a tenth part of what it would be worth now. A penny, in the Saxon times, was at least equal to a shilling now, and only fivepence made a shilling.

[1] By the common law, the sheriff was the minister of justice, and could

either to enforce or to resist it by a recourse to force. In such an age, to allow any but the officers of the State to execute it, would have led to anarchy and civil war.

The turbulence which characterized the county courts continued to disturb trials in the counties, even after a more regular administration of justice had been established, and under the itinerant justices sent by the crown into the counties, and the administration of justice was often so disturbed by local " routs,"[1] or by the influence

---

take any sufficient number of men to assist him (*Brook's Abr.* "Forcible Entree," 8; *Year-Book*, 22 *Hen. VI.*, 37). And men were accustomed to assemble with force and arms, and either to enforce what they considered justice, or to resist it. Hence, though the law allowed of personal self-defence (*Year-Book of Edward IV.*, 28), and even allowed of violence in defence of property in actual possession, even to regain possession after recent dispossession, it did not allow of violent attempts to regain possession after the wrongdoer had acquired peaceable possession (*Mirror*, chapter on "Disseisin"). Hence the statutes of forcible entry, to prevent men from making forcible entry even into their own lands, if with arms, or terror of actual bodily violence (*Year-Book*, 8 *Henry VI.*, 9). These statutes, Coke said, were in affirmance of the common law, for, says he, the law abhors violence (3 *Coke's Reports*, 12). And it was laid down that if a man came with many, even of those who were accustomed to attend upon him, it was force (*Year-Book*, 10 *Hen. VII.*, 72). And in the *Mirror* it is said that not only swords and spears, but clubs and staves, were "arms." That men did in those days gather together in numbers, armed with weapons, in order to enforce what they deemed justice, or to resist the law, is apparent from the reports in the *Year-Book*, and from contemporary history. Thus in the *Paston Letters* we find a place in dispute held by one body of armed men, and regularly besieged and assailed by another, and a man actually killed in the fray (*Letter* 281). So in the *Year-Book* of Henry VI. we find a case in which a case was adjourned from the assizes "because the parties in their own counties came with great routs of armed men, more as though they were going to battle than to an assize" (*Year-Book*, 7 *Hen. VI.*; 33 *Hen. VI.*, 9). In such a state of society to allow every suitor to enforce justice would be to allow of civil war, and lead to anarchy. Hence the doctrine was established, of necessity, that it was only the ministers of the king, the sheriff and his officers, who could use force to execute the law, although under him and in his aid, the whole county could act, and thus under the statutes of forcible entry the justices of the peace were allowed to use force to remove force (*Year-Book*, 21 *Hen. VI.*, 5; 7 *Edw. IV.*, 18).

[1] Thus, so early as the reign of Henry I., it was mentioned as a cause of failure of justice, which drew causes into the king's court (*Leges. Hen. Prim.*, c. vii.). And even when king's justices went down into the counties, it is not to be supposed the evil entirely abated, and it truly appears it had not. The *curia regis*, certainly, as early as the reign of Henry II., took cognizance of causes which previously would have gone into the counties, for Glanville wrote his Treatise upon it. And the charter of Henry III. provided that the common pleas should be taken in a fixed court, and that the evil continued, a case will show. An assize was arrayed before Sir Wm. Babington and Strange, in the county of Cumberland, and it was adjourned before them at Westminster, and Fulthorpe asked of the justices the cause of the adjourn-

of local magnates, that it was necessary to remove cases into the *curia regis*, the king's superior court.

Independently of the turbulence of the county court, there were various reasons for the removal of causes therefrom, or from other local courts, into the king's superior courts. The power of the county court, or any local court, was strictly limited by its local jurisdiction;[1] whereas the king's superior court had jurisdiction over the whole country, and could send causes for trial into any county, or summon parties to attend in any county.

Again, it was often necessary to remove causes from the local court, to avoid a failure of justice, on account

---

ment, and Babington said that it was because it was a great matter, and the parties in their own counties came with great routs of armed men, more like as though they were going to battle than to an assize ("les parties en lour propre counties, viendront ove graund routs des gents armes, plus semble pur vener a battaile que al assize"), and so for danger of the peace being disturbed; and also for that counsel were in London, and the parties could be better served in their right, the case was adjourned (*Year-Book*, 7 Hen. VI.). See *Year-Book*, 32 Hen. VI., 9, where a trial in the country was denied in a cause between the duke of Exeter and Lord Cromwell, "because there had been a great rout, and a greater would ensue if the trial should take place there, for my lord of Exeter is a great and potent prince in that county (un graund et prepotant prince")" (*Year-Book*, 32 Hen. VI., 9). The *Paston Letters* afford many instances of similar proceedings at assizes about the same period. In modern times the courts have always recognized that it is a good cause for removing a case into another county for trial, that there is a popular excitement and doubt of the possibility of fair trial.

[1] Thus in an assize, where the tenant set up a release, the witnesses of which were in divers counties, the case was adjourned to the king's court at Westminster, "which had jurisdiction over the whole country" (*Year-Book*, 7 Edw. II., p. 231). Various modes were provided for removal of causes into the superior courts, writs of "pone," "recordari," or "certiorari" (*Year-Book*, 7 Edw. IV., 23, 34 Hen. VI., fol. 43). The plaintiff might always remove a cause at his will without cause, for, of course, he would not needlessly delay his own suit, and there could be no disadvantage to the other party in removal of the case from the court of the county; but the defendant could only remove a case for good cause shown (*F. N. B. Recordare*, 79). Thus so early as *Year-Book*, 50 *Edward III.*, it was said to Belknap, J., if a stranger comes into the Cinque ports and commits a transitory trespass, and afterwards goes out of their jurisdiction, he to whom the trespass is done may have an action at the common law; for it is more for his benefit to have the suit at the common law than within the Cinque ports, for they have no power to summon any man that is out of their jurisdiction, viz., in the county of Kent, or elsewhere, into the limits of their jurisdiction. And thus an appeal of felony was held to be in Kent for a murder in their jurisdiction, "because although the Cinque ports have several liberties (i. e., local courts), yet the reason of the grant of these liberties was for the case and benefit of the inhabitants, and not for their prejudice" (*Crispe* v. *Viroll*, Yelverton's *Rep.* 13); and it would be for their prejudice if they could not follow murderers or debtors out of their own limited local jurisdiction.

of the deficiency of suitors or jurors, or the influence of one of the parties over them, from their being, most of them, or all of them, his tenants, or from the lord having an interest in the case, or other causes likely to prevent a fair trial.[1]

Nevertheless, notwithstanding the obvious advantages to be gained by suing in the king's court, it is probable that ancient usage would have longer delayed their ascendancy, but for some degree of legal compulsion to sue there, occasioned by the legal maxims and rules already alluded to. And there is every reason to believe that the exercise of this compulsion, and the strenuous assertion by the sovereign of the prerogative of a general control over the administration of justice, and the establishment of a regular judicature, arose chiefly from its being found that fees and amercements would constitute a considerable source of revenue. It is beyond a doubt that the first court was the exchequer. And the sending of itinerant justices,[2] and in the subsequent establishment of a su-

---

[1] Thus a case was removed from the local court where there were only six suitors (*Year-Book, Hen. IV.*). So where the lord of the hundred was interested, as in an assize against the mayor and commonalty of Winton (31 *Assize*, 19); so in a case as to the mayor and corporation of Coventry (*Year-Book*, 15 *Edw. IV.*, 18); so if all the inhabitants were tenants of one of the parties (*Year-Book*, 22 *Edw. IV.*, 3). In such cases the evil was avoided by removal of the case into the king's court, because then the jury could be accorded to come not from the place in question, nor even from the county at large (in which case some of the inhabitants of the place might be included), but from some other hundred (*Year-Book*, 3 *Hen. VI.*, 39; *Trials per Pais*, 109; *Gilbert's Hist. of C. P.*, 68–71; *Comberbatch*, 332; *Dance* v. *Ellden*, *Cro. Jac.*, 650).

[2] There can be no doubt that, in the commissions of these justices, especial care was given to direct their attention to any branches of the revenue, particularly fines and amercements; and so diligently did they attend to this department of their duty that we find the people at last began to dread their approach, and actually desired the periods at which they came might be lengthened (*vide Ang.-Saer.*, i., 495). This led to the discontinuance of justices itinerant, who went once or twice a year, and the substitution of justices in eyre, who went only once in seven years; but their commissions again directed their attention to the revenue, escheats, fines, forfeitures, etc. That the exchequer was the first superior court is clear, for a contemporary writer, the author of *Dialogus de Scaccario*, says it was established soon after the Conquest, and it is mentioned in the reign of Henry I. (*Mador's Exch.*, i., 204), while there is no mention of any other superior court of law except after Magna Charta, when, as common pleas were forbidden from being taken in any court which followed the king, as the exchequer did, the court of common pleas arose at Westminster. Until then, the records show that all suits between party and party which came up to the superior court of the king, came into the exchequer (*Mad. Exch.*, 686–793). The judges of that

perior court for private suits, or common pleas (as they were called), or rather that cognizance of them in the exchequer, which led to such a court, arose from this cause.

For these writs fees were charged,[1] and justice was thus, and in other ways, made a source of royal revenue, which caused it to be made a branch of royal prerogative, and secured it the care and attention of the government, in order to promote and extend that from which revenue was derived. Thus the interest of the crown happily led it to make the administration of justice its special study, and from this at first some abuses, but in the ultimate result many improvements, undoubtedly arose.

From whatever causes, however, the ordinary jurisdiction of the king's courts was upheld to the utmost by legal rules and maxims, and to a great extent, no doubt, it rested upon legal principle.[2] In pursuance of the same

court were called barons of the exchequer, and the other judges who sat there, probably to assist in deciding common pleas, were called "justices of the bench," to distinguish them from the justices itinerant. Fines were taken in the exchequer, and the records removed there about the time of Henry IV. (*Year-Book*, 37 *Hen. IV.*, 17).

[1] "The sauris regis," says Lord Coke, "est pacis vinculo," a truth which all our sovereigns, Saxon or Norman, caught with singular avidity, and grasped with great tenacity. And so soon as they found that justice could be made a source of revenue, they gave every attention to it. Fees were charged for writs, and even fines for expedition; and this is alluded to in the *Mirror* as an "abuse." Moreover, every possible occasion was taken for declaring a suitor be in mercy, as it was called — *in misericordia regis* — for any contempt of court, the effect of which was that he was liable to be amerced, and this was a further source of revenue. This is alluded to in the laws of Henry I., and there is a chapter upon it. There is also a chapter in the *Mirror* on the subject, and one of the clauses of *Magna Charta* was directed against the abuses of amercements. All this, however, tended to give the sovereign an interest in enforcing a regular administration of justice, and in establishing a regular judicature for the purpose. That this was so is shown by this, that the very worst and most rapacious of our Norman sovereigns showed a great regard for the administration of justice. Thus Hale states as to John —" This king endeavored to bring the law and the pleadings and proceedings thereof to some better order than he found it — for saving his profits, whereof he was very studious — and for the better reduction of it into order and method, we find frequently in the records of his time, fines imposed, *pro stulti loquio*, that is, mulcts imposed by the court for barbarous pleadings, whence afterwards arose the common fine, *pro pulchre placitando*, which was, indeed, no other than a fine for want of it" (*Hist. Com. Law*, 7). All this was of course illegal; and these were the kind of exactions, no doubt, intended by the article in *Magna Charta*, "Nulli vendemus, nulli negabimus, aut differemus rectum aut justitiam."

[2] So early as the reign of Henry I. the county court was called *curia regis* (*Leges Henrici Primi*, c. xi.), yet counties existed before the earliest times of

policy, it became firmly established in our courts that all jurisdiction, even in the smallest and most ancient local courts, emanated from the crown, so that even the leet, which was said to be the most ancient court in the realm — and was far more ancient than the monarchy — was said to be the king's court, as part of the justice of the realm.

Under Edward I. the principles which had been established as to the administration of justice were pursued and carried out; the jurisdiction and the judicature of the superior courts of law were settled;[1] with the impor-

---

the Saxons, and the courts of counties arose before there was any united monarchy. "Le leete est le plus ancient cour in le realme" (*Year-Book*, 7 *Hen. VI.*, 12). It was as ancient as hundreds, which undoubtedly existed before the time of the Saxons (whose earliest laws speak of them as already existing), so that it was more ancient than the monarchy itself. So of the courts baron, as ancient as manors, which belong to the time of the Romans. Yet even the leet was said to be the court of the king (*curia regis*), and so of courts in towns and boroughs, which have courts; they are entitled the court of the king (*Year-Book*, 21 *Hen. VII.*, p. 40). Yet the ancient style of the court baron is said by Lord Coke to have been the court of the lord. It also was a necessary consequence of the principle that the crown is charged with the duty of seeing that justice is administered, and that thus allegiance and protection are correlative. Where there is the duty and responsibility, there must be the power. And again, as the crown alone can enforce the execution of the sentences of courts, of necessity their power or jurisdiction must be derived therefrom. And again, as jurisdiction, civil or criminal, is coercive, it is a necessary attribute of the executive power of government, as Guizot points out. Thus Rayneval lays it down that "le pouvoir judiciaire est une emanation du pouvoir executif" (*Droit de la Nature*, c. xii.). Thus our most ancient authorities of law lay it down that all jurisdiction is from the crown. Thus Fleta, "Sine warranto jurisdictionem non habent neque coercionem" (c. xxxiv.). So as the *Mirror of Justice* said, that jurisdiction is the power to declare the law, and that it rests with the king, because he alone can enforce and execute it (c. ii., s. 3). The county courts were in theory the courts of the king, but only in theory; in reality they were mere popular assemblies; practically, a king's judge made a king's court.

[1] Hale says of this king that, "as touching the common administration of justice between party and party, and accommodating of the rules and methods and orders of proceeding, he did the most of any king since William I., and left the same as a fixed and stable rule and order of proceeding, very little differing from that which we now hold and practise, especially as to the substance and principal contexture thereof" (*Hale's Hist. of Com. Law*, c. vii., p. 158). "He established the limits of the court of common pleas, perfectly performing the direction of Magna Charta: 'Quod communia placita non sequuntur curia nostra,' and in express terms extending it to the exchequer. He settled the bounds of inferior courts, of counties, hundreds, and courts baron, which he kept within their proper limits; and so gradually the common justice of the kingdom came to be administered by men knowing in the laws, and conversant in the great courts, and before justices itinerant. He settled a speedier way for recovery of debts, not only for merchants, by the statutes *de mercatoribus*, but for other persons, by granting

tant addition of a provision for the reservation of questions of law from the circuits for the determination of a superior court; and the consequence was, that the development of law made such rapid progress in his reign that it marks an era in the history of our law.

The result of these improvements in the judicature of the country was, that in the reign of Edward I.,[1] the legal remedies for wrongs and injuries were well settled, and the course of the common law was known and established, so that it was no longer necessary for the great council of the realm to take any part in the administration of justice, which was left to take its regular course in the courts of common law, according to their respective jurisdictions, and subject to the proper correction by appeal.

Hence the reign of Edward I. is a great era or epoch in the history of our law, and hence it resulted that, as in the reign of Edward I., as Hale says,[2] the law received

---

an execution for a moiety of the lands by *elegit* (*Hist. Com. Law*, p. 160). That is to say, he established a species of recognizances or acknowledgments of debt, under which merchants could obtain summary execution without going through the ordinary formalities of an action; and as to all creditors he gave a remedy against the land of the debtors, which it was thought in these times was the surest way of enforcing or obtaining satisfaction, since in those days, all persons of any substance at all had some property in land.

[1] "Let any man," says Hale, "look over the rolls of parliament, and the petitions in parliament, of the times of Edward I. to Henry VI., and he will find hundreds of answers of petitions in parliament concerning matters determinable at common law endorsed with answers to this or the like effect: 'Suez vous a le common ley;' 'Sequatur ad communem legem;' 'Mandetur ista petitio in cancellarium, vel justiciariis de Banco;'" and so parliament refused to review judgments given in courts of law, except in the regular course, in writs of error carried through the courts of error, as to which, it may be observed, that in the reign of Edward III. statutable provision was made.

[2] "The laws did never in any one age receive so great and sudden an advancement; nay, I think it, I may safely say, that all the ages since his time have not done so much in reference to the orderly settling and establishing of the distributive justice of the kingdom as he did within his reign" (*Hist. Com. Law*, c. vii.). "Upon the whole, it appears, that the very scheme, mould and model, of the common law, especially in relation to the administration of common justice between party and party, was highly rectified and set in a much better light and order, by this king, than his predecessors left it to him; so in a very great measure it has continued the same in all succeeding ages to this day. So that the mark or epoch we are to take for the true stating of the law of England as it is, is to be considered, stated, and estimated from what it was when this king left it. But in his time it was in a great degree rude and unpolished in comparison of what it was after his reduction thereof; and on the other side, as it was thus ordered by him, so has it stood hitherto, without any great or considerable alteration, abating some few ad-

a greater advancement than in all the subsequent periods up to the time at which Hale wrote, long after the reign of Elizabeth, where our author's history closes; inasmuch, indeed, that, in the opinion of that high authority, "the very scheme, mould and model, of our law was then so settled that, in a very great measure, it continued the same in all succeeding ages;" as undoubtedly it did to the end of the reign of Elizabeth, for which reason, doubtless, it was that our author there terminated his history.

When once a regular judicature and regular administration of justice had been established, the law became developed by judicial decisions from the first rude elements of jurisprudence contained in the treatise based upon the Roman law,[1] or judicial decisions made with the aid of principles derived from the same source, and adapted by these decisions to Saxon usages and institutions.

It is remarkable by what slow degrees the most primary and important principles of law were practically carried out and enforced in this country, as for instance, that fundamental principle which lies at the basis of all civilized justice, the supremacy of law, and the unlawfulness of force or violence for the redress of wrong, or obtaining of right. This great principle, laid down in the Roman law and adopted into the Saxon, was for centuries in a great measure ignored,[2] and it was not until a much later age that it was really carried out.

It is also observable, on the other hand, how, by force

---

ditions and alterations, which succeeding times have made, which for the most part are in the subject-matter of the laws themselves, and not so much in the rules, methods, or ways of its administration" (*Hist. of Com. Law*, c. vii., p. 163).

[1] And so all these elements of law will be found to have been by degrees developed into the more complete form which our law in later ages by degrees assumed. Nor is there any more interesting branch of legal studies than the observation of this gradual process of development. This, indeed, is the great scope of legal history, and in these earlier elementary principles of law are often to be found the only true interpretation of later laws.

[2] Thus in the *Paston Letters* will be seen an account of a regular attack upon a castle in the reign of Edward IV. by a body of armed men, in order to obtain possession of it by force (vol. ii., p. 39, letter 281), and it is most remarkable that even Mr. Hallam appears to have considered it lawful. He cites Britton: "The first remedy of the disseisee is to collect a body of his friends (recoiller ducys et force), and to cast out the disseisors;" and though he notices that the statutes of Henry VI. and Richard II. are against it, he says they imply the facts which made them necessary (*Middle Ages*, vol. iii.). But Lord Coke says the statutes were only in affirmation of the common law, and if so, the common law followed the Roman.

of judicial decisions, legal principles derived from the Roman law were carried out and developed into consequences of the most vital character, so as to amount practically almost to alterations of the law, as in the instances of the judicial decisions[1] which virtually converted mere villeins into owners of their lands and tenements.

During the important reign of Edward I., which, above all others, marks a great era in the history of our law, in which, as Lord Hale observes, the very mould and model of our law and constitution were settled, the influence of the Roman law on the formation of our own is undoubted.[2] But after this reign, probably from the fact that ecclesiastics ceased to be judges, and that the laymen appointed to the judicial office were not sufficiently acquainted with it, its influence in our courts declined, and the result was unquestionably detrimental to the development of our law.

---

[1] It has been seen that in the Roman law, adopted into the Saxon and the Norman, villeins were not to be coerced into services beyond such as were established by custom. This was long afterwards deemed virtually to imply that, so long as they rendered their customary services, they could not be removed. But even in the reign of Henry VI. it was said, as Littleton tells us, that if the lord put them out, they have no other remedy than to sue their lord by petition. But he adds, Brian, chief justice in the reign of Edward IV., said that "his opinion always hath been, and always shall be, that if the tenant, by custom tendering his services, be cast out, he shall have his remedy by action;" and so was the opinion of Chief Justice Danby (*Littleton's Tenures*, c. ix.).

[2] As Mr. Hallam observes, that wise monarch encouraged its study, and the great treatise of Bracton was based upon it, which Lord Coke regards as the basis of our common law. In the early part of the reign of Edward II. it was said from the bench that the law of England was based upon the civil law. "Que respondez vous," said the chief justice, "a la loy imperial, donques sur quel ley de terre est fondue?" (*Year-Book*, 5 *Edw. II.*, fol. 148). In the next reign, however, a sergeant, afterwards chief baron, observed, when the civil law was cited, that he could not understand it (*Year-Book*, 22 *Edw. III.*, fol. 37), but Blackstone admits the judge was probably ignorant of it (*Comm.*, vol. i., p. 21), and Mr. Phillimore states that Edward I. encouraged the study of the Roman law, and that it was often quoted in the temporal courts here, but that in Edward III.'s time it was quite exploded. Selden, in *Fletam*, c. vii., s. 9, has preserved some curious instances in which it was cited prior to the reign of Edward III., in whose time he says it was "plane neglectus rejectusque," and was unknown to the practitioners in our courts, though still Mr. Phillimore thinks it exercised some indirect influence through the ecclesiastical judges or teachers. Mr. Phillimore cites with amusing contempt the sneer of "an old savage who was chief baron of the exchequer in the reign of Edward III." against the Roman law. In the reign of Richard II. the commons protested that this realm never had been nor should be governed by the civil law, quite ignorant that all that was worth anything in it was derived from the civil law.

The cause or the result of this disregard of the Roman law was great ignorance in the courts of law,[1] with such extreme narrowness of mind among the judges, that, in consequence of their contracted notions of law, suitors were driven from the courts of law, and forced to find, in an appeal to equity, that full measure of justice which was no longer to be obtained at law.

How scandalously, after discarding the civil law, our courts of law perverted justice,[2] can be shown even from

---

[1] Of this ignorance many illustrations could be given. In the reign of Henry VII. a judge said from the bench "that a hundred meant one hundred men, or one hundred vills, or *one hundred parishes!*" (*Year-Book*, 8 *Hen. VII.*, fol. 3). No man who had traced the history of our institutions from the Roman times could have fallen into such a blunder. From the *Year-Books* of Edward IV., a passage might be cited in which one of the judges, probably a little less ignorant than the rest, declared that it was entirely through ignorance the suitors were driven into equity (*Year-Book*, 21 *Edw. IV.*, fol. 21). It need hardly be stated that in the reign of Henry VIII. the jurisdiction of equity over cases of law was assisted and established by Sir T. More.

[2] Thus it was said in a court of law that "If a man promise to make me a house, and do not, I shall have a remedy in chancery, and that, but for 'mispleading' (*i. e.*, ignorance), there might be a remedy at law" (*Year-Book*, 21 *Edw. IV.*, fol. 23). So in the plainest possible cases it was constantly said that there was no remedy at law, but that there was in chancery, where the rules of the civil law were followed. Thus, for instance, if a bond was negotiable until actually cancelled in chancery, the party had no remedy against it at law (*Year-Book*, 37 *Hen. VI.*, 13). So again, in that plainest of all possible cases, that of a man who had paid a debt and omitted to take a proper acknowledgment, — it may seem scarcely credible, but it is the fact, — that if the debt were by deed, there was no remedy at law without an acquittance by deed! If a man pay a debt for which he is bound by deed without taking an acquittance by specialty (*i. e.*, by deed), *he shall have a remedy in chancery!* (*Year-Book*, 7 *Hen. VII.*, 11). That is, he was to be made to pay the debt at law twice over, and then sent to commence a suit in chancery to get the money back again! This incredible absurdity was actually vindicated at the time as the perfection of right reason! Thus it was laid down in chancery: Here we adjudge "secundum veritatem rei," and not "secundum allegata;" and if a man alleges by bill that the defendant has done a wrong to him, and the other says nothing, if we can see that he has done no wrong, the plaintiff shall recover nothing. "There are," said the chancellor, "two powers and (kinds of) processes (or procedure): s. potentia ordinata, et absoluta. Ordinata is as positive law, and has a certain order. Sed lex naturæ non habet certum ordinem: sed per quemcunque modum veritas sciri poterit; and therefore it is called absolute procedure; and in the law of nature it is required (*i. e.*, only) that the parties shall be present (or absent by contumacy), and that there shall be an examination of the truth." (*Year-Book of Edw. IV.*, fol. 15; *Bro. Abr. Jurisdiccion*, 50). Thus it was said in these times: "En le chancery (per le chancellor) home ne sera prejudice la per mispleadinge, ou pur defense de forme, mes secundum veritatem rei, et nous doyomus aduidger secundum conscienciam, et non secundum allegata, car si homo suppose per byl: que le defense ad fait tout a lui,

the language of the courts of law themselves, who admitted that justice, through their own ignorance, constantly failed at law; that they had come to regard form more than substance; that even in the plainest case justice was too often obstructed or perverted by technical rules, and that suitors were driven to seek in the court of chancery the remedy they could no longer find at law.

A rigid adherence to common law rules, sometimes not supported by any sound legal principle, but the result only of other rules, themselves entirely arbitrary,[1] and

---

a que il dit riens, si avomus conusans que il ad fait nul tort a luy, recouera riens; et sont deux powers et proces, silicet potencia ordinata et absoluta, ordinata est come ley positive, come certen ordre, sed lex naturæ non habet certum ordinem, sed per que meunique modum veritas sciri poterit, et ideo dabitur processius absolutus; et in lege nature requiritur que les partis sont presents, ou que ils sont absentes per contumacy, silicet ou ils sont garnie, et font defense et examinatio veritatis" (*Year-Book, Bro. Abr. Jurisdiccion*, 50). Thus in the *Doctor and Student*, the first question of the doctors of the law of England and conscience is, "that if a man that is bound in an obligation pay the money, but taketh no acquittance, or if he take one, and it happeneth him to lose it, that in that case he shall be compelled by the laws of England to pay the money again!" To which it is answered by the student that "it is *not* the law that a man in such case *ought of right to pay the money eftsoons*, for that would be against reason and conscience, but that there is a general rule in the law that in an action of debt on an obligation, the defendant shall not discharge himself without an acquittance in writing, which is ordained by the law to avoid a *great inconvenience that else might happen to many people*—that is, that every man by mere parol should avoid an obligation; wherefore, to avoid that inconvenience, the law hath ordained that, as the defendant is *charged* by a writing, he shall be *discharged* by writing" (c. xii.). As if this did not come practically to the same thing! It will be seen how the chancellor sophisticated the law. And if this was the law even of a chancellor, it may be imagined what the common law judges were.

[1] Take, for instance, the rules as to tenants in common, or copartners. As long ago as the reign of Henry I. they had remedy at law, for in the *Leges Henrici Primi*, founded on the civil law, we find a section (54): "De discessione sociorum civis pecuniæ," we read, "Si ab qui fuerint ita socii, ut pecuniam suam posuerint in commune, et a societate et communitate illa discedere voluerint, afferant coram testibus quicquid habent in commune dividendum, ut si opus est super sancta jurent, quod amplius non habeant, et adquisicionem et adquisitium, sicut rectum est et pactum fecerunt, dividant inter se." This shows that no difficulty could have been made at that time about any case of joint or common property, even when it was a matter of adjustment and settlement, much less when it was a question of ouster of one of the common owners by the other. But in the reign of Henry VI. it was otherwise at law. Thus *Littleton*, s. 322, and *Co. Litt.*, 323: "Albeit one tenant in common takes the whole profits, the other hath no remedy by law against him, for the taking of the whole profit is no ejectment; but if he drive out of the land any of the cattle of the other tenant in common, or do not suffer him to enter or occupy the land, this is an ejectment or expulsion, whereupon he may have an ejectment for the moiety, and recover damages for the entry,

resting rather on custom than reason, too often operated to deprive the party of his remedy at law, and remitted him to the delay and vexation of a suit in chancery.

In a later and more learned age, the age of Selden and of Spelman, the study of the civil law was revived, and the result was a great improvement in our law; and some of the most celebrated judgments afterwards delivered in our courts of law were derived from the principles of the Roman law.[1] Nor can there be any doubt that large por-

---

but not for the mesne profits. And thus one tenant in common could not have an action of trespass against the other (*Bro. Abr.*, "Tenants in Common," pl. 14; *S. P. Haywood* v. *Danes*, Salk. 4), nor account, even though the other was his bailiff (*Year-Book*, 17 *Edw. II.*, 552). So a tenant in common could not be a disseisor without an actual "ouster" of his companion (*Goodtitle*, 2; *Points*, 3; *Wilson*, 118; *Ibid.*, 391). So *Litt.*, s. 323: "If two be possessed of chattels personal in common, and one take the whole to himself out of the possession of the other, the other has no remedy but to take this from him who hath done the wrong, to occupy in common, *when he can see his time.*" So *Coke Litt.*, 200, a: "If one tenant in common takes all the chattels personal, the other has no remedy by action, *but he may take them again.*" So *Brown* v. *Hedges*, 1 Salk., 290; *Fox* v. *Hanbury*, *Cowp.*, 443.

[1] For example, the celebrated judgment of Holt in the great case which settled the law of bailments, the case of *Coggs* v. *Bernard* (1 *Lord Raymond's Rep.*, 709), which Mr. Hargreave called a most masterly view of the law of bailment (*Co. Litt.*, 896, n. 3). Sir W. Jones, in his *Treatise on Bailments*, observed that it was in a great degree based on Bracton, who was derived from Justinian, and the judgment certainly is based entirely on the civil law. A very learned writer of our own time says that equity formed an ingredient in the Roman law, and was thence infused in some degree into the common law (*Spence's Eq. Jur.*, 411). As a matter of fact there can be no doubt that there was the most remarkable resemblance between the Roman and the common law, upon a great variety of most important subjects. As to the rules of descent of real property, they were substantially the same, until the common law was altered as to real estates by the feudal system, and the custom of primogeniture, introduced, no doubt, with reference thereto. And the Roman rule was retained in substance as to personalty, and restored by the statute of distributions. Then as to lineal descent, the Roman law provided certain precautions to prevent frauds upon the real heirs, by frauds of widows pretending to be with child (*Pandects*, lib. xxv., tit. 4), and hence our common law writ, *De ventre inspiciendo*. Again, the Roman law as to services and servile tenures, and as to servitudes, formed the basis of our own law of manors and copyholds, and our whole law of easements. So as to the Roman law of limitation or prescription, which was always recognized by our law, though fully established by old statutes. The principle of the common law, on which the statutes of limitation were founded, was the presumption in favor of possession, which is derived from the Roman law (*Pand.*, lib. xliii., tit. 17). And this principle in Roman litigation, as in our own, threw the onus on the claimant until he had established his right, when the possessor had to show a better title.

Then there is the remarkable law of Ethelred. "He who sits without contest or claim on his property during life, let no one have an action against his heirs after his day" (s. 14). "Where the husband dwelt with-

tions of our law can be traced to that source, to be found in the Saxon laws, and were afterwards developed into a complicated system of rights and remedies as to real property, which, having reached to so great a pitch of refinement, was only swept away by a statute passed in our own times.

In the civil as in the criminal branch of our law, there are entire heads of law, peculiar in their character and in their terms, which have been in our law from the very earliest times, and which by their very terms are obviously derived from the Roman law.[1]

Some of the processes of our law, which we suppose to be most entirely the inventions of our common lawyers, will be found to bear such a remarkable resemblance to Roman usages as to justify the persuasion that those usages suggested them.[2]

The main importance, however, of the study of the

out claim or contest, let the wife and children dwell unassailed by litigation; but if the husband before he was dead, then let the heirs answer, as he himself should have done if he had lived" (*Canute*, c. lxxiii.), which was enacted in a law under Canute, and was retained in our law under the title of right of entry "tolled" or taken away by descent, or a continual claim, until it was abolished by the Real Property Act, 3 & 4 William IV., cap. 27. So in a law of Canute as to the effect of a judgment as to the right to land, we find the origin of the use of recoveries, which afterwards prevailed until that act. "He who has defended land (*i. e.*, against all claim) with the witness of the shire (*i. e.*, in the county court, the only court at that time), let him have it undisputed during his day, and after his day to sell and to give" (*Laws of Canute*, c. lxxx.). So of fines.

[1] Thus, for instance, the whole law as to gifts or donations, especially that peculiar one of *Donatio mortis causa* (*Cod. Just.*, lib. viii., tit. 56). So as to distress (*Cod. Just.*, lib. viii., tit. 27, "De districtione pegnorum;") and lib. x., tit. 30, "De capiuendis et distrahendis pignoribus tributorum causa;" lib. x., tit. 21, s. 1, "Res eorum que fiscalibus debitis per contumaciam satisfacere diffescerit, distrahantur." The application of the process to the levying of rent or service was easy and natural. So as to the precaution provided by the Roman law against frauds by widows upon heirs, and the writ, *De ventre inspiciendo*, which was derived from the Roman law into our own (*Pand.*, lib. xxv., tit. 4, *De inspiciendo ventre*). Savigny gives several instances of citations from the Roman law in the Saxon.

[2] The action of ejectment for instance. In the Roman law there was this usage. If the thing was immovable, there appears to have been an old ceremony of the parties going to the land, and one expelling the other from it and leading him before a magistrate (*Sandar's Introd. to the Institutes*, p. 59). Now no one can fail to be struck with the resemblance here presented to the original procedure in ejectment, the lease, and the expulsion which used to form the foundation of the action. So as to fines, learned authors are of opinion that they originated in a suggestion derived from a proceeding in the Roman law (*Cruise's Essay on Real Property*), and there is great foundation for the belief.

Roman law, with reference to its influence on the formation of our own, is in this, that it was the great fountain of legal principle, whence all of our law that was not barbarous (and which, therefore, for the most part has disappeared) was derived. And it might have been imagined that writers upon our legal history would have directed attention to this source and fountain, whence were derived the principles from which our own was developed.

This, however, has not been the case, and the only writers on our legal history, Hale, Blackstone, and our author, have either ignored the influence of the Roman law upon the formation of our own, or have, at all events, made no attempt to trace and to describe it, because they found it difficult to trace particular pieces or portions of our law to that source.

It surely must be manifest that this view is narrow and inconsistent,— narrow, because it restricts the use and scope of legal history to a mere process of precise identification of particular laws; and inconsistent, because if this were all, the study of legal history would, on the narrow practical view suggested, be of little use or value. If legal history is to be looked at only with a view to the actual law as it is, its scope is limited indeed; but in the view of the greatest writers, it has a far wider and larger scope — it teaches the principles from which laws are derived, and the processes by which they are developed; it gives the mind the best possible training, either for law or legislation, and the best possible preparative for the study either of history or law. "Il faut," said Montesquieu, " éclairer les lois par l'histoire, et l'histoire, par les lois." And if the history of law leads to the Roman law as the true source and standard of law, then the mind is directed to the study of that which is the highest human law, and the key to all human history.

Since Hale wrote and since Reeves wrote, a far wider view than theirs has been taken of legal history. That great writer, Guizot — who has, perhaps, more than either, elicited the philosophy of legal history — thus expounded its nature and advantages: " Between the development of legislation and that of society, there is an intimate correspondence; the same revolutions are accomplished therein, and in an analogous order. Let us study the history of laws during the same epoch, and let us see if they will lead us to the same result — if we shall see the same explanation arise from it. The history of laws is more difficult to understand thoroughly than that of events properly so called. Laws, from their very nature, are monuments more incomplete, less explicit, and consequently more obscure. Besides, nothing is more difficult, and yet more indispensable, than to take fast hold of and never lose the chronological thread. When we give an account of external facts, wars, invasions, etc., then chronological concatenation is simple and palpable; each event bears, as it were, its date upon its face. The actual date of laws is often correctly known, it is often known at what epoch they were decreed; but the facts which they were designed to regulate, the causes which made them to be written in one year rather than another, the necessities and social revolutions to which the legislation corresponds, this is what is almost always unknown, at least not understood, and which it is still necessary to unfold, step by step. It is from this study having been neglected, from the not having rigorously observed the chronological progress of laws in their relation to that or society, that confusion and falsehood have so often been thrown into their history. A little more attention to the chronological development of laws and of the social state would have prevented it" (*Lettres sur la Civiliz. dans France*, lect. xxv.).

It would be impossible to express more clearly or more correctly the objects, the uses, and advantages of legal history, or the history of law, and the necessity for tracing it from its earliest rise, and in every step of its course and progress.

And the same great writer, Guizot, forcibly expounded the importance of the study of the Roman laws and institutions, as a preparation for the study of those of the races they subdued. He says — "In commencing, in any quarter of Europe, the study of modern civilization, we must first investigate the state of Roman society there, at the moment when the Roman empire fell — that is to say, about the close of the fourth to the opening of the fifth century"[1] (*Lectures sur la Civilization dans France*).

---

[1] The eminent writer goes on to say: "This investigation is peculiarly necessary in the case of France. The whole of Gaul was subject to the empire and its civilization; more especially in its southern portions was

The grand feature in the character of the Roman law was its universality. This may here well be described in the eloquent language of one of the most eminent and enthusiastic of its teachers, the gifted author already alluded to:—"In consequence of the increasing power of the republic, new magistrates became necessary. Among these, one was created of the utmost importance in the history of Roman legislation; this was the *Prætor peregrinus, qui inter cives et peregrinos jus dixit*. The function of this magistrate was to adjust the disputes which might arise between citizens and foreigners. Thus a new element found its way into Roman jurisprudence. In addition to the local and positive laws by which their own society was regulated, it became necessary for the Roman judge to consider the fundamental principles of justice, from which all law derives its obligation. These principles, under the name of *jus gentium*, thus became familiar to the minds of Roman jurists, and exercised a considerable and happy influence over the institutions of Rome itself. Thus it was, that the view of the jurist became more liberal and extensive, and the notion of a law not dependent upon climate or on caste, common to man on the banks of the Ilissus, the Tiber, or the Euphrates — a covenant, as it were, between earth and heaven, which no human authority could abrogate or supersede, from which all laws derived their controlling power — was transferred from the schools of Greece to the tribunals of Rome. It became every day more and more necessary to appeal to broader principles than those which the municipal institutions of any country could supply; and these were to be found only in the *naturalis ratio*, the principles implanted in the man wherever he lived, and however he was governed" (*Phillimore's Study of the Roman Law*, p. 80). It must be manifest that a law pervaded by such grand views and such broad principles

---

thoroughly Roman. In the histories of England and Germany, Rome occupies a less prominent position; the civilization of those countries in its origin was not Roman but Germanic. It was not until a later period of their career that they really underwent the influence of the laws, the ideas, the traditions of Rome" (*Lect. sur la Civiliz. dans France*, Lect. ii.). It will have been seen, however, that this was a mistake, and that he had forgotten his own contemptuous allusion to Saxon sources of civilization; when the course of those influences is traced, it will be found to have commenced much earlier than this eminent writer supposes.

as these, must have been singularly adapted to exercise a salutary influence upon the barbarian races reduced under its rule; and that this influence must have endured even after the power of the empire was withdrawn, by the force of moral suasion, which never fails to draw men to imitate what they admire or revere. Hence we might expect to find the barbarian races — for instance, our own Britons or Saxons — so soon as the influence of Roman civilization began to tell upon them, look up to, and lay hold of, the laws and institutions of the mighty empire, whose greatness they could not but recognize even in the age of its decline. The main interest of the question as to the connection between the Roman law and our own, is, that our vast empire, over numerous races and peoples, occupies a position in the world very analogous to that of Rome, and in which a like necessity exists for recourse to principles of jurisprudence, wide and broad enough to embrace all the numerous nations subject to our sway, and enable us to rule and govern them all upon the broad ground of common principles of justice, equally applicable to them all. This was the glory of the Roman law, and for that very reason does enter largely into our own law, and that of many of the colonies or countries subject to our rule; and it is manifest that the more the attention of English lawyers is called to it, the more enlightened and enlarged will be their views of law and legislation, and the more free from the narrow bonds of mere municipal law and national prejudice.

This is undoubtedly the view taken by the ablest writers. A learned and able writer in our own time says: —"It is scarcely possible to suppose any well-read lawyer, captivated as he may be with the notion of Saxon liberty, can proceed far in the study of either system, without perceiving a striking analogy between the civil law of Rome and the common law of England, not only as to their maxims and principles, and their technical phraseology, but also their method of practice, showing how early, and to what extent one system became the instructor and guide of the other. To some minds there is a black-letter witchcraft in the expressions, 'Anglo-Saxon liberty,' 'ancient constitution,' and the like, while the chances are, that in furnishing an example they may fall into the whimsical position of seizing upon some relic of Roman jurisprudence to prove the perfection and justice of their own" (*Goldsmith's Doctrine of Equity*, p. 8).

"When we remember that the Romans held possession of this island nearly five hundred years, and during that period some of the most celebrated lawyers administered justice among the conquered Britons upon the like footing, and according to the same system adopted by the conquerors in their own country, we cannot be surprised that such an event had its due influence in stamping a character upon the future institutions of the country, more especially as the Romans also imposed their language as well as their customs upon the newly-acquired colony" (*Goldsmith's Doctrine of Equity*, p. 8).

No one can have followed the imperfect review which has here been presented of the course of our legal history without feeling that this is perfectly true.? The same view has the authority of the great writer — the historian of *Europe in the Middle Ages*,— who has left on record his opinion that the influence of the Roman law upon those who framed our own was greater than they acknowledged, or even than they knew, and he added: "A full view of the subject is still, I think, a *desideratum* in the history of the English law, which it would illustrate in a very interesting manner" (*Middle Ages*, c. viii.). It has been the endeavor of the writer, in some degree, to supply this deficiency, and at all events he has now explained the views and principles upon which the present edition has been prepared. Nor is the interest of all this merely historical, nor has it only a reference to the past. The subject has a nearer interest on this account, that within the numerous dominions or dependencies of our vast empire there are always some communities which are in a state similar to that of our own country, at some one or other of its different conditions, and are passing through periods of transition, and undergoing changes, which this country went through in ages past. Thus, for instance, in the vast dominion of India, in itself an empire, there have always been provinces which have exemplified, under some species of rule, the various states or conditions through which this country passed in early times; whether the elaborate despotism of the Roman period of occupation, the rude barbaric freedom of the Saxon popular tribunals, or the feudal system of the Normans; all these, as described by the pen of a Gibbon, or a Guizot, or a Palgrave, in our own or other countries of Europe during the earlier or middle ages of European history, will be found to have been reproduced upon the continent of India, either under native rule or under our own.

Thus the first state or condition in which we find the people of India under their Hindoo emperors, that of unmitigated despotism, so closely resembles that in which the various races of Europe were in the latter period of the Roman empire, that the passages in Gibbon or in Mill which describe them, respectively appear like remarkable historical parallels.[1]

---

[1] In Mill's *Hist. Brit. India*, vol. i., c. iv., a very similar account is given of Hindoo judicature: "As kings and their great deputies exercised the principal functions of judicature, they were too powerful to be restrained by a regard to what had been done before them by others. What judicature could pronounce, therefore, was almost always uncertain, almost always arbitrary" (p. 171). And again, in a note, "The authority of the Hindoo princes, as well as that of the vile emissaries whom they keep in the several provinces of their country, being altogether despotic, and knowing no other will but their own arbitrary will, there is nothing in India that resembles a court of justice. The civil power and judicial are generally united and exercised in each district by the collector or receiver of the imposts. This tribunal, chiefly intended for the collection of taxes, takes cognizance of all affairs, civil or criminal, within its bounds, and determines on all causes." "This was just the state of the Saxon and early Norman system, when the shire-reeve, the sheriff, the king's steward, or bailiff, originally appointed mainly to receive his dues, was also the chief judge of the county. The sheriff was ultimately deprived of all real *judicial* power, and made the mere minister of the law. And the judicial powers of the 'collector system' of magistracy in India is not approved of by the best authorities. The 'collector' commonly exercised both civil and criminal jurisdiction within the territory over which he was appointed to preside. In his criminal court he inflicted all sorts of penalties.... In his Adawlut or civil court, he decided all questions relating to property. His discretion was guided or restrained by no law, except the commentaries and customs, all in the highest degree loose and indeterminate. There was no formed and regular course of appeal from the Zemindary decisions, but the government interfered in an *arbitrary* manner. ... To the mass of the people these courts afford but little protection. The expense created by distance precluded the greater number from so much as application for justice. The judges were swayed by their hopes or their fears, their proceedings were not *controlled by any written memorial or record*. Originally questions of revenue, as well as others, belonged to the courts of the Zemindars; but a few years previous to the transfer of the revenues to the English, the decision of fiscal questions had been taken from the Zemindars, and given to an officer called the fiscal-deputy in each province" (*Mill's Hist. British India*, vol. i., b. v., c. i., p. 314, *quart. ed.*). "One of the first steps in reform was to establish supreme courts of appeal; and, of course, as a necessary condition, it was ordained that *records* of all proceedings should be made and preserved" (*Ibid.*, p. 316). The Zemindars, it is elsewhere stated, had an office and authority, comprising both an estate and a magistracy, a species of sovereignty (*Ibid.*, c. iii.). As kings and their *great deputies* exer-

In India, from very early times, there had existed a system of natural arbitration by the neighbors, which probably formed in every country the first attempt at anything like an administration of justice, and which substantially resembled our old Saxon county courts, being mere assemblies of the principal inhabitants, who took cognizance of the disputes which arose among them, and made the best settlement they could — a system suited to an early state of society, and which necessarily precedes a more regular administration of justice.[1]

Such a system was only suited to the rude and simple condition of society in which it had originally arisen; and hence, when it was attempted half a century ago to restore it in India, the experiment failed,[2] for reasons

---

cised the principal functions of judicature, what judicature would pronounce was uncertain and almost always arbitrary (vol. i., c. iv., p. 2). "For a considerable time before the establishment of British supremacy, the people of India had been unaccustomed to any regularly *organized and administered* system of law or justice. . . . The main principle that everywhere regulated the administration was *the concentration of absolute authority*, and the same individual was charged with the superintendence of revenue, justice, and police; with little to guide or restrain him, except his own perceptions and sentiments of equity. Even in the best of times the sovereign was the fountain of law and justice, . . . but the leading object of the native governments was the realization of the largest possible amount of revenue, and all persons engaged in this duty were armed with plenary powers, both as magistrates and judges; so that, in general, the people were left to the uncontrolled will of individuals" (*Mill's Hist. Brit. India, cont. by Wilson*, vol. i., 387).

[1] In the absence of courts of justice provided by the state, the people learned to abstain from litigation (*Elphinstone*, iv., 194); or "when disputes arose among them, submitted them to the arbitrament of judges chosen among themselves. This expedient had probably descended from ancient times, in what had been a recognized element of Hindoo judiciary administration, under the name of Panchayat," [this is a mistake, for in the next page the historian mentions "the Panchayat had no power to enforce its decrees, so it was not a judiciary body;"] but it had fallen into discredit in most parts of India." Although, he adds, they were not inaccessible to personal bias or corruption, and their proceedings were occasionally irregular and tedious, yet they were suited to the times, and congenial to the feelings of the people, and supplied the place of better organized and more solemn tribunals (*Hist. Brit. India*, vol. i., 339). He says, in a note, they seem to have been but clumsy instruments. He elsewhere says they were prized only so long as nothing better was to be had.

[2] The effects of the regulations, (extending the system of village Panchayats) operated to lighten the duties of the judges, and to facilitate the determination of civil suits. Some of their results, however, were unexpected, and afforded an unanswerable proof that the sentiments of the natives of India are as liable as those of other natives to vary with change of time and circumstances. The benefits so confidently anticipated from the public recognition of the Panchayat, were not realized: the supposed boon to the

which might have been anticipated by the aid of the light to be acquired from our own legal history. It was found, as indeed had been predicted, that the ancient system of rude popular arbitration had only been tolerated when nothing better was known, and because nothing better was known; and that when once the idea of a rational and intelligent administration of justice by any judicial order of men had arisen, the preventive system of natural arbitration would not be endured.

people was rejected; they would make little use of an institution interwoven, it had been imagined, inseparably with their habits and affections. The Panchayats, it appeared, had been highly prized, only *as long as nothing better was to be had.* In the absence of all other tribunals, the people were constrained to establish one for themselves, and willingly admitted its adjudication of disputes which there was no other authority to settle; while, on the other hand, the most respectable members of the community, especially interested in maintaining property and peace inviolate, and being subject to no authoritative interference or protection, willingly discharged, without any other consideration than the influence which they derived from their discharge of such functions, the duties of arbitrators and judges. But a court, the members of which had no responsibility, etc. (*Wilson's Hist. Brit. India*, vol. ii., p. 321). As the patels or head men of the villages, and the village Panchayats, were not to receive any remuneration for the performance of the duties to be assigned to them, it was anticipated that they would either decline the obligation, or fulfil it with reluctance and indifference. Connected also as they must be with the parties concerned in the cases before them, it was scarcely to be expected that they should perform their duties free from bias or partiality; and as it was part of the plan that their sentences should not be subject to appeal, there was no security against their committing gross injustice. As also they were necessarily ignorant of the laws and regulations, their judgments could not be governed by any determinate principles, and their decisions could not fail to be capricious and contradictory (*Wilson's Hist. Brit. India*, vol. ii., p. 518). Notwithstanding, however, these objections, the system was established in 1816 — with what result? "The benefits expected were not realized; the Panchayats, it appeared, had been highly prized, *only as long as nothing better was to be had.*" "In the gross and complicated mass of human passions and concerns, the primitive rights of men undergo such a variety of refractions and reflections, that it becomes absurd to talk of them as if they continued in the simplicity of their original direction. The nature of man is intricate; the objects of society are of the greatest possible complexity; and therefore no simple disposition or direction of power can be suitable either to man's nature or to the quality of his affairs. When I hear the simplicity of contrivance aimed at and boasted of in any new political constitution, I am at no loss to decide that the artificers are grossly ignorant of their trade. The simple governments are fundamentally defective. If you were to contemplate society in but one point of view, all these simple modes of polity are infinitely captivating. In effect, each would answer its single end more perfectly than the more complex is able to attain all its complex purposes. But it is better that the whole should be imperfectly answered than that while some parts are provided for with great exactness, others might be totally neglected or materially injured. The advantages of government are often balances between differences of good, compromises sometimes between good and evil,

And although some writers in our own times[1] have been disposed to admire what they called the "simple and natural" proceedings of these popular tribunals in India, they have been compelled to admit, in a great degree, their evils, especially in the absence of anything like certainty or uniformity in the administration of the law; and it has been manifest, from the tenor of their observations, that the view they had taken was comparative with reference to a system of procedure then established in this country, which was infinitely too formal and artificial, and led many to suppose that a system could not have forms without being formal, could not be regular without being technical. And these writers have

and sometimes between evil and evil" (*Burke's Reflections upon the French Revolution*).

[1] Mr. Mill, while arguing against the uncertainty of unwritten laws, admits that this uncertainty is limited by the writing down of decisions, "when, on any particular subject, a number of judges have all, with public approbation, decided in one way; and when these decisions are recorded and made known, the judge who comes after has strong motives not to depart from their example. This advantage, the Hindoo judicial system," he observes, "was deprived of, in this respect resembling our old Saxon system." Among them, the strength of the human mind has never been sufficient to recommend effectually the preservation by writing of the ceremony of judicial decision. It has never been sufficient to create such a public regard for uniformity as to constitute a material motive to a judge. And as kings and their great deputies exercised the principal functions of judicature, they were too powerful to be restrained by a regard to what others had done before them. What the judicature would pronounce, was therefore almost always uncertain, almost always arbitrary (*Mill's Hist. Brit. India*, b. ii., c. 4). It would surely be impossible to imagine a greater fallacy. Mr. Mills approved of the Hindoo and Mohammedan systems of procedure because, he says, they were so "simple and natural," merely summoning the parties, and making a direct and simple investigation. This system may do well enough for simple cases, and, as shown in the text, it has always been allowed in our law for such cases, with the advantage, however, of a central system of control in the superior courts to prevent excess or abuse of jurisdiction (p. 171, and p. 6, c. i., vol. i.). Under the Hindoo and Mohammedan systems, however, it seems to have been applied to all cases, and without control or appeal; and Mr. Mills admits that it made no provision for securing uniformity: "no provision made for the preservation by writing of judicial decisions; no regard for uniformity" (p. 171); "so that what judicature would pronounce was almost always uncertain and arbitrary" (*Ibid.*). And he admits "that the Indian system of procedure is liable to the evil of the arbitrary power with which it entrusts the judge" (p. 141, 1st ed.). His only defence for it is, that a regular — as he calls it — technical system could not avoid the same evil. But a regular system need not be technical; and may, as ours does, regard only what is substantial, and may be sufficient to guard against the evils he points out. It is due to him to add that our system of procedure has been greatly altered since he wrote; not, indeed, in its principles, but in its forms, which were infinitely too strict and technical.

admitted the advantages of a regular judicature, and a regular system of procedure, with its records and appeals, and its guarantees against error or uncertainty in law.

But when an order of judges were appointed, however inferior, yet acting in the regular discharge of a judicial duty under the authority of government, and under some sense of responsibility, the great superiority of this approach to a regular judicature, and a settled system of administration of justice, was so apparent to the people, that their ancient native tribunals were soon deserted, and the new order of judges, notwithstanding all their imperfections, were appealed to in preference.[1]

The interest and the importance of the study of our legal history may be enhanced and illustrated by some further considerations. In the numerous dominions and dependencies within the compass of our vast empire, while, on the one hand, our own law is, more or less prevalent in the greater portion of them, yet, on the other hand, there are many of them in which other systems of law are more or less prevalent; but most of these derived, like our own, from the Roman or civil law. It is manifest that to the subjects of such an empire, in whatever portion of its dominions they may live, the study of her legal history must be of great interest and advantage, whether as being itself the law under which they live, or as derived from the same law which was the parent of their own, and which was based on great principles, capable of application in every civilized community.

There is probably no empire in which the law is more honored than in our own. In this respect, again, the

---

[1] "But a court, the members of which acknowledged no responsibility, and performed their functions only for such a term or at such times as suited their own convenience; who were guided by no light except their own good sense; and who, even if incorrupt, could scarcely be impartial; who had no power to carry their own decrees into effect, and whose sentences were liable to no revision; such a court must have been a very inadequate substitute for any tribunal, the proceedings of which were regulated by fixed rules, removed from personal influence, and subject to vigilant supervision. Whatever defects might still adhere to the administration of justice through individual judges, native or European, appointed by the government, *their courts continued to be crowded, while the Panchayats were deserted, etc.* . . . The patels were mostly ignorant men, little qualified by superiority of knowledge or talent to command respect for their decisions. Recourse was rarely had to their judgments, and the chief labor fell upon the *officers appointed by the state* for the distribution of justice among the people" (*Wilson's Hist. Brit. India*, vol. ii., p. 522).

British empire resembles the Roman. A semi-barbarous people pay more regard to arms than to morals, to commerce, or to law. Thus, in Russia at this day, commerce, the law, and all civil employments, are held in no esteem (Sir A. Alison's *Hist. Europe*, vol. ii., p. 391). So the same writer says, "Nothing astonishes the Russian or Polish noblemen so much as seeing the estimation in which the civil professions, and especially the bar, are held in Great Britain" (*Hist. Europe*, vol. x., p. 566). As the Roman empire extended the study of the Roman law through its provinces, so it has been with our own; and nowhere is law more regarded than in our colonies. Thus very early in the history of our American colonies, their respect for law was remarkable. Burke was struck by it. "In no country perhaps in the world is the law so general a study" (*Burke's Works*, vol. i., p. 188). Mr. Buckle cites this remarkable testimony, and adduces more modern works to establish the same characteristic. (See Lyell's *Second Visit to the United States*, vol. i., p. 48; and Combe's *North America*, vol. ii., p. 329.) It is obvious that in such countries and colonies the study of our legal history must have a great interest.

There are, it will have been observed, many uses or objects of legal history, which, however, perhaps may be included under the two great heads mentioned by Montesquieu: the illustration of history by law, or of law by history. The former belongs rather to the general student, to the politician, the jurist, the legislator, or the statesman. The latter alone belongs specially to the lawyer.

It has been well said by an eminent luminary of the law that no man can be a good lawyer who is not well acquainted with the *history* of law. The reason is obvious enough upon reflection, for to be a lawyer, and, still more, to be a jurist, demands a thorough acquaintance with the principles of law,[1] and these can only be acquired by tracing them, so to speak, to their real source and origin, an inquiry which belongs to legal history. The principles of every part of our law are to be found in their simple, original forms, in its more ancient forms and proceedings; and though these may long ago have

---

[1] There is a passage in our author to this effect (*vide* vol. v., c. xxxv.), & *vide* p. 316.

become obsolete, the principles endure, for, as a learned judge once observed to the writer, forms may perish, but principles remain, and they only reappear in new forms more suited to the manners and exigencies of the age.[1]

Thus the old writs or proceedings of our law embodied the principles and objects which are now worked out by more modern procedure.[2] The ancient tribunals of the country are superseded by other institutions directed to the attainment of the same object, and not only the vast domain of common law, but still more complicated systems, like our systems of conveyancing or of equity, are to be deduced from simple elements to be found in the Year-Books.

It is laid down by all great writers that the only way to become a lawyer is to study the more ancient authorities of our law, and it is often otherwise impossible to master the law on a subject;[3] yet it is as impossible, with-

---

[1] For instance, advertisement in the papers now takes practically the place of proclamations in the ancient county court, or assemblies of the people.

[2] Thus the old writ of *ad quod damnum* was superseded, as to the stoppage or diversion of highways, etc., by the Highway Act, 13 Geo. III. (*Ex parte Armitage Ambler*, 204; *Dairson v. Gill* (East); *Rex v. Netherthong*, 2; *B.* and *Ald.*, 179). The whole statute law as to the liability of the hundred for damage done by rioters (going back to 1 & 6 Geo. I., and the 27 Eliz., c. xiii.), is based on the common law liability, founded on customs derived from the ancient Saxon laws (*Rex v. Clark*, 7 T. R., 496). An action on the case was held maintainable upon the 6 Geo. I., c. xvi., s. 1, by the party grieved, to recover damages against the inhabitants of the adjoining township, for trees, coppice, and underwood, unlawfully and feloniously burnt by persons unknown, though the clause directed the party grieved to recover his damages in the same manner and form as given by the stat. 13 Edw. I., st. 1, c. xlvi., *for dykes and hedges overthrown by persons in the night*, upon which the usual course of proceeding had been by the writ of noctantur (*Thornhill v. Huddersfield*, 11 East., 349). So as to the statute of *Hue and Cry* as to robbery (*Whitworth v. Grimshaw*, 2 Wils., 105; *Rex v. Halfshire*, 5 T. R., 341). These are only instances.

[3] Even although they have for ages been obsolete. Thus, for instance, on the important subject of bail in criminal cases, Lord Coke is careful and copious in expounding the enactment in the first statute of Westminster, although the writ founded thereon was, as he mentions, taken away by the subsequent act, 28 Edw. III., because (he says) "the statute of Philip and Mary concerning bail has relation to our act" (2 *Inst.*, 190). So he cites the *Mirror*, Bracton, and Britton constantly and copiously to explain our older statutes, and he frequently speaks strongly as to the necessity for a knowledge of the history of law. For instance, he says: "It is necessary not only to know the law, but also the root and reason out of which the law deriveth his life — viz., whether from the common law or from some act of parliament, lest, if he taketh it to spring from the common law, it may lead him into error" (2 *Inst.*, 296). So in another place he says, "And though this act (of 18 Edward I.), be repealed, yet it may serve in many respects to

out an acquaintance with the history of the law, to understand them, for the very reason that the forms and proceedings they mention have long been obsolete, and yet without understanding them, the statutes and the reports are unintelligible, and the sources of the principles on which the law rests are sealed and inaccessible. No part of our law can be thoroughly understood without tracing back that tradition to its origin and source. But to do so it is necessary to have the guidance afforded by legal history.

On the other hand, as one who was both a lawyer and an historian,[1] and himself well understood and applied the mutual illustration of law and history, observed, law as often illustrates history, as history elucidates law.

These, therefore, are the uses and objects of legal history, and these the ideas and views upon which this history has been edited.

---

explain the statutes of 4 Henry VII., and 32 Henry VIII., for the true understanding of the common law, and of former statutes, is the sure masterexpositor of the later" (2 *Inst.*, 518). But it is manifest that the very language and terms of the Year-Books or old statutes cannot be understood without an acquaintance with legal history. No man who has not read Britton can well understand the Year-Books; and to master the law, it is necessary to refer to the Year-Books, and often to the Roman law. Thus the liability of innkeepers and carriers can be traced back through the Year-Books (42 *Edward III.*, fol. 11; 11 *Henry IV.*, fol. 45) to the civil law (*Dig.*, lib. iv., tit. 9, leg. 3, s. 2), whence, no doubt, it was derived, by custom, into our own.

[1] Lord Bacon, who says—"It is a defect even in the best writers of history, that they do not often enough summarily set down the most memorable laws that passed in the times whereof they write, being indeed the principal acts of peace. For, though they may be had in the original books of laws themselves, yet that informeth not the judgment of king's councillors and persons of estate so well as to see them described and entered in the title and portrait of the times" (*Life of Henry VII.*, p. 46).

HISTORY OF THE ENGLISH LAW.

THE SAXONS.

THE LAWS OF THE SAXONS—THAINLAND AND REVELAND—FREEMEN—SLAVES—THE TOURN—COUNTY COURT—OTHER INFERIOR COURTS—THE WITTENAGEMOTE—NATURE OF LANDED PROPERTY—METHOD OF CONVEYANCE—DECENNARIES—CRIMINAL LAW—WERE—MURDER—LARCENY—DEADLY FEUDS—SANCTUARY—ORDEAL—TRIALS IN CIVIL SUITS—ALFRED'S DOM-BOC—COMPILATION MADE BY EDWARD THE CONFESSOR—SAXON LAWS.

THE law of England is constituted of Acts of Parliament and the custom of the realm (a); on both which courts of justice exercise their judgment; giving construction and effect to the former, and, by their interpretation, declaring what is and what is not the latter.

We possess many of these Acts of Parliament from Magna Charta, 9 Henry III., to the time of Edward III,, and from thence in a regular series to the present time. The statutes, except some very few, enacted by the legislature before that period, are lost; though, no doubt, many of the regulations made by them, having blended themselves with the custom of the realm, have been received under that denomination, since the evidence of

---

(a) This, it will be observed, is a definition rather of law, or of the "formal grounds or constituents," as Lord Hale calls them, of the law, than of legal history. And it omits what he includes among them, judicial decisions (c. 4), which he says are incorporated into the law (c. 1), together with the materials on which they proceeded, which are often lost to us, whether it be ancient statutes or usage. And as to this he points out that the canon or civil law has been, by immemorial usage, in some matters adopted into our own (c. 2). And, elsewhere, he also points out that these judicial decisions are in part themselves the result of a knowledge of the law (c. 4). It seems to follow that a history of our law ought to go back to, or be founded upon, that system of law which was the earliest civilized law known in the country, and was established here for ages. Because in that system of law it needs must be that we have the fountain whence our oldest customs were derived, the sources from which, by judicial decisions, all our subsequent law has been developed.

their parliamentary origin is destroyed (*a*). The custom of the realm, or *the Common Law*, consists of those rules and maxims concerning the persons and property of men, that have obtained by the tacit assent and usage of the inhabitants of this country; being of the same force with acts of the legislature. The only difference between the two is this, the consent and approbation of the people with respect to the one is signified by their immemorial use and practice (*b*); their approbation of, and consent to, the other is declared by parliament, to the acts of which every one is considered as virtually a party.

The common law, like our language, is of a various and motley origin; as various as the nations that have peopled this country in different parts and at different periods (*c*).

(*a*) Lord Hale says that "acts made before the reign of Richard I., and not since repealed either by contrary usage or subsequent acts, are now accounted part of the *lex non scripta*, being incorporated therein and part of the common law, and many of those things that now obtain as common law had their origin by acts or institutions, though those acts are now either not extant, or, if extant, were made before time of memory: and that this appears thus, that in many of the old acts made before time of memory (*i.e. temp.* Richard I.), and are yet extant, we find many of those laws enacted which now obtain as common law, or the custom of the realm." He says further, that these ancient acts, now ranged under the head of *leges non scriptæ*, or customary laws, are from the Saxon laws, which he cited from Lambard's Collection, and which have since been published by Wilkins, and also more lately under the title of *Anglo-Saxon Laws and Institutes*, edited by Mr. Thorpe, and next, various statutes passed in and since the reign of the Conqueror, *e. g.*, to Henry III. In these he includes the laws of William I. himself, which, he says, consist in a great degree of the laws of the Confessor, the laws of Henry I., published in the *Anglo-Saxon Laws, vide post*, p. 477, and the constitutions of Clarendon, *temp.* Henry II. Then, as regards the statutes within the time of legal memory,—that is, in and since the reign of Richard I.,—he says there is very little extant in any authentic form, and mentions nothing of importance except the Charter of King John, of which, and the other charters, he truly says that "there was great confusion, until in Magna Charta of Henry III., they obtained a full settlement, and the substance of them was solemnly enacted by parliament." So that statutory law really commences with Magna Charta.

(*b*) The author here forms the well-known maxim of the Roman law, which bases the force of custom on this principle, "Sine scripto jus venit, quod usus approbavit nam diuturni mores consensu utentam comprobat legem imitantur" (*Inst. Just.*, lib. 1, tit. 2).

(*c*) This, to some extent, is true, but to what extent, has already been considered in the Introduction. As to the Britons, as distinct from the Romans, it would be idle to speak of the "laws" of mere barbarians. The bulk and body of our law, so far as it is civil, is Roman; but so far as it is criminal, it seems to be chiefly Saxon. It would be difficult to find anything now existing in our law, except our criminal system of procedure and the form of trial by jury, which could be said to be distinctively Saxon, nor anything at all which is distinctively Danish or Norman: when our author wrote, and

Some of it is derived from the Britons (*a*), and some from the Romans (*b*), from the Saxons, the Danes, and the Normans. To recount what innovations were made by the succession of these different nations, or estimate what proportion of the customs of each go to the composing of our body of common law, would be impossible at this distance of time (*c*). As to a great part of this period, we have no monuments of antiquity to guide us in our inquiry; and the lights which gleam upon the other part afford but a dim prospect (*d*). Our conjectures can only be assisted by the history of the revolutions effected by these several nations.

Certain it is, that the Romans had establishments in this island, more or less, from the time of Claudius (*e*);

---

real actions existed, and trial by battle and wager of law had not been abolished, it might have been otherwise, though these parts of our law were, even then, obsolete.

(*a*) It has already been shown in the Introduction that the Britons before the arrival of the Romans were mere barbarians, and had no "laws" at all; so that this, to mean anything, must mean the laws of the Britons after they had become Romanized, and had to a great extent adopted Roman laws and institutions, in which sense it is in substance the Roman law. The only British laws remaining — those of Howell Dhu — are of Roman origin, having been compiled long after the Roman occupation.

(*b*) The whole of our municipal system — our manorial system — the rules of inheritance (modified, no doubt, by subsequent usage) — the general scope of our civil procedure, and the whole substance of our law, so far as it relates to civil matters, are of Roman origin. This has been shown in the Introduction.

(*c*) This is the view conveyed by Lord Hale in his history; but, in the comments already made upon it in the Introduction, it has been observed that it affords no sufficient reason for entirely ignoring the Roman law, and its influence in the formation of our own, and thus losing the light which that law sheds upon it; nor, on the other hand, losing sight in a great degree of the Saxon laws and institutions, so far as they related to criminal matters. From these sources of information it may, it is conceived, be made out, that the civil part of our law is of Roman origin, and the criminal part of it of Saxon origin. And it is a great deal to get at the *original source* of the law upon a subject.

(*d*) On the contrary, there is the Roman law, there is the Romanized British law, in the old laws of Wales, and there are the Anglo-Saxon laws, and the *Mirror of Justice* — an ancient work, embodying one still more ancient, of the time of Alfred. Of the text of the former and latter of these materials, however, the author made no use; and of the other — the Saxon laws — it will be seen that he did not sufficiently appreciate them to make a full and adequate use of them. Had he done so, he would have found a far greater degree of light than he supposed to be attainable on the subject.

(*e*) A. D. 43. Suetonius subdued the great rebellion of the Britons, A. D. 60; Agricola completed the conquest of the island, A. D. 80; and, in the pages of Tacitus, we find that the British learned the language and imitated the usages of the Romans. "Jam vero principum filios liberalibus artibus erudire et

that they did not finally leave it till the year 448 A.D., and that during a great part of that period they governed it as a Roman province, in the enjoyment of peace, and the cultivation of arts. The Roman laws were administered as the laws of the country; and at one time under prefecture of that distinguished ornament of them, *Papinian*. When these people were constrained to desert Britain, and attend to their domestic safety, the *Picts* and *Scots* broke in upon the peaceable inhabitants of the southern parts; who, unable to resist the attack, at length applied to the *Saxons* for assistance. Several tribes of Saxons landed here, and first drove the northern invaders within their own borders; then turned their arms against the Britons themselves; and having forced great numbers of them into the mountains of Wales, subjected the rest to their dominion, which gradually subsided into seven independent kingdoms (a).

The circumstances of this revolution are related to be of a kind differing from most others. The Saxons are described as a rude and bloody race; who, beyond any other tribe of northern people, set themselves to exterminate the original inhabitants, and destroy every monu-

---

ingenia Britannorum studiis Gallorum anteferre; ut qui modo linguam Romanam abnuebant, eloquentiam concupiscerent; inde etiam habitus nostri honor, et frequens toga . . . idque apud imperitos humanitas vocabuntur, cum pars servitutis esset" (*In vit. Agric.*). A century and a quarter later, we find the Emperor Severus residing at York, and elevating the great jurist, Papinian, to the prefecture. His successor, Caracalla, conferred upon all free subjects in the provinces the rights of Roman citizens. This was A. D. 220. Nearly another century elapsed before the reign of Constantine — nearly another to the reign of the second Theodosius. The Theodosian code was not long afterwards published, and another generation had elapsed before the Roman rule in Britain terminated. Thus, therefore, during more than three centuries and a half, the country was thoroughly under Roman laws and Roman institutions, and its inhabitants civilized under their influence. It is not possible but that during this long period the Romans should have deeply planted their laws and institutions in the country they ruled.

(a) This is hardly perhaps accurate, and conveys an entirely erroneous idea. Guizot points out the fallacy of supposing that the conquests of the barbarians were so sudden, so general, or so absolute as is supposed; and the idea is especially fallacious with reference to the Saxon invasions, because these invasions were successive: the contest between them and the Britons lasted for centuries, the conquests were partial and gradual, and were not quite complete when the Danish invasion took place, but ended rather in a union of the two races, by means of intermarriages and a gradual amalgamation of institutions. The contest can be traced all through the Saxon chronicles up to the tenth century, and in the course of those four or five centuries the process of amalgamation was going on.

ment and remains of their establishment (*a*). In so general a ruin, it cannot be imagined that the customs of the native Britons, or the laws ingrafted upon them by the Romans, could meet with any favor (*b*). The kingdoms of the Heptarchy were, for a time, independent of each other; and though a like state of society and manners prevailing in all of them must of course have produced the like spirit and principle of legislation in common, yet their laws must have been specifically different. Hence grew a variety of laws among the Saxons themselves (*c*). In the reign of Alfred, the Danes, who

(*a*) This was so only at first and to a limited extent. So soon as they had made sure their footing in the country they were content to render the Britons their tributaries; and it was only those who refused to become so who were exterminated or expelled. This appears from a passage in Bede, cited by Lingard — who says: "After the adventurers had formed permanent settlements, they gradually abandoned their former exterminating policy, and suffered the natives to retain their national institutions as subordinate and tributary states." Bede gives an instance of both in Edelfrid, about the year 600 — "qui terras eorum, subjugatis aut exterminatis, indigenis, aut tributarias gente Anglorum aut habitabiles fecit" (*Bede*, lxxxiv., *Lingard's Hist. Eng.*, vol. i., c. 2). Both Lingard and Sir F. Palgrave represent the Saxon sovereigns as thus rendering the Britons their tributaries.

(*b*) This inference arises from the notion, already shown to be erroneous, that the Saxon conquest was sudden and complete, instead of which it was slow and gradual; and thus, in the meantime, the two races became in a great degree united, and their institutions amalgamated, or rather the more civilized institutions of the Romanized Britons were adopted; the Saxons, still retaining also their own, which became by degrees first modified, and then, after the Conquest, superseded, as shown in the Introduction. Had the author made more use of the Saxon laws (after the conversion of the Saxons), even so early as the reign of Ina, he would have found the Briton and the Saxon put as much as possible on a footing of equality, based upon their common Christianity. The allusion here to the "customs of the native Britons," anterior to the time of the Romans, is, as already shown, with any reference to law, entirely fallacious; and instead of the laws of the Romans being ingrafted upon those customs of a barbarous race, it is manifest from history that by degrees, as the race became civilized, they adopted the laws of the Romans, not only as being the best possible laws, but as being the only laws they had any knowledge of. And for the same reason, as is amply shown by the authorities quoted in the Introduction, the Saxons, as soon as they became settled and civilized, adopted by degrees the Roman laws, discarding, by degrees, their own barbarous usages.

(*c*) This was only true temporarily, if, indeed, ever really true at all; and it certainly was never true after the country was at all settled under one rule. Nothing is more remarkable, indeed, in the early history of the country, and nothing more clearly indicates the influence of the Roman law upon the barbarians, than the tendency shown in our earliest laws to imitate its comprehensive character by forming laws for both, or all the various races in the country. Thus, as already mentioned in the laws of Ina, the earliest Saxon laws for the kingdom, there is an endeavor to apply the same laws to Britons and Saxons, and to blend both races under the same rule; so in the

had long harassed the kingdom, were by solemn treaty settled in Northumberland and the country of the East Angles, besides great numbers scattered all over the realm. The Danes were after this considered, in some measure, as a part of the nation. They were suffered to enjoy their own laws within their district; and these, when their own kings sat upon the English throne, pervaded in some degree all parts of the country.

<small>Laws of the Saxons.</small> From these various causes it happened, that towards the latter part of the Saxon times, the kingdom was governed by several different laws and local customs (*a*). The most general of all these were the three following; the *Mercian Law*, the *West-Saxon Law*, and the *Danish Law*. If any of the British or Roman customs still subsisted, they were sunk into, and lost in one of these laws (*b*); which governed the whole kingdom, and

---

subsequent treaties between the Saxon Alfred and Guthrum the Dane, or between Edmund and Canute. And Canute and the Norman Conqueror pursued the same wise policy.

(*a*) On the contrary, "towards the latter part of the Saxon times," the endeavor was, whether the monarch was Saxon or Danish, to amalgamate the laws and render them uniform and equally applicable to all. And this was so far effected that it was carried out with few and unimportant exceptions, and those exceptions rather customs, or rude usages, which would never survive the least civilization, than of anything like laws. For instance, in the laws of Canute this is very remarkable, the reason assigned being the common Christianity of the various races, both Danes and Saxons being then Christians; for he lays down a whole body of laws as equally applicable to all his subjects, without exception, and *specifies* several peculiar barbarous usages which could not even be translated out of the language of the race to which they belonged, and these, and these alone, he says, pertains to such or such a race in particular. And there is some reason to suppose that even in these instances it is rather that there were different terms in each language for the same thing, since it is obvious that they denote substantially the same thing. With these unimportant exceptions the whole bulk and body of the laws are laid down generally of the whole people, which is shown plainly by the exceptions alluded to. And at the end there is this — "And he who violates these laws, *which the king has now given to all men*, be he Danish or be he English, let him be liable," etc. (c. 84). So of the laws of the Confessor, which are general, with one or two exceptions.

(*b*) On the contrary, a general body of laws were framed, with one or two specific exceptions, applicable to the whole kingdom; but very far from containing all the law, or excluding the Roman law, which had become incorporated in the institutions of the country; on the contrary, there was much that was mentioned, and of which the existence was implied, but of which the origin is not to be found in any of these laws, and which, therefore, could only have been derived from the Roman law. Throughout the whole of these laws there is no law establishing the division of the country into counties or hundreds, or establishing courts of the hundred or county, nor manors, nor corporations, municipal or otherwise; nor rules of descent and inherit-

have since received the general appellation of *The Common Law*.

The history of this body of common law, with the divers alterations and improvements which its rules, its principles, and its practice have received at different times by acts of parliament, and by the decisions of courts, we shall endeavor to investigate and deduce in the following History.

The great obscurity in which all inquiries concerning these times are involved, renders it impossible to trace the history of laws with much certainty (*a*). For the present, we must be content if we can collect what were the outline and striking features of the Saxon jurisprudence in general; without entering into any nice discus-

ance, nor a variety of other matters, which nevertheless existed, and many of which are alluded to. The truth is, that these laws were only the written laws of the time, the *leges scriptæ;* but there was a vast deal of unwritten law, *leges non scriptæ,* incorporated in institutions long established in the country, and upon some of which it may be that barbarian laws or usages engrafted some excrescences, which soon disappeared. The greater portion of these laws are little worthy of the name; they were for the most part either precepts of morality or embody some barbarous usages, such as pecuniary compositions, the ordeal, compurgators, and the like, all which before long became obsolete, and such fragments as at all resemble law are rough and rudimentary. To suppose that these comprised the whole of the laws of the country would be an egregious fallacy; they were merely the written laws of the Saxon or Dano-Saxon races, the contributions they brought, so to speak, to the general law of the nation — happily (as already observed) before long to be discarded. And so far from the Roman law being sunk or lost in any of those barbarous laws, on the contrary, it was the Roman laws and institutions which have survived and remain to this day; while, for the most part, those rude and early attempts at law have for ages been matter rather of antiquarian research than legal study. And the only use of the study of them at all is to illustrate what Montesquieu long ago observed, that barbarous races may indeed have usages but cannot have laws, and to show that so soon as they were civilized enough to understand and appreciate regular law, they would gladly avail themselves of the resources of the Roman law, remodelling and modifying it perhaps, but still applying it to their own use.

(*a*) This obscurity was not a necessary incident of the study; for the laws of Romans, of Romanized Britons, and of Saxons and Danes have been preserved, and speak plainly enough; but the author, having ignored the Roman law, and hardly given sufficient attention to the Saxon laws, lost the greater part of the light which was available, and so felt himself here in obscurity. The author was wrong in assuming that all the law there was in this country in the time of the Saxons was comprised in the laws they put into writing; whereas these were only their first rude attempts at laws, and there was a vast deal of unwritten law practically embodied and in operation in actual existing institutions, to be found in the *Mirror of Justice* for instance, to which he did not advert; nor was he, it will be seen, sufficiently acquainted even with the written laws of the Saxons, while he avows that he had given no attention to the Roman period.

sion about the time and manner of the particular changes it might undergo during the long period before the Conquest.

If the law of a country is circumscribed in its extent by the bounds of a realm, much of its influence and operation depends on the internal divisions of it; and a history of the law would be incomplete without noticing the parts of a kingdom (*a*); so far, at least, as the process of legal proceeding is affected by provincial limits.

(*a*) Of this there can be no doubt; and therefore, as has been seen in the Introduction, the Romans always established a very complete and elaborate political organization in a conquered country, and thus Britain with other "dioceses" of the empire were divided into "provinces," and these again were sub-divided into smaller districts under "comites," or counts, and hence called "*comitates*," or counties; and there is every reason to believe that there may have been another system of division into centuries and decennaries, for the Romans had such a division in their own country, and a large portion of this country was colonized by Roman citizens, whether of Roman, Briton, or foreign origin. Such a division was found existing here soon after the Saxon times, and no Saxon law established it, though it is alluded to in the Saxons laws as existing. And though some of the Germans had a system of dividing the population into centuries, it was only numerical and military in its nature, and does not seem to have been a civil and political division, and territorial in its character, as it was among the Romans. To adapt it, however, to the purposes of settled civil government, it is obvious that it must have been founded on the number of habitations or estates of free citizens, rather than on mere numbers of men; and thus would give it a territorial character. On the other hand, it will be shown that this was a mode of division which, from its nature, as necessarily numerical, could not be formed by sub-division of counties, or other divisions merely territorial, but must rather have been formed by aggregation of estates and habitations, so that the division into counties and hundreds must have been independent. The common notion that counties, which are local, were "divided into" hundreds, which were originally numerical, and only incidentally territorial, must therefore be erroneous, and that it is so is shown by the fact, that parts of hundreds are sometimes in different counties. The basis of the division into hundreds must be sought in some independent system pre-existing: and out of which it could be formed by numerical aggregation, first into tens, and then into hundreds. Now, such a system existed among the Romans, in the manorial system, the growth of that colonial system which they applied to the cultivation of a conquered country. No grants of land would be made, except to free citizens, whether of Roman, of Briton, or of foreign birth; and these dwellings would form the basis of the division into tens and hundreds — a division which would thus be at once numerical and territorial. As the grants of land would vary in size, the hundreds would equally vary in their extent (as is found to be the case); and also would be found partly in one county and partly in another. This latter fact, indeed, might also be accounted for by the boundaries of the counties having been subsequently rearranged; but then, on the other hand, it would also show that the systems of division into counties and hundreds were distinct and independent. Further, the view here suggested as to the origin of hundreds is supported by the close connection which has always subsisted between the hundreds and the manors. From the earliest times it has been recognized

The division of England into counties is very ancient; but is said to have been reduced to its present appearance

that a hundred may be parcel of a manor, or appurtenant property to a manor (*Year-Book*, 11 Hen. IV., 89; 8 Hen. VII.). So a hundred might — *i. e.*, as a franchise, and not merely as a territory — be the property of a particular person, who, in ancient times, would probably be called or named from it, and thus there is a hundred in Devonshire named Coleridge (9 *Coke's Rep.*, s. 30), from which, no doubt, an illustrious family who have been settled there, it is known for many generations, derived their name, possibly long before the Conquest. The mention of that name reminds the editor that Sir John Coleridge, in his valuable edition of Blackstone's *Commentaries*, expresses an opinion, as Lord Coke had done long before, adverse to the common notion that Alfred divided the counties into hundreds, or indeed that any one so divided them: and he points out their irregularity of size and position as negativing that view. The view of the editor, that they were formed rather by aggregation than division, and that the counties also were so formed, is strengthened by the extreme antiquity of the court "leet" of the hundred, which, in the *Year-Book*, is seen to be "the most ancient court in the kingdom" (*Year-Book*, 7 Hen. VI., 12). It may here be observed, that from want of attention to the history of the subject, great doubt and obscurity arose as to the real meaning of a "hundred;" and in the reign of Henry VII. it was actually said from the bench that a hundred meant a hundred vills, or a hundred houses, or a hundred parishes (*Year-Book*, Hen. VII.). The latter idea of course is absurd; the two former were at variance, and were so, even as long ago as the reign of Henry VII., by reason of the changes and the increase of population; so that a hundred would contain of course far more than a hundred houses. But it was not so at the time when the country was colonized by the Romans, nor at the time of the invasion by the Saxons. The derivation suggested, however — from the manorial system, founded by the Romans — makes all plain, and reconciles these views. For although, originally, the hundred would mean a hundred free citizens, that, in the country, would mean a hundred villas, and the local and numerical division would coincide. In course of time, as the villeins became emancipated, and the villas became the centres of clusters of houses of free tenants, vills or towns would arise; and to this day, in remote parts, a farm is called a town. And though these would be of too late a formation to have been municipalities under the Roman system, they would, many of them, become "boroughs" under the Saxon system, which was, like other Saxon customs, superinduced upon the Roman institutions. "Borhs," or boroughs, under the Saxon system, were simply aggregations of freemen into tens for the purpose of mutual guarantee and self-defence; and thus, side by side with the Roman cities or municipalities, rose up the Saxon villages, towns, and boroughs. That the municipal system in England was of Roman origin, is historically clear. Lord Coke indeed states that boroughs were villas, vills, or towns, and were in former times taken for those companies of ten families, which were one another's pledge, and therefore in the Saxon laws called "borhs" or burghs (1 *Inst.*, 109). But, as already shown, the aggregation of families into tens was of Roman origin, and only adopted by the Saxons into their frankpledge system, or, rather, probably suggested it. And it is hardly necessary to say that the Roman system was essentially municipal, and encouraged municipal corporations; and it is certain that most of our cities can be traced to Roman times, while the boroughs are of later and Saxon origin. In the *Mirror*, the body of which was written in the Saxon laws, it is said that villeins are tillers of land, dwelling in upland (*i. e.*, country villages); for of vill cometh "villeins." And the derivation

by Alfred (*a*). That great prince carried his scheme yet further; and subdivided counties into *hundreds*, and hundreds again into *tythings*. This parcelling out of the kingdom into small districts, was made subservient to the well-ordering of the police, and the due administration of justice; as will be seen presently. There was another division purely ecclesiastical (*b*). *Parishes*, and even mother-

---

of it from the Roman "villa" is obvious. And as Littleton said, "Every burgh is a vill, but not *e converso*," and a vill, from villa, was originally the Roman phrase for a house in the country, while "town" was the Saxon or British word for it. And thus, as Lord Coke says, the villeins or cultivators were so called from the word "villa," being attached to the villa or country house, or the estate belonging to it, *i. e.*, the manor. Thus the whole organization of the country, political, social, or municipal, appears to have been of Roman origin.

(*a*) The popular notion had long been that he first made this division. Even in Lord Coke's time this was understood to be a fallacy, arising from a passage in William of Malmesbury, which was either erroneous, or has been misunderstood. Lord Coke pointed out that the realm was divided into shires and counties, cities and farms, by the Britons, by which he means the Roman Britons; for, he says, the Romans called the county comitatus, and the principal officer, consul; so that King Alfred's division of shires and counties was but a renovation or more exact description of the same (1 *Inst.*, 168). Thus Lord Coke cites a passage from the laws of Edward: — "Apud Britones *temporibus Romanorum* in Regno isto Britanniæ, vocabantur senatores, qui postea, temporibus Saxonum, vocabuntur Aldermani, etc." And again, "Verum quodmodo vocatur comitatus, olim apud Britones *temporibus Romanorum* in regno isto Britanniæ, vocabantur consulatus: et qui modo vocatur vice comites, tunc temporis vice consules vocabantur." Thus, in the time of the Saxons themselves, it was recognized that these primitive institutions and divisions of the country were as ancient as the times of the Romans. The truth is, that our whole system came from the Romans, and the Saxons only gave them, in some instances, new names or new arrangement. This seems indeed indicated by the way in which the author puts it.

(*b*) A parish is an ecclesiastical division, as a vill or town is a civil division; but, as, originally, where there was a vill or town, there was spiritual provision made for the inhabitants, the parish was presumed to be identical with the vill until the contrary appeared, and indeed Lord Coke lays it down that there could not be a town without a church (1 *Inst.*, 169); for a town meant at first a vill, from the villa of the lord of the manor; and though no doubt the provision was first made by lords of manors, on the other hand, a parish might contain a whole hundred, as the parish of Fountain Dean (*Skin.*, 50; Addison *v.* Otway, *Freeman's Rep.*, 218). If the hundred happened to be small, and the lords of manors poor, they might aggregate together to make a provision; and this permanent provision or endowment for a specific place or district created a parish. There can be little doubt that the manorial system was the basis of the parochial, and that the lords or owners of estates made this provision, either for churches on their own manors, or for churches for districts formed from several manors. In course of time the spiritual district thus formed for each church would be known, and thus would constitute an ecclesiastical division. So the offerings which were originally voluntary would become customary, and lastly would be rendered obligatory by law, and then would arise the necessity for some legal appropriation of the tithes

churches, were known so early as the time of King Edgar, about the year 970; for the consecration of tythes before that time being *arbitrary*, it was ordained by a law of that king,[1] that all tythes should be paid *ecclesiæ ad quam parochia pertinet.* Besides these divisions, there was another that had reference to the conditions under which the land of every one was possessed; a division which regarded the nature, description, and incidents of landed property. On this, together with that of counties, depended the bounds and extent of judicature.

The lands of the Saxons were divided into *thainland* and *reveland* (a). Land granted to

Thainland and Reveland.

---

to these ecclesiastical divisions. Hence the law of Edgar that tithe be rendered to the old church to which the district belongs, and be paid both from the lord's own demesne land and from the land of the villeins, so far as it was cultivated (*Laws of Edgar*, 1); but that if any lord had a church on his own land, he might give a third of the tithes thereto; that is, in cases where the lord had built a church on his land, subsequent to that which had by custom become the mother-church of the district (*Laws of Edgar*, c. 2). The Saxon word here used is rendered in the Latin version "parish;" and it will be observed that the earliest law relating to the subject connects the parochial endowments with the manor. The author had omitted all mention of the origin of the manorial system, which naturally would have preceded the parochial.

(a) No mention is made of this division in the Saxon laws, but it is found in Domesday. It seems, however, rather fiscal than political. Lord Coke says: — " It is to be observed that, in the book of Domesday, land holden by knights' service was called Tainland, and land holden by socage — *i.e.,* rent or certain services — was called Reveland, which appeareth in that it is said there: 'Hæc terra fuit terra regis Eduardi Tainland: sed postea conversa est in Reveland'" (1 *Inst.,* 86). Elsewhere, he says that the tains (thanes) held of the king by military service, and were freeholders, and were sometimes called *milites regis,* and their land called thane land. But *thainus regis* was a baron; and there were lesser thanes who did not hold of the king, but of great thanes (*Ibid.,* 5). Hence, it appears that thane land was originally held on knight-service from the baron, but afterwards some of it became freehold land, and included land not held of the crown, but of other proprietors. All the manors were the freeholds of the lords; their villein-tenants holding of them by servile tenures. As to the reveland, it meant land held of the king by tenure otherwise than military. Afterwards, in describing tenure by knight-service, Lord Coke says: — "In ancient times they which held by knight-service were called milites, and held by such service for the defence of the realm, and had their privileges, especially freedom from talliages or taxes" (76). In Domesday it is written: "Quod thainus vel miles regis moriens, pro relevanti dimittebat regi omnia arma sua," etc. Thus, therefore, Tainland meant land held by military service, and free from the taxes the sheriff collected, and Reveland meant land liable to such taxes. It is to be observed that there are many manors in the lands of the crown, the tenants of which, who were called tenants in ancient demesne (from their holding under portions of the ancient demesnes of the

[1] Leg. Eadg., cap. i.

the *thains,* or lords, was called *thainland:* That over which the king's officer (called in their language *shire-reve,* since *sheriff*) had jurisdiction, was called *reveland*. Again, the former being held by charter, was otherwise called *bocland* or *bookland* (a): Land of the other kind, being held

crown), owed contributions in kind for the supply of the sovereign, which were afterwards commuted by talliages; and so of the tenants in burgage — *i. e.,* tenants of houses in ancient burghs or vills on lands belonging to the demesnes of the crown (*Maddox,* 520). Now, when these were held by the thanes, they settled for these talliages; otherwise, — *i. e.,* if in the lands of the crown, — they were accounted for by the *sheriff*. In process of time the lands in ancient demesne were let out or farmed at rents, and other land not of ancient demesne were so let or farmed. Such lands as the above were held by the crown for profit, and so came under the jurisdiction of the king's fiscal officer, the sheriff (shire-reeve or steward); but land held on knight-service was held, not for profit, but the defence of the realm, and so was not deemed under the jurisdiction of the sheriff.

(a) The learned author is not quite accurate here. The earliest mention of "bocland" is in the laws of Alfred (141): "The man who has bocland, and which his kindred left him; he must not give it from his kindred, if there be writing or witness that it was forbidden by those men who at first acquired it, and by those who gave it to him, that he should do so" (*Anglo-Saxon Laws,* vol. i., p. 89). Then, in the laws of Edward (A. D. 900), it was ordained as to "one who denied justice to another, either in bocland or in folcland," that he should give him a term respecting the folcland, when he should do him justice before the reeve (the sheriff); but if he had no right either to the bocland or folcland, he who denied the right should pay a fine to the king (*Laws of Edward,* s. 2; *Ang.-Sax. Laws,* v. i., p. 161). In the same laws mention is made of "folc-right." And among the Saxon oaths there is this, which evidently refers to land: "Bequeathed it, and died he who it owned with *full folk-right,* so as it his elders lawfully got and let and left in power of him whom they well gifted; and so I have it as he gave it who had it to give, and I possess it as my own property" (*A.-S. Laws,* v. i., p. 183). By the laws of Edgar, "folk-right" was to be pronounced every term in the county court (v. 7), and if a thane had a church on his bocland, he might give a third of his tithes to its support (*A.-S. L.,* p. 263). In the laws of Ethelred it is enacted that the king should have the fines of those who had bocland (*Ibid.,* 283). By one of the laws of Canute, if an outlaw had bocland, it should be forfeited to the king (s. 13, *A.-S. Laws,* v. i., p. 383). From these passages it will be seen, (1.) that the bocland was inheritable and disposable, though it might, by special condition in the donation, be entailed or limited to the family of the donor; (2.) that as to bocland, it could become forfeited to the king by the crime of the owner, whereas this was not so as to folcland; (3.) that claims as to folcland were determined by the sheriff in the county court, whereas it should seem that claims of bocland were determinable in the king's courts. So much information on the subject is derivable from the Saxon laws themselves. Spelman describes folcland as "terra popularis quæ jure communi possidetur, sine scripto" (*Gloss.,* Folcland). In another place he distinguishes it from bocland thus: "Prædia Saxonis duplici titulo possidebant; vel scripti authoritate, quod bocland vocabunt; vel populi testimonio, quod folcland dixere" (*Ibid.,* Bocland). These definitions, it will be observed, are quite different — the former making the distinction one of tenure, the latter one rather of mere title or conveyance. Spelman, however, and Lambard,

without writing (probably by those who remained of the first inhabitants of the country), was otherwise called erroneously imagined that folcland was only possessed by the *common people;* and Blackstone still more erroneously (following Somner) supposes it was land held in villenage. It should seem that folcland was not inheritable or devisable except by special grant. But there are deeds or wills in which the owners of folcland beg that it may be permitted to descend to their sons (*Anglo-Saxon Dict.*, App. ii., 2). A learned author says:— "Folcland was the land of the folk, or people. It was the property of the community. It might be occupied in common, or possessed in severalty; and in the latter case it was probably parcelled out to individuals in the folkmote, and the grant sanctioned by the freemen who were present. But while it continued to be folcland, it could not be alienated in perpetuity; and therefore, on the expiration of the term for which it had been granted, it reverted to the community, and was again distributed by the same authority" (*Allen's Inquiry into the Rise and Growth of the Royal Prerogative,* p. 143). The definition here given remarkably resembles that of the public lands among the Romans, and affords another instance of the illustration of our ancient law derivable from the Roman. The same learned writer also points out that the folcland was assignable to the thanes on military tenure — i. e., on condition of military services — and that again resembles the public lands of the Romans. Mention is made in the Anglo-Saxon laws of land held in common by the ceorls or husbandmen (*Laws of Ina,* s. 42). Folc-right was the original unwritten understood compact or custom by which every freeman enjoyed his land, and folcland was one of those rights. The same learned author defines bocland as "land held by book or charter — that is, land which had been severed by an act of government from the folcland, and converted into an estate of perpetual inheritance. It might be held by any freeman, and most of the land of the higher thanes consisted of it. It was alienable and devisable at the will of the proprietor, and might be limited in its descent, and it was forfeited by various delinquencies to the state." He adds,— "Estates in perpetuity were usually created by charter, after the introduction of writing, and on that account bocland and land of inheritance are often used as synonymous." This, however, appears to confound title and tenure, for at a far later period feoffments in fee were common — that is, transfers of an absolute and inheritable property by mere open delivery of the land; and the learned writer indeed adds: "At an earlier period they were conferred by delivery, nor was this practice entirely laid aside after the introduction of writing." It is not therefore correct to say that all the lands of the Saxons were either folcland or bocland. When land was granted in perpetuity, it ceased to be folcland, but it could not with propriety be termed bocland, unless it was conveyed by a written instrument. The best possible definition of the term folcland is afforded in a passage in the *Mirror,* in which, describing the condition of the country in the earlier times, it says, that "some had their lands to hold by homage and by service for the defence of the realm, and some by villein customs, as to plough the lord's lands, to reap, and cut, and carry his corn and hay; and although the people have no charters, deeds, nor muniments of their lands, nevertheless, if they were ejected, they might be restored to their estates, because they could show the certainty of their services and works by the year, as those that their ancestors before them a long time had rendered;" and then it is added that King Edward in his time caused inquiry to be made of those who held of him by services, as to their lawful customs. It is mentioned also that a lord might give a villein land to hold to his heirs, even by taking his homage for it, without any deed. Thus the great body of the people held their lands with-

folcland; a distinction, which, after the feudal law was established, received other appellations of a similar import (*a*). That within the jurisdiction of the sheriff was then called *allodial;* that held of lords, *feudal.* The possessors of such as has since been called allodial were styled, in the laws of those times, *liberi*, being subject to the king alone in his political capacity; in contradistinction to tenants under the dominion of the thains, who were called *vassals*, being subject to the control also of their lord.

Freemen. The civil state of the Saxons was of this kind. The whole nation consisted of *freemen* and *slaves.* The *freemen* were divided into two orders, the *nobles* and the *ceorls* (*b*). The nobles were called *thanes,*

---

out deeds, and only by the evidence of actual possession and enjoyment upon certain known services notorious to the people, and attested by them, and therefore called folc-right," for on any question the "folc" would, in the folcmote or county court, testify about it. And as the great body of the people held their lands by the evidence of custom, this was what made them after the Conquest call so often for the customs of King Edward—*i. e.*, the customs known in his time.

(*a*) The next paragraph is obviously erroneous. It confounds two divisions or classifications which are plainly distinct and different. The one—the distinction between bocland and folcland—relates rather to the nature of the ground of the right, be it deed or be it custom; the other relates entirely to the nature and quality of the right, be it feudal or allodial in its tenure. And the author also further confounds these divisions with the distinction between thaneland and reveland, which again is quite different and distinct. There might be bocland not inheritable, there might be folcland which was. There might be feudal land which was not bocland, (indeed feudal tenure was never created by deed,) and yet would not be folcland, as not held by popular custom, but by military tenure. The fiscal jurisdiction of the sheriff, again, had nothing to do with the feudal land or allodial land; not the former, for the services were military; nor the latter, because there were no services at all; the distinction between feudal and allodial being that the one was derived from fee-od, meaning land held by way of fee or reward, and therefore reverting on failure of the same; and the other from all-od, or land not so held, but held in full, entire property without any tenure or liability to service. Allodial land meant land inheritable, and not feudal, nor subject to services, the owner being absolute owner, and subject only to the crown in its political capacity, and therefore not contradistinguished from tenants who held under tenure of services to thanes, but from tenants who held under tenure of services to the crown; that is to say, what we now call "estate in fee simple." It may be proper here to mention that in the ancient language of the law the custom of the country meant the custom of the *county*, and thus Bracton and Glanville speak of the customs of the different counties (lib. xiv., c. 8).

(*b*) This distinction is drawn much too sharply, and is indeed not accurate. There were nobles, freeholders, villeins, and slaves, all quite distinct classes. There were freemen, who were neither nobles nor ceorls. The ceorls (pronounced churls) were the villani of the Roman times and the villeins of the Normans; and they were not freeholders, but held on servile tenure; and

and were of two kinds, the *king's* thanes and the *lesser* thanes. The distinction between them seems to be, that

though they were quite different from the "theows," or slaves, they were a species of serf, and were apparently distinguished from the freemen, the *liberi homines*, who were freeholders. The distinction between "freemen," and "ceorls," and "theows," will be found drawn throughout the Anglo-Saxon laws from the earliest times, of Ethelbert (*Ang.-Saxon Laws*, v. i., p. 9). The ceorls or villani were no doubt an inferior order of freemen, and themselves had theows or slaves (*Laws of King Alfred*, 25), and they often rose to the rank of freemen by acquiring land. The "theows" or slaves were either Saxons or Britons (*Laws of Ina*, s. 24); and it should seem from direct evidence of the laws, and the resemblance in sound between the word "theowe" and "thieve," that "thieves" were made "theows," and condemned to slavery (*Laws of King Edward*, s. 29). The lesser thanes were simply freeholders, and a "ceorl" might rise to the same rank if he had acquired land to the amount considered equivalent to a qualification (*Anglo-Saxon Laws*, p. 189); so a Briton might be free, even though he had no land, and might rise to the rank of a ceorl. The highest temporary rank was that of the earl; the next was that of the king's thanes or nobles; then came the freeholders, who were the lesser or "medial" thanes, usually holding of the king's thanes (*Anglo-Saxon Laws*, v. i., pp. 192, 193). Then came the "ceorls" or villeins, and lastly the "theows" or slaves. The qualification was that of property, or rather, to be more accurate, a property qualification was required. "If a ceorl thrived, so that he had freeholds of his own, land and church and kitchen, *i. e.*, house, and a seat in a church, and did special duty in the king's hall, then he was thenceforth thought worthy of thane-right. And if a thane thrived so that he served the king, and had a thane who followed him, etc., he became a king's thane; and if a thane thrived so that he became an earl, then was he thenceforth thought worthy of earl-right. And if a merchant thrived so that he fared twice over the wide sea by his own means, then was he thought worthy of thane-right. And so of a scholar who through learning thrived so that he had holy orders," etc. (*Anglo-Saxon Laws*, v. i., p. 133). The alderman was the chief of a hundred (*Laws of Edgar*, 8), as the earl or count was of a county; and the sheriff (shire-reeve) was the deputy of the earl, and hence called viscount (*Laws of King Athelstane*, 91; *Laws of King Edgar*, 13). The grades of rank were earls, king's thanes, and lesser thanes (*Laws of Canute*, s. 72), " Taini lex est ut sit dignus rectitudine testamenti sui" (Rectitudines Singularum Personarum, *Laws of Anglo-Saxons*, p. 433).

With regard to the condition of men before the Conquest, the author omitted to notice two passages, one in BRACTON, and the other in the *Mirror*. These passages show that there were under the thanes a class of men who held land by free services or customs, who were gradually raised to the position of freeholders, and this is confirmed by the Saxon laws. The *Mirror* says that by the first conquerors — which must mean the Saxons or Danes — the earls, and barons, and knights were feoffed of lands in knight-service; and villeins of villenages, whereof some receive other lands without obligation of service, as in frankalmoigne; and some to hold by homage and service for defence of the realm; and some by villein customs, as to plough the lord's lands, to reap, cut, and carry his corn and hay, without giving of wages; and that King Edward in his time caused inquiry to be made of all such who so held and did to him such service; and *afterwards* (*i. e.*, after the Norman Conquest), many of these villeins, by wrongful distresses, were forced to do their lords other services to bring them into servitude again (c. 2, s. 28).

And this certainly agrees with a passage in Bracton which states to the

the former were next in rank to the king and independent; the latter were dependent on the king's thanes, and seem to have occupied lands of their gift, for which they paid rent, services, or attendance in war and peace. Noble descent or possession of land were the two qualifications that raised a man to the rank of thane. The inferior rank of freemen, called *ceorls*, were chiefly employed in husbandry; so much so, that a ceorl and a husbandman became almost synonymous. These persons cultivated the farms of the nobility, for which they paid rent; and they seem to have been removable at pleasure[1] (*a*). The next order of people, and a very numerous body they were, was that of the *slaves* or *villains*, a lower kind of *ceorls*[2] (*b*), who, being part of the property of their lords[3] (*c*), were incapable of holding any them-

_{Slaves.}

---

same effect: "Fuerunt in conquestu liberi homines qui libere tenuerunt tenementa sua per libera servitia, vel per liberas consuetudines, et cum per potentiores, ejecti essent postmodum reversi receperunt eadem tenementa sua tenendain villenagio, faciendam inde opera servilia sed certa et nominata, et nihilhominus libera quia licet faciant opera servilia" (*Ib.*, i., c. 11, fol. 7). Hence it appears that the ceorls were freemen, who, however, had not generally their lands on freehold tenure, but in villenage, and that they were gradually having their tenure raised to freehold by their services being rendered certain and their tenure inheritable. And this quite agrees with the Saxon laws which distinguish the ceorls from the theows or slaves; and throughout speak of them as freemen, and yet at the same time speak of them as sometimes acquiring freehold lands, which shows that though their persons were free, their lands were not so in general.

(*a*) This and what follows, it will be seen, is erroneous. The ceorls were the villeins, and they originally held lands of their lords on condition of agricultural service, which in a certain sense was servile, but in reality was not so, as the actual work was done by the theows or slaves, which our author confounds with the ceorls or villeins. The ceorls did not pay rent, and were not removable at pleasure; they went with the land, and rendered services, uncertain in their nature, and therefore opposed to rent. They were the originals of copyholders, who were deemed to hold according to the custom of the manor, and not merely according to the will of the lords; and hence, in the laws of the Conqueror, it was said, that they could not be removed at pleasure, so long as they rendered their accustomed services. Here the force of custom is seen, in modifying or creating rights. The distinction between the ceorls and the slaves will be manifest, and yet in the next sentence they are confounded.

(*b*) These slaves were *not* ceorls, but theows were slaves.

(*c*) All this applied only to the theows or slaves, not to the villeins or ceorls. Throughout, the author confounds these classes, the reason being, as appears from the authorities he cites on this subject, that he took them at second-hand, instead of consulting the laws themselves.

[1] Spelm., Feuds, p. 14.
[2] Persons of this rank were called by the Saxons *Theow*, or *Theowmen*, as appears by LL. Will. Conq., 65, 66, and in LL. Hen. I., 77, 78, servi.
[3] Spelm., Feuds, p. 14.

selves. These are the persons who are described by Sir William Temple, as "a sort of people who were in a condition of downright servitude, used and employed in the most servile works, and belonging, they, their children, and effects, to the lord of the soil, like the rest of the stock or cattle upon it" (*a*). However, the power of lords over their slaves was not absolute. If the owner beat out a slave's eye or teeth, the slave recovered his liberty.[1] If he killed him, he paid a fine to the king.[2] These slaves were of two kinds, prædial and domestic.

We shall next take notice of the judicature of the Saxons, which depended, as we before said, on the division of land. In the thainland, the thain himself was the judge (*b*): so the judge of the reveland was the *reve*, or

---

(*a*) It is not worth while to verify this quotation (for which no reference is given), since it is certainly wrong, as will be seen from what has been stated.

(*b*) That is to say in the court-baron, the court of the lord of the manor. It was only in a court-baron, or court of a manor, that (apart from every special liberty or franchise) there was any other local jurisdiction than that of the courts of the hundred of the county. On the other hand, it will be observed that the court of the lord of a manor was quite different from, and not in any way derived out of the county court, nor connected with it at all, as the hundred court was; it was rather a different jurisdiction, independent of the county court. This is noted because in a subsequent passage the author speaks of the court-baron as derived from the county court — a great mistake, arising from his not having traced the origin of the manorial system, and seen how distinct it was from the political system, to which the county belonged. So the next paragraph is incorrect in describing the sheriff as the "judge" of the county court, and his jurisdiction as arising from its being reveland — a distinction already noted as fiscal, not judicial. The sheriff was not judge of the county court, according to the Saxon theory, but the suitors or freeholders were; and so of the hundred court; but the author does not mention they were the judges. By the laws of the Saxons, the courts-baron, or the courts of the thanes or lords of manor had jurisdiction in matters arising within their manor, and between their tenants, but the general jurisdiction was in the courts of the hundred and of the county, the rule as to inferior courts being, that if the matter arose within the jurisdiction of the local court, it would be dealt with in that court, otherwise in the next higher court; and if it did not arise between parties in the hundred, then it would go to the county court. The folcmote, or county court, had general jurisdiction in matters of debt (*Laws of Alfred*, 221; *Anglo-Saxon Laws*, vol. i., 77); and the sheriffs (shire-reeves) were to hold the courts (*Laws of Edward*, 12) and were to hold the motes or assemblies every month (*Ibid.*, 11). And from the same laws it appears that the county courts had unlimited jurisdiction, even as to land, provided the matter arose between men of the county, and as to land in the same county (*Laws of Edgar*, 7; *Anglo-Saxon Laws*, v. i., p. 261). The general rule was that no man should go into the king's courts unless he could not obtain justice at home, *i. e.*, in the local courts (*Ibid.*, 217). The hundred court, or the court of the county

[1] LL. Alf., sec. 20.   [2] Ibid., 17.

shire-reve, whose great court was called the *reve-mote*, or *shire-mote*, and at other times the *folc-mote*[1] (a). The limits for the hundred, was to be held every month, and the general county court twice or thrice a year — the sheriff holding the county court in each hundred in turn, whence it was called his "tourn." So, in the laws of Canute, "Let no one apply to the king, unless he may not be entitled to justice within his hundred, and let the hundred-mote be applied to, and then again let there be a shire-mote" (*Anglo-Saxon Laws*, p. 387). The lords had jurisdiction over their own tenants in their own courts, the courts-baron of the manors; but if they were accused by others, then the hundred courts had jurisdiction; and hence, in the laws of Canute, "Let every lord have his household in his own 'burgh' (or jurisdiction), and if any one accuse his man of anything, let him answer within the hundred where he is cited" (*Anglo-Saxon Laws*, p. 395). So in the laws of the Confessor, after stating that "Justicia Regis cum legalibus hominibus provinciæ illius assit ad judicium; barones autem, qui curias suas habeant, de hominibus suis; videant ut ita agant de eis quatenus erga dominum reatum non incurrant et regem non offendant. Et si placitum de hominibus aliorum baronum oritur in curiis suis assit ad placitum justicia regis, quoniam absque eo fieri non debet. Et si barones suit qui judicia non habeant, in hundredo ubi placitum habitum fuerit, ad propinquiorem ecclesiam, ubi judicium regis erit, determinandum est, salvis rectitudinibus baronum ipsorum" (*Anglo-Saxon Laws*, p. 446). And these franchises of the lord's courts are thus explained in the same laws: "Comites, barones, et milites suos, et proprios serientes suos, sub suo frithborgo (a Saxon word, signifying jurisdiction) habebant; quod si ipsi foresfacerent et clamor vicinorum insurgent deies ipsi haberent eos ad rectum in curia sua, si habebant sacham et socham, tol et theam et enfangenthef: soche est quod si aliquis querit aliquid in terra sua, etiam furtum sua est justicia; si inventum fuerit, an non. Sache, quod si aliquis aliquem nominatim de aliqui calumpniatus fuerit et ipse negaverit, foris factura probacionis vel negacionis si evenerit, sua erit. Tol, quod nos vocamus theloneum scilicet libertatem emendi et vendendi in terra sua. Theam quod si aliquis aliquid intercubatur super aliquem, et ipse non poterat warrantum suum habere, erit forisfactura, et justicia: similiter de calumpniatore, si deficiebat, sua erit. De infangenthef justicia cognoscentis latronis sua est de homine suo si captus fuerit, super terram suam. Et ille qui non habent consuetudines quas supra diximus, ante justiciam regis faciunt rectum, etiam in hundredo, vel in wapentagiis, vel in schiris" (*Laws of Edward the Confessor*, c. 22). And if a thing was found, and a question arose, "Si dominus in cujus terra inventum est non habet consuetudines suas scilicet socham et sacham, omnia liberabit prefecto hundredo si haberi voluerit. Et si dominus ipsis habet suas consuetudines, in curia domini sui tenent rectum" (*Ibid.*).

(a) This was the county court, which was, so lately as the reign of Henry II., the only court for ordinary suits between party and party above the court of the hundred. There was also the court of the county for the hundred, which was held once in every four weeks (*Laws of Edward*, s. 11; *Anglo-Saxon Laws*, p. 165). It is there laid down that the reeve or sheriff of the county should hold a "mote" once in every four weeks; and from subsequent laws it appears that this meant in the hundred (*Laws of Edgar*, 5, p. 269). "Let the hundred-mote be attended as before, and twice a year a shire-mote." And no man was to apply to the king, unless he could not get justice in the hundred (*Canute*, 17); and twice a year there was to be the shire-mote (*Ibid.*, 18); the eldermen might preside over each hundred (*Laws of Henry*, 1, 8). And thus the hundred court was a civil court, though it

[1] Dalr., Feud. Prop., p. 11.

between the official judicature of the king's courts and the court belonging to the lord, were strictly preserved: only when the lord had no court, or refused to do justice; or when the contest was between a vassal of one and a vassal of another; then the suit was referred to the king's court, namely, to the reve-mote of the sheriff.

Though the *sheriff*, *earl*, or *elderman* (by all which names he was known) had properly the government of the county (a), a bishop was always associated with him in judicial matters. The *bishop* and *sheriff* used twice a year to go a circuit, within a month after Easter, and a month after Michaelmas; and held the great court called *the tourn*, in

was also criminal (*Laws of William*, 51). As already seen, the hundred court, like any local court, would not have jurisdiction unless the matter arose, and both parties resided, within its local limits; and hence the necessity for the larger jurisdiction of the county court or "tourn"—the former the civil, the latter the criminal jurisdiction, held by a kind of "tourn" or circuit twice a year, when all causes, civil or criminal, arising within the county could be tried. The *Mirror* says, in a part of the work the antiquity of which is obvious, "Des assemblies primes vindrent consistoires que l'un appel courts, et ces in divers lieus, et en divers manieres, dont l'un court tenoient les visconts de mois en mois; on et celes courts sont appelles counties ou les judgments si sont par les suitors, si bref ne y soit, et ceo est per gurrant de jurisdiction ordinaire. L'autre mesnes courts sont les courts de chacune sieurs del fief al foer del courts hundreds. En les quelles courts ouent connaisance de dets et de transgressions et tiels autres petits peches que ne passent my 40 s. en le valew. Et aussi elles ont connaisance de trespass et forfeitures des fief parenter ces sieurs et leur tenants. Autres mesne courts sont, que les bailiffs de Roy tenoient, en chescun hundred, de trois semaignes, et les suitors des fief tenants des hundreds" (*Le Myrrour des Justices*, c. i., s. 15). Here it will be seen that the county courts were held in various places (no doubt hundreds) once a month; which were distinguished from the great county courts, held only twice a year, answering to our assizes. And that the courts baron were distinguished from the courts of the county, or hundred, as having only jurisdiction to the amount of 40 s.; except on matters of tenancy, as to the lands within the manor.

(a) This is inaccurate. The earls, counts, or comites, were chiefs of counties; the sheriffs — vice comites or viscounts — were their deputies; and ealdermen, who answer to our modern aldermen, were chiefs of hundreds. It is only in the most general way that these latter dignities could be identified, as it is explained in the laws of the Confessor, "reve" being a general appellation. "Reve autem nomen est potestatis; est enim multiplex nomen: reve enim dicitur de scira, de hundredi, de villis; et sicut modo vocantur reves, qui habent prefecturas super alios, ita tunc temporis eldermen; non propter senectutem; sed propter sapitentiam" (*Ang.-Sax. Laws*, p. 456), and the term eldermen in this sense was general, and is sometimes applied to the chief of the connty as well as the hundred (*Law of Canute*, s. 18). But all through the laws the office of reve, or sheriff, or shire-reve, is spoken of as distinct from that of elderman or earl; which latter indeed was rather a name of dignity than of office. "Twice a year, let there be a shiremote, and let there be present the bishop of the shire and the elderman" (*Laws of Canute*, pp. 1-18; *Ang.-Sax. Laws*, p. 38).

M

every hundred in the county (*a*). This was the grand criminal court, in which all offences both ecclesiastical and civil were tried. On the examination of the former, the bishop sat as judge, and the sheriff as coadjutor, to inflict temporal punishments: in the latter, the sheriff was judge, and the bishop his assistant, to aid his sentences if necessary, by ecclesiastical censures.

The tourn.

The great court for civil business was the county court, held once every four weeks (*b*). Here the sheriff presided; but the *suitors of the court*, as they were called, that is, the freemen or landholders of the county, were the judges; and the sheriff was to execute the judgment; assisted, if need were, by the bishop. Once a year, at the Easter tourn or circuit, the sheriff and bishop were to hold also a *view of frankpledge;* that is, to see that every person above twelve years of age had taken the oaths of allegiance, and found nine *freemen pledges* for his peaceable demeanor.

County court.

Out of the tourn were derived two inferior criminal courts, the *hundred* and the *leet*, for the expeditious and easy distribution of justice, where a hundred or manor lay too remote to be conveniently visited in the course of the tourn. The hundred court was held before some bailiff; the leet before the lord of the manor's steward (*c*). Both these, though held in the

Other inferior courts.

(*a*) Here is the account of it in the *Mirror*, c. i., 16, title "de tornis." "Les Visconts d'anncient ordinances tenent assemblies generals deux fois per l'an en chescun hundred, au touts les fre tenants dedeins le hundred sont obliges devener par l'usage de leur fiefs; et pur ceo que les visconts a ceo fairie font leur tornes de hundred sont tiels venus appelles tornes des visconts; ou aux visconts appert d'enquerer de touts peches personal et de touts circumstances de peches faits en ceux hundreds, et de torts faits au roy et al commonalty del people. Trestouts fieftenants en hundred ne sont mys tenus a vener a ceux tornes Car l'Roy Hen. III. le tiene excusa ascunes persons, et dist que al tornes des visconts ni estoit mester que Archevesques, Abbes, Priors, Comites, Barons," etc. (*Mirror*, c. i., p. 16). In the reign of Henry II., however, it was laid down that the bishops and barons ought to attend these great county courts, civil and criminal; which were gradually superseded by the circuits of the king's judges. It was not until the reign of Richard II. that it was enacted that no lord, little or great, should sit upon the bench in the counties, when the king's judges were.

(*b*) This is inaccurate, *vide ante*. It was the hundred court, or the court of the county in the hundred, which was held monthly.

(*c*) This is incorrect, as will appear from what already has been stated. The court of the hundred was not derived out of any other, nor was it a criminal court only, but civil; and the reason given for it here is obviously inadequate. The principle was that justice should be as local as possible;

name of a subject, were the king's courts. Out of the county court was derived an inferior court of civil jurisdiction, called the *court baron* (a). This was held from three weeks to three weeks, and was in every respect like the county court; only the lord, to whom this franchise was granted, or his steward, presided, instead of the sheriff.

and the necessity for courts of larger jurisdiction arose, as already explained, from the necessarily limited scope of a local jurisdiction. The court of the leet was not derived from the court of the tourn; it might be the court of the manor, and a peculiar local jurisdiction. So, as to the court baron, it had nothing to do with the court of the hundred, but was the peculiar court of the manor. This has been already amply explained in the passage from the laws of the Confessor. *Barones que curias suas habent de hominibus suas, etc.*, et si placitum de hominibus aliorum baronum oritur si curiis suis assit ad placitum justicia regis, etc. It was the principle of convenience which led our ancestors to make their tribunal as local as possible, but the more local it was the more the infirmity of a local jurisdiction is made manifest, by restricting it to matters arising within that local jurisdiction, and hence the more manifest the necessity for courts of larger jurisdiction.

(a) The author, it will be observed, has confounded the court leet, or court baron, with the hundred, but it will be seen from the following case, how entirely distinct they might be. It is to be borne in mind that the word leet, or assembly, was a general term. And the court leet might either be the hundred court, or it might be the court baron. The leet means assembly or meeting, and was a general word applicable either to the hundred court or to the court of a manor. Thus in a case where, in justification of taking the plaintiff's cattle, the defendant pleaded that place was within a certain hundred and the sheriff's tourn of the hundred; and at a leet within the hundred the plaintiff was prosecuted for a nuisance and fined, the plaintiff replied that the bishop was seized of the manor, and had a right to have a leet distinct from the leet of the hundred (*Loader* v. *Samwell*, Croke, Jac., 551). It was said: — "Le Leetè est le plus ancient court in le realme" (*Year-Book*, Hen. VI., 7, 12); and there can be no doubt that though the name "leet" is Saxon, the court had its origin in the formation of the hundred in the Roman times, as the court barons were also incident to the "villa" and the manor. In the course of ages some of the land had changed hands, but the jurisdiction continued over all residents within the manor. Sicut al leete, n'est done per reason le soil, mes resiancy del person (*Year-Book*, 7 Edw. II., p. 204). It is said again that la venue a la lete est autre que soil ou court que la venue est a real jurisdiction, que de commune droit donne la viewe per reson de la person, so that it was no answer that the party held his land of another person than the lord of the leet (*Ibid.*, 276; 11 Edw. II., fol. 345). It had jurisdiction only over common nuisances (27 *assize*, 1; 22 Edward IV., 22; 4 Edward IV., 31). A particular private wrong could not be inquired of at the leet, as an assault (per Martin, J., 4; Henry VI., 10). The essence of the leet was prescription, and it was limited by prescription (2 *Inst.*, 72). The notion that the leet was the king's court was of modern origin. These local courts not being king's courts, they could not inquire of trespasses committed with force, for which a fine was due to the king (*Year-Book*, Edw. IV., 8, 15). The court leet was rather a criminal court in its nature. The court baron was the civil court of the manor.

In all these courts, justice was administered near the homes of suitors with despatch, and without much ex-
The wittenage- pense. Besides these, there was a superior
mote. court, known by the name of the *wittenagemote*, which had a concurrent jurisdiction with them (a). This court sat in the king's palace, and used to remove with his person. The judges, it is said, were the great officers of state, together with such lords as were about the court. The business of this court consisted in causes where the revenue was concerned; where any of the lords were charged with a crime; and in civil causes between them. This was the ordinary employment of the court: besides which, offences of a very heinous and public nature, committed even by persons of inferior rank, were heard here originally; and all causes in the inferior courts might be adjourned hither, on account of their difficulty or importance.

Nature of landed property. The next object of consideration is the nature of property among the Saxons: and first, of landed property. It has been a question, long debated among the learned, whether the lands of the Saxons were subject to the terms of feudal tenure, or whether tenures with all their consequences were introduced by William the Conqueror. It would hardly afford much instruction or amusement at this time, to enter deeply into an inquiry which has been already so unsuccessfully discussed, and which has divided so many great names. Lord Coke,[1] Selden,[2] Nathaniel Bacon,[3] Sir Roger Owen (b), and Tyrrell,[4] are of opinion, that tenures were

---

(a) This it should seem is a mistake. The wittenagemote appears to have been rather a council than a court, and though it is probable that, in the earlier times, the distinction between the legislative and judicial functions may not have been well drawn, yet in the time of the Confessor there are traces of the existence of a "Curia Regis," to which probably the remainder of this paragraph more properly refers or applies. At all events there is mention made of the "Justicia Regis;" and in the laws of the Conqueror, drawn up about the same time as the laws of the Confessor, this "Justicia Regis" is distinguished from the viscount or sheriff (*Laws of Conq.*, 2). The author makes no mention, however, of the rise of a regular royal judicature among the Saxons — a most important era of our legal history, since, as shown in the Introduction, such a judicature is really the parent of regular law. In the county court there was no judicial element. It was a mere popular tribunal.

(b) The author here in a note explains that he alludes to a manuscript in
[1] 1 Inst., 776.   [3] Hist. Disc., 161.
[2] Titles of Honor, 510, 511.   [4] Introd., vol. ii., p. 84.

common among the Saxons (*a*). Crag,[1] Lord Hale,[2] Somner,[3] Sir Henry Spelman,[4] Dr. Brady, and Sir Martin Wright,[5] are of opinion that feuds were first brought in and established by the Conqueror. After this difference of opinion, some later writers have taken a middle course. Blackstone,[6] Dalrymple,[7] and Sullivan,[8] endeavor to compromise the dispute, by admitting an imperfect system of feuds to have subsisted before the Conquest.

Perhaps the latter of these opinions may be nearest the truth. A system of policy that had prevailed over all parts of Europe, it is most probable, got footing in England, inhabited by persons descended from the same common stock, and possessed of the country they then enjoyed under like circumstances with the nations on the continent. But the feudal law, in the time of our Saxon kings, was in no part of Europe brought to the perfection at which it afterwards arrived; and in this country, separated from the world, and receiving by slow degrees a participation of such improvements as were made in jurisprudence on the continent, we are not to look for a complete system of feudal law. At the latter part of this period, feuds on the continent were very little more than in their infant

---

the Harleian Collection, entitled "The Antiquity and Excellency of the Common Law of England," which he says "was written with a view to maintain the popular argument of the times, that our constitution and laws were derived from the Saxons, and that the Conqueror made no alteration thereon," and he dismisses it as of no importance.

(*a*) It is a matter of historical certainty that this was so. It has already been seen that the Romans had a system of military tenure which was established in this country, and existed during all the period of the Saxon Conquest, which lasted for centuries. And it has also been seen that some such system existed in Germany. From traditions, both of our national usages and of the Romans, it was natural that the Saxons should establish a similar system of military tenures, and they undoubtedly did so. The land was assigned on condition of military service; the greater thanes held directly of the king, the lesser thanes of them; and what more was necessary to constitute in substance the feudal system? This was still more clearly the case under the Danes; and the "heriots," as described in the laws of Canute, were, for earls, king's thanes, and the lesser thanes, entirely military (*Anglo-Saxon Laws*, p. 415). The heriot was a species of relief, and involved in it the rudiments of the burdens of the feudal system. No doubt that system was, under the Saxons, in a rude and imperfect stage; and was only developed in the time of the Normans. So, also, there was forfeiture; for if a man who had land of his own forsook his lord, he forfeited it — another evidence of feuds or fiefs (*Anglo-Saxon Laws*, p. 456).

[1] Jus. Feud., lib. 1, tit. 7.
[2] Hist. Com. Law, 107.
[3] Gavel., 100.
[4] Glos. Feudum.
[5] Ten., 57.
[6] Vol. ii., p. 48.
[7] Feudal Prop., 8.
[8] Lecture 28.

state; they were seldom granted longer than for the life of the grantee.¹

Without engaging in a controversy whose extent and difficulty have eluded the greatest learning and sagacity, it will be more satisfactory to notice such few facts as we really know respecting the landed property of the Saxons. We know that their lands were liable to the *trinoda necessitas;* one of which was a *military service* on foot; another, *arcis constructio;* and another, *pontis constructio.* They were in general hereditary (*a*); and they were partible equally among all the sons (*b*). They were alienable at the pleasure of the owner; and were divisible by will. They did not escheat for felony (*c*); and the landlord had a right to seize the best beast or armor of his dead tenant as a heriot (*d*). This is the principal outline of the terms

(*a*) The bocland seems to have been so (*vide ante*), though the deed of grant might define and limit the course of descent, and hence the law of Alfred, that a man who had bocland should not alienate it from his family, if the deed provided that it should not be so alienated.

(*b*) According to the British law — that is, after the Roman occupation — the land was partible among all the sons, as is recited in the Statutum Walliæ, 12 Ed. I., *quod hæreditas partibus est inter hæredes masculos.* Among the Saxons, the laws of Canute, *cited post*, show that the estate was divided among all the *children;* and Lord Hale thinks that, until the Conquest, the descent was to all the sons, and probably to all the daughters, for which he cites the laws of the Confessor (*Ang.-Sax. Laws and Instit.*); and Selden in his notes upon Eadmerus, says, "Si quis intestatur obierit, liberi ejus hæreditaten æqualiter divident." After the Conquest, the law by degrees changed, except in Kent, where, according to the old British, or rather Roman-British law called the custom of gavelkind, all the land is still partible among all the sons. In the reign of Henry I., as Hale says, "the whole land did not descend to the eldest son, but began to look a little that way," and he cites the *Leges Henrici Primi,* c. 70, Primum patris feudum primogenitus, filius habet; upon which he observes that the eldest son, although he had jus primogenituræ, the principal fee (or estate) of his father's land, yet he had not all the land. In the reign of Henry II., as appears from Glanville (lib. 7), in ordinary freehold lands called "socage," (*i. e.*, land not held on military tenure) the jus commune, or common law, gave all the land to the eldest son, unless there were an ancient custom to the contrary, "unless the land was *antiquitus divisum.* Si ne vero non fuerit antiquitus divisum, tunc primogenitus totam hæreditatem obtinebit."

(*c*) This is a mistake, for in the law of Athelstane, it is laid down that if a thief was taken, he should forfeit all he had, though part was to be given up to his family, and the rest retained by the king (*Ang.-Sax. Laws,* 229); and a man who had bocland forfeited it *even* for outlawry (*Ibid., Laws of Canute,* 13; Henry I., 13), and if he forsook his lord (*Ibid.,* 456); so that it would not be probable that there was *not* forfeiture for felony even if there were nothing to show that there was. Lord Coke maintained that there *was.*

(*d*) In the laws of Canute, the reliefs of earls and thanes, whether king's

¹ Lib. Feud. i., tit. 1.

on which landed property was possessed among the Saxons.

It should seem that a legal transfer might be made of lands by certain ceremonies, without any char- Method of conveyance. ter or writing (*a*). Ingulphus says, *confereban-*

---

thanes or medial thanes, are described, and are entirely military in their nature, so much so, that the law is copied into the collection of laws of Henry I. They consisted of horses and their military accoutrements. There is strong evidence that the foundation of the feudal system already existed, that is, military service for the defence of the realm, and there is also the appearance of what Guizot calls the hierarchical system, which was characteristic of it.

(*a*) In the Anglo-Saxon Chronicle, A. D. 657, mention is made of a deed of grant of lands by Wulfhere, king of the East Saxons, to the monastery of Medeshewsted (Peterborough), and it is stated that the king "subscribed it with his fingers on the cross," evidently being unable to write, and being what is called a "marksman," *i. e.*, attesting an instrument only by putting his finger on his mark. The grant was thus, as the Chronicle says, executed in the presence of witnesses, "who subscribed it with their fingers on the cross, and assented to it with their fingers," and this was done in the presence of the nobles and bishops, and several ealdormen. Three centuries afterwards, the deed was found concealed in the walls of the monastery (which had been destroyed by the Danes), and it was solemnly confirmed by Edgar in the presence of prelates, nobles, and ealdormen, and the franchises of sack and sock, toll and theam, and infangenthef, were also granted (*Sax. Chronicle*, A. D. 963). It is also mentioned that the abbot of this monastery let to an ealdorman ten copy-lands, with all that lay thereto, for £50, and each year a day's entertainment, or 30 s. in money, and that, after his death, it should return to the monastery. The witnesses to this are mentioned (A. D. 777). It is added, "A copy of this grant was set forth in presence of the king, in the monastery, in the year 745." And as there is no doubt that Glastonbury monastery had large grants from early Saxon kings, and their charters have every sign of genuineness, there appears no reason to question their authenticity. As *laws* were written in the seventh century, *deeds* might well be, and there are laws of Ethelbert who reigned in the middle of that century (*Anglo-Saxon Laws and Institutes*, vol. i.). It appears, however, that these kings could not write, and probably the nobles could not, as all but the prelates signed, or rather attested, by means of marks in the form of the sign of the cross; so that they could only be cognizant of the contents of the deeds as they were read to them. And no doubt they were, when they became Christian, greatly under the influence of ecclesiastics, though, as Guizot points out, that influence was exercised in favor of civilization. In the same Chronicle mention is made of a charter of immunities granted by Ethelwulf, the father of Alfred, A. D. 846. The same grant is mentioned by Ingulphus and by Æsser, though in the year 855. The charter contained a passage which has given rise to much controversy as to tithes.

In William of Malmesbury, mention is made as early as A. D. 721 of a royal grant or charter by Ina, a Saxon king (the first of those who framed laws after becoming Christian), to the monastery of Glastonbury. It was thus: "I do grant one of those places which I possess by paternal inheritance, and hold in my demesne, for the maintenance of the monastic institution (so many hides at such a place, and so many hides at another), and I grant that all places and possessions of the monastery be free of rent, and undisturbed from all royal taxes and works which are wont to be appointed;

tur prædia nudo verbo, absque scripto vel chartâ, tantùm cum domini gladio, vel galeâ, vel cornû, vel cratere, et plurima tenementa cum strigili, cum arcu, et nonnulla cum sagittâ.[1] Thus Edward the Confessor granted to the monks of St. Edmund, in Suffolk, the manor of Brok *per cultellum;*[2] and holding by the horn, by the sword, by the arrow, and the like, were common titles of tenure. However, deeds or charters were in use (*a*). These were called *gewrite, i. e.*, writings; and the particular deed by which a free estate might be conveyed was usually called *landboc, libellus de terrâ*, a donation or grant of land.[3] The land so passed was, as has been already observed, called *bocland;* and the person who so conveyed to another was said to *gebocian* him of it. An Anglo-Saxon charter of land has also been called *telligraphum;*[4] the etymology of which mongrel term seems to imply that the land was therein described by its situation and bounds. But this appellation was probably adopted after the Conquest, as a translation of the word *landboc*. The like may be said of the term *cyrographum*, another name by which Anglo-Saxon charters were known: but those denoted by this name were of a peculiar kind; such as had the word *cyrographum* written in capital letters

---

that is to say, expeditions, and the building of forts or bridges, and cities, as is found to be empowered and granted by my predecessors in *the ancient charters of the same church:*" so that, according to this recital, there were still earlier charters in the seventh century; but these might, if they stood alone, be deemed of doubtful authority, as William was not a contemporary. Some twenty years later, however, another charter or grant by Ina's successor is set out: "I declare that all the gifts of former kings in country houses (villæ), and in villages, and lands, and farms, and mansions, according to the confirmations made, and *confirmed by autographs and the sign of the cross*, shall remain inviolate."

(*a*) It is plain, however, that deeds were in use among the Saxons, although, as even their kings could not read or write, they were executed by sealing instead of signing. The very word bocland demonstrates that they had deeds. There is a law of Alfred restraining alienation of land from the kindred where it had been acquired, by a donation in writing restraining such alienation. " De eo qui terram hæreditariam habet quam ei parentes sui demiserunt, ponimus ne illam extra cognationem suum mittere possit, si *scriptum* intersit testamenti, et testis quid eorum prohibirent qui hanc imprimis adquisierunt, et ipsorum qui dederunt ei ne hoc possit, et hoc in regis et episcopi testimonia recitetur, coram parentela sui" (*Laws of Alfred*, c. 41). It would not appear, however, that deeds of alienation were in common use. In the Saxon version of the above, the words rendered terram hæreditariam are "bocland." It is certain that deeds were used for donations to public bodies, such as monasteries.

[1] Hist. Croy. 901, Franc. 1601.
[2] Mad. Form. Diss., pa. 2.
[3] Mad. Form., 283.
[4] From *tellus* and γραφω.

either at the top or bottom of the charter, and cut through or divided by a knife.[1]

Before the time of Edward the Confessor, the usage was to ratify charters by subsigning of names accompanied with holy crosses. This was done both by the parties and witnesses. It is generally believed that Edward the Confessor was the first who brought into this kingdom the custom of affixing to charters a seal of wax. It is said, that being in Normandy, at the court of his cousin William, he there learned several Norman customs, and among others, which he transplanted hither, was this of sealing deeds with wax. Though the word *sigillum* often occurs in charters before his time, yet some great antiquarians (among whom is Sir Henry Spelman) have agreed that this did not mean a seal of *wax*, but was used synonymously for *signum*, and denoted the sign of the cross and other symbols made use of in those times.[2]

There is no evidence that the Saxons made any distinction between real and personal property; the whole property of a man was described by the general term *res*, and under that denomination was subject to the same succession *ab intestato*, and might be given or disposed of by will.

We are not to imagine that the power of disposing by will was allowed without restriction (a), for we have every reason to conclude, from the prevailing custom of the realm in the next period, that they restrained a man from totally disinheriting his children or leaving his widow without a provision. After such duties were reasonably performed the remainder of his effects were at his own disposal. Consistently with such sentiments, we find the law, with regard to the estates of intestates, delivered in these words:[3] *Sive quis incuriâ, sive morte repentinâ fuerit intestatus mortuus, dominus tamen nullam rerum suarum partem (præter eam quæ jure debetur herioti nomine)*

(a) It does not appear that wills were used among the Saxons. As already seen, deeds of alienation, *inter vivos*, were known among them, and it would seem that their alienations were usually of that nature. The law of Alfred already quoted, restraining alienations of land from the kindred, does not seem to allude to wills, but alienations *inter vivos*. It speaks of *terram hæreditariam*, and implies that land ought to descend to the children, or next of kin, at all events if it was *obtained* in the family; and the greater the regard paid for the claims of descent or relationship, the less likely is it that there would be alienations by will.

[1] Mad. Form. Diss., 2.   [2] Ibid., 27.   [3] Leg. Can., c. 68.

sibi assumito. Verùm possessiones uxori, liberis, et cognatione proximis, pro suo cuique jure distribuantur (a).

There does not appear sufficient in the monuments of Saxon antiquity to make us assured in what manner they ordered the authentication of wills (b). It may, however, be conjectured, with some probability, that cyrographated or indented copies might be left with the alderman or sheriff of the county, or with the lord who had a court or franchise, where, besides the hearing of causes, other legal proceedings, spiritual as well as temporal, were usually transacted. It is more clear (c) that in this court was made the distribution of intestates' effects, according to the proportions above laid down. From this may be derived the privilege which the lords of some manors claim at this day, to have probate of wills in their manor court without the control or interposition of the bishop.

(a) The law of Canute implies, that all property, real and personal, was distributed among the relations, for it says that if any one should die intestate, be it through neglect or sudden death, let the property be distributed justly among the wife and children and relations, according to their degrees (*Laws, Canute*, 71). This implies that there were wills at that time, and also that distribution of intestate estates was settled.

(b) There is no trace to be found of wills in the Saxon times, and all the instances of alienations or dispositions of property to be found in the Chronicles are cases of alienations *inter vivos*. If, however, wills were known, as they involved writing, and none could write or read except the ecclesiastics, it is pretty certain, *à priori*, that the wills would be authenticated by being recorded or enrolled in some ecclesiastical registry; and accordingly, as we know the registries of wills, when they afterwards became known, were ecclesiastical, the instances to the contrary were probably cases of manors originally held by ecclesiastics, or by some laymen who, for a wonder, *could* write and read, and therefore obtained this privilege for themselves, or rather for the convenience of their tenants. The law of Alfred already alluded to makes mention of authentication by the bishops and aldermen, and they both had seats in the Saxon county courts, which, however, would be most useful for a registry of wills, or for distribution of the effects of intestates, and it is probable that both would be committed, for the sake of convenience, to the bishops. Reasons would render it convenient then which would not exist in modern times. What the author means by its being "clear" that in the county courts the estates of intestates were administered, cannot be divined. There is no trace of it, and he, of course, gives us no authorities. It would appear that, by the latest laws of the Saxons, the rule of law was the distribution of the effects of an intestate among the relations; for, among the laws of the Conqueror, professedly founded upon the Saxon customs, there is this: Si quis paterfamilias casu aliquo sine testamento obirit, pueri inter si hæreditatem paternam æqualiter dividant (*Laws of the Conq.*, c. 34); and as regards real property, that was the rule of law as well as with regard to personalty. The law, however, implies that wills were sometimes used, though it is probable, in such a simple state of society, and writing being so little known, it was very rarely there was a testament, and intestacy was the rule.

(c) There is not any evidence of this.

All contracts for the buying or bartering of anything were required to be made in the presence of witnesses (a). This was as much to prevent the sale of things stolen or improperly obtained, as to preserve the memory of contracts and obligations. A law of King Ethelred ordained,[1] that if there were no witnesses to a contract the thing bargained for should be forfeited to the lord of the soil, till inquiry was made about the real ownership.

This regulation about contracts is frequently enforced in the Saxon laws, and the beneficial consequences of such strictness must have been universally felt. It had the effect of precluding questions and litigations about matters of contracts and keeping the law of property in a very plain and intelligible state.

As the forms and circumstances under which property could become a subject of debate in their courts were few and simple, so the proceedings must in a like degree have been uniform and unembarrassed. While the objects of legal inquiry admitted of little modification, and contained very little artificial learning, the freemen or landholders of the county were, no doubt, very competent

---

(a) It is desirable to make an explanation here upon a matter not quite understood by the author, and which has an important bearing upon the question of trial by jury. It is admitted that jurors, in the infancy of the system, were witnesses, and hence the origin of the rule, that they must come from the vicinage, that is, from the very "vill," or, at all events, the hundred, where the matter arose, and they were supposed to determine on their own knowledge. Hence, also, the jury arose out of the court of the hundred, and were, in fact, a certain number of the hundredors sworn, and sworn, originally, to give a verdict of their own knowledge. Now, the object of the presence here referred to was to secure that the hundredors should have knowledge of every contract made, and with that view it provided that no contract of which they had not knowledge should be deemed valid. The provision is repeated in the laws of all the Saxon kings (Edward I., Athelstane I. 10, Edward V., Edgar 6, Ethelred I. 3, Canute 24, Edward Confessor 23). The laws of Ethelred and Canute require that the witnesses shall be in the "borh," or hundred, and the laws of Edgar make the connection clearer between this provision and the trial by jury; for they required that in every borh and in every hundred, so many were to be chosen and set apart as witnesses, and in every hundred, twelve — the number, be it observed, afterwards chosen for the number of a jury. These witnesses were to be sworn to speak truly in any matter that might arise, and of them *some* were to be witnesses of every bargain made (*Laws of Edgar*, 41–45), to which the law of Ethelred adds a penalty. Now, here it is obvious that this was, in substance providing pre-appointed jurors for particular matters; for jurors were witnesses, and this law simply provided that they should have the requisite knowledge of the matter in hand. This, then, was the origin of trial by jury.

[1] Ca., 4.

judges of the matters they were to determine, and the parties themselves were equally qualified to be their own advocates. Causes were commenced by lodging a complaint, the admission of which by the officer of the court, and giving a day to the parties, constituted perhaps all the practical knowledge of the bar (*a*).

Before we speak of the criminal law of the Saxons (*b*),

(*a*) In the laws of Edgar, it is provided, under a special ordinance as to the hundred, that they meet always within four weeks, and that every man do justice to one another — that is, according to the award of his neighbors — for this is what it came to. This arbitration of neighbors, as it is the earliest form of civil jurisdiction resorted to, so it is most remarkable, that it is invariably recurred to in the age of highest civilization, as most convenient, and far preferable to hostile and formal litigation. The whole tendency of our own procedure has been for ages, and is now more strongly than ever, to encourage arbitration, and substitute it as much as possible for hostile litigation. In the same law it was ordained that in the hundred folk-right should be pronounced in every suit, and that a term be fixed when it should be fulfilled (*Edgar*, 7), and that the sheriff hold a court in each hundred once a month (*Edward*, 11).

(*b*) It might, perhaps, have been more natural and convenient to consider first the nature of the crimes and punishments defined by the Saxon law; next, the procedure for trial and punishment; and lastly, the peculiar proceedings provided by way of security of compensation in default of punishment, which is here described. But our author has inverted that order, and considered first the system of security, next the compensation, and lastly the crimes. It resulted, perhaps, from this that he failed to consider, except very cursorily, the law as to crime, apart from the system of compensation, and that this review of the subject is extremely imperfect; the more so, since he did not have recourse to the ample exposition of the Saxon criminal law contained in the *Mirror of Justice*. The peculiar system of frankpledge above explained was only a species of supplement to, or security for, the execution of the criminal law, and it had a close connection with the system of pecuniary compensation, for of course pledges could only be made responsible for such compensation. But then, as the author himself mentions further on, there were crimes which did not admit of compensation, which applied only to such personal injuries as might be regarded as rather private in their nature, and more of the nature of aggravated assaults, such as would be proper subjects of actions for compensation (although in these rude times rather more severe than in our own age), and did not apply to crimes public in their nature, as tending to endanger the public peace and general security — such as housebreaking, burning of houses, open robbery; manifest homicide, and treason. These, it was declared by the law of Canute, should not be the subject of pecuniary compensation, and were, therefore, left to ordinary criminal justice of the realm, which our author hardly describes at all. Yet a remarkably full account of it is given in the *Mirror of Justice*, which bears upon its face, in various parts of it, and especially in those parts which relate to the criminal law, traces of an origin in an earlier work of the age of Alfred. At all events, it gives the forms of indictments in all cases of serious crimes, and the mode of trial, substantially the same as in our own time; and there is probably no part of our law which has so little altered in its general course and tenor. The names given are all unmistakably Saxon; in many instances the names of the Saxon kings, under whom the cases oc-

let us take a view of that remarkable institution so necessary towards a due execution of it, that is, the police established by Alfred.

curred, are given; and in others, the names of the judges, which are all evidently Saxon, and must have been before the Conquest—since after that era the names of the judges are known, and were all Anglo-Norman. Moreover, the nature of the crimes described after, afford internal evidence that the times referred to are very early. Thus, for instance, as to treason, it is defined in a way in which it certainly would not have been defined by any lawyer after the Conquest, as including the falsification of the seal of a manor, so as to defraud the lord of the same. So as to the next section: of Burners, who are described as those who burn a city, farm, or honse, men, beasts, or other chattels feloniously, in time of peace, for hatred or revenge. And if any one *put a man into the fire,* whereby he is burnt or blemished by the fire, although he be not killed by the fire, nevertheless it is an offence for which he shall die. Now we know from the Saxon Chronicles, that ages before the Conquest men were burnt to death by their enemies, but no trace of such atrocities can be found in the later times; and it is evident that they mark a state of society characterized by savage ferocity. So under the head of Mayhem, which is described as "the deprivation of a member or the enfeeblement of it by breaking or cutting the bones of a man," whereby he is less able to combat—a crime very common among the Anglo-Saxons in their earlier and more savage ages, as is shown by the earlier of these laws, but which gradually disappeared before the Conquest, at all events became comparatively rare; but it is evident that at the time the work quoted was originally written, it was the subject of frequent judicial decision; for the author at once quotes several judicial dicta of judges, with pure Saxon names. "And *Turgis* saith that the loss of the fore-teeth is 'mayhem,' and *Sennall* saith that the loss of the eye is 'mayhem,' and *Billing* saith that rasure by turning the bones of the head is 'mayhem.'" Now it is worth observing (1.) that all these names are pure Saxon; (2.) that in two cases the dicta are reported in the present tense: "Billing saith," as if the judge were still alive at the time it was written, and the *dictum* quite recent; and (3.) it is to be noted that Billing is afterwards given as the name of a judge who was hanged by Alfred; so that, on the whole, it is manifest that these cases are as old as the age of Alfred. So again, as to the crime of larceny, it is evident that the definition given is extremely ancient, for it actually comprises all those who suffer thieves to pass when they may arrest them; "and those who steal by false measures and false weights, or in any other manner of fraud by color of merchandise." And it is curious to note that it includes cases of bailiffs, and receivers of goods, who steal in not giving their accounts, as to which the old law has, in our own times, been restored by the statutes as to embezzlement and as to fraudulent bailees. So, as to felons flying to avoid arrest, judicial dicta are given of Saxon judges, one of whom was afterwards hanged by Alfred. "*Bermond* decided that the goods of those who fled should be forfeit to the king." Now, afterwards, this very name is given as that of a judge who was hanged by Alfred. The book purports to have begun with the time of Alfred, and to have continued in the times of subsequent kings, so that it would contain cases as old as Alfred; though it also includes cases of subsequent Saxon kings up to the Conquest, and also of kings after the Conquest up to Edward I., but the ancient parts can easily be distinguished, and indeed are often expressly identified with a particular reign. Thus, as to the forms of indictment, the first given is that for treason, "according as it was done in this case in the time of King Edmund." Here, again, the

It is said that a hundred neighboring families composed *a hundred*, as the name imports; ten such
families constituted a *tything, decennary,* or *fri-*

<small>Decennaries, boroughs.</small>

names also are pure Saxon. "Rocelyn saith against Wallgrot, that at such a day, in such a year of the reign of such a king, into such a place came the said Wallgrot to this Rocelyn, and found him to be in counsel and in assistance with Ashelung, Turkille, Bollard, and others, to arrest, or to make prisoner, or to kill, our said King Edmund, and, to do the same, they were sworn to keep counsel" (*Mirror of Justice,* c. i., s. 11). Here is a precedent of an indictment for treason undoubtedly as old as the time of Edmund, who reigned in the middle of the tenth century, Alfred having died at the beginning of it. Again, treason is set forth in this manner, "as it is found in the rolls in the time of King Alfred. Bardulf here doth appeal Darling for that" (*Ibid.,* s. 13). So there are precedents given of indictments for all the felonies — murder, rape, burglary, robbery, arson, etc.; and it is to be observed, as another mark of antiquity, that burglary is to be defined as housebreaking for robbery, whether in the day or night; whereas, in our law, for ages it has been the essence of the crime that it should be committed at night. The names used are always the plainest Saxon — Osmond, Saximund, Darling, Carling, Billing, Harding, Atheling, etc. There is an indictment for heresy, which is exceedingly curious, and said to be "according to that which is found in the rolls of the ancient kings:"—" I say, Sebourge there is defamed by good people of the sin of heresy, because that he of evil art, and by belief forbidden, and by charms and enchantment, took from Brighton the flower of his ale, whereby he lost the sale thereof;" or this, "Molling is defamed, for that such a day he denied his baptism." No one will deny the extreme antiquity of these absurd indictments, in which slander, heresy, and enchantment were all mixed up together most strangely. Although, however, on this particular head of offence there may appear some absurdity, yet, speaking generally, the definitions of crimes are not only marked by sound sense, but are in substance, with some exceptions, those which prevail in our present law. Thus, under the head of distresses, it is pointed out that men may cover that robbery by distress, that is, might commit robbery under color of distress; and it is said, "ye are to distinguish whether it be by those who have power to distrain, or by others, and, if by others, then therewith an appeal of robbery:" whereof it is said "Hailif gives a notable judgment;" who Hailif was being left to the reader's presumed knowledge of him — an evident indication that the passage was written when Hailif was alive, or when his memory was recent, for he is cited just as any judge might be cited in our own day. So as to criminal procedure. On the one hand, it is manifest that the procedure described is as ancient as the Saxons, and, on the other, that it was in substance the same as in our own time. Thus it is said, "Thurmond ordained that criminal actions (prosecutions) for revenge (*i. e.,* for punishment) should cease at the year's end (s. 22):" a passage which is evidently most ancient, for the name of the judge is Saxon, and the notion of any limitation of criminal prosecution was not known in later times. Again, it is said as to indictments, "there may be exceptions against the person of the indictor, for no villein can indict any man," which shows the antiquity of the passage. Or, if the indictment be not made by the whole dozen of freemen, or if it be not sealed with the seals of the twelve jurors (s. 15), which shows that indictments were presented by juries just as they are now, at all events in the king's courts. And it is equally clear that they were tried by juries; for in a subsequent part of the work cases are given in which Alfred had executed judges for tampering

bourg, over which an officer presided, called *the head of the fribourg*.[1] Every man in the kingdom was expected to belong to some decennary, and those who did not were considered in the light of offenders, or at least of suspected persons, and were accordingly put in prison till they could get some one to take them in, or become pledge for their good behavior. In these decennaries, every man was a security for the rest, *pledging* himself that all and every of them should demean himself orderly, and stand to the inquiries and awards of justice. It was from such reciprocal engagement between the *free* members of a decennary, that this sort of community was commonly called *frankpledge*. If any one fled from justice, the term of thirty-one days was given to the decennary to produce the offender. If he did not then appear, the head of the fribourg was to take two principal persons of his own decennary, and from the three neighboring decennaries, the head and two of their members: these, together with himself, making twelve, were to purge him and his decennary from any wilfulness or privity to the offender's crime or flight: and if the head of the fribourg could not purge his decennary in this way, he and his decennary were, of themselves, to make a compensation to the party injured.

So great care was taken that persons should be well known before they were harbored, that if any one took a stranger in, and suffered him to stay three nights under

with juries, etc. "He hanged Marks, because he judged During to death by twelve men who were not sworn; he hanged Thurston, because he judged Thuringer to death by a verdict of inquest taken, *ex officio*, without issue joined; he hanged Rombold, because he judged Lischild in a case not notorious, without indictment; he hanged Fribnone, because he judged Harpen to die, whereas the jury were in doubt of the verdict, for in doubtful cases one ought rather to save than to condemn; he hanged Cordwine, because he judged Hackwy to death without the consent of all the jurors, and whereas he stood upon a jury of twelve men, and because three would have saved him against the nine. Cordwine removed the three, and put others upon the jury, upon whom Hackwy put not himself." These words are the precise words now used and recorded in a criminal trial, when the prisoner is said to put himself upon his country to be tried, as upon a jury. These extracts will suffice to show that the system of criminal law and of criminal procedure, which prevailed as far back as the time of Alfred, was in substance similar to those which prevail at this day; and there is probably no part of our law which is of such antiquity as that of our criminal procedure. It is only the systems of frankpledge and compensation which our author now proceeds to notice which are obsolete.

[1] Leg. St. Edw., 20.

his roof, and the stranger afterwards committed any crime, the person so harboring was considered as having made himself a *pledge* for him, as for one of his own family, and was, upon the absconding of the offender, to make amends to the injured person.[1]

An establishment like this contributed more effectually than any other to the prevention of crimes, as well as to the detection of offenders.

We shall now take a cursory view of the penal code of this people (a). The Saxons were particularly curious in fixing pecuniary compensations for injuries of all kinds, without leaving it to the discretion of the judge to proportion the amends to the degree of injury suffered. These penalties were more or less, according to the time or place in which the wrong was committed, or the part of the body or member which was injured.[2] The cutting off an ear was punished with the penalty of thirty shillings; if the hearing was lost, sixty

Criminal law.

(a) The author gives a very imperfect idea of it, as he confines himself to the written laws, and those of the earlier and ruder age. No doubt at first not only bodily injuries but even death could be compensated, though there is reason to suppose that this applied rather to such cases as would now be called manslaughter; hence simple homicide is spoken of, and there is no epithet used to denote what we would deem murder; while, on the other hand, in the criminal law of the Saxons, as disclosed in the *Mirror*, murder appears to have been capital. The written laws, which bear the name of Alfred, may have been the early records of ruder customs, which, at a later period of his reign, he may have altered. Certainly, the idea of his criminal law, as conveyed in the *Mirror*, is very different from what it appears in his written laws. In the written laws of Ethelred, indeed, we find that homicide and even theft are punishable even with death, unless the king allows the penalty to be redeemed (*Eth.*, vii., 15). And in the laws of Canute we find that housebreaking and mere robbery and murder are declared to be "botless," *i. e.*, not redeemable by pecuniary penalty (*Laws of Canute*, c. 651). And the punishment to be inflicted by Canute's laws are horrible; cutting off the feet or hands, the nose, the ears, or the upper lip, nay, even scalping, were allowed (c. 30). The sentences which, according to the *Mirror*, were inflicted by Alfred, were extremely severe — in some, even cutting off the hand. The laws of the Confessor, as collected under the Conqueror, contain no criminal penalties except that (borrowed from Canute) as to the murder of a Dane. But it may be gathered that, as under the Confessor, the criminal code was mitigated, for in the laws of William, professedly based upon the customs of the Confessor, the pecuniary penalties are allowed, and there is a clause prohibiting the infliction of death for the lighter offences (*Laws of Conqueror*, 140). Later in his reign, however, the Confessor adopted the more severe penalties of Canute's code. It is probable that the mildness of the Confessor's criminal justice may have been partly the cause of the fondness with which the people always spoke of his laws, and the great anxiety they always showed for the restoration of them.

[1] Leg. St. Edw., 27.   [2] Leg. Inæ, 6; Leg. Alf., 23.

shillings: so, striking out the front tooth was punished with a fine of eight shillings; the canine tooth, four shillings; the grinders, sixteen shillings:[1] if a common person was bound with chains, the amends were ten shillings; if beaten, twenty shillings; if *hung up*, thirty shillings.[2]

In the same manner injuries to property were generally considered in a criminal light; and the specific amends to be made by the wrong-doer to the injured party were fixed by law. A man who mutilated an ox's horn was to pay tenpence; if that of a cow, then only twopence. A like distinction was made between cutting off the tail of an ox or a cow.[3] To fight or make a brawl in the court or yard of a common person was punished with a fine of six shillings; to draw a sword in the same place, even though there was no fighting, with a fine of three shillings; if the party in whose yard this happened was worth six hundred shillings, the amends were treble, and they were increased further, according to the circumstances of the person whose house and domain were so violated.[4]

A system of regulations framed on this principle seems to have converted all notions of civil redress for injuries into a criminal inquiry; while the degree and circumstances attending the fact, both which it was out of the power of legislation exactly to reach, made no part of the judicial consideration; but the judge was to award the same stated fine in all cases which could be brought within the letter of the legal description. However, these penalties had so far the nature of a civil redress, that they were given in the way of compensation to the injured person.

The notion of compensation runs through the whole criminal law of the Anglo-Saxons, who allowed a sum of money as a recompense for every kind of crime, not excepting the taking away the life of a man. Every man's life had its value, called a *were*, or *capitis estimatio*. This had been various at different periods;[5] in the time, therefore, of King Athelstan, a law was made to settle the *were* of every order of persons in the state. The king, who on this occasion was only distinguished as

Were.

---

[1] Leg. Alf., 40. [3] Leg. Inæ, 59. [5] Leg. Inæ, 69.
[2] Ibid., 31. [4] Leg. Alf., 35.

a superior personage, was rated at 30,000 thrymsæ;[1] an archbishop or earl, at 15,000; a bishop or calderman, at 8,000; *belli imperator*, or *summus præfectus*, at 4,000; a priest or thane, at 2,000; a common person, at 267 thrymsæ. It seems this *were* was sometimes different in different parts of the country.[2] When any person was killed, the slayer was to make compensation to the relations of the deceased, according to such valuation. In the case of the king, half the *were* went to his relations, and half to his people. If the deceased was a stranger, or had no relations, the *were* was to be divided, half to go to the king, and half to the most intimate companion of the deceased.[3]

As the manners and notions of this people would not allow them to submit to any harsher punishment in the first instance, it was endeavored to render this as severe as possible. The *were* was not to be remitted;[4] and, to make the offender an example, as well as to prevent the effusion of blood, all his own relations were, by a law of King Edmund,[5] discharged from the obligation of abetting him against the *feud* of the relations of the deceased, whose deadly resentment he was to support *alone*, till he had paid the *were*. A person guilty of homicide was also excluded from the presence of the king.

But this *were*, in cases of homicide, and the fines that were paid in cases of theft of various kinds, were only to redeem the offender from the proper punishment of the law, which was death; and that was redeemable, not only by paying money, but by undergoing some personal pains: hence it is that we hear of a great variety of corporal punishments. A person *often* charged with theft was to lose his hand or foot.[6] There was also the pain of banishment and slavery,[7] and at one time it was enacted[8] that housebreaking, burning of houses, open robbery, manifest homicide, and treason against one's lord, should be *inexpiable* crimes; that is, not to be redeemed by any pecuniary compensation, or any pain or mutilation.

Thus far of punishments. We come now to consider

---

[1] A *thrymsa*, according to Du Fresne, was worth fourpence. According to this, 30,000 thrymsas = £500; 15,000 = £250; 8,000 = £133 6s. 8d.; 4,000 = £66 13s. 4d.; 2,000 = £33 6s. 8d.; 267 = £4 9s.
[2] Leg. Athelst., 3.
[3] Leg. Inæ, 22.
[4] Leg. Edm., 3.
[5] Ca., 8.
[6] Leg. Inæ, 18.
[7] Leg. Can., 6.
[8] Ibid., 61.

the notions they had of crimes, and their nature (a). A person present at the death of a man was looked on as *particeps criminis*, and as such was liable to a fine.[1] A

(a) It is curious that this law is not to be found among the laws of Canute; and, on the contrary, the scope and spirit of the laws (which bear the impress of great candor) is to exhibit a perfect equality between the two races; and by the previous laws the fine or penalty was the same whether a Dane or an Englishman. In the *Mirror of Justice*, however, there is this passage: — "King Canute ordained for the safeguard of the Danes whom he left in England, that if a man unknown was killed, the whole hundred should be amerced to the king by the judgment of murder," which was only an application of Alfred's law of frankpledge, that every freeman should enter into a hundred or a tithing, who wishes to be entitled to "were," in case any one should slay him (*Laws of Canute*, c. 20; *Anglo-Saxon Laws*, p. 387). And he who violates these laws, which the king has now given to all men, *be he Danish or be he English*, let him be liable to the king (*Ibid.*, 84). The only references given by the author are, it will be observed, not to that of Canute, but to the laws of the Confessor (those very laws which he in a subsequent part of this chapter describes as spurious); and in the passages to which he refers there is nothing of the kind. Sec. 15 is only to the effect that in case of murder the "vill" or the hundred shall be responsible, and section 16 is "de inventione murdre" — "murdra quidem inventa fuerunt tempore Canuti regis qui post acquisitam terram, et secum pacificatam, remisit domine exercitum suum preclari baronum de terræ; et ipsi fuerunt fide jussores erga regem quod illi quos retinent in terra primam pacem haberent. Ita quod si quis de Anglis aliquem ipsorum interficeret, si non possit defendere se judicio Dei ferro vel aquo, fieret justiciæ de eo." It will be seen that there is nothing in this to support the above version of the supposed law. In the laws of the Confessor allusion is made to a law of Canute's, simply to the effect that if a Dane were killed by an Englishman, and the latter could not defend himself by ordeal, he should suffer death, the hundred being liable to a fine if he escaped. This was applied by William to the protection of the Normans (*Laws of William the Conqueror*, c. 21); but as the law only applied if it was a Norman killed, it was taken that, so far as regarded that part of the law, unless the deceased was shown to have been an Englishman, he should be taken to have been a Frenchman (*Laws of Henry I.*, c. 75 and c. 92). So, according to Bracton, "Pro Anglico veo et de qui constare possit quod Anglicus sit, non dabitur murdrum," *i. e.*, the fine so called (*Ibid.*, c. 15, p. 135). This was the origin of presentments of Englishery, which are explained in the *Mirror*, where it is laid down that it should be inquired of what kindred or lineage those that were killed were, so that we may know by their parents whether they were of the English nation or not. And thence it is that we called that parentage Englishery, where the parentage could be found of the father's or of the mother's side; and if no Englishery be found, then it hath the judgment of murder. It is remarkable that no mention of this should have been made in the laws we have of Canute, but it may be explained, perhaps, as a mere temporary law, enacted on a special occasion in the earlier portion of the reign of Canute, and that the laws which go by his name, which were enacted in the latter part of his reign, and represent the results of his more mature and enlightened policy, deliberately excluded the law in question, as founded upon a bad principle, or tending to perpetuate feelings of jealousy between the two nations, whom it was his object to consolidate and unite.

[1] Leg. Inæ, 33; Leg. Alf., 26.

person killing a thief, unless he purged himself by oath before the relations of the deceased, relating all the circumstances of the fact, and that immediately, was to pay a fine.¹ If one in hewing a tree happened to kill a man, the relations were entitled to the tree, provided they took it within thirty days;² which was in the nature, and might perhaps be the origin of *deodands*. It does not appear that they made any distinction in the degrees of homicide;

Murder. except in one instance, which deserves particular notice; and that is where the fine called *murdrum* was to be paid. It is said, that Canute, being about to leave the kingdom, and afraid that the English might take advantage of his absence to oppress or destroy his own subjects, the Danes procured the following law in order to prevent secret homicides: That when any person was killed, and the slayer had escaped, the person killed should be always considered as a Dane, unless proved to be English by his friends or relations; and in default of such proof, that the vill should pay forty marks for the Dane's death; and, if it could not be raised in the vill, that the hundred should pay it. This singular provision, it was thought, would engage every one in the prevention or prosecution of such secret offences.³ It was upon this sort of policy that presentments of *Englishery*, as they were afterwards called, were founded.

Larceny. Larceny, called by the Saxons *stale*, might have been committed by a child of ten years old;⁴ but afterwards this crime was not imputed, unless the child was twelve years of age.⁵ If all the family of the offender were privy to the stealing, they were all to be made slaves.⁶ Where there was not that privity in a family, the mulct was, at one time, sixty shillings; at another time, one hundred and twenty shillings.⁷ Such regard was paid to the character of a wife, and the subjection she was supposed to be under to her husband, that when anything stolen was found in their house, the law considered her as no party in the stealing, unless it were manifestly in her separate custody.⁸

The more atrocious of these offenders, when they came in a body of seven, were called *theof*, or *prædones*; if more

---

¹ Leg. Inæ, 34.   ⁴ Leg. Inæ, 7.   ⁷ Leg. Athelst., 1.
² Leg. Alf., 13.   ⁵ Leg. Athelst., 1.   ⁸ Leg. Inæ, 58; Leg. Can., 74.
³ Leg. Confess., 15, 16.   ⁶ Leg. Inæ, 7.

than seven, they constituted *hlothe*, or *turma;* if more than thirty-five, they were then called *herge*, or *exercitus*.[1] These distinctions show in what manner these people carried on their depredations in the times before Alfred reformed the police.

False swearing was, at first, only punishable by a fine of one hundred and twenty shillings.[2] Afterwards,[3] false swearers were considered as no longer entitled to credit, and were obliged to purge themselves not by their own affirmation on oath, but by the ordeal: they were sometimes excommunicated.

Breaches of the peace were severely punished, as leading usually to bloodshed and death. If a person fought in the king's palace, his life was in the king's hands, unless he redeemed it with a fine;[4] and particular penalties were inflicted on those who fought in the presence of the bishop and ealderman;[5] or in the city or town where the bishop and ealderman were then holding their court.[6] A law of King Edmund's was so severe,[7] that if any one attacked another in his house, or broke the peace there, he was to forfeit everything, and his life was to be at the king's disposal. The great occasion of violent breaches of the peace, were the *deadly feuds* by which people in those times revenged the death of a relation. This method of prosecuting offenders had become so habitual to the people, that it appeared necessary even to make it a part of the penal code; and it was accordingly inserted under reasonable restrictions in a law of Alfred.[8] At length, it was thought expedient to impose additional checks on this singular piece of criminal jurisprudence. This was done by a law of Edmund;[9] which directs that somebody, in the nature of an arbiter, should be deputed to the relations of the deceased, and engage that the slayer should make compensation. He, in the meantime, was to be put into the hands of this arbiter, who was to see that sufficient sureties were taken for paying the *were* in twenty-one days; during which time there was to be peace, by mutual compact.

Deadly feuds.

Very early after the Saxons had been converted to Christianity, places of public worship were held in such

---

[1] Leg. Inæ, 13, 14, 15.
[2] Ibid., 12.
[3] Leg. Edw., 3.
[4] Leg. Alf., 7.
[5] Ibid., 15, 34.
[6] Ibid., 36.
[7] Leg. Edm.
[8] Leg. Alf., 38.
[9] Leg. Edm., 7.

reverence that a criminal flying thither was, during his stay there, allowed protection, whatever his crime might be (*a*).[1] It was usual to fly to such a place of security, to avoid the instant resentment of the aggrieved party, till provision could be made for paying the legal compensation. In a state of society like that among the Anglo-Saxons, the immunity indulged to places of worship was politic, humane, and necessary. It prevented the shedding of blood, and preserved the peace. Accordingly a penalty was inflicted on those who dared to violate this place of sanctuary by evil treating the culprit while there;[2] the *pax ecclesiæ* being more sacred, and in this instance better protected by law, than the *pax regis*. The offender might stay there thirty days,

_{Sanctuary.}

(*a*) The Saxon laws carried to the utmost extent the power, privileges, and immunities of the church, of which the sanctuary was only an instance. That particular right is expressly sanctioned in the laws of Alfred, Ethelred, and all the subsequent Saxon kings. The Saxon laws also enforced the payment of tithes, church rates, and Rome-feoh or St. Peter's pence (*Laws of Edgar, Ethelred, and Edward*). The bishops were to sit in the county courts (*Edgar*, 5; *Canute*, 18), and the preambles of the Saxon laws show that the bishops also sat in the Wittenagemote or Great Council. The law also recognized the canon or ecclesiastical rules, and as far as possible enforced them (*Laws of Ethelred and the Confessor*). Thus, in the laws of the Confessor, "Si quis sanctæ ecclesiæ pacem fregerit, episcoporum tunc est justicia. Et si eorum sententiam depigiendo, vel superbe contempnendo, parvipenderit, justicia regis mittet eum usque dum Deo primitus et rege postea satisfacerit." Any one who held of the church was not to be compelled to plead in any other than the ecclesiastical court. "Quicumque de ecclesia tenuerit, vel in feudo ecclesiæ manserit, alicubi extra curiam ecclesiasticam non placitabit, si in aliquo forisfactum habuerit donec quod absit in curia ecclesiastica de recto defecerit" (*Laws of the Confessor*, c. 4). The church was above all to be free in the appointment of her own ministers, of whatever order. No one was to reduce a church to servitude, or turn out a church minister, without the bishop's consent (*Anglo-Saxon Laws*, vol. i., p. 343). Lastly, ecclesiastical persons could not be prosecuted in the lay courts. Thus, the laws of Ethelred: "If a priest become a homicide, or otherwise commit a flagrant crime, let him forfeit his order and be an exile, or what the Pope may prescribe to him. If a priest stand in false witness, let him be cast out of the community of ecclesiastics, unless he do *as his bishop may direct him*" (*Anglo-Saxon Laws*, vol. i., p. 347). This is repeated in the laws of Canute, where it is said, "We will that men of every order submit each to the law which is becoming to him" (*Ibid.*, p. 367). If a man in holy order defile himself with a crime worthy of death, let him be seized, and *held to the bishop's doom*, according as the case may be (*Ibid.*, p. 403). And in the *Mirror of Justice* it is stated that King Alfred hanged a judge who had hanged a clerk in holy orders, who was not subject to his jurisdiction (*Mirror of Justice*, c. 5). The author, in his quotation in the next sentence, has omitted the essential words, *as the bishop may direct*.

[1] Leg. Inæ, 5.   [2] Leg. Alf., 2.

and was then to be delivered to his relations unhurt and safe.¹ Notwithstanding this regard for churches, there seems to have been no immunity granted to the persons of churchmen (a). If a clerk committed homicide, he was to be degraded from his orders, and was, moreover, to make his compensation, or suffer punishment, in the same manner as any other person (b)². The bringing of criminals to justice was very much facilitated by the police established in the reign of Alfred (c). The objects which next present themselves are the proceeding, the mode of trial, and the proof, all which were very remarkable parts of the Anglo-Saxon jurisprudence (d). The prosecutor, or accuser, as he was called,

(a) *Sed vide ante.*
(b) These are mistaken references, and the laws referred to have nothing to do with the period; but there are two of Canute's laws directly to an effect the contrary of what is stated in the text. "If a servant of the altar be a homicide or work iniquity enormously, let him forfeit both degree and order, and go walk as the Pope shall prescribe to him and do penance." And if he *would* clear himself, *i. e.*, if he elected to do so, then he was to do it in the way pointed out for priests by a former law (*Ethelred*, c. ix., 19); but if he did not do so, or practise the penance prescribed, then he was to be an outlaw (*Canute*, c. 41). In no case was he to be tried before the lay courts. So again, "If a man in holy orders do a crime worthy of death, let him be seized and held to the bishop's doom" (*Canute*, 43).
(c) The system of frankpledge, *vide ante.*
(d) The author does not give any intelligible account of it, and cites no authority about it; and it will be manifest that he had not given much attention to it, and had only attended to the two barbarous and primitive modes of procedure by compurgation and by ordeal. No authority is cited for the next proposition, that a mere accusation was sufficient to put the accused upon his defence; and it is quite contrary to the whole tenor of the later Saxon laws and the cases recorded in the *Mirror of Justice.* As early as the reign of Edgar and Ethelred mention is made of presentments by twelve sworn freemen jurors, who answered to our modern jurors; and Alfred is recorded to have hanged a judge who sentenced a man to be hanged without an indictment or presentment on oath by such jurors or sworn indictors. The laws of Ethelred begin, "that every freeman have a 'borh,' or borough, that they may present him to every justice if he be accused, but if he be infamous let him go to the ordeal," so that the ordeal was only for those who were not worthy of credit, and then only upon sworn presentment. If the man could obtain compurgation he would avoid the ordeal, which was only the ultimate resource, failing compurgation, upon a charge made by the neighbors upon oath (*Ang.-Sax. Laws*, v. i., 282). And again, the laws of Ethelred provided that in the hundred twelve thanes or freeholders were to be sworn that they would accuse no innocent man, nor conceal any guilty one (*Ibid.*, 295), which is precisely the present oath of the grand jurors. In the laws of Ethelred there is this remarkable provision set down, "and where thanes (or freeholders) are of one voice; if they disagree, let that stand which eight of them say" (*Ibid.*, 299). So, from the *Mirror of Justice,*

¹ Leg. Alf., 5.   ² Leg. Can., 36, 38.

made his charge; which, it should seem, was sufficient
alone to put the person accused on his defence. The de-

it appears that indictments were by the oaths of jurors (c. ii., s. 15), and
that it was only if there were no witness the trial by ordeal was resorted to,
and it was even then discredited and discouraged as a relic of heathenism
(c. iii., s. 23). And unless the ordeal was resorted to, the proof lay upon the
prosecutor. The subject of the criminal procedure of the Saxons, with
reference to the mode of trial, and the recourse to compurgation, ordeal, or
jurors, is one of extreme difficulty and obscurity, and as to which, it will be
observed, the author gives little, if any, assistance. After much study, the
editor ventures to propound this view, that these proceedings arose, one after
the other, by gradual growth, as the result of practical experience; and that
they arose in this order, first, simple denial on oath, then compurgation,
then ordeal, and trial by jury. If a thief were taken in the act, the case was
quite clear (*Ina*, 28), and no trial was needed (12). If the accused was not
taken in the act, then at first he was required to clear himself by his own
oath (*Ina*, 17, 46, 57) — that is, if oath-worthy (54). But it would be necessary to judge whether the man was credible, and hence some one else of
known credit might join with him, and even then it would be necessary that
some sort of tribunal should decide whether the man had cleared himself;
and hence it was said, "if he be found guilty," then there should be a penalty (*Ina*, 54). "Found guilty" could only mean found guilty by the hundred court, and hence there was a trial, and compurgation was only a species
of evidence or mode of proceeding at the trial. In the treaty between Alfred and Guthrum the practice of compurgation is brought out clearly; and
the accused, to clear himself, had to get eleven freeholders to join with him
in swearing (*Ang.-Sax. Laws*, 155). It is remarkable that no mention is
made of ordeal, and, by the *Mirror of Justice*, we find that in Alfred's time
there was trial by jury in criminal cases. It is in the laws of a later reign,
Edward's, the ordeal is first mentioned; and this is most remarkable, and
really looks as if there had been a recourse to the ordeal to solve cases of
doubt too difficult for the rude minds of that age; it was provided that he
should go to the oath, and if he failed in that, then to the ordeal (*Ibid.*). All
this was at the hundred court, and it is plain that these were sworn men to
determine the case; and that " oaths and ordeal " were used as means to assist them in determining in cases where the evidence left them in doubt, or
where they had no knowledge of the matter one way or the other. For
jurors in those early days were witnesses, and men had small capacity of
weighing evidence. Thus, therefore, the whole of these processes were
blended, and if the jurors did not know enough of the matter to enable
them to judge, and the compurgation or oaths failed to satisfy them, then
there was recourse to the ordeal, which was thus only used as the resort when
all other means of getting at the truth had failed. Mention is made of the
ordeal in the laws of the Confessor (*e. g., Ang.-Sax. Laws*, v. i., p. 445). And
after the Conquest, trial by battle prevailed, which was not less barbarous.
But as jurors grew more intelligent, and would attend to evidence, those
barbarous usages died out by degrees. That the hundred court was the
criminal tribunal, and that evidence was used when available, appears from
the later laws of Edgar. For there it is said, that if a thief denied the doom
of the hundred, and it be afterwards proved against him, he should pay a
penalty (*Edgar*, 3). But at the end of those laws the ordeal is mentioned.
Subsequent laws of Edgar provide for sworn witnesses of every transaction,
and that if a criminal charge arose out of it, they might determine the
matter by their testimony or verdict to the hundred; for if the accused said
that he had bought the things in the presence of the witnesses, and they so

fence and answer to this charge was this: If it was a matter not of great notoriety, but such as might admit of some doubt, the party *purged* himself by his oath, and the oaths of certain persons (called thence *compurgators*) vouching for his credit, and declaring the belief they had that he spoke truth. If the compurgators agreed in a favorable declaration, this was held a complete acquittal from the accusation. But if the party had been before accused of larceny or perjury, or had any otherwise been rendered infamous, and was thought not worthy of credit, he was driven to make out his innocence by an appeal to heaven in the trial by *ordeal*. This was of several kinds. The two principal were by water and iron; by water hot or cold and by hot iron; the iron was to be of one, two, or three pounds weight, and was, therefore called simple, double, or triple ordeal.

The *ordeal* was considered as a religious ceremony. The person, the water, and the iron were accordingly prepared under the direction of the priest, by exorcisms and other formalities, and the whole conducted with great solemnity. For three days before the trial the culprit was [1] to attend the priest, to be constant at mass, to make his offering, and in the meantime to sustain himself on nothing but bread, salt, water, and onions. On the day of

---

declared to the hundred, he would be absolved; but if they declare that it was not so, he would be convicted (*Edgar*, ii. 10). What was this but in effect trial by jury, seeing that the first jurors were witnesses? Thus came the law of Ethelred, that, at the hundred court, twelve freeholders were to be sworn to present no one untruly; and after this, men not credible are to go to the ordeal, and if the purgation failed, then by the compurgation (*Ethelred I.*, c. iii., s. 5). And afterwards, ordeal and oaths are mentioned together as modes of trial (*Ethelred*, v. 18). So, in the laws of Canute (c. 22), mention is made of men who never failed in oath or ordeal (*Ang.-Sax. Laws*, i., p. 389). And as to men who had failed, and were not credible, the words of the law are, "we have ordained concerning those men who were perjurers, if that were made evident, or an oath failed to them, or were not proved, that they should afterwards not be oath-worthy, but worthy of the ordeal" (*Edward*, 3). So, in the laws of a later reign, "And we have ordained, respecting the single ordeal, for those men who have been often accused, and have been found guilty, and they knew not who shall take them in pledge," etc. (*Athelst.*, 7). And then the law of ordeal is carefully and minutely laid down. This is very remarkable, and almost inexplicable; for it is after Alfred's time (when there were juries), and it looks as if the ordeal had been re-established after trial by jury; and as though the barbarian mind, unable to solve cases of doubtful character, took refuge in the ordeal, and thus revived the practice of their ignorant heathen ancestors.

[1] Leg. Athelst., 23.

trial he was to take the sacrament and swear that he was not guilty of, or privy to, the crime imputed to him. The accuser and the accused were to come to the place of trial attended with not more than twelve persons each, probably to prevent any violence or interposition; and a production of more than that number by the accused would have amounted to a conviction. The accuser was then to renew his charge upon oath, and the accused to proceed in making his purgation. If it was by hot water, he was to put his hand into it, or his whole arm, according to the degree of the offence; if it was by cold water his thumbs were tied to his toes, and in this posture he was thrown into it. If he escaped unhurt by the boiling water, which might easily be contrived by the management of the priests, or if he sunk in the cold water, which would certainly happen, he was declared innocent. If he was hurt by the boiling water, or swum in the cold, he was considered as guilty.[1]

If the trial was to be by the hot iron, his hand was first sprinkled with holy water, then, taking the iron in his hand, he walked nine feet. The method of taking his steps was particularly and curiously appointed. At the end of the stated distance he threw down the iron and hastened to the altar; then his hand was bound up for three days, at the end of which time it was to be opened; and from the appearance of any hurt, or not, he was declared in the former case guilty, and in the latter acquitted. Another method of applying this trial by hot iron, was by placing red-hot ploughshares at certain distances and requiring the delinquent to walk over them; which, if he performed unhurt, was considered as a proof of his innocence. These trials by water and fire were called *judicia Dei* (*a*).

(*a*) Or, as it is called in the *Mirror*, the miracle of God: that is, the priest was to do something which it were impossible to do without a miracle from God; " but Christianity suffered not that they be by such wicked arts cleared, if one may otherwise avoid it" (c. 7, s. 24). Nevertheless, the ordeal is mentioned in the laws of the Confessor; and the only substitute the Normans afforded for the stupid ordeal, was the brutal battle. The persuasions of the clergy, Lord Hale says, were used to the utmost to abolish it, and he thinks it died out in the reign of John; but so tenacious are an ignorant people of their barbarous usages, that it is actually mentioned at the end of the *Mirror* as "an abuse," "that purgations are not allowed by the miracle of God, where other proof faileth" (c. 5, s. 1). That was written in the time

[1] Leg. Athelst., 23.

Another method of trial was by the *offa execrata*, or Corsned, which was that by which the clergy were used to purge themselves, and which they chose, probably, as the least likely to put the party to any peril. A morsel of bread was placed on the altar with great ceremony and preparation, which the person to be tried was to eat; if it stuck in his throat, this was to be considered as a token of his guilt. Thus, in this instance and that of the cold water, a miracle was supposed to be wrought to prove the guilt of the person; in those of the hot water and hot iron the like divine interposition was expected to demonstrate his innocence. Another ordeal was that of *the cross*. This was performed by placing two sticks, one with a cross carved upon it and one without, and making the culprit choose one of them blindfolded. If he hit upon that which had the cross upon it, this piece of good fortune was looked upon as an evidence of his innocence. These seem to have been the methods of investigating truth in criminal inquiries.

It may be observed that the Anglo-Saxons made a distinction between manifest or open offences, and such as were not so public; and the degree of punishment was proportioned accordingly (*a*). It has been observed that this implied some doubt entertained by themselves of their methods of proof[1] (*a*); but, it may be remembered, that the Romans made the like distinction and inflicted only half the punishment on *furtum non manifestum*, which they did on that which was *manifestum*.

Next, as to civil causes, and the manner in which they were tried. It seems that causes in the county and other courts were heard and determined by an indefinite number of persons called *sectatores*, or suitors of court; and there is no great reason to believe that they had any juries of twelve men, which was an invention of a much later date (*b*). The *sectatores* used to give

Trial in civil suits.

---

of Edward I. As to the Norman substitute for the ordeal, the duel or battle, it was hardly obsolete until the time of Elizabeth; at all events, in civil cases; but in criminal cases, no doubt much earlier.

(*a*) There seems no sufficient authority for this. None is cited by the author.

(*b*) No authority is cited for this; and it is manifest, from the tenor of the later Saxon laws, and from the traces of the Saxon law to be found in the *Mirror of Justice*, that it is correct only as to earlier and more primitive

[1] Littl. Hen. II., vol. v., 292.

their judgment or verdict, both upon the matter of fact and of law (*a*). It may be a doubt whether they ever acted as an inquest to make inquiry of crimes and delinquents, as juries did after the Conquest.[1] In a law of King Ethelred (*b*), there is a provision that there should be twelve *thanes*, or *liberi homines* of superior consideration and parts, whose concurrence was made necessary. It should seem, however, these were rather assessors to the judge of the court than a part of the suitors, or indeed anything like a jury.[2] By all the monuments that remain of these times, it appears that the number of *sectatores* was various, according to the custom of different places, and perhaps in most instances depended on chance and convenience, but in no case is there the least reason to believe that it was confined to twelve [3] (*c*). These *sectatores* dis-

---

times. For as early as the laws of Edgar, we find provision is made for the securing of twelve men in every hundred as witnesses of transactions within the hundred; and these men were afterwards, if any question arose, either in a civil or criminal matter, to testify thereof to the hundred (*Laws of Edgar*, c. 3, s. 56). These were in truth juries; for the juries were originally witnesses, determining of their own knowledge; and the object of these laws was to provide that they should have knowledge of all matters within the hundred. Thus it came to be a fixed rule that some of the jurors must come from the hundred, who were called hundredors; and this, which was the case until modern times, shows that the jury arose out of the hundred.

(*a*) *Sed vide supra*.

(*b*) This law was, that a mote or court be held in every hundred, and that the twelve senior thanes or freeholders should go out — *i. e.*, be selected out of the hundred, and the sheriff with them, and that they should swear *that they would accuse no innocent man, nor conceal any guilty one,* the very oath which is now taken by a grand jury; and there can be no question that this was a jury; for it would be difficult to define a jury in any other way than as a selected body of men sworn to determine judicially. In the times of Edgar, it had already been enacted, that in every hundred there should be twelve men sworn as witnesses (*Edgar*, 6). And in the *Mirror of Justice* — which, there is no doubt, embodies the Dom-boc of Alfred, and certainly records many proceedings which had taken place in his time — jurors and juries are repeatedly mentioned in criminal cases. As regards civil suits, no doubt the suitor was judged in the county court, a turbulent and tumultuous body, unsuited for the administration of justices; but the necessity for having a selected number of them sworn would soon be recognized; and that, in reality, would be a jury.

(*c*) On the contrary, as will be seen from the Anglo-Saxon law, and from the *Mirror of Justice*, there is no mention made in the latter of these laws of any judicial function of the hundred court, either in civil or criminal cases, without the number twelve being alluded to; and in the instance just quoted, the author omits the words which show that the twelve men were jurors. It is evident, indeed, from his citation of Hickes, instead of the laws, that he took his authority at second-hand, and had not himself much studied the

[1] Leg. Ethel., ca. 4.   [2] Hickes' Thes. Diss. Ep., 34.   [3] Ibid., 33.

charged their office, it is thought, without any other obligation for a true performance of it than their honor, for it does not appear that they were *sworn* to make a declaration of the truth.[1] It is not improbable that the *thanes* in the counties, the citizens in boroughs, and those who were the *sectatores* in other courts, might determine all causes in like manner as peers of the realm, at this day, determine in criminal cases, without an oath. There is at least a perfect silence as to this subject in the remains of antiquity, and the most we can conjecture is that they might perhaps solemnly engage to speak the truth in all matters which should come before them, without renewing it in every particular cause.[2]

It is not unsuitable with what has been already said of the modes of proof used by these people to suppose that they admitted the oath of the defendant in civil causes, when that oath was supported by *compurgators*, who swore they believed what he said to be true. The laws requiring witnesses to all contracts supplied evidence almost in all inquiries about him; but where that was not the case, it seemed consistent enough with the established order of living in those times to allow credit to a man's oath, *when* supported by the concurring testimony of others to his credit (*a*). The small districts into which the people were

---

Saxon laws. He is equally incorrect, it will be seen, in the next statement, as to the suitors not being sworn; wherens, as will have been seen, mention is repeatedly made of those of the suitors being sworn who were really to determine, as jurors or witnesses. No doubt these decisions might be ratified by the voice of the whole body of the hundred, and in the earlier state of the Saxons this general voice might have been the only mode of decision. But it is manifest, from the later laws, that the danger and mischief of this had been made apparent, and that, therefore, *sworn* men were delegated really to determine.

(*a*) No doubt; and the practice of compurgation was the origin of "wager of law," in which the defender was examined on oath, with others; and, as Lord Coke says, "this countervailed a jury." But the author failed to see how what he said applied equally to jurors, who differed from compurgators simply in this, that the latter were called by the defendant to swear that they believed him innocent, and the former by the court, to swear whether they believed him guilty or innocent — both swearing equally upon their own knowledge. For this reason the Saxon laws, it has been seen, made provision that all transactions should be before some sworn men of the hundred, who should afterwards decide disputes arising out of the transactions they witnessed — *i. e.*, as jurors; for jurors were witnesses. Hence it was that, as the jury arose out of the hundred, and were supposed to be witnesses, and determine upon their own knowledge, it was an inflexible rule or custom,

[1] Hickes' Thes. Diss. Ep., 42.   [2] Ibid., 42.

divided, and the consequent relation which by law they bore to each other, furnished abundant opportunities for a man's character to be known, and declarations of his neighbors concerning his credibility might be received with no small degree of confidence.

It cannot be dissembled that some learned men have been of opinion, that the trial by jury was in use among the Saxons; and this point, like some others, had been maintained with great pertinaciousness by those who have labored to prove the antiquity of our juridical constitution.

This opinion may, probably, have been founded on the similitude between *sectatores* and *jurors*, an appearance which, on a superficial view, may indeed deceive (*a*). However, it may be laid down with safety that the trial by jury did not at this time exist; and if the reader will suspend his judgment till he comes to those times when the trial by jury was really established, he will then see distinctly the essential difference between *sectatores*, *compurgatores*, and *juratores*, and will agree with us in declaring that the frequent mention of *sectatores* is no proof of *juries*, properly so called, being known to our Saxon ancestors.

Thus have we attempted to give a sketch of that system of jurisprudence which subsisted among the Saxons. The materials which furnish any knowledge of it are so few and scanty, that it is with the utmost difficulty anything consistent can be collected from them (*b*). This

---

until abolished by statute, that there must be some hundredors upon a jury. And to this day, in matters of a public nature, juries may decide of their own knowledge.

(*a*) As already shown, the jurors were sworn suitors, and the suitors who really decided cases were sworn, in the later Saxon times. The author had misunderstood the provisions in the laws as to the witnesses, forgetting that, in the infancy of trial by jury, the jurors were witnesses, and determined upon their own knowledge; and he had failed also to see how one institution grew out of another in the course of experience. Thus, the original course, no doubt, was to put the defendant to purge himself by his own oath; then he was called upon to add the oaths of others; and if he failed to find a sufficient number to swear in his defence, then a certain number were sworn to determine the case. Both compurgators and jurors were simply suitors sworn; and there is no authority in the Saxon laws for saying that the hundred, after these laws were made, decided cases without some mode of inquiry by sworn men, either as compurgators or jurors. The only difference between them was, that the compurgators swore to their belief in the man's innocence, and the jurors swore to their belief that he was guilty or innocent, as the case might be — both equally swearing from knowledge.

(*b*) Unfortunately, our author was not at all aware of the materials which

must give rise to a variety of opinions, according as persons are biased by prejudices and different turns of thinking. Perhaps, after all, the clearest opinion that can be formed respecting such distant and obscure times, is not worth defending with much obstinacy.

Of this the reader will be able to judge when, in the course of this history, he finds institutions either so abundantly superinduced upon the original groundwork, or so entirely substituted in the place of it, that very little remains of the Saxon jurisprudence can be traced even in the earliest times of our known law, after the Conquest (a). The parts which alone survived that revolution seem to have been the methods of trial, some notions of criminal law, and the scheme of police. The others were gradually superseded, and at length are no longer known.

It remains now to inquire what steps were taken by

---

existed, nor was he sufficiently acquainted with those of which he was aware. Instances have already been adduced which show that he had derived his knowledge of the Saxon laws at second-hand, and had not studied them himself; and he wholly ignores the *Mirror of Justice*, which, as has been shown, contains a great deal of matter which obviously belongs to the Saxon age, and affords much information as to the Saxon system. No doubt it was rude and imperfect, and in its best time only a striving after better things; but in these attempts lie much of the interest of legal history, and in their criminal system the Saxons had made great advances. Our author had derived a very imperfect idea of the Saxon system, because he had derived it entirely from their written laws, and had missed the valuable evidence we have of their unwritten laws. It is in these, the unwritten laws of a nation, in its earlier stages of advance, that the alterations suggested by practical experience are more usually made, and therefore the course of progressive improvement is more distinctly marked. The author had failed to realize this progressive improvement, and his idea of the Saxon system is therefore imperfect.

(a) This is very true. It may indeed be said that no institutions peculiarly Saxon have survived; for although trial by jury, especially in criminal cases, virtually came to us through the Saxons, it would be an error to suppose that the principle of it was exclusively Saxon; and in substance it was known to the Romans, though no doubt it was not fully developed, until its union, so to speak, with the free popular element in the Saxon institution of the hundred court, out of which it really arose. And the whole of our criminal system of procedure, with its presentment by grand jurors, is distinctively Saxon; but this is all. The barbarous practice of the ordeal did not survive the reign of John. The practice of compurgators soon became obsolete in criminal cases, and the practice of wager of law in civil cases, which arose out of it, had been obsolete for ages long before its abolition, although its legal existence was an inconvenience. The system of "frank-pledge" also became obsolete. Nothing except the criminal system of the Saxons survived civilization.

the Anglo-Saxons in collecting and improving their laws (*a*), and what monuments they left of their legal polity.

(*a*) The author rightly speaks of these collections as confined to the laws of the Saxons. This may be the proper place in which to give some general notice of those written collection of Saxon laws to which the author here alludes. It is to be especially observed that these were by no means complete codes or bodies of law, containing all the laws existing in the country. On the contrary, it can be shown from the laws themselves — and this is the first and most important point to be observed in them — that they did not contain all the law, nor the most important part of it, the law of the most important institutions in the country. For, on the one hand, throughout these laws, there are none establishing any institutions at all; as, for instance, the municipal or the manorial, nor the divisions and organizations of the country, as counties and hundreds; and, on the other hand, there are constant allusions to some of those divisions and institutions as already existing. For instance, the earliest of these laws make mention of the ecclesiastical organizations and endowments, for they make mention of the property of the church, and of bishops, and of priests (*Ethelbert*, 1), and church scot (*Ina*, 61), and tithes (*Edgar and Ethelbert*). And so of the civil organizations — one of the earliest of their laws makes mention of counties, while not mentioning their formation. "If any one demand justice before a shire-man or other judge," — which last, no doubt, means hundredor (*Ina*, 8, 36). In the same laws mention is made of tens, which implies hundreds (*Ina*, 54). This was long before Alfred, who by a popular error is supposed to have established counties, hundreds, and tithings. So, mention is made of the manorial institution, — that is, of serfs or villeins, which implies its existence. "If any one go from his lord without leave, and steal into another shire, and he be discovered, let him go back" (*Ina*, 22, 39). This is a rough translation of an imperial edict as to the coloni; it comes between two clauses as to ceorls (churls) or husbandmen. In the Latin version, ceorl is translated "coloni," added to which there is another clause speaking of ceorls having meadow in common. All which points plainly to the state of villenage and the existence of manors. So mention is made of reeves, sheriffs, shire-reeves (*Laws of Ina*). Mention is next made of "borhs" (burghs), and pledges (*Ina*, 1). All this was before the time of Alfred, who is supposed to have been such a remarkable legislator, but whose laws, on the contrary, are very inferior to those of Ina. There is little at all new, and nothing which can be called original; and they commence indeed by a preface in which the king states that he had gathered from the laws of Ina and Ethelbert those which he thought best, and had added little of his own (*Laws of Alfred; Anglo-Saxon Laws*, p. 59). These laws established nothing, unless it were the right of sanctuary in a church (c. 5). They make mention of royal manors or farms (c. 8). They likewise mention the folcmote or court of the county or hundred (c. 22). They contain an enactment as to bocland (already quoted), implying that the distinction of such land was already known and established (c. 41); and there is no previous law about it. It may here be mentioned that these "laws" were the Saxon, called "dooms," and that thus the laws of Alfred are called "Alfred's dooms." So Edward's "dooms" or laws; they allude to bocland and folcland (the first time the latter is mentioned), and to serfs and sheriffs, and requires that each sheriff have a court once a month. So of the "dooms" or laws of Athelstane; the first thing new is the ordinance for the payment of tithes (I., 1). The next is that if a lord denied justice, the king might be appealed to (II., 3). So allusions are made to trial by ordeal, as already established (*Edw.*, 3; *Ath. I.*, 4–6). And there are specific regulations about it. So as to the county court and

We are told that the great and good King Alfred, besides the regulations he made for the better order and government of his people, seeing how various the local customs of the kingdom were, made a collection of them, and out of them composed his *Dom-boc*, or *Liber Judicialis* (a). It seems this was intended as

Alfred's Dom-boc.

---

hundred court, which had been mentioned as existing in previous laws, it is provided that the county court shall be held twice a year, and the hundred court once a month (*Edgar*, 5). So, in the laws of Canute, there is a requisition that every man be brought into a hundred and into a tithing (c. 20). It would be difficult to find anything *established* or constituted in the Saxon laws (except, indeed, the payment of tithes and church scot, and "Rome-fee," or the "hearth-penny" to St. Peter (*Laws of Ethelred, Edgar, and Canute*). With these exceptions, all the provisions in these laws are matter of mere regulation of existing institutions, and for the most part relate either to more barbarous usages, long since obsolete, or, on the other hand, to pious duties and religious obligations.

It is obvious, then, that these successive collections were not complete codes of law, nor even of the Saxon law — that is, of the whole of the law they had — nor even collections of their laws, in the sense of all their laws, but they were only collections of their written laws; that is to say, of the *new* laws they made to alter, or regulate, or enforce laws already existing, or institutions already established. Each king put forth a kind of edict, or collection of edicts, on such matters as appeared to require to be altered or enforced, and thus they afford only a kind of indirect and incidental evidence of the system of law then existing, which is not embodied or codified in these laws, but, on the contrary, is only to be collected therefrom by close examination and careful induction.

(a) It did not occur to the author that this might be the Dooms or Laws of Alfred above mentioned; and which, it will be seen, were only a compilation from a former collection of general laws better than his own. The name of Alfred has become associated with the revival of law and literature, but it is manifest that his merit must have been more in the administration of law than in legislation; and it is remarkable that, although the chroniclers speak of him in terms of high eulogy, they do not mention his laws, or those which pass under his name as the Anglo-Saxon Laws, nor the "Dom-boc," or *Liber Judicialis*, which is spoken of by the author in this passage. And the only mention made of his legislation is mistaken, and has given rise to the erroneous notion that Alfred divided the country into hundreds and tithings, an error into which the author had fallen. The notion is derived from a passage in William of Malmesbury, but it was perhaps misunderstood, and, at all events, it was corrected by Lord Coke. The chronicler says most truly that Alfred perceived that "literature had gone to decay all over the island, because *every one was occupied in the defence of his life*, and so had no time to devote to books," a sentence which *speaks* volumes as to the barbarous condition of the country at the time, and the entire insecurity of life and limb which existed; and the impression to be derived from it is confirmed by the earlier Anglo-Saxon laws, which are full of penalties against the most brutal bodily injuries. Hence, it is plain, it was the policy of Alfred to restore literature by establishing security of person, and with that view to restore the reign of law — a most remarkable illustration of the inseparable connection between law and civilization, and the absolute necessity of peace and order as agents of civilization. With this

a code for the government of his whole kingdom, and it

view, the chronicler says, "he appointed centuries, which they call hundreds, and decennaries, that is to say, tithings, so that every Englishman living according to law, must be a member of both, and if any one was accused of a crime, he was obliged immediately to produce persons from the hundred and tithing to become his surety, and whoever was unable to find surety must dread the severity of the law," *i. e.*, he had to undergo either the ordeal or some form of trial. And if any one who was impleaded made his escape either before or after he had found surety, all persons of the hundred and tithing paid a fine to the king (*William of Malmesbury*, B. 2, c. 4). Now, comparing this carefully with reference to contemporary history, it will be found that the true meaning of it, or, at all events, all that is true in it, is, that Alfred *adapted* the institution of tithings and hundreds to the object he had in view, by founding on it the Saxon institution of frankpledge, making all the inhabitants pledges for each other, a system the principle of which remains to this day, having been adopted by the act of George I., which made the hundred liable for damage done by rioters. To suppose that he *instituted* hundreds and tithings is a great error, since they were known to the Romans long before his time, and the truth is, as Lord Coke explains, he restored or renovated the institution, though even as to that it is remarkable that these things are not mentioned in the laws until Edgar. Neither Malmesbury the chronicler, nor Asser, his biographer, make any mention of the laws which pass under his name, but they both concur in one statement, that he was a strict inquirer into the sentences passed by his judges, and a *severe corrector of such as were unjust* (*Ibid.*). This statement — which is far stronger and more pointed than Asser's — is remarkably exemplified in the severe sentences of Alfred recorded in the *Mirror of Justice*, a book which, although written in its present form in the reign of Edward I., bears internal evidence of having been founded upon one originally written soon after the reign of Alfred, since almost all the names of judges or parties mentioned are unmistakably Saxon, and the names of judges under Edward are known, and were all Norman; and, moreover, it professes and purports to record what took place under Alfred, and to give a kind of comparative account of the law as it existed under Alfred and under Edward. In this respect, then, it is one of the most interesting of the sources of our legal history. And it is curious that the author should not have mentioned it here, especially as he mentions an obsolete and doubtful book, of which all trace has been lost, unless by it is meant either the collection of laws which passes under Alfred's name, or the original of that very treatise which is now under notice, and which may have been called Alfred's *Liber Judicialis*, or Book of Dooms. And for this latter supposition there is great reason, for the treatise in question bears upon the face of it evidence that it *was* founded upon an ancient book of the age of Alfred, and purporting to record a number of "Alfred's dooms"— that is, of judgments pronounced by Alfred or by judges under his authority; and these dooms appear all to have been preserved and incorporated in the work in question, and afforded such valuable and remarkable illustrations of the legal history of the period, that they may properly and usefully be here extracted; that is to say, all those passages which bear traces of being as old as Alfred. The treatise begins with a statement that the realm was divided into shires, the names of which are given, and in which it is remarkable that Warwickshire is spelled in the Saxon way, Euerwickshire. The Roman origin of our territorial divisions and civil institutions is betrayed in the statement that eighteen of the shires had been committed to counts or comites (called by the Saxons earls), and therefore had been by the Romans called comitates, as each had been com-

obtained, with great authority, during several reigns,

mitted to one of the comites; and it is stated that, "so at this day these shires are called in Latin 'comitatus,' and that which is *without* these counties belongs to the English by conquest"— a remarkable statement for more reasons than one; it may explain how it is that some counties end with the word shire and others do not, and next, it shows that the Saxons, in the main, preserved the old institutions and divisions. It then mentions the division of the country into centuries or hundreds, and tithings or decennaries — not ascribing it to Alfred. Then it states that, for the estate of the realm, King Alfred caused the earls to meet, and ordained that twice in the year, or oftener if need be, they should meet at London; "and that by this estate many ordinances were made by many kings until the time of the king that now is," *i. e.*, Edward I.; and then it states the substance of these laws, which are here stated, only as far as it appears from the Saxon laws, was really the law of the time of Alfred. The sheriffs were ordained to defend their counties, and bailiffs, in the place of centiniers or hundredors. And the sheriffs and bailiffs caused the free tenants of their bailiwick to meet in their counties and hundreds, at which justice was so done that every one so judged his neighbor by such judgment as a man could not elsewhere receive in the like cases, until such time as the customs of the realm were put into writing, and certainly established. And although a freeman commonly was not to serve without his assent, it was assented to that free tenants should meet together in their counties, hundreds, and the lord's courts, if they were not especially exempted to do such suits, and there judge their neighbors. And that right should be done from month to month in the counties, if the largeness of the counties required not a longer time; and that every three weeks right should be administered in other courts; and that every free tenant was bound to such rule, and had ordinary jurisdiction. The turns of sheriffs and view of free pledges were ordained; and it was ordained that none of the age of fourteen years or above, was to remain in the realm above forty days, if they were not first sworn to the king by an oath of fealty, and received into a decennary (B. 1., s. 2). Then afterwards (s. 15), that county courts were held monthly, and the judgment was by the suitors, and the other inferior courts were the courts of every lord, to the likeness of hundred courts, "where right was to be administered without delay" (sec. 15). And again, "the sheriffs by ancient ordinances held meetings twice in the year in every hundred," where all the freeholders within the hundred were bound to appear, and because sheriffs, to do this, made their turn of the hundreds, and such appearances are called the sheriffs' "tourns," — where it belongeth to them to inquire of all *personal offences* done within their hundreds, and of all wrongs done by the king and king's officers, and of wrongs done to the king (sec. 16). Then it "was ordained that there should be in each hundred a view of frankpledge, that is, to show the frankpledges, and if all the frankpledges had their dozens entire," whence it appeared that they were not in decennaries but in dozens, that is, that the number of each was not ten but twelve, which was, it will be observed, the number of a jury. And this meeting of the hundred was called the "leet" (sec. 17), and made presentment of nuisances, etc. Then there is this passage, which seems to show that these "leets," or assemblies, were the origin of juries: "and though the bailiffs cannot determine any action at the leet, if any be grieved by wrongful presentment, it is lawful for the bailiff or steward, by twelve of the more discreet men, to inquire of the truth, though no *decennary or juror* is not attestable with less than two juries"— treating the decennaries and grand jurors as identical (*Ibid.*). "And if any one proffer himself to swear fealty to the king, he is to be pledged in some frankpledge and first in the decennary" (sec. 17). All this is evidently of the time of Alfred, for it relates to the very constitution of frankpledge which he first established, and it connects it with the jury system. In a previous passage it is said, "The panel (of jurors) are to be of decennaries; for sheriffs at their tourns, or bailiffs at their view of frankpledge, have power by authority of their office to send for the people, which none other have without the king's consent, and that is for the keeping of the peace, and for the right of the king and the common people" (sec. 13). All this, again, relates to frank-pledge, and therefore is of the age of Alfred, and connects it with juries, and identifies decennaries with jurors. And there are numerous evidences that the book had its basis in a work composed after Alfred's time. There is mention made of a judge who is afterwards said to have been hanged by Alfred (sec. 1). There is mention made of a case decided in the time of King Edmund (Book ii., sec. 17). There are many instances of indictments, in which, without any exception, all the names are Saxon (sec. 13–22). The part of the work, however, which most unmistakably points to the time of Alfred, and most conclusively identifies it with the "doom-book" above referred to by the author, is that in which, literally, Alfred's dooms are set forth. "It is an abuse that judges and their officers who kill men by false judgment, are not destroyed as other murderers, which Alfred caused to be done, who caused forty-four judges to be hanged in one year as murderers for their false judgments." This is, as other facts show, wilfully false. "He hanged Segnor, who judged Selfe to death after sufficient acquittal. He hanged Cadwine, because he judged Hackwy to death, without the consent of all the jurors, and whereas he stood upon the jury of twelve men, and three could have saved him against the nine. Cadwine removed the three, and put others upon the jury, upon whom Hackwy put not himself. He hanged Markes, becansed he judged During to death by *twelve men who were not sworn.* He hanged Seafaule, because he judged Olding to death for not answering. He hanged Thurston, because he judged Thurnger to death by a verdict of inquest taken *ex officio* without issue joined. He hanged Athelstane, because he judged Herbert to death for an offence not mortal. He hanged Rombold, because he judged Lischild in a case not notorious, without appeal, and without indictment. He hanged Freburne, because he judged Harpin to die, *whereas the jury were in doubt in their verdict;* for in doubtful cases one ought rather to save than to condemn. He hanged Hale, because he saved Tristram the sheriff from death, who took to the king's use from another's goods against his will, forasmuch as between such taking from another against his will, and robbery, there is no difference. He hanged Bermond, because he caused Garbolt to be beheaded by his judgment in England, for that for which he was outlawed in Ireland. He hanged Alflet, because he judged a clerk to death over whom he had not cognizance. He hanged Muclin, because he hanged Helgaire by command of indictment, not special. He hanged Saxmund, because he hanged Bunold, in England, where the king's writ runneth, for a fact which he did in the same land where the king's writ did not run. He hanged the suitors of Calevot, because they had adjudged a man to death in a case not notorious, although they were guilty thereof; for no man can judge within the realm but the king or his commissioners, except those lords in whose lordships the king's writ doth not run. He hanged the suitors of Dorchester, because they judged a man to death by jurors in their liberty, for a felony which he did out of the liberty, and whereof they had not the cognizance by reason of property. He hanged the suitors of Cirencester, because they kept a man so long in prison that he died in prison, who would have acquitted himself by foreigners. In his time the suitors of Doncaster lost their jurisdiction, besides other punishments, because they held pleas forbidden by the customs of the realm to

being referred to, in a law made by King Athelstan, as an *authoritative* guide[1] (*a*).

However, this work, valuable as it was, had probably the defects of all original attempts. On that account, as well as on account of the irruption and settlement of the Danes, and the consequent prevalence of their customs, it was found necessary in the days of King Edgar to revise this compilation, or make another more full, and more suitable to the then state of the law. Compilation by Edward the Confessor. But this undertaking was left unfinished; so that the grand design of making a complete code of English law fell to the part of Edward the Confessor (*b*), who is said[2] to have collected from the Mercian, West Saxon, and Danish law, a uniform body of law to be observed throughout the kingdom.[3] From this circumstance, the character of an eminent legislator has been conferred on Edward the Confessor by posterity; who have endowed him with a sort of praise nearly allied to that of Alfred: for as one is dignified with the title of *legum Anglicanarum Conditor*, the other has been called *legum Anglicanarum Restitutor* (*c*).

---

judges and suitors to hold. In his time, Colgrin lost his franchise of enfangenthief, because he could not send a thief to the common gaol of the county, who was taken within his liberty for a felony done out of the liberty. In his time, Buttolphe lost his view of frankpledge, because he charged the jurors with other articles than those which belonged to his view. In lesser offences he did not meddle with the judgments, but removed the judges, etc. In his time every plaintiff might have a commission, and a writ to the sheriff, to the lord of the fee, or to certain justices, upon every wrong done (Book 5, sec. 1). Now, it is manifest that all this is recorded of the time of Alfred; and it shows plainly that trial by jury was fully established in criminal cases, and, no doubt, in civil cases also.

(*a*) Had the author read the laws, he would have found that there was no foundation for the statement. Athelstane makes no allusion to Alfred's laws, but simply says that such a fine shall be paid, as the doom-book may say; which may mean his own, or any other, and there were express provisions on the subject in most of the laws, as in Edward's, for instance: and not especially in those of Alfred.

(*b*) Had the author read the laws of Canute he would have seen that his collection is far more full than any other; but, as already mentioned, there was no attempt by any one to embody or codify all the laws, and these successive collections were only collections of written laws. There is no contemporary evidence that the Confessor ever made such a code as is supposed, and the idea of such a code was far beyond his age. The notion, no doubt, arose out of a misapprehension of the cause of the great regard shown by the people for the customs of his time.

(*c*) There is no more foundation for the one title than the other, nor an

[1] Ca., 5. [2] Hoveden, Hen. II., Leg. St. Edw., 35 to 36; Lamb., p. 149.
[3] 1 Bla., 66.

It is said that the *Dom-boc* of Alfred was in being about the time of Edward IV.; but we hear nothing of the fate attending the volume compiled by Edward the Confessor (a). As to the nature of the work: it seems

---

atom of contemporary authority for either. On the contrary, contemporary authority points rather to Edgar as the author or restorer of our laws, and his laws are far superior to those of Alfred, and as good as those which have come down to us as those of the Confessor. In the collection of the laws of the Confessor, made by royal authority, only a few years after his death, it is said: " Et sic auctorizati sunt leges regis Edwardi; *quæ prius adinventæ et constitutæ fuerunt tempore regis Edgari*, avi sui " (*Ang.-Sax. Laws* and *Inst.*, v. i., p. 458). Popular ideas are often not supported by authentic contemporary authority. In the next sentence, the author shows he assumes that Alfred's "dooms" had not come down to us, and in the next he shows that he equally assumed the non-existence of any of the laws of the Confessor. But on both points it will be seen he was in error.

(a) Because there was no such code. If there had been, it must have been known of in the next reign, and it would not have been necessary for the Conqueror to order a compilation of the Confessor's laws to be made, as he undoubtedly did, according to all historians, in the fourth year of his reign. This collection has come down to us, and it is headed thus: " Post quartum annum adquisicionis regis Willielmi consilio baronum suorum, fecit summoniri per universos patriæ comitatus Anglos nobiles sapientes, et in lege sua eruditos, ut eorum consuetudines ab ipsis audiret. Electis igitur de singulis totius patriæ comitatibus 12 jurejurando imprimis sanxerunt ut quoad possent recto tramite incedentes, legum suarum ac consuetudinum sancita edicerent; nil pretermittentes, nil addentes, nil prevaricando mutantes" (*Ang.-Sax. Laws*, v. i., p. 442). It would be impossible to imagine anything more apparently authentic than this collection. These laws are general in their application to the whole kingdom, with several special exceptions which are expressly mentioned. One of the first shows that the prerogative of the king to administer justice in the supreme courts was recognized, for it runs thus: " Ubicumque justicia regis vel alia quælibet justicia cujuscumque sit, tenuerit placita," etc. (*Ibid.*, p. 443). It appears that the ordeal was still resorted to, and it is laid down, " assit ad judicum minister episcopi cum clericis suis, et justicia regis cum legalibus hominibus provinciæ illius, ut videant et audiant omnia æque fiant et quos salvaverit Dominus per misericordiam suam et justicia eorum, quietis int et liberi abscedant; et quos iniquitas et injusticia sua condempnaverit, justicia regis de ipsis fieri faciat justiciam" (c. ix., p. 446). It appeared that there were civil and criminal courts in the hundreds and the counties, and also courts baron in manors. There is little in the collection relating to anything except the rights of the church and the administration of justice; there is no reference to the rights or customs of the people, except in a clause referring to their right to assemble in their counties in full "folcmote," and to elect a sheriff, and discuss public affairs (which is omitted in some copies). It is remarkable that though there is a recognition of the rights of the church, there is no recognition of the rights or institutions of the laity. It is difficult indeed to imagine any popular enthusiasm excited by anything in this collection, except as to the county assemblies; the main importance of which, however, would be as necessary for the maintenance of the rights and customs of the people. And though this collection is clearly, as far as it goes, authentic, it is not surprising, therefore, that people should have doubted whether these could be indeed the laws of Edward the Confessor, about which the people

probable, that as the Danes had now become incorporated into the body of the people, their laws were melted down into one mass with the Mercian and West Saxon; and all together composed a set of laws to govern both peoples. This, most likely, was done with equable qualifications of all these laws, so as to render submission to them, by both nations, neither strange nor oppressive. It should seem, there was throughout that book a constant intimation what was Saxon, Mercian, or Danish; as we find in the laws of William the Conqueror, which were designed to make certain alterations in those of Edward, frequent mention of them by their respective names, as different subsisting laws.

As the collection of Edward the Confessor comprised in it the whole law of the kingdom, it contained not only the unwritten customs, but the laws and statutes made by the several kings. By the loss of this volume, we are

were so anxious. But a little attention will solve the difficulty, and show that it arose from an error, already pointed out, in confounding the written laws with the unwritten; and an attentive reference to contemporary history in the chronicles will show that what the people were chiefly anxious about was the maintenance of the "customs" of the Confessor — that is, the customs which existed in his time, which were erroneously imagined to have been put into writing by him, a notion for which there is no foundation. What these customs were, and that they were not written in his time, will appear from the laws of the Conqueror, which commence thus, "Istæ sunt leges et *consuetudines* quos Willielmus rex post adquisicionem Angliæ omni populo Anglorum concessit tenendas eadem, quas predecessor suus Edwardus, servavit." And then among the "laws and customs" are these, "Coloni et terrarum exercitores non vexentur ultra debitum et statutum, nec licet dominos removere colonos a terris dummodo debita servicia persolvint." This, which was a reproduction of a law of Ina almost, the earliest Saxon king, and of an imperial edict in the time of the Roman occupation (*vide* Introduction), was a recognition of the right of the great body of the agricultural tenants all over the country, to retain their tenements so long as they rendered their services, and it would be impossible to conceive anything more vitally important to the great body of the people. There was another custom recognized, the right of inheritance, and the equal division of land, "Si quis paterfamilias casu aliquo sine testamento obierit, pueri inter se hæreditatem paternam æqualiter dividant." And there was another as to the local administration of justice in the courts of the county, or hundred: "Nemo querelam ad regem deferat nisi ei jus defecerit in hundredo vel in comitatu" (c. 43), which was a reproduction of similar provisions in Saxon laws. These two customs may have strongly interested popular feelings, through the medium rather of their prejudices than their real and solid interests; but the first-mentioned one, as to the rights of the agricultural tenantry all through the country, must have been of vital importance to the great body of the people, and a reference to these "customs" thus recognized by the Conqueror as existing under the Confessor, will amply explain the anxiety of the people about the customs of the Confessor's time.

left very much in ignorance as to the extent, scope, and nature of these customs. It is not so with the written laws of these times; for we have many of these still remaining. These remains of Saxon legislation give us some insight into the nature of their jurisprudence.

As laws, if not made to create some new regulation, are designed to restrict, amend, or enlarge some pre-existent custom or law; they always enable us to make some conjectures respecting the subject upon which they are intended to operate. From these Saxon laws we may pronounce, that matters of judicial inquiry were treated with great plainness and simplicity. Like the laws of a rude people, they are principally employed about the ordering of the police; and accordingly contain an enumeration of crimes and their punishments (a). As this

(a) No doubt this is so, and these laws are, for the most part, the mere records of the barbarous usages of a barbarous race — these written laws being the peculiar laws or usages of the Saxons themselves, which they brought here, and therefore of the rudest and most barbarous character. It has been already shown that they established no institutions, though there are recognitions of existing institutions (as, for example, the manorial and ecclesiastical); which were entirely of a rural character, and had little applicable to cities, or relating to municipal institutions; and as already shown, the earlier conquests of the Saxons would be in the rural districts, their progress would be gradual, the cities would be the last subdued, and in the rural districts the amalgamation of the races would be the most slow, and the barbarous usages most deeply rooted. Moreover, it is to be remarked of these laws that the earlier of them were local, and only related to particular kingdoms of the Heptarchy. Those of Ethelbert, for instance, relate to the province of Kent; those of Ina and Alfred to the West Saxons. It was not until after the Danish invasion that there is any indication in the laws of a general application to all England; and it is in the laws of Athelstane that first there are expressions which denote that they have that character (*Anglo-Saxon Laws*, p. 225). These laws contain internal evidence that they were framed for the whole realm, as they establish a general coinage and currency, enumerating the cities where there are to be mints, and these include all the chief cities in the country, at least as far north as London; these laws likewise include the customs of London. These laws, however, seem to indicate that the more northern and central counties were under the Danish rule, and the laws of Ethelred are said to have been made in Mercia, according to the laws of the English, and he is called King of the English (p. 305). It is only in the laws of Canute for the first time declared that they were made by the king of all England and king of the Danes (p. 359), and to be observed over all England (p. 377); and these establish one general law for all the races with special exceptions, which are specified. Thus, then, up to the time of Athelstane these laws were merely local. Athelstane was the first king of all the English, and his were the first laws for the whole of the Saxon race, but his dominion only extended over half England; and Canute was the first monarch who reigned over all England, and who framed a collection of written laws for the whole of the population of the country. His, therefore, was the first compilation of laws which could be considered gen-

makes the greater part of the Saxon laws now existing, it may fairly be concluded that the *Dom-boc* of Alfred and

eral or national: those of Alfred were entirely local; and, as to the supposed compilation by the Confessor, it has already been shown to be a mere fiction. It may be of interest here to select from these collections all the laws which appear worthy of mention. First, as to the established church: as already mentioned, the earliest of these laws mention bishops and priests, and church property, and further disclose that the bishops had seats in the national or local councils, for the laws of Ina commence with a statement that they were made with the council of the bishop and his eldermen, and the rest of the distinguished members of the witan (*Anglo-Saxon Laws*, 103). These laws ordain payment of church scot (*Ibid.*, 105; *Ina.*, 4), as do subsequent laws (*Edgar* I., 3; *Ethel.*, vi. 18; ix. 11; *Edgar*, i. 2, etc.); Tithes are ordained to be paid in the laws of Edgar (i. 3), and later laws (*Ethel.*, ix. 8; *Can.*, 8; *Ethel. I., Ed. Conf.*, 70); and the hearth-penny, or Peter's pence (*Edgar* and *Ethel.*). The earliest laws command the observance of Sundays (*Ina*, 3; *Can.*, 46; *Athels.*, i. 24; iii. 2; *Ethel.*, v. 13; vi. 22; *Edgar*, i. 5; *Can.*, 14), and mass days (*Alf.*, 43; *Edgar*, i. 5; *Can.*, 14). Throughout the laws there is an emphatic recognition on the part of the people of their common Christianity; and it is interesting to observe how, under the influence of the church, the laws bear the impress of a spirit of equality, and equal justice, to all classes and races of the people. Thus, through the laws of Ina is to be observed an evident endeavor to put the British on the same footing as the Saxons; the laws are framed generally for both races, and there are special provisions in favor of the British (*Ina*, 33–46). And so as to ranks and classes. The laws of Ina commence thus:— "First, we command that God's servants hold the lawful rule; after that, we command that the law and doom of the whole folk to be thus held." And almost the first law is, that if a theow, or slave, be made to work on Sunday, he shall be free (*Ina*, 3), and none could be put into slavery but for felony or stealing (7). There is a general provision for the whole of the people, — "If any one demand justice before a scire-man (shire-reeve, sheriff), or other judge, and cannot obtain it, and the man will not give him satisfaction, let him pay a fine, and within eight days do him justice: if one takes revenge before he demand justice, let him give up what he has taken to himself, and pay damage and a fine" (sec. 9): if any commit forcible ouster, let him give up what he has taken and pay a fine (*Ina*, 10),— laws which were evidently suggested by the Roman law, and aimed at the establishment of the supremacy of law and legal justice over that rough and legal justice which is the great characteristic of a barbarous state of society. The criminal code was, as might be expected, barbarous; a thief could not be punished with death (*Ina*, 12), unless his life could be redeemed, and an habitual thief could have his hand or foot cut off (*Ina*, 18–37). The same laws contained the first of a series of enactments which run all through the Saxon laws, requiring transactions to take place before witnesses, who should afterwards be able to testify as jurors, the jurors at first being witnesses, and proceeding according to their own knowledge. If a chapman traffic among the people, let him do so before witnesses; if stolen property be attached with a chapman, and he have not brought it before good witnesses, let him prove that he was neither party to the theft, nor thief, and pay the penalty (*Ina*, 25); and there are similar provisions in later laws of *Edward I., Ath. I.*, 10, 12; *Edm.*, c. 5; *Edj.*, 6; *Ed.*, 5; *Edg.*, 6; *Ethel. I.*, 3; *Can.*, 24; *Ed. Conf.*, 33. These provisions are important, as containing the first germ of trial by jury. The laws of Ina are the first that deserve mention. The laws of Ina contain an important recognition of the condition of serfdom, as distinguished from slavery,— "If any

19

the compilation of Edward the Confessor were mostly filled with the same kind of matter.

one go from his lord without leave, or steal himself away into another shire and be discovered, let him go where he was before, and pay a fine" (*Ina*, 39). This comes between two laws relating to "ceorls" (pronounced "churls") or husbandmen, whom the Latin version call "coloni," and who are throughout distinguished from "theows" or slaves, who held no property and could pay no penalty, and as to whom it had been provided that if they ran away they should be hanged (*Ina*, 24). These "ceorls," then, were the "coloni" of the Roman-British period; and the villains or villeins of later times, the originals of our modern copyholders. They held tenements on servile tenure, afterwards secured by custom, the tenure being that of rendering services in the way of agricultural labor or supplies. This tenure, even in those early times, was already distinguished from tenure at certain rent. For there is a subsequent law, "If a man agree for a yard of land or more (*i. e.*, for a free tenancy of it, at a rent, as distinguished from the servile tenancy of the ceorls) at a fixed rent, and plough it, if the lord desire to raise the land (*i. e.*, the rent) to him, to service and rent, he (*i. e.*, the tenant) need not take it upon him, if the lord do not give him a dwelling, and let him lose his crop," that is, let the landlord lose it, unless he gives the dwelling as an equivalent for the increase of rent. So Lambard reads it. It is still a principle of our law that if the landlord determine a tenancy at will, after the tenant has sown the land, the tenant shall have the crops, which is called the right of emblements. So much for the tenant's right. Then there are other provisions as to landlord right. "He who has so many as twenty hides, shall leave twelve hides of cultivated land when he wishes to go away; he who has ten hides, shall leave six hides of cultivated land; he who has three hides, shall leave one and a half" (*Ina*, 14, 15). These laws could not refer to the villeins, who could not "go away:" they must have referred to free tenants at certain rents. And the "ceorls," who were not slaves, though feudal serfs, could acquire property, and could lease other land than that they held in villenage, as they could have cattle, etc. "The ceorl who has hired another's yoke, if he have to pay wholly in fodder, let him do so; if he have not, let him pay half in fodder and half in other goods" (*Ina*, 60). Whence it appears that payments were in kind, and probably the rent was so paid. The ceorls evidently belonged to manors, and held pasture land of the manor in common, as copyholders do still. "If ceorls have a common meadow, or other partible land to fence, and some have fenced their part, some have not, and cattle come in, and eat up their common corn or grass, let those who own the gap compensate the others who have fenced their part, the damage which then may be done; and let them demand such justice on the cattle as may be right: but if there be a beast which breaks hedges, and goes in everywhere, and he who owns it will not, or cannot restrain, let him who finds it in his field take it and slay it, and let the owner take its skin and flesh, and forfeit all the rest" (i. 42). The point to be observed here, is the recognition and careful protection of the property of "ceorls" or villeins. So, from another of the laws of Ina, "A ceorl's close ought to be fenced: if it be unfenced, and his neighbor's cattle stray in through his own gap, he shall have nothing from the cattle; let him drive them out and bear the damage" (s. 4),—which is good law at this day, and has lately been applied in one of our courts of common law (*Singleton* v. *Williams*, 6 H. & N.). It will be observed that the laws of Ina contain the germs or elements of a great deal of good law, no doubt derived from the Roman; and which have been developed in later times, relating to the dealings and transactions of men in the affairs of life. Thus, for instance, in one of the laws of Ina we

The first of the Saxon laws, now in being, are those of King Ethelbert. These are the most ancient laws in our realm, and are said to be the most ancient in modern Europe. This king reigned from 561

Saxon Laws.

find this, "If a man buy any kind of cattle, and he then discovers any unsoundness in it within thirty days, then let him throw the cattle on his hands, or let him (the other) swear that he knew not of any unsoundness in it when he sold it to him." This law, it will be observed, made provision for a case not provided for by the contract, and it contains a principle which has been adhered to and developed in later times. (See *Burnby* v. *Bollett*, 16 M. & W.) These portions of law, indeed, were few and fragmentary, and contrast with the rudeness and barbarity of the usages by which they are accompanied; still they show the seeds and germs of something like law. And it is very remarkable that the laws next in order of time are those of Alfred, who, like Ina, was only king of the West Saxons, and are greatly inferior to his. Though he had the benefit of Ina's laws, and says he selected from his and others, the only really good laws of Ina's are omitted, and there is nothing in those laws of Alfred's beyond the barbarous usages of the Saxons, except one or two laws already alluded to, and the following "of tearing by a dog:" "If a dog tear or bite a man, for the first misdeed let six shillings be paid, if the owner gives him food; for the second time, ten shillings; for the third, thirty shillings. If, after any of these misdeeds, the dog escape, let the penalty nevertheless be paid. If the dog do more misdeeds, and the owner keep him, let him make amends according to the full sum for wounds" (*Alfred*, 24). The treaty of peace between Alfred and Guthrum applies the practice of compurgation to cases of homicide. The laws of Edward the Elder, the next in chronological order, are thought stricter, far superior, and contain the first germs and elements of civil or criminal procedure. As to civil suits, the sheriffs are to hold courts once a month (*Ed.*, 11), and do justice, and give a term to every suit (*Ed.*, 1, s. 11); and if any one denied justice to another as to land, he should give him a "term" where he should do justice before the sheriff, or pay a penalty (*Ed.*, 2). As to criminal suits, if any one was accused of theft, and no one would be compurgator for him, then he must stand to judgment (6); and men who were not "oath-worthy" or credible, were to undergo the ordeal; but, as much as possible, transactions were to be before witnesses who might afterwards testify as jurors (1). If the accused could bring forward sworn witnesses, or the oaths of credible persons in the county as compurgators, he could do so (1); otherwise, six of the men of the neighborhood where he was resident. The witnesses were sworn, and were really jurors; for jurors originally gave their verdicts of their own knowledge; the difference between the jurors and the compurgators being, that the latter swore from their knowledge of the character of the accused, and the other from their knowledge of the matter. This verdict or true testimony of sworn witnesses, men of the county, was called "shire-oath" in the Saxon laws, and they were called jurors in other contemporary laws. Thus, in the capitulary for 593, "Si litus de quo inculpatur, ad sortem ambulaverit mala sorte priserit, medietatem ingenui legem componat, et *juratores* sex medios electos dare debet" — a phrase borrowed from the Roman law, in which the magistrate was sued "judices dare," *i. e.*, "judices facti," or jurors (*vide* Introduction). The most important parts of the laws of Athelstan, the first which were framed for the whole population and dominion, relate to this subject of procedure. Thus the shire-oath is mentioned, "He who seizes cattle, let five of his neighbors be named to him, and of the five let him get one who will swear with him that he took them rightfully; and

to 636. The next are the laws of Hlothaire and Eadric, and of Wihtred, all kings of Kent. Next are those of he who will keep it to himself — *i. e.*, the claimant — let ten more be named to him, and let him get two of them to give the oath that it was born on his property" (*Athel.*, 1, 9). Then there is a provision that transactions take place in the presence of witnesses who might afterwards testify that, as jurors (10); and there are provisions for the ordeal in cases where such testimony of jurors cannot be got, nor sufficient compurgators (*Athel.*, 7). So of the laws of Edgar — (those of Edmund have nothing worth noting) — the most important provisions are those on this subject; that he who denied the doom of the hundred, and it was afterwards proved against him, should pay the penalty (*Edgar*, 3); that no one should possess unknown cattle without the testimonies of the men of the hundred (4); that the hundred court be held as before fixed, once a month, and the county court twice a year (ii. 5); that witnesses be appointed in every borough and hundred in every hundred twelve (*Supp.*, 5); and that all the transactions be before some of the witnesses, who were first to be sworn to give true testimony of all they did know, and whose testimony afterwards was to be sought in any civil or criminal matters (*Ibid.*, v. 10). So, in the laws of Ethelred, there are provisions as to witnesses (i. 3; iii. 2), and at hundred courts the twelve sworn freeholders were to take oath not to present any one untruly (*Ibid.*, 3). The laws of Ethelred, though extremely voluminous, contain nothing original, and are, for the most part, religious precepts or ordinances. As already mentioned, the laws of Canute were the first which were formed for the whole kingdom; and they are the first after those of Ina that deserve the name of a compilation of anything like laws. They are divided into ecclesiastical and secular. The first confirm all former laws as to payment of tithes, church scot, and Rome fee, or Peter's pence, and the observance of Sundays and festivals. There is a distinct ordinance against Sunday marketings and folcmote, unless it be for great necessity: "and let huntings and all other worldly works be strictly abstained from on that holy day" (*Ecc. Laws, Can.*, 15). The secular laws, ordained to be observed over all England, commence by laying down a noble principle: "Let God's justice be exalted; and henceforth let every man, both poor and rich, be esteemed worthy of folc-right, and let just doom be doomed to him" (1). And that Christian men be not for too little be condemned to death (2), nor sold out of the land (3), nor that thieves and public robbers perish unless they amend (4). Heathenism was prohibited (5). All manslayers were to pay the penalty, or be outlawed (6). One money was to pass over all the nation, without any counterfeit, and no man was to refuse it; and if any counterfeited, he was to have his hands cut off (8). And all weights and measures were to be carefully rectified, and every species of fraud was prohibited (9). Local customs were preserved (12, 14, 15); but the general laws laid down applied equally to all; and whoever was outlawed forfeited his land (16). No one was to apply to the king's court unless he could not get justice in the hundred (17). And twice a year there was to be a county court for the administration of justice (18). No man was to take a distress before he had four times demanded justice — thrice at the hundred court, and once at the county court (19). Every freeman was to be brought into a hundred and tithing (20). Every freeman who was not infamous, and had never failed in oath or ordeal, could clear himself with a single oath; others had to find compurgators, or go to the ordeal (22). No man was to buy without the witness of four men, either of the borough or the hundred (24). And every lord, *i. e.*, of a manor, was to have his household in his own "borh," or borough, *i. e.*, his own court-baron the court of his manor; but if any one accused one of his men of anything, he was to answer in the

Ina, king of the West Saxons. After the Heptarchy we have the laws of Alfred, Edward the Elder, Athelstan, Edmund, Edgar, Ethelred, and Canute. Besides these there are canons and constitutions, decrees of councils, and other acts of a public nature (*a*). These are in the

hundred court (21); the courts-baron only having jurisdiction over the tenants of the manor, and in matters arising between the tenants themselves. Housebreaking, and arson, and theft, and murder, were, by the secular law, declared not subjects of compensation — that is, they were liable to the penalties of the king's criminal justice (60). The civil offence of forcible ouster, was to be punished by restitution and compensation, and a fine to the king (64). If any one died intestate, the lord was only to have a heriot ; and let the property be distributed among wife, and children, and relations, to every one according to the degree that belongs to him (71). And where the husband dwelt without claim or contest, let the wife and children dwell in the same, unassailed by litigation. And if the husband, before he was dead, had been cited, then let the heirs answer, as himself should have done if he had lived (73). And he who has defended land (*i. e.*, against all claims) with the witness of the shire, let him have it undisputed during his day, and after his day to sell, and to give to him who is dearest to him : a law in which we see the origin of fines and recoveries — that is, alienations or acquisitions of land by proceedings in a real or feigned suit in a court. It will be seen that these laws are far superior to any that went before, and really deserve the name of a compilation of laws. And it is a remarkable instance of national prejudice that Alfred, who framed no laws worthy of the name, and even overlooked and neglected many which are valuable, and Edward the Confessor, who framed no laws, nor made any compilation of laws at all, should, by reason of false tradition, arising from national feeling, have had the reputation of legislators, while Canute, who really deserved the credit of wise and careful legislation, yet, being a Dane, has had no credit for it.

(*a*) This is the proper place in which to present a summary of the ecclesiastical laws or institutions of the Saxons, whether gathered from their municipal laws or their ecclesiastical canons or constitutions. As already mentioned, the earliest Saxon laws make mention of an episcopal church as already existing and established, and guarantee its property (*Ethelb.*, 1). There were laws of the Saxons relating to ecclesiastical matters, contained both in the secular and ecclesiastical laws enacted by the kings in their councils, and there were also ecclesiastical canons and constitutions put forth by the prelates, under the sanction of the state, but with only spiritual penalties. The latter are alone alluded to here, but as the author has omitted all notice of the laws of the Saxons relating to ecclesiastical matters, it is necessary here to present an analysis of them. It has already been mentioned that, by the Saxon political constitution, the bishops had seats in the national council, and all the laws are prefaced by a formal declaration of their consent (*Laws of Ina*). "With the counsel and teaching of the bishops and ealdermen and distinguished 'witan'" (*A.-S. Laws ; Laws of Alfred*). "Many synods assembled among the English race after they had received the faith of holy bishops and other exalted 'witan' (wise men), and they then in many synod-books wrote dooms (or law); And I, Alfred, gathered them together, and, by counsel of my 'witan,' commanded those to be written which seemed to me good" (*Ibid.*, 19). Laws of Athelstan: "I, with the counsel of the archbishop, and of my other bishops," etc.. (*Ibid.*, 193). All this was established in the great synod, at which the archbishop, with all the noblemen and "witan," etc. (*Ibid.*, 215). So the secular laws of Edmund: "I,

19*

Saxon language, and were some of them collected, in one volume in folio, by Mr. Lambard, in the time of Queen with the counsel of my 'witan,' both ecclesiastical and secular" (*Ibid.*, 247). So Edgar: "With the counsel of my 'witan'" (*Ibid.*, 263). So Ethelred: "The ordinances that the king and the ecclesiastical and lay 'witan' have done" (*Ibid.*, 305). So much for the authority of the secular laws of the Saxons, and the union of ecclesiastical and lay elements in their constitution. Next, as to the matter and substance of their secular or municipal laws, so far as they relate to spiritual or ecclesiastical things. The laws of Ina began by upholding the rule of the bishops: "First, we command that all God's servants hold their lawful rule" (1). Next, baptism was enforced with a penalty: "Let a child within three days be baptized," etc. (2). Sunday working was prohibited (3). Church scots were ordained to be paid (4). The right of church sanctuary was established (5). The laws of Alfred first upheld episcopal jurisdiction: "If one pledge himself to what is lawful, and belie himself, let him suffer what the bishop may prescribe" (1). The right of sanctuary was also upheld (2). So, as to confession, "If any man seek a cloak for any of those offences which had not been before revealed, and then confess himself, in God's name be it half forgiven (5). The abduction of a nun was made penal (8). Fighting before a bishop was made penal (15). Pledges by baptismal vows were enforced (33). Days were given as holy days for the celebration of masses (43). If a priest killed a man, all his goods were to be forfeited, and let the bishop secularize him; then let him be given up, unless the lord will compound for him (21). So the laws of Alfred and Guthrum declare that they established secular laws for these reasons, that they knew that else many men would not submit to the spiritual laws, and hence they established civil penalties, when men would not submit to the spiritual law by correction of the bishops (*A.-S. Laws*, p. 163). So church sanctuary was ordained, and any one who violated Christianity or reverenced heathenism by word or work, let him pay penalties (2). If a man in orders steal or fight, etc., let him pay penalty; and, above all, make amends before God, as the canon teaches, or yield to prison. If a masspriest misdirect the people about a festival or a fast, let him pay a penalty. If a priest refuse baptism to him who has need thereof, let him pay a penalty (3). If a man in orders foredo himself with capital crimes, let him be seized and held to the bishop's doom (4). To this it may be added that, in the *Mirror of Justice*, it is stated that Alfred hanged a judge because he judged a clerk to death over whom he had no cognizance (c. v., s. 1). And if a man guilty of death desire confession, let it never be denied him (5). If any one withhold tithes, let him pay a penalty. If any one withhold Rome's fee (*i. e.*, Peter's pence), let him pay a penalty. So if any one does not discharge church scot, or deny divine dues (6). If any one engage in Sunday marketing, let him forfeit the chattel and pay a penalty. If a freeman work on a festival, let him forfeit his freedom or pay a penalty (7). If a freeman break a lawful fast, let him pay; if a theow (slave) do so, let him suffer in his hide (*i. e.*, be flogged). The laws of Athelstan begin by enforcing tithes (*A.-S. Laws*, v. i., 145). So the laws of Edmund, which were civil and ecclesiastical, and in the ecclesiastical laws enforced the canons as to celibacy and the payment of tithes, church scot, and "Rome fee" (p. 246), in the secular laws uphold the right of church sanctuary (249). So the ecclesiastical laws of Edgar enforce tithes, church scots, and the "hearth-penny" or St. Peter's pence (p. 265), and also festivals and fasts (*Ibid.*). So the secular laws of Ethelred uphold the rights of the church. Let no man reduce a church to servitude, nor unlawfully make church-mongering, nor turn out a church minister, without the bishop's counsel (*A.-S. Laws*, p. 317). Let God's

Elizabeth, and published under the title of Ἀρχαιονομία; *sive, de priscis Anglorum legibus.* To this additions have since been made by Dr. Wilkins. These remains compose, all together, a body of Anglo-Saxon laws for civil and ecclesiastical government.

We have refrained from mentioning some laws which have gone under the name of Edward the Confessor, as they have been rejected for spurious,[1] upon the fullest consideration of antiquarians (*a*). They are in Latin, and

---

dues be paid — that is, plough alms and tithes, and "Rome fee," and church scot (308). Let Sunday festivals be rightly kept, and let marketings and folcmotes be carefully abstained from (13). And let all St. Mary's feast-tides be strictly honored (14), and all other festivals and fasts (15). And the witan have chosen that St. Edward's mass-day shall be celebrated all over England (16). And if any excommunicated man (unless a suppliant) dwell anywhere in the king's proximity before he has earnestly submitted to divine correction, let it be at the peril of himself and all his property (p. 313). The ecclesiastical laws of Canute ordained that if a priest was charged with a crime, he should clear himself in the "housel," or with the "corsned" (*vide ante*, p. 203); and if a priest was found in false witness or theft, etc., let him be cast out of the community of ecclesiastics, unless he made amends, as the bishop might direct (*A.-S. Laws*, v. i., p. 365). And tithes and church scot and "Rome fee" were to be paid (367). And Sundays were to be observed, and festivals, and fasts (376). And, by the secular law, if a servant of the altar be a homicide, or work iniquity, let him forfeit both degree and country, and go in exile, as the pope shall prescribe to him, and do penance (*Ibid.*, 401). If a man in holy orders defile himself with crime worthy of death, let him be seized and held to the bishop's doom, according as the case may be (*Ibid.*, 402). If any one with violence refuse divine dues, let him pay penalty (405). So also the laws of the Confessor contained similar provisions (443), of which the chief have been given.

(*a*) This is a mistake, unless all that the author meant was that this collection of laws was not actually made by or under the Confessor; and that it by no means contained the whole of the laws in force in his time; and, indeed, as he cites this collection himself, this is probably his real meaning, which is hardly expressed correctly by the word "spurious." The collection, upon the face of it (as already has been seen), purports to have been made in the fourth year of the Conqueror (*vide ante*, p. 214), and would hardly be less authentic on that account. But there is no doubt that it was extremely imperfect, and indeed omitted the most important portions of the laws in existence under the Confessor, because those laws were for the most part *customary*, and *unwritten*, and there would be great difficulty in collecting and embodying unwritten customs. That this was the real reason of the imperfect character of this collection, has been already shown, and will be seen from a subsequent collection of the laws of the Conqueror, in which he embodies many of the customary laws in force under the Confessor. "Istæ sunt leges et *consuetudines* quas Willielmus rex, post adquisicionem Angliæ, omni populo Anglorum concessit tenendas; æadem quas *predecessor suus Edwardus*, servavit." These laws were conceded in consequence of the clamor of the people for the customs of the Confessor, and in the meantime those customs had been better ascertained. Thus, therefore, it is rather in

[1] Spelman *voce* Ballivus.

bear evident internal marks of a later period. They are supposed to have been written, or collected, about the end of the reign of William Rufus; and are to be found in the collections of Lambard and Wilkins.

---

the laws of the Conqueror, than in this collection of the laws of the Confessor, that the most important portions of the law in force under the Confessor are to be found; those portions having previously been *unwritten* (*vide ante*, p. 215). And this is only an illustration of an observation which has already been made more than once, that the most important portions of the law in existence under the Saxons were customary and unwritten, and embodied in usages and institutions, in existence at the time of the invasion, and undoubtedly of Roman origin. The Conqueror in his laws preserved all the customs and institutions previously existing (save so far as consistent with any of his own newly-enacted laws), and this was very much what the Saxons had done before.

CHAPTER II.

WILLIAM THE CONQUEROR TO HENRY II. (a)

THE CONQUEST—SAXON LAWS CONFIRMED—THE LAWS OF WILLIAM THE CONQUEROR—TRIAL BY DUEL IN CRIMINAL QUESTIONS—ESTABLISHMENT OF TENURES—NATURE OF TENURES—DIFFERENT KINDS OF TENURES—VILLENAGE—OF ESCUAGE—CONSEQUENCES OF TENURE—OF PRIMOGENITURE—OF ALIENATION—OF JUDICATURE—THE CURIA REGIS—JUSTICES ITINERANT—THE BENCH—THE CHANCERY—JUDICATURE OF THE COUNCIL—OF THE SPIRITUAL COURT—OF THE CIVIL AND CANON LAW—DOCTRINES OF THE CANON LAW—PROBATE OF WILLS—CONSTITUTIONS OF CLARENDON—OF TRIAL BY DUEL IN CIVIL QUESTIONS—OF TRIAL BY JURY—BY THE ASSIZE—OF DEEDS—A FEOFFMENT—A FINE—OF WRITS—OF RECORDS.

THE accession of William of Normandy to the English throne makes a memorable epoch in the history of our municipal law. Some Saxon customs may be traced by the observing antiquary, even in our present body of law; but in the establishment made in this country by the Normans, are to be seen, as in their infancy, the very form and features of the English law (b). It is to the Conquest

---

(a) The author heads this and the next two chapters alike—"William the Conqueror to John;" thus treating the whole period as one, and mixing up the events of it without distinguishing the important era in the history of our law which is marked by the reign of Henry II. The second of these two chapters, however, is entirely devoted to the law as it was in the reign of Henry II., and therefore it appeared better to so entitle the chapter of that reign, and to entitle the present, William I. to Henry II.

(b) This and what follows must be taken with great qualification, and is true only to a limited extent; for, as already has been shown in the Introduction, it would be far more true to state, as Lord Hale does, that "in the establishment made in this country by Edward I. are to be seen, as at their infancy, the very form and features of English law." And this, indeed, at a future page the author himself will be found to indicate. The Conquest, by itself, effected far less direct alteration in our laws and institutions than the author appeared to suppose, and the change was infinitely more gradual and progressive than he here represents. The Normans brought the trial by battle and the feudal system; and this was all that was distinctive in their system. All the rest—all that has remained to us—was of Roman origin. Although it may have been developed in the Norman period, it was not characteristically Norman, and would have been, no doubt, in due time developed by any nation as it attained civilization, and advanced in intelligence. The laws of the Conqueror and his successors preserved the

and to the consequences of that revolution that the juridical historian is to direct his particular attention. A

laws and *customs* of the Saxons, save so far as inconsistent with any laws and institutions which he introduced. The principal change he introduced was a development of the feudal system, which was military in its character, and therefore did not interfere with civil institutions, and not necessarily with civil rights, except within the limits of its own operation. The customary rights of the agricultural tenants, who formed the main body of the people, were confirmed. There is a remarkable passage in Bracton which very well explains what occurred at the Conquest, and is the account given in the *Mirror*, which says, that at the Conquest many freeholders were forced to hold their lands in villenage; which implies that it was not a universal revolution:—" Fuerunt etiam in conquestu liberi homines qui liberè tenuerunt tenementa suaper libera servitia vel per liberas consuetudinas, et cum per potentiores ejecti essent, postmodum reversi receperunt eadam tenementa sua tenenda in villenagio, faciendo inde opera servilia: sed certa et nominata: et nihilominus liberi quia licet faciat opera servilia cum non faciunt ea ratione personarum sed ratione tenementorum" (*Bracton*, lib. 1, c. 11, fol. 7). That is, they were not villeins, though they held their land in villenage, subject to the invaders who had ejected them. It is manifest that this was not a universal, or legal, or political change, but the result of individual acts of spoliation, and probably only against the tenants of those who had forfeited their lands in war. And there is a remarkable passage in the *Mirror*, which affords an apt commentary upon the above, and a striking illustration of what occurred at the Norman, and probably at the Saxon conquest. It says that the first conquerors (and, as the work was originally written in the Saxon times, this no doubt *included* the Saxons, though, of course, it also applied to the Normans) "enfeoffed the earls, barons, knights, and villeins, some to hold by tenure for the defence of the realm, and some without obligation of service, and some to hold by villein customs, as to plough the lord's lands, to reap, cut, and carry his corn or hay. And it is said villeins are tillers of land, and of villeins, there are tillages called villenages, and that villeins became freemen if their lords granted or *gave* to them any free estate of inheritance to descend to their heirs, or if the lord *took homage from them.*" So that the land might be made freehold *without deed.* And then it is said, "And although the people have no charters, deeds, or muniments of their lands (*i. e.*, they who *so* held), nevertheless, if they are put out of their possessions wrongfully, they might be restored to their estates as before, because they could show that they knew the *certainty* of their *services and works by the year,* as those whose *ancestors* before them were astraeis (*i. e.*, serfs), for a long time" (*Ib.*). From which it plainly appears that some villeins became, by custom or implied grant, tenants in socage, or by certain plough-service, which was a freehold tenure, and so made them freemen; for it was a maxim in law that freeholders must be freemen; and, therefore, to have a freehold was to be free. This power of custom must have been of inconceivable value and importance to the great body of the people, who were thus becoming gradually emancipated, and raised from slavery to villenage or serfdom, from villenage or serfdom to freedom; and this may explain the attachment of the people to what they called the "customs of the Confessor," *i. e.*, the customs known and remembered as of his time, by the generation of men living at and after the time of the Conquest. And it is remarkable, that in the *Mirror,* immediately after the passage just quoted, follows this: " And *thereupon* (*i. e.*, upon the customary enfranchisement of villeins by their lands becoming freehold) St. Edward, in his time, caused inquiry to be made of all such who held, and did to him

new order of things then commenced. The nature of landed property was entirely changed ; the rules by which

such *services as ploughing his land,* besides their lawful customs," — *i. e.,* those who became emancipated through holding any of their land by *certain* socage or plough-service, which made it freehold, and so made them free, irrespective of other services. And it is added, "that many of them were wrongfully forced to do other services, to bring them into servitude again" (*Ib.*), which, no doubt, was after the Conquest, and caused that great cry among the people for the restoration of the customs of the Confessor — *i. e.*, of the Confessor's time. These *customs and tenures were expressly confirmed by the Conqueror.* No sudden or sweeping change in our institutions was effected, and all the municipal institutions, as well as the manorial, were maintained. So the tenure of land, except so far as regarded those who held under military tenure — that is, by knight-service, which applied only to the nobles and knights — the common freehold tenures, also the tenure in villenage, were left unaffected. The charter of the Conqueror, indeed, imposed an oath of allegiance upon all freemen; but allegiance implies protection, and the charter went on to guarantee their possessions; and though it also imposed, as a condition, readiness for military service for the defence of the realm, there is nothing to carry it further than that obligation, which already existed, and is indicated in the laws of Canute as to military reliefs (*vide ante*). The Conqueror expressly confirmed the customs of the country as to the rural tenantry, villeins, or freemen. No doubt, as Lord Hale says, the Conqueror, like all previous conquerors, took into his hands all the demesne lands of the crown (*Hist. Eng. Law*, p. 97), and no doubt, also, he seized the lands of all who had been in battle or rose in rebellion against him (*Ib.*, 97), and in regranting these lands, imposed military service as the condition of tenure. But that great authority cites Spelman, and an ancient record which he quotes, and maintains that all others were allowed to retain their lands upon the ancient tenure (98); and he cites the great case of the recovery of a large number of manors, after the Conquest, according to the ancient laws and customs of England, the record of which is set out at length by Lord Coke in his Reports, and also by Spelman, in his *Life of Eadmerus* (*Hist. Com. Law*, 98). Lord Hale shows that it was only partially the possession or the tenure of land was altered, and so as to the rule of descent; it was, he says, altered "little by little," an expression which accurately expresses the historic truth. Thus, then, the changes in the tenure of land were, in the words of Hale, introduced not at once, but by "little and little," and were not general, but, for a time, only partial and gradual. And this was the real character of all the changes introduced at the time of the Conquest, and so it has been on all similar occasions in our history ; and therefore the statements which follow can only be taken as true, subject to this important qualification. The changes that were effected, indeed, were rather by judicial than legislative authority, and were mainly the result of alterations in the system of judicature. But the statement that a new system of judicature was created, for example, is not correct, and is calculated to mislead ; for, as already pointed out in the Introduction, nothing is so remarkable in our legal history at this era as the absence of any apparent change in our legal system, and the skill with which it was modified without being changed: which will be seen in the history of this and the next reigns.

It is to be observed, with regard to the estates of the church, it is clear that their tenures were not altered; for Glanville, who was chief justiciary under Henry II., distinctly states in his celebrated *Treatise* that the baronies of the bishoprics "are held in frankalmogne" (lib. vii., c. 1). Littleton quite confirms this, and Lord Hale, as already has been seen, strongly con-

personal property was directed, were modified; a new system of judicature was erected; new modes of redress contests the notion that there had been any general alteration in the tenure of the land of the kingdom at the Conquest. If, therefore, Blackstone stated "that the Conqueror thought fit to change the spiritual tenure of frankalmogne, under which the bishops had their lands during the Saxon government, into the feudal tenure by barony" (2 *Bla. Comm.*, 156), all that is important is his distinct admission that the tenure was so *before* the Conquest; the testimony of Glanville, of Bracton, of Littleton, and of Hale is overwhelming to show that the tenure had not been legally changed. The changes produced in the laws after the Conquest being the result rather of judicial than legislative changes, it would have been better to have first given some account of those improvements in the judicature which led to these results. Instead of this, however, the author has given, without any authority, a theory of sudden change, including the sudden institution of a *curia regis*, to which he seems to ascribe great importance; whereas, the ordinary justice of the country, court and criminal, being local, and remaining so for a long time, it was in the local judicature the most important changes took place, and those very gradually and by degrees. Towards the end of the chapter the author gives some account of a change instituted in the proceedings of the county court, which led to a result not less important than the establishment of trial by jury in all cases; but he failed to notice the not less important fact that it was before the king's justiciary the court was held, and that *he* directed the jury to be sworn, and thus effected this important change. That was one instance of the important changes effected, not by legislation, but by judicial decision, and therefore gradually and by degrees. And in the order of time and events these changes in the judicature which produced these results, and then those changes which they produced, should have been recorded. Moreover, these changes for the most part did not take place in the reign of the Conqueror, nor of his successor; and though the beginnings of some of them took place in this reign, they were for the most part commenced in the reign of Henry I., and carried out in that of Henry II. Both of these reigns constitute eras or epochs in our legal history far more important than that of the conqueror, whose conquest was rather a political than a legal event, and made no sudden or immediate general change in the laws or institutions of the country; and though the Conquest led to these changes, it was indirectly and almost accidentally, and chiefly by the gradual development of legal principles in judicial decisions. It was not, therefore, the *direct* effect of the Conquest so much as its indirect and accidental consequences which produced these changes, and thus it is they were so gradual and progressive. This would have been seen more clearly had the author separated the reigns of the Conqueror and his successor from those of Henry I. and Henry II. The course of progression would then have been displayed, which it is the great object of legal history to exhibit. Instead, however, of that course, he has treated those three important reigns all together, and has thus produced great confusion, lost the chronological order of events, and missed the progression they illustrate. For example, he does not deal distinctly and separately with the reign of Henry I., and that elaborate body of laws of his reign, of which we have a most valuable collection, which is noticed and cited by Lord Hale, and is once or twice cited by our author, but of which he offers no account. Yet it is most important, as the middle stage between the state of our laws and institutions at the time of the Conquest and for some time after it, and that period of development which they had reached in the reign of Henry II., under the auspices of Glanville.

It is not easy to supply in notes deficiencies so extensive, still less easy is

ceived; new forms of proceeding were devised; the rank and condition of individuals became entirely new; the whole constitution was altered; and after fluctuating on a singular policy, pregnant with the most opposite consequences of freedom and slavery, by degrees settled into peace and orderly government. In short, a state of things then took place, from which, after innumerable alterations, arose the present frame of English jurisprudence.

It has long been a debated question, in what manner William was the *conqueror* of this island; nor has the discussion been confined to historians and antiquaries: the adherents of modern parties did, at one time, warmly interest themselves in the decision of a point, which they considered as involving consequences very material to the political opinions they avowed. The lovers of high monarchical authority thought they derived a very ancient and rightful title to all kinds of prerogative in the king, by maintaining that William made the people of this country submit, as a conquered nation, to his absolute will. The friends of liberty, admitting as it should seem, in some measure, the consequences of such a claim, contended as firmly that William never assumed such powers, and was in truth no conqueror. Attempts have been made to explain the term *conquest* in such a manner as to get rid of any unfavorable conclusions from the word. It is said to have been a conquest over Harold, and not over the kingdom; that conquest signifies *acquest*, or new acquired feudal rights;[1] with other explications of the like design and import; so important a matter was it esteemed to ascertain the true nature of this event in our history; as if the tyranny of a prince who lived seven hundred years ago, could be a precedent for the oppres-

---

it to supply the lack of proper order and arrangement. All that can be done is to introduce, wherever an occasion occurs, any omitted matter which tends to supply these deficiencies, and fill up the gaps and missing steps in the course of the legal history. In order, also, to draw some distinction between the reigns, and especially to mark the important era of the reign of Henry II., the titles of this and the two following chapters have been altered. The author had entitled them all "William the Conqueror to John;" but as the most important portions of the first relate to the reign of Henry II., and the other two entirely so, it has been thought better to entitle the first "William I. to Henry II.," and the other two, "Henry II." and "Henry II. to John."

[1] In the law of Scotland, at this day, *feuda nova*, or, as we call it, lands taken by purchase, are termed *feus of* CONQUEST.—*Ersk. Prin.*, b. 3, tit. 8, s. 6.

sions of his successors; or any length of time could establish a prescription against the inalienable rights of mankind. The present prevailing notions of free government are founded on better grounds than the examples of former ages, when our constitution was agitated by many irregular and violent movements; they are founded on a rational consideration of the ends of all government, the good of the whole community. To leave such useless disquisitions, let it suffice to relate the fact: that William put off the character of an invader as soon as he conveniently could; and took all measures to quiet the kingdom in the enjoyment of its own laws, and a due administration of justice.

We are told, that in the fourth year of his reign, at Berkhamstead, in the presence of Lanfranc, Archbishop of Canterbury, he solemnly swore that he would observe the good and approved ancient laws of the kingdom, particularly those of Edward the Confessor; and he ordered that twelve Saxons in each county should make inquiry, and certify what those laws were (*a*).

Saxon laws confirmed.

When the result of this inquiry was laid before William, and he had set himself to consider the different laws of the kingdom more particularly; he showed a disposition to give a preference to the Danish, as more conformable with those of Normandy; being sprung from the same root, and better suited to the genius of his own subjects. This alarmed the English, who wished to have no

---

(*a*) What took place is thus described in the preamble to the collection of laws which was the result of the inquiry, "Post quartum annum adquisicionis regis Willielmi istius terræ, consilio baronum suorum fecit summonire peruniversos patriæ comitatus, Anglos nobiles sapientes et in lege sua eruditos, ut eorum consuetudines ab ipsis audiret. Electis igitur de singulis totius patriæ comitatibus xii jurejurando, imprimis sanxerunt ut quoad possent, recto tramite incidentes legum suarum ac consuetudinum sancita edicerent, nil pretermittentes, nil addentes, nil prevaricando mutantes." It is impossible to imagine anything more authentic, and yet the author elsewhere terms the collection "spurious," by which, however, probably he meant no more than that the laws were not enacted in this form under the Confessor, which, no doubt, is the case, for they purport, on the face of them, to be a collection of *laws and customs;* still, there is a suspicious omission of matters important to the people. The first ten articles relate to the rights of the church, and the chief of these have already been noticed. The franchises of the nobility are mentioned, and the courts of the county and hundred. This is all that need be mentioned. The laws of the Conqueror himself were far more important.

more of that law imposed, than what had been incorporated into their customs by Edward the Confessor. They beseeched him not to recede from his solemn engagement; and conjured him by the soul of Edward, who had bequeathed him his present sovereignty, to confirm the English in possession of their laws, as they stood at the death of the Confessor. To this William at length consented, and, in a general council,[1] solemnly ordained (*a*), that the laws of Edward, with such alterations and additions as he himself had made to them, should in all things be observed.

In this manner was the system of Saxon jurisprudence confirmed as the law of the country; and from thenceforth it continued the basis of the common law, upon which every subsequent alteration was to operate.

Though these alterations soon grew very considerable, yet the direct and open change by positive laws was not great. The laws of William are in *pari materiâ* with those that remain of the Saxon kings, except such as introduced the feudal constitution, and the trial by duel. But a revolution was effected through other means, and that by

---

(*a*) These really did contain important guarantees. It has been seen that there was no alteration as to the tenure of land, save so far as military tenure was already obligatory, or might be made so by actual grant of land on such tenure, or so far as all tenures were conditional upon allegiance and the defence of the realm. Then the laws of the Conqueror commenced thus, "Istæ sunt leges et consuetudinus quas Willielmus rex, post adquisicionem Angliæ omni populo Anglorum concessit tenendas, eidem quas predecessor suus servavit." And among them was expressly mentioned the customary rights (1) of the agricultural tenantry holding tenure or villenage, who formed the great body of the people, "Coloni et terrarum exercitores *non rexentur ultra debitum et statutum, nec licet dominis remorere colonos a terris, dummodo debita servicia persolorant*" (*A.-S. Laws*, 431, c. 1; *Laws of W. Conq.*, c. 29). So the (2) burdens imposed by way of relief were defined, not only as to the knights, and barons, and landholders, but as to the villeins, or leaseholders. "Relevium villani melius averium," "qui terram ad censum annum tenet sit ejus relevium quantum unius anni census" (*Ib.*, 477). The jurisdiction of the (3) county and hundred courts was upheld, "Nemo querelam ad regem deferat, nisi ei jus defecerit in hundredo vel in comitatu" (*Ib.*, 485). Oppressive (4) distresses to enforce legal claims were repressed, "Nullus naminm capiat nisi recto in hundredo vel comitatu tertii postulaverit" (c. 44). The rights (5) of relations to the effects of an intestate was admitted, "Si quis pater familias casu aliquo sine testamento obierit pueri inter se hæreditatem paternam æqualiter dividant" (c. 34). Criminal procedure, according to the Saxon (6) law, was simplified and improved: if a freeman was accused of theft, he might, if a good character, purge himself by his own oath; otherwise, by that of twelve compurgators: and capital punishment was confined to the graver cases.

[1] Leg. Conq., 63.

slow and imperceptible degrees. The Normans brought over with them a disposition to favor the institutions to which they had been used in their own country; and the comparative state of the two people enabled them to succeed in the attempt. Having, from their continental situation, had greater opportunities of improving their polity and manners, they had very far surpassed the Saxons in knowledge and refinement. This was discoverable in their laws, which were conceived and explained with some degree of artificial reasoning. Though this jurisprudence was simple compared with what it grew to in after times, it was conceived on principles susceptible of the inferences and consequences afterwards really deduced from it.

The doctrine of tenures being once established by an express law, all the foreign learning concerning them of course followed (*a*). The other parts also of the Norman jurisprudence, their rules of property and methods of proceeding, soon began to prevail; they were referred to and debated upon as the native custom of this realm, or very fit to be ingrafted into it; and, being once introduced and discussed in the king's courts, which were framed upon the Norman plan, and presided over by Norman lawyers, they gradually became a part of the common law of England.

The revolution effected by these means was very important indeed. Besides tenures, with all their incidents and properties, the *aula*, or *curia regis*, was established (*b*),

---

(*a*) It is presumed the author means military tenures, *sed vide ante*. This and the other modes of tenure existed in this country before the Conquest, as will have been seen from the Saxon laws. The whole of these passages are illustrations of the substitution of theories in place of historical verities. The theory of the author was, that the English law was moulded on the Norman; and he deduced his theory from what seemed to him, no doubt, a strong probability. But there are those formidable *facts* and dates: (1) that the British had in the ninth century a system of law and legal procedure as elaborate and complete as that of this country a century after the Conquest; (2) that the Normans had no collection of laws until after ours was thus elaborated; (3) that the *Grand Constumier* of Normandy is subsequent in date to the great treatise of Glanville, and is plainly founded thereon. And Hale, therefore, was of opinion that the Norman law was rather borrowed from ours than ours from the Norman. And that *both* were founded upon the Roman appears equally clear.

(*b*) It will be observed that the author cites no authority for these statements, and they are far too extreme. There is no evidence that a "curia regis" was established in this reign, and certainly not all at once; though there is an allusion in William's laws to the Justitiarius Regis (*A.-S. Laws*,

as was the law of estates, the use of sealed charters, the trial by jury of twelve men, and the separate jurisdiction of the ecclesiastical judge. These were almost instant consequences of the Conquest. The other branches of the Norman law soon followed upon the like tacit admission, that they constituted a part of the common law of the realm.

We shall now consider those laws which were made by William the Conqueror, and have constantly gone under his name (*a*). The regulations made by these laws seem, most of them, very

The laws of William the Conqueror.

---

c. i., 46), which cannot mean the sheriff, who is called Justicia Regis in the Laws of the Confessor, because it may fairly be supposed in the Laws of the Conqueror that the sheriff is convicted before the justiciary of some misconduct. But that evidently implies an extraordinary jurisdiction, and, as already mentioned, the Conqueror's laws had already enacted quod nemo querlam ad regem deferat nisi ei jus defecerit in hundredo vel comitatu, (c. 43), so that it is clear there was no curia regis with ordinary or primary jurisdiction, and that quite agrees with what the *Mirror* says, speaking of the era of the Conquest — that remedial writs directed the *sheriffs* to decide cases. "It was ordained that every plaintiff have a remedial writ to the sheriff, — questus est nobis quod, etc., et ideo tibi (vices nostras in hac parte committentes) præcipimus quod causam illam audias et legitime fine decidas" (c. ii., 3). No other remedial writ is mentioned, and no curia regis, except the exchequer, which is described as constituted for matters of revenue, and rather as an office than a court, to "affeer" or assess amercements. The amercements, indeed, are alluded to as imposed in the king's court, but even in the laws of Henry I. the county court is called the curia regis (c. 7), and no other curia regis is alluded to; so that not only is there no evidence of the establishment of a curia regis at this time, but there is evidence that there was *no* such court. As to trial by jury also, it was, as will be seen, of very slow growth into a real trial by jurors on *evidence*, and for ages the jury were only witnesses. As to estates, they have already been alluded to; as to deeds, they were known long before the Conquest.

(*a*) The laws of the Conqueror are (as the author states further on) divided into separate portions, the first consisting of fifty chapters or sections, professedly (and to a great extent really) based upon the customs and laws of the Confessor, and have already been noticed; and the author, it will be observed, of these most important portions has taken no notice. The next portion consists of laws which he himself, apparently at a later period, enacted, and which contain more political constitutions, of a more severe character, and more of the nature of the laws of Canute. These, it is to be observed, are numbered on with the others in the versions of the laws which the author cites, so that sec. 1 of the second series is cited by him as 51, and so on; whereas in the last edition of the Anglo-Saxon laws they are separated in their numeration. In these, however, there is the important clause, that the laws of Edward, *i. e.*, of Edward's time, should be observed, except so far as altered by any of the new laws. "Hoc quoque præcipimus ut omnes habeant et teneant leges Edwardi regis in omnibus rebus adauctis hiis quas constituimus ad utilitatem Anglorum" (c. 13). The political constitutions the author notices farther on, and commences with those which are of a more municipal character. But in these he omits to notice the most

20*

little worthy of curiosity, as differing in nothing from the subject of many Saxon constitutions. They make some alterations in the value of *weregilds* and penalties. They sometimes merely enforce or reënact what was before the law of the realm, taking notice of the differences observed by the three great governing politics, the West-Saxon, Danish, and Mercian. The parts of these laws which are most material are the following: —

The *relief*, or consideration to be paid to the superior upon succeeding to the inheritance, was settled in the case of an earl, baron, and vavasor,— the first at eight horses, the second at four, and the last at one; these were

---

important—as the important laws relating to the "coloni," or villani, the tenants of manors, which have already been noticed, and to which it is here important to add an important law as to the servi, contained in the latter series. "Si servi permanserint sine calumpnia per annum et diem in civitatibus nostris vel in burgis vel muro vallatis, vel in castris nostris, a die illa liberi efficianter: et liberi a jugo servitutis sine sunt in perpetuum" (c. 16), upon which this important point is to be noted: that the "servi" are here distinguished from the villeins mentioned in the former series; these villeins being tenants in villenage; the servi, if not slaves, at all events are villeins in the sense of a personal, through predial servitude. It is very important to observe this distinction, which the author altogether loses sight of, confounding villeins with tenants in villenage, or even slaves with villeins. This law of the Conqueror may be best illustrated by some passages in the *Mirror*, as to the villeins and their emancipation. It is particularly pointed out that all villeins are not slaves, but that they are regardant or attached to the possessions of their lords; that they are tillers of land, dwellings in upland (*i. e.*, country) villages, for of vill, it is said, cometh villeins, as of burghs, burgess, and of city, citizen; and of villeins there are tillages, called villenages. Thus it is said that villeins become free in various ways, and, among others, by the lords allowing them to remain for a whole year within a city or upon the king's "demesnes," *i. e.*, in a borough, for a borough was a town built upon part of the demesnes of the king, and owing him real service; whence came tenancy in burgage, which thus can be traced back to the Conquest. In the present law, boroughs, which are Saxon, are distinguished from cities, which are Roman, there being, it is noticed, none of our cities not of Roman origin. Another thing to be noted upon the law is, that as the Saxons found the municipal system here established, and merely adopted it, so of the Conqueror, who found the Roman cities, and the Saxon boroughs, and encouraged them. Another law upheld and enforced the frankpledge system, which was the laws of the boroughs, the Saxon "borh," or pledge, being in part the origin of the borough, and the same term. The Conqueror was careful of the police of the realm, and there was a law enforcing upon all the municipal or civil authorities the duty of maintaining it. "Statuimus etiam, et firmiter præcipimus, ut omnes civitates, et burgi, et castella et hundreda totius regni nostri singulis noctibus vigilentur et custodiantur pro maleficis et inimicis; prout vice comites et aldermanni et prepositi, et ceteri ballivi et ministri nostri melius per commune consilium ut utilitatem regni providebunt" (c. 6). And one weight and measure were established throughout the realm.

to be caparisoned with coats of mail, helmets, shields, and other warlike accoutrements.¹ The relief of those who held by a certain rent was to be one year's rent,² and that of a slave, or, as he was now called, a *villain*, was to be his best beast.³ It was directed, that if a man died intestate, his children should divide the inheritance equally.⁴ It was strictly enjoined that no one omit paying the due services to his lord, on pretence of any former indulgence.⁵ A regulation was made respecting *namium*, or, as it has since been called, a *distress*, a kind of remedy which, according to some, was introduced by the Normans, and according to others was before in use here. It was directed,⁶ that a *namium* should not be taken till right had been demanded three times in the county or hundred court; and if the party did not appear on the fourth day appointed, that the complainant should have leave of court to take a *namium* or distress sufficient to make him full amends. Thus this summary remedy was considered only in the light of a compulsory process, and was therefore called *districtio* (and thence in after-times *distress*), from *distringere*, which in the barbarous latinity of those days, signified *to compel*. The remarkable law made by Canute in protection of his Danes was adopted by William, in favor of his own subjects. He ordained⁷ that where a Frenchman⁸ was killed, and the people of the hundred had not apprehended the slayer and brought him to justice within eight days, they should pay forty-seven marks, which fine was called *murdrum*. By virtue of this, presentments of *Englishery* were made; and all the former law upon the subject was continued, with the single difference of putting *Frenchman* in the place of *Dane*. William forbade all punishments by hanging, or any other kind of death;⁹ and substituted in the place of it several kinds of mutilation; as the putting out of eyes, cutting off the hands or feet, and castration. This alteration was made, says the law, that the trunk may remain a living mark of the offender's wickedness and treachery.

There are some laws of William which establish the trial by *duel*, and sketch out certain rules for the application of it.¹⁰ By one law, the same liberty is given to an

---

¹ 229 Conq., 22, 23, 24. ³ 29. ⁵ 34. ⁷ 26. ⁹ 229 Conq., 67.
² 40. ⁴ 38. ⁶ 42. ⁸ Francigena. ¹⁰ 68.

Englishman, which every Frenchman had in his own country, to accuse or appeal a Frenchman, by duel, of theft, homicide, or any other crime, which before that time used to be tried either by the ordeal or duel. If an Englishman declined the duel, then the Frenchman was at liberty to purge himself by the oaths of witnesses, according to the law of Normandy. On the other hand, if a Frenchman [1] appealed an Englishman by duel, the Englishman was to be allowed his election, either to defend himself by duel or by ordeal, or even by witnesses; and if either of them were infirm, and could not or would not maintain the combat himself, he might appoint a champion. If a Frenchman [2] was vanquished, he was to pay to the king sixty shillings. In case of outlawry,[3] the king ordained, that an Englishman should purge himself by *ordeal;* but that a Frenchman appealed by an Englishman in such a case, should make out his innocence by a duel. However, if the Englishman should *be afraid,*[4] says the law, to stand the trial by duel, the Frenchman shall purge himself *pleno juramento,* that is, by oaths of compurgators.

Thus was the trial by duel formally established in criminal inquiries; but with such qualifications annexed, as show a regard to the prejudices which both people had in favor of their own customs. The trial by duel in civil causes (a) does not appear to have been introduced by any

---

(a) There is one of the laws of William which has escaped the observation of the author, and apparently had reference to trial by jury — jurors in those days being, it will be borne in mind, witnesses This law is in accordance with a series of similar Saxon laws, the origin of which evidently was to provide for trial by jurors, by providing witnesses of transactions who might afterwards be jurors. Hence the present law —"ne venditio et eruptio fiat, nisi coram testibus, et in civitatibus. Interdicimus ut nulla viva pecunia vendatur aut ematur, nisi inter civitates, et hoc ante tres fideles testes," (c. 10). This law probably had a twofold bearing, in favor of cities and of trade, and also in favor of the administration of justice, by providing pre-appointed witnesses who might be jurors. It is to be borne in mind that ordeal or battle were only resorted to from *default* of witnesses who might be jurors. If there were no witnesses, there could be no trial by jury; and hence the recourse to other modes of trial, from an apparent necessity. From the *Mirror* it plainly appears that this was so, and that the duel, like the ordeal, was considered a mode of *trial,* and only resorted to in default of a better, and that the duel was considered less absurd than the ordeal, the parties being each *sworn* to the truth of their respective cases, and then attesting the

[1] 229 Conq., 69.
[2] 70. In these and other passages the word is *Francigena.*
[3] *De omnibus rebus utlagariæ,* 71. [4] *Non audeat.*

particular law; but when this opening was made, it soon began generally to prevail; and indeed, after such a precedent, it had more color of legal authority than the numerous other innovations derived from that nation.

It was declared by a law of William[1] (a), that all free

---

truth of their oath by their persons; wherefore this mode of trial was called "juramentum duelli." "There are, it is said, many manner of proofs, by record, by battle, by witnesses" (*i. e.*, jurors). "And the usage of battle is allowable by the law, so that the proof in felony and other cases is often by battle, according to the diversities of the case. For in *felony* none can contest for another; but in *actions* it is lawful for the plaintiff to make their battles by their bodies or by *lawful witnesses*, because in real actions none can be witness for himself; and no man is bound to discover his real right," (the parties in the duel being, as already stated, *sworn* to the truth of what they contended for.) Combats, it is added, may be in other cases than felonies, "for if a man hath done any falsity to one, for which he is appealed, and denies it, it is lawful for *one to prove the action either by jury*, or by any body, or by the *body of a witness*." "And so it is in cases where you deny your gift, bailment, pledge, or deed, and in cases where the battle could not be joined, *nor was there any witness*, the people in personal actions *used* to help themselves by a miracle of God (the ordeal); and if the defendant could not give battle, and if the plaintiff had no witnesses to prove his action (so that there could not be a trial by jury, the jurors being witnesses), then the defendant might clear his credit by the miracle, or leave the proof to the plaintiff, for Christianity suffered not that they be by such wicked arts cleared, if one may otherwise avoid it." And then it is stated that whoever waged the battle was *sworn* to the truth of that for which he contended, so that he was a juror. Thus, therefore, the ordeal was regarded as a mode of trial by jurors.

(a) This is only one of several political constitutions, and it is important that they should be considered all together. They are the first in the second series of the Conqueror's laws, and amply exhibit his most matured policy. At the outset, in the first article, he propounds the wise scheme of a just and impartial rule over all classes and races of his subjects, with the view of blending them in one kingdom, on the basis of their common faith, "Statuimus imprimis super omnia unum Deum per totum regnum nostrum venerari, unam fidem semper inviolatam custodiri, pacem et secritatem et concordiam judiciam, et justiciam, inter Anglos et Normannos, Francos, et Britones, etc.; et inter omnes nobis, subjectos per universam monarchiam regni Britanniæ, firmiter et inviolabiter observari." Then comes article 52, extracted by the author. Next is an article placing all the subjects of the realm under the king's protection, "ut omnes homines sint sub protectione et in pace nostra per universum regnum." Allegiance and protection being correlative, they are thus closely connected in the laws. Then comes the clause of immunity: "Ut omnes liberi homines totius monarchiæ regni nostri habeant et teneant terras suas et possessiones suas bene et in pace, libere ab omni exactione in justa, et ab omni tallagio, ita quod nihil ab eis exigatur vel capiatur, nisi, servicium suum liberum, quod de jure nobis facere debent, et facera tenentur, et prout statutum est eis, et illis a nobis datum et concessum, jure hæreditario in perpetuum." Then comes c. 58, which the author extracts in the text, and then another, which he omits, and which is important for its construction, "Ut omnes liberi homines sint fratres conjurati

[1] 229 Conq., 55.

men should enjoy their lands and possessions free from unjust exactions and talliages; so that nothing be taken from them but what was due by reason of services, to which they were bound. What those services were, we are now going to consider.

Establishment of tenures.

The most remarkable of William's laws are cap. 52 and 58. The tenor of the 52d is this: *Statuimus et omnes liberi homines fœdere et sacramento affirment, quòd intra et extra universum regnum Angliæ (quod olim vocabatur regnum Britanniæ) Wilhelmo suo domino fideles esse velint; terras et honores illius fidelitate ubique servare cum eo, et contra inimicos, et alienigenas defendere.* The interpretation put upon this law is, that all owners of land are thereby required to engage and swear, that they become vassals or tenants, and as such will be faithful to William, as lord, in respect of the *dominium* (upon the feudal notion) residing in a feudal lord;[1] that they would swear, everywhere faithfully to maintain and defend their lord's territories and title as well as his person; and give him all possible assistance against his enemies, whether foreign or domestic.[2] These engagements and obligations being the fundamental principles of the feudal state, it was said that when such were required from every freeman to the king, that polity was in effect established.

As the enacting language of this law is in the first person plural, *statuimus*, and the king is spoken of in the third person, some writers think it must be considered as an act of the legislature. A regulation that was at

---

ad monarchiam nostram et ad regnum nostrum pro viribus suis et facultatibus, contra inimicos pro posse suo defendendum, et viriliter servandum; et pacem, et dignatatem coronæ nostræ integram observandum; et al judicium rectum, et justiciam constanter omnibus modis pro posse suo sine dolo et sine dilatione faciendam." The scope of the whole seems to be simply allegiance and protection, and the defence of the realm, by means of knight-service, for the defence of the kingdom; and possibly also, at the desire of many of the owners, it changed their former tenure into knight-service; which introduction of new tenures, however, was not done without the consent of the council of the realm, as appears by the provisions already quoted, whereby it appears, says Hale, that there were two kinds of military provisions — one that was set upon all freeholds by common consent of freeholders, and was called assize of arms, and the other was by tenure, upon the infuedation of the tenant, and was sometimes called knight-service. And hence it came to pass that these estates descended to the eldest son (*Hist. C. L.*, 222). And by "little and little," says Hale, "this rule of descent was introduced into the other lands of the kingdom" (*Ibid.*).

[1] Wright, Ten., 68.   [2] Ibid., 68.

once to overturn the whole law of the kingdom with regard to land, could not well be hazarded on any other authority; and indeed chap. 58 of these laws, which dilates more largely upon the subject of this, refers to it as ordained *per commune concilium.*

The terms of this law are very general; and probably it was purposely so conceived, in order to conceal the consequences that were intended to be founded thereon. The people of the country received with content a law which they looked upon in no other light than as compelling them to swear allegiance to William. The nation in general, by complying with it, probably meant no more than the terms apparently imported, namely, that they obliged themselves to submit, and be faithful to William, as their lord, or king, to maintain his title and defend his territory.[1] But the persons who penned that law, and William who promoted it, had deeper views, which were a little more explained in his 58th law. This constitution runs in these words: *Statuimus etiam, et firmiter præcipimus, ut omnes comites et barones, et milites, et servientes, et universi liberi homines totius regni nostri prædicti habeant et teneant se semper bene in armis et in equis, ut decet, et oportet; et quòd sint semper prompti, et bene parati ad servitium suum integrum nobis explendum, et peragendum, cùm semper opus fuerit, secundum quod nobis* DE FEODIS *debent et tenementis suis de jure facere, et sicut illis statuimus per commune concilium totius regni nostri prædicti, et illis dedimus et concessimus in fœdo, jure hæreditario* (a).

(a) Lord Hale, commenting upon this, observes that it related to the assize of arms, and to services reserved upon grants made out of the crown lands, who held on knight-service: and he adds that these laws were not imposed *ad libitum regis,* but were such as were settled by the common consent of the realm (*Ibid.,* 107). So Hale observes elsewhere that the laws of the Conqueror confirmed the Saxon rule of descent, "Si quis intestatus obierit liberi ejus hæreditatem æqualiter divident," and goes on to point out that this led to some evils, "as it weakened the strength of the kingdom, for, by frequent parcelling and subdividing of inheritances, they became so divided that there were few persons of able estates left to undergo public charges. And, therefore, William having got into his hands the demesnes of the crown, and also many and great possessions of those that opposed him, disposed of their lands, or great part of them, to those that adhered to him, and reserved certain honorary tenures." That is to say, as far as he could, he established tenure by military service. Lord Hale's view of the meaning of the constitution, it has already been shown, is correct — viz., that it applied only to the assize of arms, or those who held of the king, either part of his demesnes, or forfeited land granted by him on military tenure. And this view is up-

[1] Wright Ten., 79.

By this law the nature of the service to be performed is expressly mentioned, namely, knight-service on horseback; and the term of each feudal grant was declared to be *jure hæreditario* (*a*). This latter circumstance must have had a very considerable effect in quieting the minds of men respecting the nature of this new establishment. The Saxon feuds, being perhaps beneficiary, and only for life, were at once converted into inheritances; and the Normans obtained a more permanent interest in their new property, than probably they had before enjoyed in their ancient feuds.

---

held by a reference to a passage in the *Leges Henrici Primi;* which, though the author refers once or twice to the laws, he had not observed:—had he read them, he would not have failed to notice it. The passage here referred to is in c. 2, entitled "De confirmatione legum Edwardi Regis:" "Militibus, qui per loricas terras suas deserviunt (or defendunt) terras dominicarum carucarum suarum quietas ab omnibus gildis et ab omni operæ proprio, dono meo concedo, sicut tam magno gravamine allevati sunt, ita equis et arma se bene istruant, ut *apti et parati sunt* ad servitium meum et *ad defensionem regni mei*," which implies merely that they should be ready for military service when required for the defence of the realm, but was equally obligatory before the Conquest, as appears from the obligation to render military "relief" on the death of a noble or knight (*vide Leges Can.*, 32). It is evident that this passage quite confirms Lord Hale's view.

✝ (*a*) The author failed to observe that, from the nature of feuds or fiefs, they necessarily implied a *donation* of land; in that, it is manifest that Hale was right in his view that any alteration in tenure could only have applied either to the demesne lands of the crown, or to forfeited lands regranted by the crown. As Guizot points out, when the feuds were created the lands were given, and the Conqueror could only give lands which were his to give, and Hale conclusively shows that there was nothing like a general confiscation. The definition of "feudal" and allodial is very simple, as Guizot gives it. It is fe-od land, or property held as fee or reward; and all-od land, or land held unconditionally and absolutely in full property. Guizot also points out that the word *beneficium*, which preceded fe-od or fief, and meant the same thing, likewise on the face of it imported an estate or land received from a superior, and on the tenure of some service. He refutes the idea held by Montesquieu, Robertson, and apparently by Reeve, that benefices were revocable or temporary, and shows that they were hereditary; although some may have been temporary, or for life, as well as hereditary. And he accounts for the gifts ("reliefs") rendered on the death of the holder, by the desire to secure a confirmation and protection of the inheritance from the superior. For some centuries before the era of the Conquest, he thinks freehold or allodial property was becoming beneficiary, and estates became changed into fiefs or feuds, mainly from a sense of weakness and desire for protection, which was gained by becoming a member of the great feudal hierarchy or organization under which the obligations of lord and vassal were correlative; and the lord was bound to protect the vassal, as the vassal was bound to protect his lord (*Lect. sur la Civ. en France*, lect. i.). This explains the spread of the feudal system, which, however, existed in its essence and substance before the Conquest, since "reliefs" and military reliefs were rendered, and were defined by the laws of Canute.

From these two statutes were deduced the consequences of tenure: from these a new system of law sprang up (*a*), by which the landed property of the kingdom was entirely governed till the middle of the last century, and is, in some degree, influenced even at this day. The Norman lawyers, who were versed in this kind of learning, exercised their talents in explaining its doctrines, its rules, and its maxims; and at length established, upon artificial reasoning, most of the refinements of feudal jurisprudence.

By the operation of these two statutes, the Saxon distinction between bocland and folcland, charter-land and allodial (*b*), with the *trinoda necessitas*, and other incidents, was totally abolished; and all the *liberi homines* of the kingdom, on a sudden, became possessed of their land under a tenure which bound them, in a feudal light, mediately or immediately to the king. Thus, if *A.* had

---

(*a*) This is an error, for, as already shown, the system existed in substance before the Conquest, and, as Guizot shows, had been growing for ages. The prevailing error of the author is to lose sight of the *progressive* growth and development of institutions. . . . .

(*b*) It has already been shown that our author confused these distinctions. There was nothing in the above "statutes," or in any change effected at the Conquest, to alter them. Bocland meant land held by deed, which might or might not be hereditary, or allodial; for allodial land, *i. e.*, common freehold land, might of course be conveyed by deed, and it was indeed that kind of land which was chiefly so conveyed. Feudal land was not so conveyed or transferred, and, on the other hand, folcland, or land held by custom, *might* be hereditary (as is the case with "customary freeholds" at this day), though usually and originally not so. There was nothing in the feudal system to abolish or alter these qualities of land. Feudal was indeed opposed to allodial, although, as already shown, allodial land could be converted into feudal; and so of lands already in the hand of the crown. The notion that the Saxon distinction between bocland and folcland was abolished, is an entire error. In the laws of Henry I., which, at all events, are an extemporaneous exposition of what was understood to be the law at that time, bocland is mentioned more than once; and there is a remarkable passage in the *Mirror*, already quoted, in which folcland is distinctly described: "And although it be that the people have no charter deeds nor muniments of their lands, nevertheless, if they were ejected, or put out of possession wrongfully by bringing an assize (the remedy for a *freehold*), they might be restored to their estates as before, because they could show the certainty of their services; and therefore it is said that St. Edward caused an inquiry to be made of such as so held by custom." The *origin* of this kind of tenure is also explained in a previous passage, in which it is said that only if a lord granted or gave to a villein a state of inheritance, or even took his homage for it, then he would have such an estate, and be free; yet he would have no deed to show, and the condition of his estate would only be known by common custom. This was the origin of all the *common* freehold estates of the kingdom as distinguished from those which were originally of military tenure. To suppose it therefore abolished at the Conquest was an egregious error.

received his land of the king (*a*), and *B.* had received his of *A.*, *B.* now held his land of *A.* on the same terms, and under the same obligations, that *A.* held his of the king (*b*); each considering himself under the reciprocal obligation of lord and tenant. In this manner it became a maxim of our law, that all land was held mediately or immediately of the king, in whom resided the *dominium directum;* while the subject enjoyed only the *dominium utile*, or the present cultivation and fruits of it (*c*).

This position led to consequences of the greatest importance. Military service being required by an express statute (*d*), the other effects of tenure were deductions from the nature of that establishment. As all the king's tenants were supposed to have received their lands by the gift of the king, it seemed not unreasonable that, upon the death of an ancestor, the heir should purchase a continuance of the king's favor, by paying a sum of money, called *a relief*, for entering into the estate (*e*). As he would be bound to the same service

Nature of tenures.

(*a*) But then, in order to *grant* it, the king must *have* it, and he could only have it either because originally belonging to the crown, or because forfeited to the crown by rebellion, treason, or some other cause of escheat. The notion of any statute having altogether altered the tenure of all the lands in the kingdom had been refuted by Hale, and is entirely visionary.

(*b*) This, it is conceived, is an entire error; that is, it would not necessarily be so. A person holding by knight-service could grant out land to knights on like tenure, and they to ordinary freeholders on what was called socage tenure, *i. e.*, a *certain* rent, either in corn or kind. The baron would be bound to the king to furnish so many knights, and the knights to the barons to render their military service, but the socage tenants would be bound to their lords to render their own proper services.

(*c*) This is hardly accurate, and seems to confound *usufructus* with *proprietas*. *Dominium directum* meant rather political rule; *dominium utile* meant absolute property.

(*d*) *Sed quære, vide suprâ.*

(*e*) But the author had failed to observe, that as to reliefs, they were required to be rendered before the Conquest, on the death of any noble or knight, and were military in their nature, consisting of arms, and horses, and trappings. (This appears from the laws of Canute, c. 71.) This implied an obligation to be ready to render military service when required for the defence of the realm, and this was all that was really involved in the feudal system, so far as it was lawful or legitimate. This appears plainly from a passage in the *Leges Henrici Primi*, c. xiv., De relevacionibus. This, in the first place, is taken entirely from the Laws of Canute, c. 72, which, as already shown, disposes entirely of the idea of any sudden change of tenures at the Conquest. In the laws of Canute and of Henry alike, the reliefs are described as those of earls — called comites in the Latin version of Henry — and king's thanes, or barons, who, as Lord Coke says, whether king's thanes — *i. e.*, those who held lands of the king — or "thaines mediocres," held as

to which his ancestor was liable, and which was the only return that could be made in consideration of his enjoying the property, it seemed reasonable that the king should judge whether he was capable, by his years, of performing the services: if not, that *he*, as lord, should have the *custody of the land* during the infancy; by the produce of which he might provide himself with a sufficient substitute, and in the meantime have the care or *wardship* of the infant's person, in order to educate him in a manner becoming the character he was to support as his tenant. If the ward was a female, it seemed equally material to the lord, that she should connect herself in marriage with a proper person; so that the disposal of her in *marriage* was also thought naturally to belong to the lord.

The obligation between lord and tenant so united their interests, that the tenant was likewise bound to afford *aid* to his lord, by payment of money on certain emergent calls respecting himself or his family; namely, *when he married his daughter, when he made his son a knight, or when he was taken a prisoner.*

Besides these incidents, it was held that land should

---

knights, by the obligation to military service when required for the defence of the realm. No doubt, after the Conquest, the tenure by military service was developed, and indeed abused and perverted, into the system of exaction known as the "feudal system;" and this indeed appears from the laws of Henry, for the charter states, "Si quis baronum meorum sive aliorum qui de me tenent, mortuus fuerit, heres suus non redimet terram suam sicut *faciebat tempore fratris mei, sed legitima et justa releracione relerabit eam.* Similiter et homines baronum meorum, legitima et justa relevacione relevabunt terras suas de dominis suis." So as to marriages, " Et si quis baronum vel hominum meorum filium suam nubitum tradere voluerit, sive sororem, mecum inde loquitur. Sed neque ego aliquid de suo pro hac licencia accipiam, neque ei defendam quin eam det, excepto si eam jungere vellet inimico meo. Et si mortuo barone vel alio homine meo, filia hæres remanserit, illam dabo consilio baronum meorum cum terra sua. Et si, mortuo marito, uxor ejus remanserit, et sine liberis fuerit, dotem et maritagionem suam habebit, et etiam non dabo marito, nisi secundum velle suum. Si vero uxor cum liberis remanserit, et terræ et liberorum custos erit, sive uxor sive alius propinquorum, qui justus esse debebit; et precipio ut barones mei similater se contineant erga filios, vel filias, vel uxores hominum suorum" (*Leges Hen. Pri.*, c. 1.; *A.-S. Laws*, c. i., p. 499). This shows that the pretended incidents of the feudal system, beyond reliefs (which were rendered before the Conquest), were mere abuses and usurpations, and recognized as such, so soon after the Conquest as the reign of Henry I. It also shows that there could not have been any such general alteration in the tenures of the kingdom as the author appears to have supposed, and he himself elsewhere in a note contests the notion that the feudal system was in this country established so fully as it existed abroad. *Vide post*, p. 259, *in notis.*

escheat, or fall back into the hands of the lord, for want of heirs of the tenant, or for the commission of certain crimes; and, in cases of treason, that it should come into the hands of the king by *forfeiture*.

These were the fruits and consequences the king expected to receive from the doctrine of tenure; these he demanded as lord from his tenants; and they, in the character of lords, exacted many of the like kind from theirs. In this manner was the feudal bond riveted on the landed property of the whole kingdom.

Thus far of the nature of tenures in general: but tenure was of two kinds: tenure by *knight-service*, and tenure by *socage*. Tenure by knight-service was, in its institution, purely military, and the genuine effect of the feudal establishment in England; the services were occasional, though not altogether uncertain, each service being confined to forty days.[1] This tenure was subject to *relief*, *aid*, *escheat*, *wardship*, and *marriage*. Socage was a tenure by any conventional service not military (*a*). Knight-service contained in it two species of military tenure: *grand* and *petit serjeanty* (*b*). Under tenure in socage may be ranked two species: *burgage*, and even *gavelkind*, though the latter has many qualities different from common socage. Besides these, there was a tenure called

_{Different kinds of tenure.}

(*a*) Any certain service, so that the service be not knight-service, as rent (*Littleton*, c. v.). It is said that the reason why such tenure is so called is because *socagium est servitium sociæ*, and "*soca idem est quod caruca*," a soke or plough. "In ancient times a great part of the tenants, who held of their lords by socage, ought to come with their ploughs to plough and sow the demesnes of their lords. And for that such works were done for the sustenance of their lords, they were quit against the lord of all manner of service. And because the services were done with their ploughs, the tenure was called tenure in socage. And afterwards these services were changed into annual rents, but the name remains. And if a man holdeth of his lord by escuage certain, it is tenure in socage, and not knight-service. But where the sum the tenant shall pay for escuage is uncertain, it is knight-service (*Ibid.*). And where the tenant is to pay a certain sum for castle-guard, it is socage tenure; but if he has to do castle-guard, it is knight-service." (*Ibid.*)

(*b*) This is an error. Tenure by petit serjeanty was where a man held of the king to yield to him yearly a bow, or a sword, or a dagger, or a lance, or a pair of gloves, or spears, or an arrow, or to do such several things belonging to war; and such service is socage in effect; because the tenant ought not to go, nor to do anything in person, touching war, but only to render certain things. And both species of serjeanty were only tenures of the king (*Littleton*, c. ix.), but knight-service might be of any lord (c. iv.). Again, grand serjeanty for the most part was for service within the realm; knight-service might be out of the realm (*Ibid.*, c. viii.).

[1] Wright, Ten., 140.

frankalmogne (a). This was the tenure by which religious houses and religious persons held their lands; and was so called, because lands became thereby exempt from all service except that of prayer and religious duties. Such persons were also said to hold *in liberâ eleemosynâ*, or in free alms.

Thus far of free tenure, by which the *liberi homines* of the kingdom became either tenants by knight-service, or in common socage. It is thought that the condition of the lower order of *ceorls*, who among the Saxons were in a state of bondage (b), received an improvement under this new polity. Nothing is more likely[1] (c) than that the Normans, who were strangers to any other than a feudal state, should, to a certain degree, enfranchise such of those wretched persons as came into their power, by permitting them to do *fealty* for the scanty subsistence which they were allowed to raise on their precarious possessions, and that they were permitted to retain their possession on performing the ancient services (d). But, by doing fealty,

---

(a) Here again the author confounds two different distinctions. Tenure in burgage could not be tenure in socage, which was plough-service, but it was of its nature, being certain; and as socage often was commuted for rent, for it was tenure in an ancient borough, under a rent to the king. Gavelkind was a customary right of descent, under which all the sons took, and related to the inheritable quality, not to the mode of tenure, or nature of services, though no doubt, for an obvious reason, gavelkind would always be socage.

(b) This is an error. *Vide ante*. The ceorls were not slaves.

(c) Nothing in the world less likely than that the conquerors should seek to do good to any class; on the contrary, Bracton tells us that in many cases they dispossessed the former owners, and made them hold their lands in villenage (lib. i., c. 11, f. 7). So that what the Normans did was not to raise villeins into free tenants, but to make freeholders into villeins. And so the *Mirror* says (c. 1). There can be no doubt, however, that the natural effect of this was that there were a superior order of tenants in villenage, who, as Bracton says, although they held in villenage, were not villeins, and that as time went on they by degrees got their lands emancipated (they themselves becoming freemen), the tenure being turned into freehold by its being rendered certain and inheritable. Bracton indeed distinctly says the service was certain (being plough-service); and the *Mirror* says that if the lord received homage from the tenant, he became a freeholder. *Vide ante*.

(d) It has been seen that the laws of the Conqueror, confirming the customs of the country under the Confessor, simply maintained the customary rights of ceorls. The Conqueror declared in effect that the customary rights of the "ceorls" or villeins — the "villani" or coloni — should be maintained, "Coloni et terrarum exercitores non vexentur ultra debitum et statutum; nec licet dominis removere colonos a terras dummodo debita servicia persolvant" (*Laws of the Conqueror*, c. xxix.). That these were the villeins is clear, for the next chapter calls them nativi, "nativi non recedentia terras suis," etc.,

[1] Wright, Ten., 216.

the nature of their possession was, in construction of the new law, altered for the better; they were by that advanced to the character of *tenants*, and the improved state in which they were now placed was called the tenure of *villenage* (a). Elevated to this consid-

Villenage.

and the next again calls them coloni, as they are called in the Latin version of the laws of Ina. The above law of William is almost a translation of an imperial edict as to the coloni. The effect was that these customary rights were established, so that it was afterwards held that they could not be ejected so long as they rendered their customary service (*Litt.*, c. ix.).

(a) It is evident from what follows, and from other passages, that the author supposed all the ceorls or villeins were originally slaves, and only rose to tenure in villenage by degrees. This was not so, though no doubt in the course of time slaves rose to be villeins; but all villeins were tenants in villenage, though all tenants in villenage were not villeins, as freemen might hold lands in villenage. This is all explained in the *Mirror*, and to understand it is one of the most important points in our legal history. The *Mirror* always distinguishes slaves from villeins, and says that villeins were "regardant," attached to manors, but that they held tillages or land in villenage. There is a remarkable passage in the *Mirror*, evidently written soon after the Conquest, and, at all events, written of that time, which shows exactly what was then the state of tenures. In the time of the first conquerors, it is said the earls were enfeoffed of earldoms, barons of baronies, knights of knights-fee, *villeins of villenages*, burgesses of boroughs, whereof some received their lands, to hold by homage and by service for all time of the realm; and some by villein customs, as to plough the lord's lands, to reap, cut, and carry his corn or hay, and such manner of service (*Mirror*, c. ii., s. 28). It appears that the services of the villeins varied; some plough-service, some to carry corn or manure; but all the tenants held some tenements in villenage, if it was only their cottages, for they all lived upon the manors, and all alike were tenants of manors; but these customs differed, and whether the custom was to render service, which was low and vile, or honorable, as plough-service, the tenure was tenure in villenage. But plough-service being of a higher character, and requiring some skill as well as labor, those who paid in such service gradually rose to be freeholders; and all freehold tenure was originally, when not military, in socage. The truth is, that all through the Saxon times there had been a gradual, progressive improvement in society, and there can be no doubt that the "ceorls" had become, many of them, tenants in socage, or freeholders, and the villeins had become by enfranchisement free tenants of manors, and the theows, or slaves, had become villeins. This progress in society is one of the most interesting features in the legal history of those times. Our common freehold estates arose out of villenage. The passage above cited from the *Mirror* bears internal evidence of having been written soon after the Conquest, and, at all events, clearly refers to that time; and it shows that at the time of the Conquest there were no freehold tenures, save either such as were military, or arose out of villenage, for freehold tenures are not mentioned in the above enumeration as a distinct tenure. And it also appears that the process of gradual emancipation of the land of the villeins, and alteration by usage into freehold land, had begun before the Conquest, and it would seem that under the Confessor it was promoted and extended, as he ordered a careful record to be made of those who held by plough-service, which was the origin of these freeholds; but that after the Conquest many of these freeholders were coerced into villenage again. This remarkable passage fully illustrates what historians have

eration, they were treated with less wantonness by the lords, who, after receiving their *fealty*, could not in honor or conscience deprive them of their possessions while they performed their services. But the conscience and honor of their lord was their only support. However, the acquiescence of the lord, in suffering the descendants of such persons to succeed to the land, in a course of years advanced the pretensions of the tenant in opposition to the absolute right of the lord, till at length this forbearance grew into a permanent and legal interest, which, in after-times, was called *copyhold tenure*.[1]

Copyholds.

The military service due from tenants underwent an alteration in the reign of Henry II. The attendance of a knight only for forty days was very inadequate to the grand purposes of war, which, besides the delay from unavoidable accidents, often consisted in many tedious operations before an expedition could accomplish its end; while, on the other hand, that short service was highly inconvenient to the tenant, who, perhaps, came from the northern parts of this kingdom to perform his service in a province of France.

Sensible of these inconveniences, Henry II., in the fourth year of his reign, devised a commutation for these services, to which was given the name of *escuage*, or *sculage* (a). He published an order,

Of escuage.

---

in vain sought to explain — the anxiety the great body of the people showed for the maintenance of the customs of the Confessor, *i. e.*, the customs existing in his time. They were the customs by which the people held their lands. Our copyhold arose out of villenage. There is another passage in the *Mirror*, which clearly shows that the villeins were copyholders, even though of the lowest order. "Another thing to be noted is that no more than the long tenure of copyhold land maketh a freeman a villein, the long tenure of land maketh a villein a freeman, for freedom is never lost by prescription or lapse of time" (c. ii., s. 22). And again, it is there said that a man might say in his claim of villenage that the services he did were rendered for the service of villein lands which he held, and not by service of blood (*Ibid.*). Elsewhere it is laid down that those are villeins who are born in that state, or adjudged to be so in a suit *de nativo habendo* (*Ibid.*, c. xi., s. 28). It is obvious that as there were no new creations of villenage after the last conquest by the Normans, both the modes resolved themselves into the former, the suit only being the legal way of adjudging that a man was a villein by birth; and there could at that time be no villeins but by birth. Perhaps they were originally slaves, but in the *Mirror* it is carefully laid down, that all villeins are not slaves, though attached to the land (*Ibid.*).

(a) This had already arisen out of tenure by knight-service, and what Henry did was to compound for the commutation. Originally, if a knight

[1] Wright, Ten., 220.

that such of his tenants as would pay a certain sum should be exempted from service, either in person or by deputy, in the expedition he then meditated against Tholouse. This sort of compromise was afterwards continued, and *tenure by escuage* became a new species of military tenure, springing from the advantage some tenants by knight-service had taken of this proposition[1] made by the king.

In the same reign a remission of the old service, which had in some degree been conceded by Henry I.(a) was

---

failed to attend, his feud was seized; afterwards, this was changed into an escuage or scutage, *i. e.*, a fine levied *per scutagium:* and, in like manner, the knight could levy escuage on his military tenants. It became a practice after the Conquest to essoin or excuse their personal attendance, as on the ground of sickness, etc., a phrase afterwards imported into legal proceedings, with reference to excuse for non-attendance in court upon legal process, and in this sense it is used in *Leges Hen.*, c. xli., s. 2, "Qui ad hundretum sub monitus non venerit, nisi soinus legalis eum detinet," etc. (*Anglo-Saxon Laws*, v. i., p. 549). So as to summons of a person out of the county a certain time was allowed, "Et ultra non procedit ubicunque fuerit in Anglia, nisi competens detineat eum soinus" (*Ibid.*, c. xli., lxi.; c. vii.). "Si qui ad comitatum venire noluerit, nisi competens soinus eum detineat," etc. (*Ibid.*, c. xxix., s. 3). But though the common law was that the tenant might excuse his personal attendance, he was bound to find a substitute, as was decided in a case cited by Littleton, *temp.* Edward III., and hence the commutation or composition made by Henry I. (*vide Littleton*, c. iii.). Afterwards the scutage was assessed by the barons, before they went on the war, and ultimately it was assessed by parliament. The barons could levy escuage upon their tenants, and there are instances of distringases for it (*Madd.*, 470, 471). There were talliages assessed on the tenant in ancient demesnes, and on the tenants in burgage. These also were at first assessed by the king's officers, but ultimately all these impositions were assessed by the representatives of these various bodies, assembled in the common council of the realm, which led to a parliament.

(a) The author gives no reference; but probably refers to the charter of Henry confirming the customs of the country. This is the proper place to present an analysis of the *Leges Henrici Primi*, which are above alluded to, and have already been mentioned as quoted by our author, but of which he gives no account, and of which, it is plain, he had only derived his knowledge at second-hand, through some citations of it in other works; as, for instance, in Hale. Had he read them, they would have preserved him from many errors. He has sometimes attempted to represent them as worthless, on the ground that they were probably compiled after the death of the king whose name they bear, an obvious fallacy, already exposed with reference to the compilation of the laws of the Confessor, which no doubt was made under the Conqueror, but is none the less authentic on that account. Hale treats the compilation as authentic, and says, "these laws of Henry I. are a kind of miscellany, made up of the ancient laws of the Confessor and the Conqueror, and certain parts of the canon and civil law, and of other provisions which custom and the prudence of the king and council had thought upon, chosen, and put together" (*Ibid.*, 161). And this may have been so, although the actual compilation was not made until after the close of the reign. Else-

[1] A. D. 1159. *Vide* Spelman, Cod. in Wilk. Leg., p. 321.

ratified to socage tenants, who grew now into the habit of paying a certain sum in money instead of rents in kind.

where Hale calls these laws of Henry I., "obsolete, and disordered, and confused, rather than settled legal institutions;" and no doubt this is true, and the law was in a state of transition. Still, no doubt, it contains a great deal of what was law at the time; and Hale cites it, for instance, as to the law of descent (*Ibid.*, 224); so the author cites it once or twice — his quotations, however, being evidently borrowed from Hale, he himself making no other citations from the laws. No doubt, it is not entirely a collection of *laws*: it is also a treatise upon or exposition of the laws as then understood — in that respect resembling the treatise of Glanville; but it is *also* a collection of laws, and one of great interest and importance, as illustrating an important period of transition in the history of our laws, between the barbarism of the Saxon institutions and the more advanced developments of Glanville and Bracton, in the reign of Henry II. The compilation begins with the charter of Henry I., which commences with a confession of exactions and oppressions, civil and ecclesiastical, of great constitutional importance: — "Quia regnum oppressum erat injustis exactionibus, ego sanctam Dei ecclesiam liberam facio; ita quod nec vendam *nec ad firmam ponam*, nec, mortuo archiepiscopo, sive episcopo, aliquid accipiam de dominio ecclesiæ vel hominibus ejus, donec successor in eam ingrediatur. Ex omnes malas consuetudines quibus regnum Anglia opprimebantur inde aufero, quas malas consuetudines exparte suppono." Then came the confession of feudal exactions already mentioned. Next comes a most important provision as to inheritance by testament or intestacy: — "Si quis baronum vel hominum meorum infirmabitur, sicut ipse dabit, vel dare disponet pecuniam suam, ita datam esse concedo. Quod si ipse preventus, pecuniam suam non dederit, nec dare disposuerit, uxor sua, sive liberi, aut parentes, aut legitimi homines ejus, eam pro anima ejus dividant, sicut eis melius visum fuerit." In a subsequent chapter of the "Laws," there is this, which our author, after Hale, quotes as law at the time, though it has escaped their observation that this chapter is headed "Consuetudo West Sexe:" — "Primo patris feodum primogenitus filius habeat, emptiones vero vel deinceps acquisiciones suas det ecu magis velit. Si bocland habeat quam ei parentes dederint, non mittat eum extra cognationem suam." — (*Leges Hen. Pri.*, c. lxx., s. 21; *A.-S. Laws*, v. i., p. 575.) Then come the provisions as to military service, already extracted, and then the general confirmation of the laws and customs of the Confessor, with the alterations of the Conqueror. This would include the customs of socage and villenage, and perhaps may be what the author alludes to. The next chapter contains the charter to the city of London. Then follow a great many chapters, nearly a hundred in number, all of them of some length, and containing often as many as twenty heads and sections, in which, no doubt, are combined actual laws (as, for instance, that as to intestacy, c. lxx., already extracted), and likewise *expositions* of the grounds and principles of law as then understood and applied: these portions borrowing largely from the Roman and canon law — whole passages being copied therefrom, and entire edicts set out. All this illustrates the Roman origin of our law, because the treatise of Glanville, which is built upon the foundations thus laid down, along with that of Bracton, borrowed from Justinian, form, it is admitted, the bases of our common law. It is, of course, impossible to do more than give an analysis of this elaborate compilation; but it is necessary to point out that it deals copiously with procedure, civil and criminal, courts, jurisdictions, etc. The general tenor of it supports the account given by Lord Hale, that the king composed the collection (*i. e.*, caused it to be composed), and *added* his own laws, "whereof some seem to taste of the

Having so far considered the quality or conditions of tenure, as introduced by the Norman system, let us now examine the nature of that *estate* or in-

>Consequences of tenure.

canon law." — (*Hist. Com. Law.*) As to which, it may be said, that they more than "taste," seeing that entire chapters are taken from the civil or the canon law, especially as to the nature of jurisdictions, of judicature, and of procedure. Thus, c. iii., "De Causarum Pertractione vel Distinctione," treats of the nature of causes, and so of the next head; then s. 5, "De Causarum Proprietatibus." These seem rather in the nature of expositions of principles; 6 treats of the division of counties, etc. Then, s. 7, "De Generalibus Placitis Comitatuum:" — "Sicut anti qua fuerit institutione formatum salutari regis imperio, vera nuper est recordatione firmatum, generalia comitatuum placita certis locis et vicibus et diffinito tempore, per singulas Angliæ provincias, convenire debere, nec ullis ultra fatigationibus agitare, nisi propria regis necessitas, vel commune regni commodum sepius adjiciat. Intersint autem *episcopi, comites, barones, etc.*, diligenter intendentes, ne malorum impunitas, vel graviorum pravitas, vel judicum subversio, solita miseros laceratione conficiant. Agantur itaque primo debita vere Christianitatis jura, secundo regis placita, postremo causæ singulorum dignis satisfactionibus expleantur, et quoscunque scyresmot discordantes inveniet, vel amore congreget, vel sequestret judicio . . . Si uterque necessario desit, prepositus et sacerdos, et quatuor de melioribus villæ assint pro omnibus, qui nominatim non erunt ad placitum submoniti. Idem in hundredo decrevimus observandum, de locis et vicibus, et judicum observantiis, de causis singulorum justis examinationibus, audiendis, de domini et dapiferi, vel sacerdotis et meliorum hominum præsentia" (c. vii.). All this refers to the courts of the country and the hundred. But in a subsequent chapter (iii.) the *county court is called curia regis.* The next relates to the court of the hundred, and of decennaries: — "Presit autem singulis hominum novenis decimus, et toti simul hundredo unus de melioribus, et vocetur aldermanus, qui Dei leges et hominum jura vigilanti studeat observantia promovere;" whence we see how ancient is the usage of aldermen sitting as magistrates; and it is to be observed, that although in our days the office and the phrase are applied only to municipal magistrates, in ancient times they applied equally to rural; and, as Lord Coke long afterwards explained, a "ward in a city is as a hundred in a county." Thus, then, the Saxon system of local administration of justice was distinctly upheld; and one of the most interesting and important questions arising upon these laws, is whether they afford any trace of *any other* courts for the administration of ordinary justice between subject and subject, and especially of the establishment of a *curia regis* for that object. Then comes a chapter (ix.), "De Qualitate Causarum," which distinguishes the nature of various causes, and as to ordinary causes says: — "Et omnes causa terminetur vel hundredo, vel comitatu, vel halimoto, vel dominorum curiis," *i. e.*, either in courts-baron, or the hundred courts, or the county courts (s. 4). And in conclusion, it points out how some causes concern the king: "Soca vero placitorum alia, proprie pertinet ad fiscum regium, et singulariter, alia participatione, alia pertinent vicecomitibus et ministris regis, in firma sua, alia pertinet baronibus socham et sacham (*i. e.*, domestic jurisdiction), habentibus." Then c. x., "De Jure Regis," treats of causes which concern the king, and his rights: — "Hæc sunt jura quæ rex solus et super omnes homines habet in terra sua, commoda pacis et securitatis institutione retenta, infractio pacis regis — murdrum, utlagaria (outlawry) incendium, robaria, etc., injustum judicium: *defectus justitiæ*" — an important head, under which a large number of cases were brought into the

terest a person might have in land, together with such incidents of ownership as naturally occur upon reflecting king's superior courts when they were established, on the ground of a failure of justice in the local tribunals: — "Hæc sunt dominica placita Regis: nec pertinent vicecomitibus vel ministris ejus, sine diffinitis prælocutionibus in firma sua." Then, c. xi., "De Placitis Ecclesiæ pertinentibus ad Regem," treats of ecclesiastical causes coming under the jurisdiction of the crown: — "Sunt alia quædam placita Christianetatis in quibus rex partem habet," and then it contains many, considered common to the king and the bishops, as some cases of tithes, withholding of Rome's fee (Peter's pence), and church scots, the killing of ecclesiastics, etc. Under this head occurs the following, very important with reference to subsequent disputes, as a recognition of the canon law: — "Qui ordinis infracturam faciet, emendet hoc, secundum ordinis dignitatem: Ubicumque recusabitur lex Dei justé servari, secundum dictionem episcopi, cogi oportebit per mundanam protestatem; et omnis emendatio communiter emendatur Christo (i. e., by the church), et rex." This is explained to mean that the king may take pecuniary penalties, "permissum est pecuniam emendationem capere, secundum legem patriæ," that is, if the act were at once an offence against the secular law and the ecclesiastical. The lay and spiritual tribunals might both proceed according to their respective jurisdictions, and that of the latter would be enforced by the former. And in another chapter (xxi.), the same thing is expressed, that the king has a part in these classes of cases, "Si cogi oporteat per mundanam potestatem, ut rectum fiat" (A.-S. Laws, v. i., p. 528). All this, be it observed, is mainly a compilation of the Saxon laws upon the subject, which, according to the Conqueror's charters, were all confirmed. After another chapter on a similar subject, comes one to which the Norman sovereigns attached great interest, and which became the subject of gross extortions, and therefore the subject of a clause in Magna Charta: — "Quæ placita mittunt homines in misericordiæ Regis," i. e., made them liable to fine or amercement at the suit of the king. "Hæc mittunt hominem in misericordia regis, infractio pacis, contemptus brevium suorum, utlagaria; et qui eam faciet in jure regio sit, et si bocland habeat, in manum regis veniat, furtum probatum, et morte dignum: et murdrum." Then the clause as to reliefs is precisely the same as Canute's law on the subject, which seems to show that the system of military service was not altered. Then, c. xvi., "De Pace Curiæ Regis," at first sight might seem to relate to a court of justice; but it is very clear, that it does not so, as it makes no allusion to a tribunal, and merely alludes to the limit within which an offence of violence, committed within the precincts of the royal residence, shall be deemed an infraction of the peace of the king. "Tam longe debet esse pax regis a porta sua ubi residens erit," etc. (c. 16). After one or two others of no importance comes c. xix., "De Justitia Regis," i. e., quæ ad justitiam vel indulgentiam regis et fiscum censentur, cum appendiciis suis; nec, sine diffinitis prælocutionibus pertinent vicecomitibus, vel prepositis ejus, in firma sua." Then c. xxiv., "De Judicis Fiscalis Juræ," says that "Super barones socnam suam (domestic jurisdiction) habentes, habet judex fiscalis justitiæ legis observantiam, et quicquid peccabitur in eorum personam; nemo enim forisfacturam sui ipsuis habuit sed fortasse dominus ejus;" c. xxv., "De Privilegis Procerum Angliæ," (in which Spelman thinks the Proceres mean the lords of manors) "si exurgat placitum inter homines alicujus baronum socnam habentium, tractetur placitum in curia domini sui, de causa communi," i. e., in the county court, which, in c. xxxi., is called "curia regis." Then, in c. xxix., "Qui debent esse Judices Regis," "regis judices sunt barones comitatus" (which Spelman and Coke consider to mean the freeholders of the county)

on property. The polity of tenures tended to restrict men in the use of that, which, to all outward appearance, "qui liberas in eis terras habent, per quos debent causæ singulorum tractari," as opposed to villeins and mean persons. And then it enacts that "Qui ad comitatum secundum legem submonitus, venire voluerit, culpa sit," etc. Then, c. xxxi., "De Capitalibus Placitis," is very remarkable as to the judicature of the time: "In summis et capitalibus placitis unus hundretus vel comitatus judicetur a duobus, non unus duos judicet. Si inter judices studia diversa sint, ut alii sic, alii aliter fuisse contendant, vincat sententia meliorum, et cui justitia magis acquieverit. Interesse comitatui debent episcopi, comites, etc., quæ Dei legis et seculi negotia justa consideratione diffiniant Recordationem curiæ regis nulli negari licet, alias licebit, per intelligibiles homines placiti: unusquisque per pares suos judicandus est, et ejusdem provinciæ." This shows that the county court was called "curia regis," and that in it sat the bishops and the barons, as judges, but that they were not the triers, and it was open to them to have the aid of jurors or witnesses, upon whose findings they could determine. Indeed, it is clear, that causes were tried by the vicinage. Thus in c. xxxiii., "De Placiti Tractando;" "Si quis in curia sua vel in quibuslibet agendorum locis, placitum tractandum habeat, convocet pares et vicinos suos, ut inforciato judicio, gratuitam, et cui contradici non possit, justiciam exhibeat. Defectus quippe justitiæ, et violenta recti eorum destitutio est, qui causas protahant in jus regium." Here we see very clearly exhibited the benefits and the faults of the local system of judicature then existing — the benefits of local knowledge, and the mischief of local partisanship. So, in c. xxxii., "De Placito Tractando in Justo Judicio." Another, c. xli., shows that a man could be summoned in one county to a suit in the court of another, the time for appearance being lengthened according to the distance from the court — whether one, two, three, or four shires intervened. So much as to the local jurisdiction of the old local tribunals. But in subsequent chapters there appear to be allusions to the jurisdiction of the justices itinerant, who, we know from records in the Exchequer, went their circuits regularly at least as early as the 18th of Hen. I., and whose itinera had certainly commenced under the Conqueror, in whose reign several cases occurred of trials in the county court before the king's justiciaries (*vide post*). In c. xlii. there is mention made of summons "a rege vel justicia ejus." So c. xlvi., "Si quis a domino suo vel justicia implacitetur." And c. liii., "Qui secundum legem submonitus a justicia regis ad comitatum venire supersederit, reus sit," etc., which appears to refer to the summonses issued by the justices itinerant. It appears from various other chapters that the king's justices — perhaps itinerant justices — took cognizance of the pleas of the crown. Thus, c. lii., "De proprio placito regis. Si quis de placito proprio regis implacitetur a justicia ejus, non debet justiciæ vadium recti denegare." It appears from other chapters that it was well established that pleas could only be taken in the counties. Thus c. xlvi., "Si quis a justicia implacititur, submoneatur in eodem comitatu." Hence it would be necessary to send justices of the king into the counties, and therefore it would be necessary that they should have power to summon the men of the county; and thus it is provided, "Qui secundum legem submonitus a justicia regis ad comitatum venire supersederit reus sit," etc. (c. liii.). "Clericus per consilium prelati sui vadium dare debet, cum dederit in accusatione" (c. lii.). The hundred court was to be held monthly, and the county court twice a year, like the modern circuits (c. li.). No one without legal authority was either to take or to rescue distresses, or what would in later times have been called levies under a distringas, in order to enforce appearance. "Nulli sine judicio vel licentia, namiare liceat alium in suo

was their own. When the land of the Saxons was converted from allodial to feudal, as above described, it could

vel alterius. Nemo justiciæ vel domino sum namium excutere presumat, si justi vel injusti conjuatur, sed jeste repetet plegium offerat et terminum satisfaciendi. Si vicecomes namium capiat, ad propinquiorem regis curiam dimittat, nec vendat ipsa die (c. li.). Si quis vadium recti justiciæ denegaverit, tertio interrogatus, overseunesse culpa sit, et ex judicio licet retineri eum, donec plegios inveniat, vel satisfaciat" (c. lii.), where we see the origin of outlawry, arrest, and bail. Then there is a chapter about settlement of copartnership accounts (c. lv.); and another as to how differences are to be settled between landlords and their tenants, whether as tenants of the manor, or as lessees; and how complaints against stewards of manors are to be tried (c. lvi.). Then there is a chapter as to differences between neighbors as to boundaries, which are to be settled either in the lord's court or the hundred — some enactment analogous to which might be very beneficial in our own times. These specimens may suffice to show that this compilation of laws mark an important era in our legal history, and are indicative of a state of transition to a higher development of law. It would be difficult to find any later laws of which the germs are not to be found in this compilation. It is to be observed that this compilation is not the only source from which laws of Henry I. may be collected. In the *Mirror of Justice* there are several laws of Henry I. mentioned, as that "those who survived their wives who were with child by them should hold their wives' inheritance for ever" (c. i., s. 34); which is quite different from the "tenancy by the courtesy,"as it afterwards was settled. So it is stated as to civil procedure, that whereas it was at first defined that plaintiffs should have security, Henry I. put the mitigation in favor of poor plaintiffs, that it should be according to their ability (*Ibid.*). So it is stated, that in the time of Henry I. it was ordained and assented to that jurors sworn upon assizes and the like, should not take fees (*Ibid.*, c. ii., s. 14), which shows that juries were, in his time, used in civil cases. So, as to process in civil actions, it is said that it was ordained by Henry I. that offenders should first be arrested until they found bail, and then distrained by their lands to value of the demand; and if they then made default, that their land should be delivered to the plaintiff until they had made satisfaction (s. 24), which is remarkable as showing that the subsequent statutes as to arrest and bail, only followed a previous practice. Afterwards it is stated, that in personal actions defaults were to be punished thus: that defendants were distrained to the value of their demand, and afterwards, for default after default, judgment was given for the plaintiff. This usage was changed in the time of Henry I., that no freeman was to be distrained by his body for an action, personal, venial, so long as he had lands; in which case the judgment by default was of force till the time of Henry III., that the plaintiff should receive his seisin of the land, to hold until satisfaction was made (c. iii., s. 5). Several laws of Henry I. are mentioned in the *Mirror* as to criminal procedure. Thus it is said that Canute "used to judge mainpernors according as their principals, when their principals appeared not in judgment;" but Henry I. made this difference, that the ordinance of Canute should stand against mainpernors who were consenting to the fact (c. ii., s. 15). So it is mentioned that he moderated the law as to forfeiture of lands on conviction of felony (*Ibid.*). These citations are of interest, as showing the law in a course of gradual progress and development, by means of judicial decisions, or legal ordinances of the king in council. It is stated in the *Mirror* to have been ordained by Henry I. that none should be arrested nor imprisoned for slander (*i. e.*, on charge) of mortal offence (*i. e.*, felony) before he was indicted thereof by the oaths of honest men, before those who had authority to take

{no longer be alienated without the consent of the lord, nor could it be disposed of by will. These, with other shackles, sat heavy upon the possessors of land; nor were at last removed, but by frequent and gradual alterations, during a course of several centuries. The history of these alterations in the descent, alienation, and other properties of feuds, is wrapt in obscurity during this early period; however, we will endeavor to trace such circumstances relating to it as can be collected from the scanty remains of antiquity.

By the introduction of tenures, there is no doubt but *primogeniture*, or a descent of land to the eldest son, began to prevail; yet it is found, that as low down as the reign of Henry I.,[1] the right of primogeniture was so feeble, that, if there were more than one son, the succession was divided, and the eldest son took only the *primum patris fœdum;*[2] the rest being left to descend to the younger son or sons: but this soon went out

Of primogeniture.

---

such indictments, and then they were to be seized by their bodies and kept in prison till they cleared themselves of the charge before the king or his justices (book i., c. ii., s. 20); a most important law, remaining to this day, save so far as it is altered by the statutable power of justices of the peace, a change which belongs to the age of Edward I. It may be convenient here to mention the subsequent charters up to Henry II. (*See Blackstone's Charters.*) Stephen, at his accession, granted a charter that the church should be free, and that he would not act in ecclesiastical affairs uncanonically, and that the dignities and customs of churches, as held by ancient tenure, should remain inviolable; and that, while episcopal sees should remain vacant of pastors, they and all their possessions should be committed to the care and keeping of ecclesiastics, or other honest men of the church, until a pastor should be canonically appointed. He declared that he would abolish all injustice and exactions introduced by sheriffs or others, and that he would observe and cause to be observed all the good and ancient laws and customs in civil or criminal matters. He also granted another charter, which granted and confirmed to the barons and people all the liberties and good laws and customs which had been confirmed by Henry I., and were held in the time of the Confessor. Henry II. granted a charter briefly to the like effect: "I have granted and restored and confirmed to the church, and to all my barons and tenants, all the customs which Henry I. granted to them. In like manner, all evil customs which he abolished, I grant to be abolished. And I will that the church, and all my barons and tenants, do hold all their usages, liberties, and free customs freely and peaceably, and as freely and fully and securely as Henry I. confirmed to them by his charter." To understand the "evil customs" as to the laity, it is only necessary to refer back to the charter of Henry I. To understand the "evil customs" as to the church, it is necessary to mention that the Conqueror and his sons were in the habit of keeping sees vacant for years, in order to take the revenues. At the death of William II. he held several sees so vacant (*Lingard*, vol. i., p. 272; vol. ii., c. 3).

[1] Leges, 17. [2] Hale's Hist. Com. Law, 255.

of use, or was altered by some statute now lost; for in the reign of Henry II. the eldest son was considered as sole heir: and so fixed was his right of succession to an inheritance held by his ancestors, that it could not be disappointed by alienation. Thus stood the law with regard to tenures by knight-service; but the same reasons not holding with respect to socage-lands, they were not subject to the same law; for so late as the reign of Henry II. the sons succeeded to socage-lands *in capita* equally; but the capital messuage was to go to the eldest son; for which, however, he was to make proportionate recompense to the others. But this partible inheritance in socage-land was not universal; for, if it was not by custom divisible,[1] the eldest son was heir to the whole. Both in knight's-service and socage, if a person died leaving only daughters, they all succeeded jointly and equally, the capital messuage being given to the eldest daughter, upon the terms above-mentioned.

The right of *representation* in prejudice of proximity of blood, though, perhaps, not an unlikely consequence of the legal notion of primogeniture, did not so soon establish itself. The minds of men revolted at a rule which gave the inheritance to an infant, only because he represented the person of his father, in exclusion of the uncle, who was nearer of blood to the grandfather, from whom the fee descended; especially when regard must be had to the calls of military service, which an infant tenant was not capable of performing. If to these considerations we add the little tenderness that was shown to the titles of such feeble claimants in those days of violence and oppression, we can easily account for the slow progress which was made towards establishing the right of representation.

With all these reasons against it, representation was not admitted as a rule of descent, even so low down as the reign of Henry II. Glanville states this very point, as a matter concerning which there was a variety of opinions in his time. A man, says he, dies leaving a younger son, and a grandson by his elder son; and it was a question between the son and the grandson who should succeed. Glanville seems to think, that if the eldest son had been *foris-familiated*, that is, provided for by a certain appoint-

---

[1] Si non antiquitùs divisum, Glanv., lib. 7, c. 3.

ment of land at his own request, the grandson should have no claim against his uncle respecting the remainder of the inheritance of the grandfather; though perhaps the eldest son might himself, had he survived.[1]

As the descent of crowns kept pace with the descent of private feuds, we may, from this doubt in Glanville, be able to account for the conduct of King John in excluding his nephew Arthur from the throne; and from the different opinions which were then held concerning it, we may collect, that he had some color of right and law for what he did; the rules of inheritance, as to the point then in question, not being precisely ascertained and settled. In France, where the right of representation had more generally obtained, that king was clearly esteemed an usurper; and as such, his title denied and opposed. In England, where that mode of descent had not yet been fully fixed, he was more generally held to be in lawful possession; or, at least, the objection to his right was such as admitted much debate and question. At what precise time these doubts were removed, and representation became universally regarded as a rule of descent, can only be conjectured. Probably, in the latter part of this very reign, when such a notorious event was recent, and had brought the subject under examination, our law of descents received this new modification from the Continent.[2]

When the succession of collaterals first took place, and when representation amongst collaterals, is involved in equal obscurity; we only know, that in the time of Henry II. the law was settled in this manner. In default of lineal descendants, the brothers and sisters came in; and if they were dead, their children; then the uncles,[3] and their children; and lastly, the aunts,[4] and their children: observing still the above distinction between knight's-service and socage, and between males and females.[5]

The law of feuds prevailed in this country as a custom, grounded upon the admission of the 52d and 58th laws of William the Conqueror. The particular rules and maxims of it gained footing imperceptibly, borrowed, perhaps, from foreign systems, but more commonly deduced by the analogy of technical reasoning. The effect of them upon our land is seen and known; but their

---

[1] Lib. 7, c. 3. [2] Dalr., Feud., 212. [3] *Avunculi.* [4] *Materteræ.*
[5] Glanv., lib. 7, c. 4.

source, or the time of their origin, is too remote and obscure to be pursued at this day.[1]

The restraint on alienation was a striking part of the feudal polity. This restraint was partly in favor of the superior lord, and partly in favor of the heir of the tenant. Whichsoever of these considerations imposed the first restriction, it is certain the first relaxation of it contained a caution that regarded the interest of the heir. A law of Henry I. says, *Acquisitiones suas det cui magis velit; si Bocland autem habeat, quam ei parentes sui dederint, non mittat eam extra cognationem suam.*[2] This permission, which enabled a man to disappoint his children of his lands *purchased*, was qualified in the time of Henry II.; for then it was laid down for law, that a man should alien only part of his purchased land, and not the whole, because he should not *filium suum hæredem exhæredare.* But if he had neither son nor daughter, he might then alien a part, or even the whole, in fee.[3] And though he had children, he might alien all his purchased lands; *provided* he had also lands by inheritance, out of which his children might be portioned. It was thought reasonable, that a man should have liberty to dispose of such lands as he had, by his own purchase, procured to himself; but the genius of this law would not so far dispense with its usual strictness, as to allow him altogether to disinherit his children.

The alienation of purchased lands led to the alienation of lands coming by descent; but this was under certain qualifications, and not without the like restraints, which we have before mentioned in the case of purchased lands. Part only of an inheritance, which had descended through the family, could, in the reign of Henry II., be given to whomsoever the owner pleased; so that, upon the whole, a person in his lifetime might, in some cases, dispose of all his purchased lands, and a reasonable part of those taken by descent, but could give neither of them by will.[4]

It is an opinion, that[5] alienation first became frequent in burgage-tenures (a). It seems as if the holding in them

---

(a) "Tenure in burgage is where an ancient borough is of which the king
[1] *Ingrediturque solo, et caput inter nubila condit.* [4] Ibid.
[2] Leg. Hen. I., 70. [*Vide ante*, p. 241.] [5] Dalr., Feud. Prop., 99.
[3] Glanv., lib. 7, c. 3.

was never very strict; and, as persons living in that sort of society sooner got loose from an habitual reverence for tenure, and, from their occupation, stood in need of a more exchangeable property, it is probable alienations might happen there more early than among other tenants.

When alienations had become established in burgage-tenures, the alienation of purchased lands in many instances, and of lands, descended in some, was by degrees permitted, as we have before seen. All these alterations broke in upon the original notion of tenure and its qualities; and in the reign of King John prevailed to such a degree, as to occasion the restrictions imposed by the

---

is lord, and they that have tenements within the borough hold of the king, that every tenant ought to pay to the king a certain rent. And so it is where another lord — spiritual or temporal — is lord of a borough, and the tenants of such a borough hold of their lord, to pay each a certain rent" (*Littleton*, c. x.). It appears from this that the origin of boroughs were "vills," or "towns," terms which originally meant a house and estate in the country, the Roman "villa" being the original, and the British or Saxon "town" meaning originally a single house or farm in the country, whence to this day the phrase is sometimes used in that sense. Then, as the lord gave leave to tenants to erect houses on payment of rent, a town, in the more modern sense, arose. And so, as Littleton says, every borough is a town, though every town is not a borough (*Ibid.*); for two or three houses may make a town or township, but a borough implies something of more importance; "for," says he, "of such old towns called boroughs came the burgesses of the parliament when the king hath summoned his parliament" (*Ibid.*). And as the word "borough" is simply the Saxon word "borh," or burgh, which, all through the Saxon laws, is used in the sense of an assemblage of inhabitants within the same "frankpledge," the "boroughs" must be as old as the Saxons. On the other hand, it is manifest that many towns must be much older, especially such as are, or once were cities; and that such places as have always been, or were anciently called cities, such as London and York, although, it may be, no longer called cities, or, perhaps, now comparatively deserted, were of Roman origin, being the "municipia," or municipal colonies, and "civitates," established during the Roman occupation. And, therefore, Littleton, ignoring, like other sages of the common law, what is of Roman origin, was in error when he wrote that boroughs are older than cities. That which distinguishes boroughs from other and more modern towns is, as he says, "ancient custom or prescription." "And the greater part of such boroughs have divers customs and usages which be not had in other towns; for some have a custom that if a man have issue many sons, and dieth, the youngest son shall inherit within the borough, which custom is called Borough-English. And so in some boroughs by custom the wife shall have for her dower all the tenements which were her husband's. Also in some boroughs, by the custom, a man may devise by his testament his lands and tenements within the borough. And this course is the custom. And no custom is to be allowed but such as hath been used by title of prescription — that is, from time out of mind. And many other customs and usages have such ancient boroughs" (*Ibid.*). But cities such as London and York have customs still more ancient, derived from the Romans.— *Vide Bro. Abr.*, "Custom," pl. 25, 10.

Great Charter. Thus far of tenures and their incidents, of which we shall take our leave for the present.[1] The judicature of the kingdom was thrown into a system conformable to the new polity (a). The objects which

(a) This subject, which lies at the basis of all others, as regards changes of the law during the period in question, seeing that the changes were mainly the result of judicial authority, our author has not sufficiently brought out. As already has been shown in the Introduction, it was seen that the laws could only be altered in that way, gradually and by judicial authority, and that with this view the judicature and procedure must both be improved. The difficulty was, however, that the people clung with tenacity to their old institutions, and especially to the old turbulent popular tribunals, the courts of the hundreds and the county, the evils of which are alluded to in the laws of Henry I., which have been cited, and are described by Lord Hale (*History of the Common Law*, p. 7), from whom our author borrows some passages in a subsequent page (*vide post*). The difficulty was solved in this way: the old tribunals, or at least the old *assemblies* were retained, and they

[1] Such is the shape which the feudal polity, after its introduction into this country, gradually assumed. [The author here introduced a long note excusing his not having entered into the foreign feudal system, concluding thus:] — Feuds, properly so called, namely those at the will of the lord, were no part of the system established by William; his famous law expressly declares that he had granted them *jure hæreditario*. The uncertain casualties of tenures were soon ascertained by express charters of liberties, repeatedly granted by our Norman kings. On the death of the ancestor, the fee was cast upon the heir by construction of law, who entered as into a patrimonial, not a feudal property. Such was the law of English tenures, at their earliest appearance; and to this it is to be attributed, that through all our law-books and reports, from Bracton to Coke, and further down, there is no allusion, no reasoning, that bears any relation to feuds or feudal law, in this sense of it; and those who have arraigned Lord Coke for his silence on this head, have passed, in my mind, a very hasty judgment on the extent of that great lawyer's learning. . . .

The lawyers of this country, like the people, impatient of foreign innovations, soon moulded the institutions of Normandy into a new shape, and formed a system of feuds of their own. The usage and custom of the country became the guide of our courts; who have invariably rejected with disdain all arguments from the practice of other countries. [This view is in accordance with that of Hale, who, as will have been seen, denied that there had been any such sweeping alteration of the tenures of the land as some had supposed.]

For a knowledge of the feudal system, as far as concerns an English lawyer, we are to look no farther than Glanville, Bracton, and Littleton. And as far as it is to be collected from the works of these and other English lawyers, *the feudal system of England* respecting landed property is discussed in this and the subsequent parts of this History (as I should think) at as great length as could conveniently be done consistent with the plan of such a work.

The design of this History seemed to make it absolutely necessary to adhere to this plan. To investigate the first principles of our law, and to pursue them through all the modifications and applications, all the additions and changes to which they were subjected in different periods of time, is an inquiry that called upon the writer rather to reduce and simplify his materials, than to seek for new ones, or extend his views.

first present themselves, on contemplating the introduction of Norman judicature, are the separation of the ec-

were, at the same time, slowly and by degrees so far modified, as to deprive them of real power, until, at length, becoming first virtually superseded and then obsolete, they were practically, except in trivial cases, abolished. The mode in which this was effected, — which constitutes one of the most curious, interesting, and important events in the course of our legal history, — was altogether lost sight of by our author, so that, the essential point in the legal history of the period having been missed, all the rest is lost in confusion and obscurity. It was effected in this way. The sheriff, it will be recollected, presided in these assemblies, and he was the criminal judge. Criminal justice, it will be borne in mind, was, as is noticed in the laws of Henry I., necessarily local, and administered in the counties (as it is to this day), and civil justice was most conveniently so. And no doubt it was this in a great degree which made the people cling so to their local, popular, tribunals; and if they could be made to see that justice could be *better* administered, and yet by local tribunals, they would not be so likely to cling to these popular institutions. So it was managed thus. In the first place, the king appointed, as his judges, barons or knights, or ecclesiastics, men *fit to be judges*; next he appointed them *sheriffs*, so that there was one great point gained, that there were fit and proper judges both in the civil and criminal courts of the county. Of the fact there is no doubt, owing to the learned industry of Mr. Foss; see many instances of it in his *Lives of the Judges*, vol. i., pp. 377, 189, 186, 264. And he shows that even chief justiciaries were sometimes sheriffs, and that a sheriff often held several counties, and for several years (*Ibid.*, pp. 264, 392, 373, 343). Or again, if the sheriff was an able man, the king made him his justice or justiciary. Or again, learned and able men, at first chiefly ecclesiastics, were sent down by royal commission, or writ, to convene and preside at a county court. These men, having some notion of what a civilized system of procedure should be, would, of course, be shocked at the spectacle of a turbulent county court, and would revolt from the idea of such a noisy, tumultuous assembly being deemed a court of justice. And their first object would be to improve it. The way in which to do so was simple and easy enough, and was indeed already pointed out by rude beginnings in the Saxon laws, or the usages introduced, at all events in criminal cases, by Alfred — that is, the *swearing of a certain number of men as judges;* in short, the empanelling a *jury* to try the case under the direction of a skilled and learned judge. And, accordingly, early in the reign of the Conqueror this was attempted, and the experiment was tried with great success in what Lord Coke, Selden, and Lord Hale all cite as the "great case," or "famous case," of the suit by the Archbishop of Canterbury against Odo, Bishop of Bayeux, to recover a number of manors in the county of Kent — a case tried at a county court on Penendon Heath, with the aid of a jury, that is, of twelve men out of the county, *sworn* to decide truly on their knowledge. Lord Coke sets out the whole record in the Preface to the 9th Part of his Reports, and Selden sets it out in his Notes on *Eadmerus.* And although, as the *judgment* was that of the county *court*, it is so stated in the record, there is no doubt from contemporary history that twelve men were sworn, and that made it a trial by jury. Our author mentions the case in a subsequent portion of this chapter; but misses its main point, and fails to observe how it happened that a bishop presided at the court — not the bishop of the county, but a foreign bishop, whose authority could only have been derived from royal commission. That this was not the only instance of the kind, is shown by Mr. Foss, who cites another case (*Lives of the Judges*, vol. i., p. 26). There also the king sent a foreign prelate down as justiciary

clesiastical from the temporal court, and the establishment of the *curia regis*. By an ordinance of William the

into the county, and he empanelled a jury (*Ibid.*). Sir James Mackintosh cites the former case, and says, "it has much the appearance of the dawn of trial by jury" (*History of England*, vol. i., p. 275). And as, in each instance, the judge fined one jury for giving a wrong verdict, and empanelled another, that eminent historian truly observes that there was a new trial, which implies a power in the judge to instruct the jury on the law. And it is indeed stated in the record of the first case, that a bishop, as eminently skilled in the law, came by the king's command to instruct the jury as to the customs of the realm, i. e., the law. The substantial resemblance between this proceeding and a modern assize is manifest. It is difficult to see in what the two proceedings differed. For the county assizes, at this day, sit under commissions issued into the different counties, each commission is *for the county;* under it the sheriff convenes the gentlemen of the county as the grand jurors, and the farmers and traders, the representatives of the ancient freeholders, the suitors at the county court, as jurors. There is still the sheriff and the county court, there is the king's judge and the jury; and the only difference between that proceeding, and the one which took place on Penenden Heath eight hundred years ago, is, that the jurors then gave their verdict of their own knowledge. At a later time, the curia regis gradually arose, taking cognizance first of cases between the crown and the subject, which arose in the exchequer, and then of cases between subject and subject, such as afterwards came into the common pleas. The notion that all this had any connection with feudality is mere error. It was the progressive growth of law. The judges who sat in that high court often went into the counties to hold the courts there, and the justices, who had acquired experience in the counties, were called to that high court. The serjeants-at-law, then beginning to be known, sat with the sheriff or justiciary in the county courts; and the most learned and eminent men in the kingdom, laymen or ecclesiastics, were appointed to serve the crown as judges, either in the curia regis, or the courts of the counties. All this will be found described in the first vol. of the *Lives of the Judges*, by Mr. Foss, and its effect upon the administration of justice must be too obvious to require to be pointed out. It is manifest that the decisions of these judges, either in the counties or in the curia regis, must have had a great effect in moulding procedure, and improving the law. And we have scattered through the *Mirror of Justice*, numerous judicial decisions and many "ordinances," which no doubt were no more than judicial decisions, of a most important character, and gradually modifying and improving the law, until it reached, in the reign of Henry II., the form in which we have it presented to us in the learned treatises of Glanville and of Bracton. From the 18th Henry I., the records of the exchequer prove that king's justices went into the counties on their circuits or itineracies; and there can be no doubt that from the time of the great case of the Archbishop of Canterbury, that course of proceeding was preserved. The result was that the county court in its old form lost its repute, and the way was prepared for a practice which virtually destroyed it, except for comparatively small cases. That was the practice of requiring the suitor to take out a writ to the sheriff in any case above the value of forty shillings, which was the ancient limit, according to the *Mirror*, of the jurisdiction, not of the county courts, but of the courts baron (*vide ante*). Writs used to be sued to compel the sheriff to proceed, and now it was said they were required to enable him to proceed. The effect was, that the suitor, in all cases above the amount, had a writ out of the king's court, and had to pay a fee for it, no doubt as great as he would have to pay for a writ in the king's court.

Conqueror, the bishop, with all ecclesiastical causes, was separated from the sheriff (*a*); and the calderman, or earl, receiving a feudal character, began to hold his county court as the feudal lords did theirs (*b*). This was done

---

The *Mirror* makes this a great grievance; money at that time being extremely scarce. The natural result was, that the suitors in the more important cases preferred to sue in the king's court; added to which, the king's courts would remove the suits, if at all important. Hence the county court declined in credit. In the reign of Henry I., when it was endeavored to improve it, the bishops and barons were desired to attend it (*Leges Henrici Primi*, c. ii.); but in that reign, and that of Henry II., the king's judges had long gone into the counties on their circuits, and as it was inconvenient always to make the sheriffs judges, or judges sheriffs, they convened the counties under special commissions at county courts, independent of the sittings held by the sheriff, and, of course, empanelled juries. (They were enabled to convene the men of the county by the laws of Henry I., and could easily direct juries to be empanelled.) Thus, in the reign of Henry III., the old county courts had so far declined that the bishops and barons were excused from attendance (*Mirror*, c. i.); and, on the other hand, the resemblance between the old county courts and the new courts held by king's judges were so great that the chief men of the county considered they were entitled to sit as if they formed a part of it. In the reign of Richard II. this was prohibited, and it was ordained that no lord, or other in the county, little or great, shall sit upon the bench with the justices, to take assizes in their sessions in the counties of England (20 *Richard II.*, c. iii.). Thus, then, the assizes held by the king's judges finally superseded the old county court, which, though in law retaining its jurisdiction, in practice virtually lost it. The change, it will be observed, took not less than three centuries of progressive innovation, and gradual alteration, to effect it; and throughout the whole period there was no violent or sudden change, and the alteration was effected so silently and quietly that probably the people at that period hardly observed it. It is obvious that the effect of this improvement in the judicature and in the procedure for the administration of justice, must have had an equally powerful, though equally unobserved, effect in gradually moulding and modifying the law.

(*a*) This is not correct: it was not the bishop who was removed from the county court, it was the ecclesiastical causes which were removed from it to a separate court of the bishop; the reason assigned being that it was not becoming that the laity should meddle in ecclesiastical matters. The edict was, " Ne ullus vicecomes, aut prepositus seu minister regis, nec aliquis laicus homo, de legibus quæ ad episcopum pertinent, se intromittant, nec aliquis lacius homo alium hominem, sine justicia episcopi ad judicium adducat" (*A.-S. L.*, v. i., 495). There was no idea of removing the bishop from the county court; and, on the contrary, in the "Leges Henrici Primi" we find it carefully provided, " Interesse comitatui debent episcopi comites, et ceteræ potestates, quæ Dei leges et seculi negotia justa consideratione diffiniant" (c. xxxi., *A.-S. L.*, c. i., p. 534); and again, c. vii., " Intersint autem episcopes, comites, etc., deligenter intendentes," etc. (*Ibid.*, 514).

(*b*) This is a still greater mistake. The calderman was the hundredor, and the earl was the Roman "comes," or chief of a county — our lord-lieutenant. The sheriff was, as the Latin word indicates, the deputy of the earl or count, —the viscount; and he only convened and presided at the county court, at which the freeholders were the judges. There was no alteration in the constitution of the county court, and it could not possibly have any connection

by the *sheriff*, who, soon after the Conquest, if not before, grew to be a different person from the *earl* (a). The periodical circuits henceforth ceased, and the county court and tourn were held in a certain place. In the former, the *vicecomes* or sheriff, acting for the earl, used to preside, and the freeholders, as before, were judges of the court. The latter, notwithstanding the absence of the bishop, soon after received new splendor and importance from a law of Henry I. (b), which required all persons, as well peers as commoners, clergy as well as laity, to give attendance there, to hear a charge from the sheriff, and to take the oath of allegiance to the king. This obliged the greatest lords of the kingdom to submit to frequent remembrances of their subordinate station; and so contributed to draw closer the bands of political union. In other respects, these old Saxon courts seemed to continue in their original state. In the county court were held civil pleas; and in the tourn were made all criminal inquiries (c). Every manor had its court baron,

Of judicature.

with feudality, for it was simply a popular assembly. The lords always held their courts in their courts baron, quite independently of the courts of the hundred or county; they were distinct jurisdictions, and therefore no alteration in their tenures, or in the tenures of those who would suit and serve in other courts, could have anything to do with the courts of the county.

(a) This always had been so. The earl was the count, and the sheriff the viscount.

(b) The author cites no authority, and there are only two sources whence laws of Henry I. can be derived: the "Leges Henrici Primi," printed in the *Anglo-Saxon Laws*, c. i., p. 510, and mentioned in the Introduction as a compilation made shortly after the death of that king; and the *Mirror of Justice*, which mentions many laws of the kings between the Conquest and the reign of Edward I. . The former, the "Leges Henrici Primi," contains the following as to the county court: —"Intersint episcopi, comites, etc., deligentur intendentes," etc. (c. vii.); and again, "Interesse comitatui debent episcopi, comites, et ceteræ potestates," etc. (c. xxxi.). But in the *Mirror* it is stated that Henry III. excused the bishops, earls, barons, etc., from attendance at the county court (c. i., s. 16). It is to be observed that, under Henry I. and Henry II., the king's judges went into the counties twice a year to try cases, which superseded the county courts; and, in the reign of Richard II., it was enacted that no lord, great or little, should sit upon the bench with the king's judges.

(c) As already mentioned, the "leet" was the court of the hundred for criminal matters, and was restricted to common nuisances and the like (27 *Assize;* 22 *Edward IV.*, 22, 4; *Ibid.* 4, 31). A particular private wrong could not be inquired of there as an assault (per *Martin J.;* 4 *Henry VI.*, 10). Trespass would not lie in a court baron, at common law, where force was used (*Year-Book*, 8; *Edw. IV.*, 15); and the sheriff could not inquire in his tourn of any new matter made punishable by statute, but only of public nuisances (1 *Richard*, 3). The tourn or leet shall not inquire of matters

where the lord was to hold plea and transact matters respecting certain rights and claims of his own tenants, and for the punishment of nuisances and misdemeanors arising within the manor; from all which courts, on failure of justice, there lay an appeal to the sheriff's court, and from thence to the king's supreme court. Many lords had franchises to hold hundred and other courts, both civil and criminal; and there are some few instances, where the crown had granted to a great lord *jura regalia* of a certain district; erecting it into a county palatine, distinct from, and exclusive of, all jurisdiction of the king's courts. William granted the county of Chester to *Hugh Lupus; hunc totum comitatum tenendum sibi et hæredibus ita liberè ad gladium sicut ipse rex tenebat Angliam ad coronam.* The like ample grant was soon after made of the bishopric of Durham to that prelate; and in later times grew up the franchise of Ely and Hexham, the counties palatine of Lancaster and Pembroke.[1]

The supreme court of ordinary judicature established by William the Conqueror, was the *aula regis*, or *curia regis;* so called, because it was held in the king's palace, before himself, or his justices, of whom the *summus justitiarius totius Angliæ* was chief. There was also the exchequer, called *curia regis ad scaccarium;*[2] which was held likewise in the king's palace, either before the king or his grand justiciary; and though in effect a member of the *curia regis*, was expressly distinguished from it. In what manner the grand justiciary, who presided in both these courts, ordered or distributed between them the several pleas instituted there, or in what manner these pleas were conducted, it is difficult at this distance of time precisely to determine. Respecting the nature of this obsolete judicature, little more can be hoped than such conjectures as may be founded on the few remaining monuments of antiquity.[3]

The curia regis consisted of the following persons: the king himself was properly head, and next to him was the grand justiciary, who, in his absence, was the supreme head of the court; the other members of this court were

_{The curia regis.}

---

given by statute, unless it is expressly said that they shall be inquired of at the tourn or leet (*Year-Book,* 4; *Edw. IV.,* 31), because their jurisdiction was by prescription, and it could only apply to things ancient.
[1] *Vide* 4 Inst., 211.   [2] Wilk., Leg. Sax., 288.   [3] Mad., Ex., 57.

the great officers of the king's palace; such as the treasurer, chancellor, chamberlain, steward, marshal, constable, and the barons of the realm. To these were associated certain persons called *justitiæ*, or *justitiarii*, to the number of five or six: on whom, with the grand justiciary, the burden of judicature principally fell; the barons seldom appearing there, as little valuing a privilege attended with labor, and the discussion of questions ill-suited to their martial education (*a*). The justices were the part of this

(*a*) The author cites no contemporary authority for all this; and there is great doubt as to the existence and constitution of any such court, unless it was the exchequer, which was not, originally, a court of ordinary jurisdiction. The *Mirror of Justice*, in the earliest and most ancient part of it, makes no mention of "curia regis" in that sense: and, on the contrary, states that it was ordained that freemen should judge their neighbors in the county courts and the courts of the hundred; and though it is said that plaintiffs could have remedial writs from the chancery, the form of such writs is given, and it is directed to the sheriff to compel him to decide the case; all which quite agrees with what appears even in the " Leges Henrici Primi," already largely quoted. There is no allusion to the exchequer any more than to the chancery, except as an office. The exchequer, it is said, was ordained that the barons might assess the amercements. Nothing is said in this, the earlier and more ancient chapter, of any king's court of justice, except the county court, which is called curia regis in the Laws of Henry I., as we have seen. What is said in subsequent portions of the *Mirror* may refer to later times, after Magna Charta. In the laws of Henry I.— the only source of information on the subject, except the *Mirror* (which only mentions the exchequer, in any passage which can be referred to a period anterior to the Great Charter) — the phrase " curia regis " is only once used, and then evidently applies to the county courts. In a chapter (xxix.) headed, "Qui debent esse judices regis," it is said, "regis judices sunt barones comitatus;" and then it goes on to treat of the county court, and then the next chapter (xxx.) is headed, " De libertate procerum in placito comitatuum;" and the next (c. xxxi.) directs that the barons should sit in the county court. "Interesse comitatui debent comites, episcopi," etc.; and then it is said, "Recordationem curia regis nulli negace licet," which plainly means the county court, there being no other mentioned. It will be observed the author cites no authority to sustain his statements save Madox, whose work is dedicated to the exchequer. There is no reason to believe that there was before the Great Charter any proper king's court but the exchequer. In the chapter in the *Mirror of Justice*, headed, " Del Roy Alfred," in treating of the courts, the exchequer is mentioned as " curia regis," but only as an *office;* and no other king's court is alluded to. "Ordeine fuit l'exchequer en manner come ensuist perles peines pecunielles de comities et de baronnes en certaine, et aussi d' toutes comities et baronnes entirrs ou dismembers, et que ceux amerciaments pussent afferred perles barons del exchequer, et que envoiast les estreates d' leur amerciaments al exchequer ou que ils pussent amercies en le court le roy." The exchequer was ordained for pecuniary penalties of baronies and earldoms; and the amercements were "affeered" (assessed) by the barons of the exchequer, though they might be amerced in the king's court — *i. e.*, in the county court, which, in the laws of Henry I., is so called. The *Mirror*, even in a passage not so ancient, says, "the exchequer is a place which was ordained only for the king's revenue; where

court that was principally considered, as appears by the return of writs, which was *coram me vel justitiis meis;* unless that appellation may be supposed to include every member thereof in his judicial capacity.

All kinds of pleas, civil and criminal, were cognizable in this high court;[1] and not only pleas, but other legal business arising between parties was there transacted. Feoffments, releases, conventions, and concords of divers kinds were there made, especially in cases that required more than common solemnity.[2] Many pleas, from their great importance, were proper subjects of inquiry there; others were brought by special permission of the king and his justices.

---

two knights, two clerks, and two learned men in the law are assigned to hear and determine wrongs done to the king and crown in right of his fees, and the penalties and accounts of bailiffs and receivers of the king's moneys, and the administrators of his goods, by the oversight of one chief who is the treasurer of England. The two knights, usually called two barons, were for to affeer the amercements of earls and barons, the tenants of earldoms and baronies; so that none be amerced but by his peers" (c. i., s. 14). Then afterwards, there is a passage more modern, "The barons of the exchequer have jurisdiction over receivers, and the king's bailiffs, and of alienations of lands and rights belonging to the king and to the rights of the crown. The court has a seal assigned to it and a keeper" (c. iv., s. 3). It is known that there was a royal seal before the Conquest, kept in the exchequer, and the writs of chancery were sealed there (*Madox, Exch.,* i. 194). If there was any "curia regis" at the time, it was the exchequer, apart from the personal authority of the king. In a work of the time of Henry II., "Dialogus de Scaccario," the exchequer is said to have been erected at the time of the Conquest. Gervasius Tilburiensis says, "Nulli licet statuta scaccarii infringere, vel quamvis temeritate resistere; habet hoc enim quiddam commune cum ipsa domini regis curia in quâ ipse in propriâ personâ jura dicit"—which shows, that even so late as the time of Henry II. the authority exercised by the king in *curia regis* was *in propriâ personâ;* and appears to imply that even then there was no regular judicature except in the exchequer. The roll of the exchequer commences in the reign of Henry I., and previous to that time there is no distinct evidence of a permanent office even of chief justiciary, as the person appointed to such office appears to have often exercised indiscriminately the functions of chancellor and chief of the exchequer. So lately as the time of John, common suits came into the exchequer, before the king and his barons and justices then present (Manning's *Serviens ad Legem,* xix., and Dugdale's *Orig. Jurid.,* 49, 50); and, on the other hand, there is no evidence of any king's court but the exchequer, until after Magna Charta, which said that common pleas should not be decided in a court which followed the king's person, as the exchequer did. The probability is that some ambiguity has arisen as to the sense in which the word "curia" was used, and that at first it meant the king's court, in the sense of his residence, where he sometimes in person sat, with the chief justiciary and chancellor, attending to complaints of grievances, originally as to revenue; hence *arose* a court of *justice.*

[1] Mad., Ex., 70.   [2] Ibid., 77.

The course of application to the *curia regis* was of this nature. The party suing paid, or undertook to pay, to the king a fine to have *justitiam et rectum* in his court: and thereupon he obtained a writ or precept, by means of which he commenced his suit; and the justices were authorized to hear and determine his claim. These writs were made out in the name and under the seal of the king, but with the *teste* of the grand justiciary; for the making and issuing of which (as well as for other offices) the king used to have near his person some great man, usually an ecclesiastic, who was called his *chancellor*, and had the keeping of his seal: under the chancellor were kept clerks for making these writs (*a*). It was probably this office of the chancellor that rendered him a necessary member of the *curia regis;* to which, in fact, and to the

(*a*) The author, it will be observed, does not cite any authority for all this; and was not aware of the contents of the *Mirror of Justice*, a work already alluded to as founded on one of the age of Alfred, and containing the whole of our judicial procedure, as it existed from the time of the Conquest to the reign of Edward I., when it was completed. It is very observable that this ancient work makes no mention of any "curia regis," of which so much is said by the author, unless it be the exchequer. The chancery, however, is mentioned as *officina brevium*, and the exchequer as the court or office of *brevium;* and it may be observed that in the history of all countries it will be probably found that fiscal tribunals or functionaries are the most ancient institutions, and that other judicial institutions have often arisen out of them. Instead of the curia regis being divided into the exchequer and other courts, it rather appears that the exchequer was the original court, and that the others arose out of it. In the *Mirror* it is said, It was ordained that every one have a remedial writ from the king's chancery, according to his plaint: "Ordeine fuit que chescun eyt de chancery l'roy brief remedial a sa plaint" (i. 12). But the form of such writ given is directed to the sheriff to compel him to decide the case. So elsewhere it is said, "that jurisdiction was assigned by the king, by his commissions, or writs" — phrases used indiscriminately — "and without a writ he cannot give jurisdiction." But there were the itinerant justices, as appears elsewhere. "And so our ancestors appointed a seal and a chancellor to the same, to give remedial writs without delay." These writs, it is said, used to be written in English by a clerk of the chancery; and sometimes were directed to the lord of the fee; sometimes to the justices in eyre (the commissions); sometimes to the sheriffs, etc., (c. iv., s. 2). And the writs not returnable before the king are returnable in chancery (*Ib.*, s. 3). But in the laws of Henry I., the county court is called the king's court, "curia regis;" and when, in these times, the king's justice is mentioned, it meant the itinerant justices. Thus it is said in the *Mirror*, that a cause concerning the freehold would be suspended until the coming of the king's justice into the county (c. ii., s. 28). The curia regis, if there was such a court, was the exchequer; which had not originally any ordinary jurisdiction, and the judges of which were called justices of the bench, to distinguish them from the itinerant justices. The common suits came at last into the exchequer, and then, when Magna Charta said they should not follow the king, as the exchequer did, the court of common pleas arose.

justices, and not to the king, suitors made their complaint, and, upon paying the usual fine, were referred to the chancellor to furnish them with a writ.

As the old establishment of the Saxons for determining common pleas in the county court was continued, very few of those causes were brought into the *curia regis* (*a*). While men could have justice administered so near their homes, there was no temptation to undergo the extraordinary expense and trouble of commencing actions before this high tribunal; but the partiality with which justice was administered in the courts of arbitrary and potent lords, often left the king's subjects without prospect of redress in the inferior jurisdictions: the king and the *curia regis* became then an asylum to the weak. It is not remarkable, that suitors coming to a court under such circumstances should consent to purchase the means of redress by paying a fine. Upon such terms was the *curia regis* open to all complainants: and the institution of suits was eagerly encouraged by the officers of that court.

The exchequer was a sort of *subaltern* court, resembling in its model that which was more properly called the *curia regis* (*b*). Here, likewise, the grand justiciary,

---

(*a*) It was a law of the Saxons, confirmed at the Conquest, that no man *could* go out of the county court unless on the ground that a failure of justice was inevitable there. Thus, in the laws of William the Conqueror, "Nemo querelam ad regem deferat nisi ei jus defecerit, in hundreti vel in comitatu" (c. 43). This, which embodied the Saxon law, was embodied in the Laws of Henry I., and it is there expounded what causes led to a failure of justice, and drew causes into the king's cognizance (c. 33, De placito tractando). "Defectus justitiæ, et violenti recti eorum destitutio, est qui causas protrahunt in jus regium." That is to say, there was then a ground of complaint to the king's extraordinary jurisdiction by reason of his prerogative; for under the head, "De jure Regis," is "defectus justitiæ" (c. x.). Therefore there was no ordinary jurisdiction between subject and subject, except in the county court; and no curia regis open to suitors; the remedy being, so far as appears, to send down a justice of the king to hear the trial. In the reign of Henry II., the chancellor had obtained some kind of judicial jurisdiction; for a contemporary states that he became a remembrancer in the chancery under the celebrated A'Becket, and, when he sat to hear and determine causes, was a reader of the bills and petitions (Fitz-Stephen's *Description of London* (pub. 1772), p. 19). But this may have been any of the "bills" or "petitions" for writs at common law, just as in the king's bench the ancient mode of exercising jurisdiction was upon "bill" of complaint; and the rolls of parliament, as late as the reign of Edward I., contained many instances of petitions in respect of matters which were redressed at common law.

(*b*) The reasons have already been given for holding that there was at this time no curia regis in the sense of a regular judicial tribunal, unless, indeed, it was the exchequer, in which, beyond all doubt, the king and his barons, and great officers of the palace presided. The persons who were justices in the *curia regis*, acted in the same capacity here; this court being very little else than the *curia regis* sitting in another place, namely, *ad scaccarium;* only it happened, that the justices, when they sat at the exchequer, were more usually called *barons*. The administration of justice in those days was so commonly attendant on the rank and character of a baron that *baro* and *justitiarius* were often used synonymously.[1]

Affairs of the revenue were the principal objects of consideration in the court of exchequer. The superintendence of this was the chief care of the justiciary and barons: the cognizance of a great number of matters followed as incident thereto; as the king's revenue was, in some way or other, concerned in the fees, lands, rights, and chattels of the subject; and ultimately in almost everything he possessed.

However, it is thought the court of exchequer was not so confined to the peculiar business assigned it, and its incidents, as not to entertain such suits of a general nature as were usually brought in the *curia regis*:[2] and it is probable, this usage of holding common pleas at the exchequer continued till the time when common pleas were separated[3] from the *curia regis;* and that both courts ceased to hold plea of common suits at the same time, and by the same prohibition. Other legal business, like that in the *curia regis*, was also transacted at the exchequer: charters of feoffment, confirmation, and release, final concords, and other conventions, were executed there before the barons;[4] all which, added to the consideration that the constituent members were the same, put the court of exchequer very nearly on an equality with the *curia regis*.

---

barons, and justices gave redress in common suits as well as in matters of complaint as to the crown, as early as the reign of Henry II., and possibly earlier. Thus it is stated that the prior and monks of Abingdon appealed to Ranulph de Glanville in the reign of Henry II., respecting the king's seizure of their possessions, and that he was sitting in the exchequer (Dugdale's *Orig. Jurid.*, 49). So cases are stated, as late as the reign of John, in which parties claimed redress for *private* wrongs in the exchequer (Manning's *Serviens ad Legem.*, p. 171). In the *Abbreviatio Placitorum*, which contains the earliest records — except the Rolls themselves — many such cases will be found, and none *except* in the exchequer prior to Magna Charta.

[1] Mad., Ex., 134.   [2] Mad., Ex., 141.   [3] By the Great Charter.
            [4] Mad., Ex., 145.

By the multifarious and increasing business of these two courts, the grand justiciary and his assessors on the bench found themselves fully occupied; and as the application to these courts became more frequent, it was judged necessary, both in aid of themselves and relief of suitors, to erect some other tribunal of the same nature. Justices itinerant. Accordingly justices were appointed to go *itinera*, or circuits through the kingdom, and determine pleas in the several counties (*a*). To these new tribunals was given a very comprehensive jurisdiction. As they were a sort of emanations from the *curia regis* and exchequer, and were substituted in some measure in their place (except with the reservation of appeal thereto) they were endowed with all the authorities and powers of those courts. These *justices itinerant* or *errant*, in their

(*a*) It will be obvious, from what has already been stated, that the reasons here assigned for the institution of the circuit court is quite wrong, and the inference from it erroneous. It has been seen that, as the ordinary justice of the realm was strictly local, the king's judges had to go into the counties to hold courts, and the metropolitan county formed no exception; if, indeed, there was any metropolis then, in our modern sense of the term, and not rather several chief cities or royal residences, where the court or council sat, following the person of the king; whence the necessity for the provision in Magna Charta that the common pleas should be fixed at Westminster. The constitution of the country, therefore, did not, for the ordinary justice of the realm, provide any courts other than those of the counties, and hence the necessity for remoulding them by sending down justices into the counties. This, then, was the original and most ancient form of a regular royal judicature, as far as regards the ordinary justice of the realm, civil or criminal; and there was no curia regis except the exchequer, the court for the extraordinary jurisdiction of the revenue, and perhaps a kind of royal council for matters partly political, partly judicial. It was not until some time after the itinerant justices had exercised their jurisdiction in the counties that the exchequer exercised jurisdiction in cases between subject and subject, and some time afterwards we find the court of common pleas. Thus, therefore, the order of events was exactly the contrary of what the author supposed, and it was not until the necessity had arisen for settling the issues in cases of importance, and a regular procedure was devised for the purpose, that the superior courts, as they are now called, began to rise in importance, and take cognizance of common causes, in order to determine matters of law. It was quite in accordance with the policy which had sent king's judges into the counties to empanel parties, and direct them as to the law, to provide a judicature to settle the matters in dispute, to separate matters of law, and determine them before sending the case into the county for trial, when perhaps there was nothing to try, and the question resolved itself into one of law. Hence it is not until some time after the itinera (which commenced soon after the Conquest) had shown the necessity of this, that we find superior courts engaged in deciding matters of law in suits between subject and subject. It is not until the time of Glanville, who was chief justiciary under Henry II., and probably himself brought about the change, that we find a curia regis as a regular judicial tribunal.

several *itinera*, or *eyres*, held plea of all causes, whether civil or criminal, and in most respects discharged the office of both the superior courts. The characters of the persons entrusted with this jurisdiction were equal to the high authority they exercised; the same persons who were justices in the king's court being, amongst others, justices itinerant. They acted under the king's writ in nature of a commission; and they went generally from seven years to seven years; though their circuits sometimes returned at shorter intervals. Their circuits became a kind of limitation in criminal prosecutions, as no one could be indicted for anything done before the preceding *eyre.*

The administration of justice in the county and other inferior courts, notwithstanding some striking advantages, was certainly pregnant with great evils (*a*). The freeholders of the county, who were the judges, were seldom learned in the law; for although not only they, but bishops, barons, and other great men, were, by a law of Henry I., appointed to attend the county court (by which they might, after time and observation, qualify themselves to act in the office of magistrates), the study and knowledge of the laws was confined to a very few. Again, the determination of so many independent judges, presiding in the several inferior courts dispersed about the country, bred great variety in the laws, which, in process of time, would have habituated different counties to different rules and customs, and the nation would have been governed by a variety of provincial laws. Besides these inherent defects, it was found that matters were there carried by party and passion. The freeholders, often previously acquainted with the subjects of contro-

(*a*) What follows, which is in substance taken from Lord Hale's history, is quite in accordance with what may be gathered from the language used in the Laws of Henry I. already quoted. "Defectus justiciæ, et violenti recti eorum destitutio, est qui causas protrahunt in jus regium" (c. 33). And elsewhere, "Et si quisquam, violenta recti destitutione, in hundretis vel congruis agendorum locis causam suam ita turbaverit, ut ad comitatus audientiam pertrahatur, perdat eum, etc. Si uterque necessario desit, prepositus et sacerdos, et quatuor de melioribus villæ assint pro omnibus qui nominatim non erunt ad placitum submoniti. Idem in hundreto decrevimus observandum de causis singulis, justis examinationibus audiendis de domini vel prepositi et meliorum hominum præsentia" (c. 7). The object was to get causes submitted to a select body of the better sort of freeholders, sworn to decide the case; which *was a jury.* At the end of the chapter, the author cites an instance of this, — already mentioned.

versy, or with the parties, became heated and interested in causes; which, added to the influence of great men, on whom they were too much dependent by tenure of service, rendered these courts extremely unfit for cool deliberation and impartial judgment. Nor were these difficulties remedied by the power of bringing writs of false judgment, and thereby removing a cause into the *curia regis*, though the penalty of amercement on the suitors of the county court, for errors in judgment, was sufficiently severe. If these objections lay against the king's courts in the county, much more did they against those of great lords; who made the awards of justice subservient to their own schemes of power and aggrandizement.

Besides these, there were reasons of a political nature which dictated an establishment of this kind; this was, to obviate the mischiefs arising to the just prerogatives of the crown from the many hereditary jurisdictions introduced under the Norman system. A judicial authority exercised by subjects in their own names, must considerably weaken the power of the prince; one of whose most valuable royalties, and that which most conciliates the confidence and good inclinations of his people, is the power of providing that justice should be duly administered to every individual. Though the appeal from the hundred to the court of the sheriff (an officer of the king) so far kept a check upon the jurisdiction of lords, yet it was still to be wished that the inconvenience of appeals should be precluded, and that justice should be administered in the first instance by judges deriving their commission from the king.[1] If these reasons induced the crown to promote such an institution as this; the state of things in the country was sufficient reason with the people to desire, with the most ardent wishes, the occasional visits of a regal jurisdiction, like that of the *eyre*.

It is not easy to determine the exact period when this establishment of *justices itinerant* was first made (a). It

---

(a) The rolls of the exchequer show that they went regularly as early as 18 Henry I., and there is every reason to believe they went earlier, and soon after the Conquest. Instances indeed occur under the Conqueror, in which prelates were sent down into the counties under the king's writ or commission to hear causes tried in the county courts. The celebrated case in Kent, mentioned by the author, is mentioned in Dugdale's *Orig. Jurid.*, 21; and the record is given at length by Lord Coke, and by Selden in his notes to *Eadme-*

[1] Litt. Hen. II., vol. v., 273.

has long been the common opinion, that they were first appointed in the council held at Nottingham, or, as some say, at Northampton, in the twenty-second year of Henry II., A.D. 1176, when the king, by the advice of the great council, divided the realm into six circuits, and sent out three justices in each to administer justice.

It is true, that the first mention of these justices, in our old historians, is under this year; but it has been proved from the authority of records in the exchequer,[1] that there had been justices itinerant, to hear and determine civil and criminal causes, in the eighteenth year of the reign of Henry I., and likewise justices in eyre for the pleas of the forest. It also appears by the same authority, that in the twelfth, and from thence to the seventeenth of King Henry II., A.D. 1171, justices of both kinds had been constantly sent into the several counties. It is thought,[2] that the first appointment of justices itinerant was made by Henry I., in imitation of a like institution in France, introduced by Louis le Gros;[3] that in the reign of King Stephen, continually agitated by intestine commotions, this new-adopted improvement was dropped; and was again revived by Henry II., who at length fixed it as a part of our legal constitution. It appears from the records above alluded to, that during great part of the reign of Henry II., pleas were held in the counties by the justices itinerant from year to year.

The *itinera*, or circuits appointed at the council of Northampton, were six: on each of which went three justices. The counties assigned to each of these circuits were as

---

rus. And, as already seen, the Laws of Henry I. make mention of summons by the king's justices to the men of the county to attend them in these sittings in the counties, "Qui ad comitatem secundum legem submonitus, venire noluerit, culpa sit," etc. (*Leg. Hen. Pr.*, c. xxix.). So, under the head " De summonitionibus,"—"qui summonitionem regis susceperit, et dimiserit," etc. (c. xlii.). So "De superessione comitatus,— Qui secundum legem submonitus a justicia regis ad comitatum venire supersederit," etc. (liii.). That the form of commission as given in Bracton had been framed with reference to these laws will be manifest, "Sciatis quod constituimus vos justiciarum, nostrum, una cum dilectis, et fidelibus, etc., ad itinerandum per comitatum; ut de omnibus assisis et placitis, tam coronæ nostræ quam aliis, secundum quod in brevi de generali summonitione inde vobis directo plenius continetur." A general writ of summons was addressed to all the justices (Dug. *Orig. Jurid.*, 52).

[1] Mad., Ex., 96. [2] Litt. Hen. II., vol. iv., 271.
[3] But see Schmidt des Deutchen Geschichte, vol. i., 586, and the Missi appointed by Charles the Great, vol. ii., 121.

follow: in one, the counties of *Norfolk, Suffolk, Cambridge, Huntingdon, Bedford, Buckingham, Essex, Hertford;* in another, *Lincoln, Nottingham, Derby, Stafford, Warwick, Northampton, Leicester;* in another, *Kent, Surrey, Southampton, Sussex, Berks, Oxford;* in another, *Hereford, Gloucester, Worcester, Salop;* in another, *Wilts, Dorset, Somerset, Devon, Cornwall;* in another, *York, Richmond, Lancaster, Copland, Westmoreland, Northumberland, Cumberland.*

About three years after this (A.D. 1179), some alteration was made in this arrangement of *itinera;* for, at a great council held at Windsor, the kingdom was parcelled out into four circuits only, in the following order: in the first were the counties of *Southampton, Wilts, Gloucester, Dorset, Somerset, Devon, Cornwall, Berks, Oxford;* in the second, *Cambridge, Huntingdon, Northampton, Leicester, Warwick, Worcester, Hereford, Stafford, Salop;* in the third, *Norfolk, Suffolk, Essex, Hertford, Middlesex* (the county of *Middlesex* not being included in the former division at all), *Kent, Surrey, Sussex, Buckingham, Bedford;* in the fourth, *Nottingham, Derby, York, Northumberland, Westmoreland, Cumberland, Lancaster.* As each of these *itinera* contained more counties than the former division, they had also more justices assigned; the first three had each five justices; and the last, which was much the greatest circuit, had six.[1] There is no mention of any further alteration of the circuits during the period of which we are now treating.

The justices appointed in the year 1176, were directed (a) and empowered to do, in their *itinera*, all things of

(a) The author hardly gives the meaning accurately, "Quid justiciæ faciant omnes justicias, et rectitudines spectantes ad Dominuam Regis, et ad coronam suam per breve domini regis vel illorum qui in ejus loco erunt de feodo dimidii militis et infra; nisi tam grandis sit querela quod non possit deduci sine domino rege, vel talis quam justicæ ei reponunt pro dubitatione sua, vel ad illos qui a loco ejus erunt," *i. e.*, the chief justiciaries or justices of the *curia regis,* for it was held in the time of John that all pleas held before the king's justices were held before him and held before the chief justiciary (*Abbreviatio Placitorum, in anno* 2 Johan.). And there was a distinction between them and the itinerant justices. The justices itinerant could only hold pleas of lands by writ, and cases even under the value mentioned could be sent to the king's superior courts, "pro dubitatione," *i. e.*, for their difficulty. It may be mentioned here that in the *Abbreviatio Placitorum,* and also scattered through Bracton and the *Mirror,* are many brief abstracts and reports of cases decided before these justices itinerant, whose judicial labors tended immensely to develop the law, and especially to improve procedure. Thus, in

[1] *Vide* Leg. Ang.-Sax., p. 332, 333.

right and justice which belonged to the king and his crown, whether commenced by the king's writ or that of his vicegerent, where the property in question was not more than half a knight's fee; unless the matter was of such importance that it could not be determined but before the king; or the justices themselves, on account of any difficulty therein, chose to refer it to the king, or, in

---

the *Mirror* (c. 4, s. 21), mention is made of the course taken by Martin de Pateshall, a very able justice itinerant of those days, whose writings as usual are also repeatedly reported in Bracton. These are the earliest law reports in our language.

It is to be observed that these circuits of the itinerant justices are not to be confounded with the circuits of the judges of the superior courts afterwards held; for these itinerant justices were, as will have been seen, of an inferior grade to the judges of the king's superior court; whereas, in later times, the judges themselves went circuit, as they still do now. The itinerant justices were a far more numerous body, but they formed a fine judicial school from whence the king's superior courts were constantly recruited; and, on the other hand, sometimes the judges of the superior courts may have gone the itineraries. These justices itinerary, who were sometimes the sheriffs, were a kind of intermediate grade or order between the sheriff and the superior courts. The sheriff himself was often made a king's justice by the king's writ, for the purpose of trying a particular case touching the freehold, or of greater amount than his ordinary jurisdiction; and then, as Bracton says, he acted as justice of the king. The itinerant justices marked the next step in the improvement of our judicature. And it is extremely interesting to observe by what slow and gradual steps the improvement was effected, which, it will be seen, was a necessary step in the improvement of the *law*. A study of their decisions, as stated by Bracton in his great *Treatise*, will illustrate this; and the very fact that this great lawyer should so have cited them, strongly shows the influence and effect they had in improving the law. He cites them throughout his work, and almost on every page one or more such citations occur. They are cited by the county, and the year of the king, with the name of the case, "Ut probatum in rotulo de termino Paschæ anno regis Henrici decimo sexto, in comitatu Oxoniæ de Fray Pinchard," etc. (fol. 367). He often cites the celebrated Martin de Pateshall, mentioned in the *Mirror*, and cites a case "de ultimo itinere, Martin de Pateshall, in comitatu suff." (f. 32). The circuits of the itinerant justices are set down in Hoveden, p. 337, and are quoted in Hale's *History of the Common Law*, p. 143. Bracton, in his book *De Corona*, treats largely of the authority of the justices itinerant, and sets forth the terms of their commission (lib. iii., c. 17, fol. 115), which extended to all pleas of the crown and all its franchises, etc. Upon reading the commission, it is suggested that the senior justice shall deliver a kind of charge to the men of the county (the grand jury), as Martin de Pateshall was used to do, "Si justitiarus placuerit, quidam major eorum et discretior publicè coram omnibus proponat quæ sit causa adventus eorum, et quæ sit utilitas itinerationis et quæ commoditas si pax obsevetur et proponi solent verba ista per Martin de Pateshall. In primis, de pace domini regis et justitia ejus violata per murdritores et robbatores, et burglatores," etc. (*Ibid.*) They were to try with juries, for it is said, "Etiam possunt juratores xii de alio itinere, argui de perjurio, ut in anno regis Hen. nono, de quodam Henrico Romband in comitatu Hertford" (*Ibid.*, f. 117); and though flight afforded a presumption of guilt, yet evidence was heard (*Ibid.*, fol. 128).

his absence, to those who were acting for him. They were commanded to make inquisition concerning robbers, and other offenders, in the counties through which they went; they were to take care of the profits of the crown, in its landed estates and feudal rights of various sorts, as escheats, wardships, and the like; they were to inquire into castle-guards, and send the king information from what persons they were due, in what places, and to what amount; they were to see that the castles which the great council had advised the king to destroy were demolished, under pain of being themselves prosecuted in the king's court; they were to inquire what persons were gone out of the realm, that if they did not return by a certain day to take their trial in the king's court, they might be outlawed; they were to receive, within a certain limited term, from all who would stay in the kingdom, of every rank and condition (not even excepting those who held by tenures of villenage), oaths of fealty to the king, which if any man refused to make, they were to cause him to be apprehended as the king's enemy; and, moreover, they were to oblige all persons from whom homage was owing, and who had not yet done it, to do it to the king within a certain time, which the justices themselves were to fix.

The principal part of these injunctions was given in consequence of the late civil war; but some Constitutions made at Clarendon, relating both to civil and criminal justice, were renewed at this same council at Northampton; and the justices itinerant then appointed were sworn to observe and execute those regulations in every point (*a*). Amongst other provisions of this statute, the justices were to cause recognition to be made whether a man died seized of land concerning which any doubt had arisen;

(*a*) It is to be observed that it appears from the *Mirror*, and from some passages in the chronicles, that there had been an ancient usage, even before the Conquest, for the kings, at first in person, and afterwards by their justiciaries, to go once in seven years into the counties, to observe and enforce the course of justice, and these circuits were called "eyres," or "iters," for which the more frequent itineraries of justices were substituted. These justices, however, had other things to do beside administer justice. They had also to look after fines and amercements and forfeitures for the crown, and there is reason to believe that this, rather than a zeal for justice, caused them to be sent on these missions, where they became so intolerable in their exactions that the people petitioned that they should not be sent so often; but only, as the "justices in eyre" had been — once in seven years.

and they were likewise to make recognition *de novis disseisinis*.[1]

This was the whole authority given to the justices itinerant by the statute of Northampton; how the objects of their jurisdiction were multiplied will presently appear, when we come to mention those schedules, called *capitula itineris*, which used to be delivered to the justices for their direction. In executing the king's commission, the plan of this institution was improved still further, for, that justice might not always be delayed in criminal cases till the justices itinerant came into the country, commissions used to be occasionally issued, empowering the justices therein named to make a *delivery of the gaol* specified in the commission; that is, they were by due legal examination, to determine the fate of all the prisoners, ordering a discharge of such who were acquitted upon trial, and continuing in further custody, or otherwise directing punishments to be inflicted on those who should have been convicted of any crime. But when these commissions were first brought into use, it does not appear.

It was some time after the appointment of justices itinerant that a court made its appearance under the name of *bancum* or *bench*, as distinguished from the *curia regis* (a). This court, like that of the justices in eyre, was probably erected in aid of the *curia regis;* and it is observable that the *curia regis* ceased to entertain common pleas in its ordinary course much about the same time when the *bancum*, or *bench*, is supposed to have been erected. It is not likely this alteration was

The bench.

(a) It is conceived that this is erroneous, and that the phrase justices of the bench meant justices of the *curia regis* (*i.e.*, as is believed, the exchequer), to distinguish them from the justices *itinerant*, who were an inferior grade or order, and were not, moreover, permanent judges, but were only appointed for particular *itinera* or circuits, and were not always the regular judges, nor indeed at first were any so. Hence naturally the regular judges of the king's supreme court were called justices of the *bench*. In the *Abbreviatio Placitorum* in anno 2 Johannis, is a case in which the Abbot of Leicester, being sued before the justices of the bench, pleaded a charter of exemption from suit, except before the king or his chief justiciary; and it was held that pleas heard before the justices of the *bench* were in law heard before the king. It was otherwise of justices itinerant, and it was to them the charter applied. Common pleas were then heard before the *curia regis, i.e.*, the exchequer; numerous records attest this, anterior to the time of the Great Charter.

[1] Litt. Hen. II., vol. iv., 275, 406.

made *uno ictu*, but by degrees. It had evidently been the usage to hold pleas in the *bank* before the charter of King John, as *justitiarii nostri de banco* are therein mentioned; so that the clause declaring that *communia placita non sequantur curiam nostram, sed teneantur in certo loco*, can no otherwise be understood, than as contributing to settle and confirm what had been begun before. In truth, the existence of the *bench*, and of the *justitiarii de banco*, appears from records in the reign of Richard I. At that period certain descriptions came in use which were not before known, and which plainly and clearly mark the existence of such a court; such as, *curia regis apud Westmonasterium, justitiarii regis apud Westmonasterium*, or *de Westmonasterio, bancum*, and *justitiarii de banco;*[1] from all of which it may be collected, that common pleas were at this time moving off from the *curia regis*, and were frequently determined in a certain place, whose style was meant to be described in those expressions.

It has been observed,[2] that after the erection of the bank, the style of the superior court began to alter; and the proceedings there were frequently said to be *coram rege*, or *coram domino rege;* and in subsequent times the court was styled *curia regis coram ipso rege*, or *coram nobis*, or *coram domino rege ubicunque fuerit*, etc., as at this day.[3] However, it was still called *aula regis, curia regis, curia nostra, curia magna*.

As the exchequer was a member of the *curia regis*, and a place for determining the same sort of common pleas as were usually brought in the *curia regis*, the separation of such pleas from that court did considerably affect the exchequer. The clause in King John's charter equally concerned both courts: *curiam nostram* meant the exchequer, as well as the court properly so called.

Thus have we seen this grand institution of the Normans dilating its influence over the whole kingdom, encroaching on the ancient local tribunals of the people, by drawing into its sphere all descriptions of causes and questions; till having exerted, as it were, its last effort, in sending forth the new establishments of justices itinerant and justices of the bench, it disappeared by degrees from the observation of men, and almost from the records of antiquity, having deposited in its retirement the three

---

[1] Mad., Ex., 539, 540.   [2] Ibid., 543.   [3] Ibid., 544.

courts of common law now seen in Westminster Hall: the court *coram ipso rege*, since called *the king's bench;* the bench, now called *the common pleas;* and the modern court of *exchequer.*

The court of chancery probably acquired a separate existence much about the same time. The business of the chancellor was to make out writs that concerned proceedings pending in the *curia regis* and the exchequer (a). He used to seal and supervise the king's charters, and, whenever there arose a debate concerning the efficacy or policy of royal grants, it was to his judgment and discretion that a decision upon them was referred. He used to sit with the chief justiciary and other barons in the *curia regis* and at the exchequer, in matters of ordinary judicature and on questions of revenue; though it was to the latter court he seemed mostly allied in his judicial capacity.[1] Mr. Madox, observing that the rolls of chancery begin in the reigns of Richard and John to be distinct from those of the exchequer (a method of arrangement not observed before),[2] is inclined

The chancery.

(a) This was the original province of the chancellor, and the chancery was an office ages before it was a court, though the chancellor was a member of the "curia regis." The chancery was *officina brevium*, and in a chapter in the *Mirror of Justice*, headed "Del Roy Alfred," is so described: "Ordeine fuist que chescun eyt del chancery l'Roy brief remedial a sa pleint, sans nul difficulty, et que chescun ust l'process de la jour de son plea sans le seale l'Judge ou de la partie." And then, after mentioning the exchequer as the "Court le Roy:" "Ordeine fuit que le court le Roy soit overt a touts plaintiffs per que ils ussent sans delay briefs remedials aussi lieu sur le Roy come sur autre del people d'chescun injury." And a specimen of such a writ is given: "Ordeine fuit que chescun plaintiff ust brief remedial a son Viscount ou al Seignior del fee en cest forme. Questus est nobis quod D., etc., et ideo tibi (vices nostras in hac parte committentes) precipimus quod causam illam audias et legitimo fine decidas." Now the antiquity of this chapter of the *Mirror* is manifest; first, from the very form of this writ, which commands the sheriff himself to decide the cause, and does not mention any writ to bring the case into the king's court, as in later times was the course, but is obviously only designed to compel the sheriff to hear the case in the county court; so that it is obvious that, at that time, the "curia regis" did not itself, in the first instance, hear common pleas between party and party; the old Saxon system of local jurisdiction still continued. Next, the antiquity of the passage appears from its mentioning the exchequer as the only "curia regis" then known, so that the passage must have been written before the Magna Charta. Bracton, writing after the charter, speaks of the sheriff as deciding, under a writ like the above, called a *Justicies*, causes he could not, *ex officio*, decide, which marks a great change, for it is manifest from the chapter in the *Mirror* that there was originally no other court but that of the county, for common suits, in the first instance.

[1] Mad., Ex., 131.   [2] Ibid., 132.

to think that the chancellor began about that time to act separately from the exchequer. In this conjecture he strengthens himself by a corroborating fact, as he imagines. In the absence of King Richard out of the realm, William de Longchamp, chief justiciary and chancellor, was removed from the former office by the intrigues and management of John earl of Morton, the king's brother. After this, it is thought, he might discontinue his attendance at the exchequer; and the business of the chancery, which before used to be done there, might be transferred by him to another place, and put into a new method; in which it might be judged proper and convenient to continue it ever after, separate and independent.

If this conjecture may be admitted, concerning an establishment beyond the reach of historic evidence, the court of chancery was erected into a distinct court nearly at the same time when the other three received their present form and jurisdiction; which will go a great way towards justifying one part of the maxim of the common lawyers, that the four courts of Westminster Hall are all of equal antiquity; though it *refutes* the other part of it, that they have been the same as they now are from time immemorial.

The chancery was the *officina justitiæ*, the manufactory, if it may be so called, of justice, where original writs were framed and sealed, and whither suitors were obliged to resort to purchase them in order to commence actions, and so obtain legal redress. For this purpose the chancery was open all the year; writs issued from thence at all times, and the fountain of justice was always accessible to the king's subjects. The manner in which the business there was conducted seems to have been this: the party complaining to the justices of the king's court for relief, used to be referred to the chancellor (in person, perhaps, originally), and related to him the nature of his injury, and prayed some method of redress. Upon this, the chancellor framed a writ applicable to the complainant's case, and conceived so, as to obtain him the specific redress he wanted. When this had been long the practice, such a variety of forms had been devised, that there seldom arose a case in which it was required to exercise much judgment; the old forms were adhered to, and became precedents of established authority in the chancellor's office. After this, the making of writs grew to be a matter of course; and the business there increasing, it was at length confided to the chancellor's clerks, called *clerici cancellariæ*, and since *curstores cancellariæ*. A strict observance of the old forms had rendered them so sacred, that at length any alteration of them was esteemed an alteration of the law, and therefore could not be done but by the great council. It became not unusual in those times for a plaintiff, when no writ could be found in chancery that suited his case, to apply to parliament for a new one.

Thus far the chancellor seemed to act as a kind of officer of justice, ministering to the judicial authority of the king's courts. The chancellor's character continued the same, after this separation, as it had been before, without any present increase or diminution. In the reign of Henry II. he was called the second person in the government, by whose advice and direction all things were ordered. He had the keeping of the king's seal; and, beside the sealing of writs, sealed all charters, treaties, and public instruments. He had the conduct of foreign affairs, and seems to have acted in that department which is now filled by the secretaries of state. He was chief of the king's chaplains, and presided over his chapel. His rank in the council was high; but the great justiciary had precedence of him.[1] He is said to have had the presentation to all the king's churches, and the visitation of all royal foundations, with the custody of the temporalties of bishops; but those writers who have taken upon them to speak fully of the office of chancellor, say nothing of any judicial authority exercised by him at this time. In the *curia regis* he was rather an officer than judge; but as he assisted there, so he was sometimes associated with the justices in eyre.[2] There is no notice, even in writers of a later date than this, neither in *Bracton* nor *Fleta*, that the chancellor, after he sat separate from the exchequer, exercised any judicial authority, or that the chancery was properly *a court;* but it is always spoken of as an *office* merely, bearing a certain relation to the administration of justice, in the making and sealing of writs.

Notwithstanding the hereditary lords absented themselves so entirely from the *curia regis*, they still retained an inherent right of judicature, which   *Judicature of the council.*

---

[1] Mad., Ex., 42, 43; Litt. Hen. II., vol. ii., 312.   [2] Mad., Ex., 42.

resided in them as constituent members of the council of the king and kingdom. When the *curia regis* was divided, and the departments of ordinary judicature were branched out in the manner we have just seen, the peculiar character of this council, now separated and retired within itself, became more distinguishable.

This council was of two kinds and capacities: in one, it was the national assembly, usually called *magnum concilium*, or *commune concilium regni* (a); in the other, it was simply the *council*, and consisted of certain persons selected from that body, together with the great officers of state, the justices, and others whom the king pleased to take into a participation of his secret measures, as persons by whose advice he thought he should be best assisted in affairs of importance. This last assembly of persons, as they were a branch of the other, and had the king at their head, were considered as retaining some of the powers exercised by the whole council. As they both retained the same appellation, and the king presided in both, there was no difference in the style of them as courts; they were each *coram rege in concilio*, or *coram ipso rege in concilio*, till the reign of Edward I., when the term *parliament* was first applied to the national council; and then the former was styled *coram rege in parliamento*.

The judicial authority of the barons, which still resided with them after the dissolution of the *curia regis*, was this: they were the court of last resort in all cases of error; they explained doubtful points of law, and interpreted their own acts; for which purpose the justices used commonly to refer to the great council matters of difficulty depending before them in the courts below. They heard causes commenced originally there, and made awards thereupon; and they tried criminal accusations brought against their own members.

(a) All that relates to the subject of *concilio regni*, or *concilio regis*, or *curia regis*, which in early times very likely meant very much the same thing, is involved in obscurity. The author, it will be observed, cites no contemporary authority, and it is believed that all that exists has already been cited in the notes, except, perhaps, a passage in Glanville, in which, speaking of the assize or trial of real actions, he says, "Est autem assisa regale, quoddam beneficium clementia principis, de concilio procerum populis indultum;" to which, perhaps, it may be added that several passages in the *Mirror* speak of ordinances of kings on the subject of the law, or the administration of justices, which no doubt meant ordinances made by the king, with the counsel of his chief officers of state, the principal barons, etc.

The *council*, properly so called, seems to have had a more ordinary and more comprehensive jurisdiction than the *commune concilium;* which it was enabled to exercise more frequently, as it might be, and was continually summoned; while the other was called only on emergencies. In the court held *coram rege in concilio*, there seems to have resided a certain supreme administration of justice, in respect of all matters which were not cognizable in the courts below: this jurisdiction was both civil and criminal. They entertained inquiries concerning property for which the ordinary course of common-law proceeding had provided no redress, and used to decide *ex æquo et bono*, upon principles of equity and general law. All offences of a very exorbitant kind were proper objects of their criminal animadversion. If the persons who had taken part in any public disorder were of a rank or description not to be made amenable to the usual process, or the occasion called for something more exemplary than the animadversion which could be made by ordinary justices, these were reasons for bringing inquiries before the council: in these and some other instances, as well touching its civil as criminal jurisdiction, it acted only in concurrence with, and in aid of, the courts below.

Thus was the administration of justice still kept, as it were, in the hands of the king, who, notwithstanding the dissolution of his great court, where he presided, was still, in construction of law, supposed to be present in all those which were derived out of it. The style of the great council was *coram rege in concilio*, as was that of his ordinary council for advice. The chancery, when it afterwards became a court, was *coram rege in cancellariâ;* and the principal new court which had sprung out of the *curia regis*, was *coram ipso rege*, and *coram rege ubicunque fuerit in Angliâ*.

The separation of ecclesiastical causes from civil, was not the least remarkable part of the revolution our laws underwent at the Conquest (*a*). The <small>Of the spiritual court.</small>

(*a*) There is no subject upon which the author fell into greater error than this. It was a complete fallacy to suppose that the separation of ecclesiastical causes from civil first took place on the occasion of the decree here adverted to, which merely enforced it. The distinction between ecclesiastical and secular causes is drawn throughout the Saxon laws with great acuteness, as has been shown. Several of the kings were so careful to draw it, that they separated their ordinances ecclesiastical, made either in synods or coun-

joint jurisdiction exercised in the Saxon times by the bishop and sheriff was dissolved, as has been before mentioned, by an ordinance of William; and the bishop was thenceforth to hold his court separate from that of the sheriff.[1]

cils, from their secular laws, made in the council. (See the laws of Edgar, Ethelred, Athelstan, and Canute, *Ang.-Sax. Laws*, vol. i.). And these again were distinguished from the canons and constitutions of the prelates, made of their own authority in ecclesiastical synods, which form quite a distinct collection (*Ang.-Sax. Laws*, v. ii.). And it was likewise distinctly recognized that the administration of the ecclesiastical law belonged to the bishops, though it might be enforced by the secular law: Thus Edward lays down in his ecclesiastical laws that men in holy orders who were immoral were worthy of what the canon had ordained — that is, to forfeit their possessions (*A.-S. L.*, v. i., p. 245). So, if any one committed homicide, he was not to come into the king's presence until he had done penance, as the bishop might teach (*Laws Ed. Ecc.*, 3; *Ibid.*, p. 257); and then, in the secular laws, this is enforced further (*Ibid.*, p. 249). So the laws of Ethelred speak of fines as secular correction for divine purposes (*Ibid.*, p. 319). So the ecclesiastical laws of Canute lay down that men of every order submit each to the law which is becoming to him (*Ibid.*, p. 315); and then the secular law says that if a man in holy orders commit a crime worthy of death, let him be seized and held to the bishop's doom (*Ibid.*, 403). And so Alfred hanged a judge who judged a clerk to death over whom he had not cognizance (*Mirror*, c. v., 213-235). So the distinction was drawn clearly in the laws of the Confessor, collected by the Conqueror: "A sancta ecclesia, per quam rex et regnum solide subsistere haberent, pacem et libertatem concionati sunt dicentes" (c. i.). "Et si aliquis excommunicatus ad emendacium, ad episcopum venerit, absolutus eundo et redeundo pacem, Dei et Sanctæ ecclesiæ habeat. Et si pro justicia episcopi emendare noluerit, ostendat regi, ut rex constringat forisfactorem, ut emendet cui forisfecit, et episcopi et sibi" (c. ii.). "Quicunque de ecclesia tenuerit, vel in feudo ecclesiæ manserit, alicubi extra curiam ecclesiasticam non placitabit; si in aliquo forisfactum habuerit, donec, quod absit, in curia ecclesiastica de recto defecerit" (c. iv.). "Si quis sanctæ ecclesiæ pacem fregerit, episcoporum tum est justicia" (*Ibid.*, p. 444). The distinction, then, was well established, and was not now first drawn, but only enforced; and enforced, not by taking the bishop from the county court, but by taking the ecclesiastical causes from that court, and remitting them to the court of the bishop. The edict, therefore, was in aid of episcopal jurisdiction, and merely enforced the existing law. It did not purport to be, nor was it, a new law; it was a charter declaratory of and enforcing the established law of the land, that spiritual matters were for the bishop. It recited that it was issued with the consent and counsel of the prelates, and it concludes thus: "Hoc etiam interdico, ut aliquis laicus homo, de legibus quæ ad episcopum pertinent se intromittant, nec aliquis laicus homo alium hominem sine justicia episcopi ad judicium adducat" (*A.-S. L.*, v. i., p. 496). "The language of the charter," says Sir J. Mackintosh, "and probably its immediate effect, was favorable to clerical independence" (*Hist. Eng.*, v. i., p. 113). It is true that the acute historian — for once in error, and not aware of subsequent laws recognizing and even enforcing the attendance of the prelates in the county courts — went on to observe that the effect was to withdraw them from the courts; a manifest mistake. The bishops continued to sit in the court (*Leges Henrici Primi*, c. vii., 11).

[1] Wilk., Leg. Sax., 292; Seld., Tithes.

This ordinance of William is comprised in a charter relating to the bishopric of Lincoln; and therein he commanded "that no bishop or archdeacon should thenceforward hold plea *de legibus episcopalibus* in the hundred court, nor submit to the judgment of secular persons any cause which related to the cure of souls; but that whoever was proceeded against for any cause or offence according to the episcopal law, should resort to some place which the bishop should appoint, and there answer to the charge, and do what was right[1] towards God and the bishop, not according to the law used in the hundred, but according to the canons and the episcopal law." In support of the bishop's jurisdiction, it was moreover ordained, "that should any one, after three notices, refuse to obey the process of that court, and make submission, he should be excommunicated; and, if need were, the assistance of the king or the sheriff might be called in. The king, moreover, strictly charged and commanded, that no sheriff, *præpositus sive minister regis*, nor any layman whatsoever, should intromit in any matter of judicature that belonged to the bishop."[2] This is the whole of that famous charter.

When the spiritual court was once divided from the temporal, different principles and maxims began to prevail in that tribunal. The bishop thought it noways unsuitable, that subjects of a different nature from those concerning which the temporal courts decided, should be adjudged by different laws; and, being now out of the influence and immediate superintendence of the temporal judges, he was very successful in introducing, applying, and gaining prescription for the favorite system of pontifical law, to which every churchman, from education and habit, had a strong partiality. The body of canon law soon exceeded the bounds which a concern for the government of the church would naturally affix to it. Instead of confining their regulations to sacred things, the canonists laid down rules for the ordering of all matters of a temporal nature, whether civil or criminal (*a*). The

---

(*a*) Only *in foro conscientiæ*, and as part of the great moral duty of justice; in order to ascertain breaches of it, with a view to spiritual correction. In times when there was really no law, this was very necessary; and the Roman ecclesiastics founded upon the Roman law a system of Christian jurispru-

[1] *Faciat rectum.*   [2] Wilk., Leg. Ang.-Sax., pp. 292, 293.

buying and selling of land, leasing, mortgaging, contracts, the descent of inheritance; the prosecution and punish-

dence of great use and value, which had, as already has been shown, had a great influence on the formation of our own law. Moreover, it should be observed that the law of England fully recognized the canon law for the purposes of spiritual correction, and, indeed, to a great extent enforced it. This has been already shown in the Saxon laws, being confirmed by the Conqueror, and it will have been seen that these laws repeatedly recognized the canon law and the right of the bishops to apply it in the exercise of their spiritual authority. So the law of the Conqueror, already alluded to, distinctly recognized this spiritual jurisdiction and canon law, for it directed —" nt nullus episcopus, de legibus episcopalibus, amplius in hundreto placita teneant, nec causam quæ ad regimen animarum pertinet, ad judicium secularium hominem aducant: sed quicunque secundum episcopales leges, de quacunque causa vel culpa, interpellatus fuerit, ad locum quem ad hoc episcopus elegerit veniat, ibique de causa vel culpa sua respondeat: et non secundum hundret, sed secundum canones et episcopales leges, rectum Deo et episcopo suo faciat." So that the very object of the separation of the ecclesiastical orders from the secular, was to *enable* the ecclesiastical court to administer a law *different* from the secular law; and having its own sentences and penalties; those, of course, consisting only of the deprivation of spiritual privileges, so far as the *church* was concerned; and hence it was that the same law went on to provide, that if a party set at nought the episcopal sentence, he might be excommunicated, and that then to vindicate this sentence the temporal power might be called in —" et si opus fuerit ad hoc vindicandum, fortitudo et justicia regis vel vicecomitis adhibeatur." This, which was only in accordance with the Saxon laws, collected by the Conqueror (see the *Laws of the Conqueror*, c. vi.), was going further than the canon laws, which only of themselves deal with spiritual privileges, and can only enforce the sentence by deprivation of those privileges. But as the temporal law upheld the ecclesiastical courts in the exercise of their jurisdiction, even where the law they administered was different from the secular law on the subject, it could be no ground of objection, as the author appears here to imply, that their law was different. It was necessarily so, because it was *in foro conscientiæ:* and every one knows that, quite apart from peculiar religious obligations, the measure of justice prescribed by conscience, is often larger than the measure prescribed by law. In so far as great offences against national law were concerned, as murder or robbery, there might be no difference between the spiritual law and the secular law, though as to the mode of trial there would be great difference; and men of any education, or acquaintance with the principles of intelligent procedure, could hardly do otherwise than revolt at the absurdity of the ordeal, or the brutality of the trial by battle. And accordingly, in the *Mirror*, it is said —"that Christianity suffered not that men be by such wicked arts cleared, if one may otherwise avoid it" (c. iii., s. 23). And all through the Saxon laws it has been seen there was a gradual endeavor to get rid of the ordeal, by making it only the last resort, in failure of other modes of trial, and by the end of the reign of John it was obsolete. But it prevailed all through the reign of Henry II., and trial by battle prevailed much longer. And while the law was in this barbarous state, it is not to be wondered at that the ecclesiastics, while, on the one hand, it was their utmost endeavor to improve it, as to the laity, should, on the other hand, object to its application to the clergy. Hence, it has been seen, it was undoubted law under the Saxons that a "clerk" or ecclesiastic, was not liable to trial in the temporal courts; and thus it is recorded, in the *Mirror*, that Alfred hanged a judge who had

ment of murder, theft, receiving of thieves, frauds; these, and many other objects of temporal judicature, are provided for by the canon law; by which, and which alone, it was meant the clergy should be governed as a distinct people from the laity. This scheme of distinct government was, perhaps, not without some example in the practice of the primitive times; when it was recommended that Christian men should accommodate differences among themselves, without bringing scandal on the church by exposing their quarrels to the view of temporal judges. For this purpose, bishops had their *episcoporum ecdici*, or church-lawyers; and, in after times, their officials or chancellors; and when the empire had become Christian, the like practice continued, for similar reasons, with regard to the clergy (*a*). But this, which was in its design nothing more than a sort of compact between the individuals of a fraternity, was exalted into a claim of

caused execution to be done upon a "clerk," because he had no power over him. While as to the property of the church, it was equally clear that the secular courts had no jurisdiction. Thus, one of the laws of the Confessor was—"quicumque de ecclesia tenuerit, vel in feudo ecclesiæ manserit, alicubi extra curiam ecclesiasticam non placitabit, si in aliquo forisfactum habuerit, donec quod absit, in curia ecclesiastica de recto deficerit" (c. 4). In an age when the administration of justice was still so turbulent and barbarous, it was natural that the property and persons of ecclesiastics should be exempt from it. On the other hand, from a similar cause, some matters, even of a secular character, came under the cognizance of civil courts, as, for example, testaments. In an age when none but the ecclesiastics could read or write, it was a matter of necessity that testaments should be entrusted to their care, and it was natural that the cognate subject of intestacy should also be confided to them, on account of their being acquainted with the rules of descent, and capable of making a proper division of the property among all the next of kin; a matter sometimes of much nicety. These two heads, however, of civil jurisdiction, the exclusive jurisdiction over ecclesiastics, and the special jurisdiction over testaments and intestacy, were obviously exceptional; and arose out of the barbarism of the age. Abstracting these, what remained of the ecclesiastical jurisdiction was entirely *in foro conscientiæ*, and a matter of mere spiritual censure or correction. The sentences of the church could only be enforced by deprivation of spiritual privileges, and its highest punishment was excommunication, which was merely putting out of the communion and society of the church a person who set at nought its laws. The author observes truly, a little further on, that the canon law first known in the country was formed by permission and under authority of the government, and seemed to be supported by arguments of expediency. The existence of a church called for a set of regulations for the direction and order of its various functions. This was admitted, and under that notion a body of canonical law had been suffered to grow up for a long course of years.

(*a*) That the Roman law, and the Saxon law following it, went much further than this, has already been shown.

distinct jurisdiction, exclusive of the temporal courts, for all persons who came under the title of clerks, and for many objects which were said to be of a spiritual nature (*a*). This attempt was favored by the separation now made, in this country, between the spiritual and temporal judges.

(*a*) That this was the law of England has already been shown from the Saxon laws, and can be shown from Bracton, who, writing in the reign of Henry III., having lived and died after the reign of Henry II., laid it down distinctly, that even in cases of murder the king's justices had no power to try clerks, for that they could not be touched in life or limb until degraded, and that the king's courts could not degrade them, and therefore they could not try those whom they could not punish, wherefore they were to be delivered to the bishop. "Et ideo si petatur, erit liberandus curiæ Christianititis — quia non habebit Rex de eo prisonam quem judicare non potest, nec clericos degradare, quia non potest eos ad ordines promovere" (*De Corona*, lib. iii., c. ix., p. 124). And Bracton goes on to say that the punishment of degradation ought to suffice, as the man ought not to be punished twice for the same offence, the very point used by Archbishop A'Becket in the case which gave rise to the claim of civil jurisdiction. "Cum autem clericus sic de crimine convictus degradetur — non sequitur alia pœna pro uno delicto, vel pluribus ante degradationem perpetratis. Satis enim sufficit ei pro pœna degradatio: quæ est magna capitis diminutio," though he goes on to say that if the bishop would not put him to his purgation in the matter, etc. Bracton mentions that in a case of apostacy which had happened in the time of "the good Archbishop (Becket)," a priest who had apostatized and had been degraded, was burnt by the lay authorities. "Statim fuit igne traditus per manum laicalem." This was according to the ancient law of the country, as shown by the *Mirror of Justice*, a striking illustration of the barbarism of the age. It was an age, however, in which, as also appears by the *Mirror*, men often burnt others to death, and, literally, "put them into the fire," as the book says, "for hatred and revenge," (c. ii., p. 8), so that there was a distinct head of the criminal law about "*burners*,"— those who burn houses or *men* for hatred and revenge. "And if any one put a man into the fire," etc. In an age in which men burnt each other alive for revenge, they were not likely to scruple at doing it by way of punishment. The criminal code of the Saxons and Normans was dreadfully cruel; mutilation was ordained by Canute and the Conqueror, and enacted by Henry II. with peculiar cruelty, *men's feet being cut off*, and as apostates were burnt, poisoners were boiled. It seems scarcely credible, but is the fact, that the punishment of burning women for murdering their husbands was legal, down to the end of the last century; so difficult is it to eradicate customs which have once got established in the institutions of a country. The criminal procedure of that age was, moreover, as odious and barbarous as the civil. The absurd ordeal was the resort of ignorance in quest of truth, and although, as Lord Hale says, "by means of the persuasions of the clergy, it died out in the reign of John, it was used all through the reign of Henry II. and his sons." It is necessary to understand this, in order to enter into the reasons which induced the Saxon kings to exempt clerics from their barbarous code and still more barbarous trial, and to secure them an ecclesiastical tribunal, which followed a more intelligent procedure and adopted more merciful punishments. It need hardly be added that the law as laid down by Bracton, did not apply to subsequent offences, committed after degradation.

In the gradual increase of this clerical judicature, separate from the temporal courts, we see the means by which the ecclesiastics, in after times, were enabled to perfect their scheme of independent sovereignty, in the midst of secular dominion; whereby they assumed powers dangerous to the crown and the political freedom of the state.

The increase of the clergy in power and consequence was owing to the influence of the civil and canon law. With these instruments they ventured to encounter the established authority of the municipal law, whose dictates were so opposite to their grand schemes of ecclesiastical sovereignty.

Such an entire destruction had been made of every establishment by the Saxon invaders, that the Roman law was quite eradicated (a). The only remains of this law that could be picked up in the Saxon times, were from the code of Theodosius, and such scraps of Gaius, Paulus, and Ulpian, as still existed in some mutilated parts of the Pandects[1] (b). These remnants

Of the civil and canon law.

▲ (a) It has already been shown how utterly erroneous this notion is, arising from an entirely wrong idea of the nature and character of the Saxon invasion, or rather invasions; for they were numerous, local, and partial, and the Saxon conquest was so gradual, that it took centuries before it was completed, and was scarcely so, when the Danish invasion commenced; and during this long period there was ample time for an amalgamation of races, and an adoption of institutions. It has been seen that, so soon as the Saxons got settled in any part of the country, which was at first almost always in a rural district, they at once ceased to destroy what they wished rather to enjoy, and were soon content with making the former inhabitants their tributaries; and as the existing Roman institutions afforded the most convenient mode of so doing, they, of course, retained them. The Saxon conqueror seized the Roman manor, and made the owner his tributary, and all things went on as before. That the manorial system was adopted by the Saxons, has been shown from the Saxon laws as to the coloni, or tenants of the manor, and the manorial institutions pervaded the whole of the country. As to the municipal institutions of the cities, there is no trace of their being interfered with, while there is evidence that they were adopted. The conquest of the cities were, for reasons already glanced at and pointed out by Guizot, the latest of the conquests of the invaders; and they were by that time so far civilized, as to be capable of appreciating their institutions. We find, in the earliest of the Saxon laws, after the cities were subdued, a recognition of their privileges (see the Laws of Athelstan, which make mention of most of the chief cities of the country south of London, and comprise a distinct enumeration of the customs of London—(*Anglo-Sax. Laws*, v. i., p. 234); and we find afterwards, among the Saxons, those guilds or trade corporations which the Romans had established in the cities.

(b) The author very much underrates the extent and copiousness of the Code of Theodosius, and he entirely ignores the elements of tradition and cus-

[1] Duck de aut., 299.

of the civil law, like other learning, were mostly in the hands of ecclesiastics, who studied them with diligence. It was from these that they formed a style, and learned a method, by which to frame their own constitutions; which were now growing to some magnitude and consequence, and began to claim notice as a separate system of law of themselves.

During the reigns of William the Conqueror and Rufus, we hear nothing in this country of the civil law[1] (a);

---

tom as a means of transmitting the Roman law. There can be no doubt, as has been shown in the Introduction, that during the four centuries of the Roman occupation, a vast deal of Roman law had got into the customs, especially of cities; and much of it, too, was embodied in traditional ideas of law. "It is essential to observe," says our great historian, Sir J. Mackintosh, "that the Roman law never lost its authority in the countries which formed the western empire. All Europe obeyed a great part of the Roman law, which had been incorporated with their own usages, when these last were first reduced to writing after the Conquest. The Roman provincials retained it altogether as their hereditary rule. The only historical question regards, not the obligation of the Roman law, but the period of its being taught and studied as a science. It is not likely that such a study could have been entirely omitted in Roman cities, and where there were probably many who claimed the exercise of Roman law." (In a note, he mentions instances of English prelates who had studied the Roman law from the eighth century downwards. Thus, a Bishop of Salisbury studied the Roman law at York: — "Legem Romanorum jura medullitus remari, et jurisconsultorum secreta imis præcordiis scrutari." Alcuin describes the same school, at York, in the ninth century.) "But the Roman jurisprudence did not become a general branch of study till after the foundation of universities for systematic instruction in that and other parts of knowledge. It soon made its way into England, and was taught with applause by Vacarius, at Oxford, about the middle of the twelfth century, as we are told by his pupil, John of Salisbury" (*Mack. Hist. Eng.*, vol. i., p. 173). Hallam and Guizot give similar testimony (*Lect. Sur la Civilis.*). At the time of the Conquest, as Mr. Foss states, and for a long time afterwards, our chancellors and justiciaries were Roman ecclesiastics; finally, we find the whole civil and ecclesiastical organization of the country under the Saxons as they existed during the Roman occupation — counties and hundreds, dioceses and parishes. Nothing, therefore, could be more utterly contrary to historic truth than the statement in the text; for, of course, law is best embodied in institutions; and if the institutions remain, the law they embody must also remain. But there is, as has been seen in the Saxon laws themselves, abundant evidence of the existence of some knowledge, obscure and imperfect though it may have been, of the Roman law, since some of the main principles of that law are to be found — no doubt, in scraps and fragments — in the fabric of those laws; while, in the first compilation of laws formed after the era of the Conquest — under one of the sons of the Conqueror, Henry I. — we find that, as Lord Hale says, "they taste of the civil and canon law," and whole passages are taken therefrom. The idea that the Roman law had perished or disappeared, is therefore entirely erroneous.

(a) On the contrary, the laws of the Conqueror repeatedly make mention

[1] Duck de aut., 307.

though the institute, the code, and the novels of Justinian, had been taught in the school of *Irnerius*, at Bologna, and there were even some imperfect copies of the Pandects in France; yet the study of the civil law did not go on with spirit; nor was that system of jurisprudence regarded with the universal reverence which it acquired afterwards, when a complete copy of the Pandects was found at Amalfi, A. D. 1137, at the time that city was taken by the Pisans[1] (a).

The canon law first known in this country was formed by permission and under authority of the government, and seemed to be supported by arguments of expediency. The existence of a church, with the gradation and subordination of governors and governed, called for a set of

of ecclesiastical courts and the canon law. Thus, the law already alluded to, enforcing the exclusive jurisdiction of the bishops over canonical offences: "Nec causam quæ at regimen animarum pertinet, ad judicium seculariam hominem adducant; sed quicunque, secundem episcopales leges, de quacunque causa vel culpa interpellatus fuerit; secundum *canones et episcopales leges*, rectum Deo et episcopo suo faciat" (*Anglo-Saxon Laws*, vol. i., p. 495).

(a) This is the absurd idea, borrowed from Blackstone, that the study of the Roman law, all of a sudden began on the occasion of the discovery of a particular book; as if the book would have any interest, if the subject had not *already* been studied and appreciated. The object of diffusing this idea was obviously to excite a prejudice against the Roman law, by creating a notion of its novelty, and obscuring the fact that the law of England was founded upon it. The great object of the commentator was to enhance and aggrandize the credit of the common law, as of English growth, in order to vindicate the foundation of a professorship of it, as distinct from the Roman law; and hence he entirely ignores the Roman origin of our law, and endeavors to represent the introduction of the Roman law as comparatively modern and novel. But the idea is derided by later and more honest writers. Thus Sir J. Mackintosh says, "It was indeed a most improbable supposition that a manuscript found at the sack of Amalfi, not adopted by public anthority, should suddenly prevail over all other laws in the greater part of Europe" (*History of England*, v. i., p. 173). So the great historian of Europe says, "The revival of the study of jurisprudence, as derived from the laws of Justinian, has generally been ascribed to the discovery of a copy of the Pandects. The fact, though not improbable, seems not to rest upon sufficient evidence; but its truth is the less material, as it appears to be unequivocally proved, that the study of Justinian's system had recommenced before that era. Early in the twelfth century, a professor opened a school of civil law at Bologna, where he commented, if not on the Pandects, yet on the other books — the Institutes and the Code — which were sufficient to teach the principles and inspire the love of that comprehensive jurisprudence. The study of the law having thus revived, made surprising progress" (*Middle Ages*, c. 8). And he says "that the body of the law was absolutely unknown in the west during any period, seems to have been too hastily supposed" (*Ibid.*), for which he cites Selden, ad Fletam.

[1] Giann., Hist. Nap., lib. 11, ca. 2, vol. ii., p. 119.

regulations for the direction and order of its various functions. This was admitted; and under that notion a body of canonical jurisprudence had been suffered to grow up for a long course of years. In a national synod held A.D. 670, the *codex canonum vetus ecclesiæ Romanæ* was received by the clergy.[1] It appears also by the before-mentioned charter to the Bishop of Lincoln, that *William the Conqueror, with the advice and assent of his great council, had reviewed and reformed the episcopal laws that were in use till his time in England. It is beyond dispute that a canon law of some kind had been long established here by the sanction of the legislature; as may be seen in Mr. Lambard's Collection of Saxon Constitutions [3](a). These

(a) It is here obviously necessary to take some notice of these canons and canonical constitutions, because the author gives no account of them, and goes on to argue on an assumption or supposition of their character. An analysis has already been given of the laws of the Saxons, ecclesiastical and secular, upon subjects connected with religion. Of these the learned editor of the *Anglo-Saxon Laws and Institutes* observes, "All ordinances proceeding from the king and wittenagemote, whether of a secular or ecclesiastical character, are considered as laws, and inserted in their places in the first part of the work. Those without such sanction, and of a nature strictly ecclesiastical, are placed among the *Monumenta Ecclesiastica*, vol. 1, pref., xiv., and these are in the second volume of that valuable work. It will be observed that the former — the laws — were enforced by temporal penalties, and the latter, as our author observes, were framed with the sanction of the government; and, although not directly enforced by the secular power, were so indirectly, in this way that excommunication was recognized, and men were coerced into observance of ecclesiastical censures. The principal of these *Monumenta Ecclesiastica* are the pœnitentials of Theodore, Archbishop of Canterbury, at the close of the seventh century, and Egbert, archbishop, towards the close of the eighth century; together with a body of canons, enacted under Edgar, in the tenth century. The first thing that occurs to the reader is the indirect but effective sanction the recognition these canons must have given to the sanctity of confession. For, among the first things mentioned in the earliest of these documents is the imposition of ecclesiastical penance for murder and other capital crimes, which, of course, implies that there had been confession of the crimes, and also (as murder was capitally punishable by the secular law) the concealment of the confession, " Pro capitalibus criminibus, *i. e.*, sacrilegiis, homicidiis, et his similibus, sancti patres nostri spatium pœnitentiæ, secundum mensuram et secundum ordinem cujusquæ, constituerunt" (*Pœn. Theod.*, c. 2); and all through these canons are to be seen impositions of penance for crimes, by the secular law punishable with death. It is true that by the early Saxon laws pecuniary compensation was allowed in cases of homicide (though it is by no means clear that this applied to deliberate murder, and not to cases of manslaughter), but even then the recognition of the ecclesiastical law was not less decided in another way. For in the laws of Edward — secular and ecclesiastical — it is provided that in any case of homicide the party should not come into the king's presence until he

[1] Seld., Notes to Eadm. [2] Wilk., Leg. Ang.-Sax., p. 292.
[3] Duck de aut., 98.

ancient canons were probably not so prejudicial to the rights of the sovereign and the state; for which reason,

had done penance as the bishop had directed (*A.-S. L.*, v. i., pp. 247-249). It has been seen, too, that habitual thieves were punishable with death from the earliest times among the Saxons, and were so at the time of this penitential. In the laws of Canute it is mentioned that mere manslayers might make compensation, but that murderers were to be given up to the kinsmen of the deceased; and it is to be observed, also, that even where compensation was allowed, if the guilty party could not pay it, he was liable to be punished capitally in cases of homicide, and so in cases of theft, which were capital. Yet all through the penitentials, crimes punishable with death are treated of as subjects of canonical penance for a long course of years, plainly implying secrecy; and these canons were, as the author observes, established with the sanction of the state. Thus, in the penitential of Theodore, "Synodus Romanæ decrevit parricidium faciens xiii. annis pœnitere, et semper religiose vivere" (*Pœn. Theod.*, c. 3). So, in the later canons enacted under Edgar, "We enjoin that every priest shrive and prescribe penance to those who confess to him" (c. 65; *A.-S. L.*, v. 2, p. 259). And then in the *Modus Imponendi Pœnitentiam*, "Quod episcopus sit in sede episcopali sui . . . tunc unusquisque eorum hominum que capitalibus criminibus polluti sunt, in provincia ista eo die ad illum accedere debet, et peccata sua illi profiteri, et ille tum præscribit eis pœnetentiam, cuique pro ratione delicti sui, eos qui eo digni sunt ab ecclesiastica communitate segregat. Laicus qui alium sine culpa occiderit, vii. annos jejunet" (*Ib.*, p. 267). "Si quis servum suum, sine culpa, occiderit, pro furore suo, iii. annos jejunet" (*Ib.*, p. 269). In both these cases, the homicide is supposed to have been without fault in the slain person, and thus to be wilful murder; and yet not a word is said as to the obligation of the priest to disclose the crime, and it is, on the contrary, clearly implied that he is to conceal it, or how could the criminal do penance for a long course of years? So again in these canons, penned, be it observed, as our author remarks, with the sanction of the state, there is the most distinct recognition of the right of the church to enforce its own laws, although different from the law of the state. This is plainly expressed in the passage above cited, in which it is said that the bishop is to excommunicate in such cases as he thinks fit, and, among the cases specified in the canons as fit for excommunication, are some which would be no offence against the secular law, "Si mulier aliqua viro desponsata sit, non est permissum ut aliquis alius vir illam ei auferat; si fecerit hoc quis, excommunicetur" (*Ib.*, p. 271). Numerous other instances could be adduced, but one is as good as a hundred to establish a principle; and it is manifest, not only from the canons framed with the sanction of the state, but from the secular or ecclesiastical laws established by the state, that there was a recognition of the right of the bishops to enforce, by their spiritual powers, the laws of the church, even when different from that of the state. There were, of course, no cases in which they were expressly opposed, because, by reason of the union of the church and state, the bishops, sitting in the national council, the secular laws were framed in unison with those of the church, but this only made the law stronger. And it is to be observed that, though there may have been no laws opposed to those of the church, there were many cases of difference between the laws; and thus, in a certain sense, they were opposed, as in the instance above mentioned, and many others, over which the secular law virtually allowed an act, and the spiritual law forbade it. And, as already observed, the church framing her laws *in foro conscientiæ*, and the measure of justice by the law of conscience being often much larger than that of law, there were innumerable cases in which the law of the church and of the land were different, and in

25 *

as well as on account of the appearance they bore of municipal regulations, made at home for the government a sense opposed. Nevertheless, the right of the church to enforce her own laws by her own censures was recognized, even where the state declined to enforce them. And further, in these canons, as in the secular laws, the exclusive jurisdiction of the ecclesiastical courts over clerical persons and property, was distinctly recognized. Thus in the canons of Edgar, "Si quis ordinatum hominem occiderit, discedat, à patria sua, et ita faciat, ut papa ei indicaverit et usque pœniteat" (*A.-S. L.*, c. ii., p. 273). Now, here, the canons being framed with the sanction of the state, it is an implied yet distinct recognition not only of episcopal, but of papal jurisdiction, under the sacrament of penance, in a case of homicide on an ecclesiastic. And in the laws of Ethelred and Canute, this canon of Edgar is actually enacted into law. So in the case of homicide *by* an ecclesiastic. In the laws of Ethelred it is enacted, "If a servant of the altar be a homicide, or work enormous iniquity, let him forfeit degree and country, and go into exile as far as the pope shall prescribe to him, and do penance." "And if he will clear himself (*i. e.*, if he elects to be tried by the temporal law), let him clear himself with the ordeal; and unless he begin amendment within thirty days, let him be an outlaw" (*Laws of Ethelred*, c. 26; *A.-S. L.*, vi. 347; *Laws of Canute*, c. 41, p. 401). Now, here it will be observed, that, first the canon of Edgar is enacted into law as regards the spiritual jurisdiction (no doubt for the purpose of enforcing it, for, of course, the bishop could not enforce a sentence of exile), and then it is provided that if the priest desires to have a trial by the secular law, he may do so; only, if he does not either obey the bishop or stand a trial, he is to be outlawed. That this is the meaning is clear from what follows: "If a man in holy orders defile himself with a crime worthy of death, let him be seized, and *held to the bishop's doom*" (*Ib.*, p. 403). The power of the church to enforce her own laws by her own censures is abundantly recognized in various passages both of the ecclesiastical and secular laws, which draw a clear distinction between this and the power of the state to enforce the laws of the church by secular penalties. Thus, in the Civil and Ecclesiastical Institutes (*A.-S. L.*, v. ii., p. 319), the distinction is drawn clearly. "It is incumbent on bishops patiently to endure what they themselves cannot amend until it shall have been announced to the king, and let him then get amends for the offence against God which the bishop cannot, if he will rightly execute God's law." That is to say, it is optional in the state to do this or not; and if it does not do so, then the church can only enforce her laws by spiritual censures and the deprivation of religious privileges and communion, or by excommunication. So in the laws of Ethelred the distinction is drawn most clearly when it is said, that if for a spiritual offence a pecuniary penalty shall arise, as wise secular law may have established, it belongs lawfully to the direction of the bishops, as *a secular correction for spiritual purposes* (*A.-S. L.*, v. i., p. 329). And the excommunication was enforced by exclusion from the presence of royalty (*Ib.*, 313). And wise were those secular witan who first *added* secular laws to the divine (*Ib.*, 335), that thus men might be compelled to do right (p. 349). It is added, that when, after Edgar, what before was in common in secular government was separated, the laws were impaired (*Ib.*). In the laws of Canute, the union of secular and spiritual law is found restored, and the secular laws enforce clerical sentences, and punish such offences, as in cases of adultery and incest (*Ib.*, p. 405). But the exclusive jurisdiction of the bishop to enforce the law of the church by spiritual censures is all along upheld; and the distinction is clearly drawn in the laws of the Confessor, collected by the Conqueror, "Et si aliquis excommunicatus ad emendacionem ad episcopum

of the church, they had never excited any complaint or jealousy.

venerit, absolutus pacem habeat. Quod si aliquis ei forisfecerit, episcopus faciat suam justitiam. Et si pro justitia episcopi emendare noluerit, ostendat regi, et rex constringat forisfactorem ut emendet cui forisfecit, et episcopo, et sibi" (*Ib.*, p. 443). The language of this law, it will be seen, is, on the one hand, almost the same as that of the Civil and Ecclesiastical Institutes above extracted, and, on the other hand, it quite corresponds with the law of the Conqueror, also above quoted, and which recognizes that, in matters pertaining to the correction of souls, no secular judge should intermeddle, and that when any one was, according to episcopal laws, accused of a fault or offence, it should be determined by the bishop according to the canons; "quicunque secundum episcopales leges de quacunque causa vel culpa interpellatus fuerit, *secundum canones* et episcopales leges, recti Dei et episcopi suo faciat" (*A.-S. L.*, v. i., p. 465). So in the *Leges Henrici Primi*, which are the most authentic contemporary exposition of what the law was supposed to be, there is a chapter headed "De Placitis Ecclesia pertinentibus ad Regem," and these relate to matters partly temporal, or to cases of secular correction of spiritual offences. "Sunt alia quædam placita Christianitatis in quibus rex partem habet hoc modo." This of itself implies that, as a rule, matters ecclesiastical or spiritual are not for the crown. "Si rex paciatur ut qui in ecclesia fecerit homicidium, ad emendacionem veniat, primo episcopo et regi precium reddat; et ita se inlegiat; deinde componat de pace ecclesiæ, et reconciliationem ecclesiæ quærat" (*A.-S. L.*, v. i., p. 521). Then there are penalties for non-payment of tithes, church-scot, and Peter's pence, or "Rome-fee," as it was called (*Ib.*). Then certain offences, as adultery and perjury, are dealt with as common to episcopal and regal jurisdiction. Then there is an enactment taken from the Saxon laws, that if any one guilty of a crime worthy of death desires confession, it is not to be denied to him; and as the law of the church, it was notorious, regarded confession as sacred, this was an implied recognition of the sanctity of confession: "Si quis mortis reus confessionem desideret, nunquam negatur ei" (*Ib.*, p. 521). Then there is a distinct recognition of the independent power of the church to declare and enforce her own laws by her own censures, and the duty of the state to enforce them by its secular powers: "Ubicunque recusabitur lex Dei juste servari, *secundum dictionem episcopi*, cogi oportebit per mundanam potestatem" (*Ib.*, 522). The two kinds of power, it will be observed, are clearly distinguished, and the power of secular punishment, for spiritual offences, is put as the province of the state: "In causis emendalibus permissum est, ut terreni domini audeant, pecunialem emendacionem capere, secundum legem terræ" (*Ib.*, p. 522). Thus, then, the law was recognized to be at the end of the reign of Henry I., embodying what had been the law all through the Saxon age, viz., that the bishops had the sole jurisdiction in matters ecclesiastical (which were held to include not only spiritual offences by laymen, but all offences of ecclesiastics, and all matters relating to ecclesiastical property), and that they had an independent power to enforce the canons and laws of the church by the censures of the church, leaving to the state to enforce them or not, as the state might think proper; the province of the state, however, being entirely limited to that. It would be impossible to find in the canon law any more extreme views upon the subject of the power of the Roman church, and the subordination of royal power to her — in a country which acknowledges the Roman church — than are to be found in the Saxon laws. Thus, in the last collection of them, the collection of the laws of the Confessor, made under the auspices of the Conqueror himself, and therefore undoubtedly authentic, "Rex autem, qui vicarius Summi Regis est, ad hoc est constitutus, ut regnum terrenum, et populum

But a compilation of canon law was made by *Ivo de Chartres*, in the time of Henry I. containing many extrava-

Domini, et super omnia, sanctam veneretur ecclesiam, et regat, et ab injuriosis defendat, et maleficos ab ea evellat, et destruat, et penitus disperdat. Quod nisi fecerit, nec nomen regis in eo constabit, verum testante Papa Joanne, nomen regis perdit" (*Leges Edwardi Regis*, art. 17 apud *Wilkins*, i., 312). This went further than the Decretum of Gratian, founded on the decree of Pope John VIII., which only said that a king who refused to fulfil his duty to the church might be excommunicated: but it only applied to princes, upon whom such conditions were imposed by the law and constitution of the land. Then, as to the immunities of the clergy: "Cum clerico qui uxorem habeat, et firmam teneat laicorum, et rebus extrinsecis seculariter deditus sit, seculariter est disceptandum. De illis qui ad sacros ordines pertinent, et eis qui sacris ordinibus promoti sunt, coram prelatis suis est agendum, de omnibus inculpationibus, maximis vel minoribus" (*Leg. Hen. Pr.*, c. lvii., s. 91). But in the *Mirror of Justice* it is laid down that it is a good exception to lay jurisdiction, that the judge has no power of the person of a clerk, by reason of the privileges of the church (c. xxxi., 1). "In the privilege of clergy, as if a clerk be ordered in court before a lay judge to answer to an action for a personal trespass, and especially in a case criminal and mortal, plead that he is a clerk, the judge hath no further cognizance of the case; for the church is so enfranchised that no lay judge can have jurisdiction over a clerk" (*Ib.*, s. 4). It is indeed added that it rebutted the privilege to show that the clerk was bigamous, or a murderer, or a perjurer, or in such a condition that the church ought not to protect him against the king's peace; but this was evidently added after the controversy with Archbishop A'Becket: for of course it would render the privilege nugatory.

In the canons of the Archbishop Egbert, compiled from all the canons then extant, were these: "Ut sine auctoritate vel consensu episcoporum, presbyteri, in quibuslibet ecclesiis, nec constituantur nec expellantur" (c. 21; *Ang.-Sax. Laws*, v. ii., p. 100). "Si quis episcopus aut presbyter, per pecunias hanc obtinuerit dignitatem, dejiciatur, et ipse et ordinator ejus" (*Ibid.*, c. 43, p. 104). "Si in qualibet provincia ortæ fuerint quæstiones, ad majorem sedem, vel synodum, seu etiam ad apostolicam sedem Romæ, referantur" (*Ibid.*, c. 49, p. 104). "Tempore Constantini Augusti, congregavit Silvester papa synodum Romæ cum episcopis, quorum consensu et subscriptione constitum est, ut nullus laicus clerico crimen audeat inferre. Testimonium ergo laici adversus clericum non recipiatur" (*Ibid.*, c. 144, p. 121). This, it will be observed, is founded upon the Roman canon; which is taken as beyond a doubt, that no cleric could be accused by a layman; *à multo fortiori*, he could not be tried by a laic. It would be difficult to find anything in the later canons which went beyond these. In the Penitential of Archbishop Egbert, it is laid down, as to offences of the clergy, "Si presbyter vitiatus esset capitalibus criminibus, postquam ordinatus sit, non ei licebit ministerium ullum ad altare Dei facere, sed maneat alioquin cum clericis, et si resipiscere velit, emendet prout episcopus ei præscripserit" (*Pen. Egb., Ang.-Sax. Laws*, v. ii., p. 197). "Si presbyter vel diaconus hominem occiderit, vel perjuraverit, perdant ordinem suum; et si ad emendationem se convertere velint emendant juxta sententiam episcopi" (*Ibid.*, c. 3). So that if a priest committed murder or perjury, he was degraded, and perhaps, in strict law, he would be liable to be tried for the murder, having lost his clerical privilege, a consideration which may have a bearing on the subsequent controversy between Henry II. and Becket. At the same time, it is plainly implied as the intention of the canons, that for the first offence deg-

gant opinions (a), calculated to advance the dominion of the pope, and the pretensions of the clergy. After this,

radation was to be the punishment. For an offence after degradation, of course the man would be liable to the criminal law.

The two points upon which it is represented by the author that the later canon law departed from or unduly developed the earlier, are the exclusive jurisdiction of the church over ecclesiastics, and the extension of the canon law to secular affairs. As to the former, the canons of Edgar declare both in the clearest manner, "We enjoin that no dispute between priests be referred to secular courts; but let them adjust it among themselves, or *refer it to the bishop*, if needful" (*Ang.-Sax. Laws*, v. ii., p. 247). "And we enjoin that every priest declare in the synod if in his district he knows any man contumacious to God, or sunk in sin, whom he cannot incline to amends, or care not for worldly opinion" (*Ibid.*). And in the Civil and Ecclesiastical Institutes it is laid down, "To a bishop belongs every direction, both in divine and worldly things. He shall in the first place inform men in orders, so that each of them may know what properly it behoves them to do, and also what they have to enjoin to secular men. He shall not consent to any injustice, nor false weights or measures; but it is fitting that every legal right go by his counsel, and that every balance and measure be by his sanction very exact, lest any man should wrong another, and thereby sin" (*Ibid.*, 313). These latter words clearly convey the whole scope of the canon laws, and the principle on which it entered into secular matters; that is, entirely *in foro conscientiæ*, and with a view to spiritual correction. And this, unless so far as the state chose to enforce it, was, of course, entirely of voluntary observance, and had no force or obligation save in conscience; in other words, to the extent to which a man's own conscience or moral sense impelled him to observe it. It was a purely moral power, and had no connection with the domain of the municipal law, except so far as enforced by the state, which was its own voluntary act, resulting from the collective conscience of the community, and a sense that it was right so to enforce it. To represent the canon law, therefore, as encroaching, by reason of its extension, upon the municipal law, shows an entire misapprehension. These domains were so entirely distinct and independent, that the greatest possible extension or development of the former could not encroach upon the latter. How could moral law encroach on municipal? The canon law was entirely moral law, resting on religious liberty and spiritual sanctions; and so far as the state did not interfere, a man was free to regard it or disregard it as he pleased. In the only matters on which there was an appearance of interference with the secular law, the claim of exclusive jurisdiction over ecclesiastical persons and property, the canon law followed the municipal law; for, as already seen, it had been the law for ages, and a law in those times extremely rational, although the reasons upon which it rested have long since disappeared. To represent these claims, therefore, as encroachments, is an historical error. In point of fact, they were not encroachments, for they rested on the consent of the state. And to the full extent, in all other respects, the legality of canon law and civil jurisdiction was recognized by the law.

(a) The learned author did not appreciate the grounds on which the canon law rested. The popes themselves, whose decrees formed the bases of the decretals, always put the exercise of their authority either upon the ground of spiritual direction to men as the members of the church, and acknowledging her spiritual authority, or upon the authority derived from the acknowledgment and the recognition of the church by the state. Thus, for instance, Pope Gregory VII. based his decree, deposing the emperor, upon

and about fourteen years after the discovery of the Pandects, in the year 1151, a more complete collection of authority derived from human laws — the laws of the empire, as well as upon his spiritual authority over the emperor as a member of the church, "propter quæ (*i. e.*, sceleribus suis) eum excommunicari, non solùm usque ad dignam satisfactionem, sed ab omni honore regni, debere destitui, divinarum et humanarum legum testatur auctoritas" (*Vita Greg. VIII., Benried,* c. lxxviii.; *Muratori, Rer. Ital. Script.,* tom. iii., part 1, p. 357). Rightly or wrongly, it was the view of the popes, and of most people in those days, that the laws of the empire gave the pope the power to declare this; and so it was professedly based upon human laws. So Pope Innocent III., by whom the pretensions of the Roman see were certainly pressed as far as by any pontiff, put it entirely upon his pastoral power over members of the church, and upon his acknowledged function as its head, and *disclaimed any temporal power except as far as conferred by the laws of the state.* "Non enim intendimus judicare de feudo, cujus ad ipsum (regem Galliæ), spectat judicium, nisi forte jure communi, per speciale privilegium vel contrariam consuetudinem, aliquid sit detractum; sed decernere de peccato, cujus ad nos pertinet sine dubitatione censura, quam in quemlibet exercere possumus et debemus" (*Decretal,* lib. ii., tit. 1; *De Judiciis,* c. xiii.). According to this, it is obvious the papal power was one of mere spiritual direction, *in foro conscientiæ,* resting only on moral sanction; or it was an emanation from the secular law, derived from state concession; in either case, no assumption antagonistic to state power. The excommunication was pronounced under the former power; its effect, as to deposition, entirely depended upon the latter — that is, upon the laws of the state. It was a consequence of excommunication, according to the belief of the age, founded on the laws of the empire, with reference to the oath, and the condition of allegiance. And as the former was based upon the acknowledgment of the spiritual authority of the church and of the pope as its head, it could make no pretensions to the exercise of the jurisdiction where that authority was not acknowledged; so that it rested entirely on voluntary acknowledgment. The pope simply administered the laws of the church as its head, between those who acknowledged those laws, and acknowledged him as its head. Moreover, at the age when this jurisdiction was exercised, it was so entirely in accordance with the popular belief, that it was the expression of the popular will. Voltaire admits this general belief. Speaking of the great struggle with the empire, he says, "Vous en verrez l'unique origine dans la populace; c'est elle qui donne le mouvement à la superstition" (*Essai sur les Mœurs,* tom. iii., c. xlvi.). He terms it, indeed, a superstitious feeling, but he admits its universality in that age; and it has been seen that it had a strong foundation in the laws of the empire. The princes themselves, he elsewhere says, admitted the jurisdiction, they everywhere had recourse to it (*Ibid.,* tom. iii., c. lxiv.). It can scarcely be deemed surprising that the papacy should, in such an age, have exercised a jurisdiction with which it appeared to be invested by the traditions of ancient law, by popular belief, and even by the acknowledgment of sovereigns. Quoting the language of the popes in the middle ages, Voltaire says, "Quelques téméraires que paraissent les entreprises, elles sont toujours la suite des opinions dominantes. Il faut certainement que l'ignorance eût mis alors dans beaucoup de têtes que l'église était la maitresse des royaumes, puisque le pape ecrivait toujours de ce style" (*Essai sur les Mœurs,* tom iii., c. xlvi.). It might be the result of ignorance; and no doubt, in that age, the clergy possessed most of the knowledge, and therefore most of the influence; but the fact is beyond dispute, that these were the dominant and prevalent opinions of the age, and that therefore, in the exercise of this jurisdiction, the

canon law was made by *Gratian*, a Benedictine monk of Bologna, and was published under the title of *Decretum:*

papacy acted as much in accordance with public opinion, as it would now be acting in defiance of it, were it to pursue a similar course. Even in that age, the popes never went in temporal matters beyond public opinion. Thus the popes knew the distinction between excommunication and deposition, and while they asserted the former power upon all occasions, and in every age, over the members of the church, of which they were the leaders, they never pronounced a prince deposed except when they knew they only registered the public voice. Thus, so early as the sixteenth century, at the very foundation of our Saxon monarchy, the pontiff, to whom the Saxons owed their conversion, Gregory the Great, declared, "Si quis regum, sacerdotum, judicum, personarumque sæcularium hanc constitutionis nostræ paginam agnoscens, contra eam venire tentaverit, *potestatis honorisque sui dignitate careat*, reumque se divino judicio existere de perpetratà iniquitate cognoscat" (*Greg. Epist.*, lib. xiii.; *Epist.*, viii. 9, 10). Thus Gregory VII., having pronounced excommunication, declared deposition as the consequence, according to the law of the empire, knowing that public opinion supported that view. But as Voltaire points out in a subsequent case, the pontiff pronounced excommunication, but not deposition. "Il est tres remarquable que dans ces longues dissensions le pape Alexandre III. qui avait fait souvent cette cérémonie d'excommunier l'empereur, n'alla jamais qui-qu' à le deposer." He adds, "Cette conduite ne prouve-t-elle pas non seulement beaucoup de sagesse dans ce pontiffe; mais une condamnatione générale des excès de Grégorie VII." (*Essai sur les Mœurs*, tom. iii., c. xlviii.); but Voltaire forgot that the popes well knew they had no proper power to depose, as they deemed they had to excommunicate, and that the deposition was another matter altogether, which must depend upon public opinion, and the circumstances of the times; and he admits the sagacity of the pontiff in the course which he pursued on the occasion. What, however, is most important is, that the popes knew and observed the distinction between the power of spiritual direction and power of temporal rule, which could only be derived from the consent of the state, and the general voice of the people; and could only be properly exercised for their protection, or in support of justice, of liberty and of law. That it would, so far as it was so exercised, not be in opposition to, but in favor of, liberty and law, is admitted by Voltaire, and by the most enlightened historians of our own or any other country. Thus Voltaire says, speaking of the struggle between the pope and our Henry II., "L'intérêt du genre humain demande un frein qui retienne les souverains, et qui mette à couvert la vie des peuples. Ce frein de la religion aurait pu être *par une convention universelle dans la main des papes.* Les premiers pontifes en ne se mêlant des querelles temporelles, que pour les appaiser, en avertissant les rois et les peuples de leurs devoirs, en reprenant leurs crimes, en reservent les excommunications pour les grands attentats, auraient toujours été regardés comme des images de Dieu sur la terre, mais les hommes sont reduits à n'avoir pour leur défense que les lois et les mœurs de leurs pays, lois souvent méprisées, et mœurs la souvent corrompues" (*Essai sur les Mœurs*, tom. iii., c. i.). It has always been forgotten, that, rightly or wrongly, the popes, in their contests with the emperor, always maintained and based their jurisdiction upon the fact, that the emperor had taken oaths of fidelity to them, and had contracted, owing to the peculiar relations of Italy and Germany, feudal obligations to them; and the fact is beyond dispute, that the emperor did take oaths of fidelity to the popes, which are inserted in the "Decretum of Gratian," and to be found in the *Corpus Juris Canonici*, and this oath is admitted by Bossuet to imply at

it was made in imitation of the Pandects, and was a *digest* of the whole *pontifical* canon law. This is a collection of

all events a great degree of obedience or submission. It is not material here whether the papacy was right or wrong in its view. The important point to keep in view, in its bearing on legal history is, that the papacy always based its temporal jurisdiction upon this assumption, *i. e.*, upon the assumption of an acknowledgment of it, just as the popes based their spiritual jurisdiction on the acknowledgment of it, and the recognition of them as the heads of the church. That the deposition of a sovereign was a consequence of his excommunication was the general belief in this, as in every other country in that age. Thus, in the reign of Henry II., John of Salisbury, whom Sir J. Mackintosh describes as far beyond his age in learning, and who was an attached friend and adviser of Archbishop à Becket, held that as an admitted principle, and so speaks of the pope as "Vicarius Petri, a Domino constitutus super gentes et super regna" (*Joannes Salis.*, ep. 210; *Biblioth. Patrum.*, tom. xxiii.). Nay, more, kings themselves — as our Henry among the number — admitted the jurisdiction, and only disputed its exercise; this is manifest from the contemporary accounts left by that eminent prelate, or the letters of the archbishop, for it appears that when Cardinal Gratian asserted it in his conferences with the king, the latter, so far from resenting or protesting against it, desired the council to testify his desire or reconciliation, "rex rogavit ut testificarentur vires quanta et qualia obtulerat, restitutionem scilicet archiepiscopatus et pacis" (*Ep. Fl.*, lib. iii., ep. 61). This being the view of the popes themselves, it is to be expected that they would also be the views of the compilers of these decretals, Ivo and Gratian, and so it is; and these ancient authorities on the canon law base their doctrine as to the jurisdiction of the church, primarily, on its "directive" authority, purely spiritual and voluntary, and exercised only *in foro conscientiæ*, and, secondarily, on its recognition by the civil law itself (*Ironis Decretum*, part v., c. 378). And in his letter to our Henry I., although he asserts that the temporal power ought to be subject to the spiritual, he shows his consciousness that, to the extent to which it is so, it must be the concession of the state. "Celsitudinem vestram *obsecrando* monemus, quatenus in *regno vobis commissi verbum Dei currere permittatis*, et regnum terrenum cœlesti regno, quod ecclesiæ commissum est, subditum esse debere semper cogitetis; sicut enim sensus animalis subditus debet esse rationi, ita potestas terrena subdita esse debet ecclesiastico regimini" (*Ivo de Chartres*, epist. 101) — language which, no doubt, (naturally enough, in an age when ecclesiastics had all the knowledge), implies that the church represented the intellectual power of the age, and ought to be superior; but at the same time also implying that it could only be so by the concession of the state, and that it was not the prerogative of the church by divine right. So Gratian's doctrine is in substance the same (*Gratiani Decretum*, part i., dist. 96, c. x.). The contrary notion, founded on an isolated sentence—"A fidelitatis etiam juramento Romanus pontifex nonnullos absolvit, cum aliquos à sua dignitate deponit" (*Ibid.*, causa xv., quæst. vi., c. iii.) — is disproved by the context, and the whole texture and tenor of the authorities he cites. So Hugo de St. Victor, who thus distinguishes the temporal and spiritual powers: "Secundum causam justitia determinatur, ut videlicet negotia sæcularia à potestate terrena, spiritualia vero et ecclesiastica, à spirituali potestate examinentur; sæcularis autem potestas caput habet regem, ab illo per subjectas potestates, et duces, et comites, et præfectos, et magistratus alios descendens; qui tamen omnes à prima potestate auctoritatem sumunt, in eo quod subjectis, prælati existunt" (*Ibid.*, c. viii.). The interest of all this here, and its bearing on the history of the English law is, that the doctrines thus laid down formed

opinions and decisions, extracted from sayings of the fathers, canons of councils, and, above all, from decretal

the basis of those denounced in the text, and were afterwards the subject of the great contest between the church and state in the reign of Henry II., which forms one of the most memorable epochs in our legal history; and that much the same doctrines will be found laid down in Bracton, who, more than any other ancient author, is regarded by Lord Coke himself as the parent of the English law. Enough has now been stated to enable the reader to form a judgment upon that great controversy, and to appreciate the above observations of our author. All that he has to bear in mind, however, is, that the question as to the merits of that controversy depends not upon the ideas now entertained, but upon those which were entertained in the age in which it arose. So far from the canonical law or the writers upon it being so extreme in their views as is represented by the author, the very canonist whom he cites as the chief expounder of the extravagant doctrines he denounces — Ivo of Chartres — vindicated the right of the pope to pronounce the sentence of excommunication against sovereigns, as founded on the laws of the state, as well as of the church (*Ironis Decretum*, part v., c. ccclxxviii.). And in his letter to our Henry I., already quoted, this eminent prelate only puts it upon the ground of the union between the church and the state, and of liberty allowed to the church to carry out its discipline in a country where the church and its discipline are acknowledged. And while he implies the subordination of the temporal to the spiritual, in the sense of what theologians call the directive power, he says not a word which implies a jurisdiction of divine right over temporalities; but teaches that this is founded on divine and human laws (*Ivo de Chartres*, epist. 106). All this, it is evident, was not understood by the author, in whose exaggerated representation may be observed the influence of prejudice, arising from that cause. It is in very different language Hallam writes. Speaking of the civil law, he says: "Some of the more ancient ecclesiastics, as Hincmar, and Ivo of Chartres, occasionally refer to it, and bear witness to the regard which the Roman church had uniformly paid to its decisions" (*Midd. Ages*, c. viii.). And our author himself says, a little further on, that the canon law was founded on the civil. Not having read the laws of Henry I., he was not aware that not only, as Hale says, they "had a taste of the canon and civil law," but that whole passages are taken from the canon law — that is, the later canon law, which he denounces as so full of what was "extravagant," though Hale had observed nothing in those laws to provoke animadversion; and the compilation forms the foundation for the great treatise of Glanville, the basis of our common law. The foundation of the canon law is laid in the decrees of councils, and in the rescripts, or decretal epistles of the popes to questions propounded upon emergent doubts relative to matters of discipline and ecclesiastical economy. As the jurisdiction of the spiritual tribunals increased, and extended to a variety of persons and causes, it became almost necessary to establish a uniform system for the regulation of their decisions. After several more compilations had appeared, Gratian, an Italian monk, published, about the year 1140, his *Decretum*, or general collection of canons, papal epistles, and sentences of fathers, arranged and digested into titles and chapters, in imitation of the Pandects, which, very little before, had begun to be studied with great diligence (*Midd. Ages*, c. vii.). But he adds that Gregory IX. caused the five books of decretals to be published in 1234, and that these form the most essential part of the canon law, the *Decretum* of Gratian being obsolete. "In these books," he says, "we find a regular and copious system of jurisprudence, derived in great degree from the civil law, but with considerable deviation, and possibly

epistles of popes; all tending to exalt the clerical state, and to exempt the clergy from secular subordination. The applause this book received from the see of Rome

improvement" (*Ibid.*). And a sixth was afterwards added, containing subsequent decisions. Of the body of canon law, Hallam observes: "The superiority of the ecclesiastical to temporal power, or, at least, the absolute independence of the former, may be considered the key-note which regulates it," and then he cites several passages, which, it may be presumed, were about the strongest he could select, by every one of which, it will be seen, the proposition is limited to spiritual or ecclesiastical matters. "Constitutiones principum *ecclesiasticis* constitutionibus, non præeminent, sed obsequuntur" (*Dec.*, dist. 10). "Statutum generale laicorum *ad ecclesias vel ad ecclesiasticas personas vel eorum bona*, in eorum præjudicium non extenditur" (*Decretal*, l. i., tit. ii., c. x.). " Quæcunque à principibus in *ordinibus vel in ecclesiasticis* rebus decreta inveniuntur, nullius auctoritatits esse monstrantur" (*Decretum*, dist. 96). The historian gives his readers the opportunity of observing this by quoting the terms of the decretals. And although he goes on to say, "It is expressly declared that subjects owe no allegiance to an excommunicated lord, if, after admonition, he be not reconciled to the church," and cites the following rubric from the decretals (i. 5, tit. xxxvii., c. xii.):—"Domino excommunicata manente subditi fidelitatem non debent; et si longo tempore in eâ perstiterent, et monitus non pareat ecclesiæ, ab ejus debito absolvuntur"—the historian has the candor to add: "I must acknowledge that the decretal epistle of the pope scarcely warrants this general proposition of the rubric, though it seems to lead to it." And though he quotes another rubric: —"Papa imperatorem deponere potest, ex causis legitimis" (c. ii., tit. xiii., c. 2), he adds, "The rubrics to the decretals are not, perhaps, of direct authority as part of the law, but they express its sense." And no doubt, at the period now in question, these papal pretensions were maintained. But then they were maintained, in the first place, as against sovereigns, who professed to be subject to the Roman see, as members of the Roman church, of which that see was the head, and who acknowledged the authority of the pope as the vicegerent of Christ; and, in the next place, these pretensions were entirely in accordance with national law, and proceeded upon premises laid down in that law. This has already been amply shown, so far as regards this country, from the Saxon laws, in which the authority of the pope is recognized in many ways: by the payment of Peter's pence, or Rome's fee, as it was called, which is enforced all through the Saxon laws up to the Conquest; by recognition of the papal authority, not only in matters in their nature ecclesiastical, at variance with secular law, but even as regards the clergy, in matters in their own nature properly municipal: as in cases of murder by a priest; and, in short, by his being practically and expressly recognized as the supreme spiritual authority. All that was done in the most extreme or extravagant pretensions of the canon law, with respect to papal or civil authority, was simply to carry out these premises, granted by municipal law itself, to their extreme logical conclusions. And no authority can be found (it is believed) for any such pretensions, except as to states which had made such concessions and laid down such premises. Whence it is that, in modern times, when such principles are not admitted, we hear of no such pretensions. But it is most important, in forming a judgment upon the acts or conduct of men in distant times, to take into consideration the circumstances under which they took place; and in judging of the contest between the civil and ecclesiastical power at this period, it is necessary to bear in mind *the premises admitted at the time on both sides*, which the author has failed to observe.

and the clergy, raised it soon above all former collections; and it became the grand code of ecclesiastical law, upon which the popish hierarchy rested all its hopes and pretensions.

The canon and civil law had before been studied and professed by the same persons; and the union of these two laws was now drawn closer. The canon law was from the beginning under great obligations to the civil; the very form in which it now appeared was evidently borrowed from thence; and whatever was most excellent in it, was acknowledged to be copied from that model (*a*).

(*a*) It may be of interest here to present an analysis of the canon law, or of the contents of the decretals, their chief and most authentic source, from which may be derived, in some degree, a just idea of their nature, and also how far our own laws may have derived advantage therefrom. Lord Hale states, as to the laws of Henry I., that they have a "taste" of the canon law. He might have gone further, and said that entire passages are taken therefrom, and that large portions — most of that which relates to the important subject of the *principles* of procedure, were founded thereon; and further, that these laws form the basis of the treatises of Glanville, Bracton, and the *Mirror of Justice*, the most authentic sources of our own law. So that the author, in deriding or denouncing the canon law (of which it has been shown he knew little or nothing), was really deriding and denouncing the sources whence our own law, in a great degree, was derived. The canon law was simply the civil law adapted to the use of a country acknowledging the Roman church as the head. The first book of the decretal treats, in the first place, therefore, of the doctrines of that church, the acknowledgment of which is presumed and supposed to be the basis of all the rest. It was in forgetfulness of this that the fundamental fallacy of our author lay. The canon law professes, at the outset, to be the canon law of countries which acknowledge the Roman church. The next book treats of rescripts, constitutions, and customs, and their authority; then the law as to election, confirmation, and consecration of bishops, the resignation or renunciation of benefices, and other purely ecclesiastical matters; and as to discipline of the clergy. Next there comes a head of ecclesiastical law, which formed the basis of our law of legal terms; and that was the law as to the *Pax Dei* or *Pax Ecclesiæ* — the peace of the church — *i. e.*, sacred periods, during which war or litigation ought not to be allowed, and which the ecclesiastical authorities, therefore, were to procure to be observed, so far as it was possible for them to do so; and accordingly, in order to enforce observance of these periods or intervals, they were to issue excommunications against those — that is, members of the Roman church — who failed to observe them. It may here be observed that excommunication, as the phrase itself implies, was simply a putting out of communion — *i. e.*, the communion of the Roman church; whence, of course, it followed that it did not *apply*, except to members of that church, nor *affect* those who did not care to be so. Under this purely spiritual penalty, the periods of the peace of the church were observed; and during those periods, neither priests nor laymen, nor chartmen nor rustics, either going to the field, or being in the field, or coming from the field (the origin of our legal phrase as to privilege from arrest — *eundo et redeundo*), or the cattle with which they ploughed,'could be arrested or seized. Again, it was laid down to be the duty of judges, before men entered into a lawsuit,

These two systems now became so connected, and in so near a degree of relation, that a learned writer says, the

to persuade the parties by private covenants and agreements, to compound the controversy between them; and this, there is little doubt, led to the devising of fines, or concords in court, which became used in the time of Henry I., and which the learned Hargreave considered were originally real concords of really existing suits. So also, there can be little doubt that this led to the encouragement of arbitration in our courts, which is to be observed from the very earliest records of these proceedings. Various rules and principles are laid down as to arbitrations and arbitrators, which form the basis of our rules of law upon the subject. And be it observed, that for a century or two after the Conquest, during which our law was moulded, the chancellors and chief judges were ecclesiastics, and *took their ideas of law from these very volumes now under analysis*. Again, if, pending a suit, a party alienated away the subject-matter, he was nevertheless held liable to answer for it as though he were still owner of it; and this, again, formed the basis of our rules of law or equity as to *lis pendens*, or fraudulent alienations, pending a suit. In short, the greater portion of this first book of the Decretals deals, and deals admirably, with the subject of litigation. The second book expounds the principles of *procedure* and judicature, a competent court, a proper citation, and declaration of the cause of suit. Then came the "exceptions," a phrase borrowed from the Roman civil law, and from the civil and canonical law, adopted by our earliest legal authors — Glanville, Bracton, and the *Mirror*, and in the statute of Westm. Then the nature and the order of rights is laid down: as, that rights or causes which convey possession — causes "possessory," as they were and are called — are first to be determined before a right of property, and that he who has been forcibly expelled from or deprived of property, is first to be *restored* to the thing or place of which he has been thus deprived, even although he has no other than a possessor's right, and has *not* the right of property — a principle founded upon the doctrine of the Roman law, which has already been noticed, and forming the basis of our whole law of disseisin or forcible dispossession of property, of which the possessor can obtain restitution irrespective of actual strict right. Then, as to the procedure for the elimination of the question in dispute; if the facts were admitted then, it was pointed out, it became a question of law for the judge, and not a question of fact; and the judge, upon the admitted facts, was to pronounce judgment — a principle, that of the separation of the law from the fact, which, as Sir James Mackintosh observed, formed the basis of our whole system of procedure, and which, he adds, it is impossible not to admire (*Hist. Eng.*, v. i.); although it is true, that afterwards, under *lay* judges, often so ignorant as to mistake technicality for subtlety, the system was rather perverted. If the facts were not admitted, then they were to be determined by witnesses, instead of by the absurd ordeal or the brutal duel, and after proofs on either side, judgment was to be given on the facts thus ascertained, with provision for appeal. With some alterations as to the *mode* of taking evidence, this system formed the basis of our system of trial, superadding the jury in common law cases, though not, until ages later, making them judges of evidence, not mere witnesses; while, in some of our courts, the canonical system of trial continued until our own time. The third book of the Decretals treats of such civil matters and causes as were deemed to be triable in the ecclesiastical courts — as the conduct of ecclesiastics, non-residence, and the like. So it treats of the possessions of the church, and when they may be alienated, etc. It treats also of wills and testaments, and of succession in cases of intestacy; of tithes, and of first-fruits; of the right of patronage, etc. And it is laid down that

one could not subsist without the other. They afforded each other a mutual support; they had the same professors; and it was requisite to the fame and preferment of a churchman, that he should be both a civilian and a canonist.

When these two laws were brought into this high repute, *Vacarius* came into England, and, A. D. 1149, towards the end of Stephen's reign began to read lectures, at Oxford, on the canon and civil law. Upon this an alarm was raised, and the king, apprehensive of the consequences to which these new doctrines might lead, in the year 1152, or thereabouts, is said to have forbid the reading of books of the canon law [1] (a); a prohibition that could not be meant to extend to that canon law which had long been admitted and ratified, but probably only to the novel and bold opinions contained in the collection

---

ecclesiastical persons are not to trouble themselves about civil matters, contrary to their office and profession; in accordance with which, under Henry II., Archbishop A'Becket gave up the chancellorship; and the Roman see objected strongly to ecclesiastics taking political and judicial office, although in an age when few of the laity were competent for civil offices, it was necessarily, to a great extent, tolerated that ecclesiastics should hold them. The fourth book treats of matters matrimonial, and of legitimacy, as to which the canon law was assumed to be that marriage legitimated previous issue. The fifth book treats of such *criminal* matters as are dealt with in the ecclesiastical courts, expounding offences according to their moral and religious aspect, as *in foro conscientiæ.* The decrees — that is, general, not made at any suit — were first collected by Ivo of Chartres, A. D. 1114, and were completed by Gratian in 1149. The first volume of the Decretals, which were royal epistles at the suit or instance of some party for the determination of any controversy, were put forth in 1231, and ordered to be read in schools. The second was half a century later; but, as our author elsewhere observes, many of the decrees or decretals had obtained currency long before they were collected.

(a) But Selden, recording this, adds — "Sed parùm valuit Stephani prohibitis nam eo magis invaluit virtus legis, *Deo favente,* quo eum amplius nitebatur impietas subvertere," (*Dissert. ad Flet.,* c. vii., p. 6). And Sir J. Mackintosh says, that "the civil law was taught *with applause* by Vacarius, as we are told by his pupil, John of Salisbury — the friend of Becket, distinguished in the learning of the age," (*History of England,* v. i.). And elsewhere the historian speaks with just contempt of Stephen as "a captain of banditti" (*Ibid., Steph.*). That the study of the law should have been forbidden by such a man, is its highest praise. Mr. Hallam's account of the matter is this: "The students of scholastic theology opposed themselves, from some unexplained reason, to this new jurisprudence, and these lectures were prohibited" (*Midd. Ages,* c. viii.). The prohibition, doubtless, arose from that jealousy which was incident to an ignorant age; the name of the Roman law associating it with the pretensions of the papal power, which began to be viewed with hostility.

[1] Joh. Salisb. de nug. curia.

of *Ivo de Chartres*, and more particular that lately made by *Gratian*.

Indeed the use of the canon law became now a subject of very serious consideration. The canons before admitted here were very ancient; many of them had received a legislative sanction, and by long continuance they had ingrafted themselves into the constitution of the country; but a set of opinions entirely new was advanced by the publication of the *Decretum*, which, from the parade of the work and the support it received from the see of Rome, had the appearance of a promulgation of laws imposed on the Christian world by the sole and supreme authority of the pope. From a question on the *utility*, as it had been before in some respects, it became now a question upon the *authority* of these laws.[1] The contest between the secular and ecclesiastical state was thenceforward more violent, as the points upon which it arose were more important.

Notwithstanding the prohibition of King Stephen, the study of the civil and canon law was universally promoted by the clergy. Educated in opinions calculated to promote the benefit and emolument of their own order, it was not much to be wondered, that they struck in with the designs of the pope, and stood firmly upon the maintenance of their own pretended rights and privileges.

The active spirit of the clergy did not want instruments to work with: the body of canon law lately published by *Gratian* furnished authority and arguments for every species of usurpation.

Doctrines of the canon law. The doctrines of the canon law, as delivered in the *Decretum*, tended to mark more strongly the distinction between clergy and laity, and the great deference due to the former. It is there laid down, that a custom against the decree of a pope is void; and that all men must observe the pope's command (*a*). It is

(*a*) That is, all members of the Roman church, who acknowledge him as the head of their church, and in matters which involve religious or ecclesiastical questions. These important qualifications are omitted by the author, and make all the difference in the world. That a custom, against a decree of the pope, should have been held void, in a country acknowledging the pope as the head of its church, was only natural, seeing that the papal decrees were only upon such matters in which religious questions or ecclesiastical interests were involved. There would surely have been an absurd inconsistency in holding, in such a country, that a custom, contrary to what the head of its church declared on such subject, was nevertheless valid.

[1] Litt. Hen. II., vol. ii., 471.

made an anathema to sue a clergyman before a lay judge; if a lay judge condemn or destroy a clerk, he is to be excommunicated; a clerk may implead a layman before what judge he pleases; judges who compel a clerk to answer to a suit before them, shall be excommunicated; a layman cannot give evidence against a clerk; with numberless extravagancies of the same kind (*a*). Such notions did the canonists propagate for law respecting churchmen, in the reigns of Henry II., of Richard, and of John.

Indeed it was not till these doctrines had generally prevailed that the separate establishment of ecclesiastical judicature. gained much strength. It was not till the publication of the *Decretum*, and the growing authority of the canons had given some order, consistence, and stability to spiritual government, that the exclusive jurisdiction of these courts was an object of very important consideration, or that their claims were urged to any great extent.

Some causes, apparently clerical, had continued to hang about the temporal courts, particularly those concerning tithes; which, being the issues of freehold property, and so partaking of its nature, could hardly be considered as merely spiritual.[1] Accordingly such pleas were held both in the ecclesiastical and temporal courts till the time of Henry II. After that, tithes came under the notice of our courts of common law only in an indirect proceeding; such as on prohibitions, writs of right of advowson, or by *scire facias*,[2] an ancient proceeding since abolished by parliament.[3] The prerogatives of the hierarchy, and the jurisdiction of the ecclesiastical courts assisted each other in extending their influence. The courts grew in authority and the bishops rose in their pretensions.

Amongst other attempts to aggrandize themselves, the

(*a*) "Extravagancies," nevertheless, to be found in the Saxon laws, as already has been shown, and all of which, except so far as expressly altered, were repeatedly confirmed at the Conquest. It is obvious that in that age they were not considered "extravancies," and that is the important point. That they would be so now is certain, for many reasons; but there is no greater extravagance of absurdity than making the ideas, the circumstances, the impressions of a modern age the standard or the measure of another and a distant age. Yet this form of fallacy is prevalent in most histories of the middle ages. That it has been even to some extent avoided by such writers as Sir J. Mackintosh and Mr. Hallam, is one of the greatest of their many merits. But it was not always avoided by our author.

[1] Seld., Tithes, 387.   [2] Ibid., 422.   [3] By Stat. Edw. III.

clergy did not omit so valuable a subject of acquisition as benefices. A benefice, being an eleemosynary provision for a person who officiated in the discharge of religious duties, was originally in the sole disposal of the founder, and was conferred, like other donations, by investiture; but the bishops, as having the superintendence over spiritual things, claimed a right of control over these gifts (a). This occasioned a contest between patrons and

(a) This is not a correct representation. The bishops claimed what they had always had, the right of appointing the clergy, just as the pope, as the head of the church, claimed the right of appointing the bishops, on the general principle that these offices were all pastoral, and purely spiritual. Nor was this claim disputed until they had long become the subject of *endowments*, nor even then until after the feudal system had become firmly established; and it was then insisted that the temporalities were benefices, or were fiefs, in the feudal sense, and subject to feudal incidents, one of which was the right of the crown, or the patron, to confer them (so as to secure a veto upon the appointment), and also to have the custody of them when vacant, so that by combining the veto with the power of possession during vacancy, the king might secure the possession of the temporalities until he coerced the pope into the appointment of some corrupt prelate, with whom he could make his own arrangements as regarded the inferior clergy. What they would come to, no one with the least knowledge of history can doubt; and it is thus described by Sir J. Mackintosh : "The power of nomination (for such it was) had been converted by secular powers into an indecent and scandalous means of raising money, by setting up for sale the dignities and benefices of the church" (*Hist. of Eng.*, vol. i., p. 347). This, the historian says, was the result of the claim of the king, which "involved a previous negative on every choice, and, in effect, amounted to the ecclesiastical patronage of Europe" (*Ibid.*). So Mr. Hallam says, "The sovereigns, the lay patrons, the prelates, made their powers of nomination and investiture subservient to the grossest rapacity," to which he ought to have added, *the prelates appointed by the sovereign;* the great object was the struggle, on the part of the sovereign, to get control over the appointment of the bishops, so as to be enabled to obtain, by corrupt arrangement with them, control over the appointment of the clergy. And this, indeed, was the next important feature in the matter; for, of course, to have all Christendom covered with a corrupt and ignorant clergy, would have been destructive of Christianity. And Mr. Hallam says, "Through bribery, or through corrupt agreements with princes, a large proportion of the bishops had no valid tenure in their sees. The case was perhaps worse with the inferior clerks" (*Midd. Ages*, c. v.). As to the importance of the question, therefore, there can be no doubt; neither can there be any doubt in the mind of any lawyer as to the utter absence of any pretence for the claim set up by the sovereigns. This can be shown in many ways. The shortest and clearest way, perhaps, is to refer to the general principle already alluded to, that these offices were pastoral and purely spiritual, and that by the constitution of any country acknowledging the Roman church, and the pope as the head of it, and as the supreme pastor, the nomination of episcopal pastors must pertain to him, and of parochial pastors to the bishops. And, as already noticed, this claim was not disputed, until some time after the Conquest, nor until after the establishment of the feudal system, when the grossest oppressions and exactions took place; as was noticed and acknowledged in the *Leges Henrici Primi—*

the bishops for many years; till at length the ancient way of investiture entirely ceased about the reigns of kings Richard and John, and lay patrons became obliged first to present their clerks to the bishop, who, according to his discretion, gave them *institution*.[1] A like method of filling vacant bishoprics was claimed by the pope; but the spirited resistance of some of our kings defeated all

"Quia regnum oppressum erat, injustis exactionibus: ego sanctam Deo ecclesiam liberam facio, ita quod *nec vendam, nec ad firmam ponam; nec, mortui archiepiscopo sive episcopo*, vel abbate, aliquid accipiam de *dominio ecclesiæ donec successor in eam ingrediatur*" (*Anglo-Saxon Laws*, vol. i., p. 498). So that it is certain, as it is solemnly recited in a legal record, that these things had been done by the conqueror and his sons; the voice of contemporary history (in the chronicles) also abundantly attests it, and it there appears that, as above stated, kings set up a claim to practise upon the endowments of the church the same exactions and oppressions which they practised on the other estates of the realm, upon the pretence that the feudal principles applied. That this pretence was false and unfounded, has already been shown from Littleton, who, long after these controversies was over, laid it down as undoubted law, that in tenure by frankalmoigne (which is the tenure of bishoprics and other benefices), there is *no temporal service due at all, as the service is purely spiritual*. And, as already has been shown, the whole scope and tenor of the Saxon law was to leave to the church the control of what was spiritual. It is fully admitted by all the writers who uphold the royal claim now, and is implied by our author in his use of the feudal word, investiture, that it was based upon feudal principles, and, therefore, was unfounded. The pretence that because the *endowment* was temporal, the benefice became no less clearly fallacious, for it was a well-known maxim that the principal draws it to the accessory, not the accessory the principal. And this, in fact, was the whole point of the question, whether the spiritual was to yield to the temporal, or the temporal to the spiritual. Of course, the rapacious sovereigns who ravened after church spoil, and kept sees vacant in order to enjoy it, or to force the pope to sanction the appointment of corrupt men, who would allow them to share the plunder of the diocese, and farm out benefices to the highest bidders; of course they deemed the temporalities the most important, and cared little for the spiritualities. But the original donors, who were not merely sovereigns, but multitudes of other persons (as the statutes state), gave the endowments in aid of the spiritualities and in support of the church, not for her enslavement and subjection. They gave to the church as she then existed, viz., free, and under the spiritual care of her pastors; and it would be irrational to suppose that they meant their donations to be the foundation of future usurpations. That, therefore, which the author, unaware of the contents of Henry I.'s charter, represents as an innovation introduced in the reigns of Richard and John, had been the original usage, and had been wrongly violated by the Conqueror and his sons, as Henry I. confessed. It will be apparent that the great, the fundamental question was as to the appointment of the bishops; for if the king could either appoint them at his pleasure or keep the temporalities of the sees in his hands until his nominee was admitted, the whole of the diocese would virtually be in his hands; and such kings as then reigned were capable, as the chronicles show, of any amount of corruption, plunder, or oppression.

[1] Seld., Tithes, 383.

his attempts, though, as usual, he never receded from the pretended right.

The appointment, however, to bishoprics, was, to a degree, put under the control of the pope (a). In the time of Henry I. a bishop elect was to receive *investiture* of his temporalities from the king, of whom all bishops held their lands as baronies (b). This was performed by the king's delivering to the bishop a ring and crosier, as symbols of his spiritual marriage to the church and of his pastoral office; and hence called investiture *per annulum et baculum :* after this the bishop used to do *homage* to the king, as to his liege lord. But that king finding it expedient to give way to the demands of the pope (c), resigned this power and ceremony of investiture, and only required that bishops should do homage for their temporalities: and King John, to obtain the protection of the pope, was contented to give up, by charter, to all monasteries and cathedrals, the free right of electing their prelates, whether abbots or bishops. He reserved only to the crown the custody of the temporalities during the vacancy; the form of granting a license to proceed to election (since called a *congé d'élire*), on refusal whereof the electors might make their election without it; and the right of approbation afterwards, which was not to be denied without a reasonable and lawful cause (d). This

---

(a) Had always been so, as the charter of Henry I. admits, of which the author was not aware, *vide ante.*

(b) Not so at all. Quite the contrary. There was the fallacy. The baronies were held on secular tenure, which was feudal; the bishoprics were held on spiritual tenure, which was *not* feudal. Thus Littleton says, "They who hold in frankalmoigne shall do no fealty to their lord, because the very words *exclude the lord* to have any earthly or temporal service, but to have only divine and spiritual service" (c. vi.). Glanville had laid down the same law, under Henry II.

(c) The charter of Henry I. has been already quoted, in which he acknowledges that his claims had been abominable and oppressive exactions. He had kept bishoprics vacant, in order to exact money, or the admission of his own nominees. Of course he cared not about the ceremony; it was the power of nomination and the right of patronage, which he strove to obtain, for the sake of these exactions.

(d) Thus, then, after all, the position taken by the church has been admitted to have been in substance right; for at this moment, even in this country, the letter of the law allows of free clerical choice in the election of bishops; and if the law is only a *dead* letter, it is only because, by reason of the separation from Rome, there is no supreme ecclesiastical authority to whom the clerical choice can be referred, and all authority is virtually merged in the royal prerogative. In the period referred to, however, the papal supremacy was in full force, and was *acknowledged* by the law and con-

grant was expressly recognized and confirmed by King John's *Magna Charta;* was again established by stat. 25 Edw. III., st. 6, c. 3; and continued the law and practice till the time of Henry VIII.

To return to the practice of ecclesiastical judicature. There were two subjects of jurisdiction which the spiritual court gradually drew to itself and endeavored to appropriate: these were *marriages* and *wills;* which latter led to the cognizance of *legacies*, and the disposal of *intestates' effects.*

Marriage, being a contract dictated and sanctioned by the law of nature, and entitling the parties to certain civil rights, seems to have nothing in it of spiritual cognizance; but the church of Rome having converted it into a sacrament, it became entirely a spiritual contract, and as such fell naturally within the ecclesiastical jurisdiction, very soon after its separation from the secular court; it followed almost of consequence (*a*) that the

stitutions of this country; and, therefore, as it is at this moment admitted that the election of a bishop ought to be a matter of free clerical choice, it is properly of a spiritual nature, and, therefore, according to the principles of the period in question, the papal claim was right.

(*a*) All this is put as if it arose about the same time. "The jurisdiction over matrimonial causes granted to bishops by Christian emperors was a very natural consequence of the religious rites with which marriage was solemnized, and the character of a sacrament, or eminently sacred rite, attributed to that important union" (Mackintosh's *Hist. Eng.*, vol. i., p. 208). The rite of marriage was certainly, as Sir J. Mackintosh says, considered of the most sacred character from the earliest times in this country, for in the Penitential of Theodore it is said, "Presbyter debet messam agere et benedicere ambos, sicut in libro sacramentorum continetur" (*Pen. Theod.*, c. xvii., s. 9). At the same time, it is curious that there is in that same Penetential this remarkable provision, "Si mulier discesserit a viro suo, despiciens eum, nolens revertere et reconciliari viro, post v. annos, cum consensu episcopi; ipse aliam accipiat uxorem" (*Ibid.*, c. xix., s. 23). There is no doubt, however, that any Roman counsel or canonist would condemn this as unsound; and it is well known that the whole spirit of the Roman system is, and always was, to treat marriage as sacred, and indeed sacramental; and the union as indissoluble. This being so, it was surely very natural that it should be deemed of ecclesiastical cognizance.

It is to be observed that in the *Mirror of Justice* marriage is treated as a contract, but one perpetual (c. ii., s. 27), indissoluble (c. iii., s. 5), and of ecclesiastical cognizance. "A contract is a speech between two parties that a thing is to be done, of which there are many kinds, whereof *some are perpetual*, as those of matrimony" (c. ii., s. 27). "And note that matrimony is the lawful order of joining together of a Christian man and woman, by their assents; and as of the deity and humanity of Christ, there is made an *indissoluble* unity, so *was matrimony*, and according to such unity was such coupling found to be; and therefore none can remain in that unity who takes to himself a plurality" (c. iii., s. 5). It is added that bigamy is triable in

spiritual court should likewise determine questions of *legitimacy* and *bastardy*.

Cases of wills and intestacy, as they were, in their nature, less allied to the spiritual function, did not entirely submit to the ecclesiastical jurisdiction. It appears from Glanville, that in the reign of Henry II. the jurisdiction of personal legacies was in the temporal courts.[1] But notwithstanding this, if there was a question in the temporal court, whether a testament was a true one or not; whether it was duly made, or whether the thing demanded was really bequeathed; such plea was to be heard and determined by the court Christian; because, says our author, *all pleas upon testaments are properly cognizable before the ecclesiastical judge*.[2] Thus, the validity of a testament, or the bequest of a legacy, was to be certified by the spiritual court: nevertheless, as in cases of *bastardy* the court Christian

Probate of wills.

---

the lay court; but if the jury doubt thereof, in the case of a clerk, then the ordinary is to certify the same as in the case of matrimony, when it is denied (*Ibid.*). It is very remarkable that it appears from the Saxon laws, and from this part of the *Mirror* (which is evidently as old as the Saxon time), that priests were allowed to marry, for it is said that a clerk's claim of privilege might be met by showing that he was "bigamous," either by having twice married, or by having married two wives at the same time (*Ibid.*). And it is plainly implied that his *merely having married* would be no offence. And in the Saxon laws there appears no prohibition of clerical marriages; the language of the Saxon canons on the subject rather imply the legality of such marriages, for it is put rather as a matter of continence becoming to the sacred state, than of utter disability to contract marriage, "Lex continentiæ est altaris ministris quæ episcopis aut presbyteris, qui cum essent laici, licete uxores ducere et filios procreare potuerunt, sed cum ad prædictos gradus pervenerint, cœpit eis non licere quod licuit. Unde et de carnali fit spirituale connubium. Oportet eos nec demittere uxores, et quasi non habeant sic habere, quo salva sit charitas connubiorum et cesset operatio nuptiarum" (*Capit. Theod., Ang.-Sax. Laws*, v. ii., p. 74). In the canons indeed it was laid down that if a priest married, he should forfeit his order, "Si presbyter vel diaconus uxorem duxerit, perdat ordinem suum; et si postea fornicati fuerunt, non solum ordine priventur, sed etiam jejunent juxta sententiam episcopi" (*Pen. Egb.*, lib. iii., c. 1; *Ang.-Sax. Laws*, v. ii., p. 197); but this appears to imply that the marriage was valid, or why should it be a deprivation of the order? and the prohibition of intercourse would be mere penitential discipline. In the *Institutes of Polity* it is said that marriage is not allowed to the clergy (*Ibid.*, p. 335); but then afterwards it is said that a priest's wife is a snare (*Ibid.*, p. 337). In the Saxon ecclesiastical laws there are repeated declarations that the clergy ought not to marry (*Can. Eccl. Laws*, c. 1; *Ang.-Sax. Laws*, v. i., p. 365); but it is doubtful whether by the secular law the marriages were illegal and void. It was undoubtedly considered indecent, and a cause of deprivation. But the *Mirror* appears to imply that a clerk might be married legally.

[1] Lib. 7, c. 6, 7.   [2] Ibid.

did nothing more than answer the mere question, whether bastard or not, and the consequence of *descent* and title was left to be determined at common law; so were the consequences of a testament, as the recovery and payment of legacies, to be heard and determined in the temporal courts.

By the manner in which Glanville speaks of the *probate* of wills, it seems as if that course of authenticating wills had been long in use. The beginning, or steps, by which this innovation established itself, it is not easy to trace (*a*): it lies buried in that obscurity which involves not only the origin of our municipal customs, but the encroachments gradually made upon them by the civil and canon law.

When the ecclesiastical court had once the probate of wills, it appeared no very great enlargement of jurisdiction to add the power of enforcing the execution of them, in payment of legacies. But there are no testimonies of those times that warrant us to conclude, that this had generally obtained before the reign of Henry III.[1]

It seems doubtful, whether the mode used by the Saxons for the distribution of the estates of *intestates* continued during the whole of this period. A law of Henry I. says, that upon a person dying intestate, those who were entitled to succeed should divide his effects *pro animâ ejus* (*b*). This is the first mention in our law of a

---
(*a*) On the contrary, it is perfectly easy, when reference is made to the Roman law, which had long ago provided a regular mode of authenticating wills, doubtless established in this country during their occupation, and virtually the same as that found adopted here; the courts of the bishops being substituted as the places of registry, for the obvious reason that in those days ecclesiastics were the only persons who could read and write. The existence of a custom in some manors for the lord to have the registry is easily explained, either by the supposition that the manor at one time belonged to ecclesiastics, or that the lord had the exceptional endowment of being able to read and write, and so acquired this privilege. In some of our most ancient cities, as York and London, there are customs as to wills probably as old as the Romans.

(*b*) There was no such law; and if there had been, it could not have been carried out consistently with canon law, which requires that the obligations of justice should first be satisfied before those of piety. The " law of Henry " was the *charter* of that king, recognizing and promising to observe the law of the land settled long before the Conquest, and recognized in the laws of Canute, that the effects of an estate should, in certain proportions, " be *divided among his relations*" (*Laws of Canute*, s. 73). This meaning, of course, his *available* effects, after payment of debts. " Si quis preventus, pecuniam suam

[1] Seld., Works, vol. iii., 1672.

disposition of an intestate's effects for the benefit of his soul; but there is no mention of the control or intermeddling of the bishop, either in this law, or, even later than this, in Glanville; although he expressly mentions the jurisdiction of the church as to testaments.

In King John's charter it was expressly provided, that if any freeman died intestate, his chattels should be disposed of by the hands of his next of kin *per visum ecclesiæ*, by the advice and direction of the ordinary, saving to all creditors their debts (*a*). This clause, it is said, was word for word in the charter 9 Hen. III., and is to be seen in several manuscripts of it;[1] but being left out of the exemplification of this charter on the roll 25 Edw. I., from which is copied the *Magna Charta* in our statute-books, it is not now found there. The provision was probably inserted by the contrivance of the bishops, who, with Pandolfo, the pope's nuncio, were with John at Runnymede (*b*). There was not wanting color for a provision like this; for as the statute of Henry I. before alluded to, had expressly said, that the distribution was to be *pro animâ intestati*, the bishops seemed, by their holy function, to be best qualified to see this office performed with fidelity. Hence it was that, in after-times, this power was delegated by the ordinary to the next of kin, in letters or otherwise; an authority grounded upon these words of the charter, *per visum ecclesiæ*;[2] though there are

non dederit nec dare disposuerit, uxor sua, sive liberi eam pro anima ejus dividant, sicut eis melius visum fuerit" (*Leges Hen. Prim.*, c. i., p. 7). That is, *divide* his effects according to what in *their* judgment would be right and proper, and for the benefit of his soul; and according to canon law and common sense this would imply that they, his nearest relations, should have the reasonable share the law allowed them. And no one will doubt that they took proper care of their own interest. Then the *charter* of John conceded, in pursuance of the charter of Henry, and in order to secure to the relatives their due share of the effects: "Si aliquis liber homo intestatus decesserit, catalla sua per *manus* propinquorum parentum et amicorum suorum, per *visum ecclesiæ*, *distribuantur:* salvis unicumque debitis quæ defunctus ei debebat" (*Charter of John*, c. 27). That is to say, that the effects, after payment of debts, should be *distributed according to law*, that law being, that the greater part, as Glanville states, should be distributed among the relatives, and the residue be applicable for the benefit of the soul of the deceased, according to the ideas and the belief of that age; but this, *after* payment of just debts.

(*a*) Here, again, the charter was *not* so. It was that the effects should be *distributed* among the relatives as provided by law, *vide supra*.
(*b*) A provision for distribution of the effects according to law, *vide supra*.

[1] Seld., Works, vol. iii., 1676.   [2] Ibid., 1679.

no documents that assure us this law was put in force during the reign of King John.

In the reign of Stephen the clergy began to draw into the spiritual court the trial of persons *pro læsione fidei*, that is, for breach of faith in civil contracts. By means of this they took cognizance of many matters of contract which belonged properly to the temporal court. This was the boldest stretch which that tribunal ever made to extend its authority, and would, in time, have drawn within its jurisdiction most of the transactions of mankind. The pretence on which they founded this claim was probably this: that oaths and faith solemnly plighted being of a religious nature, the breach of them more properly belonged to the spiritual than to the lay tribunal.

The circumstances of the times tended very much to encourage the clergy in their scheme of opposition to the secular power. The provision for the clergy was in those days very precarious, and left them at the mercy of their patrons. Being, in general, from their function, considered as a sacred body of people, when oppressed and ill-treated by potent lords, they drew the compassion of many, and particularly the support of their bishops; who, in their turn, receiving as little favor from kings, were continually increasing their store of merit with the sovereign pontiff by the many struggles they engaged in on their own account, and on account of their inferior brethren. The pope, no ungrateful sovereign, always distinguished his zeal in supporting his bishops as they did in supporting the lower clergy; till the several orders of ecclesiastics, united in a common cause, and sharpened against the laity by long contention, encouraged each other, by every motive of defence and aggrandizement, to contribute in their stations to promote the power of the church. The pope having made use of the bishops to gain and govern the clergy, united all their powers to establish a dominion over the laity; and no occasion was let pass in which any of them could snatch an advantage (*a*).

Henry I. being seated on the throne by a doubtful title, thought it prudent to gain the clerical part of his subjects

---

(*a*) All this is mere general assertion, not founded upon any authority, nor supported by any, and the value of it may be estimated from the degree of verity to be found in the next statement.

by some concessions (a). Stephen, who owed his authority entirely to them, went further (b). By these means they acquired such confirmed strength and habitual reverence from the people, that notwithstanding all the power of Henry II., and the spirit with which he asserted his sovereignty and independence, the contest he had with Becket tended to an issue directly contrary to that which he had promised himself; so that, after some concessions and connivance, to which he submitted in fits of repentance, his reign ended in a firm establishment of the clergy in most of their extraordinary claims of privilege and jurisdiction.

The contest that Henry II. had with Becket concerning the limits of ecclesiastical power, fills up a great part of that king's reign. To give weight to his side of the contest, and, instead of debating, to effect a clear decision, Henry procured an act of the legislature formally enacting the principal points of controversy for which he contended (c). This was the famous *Constitutions of Clarendon.*

(a) So far from it, that as he himself acknowledged, there had been great oppressions and exactions, and he only promised not to continue them, "Quia regnum Anglia oppressum erat, injustis exactionibus; ego sanctam Dei ecclesiam liberam facio, ita quod nec vendam nec ad firmam ponam ; nec, mortuo archiepiscopo, sive episcopo aliquid aliquam de dominio ecclesiæ donec successor in eam ingrediatur. Et omnes malos consuetudines qualis regnum Anglia opprimebantur, inde aufero" (*Leges Henrici Primi*, 1). But how far he kept his promise, let contemporary history tell. When Rufus died, says William of Malmesbury, three bishoprics were in his hands; in a few years Henry had *five*. And when after the controversy about investiture he yielded, so far from acting upon considerations of policy, the chronicler states that he had held out mainly in consequence of the persuasions of his nobles, who, of course, were desirous of prolonging the reign of ravage and rapine. Upon the relinquishment by the king of his unfounded claim, no less than five bishops were consecrated, whose sees had been kept vacant in order to enable the king to plunder their temporalities (*William of Malmesbury*, b. ii., A. D. 1107).

(b) Went much further in exaction and oppression. Sir J. Mackintosh terms him a captain of banditti (*Hist. Eng.*). He plundered the church without mercy.

(c) The author here, as Henry had done, begged the whole question, and, like the king, would decide the case without debating it. It is impossible to form a judgment upon the merits of this most memorable controversy, merely by looking at these Constitutions, without attending to the previous events. This would be necessary even if the Constitutions could really be considered as in the nature of a statute or an act of parliament. For though they would of course determine the question as a matter of law, that would still leave the question open as a matter of legal history, what was their real nature and origin, and what their real meaning, and whether they were an

At a great council held at Clarendon, A. D. 1164, in the 10th year of his reign a code of laws was brought forward by the king under the title

Constitutions of Clarendon.

alteration of the law or not. But whether they were indeed of the nature of a statute, or were rather a mere device of a despotic monarch to give the color of authority to his aggressive tyranny, is a question which itself must depend upon all the surrounding facts and circumstances of the case. And the first thing to carry clearly and carefully in mind is this, as in any other legal controversy, what was the state of the law when the controversy arose? The next thing is to have a clear knowledge of the facts, so far as they throw any light upon the controversy. Now, as to the law, the reader has the means of forming a judgment by referring back to those copious quotations from the Saxon laws which have already been given, and which were all confirmed by the Conqueror and his successor, Henry I., especially as to the rights and liberties of the church. This is of the more importance, because the archbishop was of Saxon origin, and would no doubt have a strong attachment to the laws of his Saxon ancestors. By those laws, in a legal point of view, he must be judged. Mackintosh, with characteristic candor, appears to allow that the only way to judge fairly of Becket is to put ourselves as much as possible in the position in which he was at the time of these events, and admit that the archbishop sincerely supposed and believed that he was in the right as to the law of the land at the time. It is to be observed that Becket, before he was archbishop, had been eight years chancellor, and that he had also acted for years as justiciary (Foss's *Lives of Judges*, vol. i., p. 198), and that under his auspices the administration of justice had greatly improved (*Ibid.*). It is manifest that such a man must have known the Saxon laws, and the charters confirming them, and of course was well aware of what had taken place in the reign of Henry I., when the rights of the church as to the episcopate were established. That being so, the probability is that he would know what the law was; and, at all events, it is manifest that to enable us to judge of his conduct, the first great question is *what the law was*? This the reader can judge for himself from the citations already given; and it need only be said that it is conceived they show that the law was clear that the church should be free — that is, free in her elections, and free in her sentences, and free from all secular jurisdiction. Controversies had, however, arisen between the crown and the church in the reign of Henry I. as to the right of the crown to give investiture of bishoprics, on the pretence that they were baronies, and so held of the crown, like feudal benefices. The effect of this would have been to give the crown virtually the control over the episcopate, as it could exercise a *reto* upon any election by refusing investiture, and thus keep sees vacant for any time. And as the crown claimed and exercised the right of custody of vacant sees, and received and enjoyed all the temporalities, it is manifest that there was the strongest motive to abuse the power thus claimed; nor is there any doubt that, as a fact in history, it was so abused. After a great struggle, in the reign of Henry I. the claim of investiture was relinquished by the crown, but it still claimed the right of custody of vacant sees. What that law was has been shown, and the reader can refer back to the statement of it, and see how far it recognized the canon law and the rights of the church. It is most natural to refer also to the terms of the charters, as to the church, and especially as to its bishoprics. The charter of Henry I. acknowledged that the church and the country had been oppressed by most grievous extortions, especially in the selling of bishoprics or benefices: "Quia regnum oppressum erat injustis exactionibus, ego sanctam ecclesiam liberam faciam *ita quod nec vendam, nec ad firmam po-*

of *the ancient customs of the realm;* and as Becket had
solemnly promised he would observe what were really

nam, nec, mortuo archiepiscopo sive episcopo, vel abbate, aliquid accepiam
de dominio ecclesiæ, donec successor in eam ingrediatur" (c. 1). This was
a confession that the Conqueror and his sons had interfered with the liberties of the church, and had made the vacancies of sees the occasion of
enormous oppressions and exactions. It was also a distinct acknowledgment
that these practices were illegal. Thus the liberty of the church meant, and
that is included, liberty to proceed to give elections of bishops, so as to put
an end to vacancies in the sees, appears from subsequent charters. That of
Stephen declared, "I promise to do nothing in the church or in ecclesiastical
affairs simonically, nor will I permit it to be done. I defend and confirm
that the power, possessions, and dignities of ecclesiastical persons, and all
clerks, and the distribution of their goods, shall be in the hands of the
bishops. And I grant and establish that the dignities of churches, confirmed
by this privilege and the ancient customs, shall remain inviolable." (See
Blackstone's *Charters.*) Then Stephen granted a further charter of all those
liberties and good laws and customs which Henry I. had granted, and which
were held in the time of King Edward. Then Henry II. himself had granted
a charter, which was in these terms: "I have granted and restored, and confirmed to the church all the customs which King Henry I. gave and granted
to them, and abolished all *evil customs* which he abolished, and I will that
the church do have and hold all usages, liberties, and free customs as freely
and fully as he granted to them," so that there had been under the Conqueror
and his successors certain usages introduced contrary to ancient usages, and
contrary to the law. And closely connected with, and indeed disclosed in
the charters, are the facts of history to which they had reference, that the
Norman sovereigns had been in the habit of *keeping sees vacant in order to
enjoy their temporalities,* and to extort money for the liberty to come to an
election, or even assent to the nomination of a corrupt and vicious prelate,
who would be willing to collude with the king in the plunder and corruption of his diocese. It is an undoubted fact that Henry and his predecessors
thus held sees vacant — sometimes as many as five or six at a time — and
plundered them meanwhile (Lingard's *Eng. Hist.,* v. i., c. 3), and in the intervals, valuable possessions of the church were alienated to royal favorites.
It appears, however, that so soon as A'Becket was made archbishop, he showed
himself resolute in recovering the lost possessions of the church, and that he
at once claimed a barony belonging to his see, which had for some time been
in the possession of one of the king's most powerful and favored vassals. If
this claim had not been warranted by law, it could and would have been contested, and as it was not, it may be presumed that it was valid. The archbishop also presented to a living (of Eynsford) belonging to a manor which,
beyond all doubt, belonged to his see; the fact is admitted by Hume (*Hist.
Eng.,* v. i., c. 8, p. 34), and it appears from the record of the great suit by
the Archbishop of Canterbury in the time of the Conqueror, to which allusion has been made more than once (*vide ante,* p. 260). One of the king's
military tenants who had possession of the manor forcibly expelled the presentee, pretending to be patron. Whether he was so or not, however, is not
material, for of course the forcible ejection of the archbishop's nominee was
not a proper way of deciding a question of church patronage, and was, moreover, a high contempt of the head of his church. The archbishop accordingly excommunicated him: the king sent orders to the archbishop to take
the sentence off. The archbishop refused, replying that it was not for the
king to prescribe whom he should or should not excommunicate. No one
who has given the least attention to the laws of that time can doubt that the

such, the king procured the principal propositions in dispute to be enacted, and declared by the council under that archbishop was right. The refusal, however, it is clear from the result, greatly offended the monarch, and he soon afterwards seized upon another ground of dispute, in which he was equally in the wrong; and in which his object — as his subsequent conduct showed — was to acquire greater power over the clergy. In the time of the archbishop's predecessor, one of the priests of his province had been accused of homicide, and tried before his bishop, according to the law still in force. One of the king's justices in circuit took occasion, the priest being in court, to denounce him as a murderer; the priest uttered expressions of anger and contempt, for which he was tried, and severely punished. The king, however, then insisted that henceforth the clergy should, after they had been first degraded by the sentence of the spiritual judge, be afterwards delivered over to the lay tribunal to be tried according to the secular law. This, it is plain, would be an alteration of the law, and the king's language, as Lingard observes, in making it, showed that he knew it was so, "Peto et volo ut tuo, Domine Cantuarensis, et coepiscoporum tuorum consilio." And it was obvious that it would have enabled him easily — by means of servile judges — to get rid of an obnoxious prelate. The prelates objected, on the double ground that it would be punishing a man twice for the same offence, and that it would be placing the English clergy in a different position from that which the clergy occupied all over Europe. It was then that the king demanded of them if they would observe "the ancient customs of the realm." This, as Lingard observes, was a captious question, for it left all open what were the "customs" intended; and it might be that what the king intended were the evil customs as to the church, which the Conqueror and his sons had introduced, and which Henry I. had renounced, and there is abundant reason to believe that this was so, from the very nature of the demand, from the circumstances under which it was made, and from what soon afterwards followed. The demand had no reference to the immediate subject of dispute, the jurisdiction over clerks, for it was not pretended that there had been any custom upon that matter at all in favor of the claim to lay jurisdiction. There had, however, been customs — evil customs though they had been admitted to be — which had for some time been in existence, though again and again renounced, and these customs were of immense practical importance to the king; while the jurisdiction over clerks was probably a matter of little concern to him. For the effect of these customs, it will have been seen, was, that the king kept sees vacant for the sake of plundering the temporalities, and also of enforcing the admission of corrupt and servile prelates who might connive at his doing so. The controversy with the archbishop, be it observed, had begun with his endeavor to recover the temporalities of his see. The king would, no doubt, foresee that such a man was likely to prove an independent and determined antagonist in any plans of church spoliation he might contemplate, and therefore it would be of the most vital importance to the king to commit the prelates, and especially the archbishop, to some vague admission of customs which might appear to cover their encroachment. Moreover, the actual facts and circumstances of the time show that this was really what the king was aiming at, for it appears that he had in his hands, a few years after this, an archbishopric, five bishoprics, and three abbeys; and a few years later, no less than seven bishoprics, and an archbishopric, besides several abbeys, and had divided the greater part of one of the bishoprics among his knights (Lingard, *Hist. Eng.*, v. ii., c. 3). This was exactly the course the Conqueror and his sons had pursued, and was the very course Henry I. had renounced; it was grossly illegal, yet it might,

denomination. Nothing will enable us to judge so well of the pretensions of the clergy, as a perusal of these Constitutions; they shall therefore be stated at length. They are contained in sixteen articles; ten of which were considered by the see of Rome as so hostile to the rights of the clergy, that Pope Alexander in full consistory passed a solemn condemnation on them; the other six he *tolerated not as good, but less evil.* These six articles were the 2d, 6th, 11th, 13th, 14th, and 16th.

The 2d, Churches belonging to the see of our lord the king cannot be given away in perpetuity, without the consent and grant of the king. 6th, Laymen ought not

---

perhaps, with some color, be pretended that it was a custom. There can be no doubt, therefore, that it was this the king was aiming at, and it affords an explanation of his sudden demand on the prelates for a recognition of his customs. The prelates replied that they could only assent, saving the rights of their order; an answer which, of course, foiled the wily monarch. He was enraged, and at last extorted an assent to the customs, and a council was summoned at Clarendon, at which these customs were drawn up, and one of them was, *that the custody of every vacant bishopric, archbishopric, or abbey should be given, and its revenues, during the occupancy,* paid to the king, and that the election ought to be by the king's writ: the effect of which was to establish the vicious and pernicious practice renounced by Henry I., and to enable the king to keep sees vacant as long as he pleased, thus receiving the revenues all the time, which of course would be the strongest inducement to prolong the vacancy. Then it was claimed that the proceedings of the clergymen should be in the king's court, an undoubted innovation. So of the next, that there should be no excommunication of any of the king's principal tenants or officers without application to him, which, of course, deprived the church of its only weapon of defence against the greatest plunderers of the age, and was also an undoubted innovation on the ancient law, which left the bishops full power of excommunication. Two other articles were directed against appeals to the see of Rome, and another gave the king's courts jurisdiction in various ecclesiastical matters, advowsons, etc. The archbishops, not at first apparently understanding them, signed the Constitutions; but the pope disallowed most of them, and the archbishop then resisted. It may be of interest to present the archbishop's view of the question, conveyed in a letter to the king: "Ecclesia Dei in duobus constat ordinibus, clero et populo. In clero sunt apostoli, apostoliciviri; episcopi, et cœteri doctores ecclesiæ, quibus cummissa est cura et regnum ipsius ecclesiæ: qui tractare habent negotia ecclesiastica: ut totium reducatur ad salutem animarum. In populo sunt reges, principes, duces, comites, et aliæ potestates, qui sæcularia habent tractare negotia, ut totam reducant ad pacem et unitatem ecclesiæ. Et quia certum est reges potestatem suam accipere ab ecclesia, non ipsum ab illissed a Christo, ut salvâ pace vestâ loquar non habetis episcopis præcipere, absolvere aliquem, vel excommunicare, trahere clericos ad sæcularia examina, judicare de ecclesiis ne decimis, interdicere episcopis ne tractent causas de transgressione fidei, vel juramenta, et multa in hunc modum, quæ scripta, inter consuetudines vestras quas dicitis avitus" (*Epi. St. Thomæ Const. Ep.*, lib. i., *Ep.* 6). This, too, accords with the law as afterwards laid down by Bracton.

to be accused, unless by certain and legal accusers and witnesses, in presence of the bishop, so as that the archdeacon may not lose his right, nor anything which should thereby accrue to him; and if the offending persons be such as none will or dare accuse them, the sheriff, being thereto required by the bishop, shall swear twelve lawful men of the vicinage or town before the bishop, to declare the truth according to their conscience. 11th, Archbishops, bishops, and all dignified clergymen,[1] who hold of the king and chief, have their possessions from the king as a barony, and answer thereupon to the king's justices and officers, and follow and perform all royal customs and rights, and, like other barons, ought to be present at the trials of the king's court, with the barons, till the judgment proceeds to loss of members, or death. 13th, If any nobleman of the realm shall forcibly resist the archbishop, bishop, or archdeacon, in doing justice upon him or his, the king ought to bring them to justice; and if any shall forcibly resist the king in his judicature, the archbishops, bishops, and archdeacons ought to bring him to justice, that he may make satisfaction to our lord the king. 14th, The chattels of those who are under forfeiture to the king, ought not to be detained in any church or churchyard against the king's justice, because they belong to the king, whether they are found within churches, or without. 16th, The sons of villeins ought not to be ordained without the consent of their lords, in whose lands they are known to have been born.

Thus was the pope pleased to tolerate such of these articles as either did not at all affect the clerical state, or rather contributed to aid and support it; and were thrown in, probably, to qualify and temper those which were evidently hostile to the ecclesiastical sovereignty. The ten which were condemned by the pope, were as follows:

The 1st, If any dispute shall arise concerning the advowson and presentation of churches between laymen, or between ecclesiastics and laymen, or between ecclesiastics, let it be tried and determined in the court of our lord the king. 3d, Ecclesiastics charged and accused of any matter, and being summoned by the king's justice, shall come

---
[1] So *universæ personæ* is construed by Lord Littleton in his Hen. II., vol. iv., 370.

into his court to answer there concerning that which it shall appear to the king's court is cognizable there; and shall answer in the ecclesiastical court concerning that which it shall appear is cognizable there; so that the king's justice shall send to the court of holy church, to see in what manner the cause shall be tried there; and if an ecclesiastic shall be convicted, or confess his crime, the church ought not any longer to give him protection. 4th, It is unlawful for archbishops, bishops, or any dignified clergymen of the realm, to go out of the realm without the king's license; and if they go, they shall, if it so please the king, give security that they will not, either in going, staying, or returning, procure any evil or damage to the king or kingdom. 5th, Persons excommunicated ought not to give any security by way of deposit, nor take any oath, but only find gage and pledge to stand to the judgment of the church, in order to absolution. 7th, No tenant *in capite* of the king, nor any of the officers of his household, or of his demesne, shall be excommunicated; nor shall the lands of any of them be put under an interdict, unless application shall first have been made to our lord the king, if he be in the kingdom, and if not, to his justice, that he may do right concerning such person; and in such manner, as that which shall belong to the king's court shall be there determined, and what shall belong to the ecclesiastical court shall be sent thither to be there determined. 8th, Concerning appeals, if any shall arise, they ought to proceed from the archdeacon to the bishop, and from the bishop to the archbishop: and if the archbishop shall fail in doing justice, the cause shall at last be brought to our lord the king, that, by his precept, the dispute may be determined in the archbishop's court; so that it ought not to proceed any further without the king's consent. 9th, If there shall arise any dispute between an ecclesiastic and a layman, or between a layman and an ecclesiastic, about any tenement which the ecclesiastic pretends to hold *in eleemosynâ*, and the layman pretends to be a lay fee, it shall be determined by the judgment of the king's chief justice, upon a recognition of twelve lawful men, *utrùm tenementum sit pertinens ad eleemosynam, sive ad fœdum laicum.* And if it be found to be *in eleemosynâ*, then it shall be pleaded in the ecclesiastical court; but if a lay fee, then in the king's court, unless both parties claim to hold of the same bishop or baron; and if they do, then the plea shall be in his court; provided, that by such recognition, the party who was first seized shall not lose his seisin till the plea has been finally determined. 10th, Whosoever is of any city, or castle, or borough, or demesne manor of our lord the king, if he shall be cited by the archdeacon or bishop for any offence, and shall refuse to answer to such citation, may be put under an interdict; but he ought not to be excommunicated till the king's chief officer of the town be applied to, that he may, by due course of law, compel him to answer accordingly; and if the king's officer shall fail therein, such officer shall be *in misericordiâ regis;* and then the bishop may compel the person accused by ecclesiastical justice. 12th, Pleas of debt, *quæ fide interpositâ debentur, vel absque interpositione fidei,* whether due by faith solemnly pledged, or without faith so pledged, belong to the king's judicature. 15th, When an archbishopric, or bishopric, or abbey, or priory of royal foundation, shall be vacant, it ought to be in the hands of the king, and he shall receive all the rents and issues thereof, as of his demesne. And when such church is to be filled, the king ought to send for the principal clergy thereof, and the election ought to be made in the king's chapel, with the king's assent, and the advice of such of the prelates of the kingdom as he shall call for that purpose;[1] and the person elect shall there do homage and fealty to the king as his liege lord, of life, limb, and worldly honor (saving his order), before he be consecrated.[2]

These Constitutions were calculated to give a rational limitation to the secular and ecclesiastical judicature; and furnished a basis on which these separate jurisdictions might have been founded, without any inconvenience to the nation, or diminution of the temporal authority; and they were with that view confirmed, A.D. 1176, at a council held at Northampton (*a*). But the king, overcome

---

(*a*) As to this, the author was in error. Before the council, the king had written to the pope, promising to withdraw any customs hostile to the liber-

[1] *Debet fieri electio assensu domini regis, et consilio personarum regni quas ad hoc faciendum vocaverit.*

[2] *Vide* Wilk., Ang.-Sax. Leg., p. 321, and also in Litt. Hen. II., vol. iv., 414, a copy of these Constitutions from the Cottonian manuscript of Becket's Life and Epistles, which is probably the most ancient and correct copy of them.

with shame for the murder of Becket, with which he was
charged, and struck with a panic of superstition, gave way

ties of his clergy, and to allow freedom of canonical election (*Hoved.*, 302;
Ep. S. Tho. ii., 119, 122, 289). At the council of Northampton, the four
points above mentioned were granted or conceded to the church as declaratory enactments, but nothing is said as to the confirmation of the constitutions of Clarendon, which would have been grossly inconsistent with the
king's promise of withdrawal, made just before. It is, indeed, stated by
Gervase that the *assize* of Clarendon was ordered to be enforced, but that
was quite different from the *constitutions* of Clarendon; it was the code of
instructions to the itinerant justices, and is given by Hoveden (413) in his
account of the council of Northampton, and is quoted by our author towards
the end of the chapter. (The council of Northampton was in 1171.) On
the other hand, it does not appear that at this council the constitutions of
Clarendon were expressly repealed, and Dr. Lingard says of the previous
interval which had elapsed: "During the interval, the constitutions of Clarendon, though still unrepealed, were not enforced" (*Hist. Eng.*, v. ii., p. 97).
In the absence of any express repeal, they would remain, and their force
and effect would depend either upon their original validity, or upon their
subsequent adoption into the customary or unwritten law of the realm. As
to the first, it seems certain, from the accounts of all historians, that coercion,
by bodily terror, was used by the king upon the prelates, and that is quite
enough to destroy the statutory authority of these constitutions. But it is
not so clear that a great deal of them were not subsequently, by actual use
and adoption, incorporated in the customary or unwritten law of the realm.
For the present, it seems sufficient to point out that there was *not* any confirmation at the council of Northampton. One of the most important points
in our legal history, upon which, it will be observed, our author throws but
little light, is, whether, or how far, these celebrated constitutions are to be
regarded as law. Of course, if they really were freely agreed to by king, by
lords, and by prelates—*i. e.*, by a majority of them, present at a lawful
council or assembly, lawfully convened by the sovereign for the purpose of
legislation, and freely and really exercising their functions as legislators,
they would substantially be statutory enactments; but if, on the contrary, the
"council" was only an assembly of barons, under the influence of the king,
to which the prelates were compulsorily called, not to consider freely, as
legislators, but to be coerced to consent to ordinances predetermined, and
forced upon them by the royal power, there would be nothing legislative in
them; they would be the mere edicts of a tyrant. That threats and coercion
were used, all historians agree, and therefore it seems idle to treat these constitutions as "statutes," in the proper sense of the term; and the very fact
that the king seems to have sought a confirmation of some of them at the
council of Northampton shows his consciousness that they were not so, for, if
already laws, or legal statutes, they would require no confirmation, added to
which, it is stated by the author, in accordance with all histories, that the
king at all events professed to withdraw them, which, again, he could not do
if they were legal statutes. On the other hand, it is clear that although, if
they were not legal statutes strictly, they would not require to be repealed,
since they had no legal existence; it would be natural, and practically necessary, since the king had *said* they were statutes, that he should publicly
withdraw them. It should seem that, in the absence either of any express
confirmation, or any express adoption at the council of Northampton, they
remained unrepealed and unconfirmed; and therefore that (their original in-
validity being clear) their actual validity would depend upon the extent to
which they were subsequently adopted by use and custom into the law of

to the torrent, and endeavored to reconcile himself to the holy see by an ample concurrence with all its demands;

the land. And such seems to have been Hale's view, for, having mentioned them as acts of parliament before the time of legal memory, he says: "Of these, as we have no authentic records, but only transcripts in ancient historians, or other books, they obtain at this day no further than as by usage and custom they are, as it were, engrafted into the body of the common law, and made a part thereof" (*Hist. Com. Law*, p. 7). This seems to be the sound conclusion, for another reason, that, if these constitutions were to be taken as statutes of the realm, in full force, there would have been nothing left to enact at the era of the separation from Rome, since their clear effect was to render the king absolute. All appeals to Rome were abolished, save at his will and pleasure, and he would have entirely in his power the whole episcopate of the realm. And the only two really effective modes in which the Roman supremacy could be exercised would be by the power of appeal and the control over the episcopate. Yet it never occurred to any one in the reign of Henry VIII. that all this had already been done by statute, centuries before. And, on the other hand, we know that, in the meantime, during the whole of that long interval, the Roman See had exercised its appellate jurisdiction, and its control over the episcopate. On the other hand, we also know that, during that long interval, without any other statutory enactment, certain parts of the law were altered, and in accordance with these constitutions of Clarendon. Thus, for instance, clerks became subject to secular jurisdiction, though privilege of clergy remained to our own age. This could not be by the constitutions, for in the council of Northampton, *that* article had been implicitly repealed (*vide ante*) by a contrary enactment. It could, therefore, only have been by usage insensibly growing up, in accordance with the general feeling of the country; and as the administration of justice improved, there would of course be no reason for the maintenance of the privilege, which only rested on the barbarous character of the criminal procedure of that age. It will be observed that Henry II. had also expressly enacted at the council of Northampton that clerks should not be subject to the duel, and we also know that after the reign of John the ordeal became obsolete. After this era it would be natural that the clerical exemption from secular jurisdiction should also die out. That it was the law, however, there can be no doubt, and this may be the most fitting place to present such passages from the *Mirror of Justice* (a work completed after this period) as serve to illustrate what the law was virtually taken to be after this period upon the points in controversy. This will show how far these celebrated constitutions had been actually incorporated by use and adoption into the common law or custom of the realm. First, as to the subject just referred to, exemption of ecclesiastical persons or property from the jurisdiction of the lay tribunals. Treating of exceptions, the *Mirror* says: "One as to the power of the judge, and that may be by reason of the two kinds of jurisdictions, or because the king or his judge hath no power in the cause, as it is of the person of a clerk, by reason of the privileges of the church" (c. iii., s. 3). So, in the next section, of exception of clergy: "For the privilege of clergy — as, if a clerk be ordered in court before a lay judge to answer to an action for a personal mishap, and especially in a case criminal and mortal, plead that he is a clerk, the judge hath no further cognizance of the cause, for the church is so enfranchised that no lay judge can have jurisdiction over a clerk. Nevertheless, to give actions to plaintiffs against accessories in appeals and indictments, it belongeth to the judge to inquire, by the oaths of honest men, in the presence of the clerk, whether he be guilty or not, and if he be guilty, then to be delivered to his ordinary" (*Ib.*, s.

28

at least he desisted from executing those laws for which he had so many years been contending. It appears, more-

4). It is, indeed, added in the next section that the privilege might be rebutted by proof that the clerk had forfeited it by what was called "bigamy" —*i. e.*, by marrying a widow, or too many wives, a curious relic of the old Saxon law which allowed priests to enter into marriage; for, although it is explained that in a clerk, who could only marry once, the offence of bigamy was committed as well by marrying twice, or by marrying a widow, as by marrying more women than one, it is implied that there would be no loss of privilege merely by his being married. This seems to refer the passage to the Saxon age, because after the Conquest a stricter discipline was introduced, and priests were not allowed to marry; but then, in that view, it only makes the case stronger and clearer in favor of the archbishop in his great contest with Henry II., because it shows that, from the Saxon times, clerks had been privileged, which, indeed, has already been shown from the Saxon laws. So much as to personal exemptions of clerks from lay jurisdiction. Then, as to ecclesiastical rights, as advowsons, patronage of episcopal bishoprics or benefices, and the like, it is to be observed that in the *Mirror*, in a chapter which mentions Edward I., and therefore was composed or edited long after the period now in question, all the branches or heads of royal rights or jurisdiction being mentioned, there is no mention of bishoprics (c. i., s. 3). And so, in a subsequent section expounding the nature of legal jurisdiction, it is confined to matters of a secular nature (c. iv., s. 3). On the other hand, in the "Treatise of Glanville," written at the end of the reign of Henry II., there is a book upon "ecclesiastical advowsons" (lib. iii.), which he treats of as decided in the king's courts. But then this only refers to the right of patronage, and it is stated that if the clerk admitted the claimant to be patron, and claimed to have been instituted upon his presentation, and that was denied, it was to be decided before the ecclesiastical judge (c. ix.). And if the clerk named another party as patron, who appeared, and disclaimed, then, again, the suit would cease in the king's court, and be dismissed between the patron and the clerk in the ecclesiastical court. In short, questions as to patronage were deemed to pertain to the king's court: questions as to institution, or presentation, to the ecclesiastical court. In other words, questions between patrons would be tried in the king's court, and questions between patron and clerk in the ecclesiastical court. It is further stated that, in case of vacancy, and default of the patron to present, the presentation fell into the hands of the king. If the party under whom the clerk claimed pressed his claim to the patronage, and was defeated, then in the king's court nothing more could be done in the matter; but the patron who had recovered the right of advowson could proceed against the clerk in the ecclesiastical court before the bishop, with this restriction, that if at the time of presentation the parson presenting was considered to be patron, the clerk should continue to hold. For (says Glanville) upon this subject a statute was passed in the reign of the present king (Henry II.) concerning those clerks who have obtained livings upon the presentation of patrons, or have, in time of war, violently intruded themselves into ecclesiastical advowsons, and, by such statute, it is provided that clerks thus presented should not lose their churches during their lives (*Ibid.*, c. x.). Elsewhere it is laid down, "that, according to the custom of the realm, no one is bound to answer in his lord's court concerning his freehold, without the king's precept. But if the plea should be between two clerks concerning a tenement-hold in frankalmoigne of an ecclesiastical fee, or if the tenant, a clerk, hold an ecclesiastical fee in frankalmoigne, whoever may be claimant, the plea concerning the right ought to be in the ecclesiastical court, unless a question should arise whether the fee be eccle-

over, from a letter which he sent to the pope by the hand of *Hugo Petrileo*, the legate, that, *notwithstanding the opposition of the greatest and wisest men in his kingdom*, he had, at the intercession of the legate, and out of reverence and devotion to the see of Rome, made the following concessions: That no clerk should, for the future, be brought personally before a secular judge for any crime or transgression[1] whatsoever, except only for offences against the forest laws, or in case of a lay fee for which lay service was due to the king, or to some other secular person. He promised that any person convicted, or making confession before his justice, in the presence of the bishop, or his official, of having knowingly and premeditatedly killed a clerk, should, besides the usual punishment for killing a layman, forfeit all his land of inheritance for ever.[2] He also promised, that clerks should not be compelled to submit to the trial by duel; and moreover, he promised not to retain in his hands vacant bishoprics or abbeys beyond the term of one year, unless from urgent necessity, and evident cause of delay, not falsely pretended.[3] It is said,[4] that Henry, by charter, granted to the clergy the cognizance of causes matrimonial; but neither this nor any other of the foregoing concessions were enacted by authority of parliament, during any part of this king's reign; nor did he himself observe them, except in not compelling criminal clerks to appear before a lay judge, as before stipulated, and in exempting them in all cases from the trial

---

siastical or lay" (lib. xiii., c. xxv.), which, it is afterwards said, is to be decided in the king's court (c. x., s. 3). But before the statute of Westminster II., Lord Coke says, "no *juris utrum* lay for one parson against another, because it was, in that case, the right of the church" (2 *Inst.*, 407). Thus, then, it came to this, that questions of right between laymen were decided in the king's courts; questions between laymen and clergymen, or between clergymen on matters ecclesiastical, were tried in the ecclesiastical courts. With regard to the bishoprics, it need hardly be observed that, as the question then would be between the king and the pope, they could not come into the king's courts; and though, according to analogy, those questions would be determinable in the papal courts, yet it is equally obvious that, as the pope could not enforce his decision except by excommunication, the extent to which it was regarded would virtually depend upon the extent to which the king could safely disregard it — *i. e.*, in the opinion of the age.

[1] *De aliquo foris-facto.*
[2] What extraordinary penalty was this, when laymen, at that time, forfeited their lands in cases of felony?
[3] Wilk., Leg. Ang.-Sax., p. 381; Litt. Hist. Hen. II., vol. iv., pp. 265, 296.
[4] Sir Roger Owen MSS., p. 397.

by duel. The statutes of Clarendon concerning ecclesiastical matters subsisted unrepealed and confirmed; but were suspended in part by a temporary connivance of the executive power.[1]

The establishment which the clergy gained in this reign was not weakened in those of his successors. Richard I. was redeemed from his captivity by the aid of his subjects; among whom the zeal of the ecclesiastics, who readily converted their plate and other valuables to the ransom of their king, was particularly distinguished. This gave them everything to hope from the king's gratitude; nor were they disappointed in their expectations. The feudal subjection under which John laid his kingdom to the pope, ratified every clerical innovation, and seemed to justify the distinctions before claimed by the churchmen.

In this manner did the influence of the civil and canon law gradually increase; but these laws were not confined to the ecclesiastical courts, where they were professedly the only rules of decision: they, by degrees, interwove themselves into the municipal law, and furnished it with helps towards improving its native stock. The law of personal property was in a great measure borrowed from the imperial, and the rules of the descent of lands wholly from the canon law: to these might be added many other instances of imitation, too long to be enumerated in the present work.

These two laws, as the Norman had before, obtained here by sufferance and long usage. Such parts of them as were fitting and expedient, were quietly permitted to grow into practice; while such as were of an extravagant kind occasioned clamor, were called usurpations, and, as such, were strongly opposed. What was suffered to establish itself, either in the clerical courts, or by mingling with the secular customs, became so far part of the common law of the realm, equally with the Norman; for though of later birth, it had gained its authority by the same title, a length of immemorial prescription.[2]

---

[1] Sir Roger Owen says the king obtained a parliamentary repeal of the constitutions of Clarendon.—MSS., p. 404.

[2] This is all that I thought necessary to state concerning the prevalence of the civil and canon law, and the influence they both had upon the common custom of the realm; and I have heard no complaint, as in the case of

It had been a very ancient custom among the Normans, both in their own country and in France, to try titles to land, and other questions, by *duel*. When William had ordained that this martial practice of his own country should be observed here in criminal trials, it became very easy to introduce it into civil ones; and being only used in the *curia regis*, it had not, among the other novelties of that court, as it certainly would have had in the county court, or any other of the ancient tribunes of Saxon original, the appearance of so singular an innovation.

Of trial by duel in civil questions.

With all its absurdity, this mode of trial was not with-

---

feuds, that this part of the work is at all defective; indeed, I should not wonder if some thought even this short sketch too prolix, so much are our studies and opinions directed by fashion. But it seems to me, if the illustration of our ancient law had been the sole object of attention, and not a prepossession in favor of a topic that happened to be in vogue, that the same censure would be at least as applicable in one as in the other case.

A comparison of our law with those two systems of jurisprudence, would, in my mind, be an inquiry of equal curiosity, and much more to the purpose of a history of the English law, than the same process when applied to the so-much-admired systems of foreign feuds. This is sufficiently evinced by the cursory remarks already made respecting these two laws. It further appears by the works of Glanville, Bracton, and other old authors, who certainly wrote the law of their time, and not their own inventions, as has been too often and too inconsiderately said; and it is confirmed by marks of conformity, or imitation, in instances where no suspicion of fabrication was ever entertained.

The civil and canon law seem in a particular manner to be objects of curiosity to an English lawyer; they have long been domesticated in this country; were taught at our universities as a part of a learned education, and the road to academic honors; they have entered into competition with the common law; and, though unsuccessful in the struggle, were still thought worthy to be retained in our ecclesiastical courts, and there became the model by which our national canons and provincial constitutions were framed. These two laws, therefore, stand in a much nearer relation to the common law than the feudal law of Lombardy, or of any foreign country; none of which can boast any pretensions equal to those above mentioned.

Notwithstanding this close affinity between the civil and canon law and our own, I thought, that to enter into a particular comparison of such parts of those laws as seemed more remarkably to relate to the common law, was an inquiry not strictly within the compass of the present History; and therefore I declined it, for reasons similar to those I have before given with regard to foreign feuds.

I cannot, however, leave this subject without expressing a wish, that the early connection of our law with the civil and canon law was more fully investigated than it has yet been. The history and present state of those two laws in this country, and of our own national canon law, seem also to have been not yet sufficiently developed. To this it may be answered, that there is at least as great want of curiosity upon this topic as of information; and I am sure I do not pretend to determine which of these is the cause, and which the effect, of the other.

28*

out some marks of a rational reliance on testimony, and vouchers for the truth of what was in dispute; for it was never awarded without the oath of a credible witness, who would venture his life in the duel for the truth of what he swore. "I am ready," says the party litigant, "to prove it by my freeman John, whom his father on his death-bed enjoined, by the duty he owed him, that if at any time he should hear of a suit for this land, he should hazard himself in a *duel* for it, as for that which his father had *seen and heard.*"[1] Thus the champion of the demandant was such a one as might be a fit witness; and on that account the demandant could never engage in the combat himself; but the other party, who was defendant, or tenant in the suit, might engage either in his own person or by that of another.

It is difficult to say what matters were, at one time, submitted to this mode of trial (a). Perhaps at first all

---

(a) If the author had read the *Mirror*, he would have found a full exposition of the matter: "There are many modes of proof: sometimes by records; sometimes by battle; sometimes by witnesses." Then as to trial by battle, the proof of felony and other causes is done by combat of two according to the diversities of actions; for as there is a personal action and a real, there is a personal combat and a real; personal in personal actions, real in real actions. And these combats are different in this, that in a personal combat for felony, none can combat for another; but in actions personal and venial, it is lawful for the plaintiffs to make their battles by their bodies, or by loyal witnesses, as in the writ of right real combats — because none can be witness for himself, and no one is bound to discover his real right; and though they make their combats for the plaintiffs by witnesses, the defendants may defend their own right by their own bodies, or the bodies of their freemen. And in appeals none can combat for another; but it is otherwise in real actions. The battle of two men sufficeth to declare the truth, so that victory is holden for truth. Combats are made in many other cases than felonies; for if a man hath done any falsity in deed or in word, whereof he is impeached, and he deny it, it is lawful for one to prove the action, either by jury, or by the body of one witness"—*i. e.*, by battle. And it may be observed here, that trial by jury here plainly means trial by witnesses—as there is no previous mention of jurors otherwise than as witnesses; and at first, jurors were witnesses, whence it followed that if there were no witnesses, there could be no trial by jury; and hence the difficulty arose, to meet which, the trial by battle or by ordeal was resorted to. "And in cases, where battle could not be joined, nor was there any witnesses, the people in personal actions were to help themselves by the miracle of God, in this manner; as, if the defendant were a woman," etc. (*Ibid.*).

[1] Ariosto, in the true spirit of the old jurisprudence, as well as of chivalry, makes Rinaldo refer to the proof by arms, as equal to if not *stronger* than that by testimony:

Col testimonio, io vo', che l'arme sieno:
Che ora, e in ogni tempo, che ti piace,
Te n'abbiano a far prova piu verace.

Orl. Fur., cant. 31, stanz. 102.

questions of fact might, at the option of the demandant, have been tried by duel. In the reign of Henry II. it was decisive in pleas concerning freehold; in 'writs of right; in warranty of land, or of goods sold; debts upon mortgage or promise; sureties denying their suretyship; the validity of charters; the manumission of a villein; questions concerning service: all these might have been tried by duel.[1]

Notwithstanding the general bent of this people to admit the propriety of a trial so suitable to their martial genius, there must have been men of gravity and learning amongst them at all times; and persons of that character would always reprobate so ineffectual and cruel a proceeding. Considerations of this kind at last effected a change.

We find in the reign of Henry II. that many questions of fact relating to property were tried by twelve *liberos et legales homines juratos*, *sworn* to speak the truth; who were summoned by the sheriff for that purpose. This tribunal was in some cases called *assisa*, from *assidere*, as it is said, because they sat together; though it is most probable, and indeed seems intimated by the manner in which Glanville often expresses himself, that it was emphatically so called from the *assisa* (as laws were then termed), by which the application of this trial was, in many instances, ordained. On other occasions this trial was called *jurata*, from the *juratos*, or *juratores*, who composed it. Of the origin of this trial by twelve jurors, and the introduction of it into this country, we shall next inquire.

_{Of trial by jury.}

The trial *per duodecim juratos*, called *nambda*, had obtained among the *Scandinavians* at a very early period; but having gone into disuse, was revived, and more firmly established by a law of *Reignerus*, surnamed *Lodbrog*, about the year A. D. 820.[2] It was about seventy years after this law, that *Rollo* led his people into *Normandy*, and, among other customs, carried with him this method of trial; it was used there in all causes that were of small importance. When the Normans had transplanted themselves into England, they were desirous of legitimating this, as they did other parts of their jurisprudence; and they endeavored to substitute it in the place of the Saxon

---
[1] Glanv., passim.   [2] Hick., Thes. Diss., Epist. 38–40.

sectatores, to which tribunal it bore some show of affinity (*a*).

The earliest mention we find of anything like a *jury*, was in the reign of William the Conqueror, in a cause upon a question of land, where *Gundulph*, Bishop of *Rochester*, was a party. The king had referred it to the county, that is, to the *sectatores*, to determine in their county courts, as the course then was, according to the Saxon establishment; and the *sectatores* gave their opinion of the matter. But *Odo*, Bishop of *Bayeux*, who presided at the hearing of the cause, not satisfied with their determination, directed, that if they were still confident that they spoke truth, and persisted in the same opinion, they should choose *twelve* from among themselves, who should confirm it upon their *oaths*[1] (*b*). It seems as if the bishop had here

---

(*a*) "There are scarcely any authentic materials for its early history. It seems most probably to have arisen from the confluence of several causes. Perhaps the first conception of it may have been suggested by the very simple expedient of referring a cause by the county court to a select committee of their number, who were required to be twelve, for no reason or even cause that has been discovered. In civil cases, the obvious analogy of arbitration might have contributed to the adopting of juries. Judges, unacquainted with, and incapable of a patient inquiry into facts, might find it safer, as it was easier, to trust to a sort of general testimony given by twelve unexceptionable neighbors, on the litigated question. There are many traces in this institution which indicate that jurors must, in some manner, have been regarded in the same light with witnesses. Neighborhood, for instance, which might be dangerous to the impartiality of a judge, is advantageous to the knowledge of a witness; and it is still a sort of legal theory, that jurors have the dangerous power of finding a verdict from their own knowledge" (Mackintosh's *History of England*, vol. i., p. 273).

(*b*) It has already been seen that the author is entirely in error on this subject, and that before the Norman Conquest, trial by juries — that is, by a number of the freeholders or suitors of the county, sworn from among the rest, to declare the truth according to their knowledge of it — was used both in civil and criminal cases. It may not have been always by twelve jurors, though it appears plainly that juries in criminal cases consisted of twelve in the time of Alfred; and the number twelve is so often mentioned in the Saxon laws, that there is reason to believe that the juries were so constituted both in civil and criminal cases. But it would appear that even in criminal cases it was not a fixed practice to have juries; as in criminal cases there were other modes of trial, and in civil cases the county might or might not have recourse to it. That which the author failed to understand was that the suitors were the judges of the court, and that they used various modes of assisting themselves in their determination, among others, trial by jury; the jurors of cases being in those days *not* judges, but witnesses. It followed, that if it happened that no suitors had any knowledge of the matter, there could be no jurors; for jurors were sworn to declare the truth of their own knowledge. Hence, in criminal cases, the resort to the ordeal in the

[1] Text. Roff. apud Hickes, *ut sup.*

taken a step which was not in the usual way of proceeding, but which he ventured upon in conformity with the practice of his own country; the general law of England being, that a judicial inquiry concerning a fact should be collected *per omnes comitatûs probos homines* (a). Thus it appears, that in a cause where this same *Odo* was one party, and Archbishop *Lanfranc* the other, the king directed TOTUM *comitatum considere;* that all men of the county, as well French as English, (particularly the latter) that were learned in the law and custom of the realm, should be convened: upon which they all met at *Pinendena*, and there it was determined AB OMNIBUS *illis probis*, and agreed and adjudged *à toto comitatu.* In the reign of William Rufus, in a cause between the monastery of *Croyland* and *Evan Talbois*, in the county court, there is no mention of a jury; and so late as the reign of *Stephen*, in a cause between the monks of Christ-Church, Canterbury, and *Radulph Picot*, it appears from the acts of the court,[1] that it was determined *per judicium* TOTIUS COMITATUS.[2]

This trial by an indefinite number of *sectatores* or *suitors* of court (b) continued for many years after the Conquest:

---

absence of jurors, or compurgators; hence, in civil cases, the care taken to provide jurors by having witnesses for all transactions, who might afterwards be jurors. Hence, also, in cases where, from their nature, there could not be certain personal knowledge, or only from uncertain memory, as in cases of claims of land, resting on past events, at some distance of time; suits in the county court would be determined more by clamor or partisanship, than by evidence or consideration.

(a) And it is one of the most curious instances of the extreme antiquity of judicial forms of expression, and the evidence they afford of ancient usages, that until recently the phrase used as to trial by jury in civil cases (and it still is so in criminal cases), was, that the party put himself upon the country — *i. e.*, the county, or the men of the county. This is a relic of that ancient jurisdiction of the county court, out of which, by a course of change which has been amply described, the trial by jury arose. And when the jury was first used, as the general body of the freeholders, the suitors were the judges, and the jurors were only witnesses; the record would continue to state that the case was determined by the men of the county. The author failed to observe this, and hence draws a totally wrong inference from the fact that the records so state it. As it did so in cases where there are known to have been juries, of course it affords no evidence that juries were not used even where the fact is not known.

(b) Here, again, we observe that the author had fallen into some confusion upon the subject. The suitors did not try the cases, they were the judges, and they resorted to various modes of trial; of which trial by jurors was one — the jurors being any of their own body who had knowledge of the matter, and were sworn to declare the truth about it. Hence trial by jurors did not, as the author supposes, exclude the suitors, and was for ages used at county courts.

[1] Bib. Cott. Faustina, A. 3, 11, 31. [2] Hickes, Thes. Diss., Ep. 36.

these are the persons meant by the terms *pares curiæ*, and *judicium parium*, so often found in writings of this period. Successive attempts gradually introduced jurors to the exclusion of the *sectatores* (a); and a variety of practice, no doubt, prevailed till the Norman law was thoroughly established.¹ It was not till the reign of Henry II. that the trial by jurors became general; and by that time, the king's itinerant courts, in which there were no *pares curiæ* (b), had attracted so many of the county causes, that the *sectatores* were rarely called into action.²

<small>Of trial by the assize.</small> The sudden progress then made in bringing this trial into common use, must be attributed to the law enacted by that king. As this law has not come down to us, we are ignorant at what part of his reign it was passed, and what was the precise extent of its regulation: we can only collect such intimation as is given us by contemporary authorities, the chief of which is Glanville, who makes frequent allusion to it. It is called by him *assisa*, as all laws then were, and *regalis constitutio;* at other times, *regale quoddam beneficium, clementiâ principis de concilio procerum populis indultum*. It seems as if this law ordained, that all questions of *seisin* of land should be tried by a recognition of twelve good and lawful men, sworn to speak the truth; and also that in questions *of right* to land, the tenant might elect to have the matter tried by twelve good and lawful knights instead of the duel. It appears that some incidental points in a cause, that were neither questions of mere *right*, nor of *seisin* of land, were tried by a recognition of twelve men; and we find that in all these cases, the proceeding was called *per assisam*, and *per recognitionem;* and the persons

---

(a) Jurors did not exclude the suitors; the suitors were judges, the jurors witnesses.

(b) What the author means is, that the suitors as judges were superseded by the king's justices, who still held their courts in the counties, and either in the old county court assemblies, or at special assemblies of the counties, and by the king's commissions. So enduring is custom, and so closely did the people cling to the idea that the body of the freeholders were judges, that it was not until the reign of Richard II. they were actually excluded from the bench where the king's justices sat.

¹ The following law of Henry I. seems to be in support of the ancient usage: *Unusquisque* PER PARES SUOS *judicandus est, et ejusdem provinciæ;* PEREGRINA *viro judicia modis omnibus submovemus.* Leg., 31.

² Persons of a new character, under the name of *secta*, and *sectatores*, in a subsequent period, made a necessary part of most actions brought in the king's courts, as will be seen hereafter.

composing it were called *juratores, jurati, recognitores assisæ;* and collectively *assisa,* and *recognitio:* only the twelve jurors in questions of right were distinguished with the appellation of *magna assisa;* probably because they were *knights,* and were brought together also with more ceremony, being not summoned immediately by the sheriff, as the others were, but elected by four knights, who for that purpose had been before summoned by the sheriff. We are also told, that the law by which these proceedings were directed, had ordained a very heavy penalty on *jurors* who were convicted of having sworn falsely in any of the above instances.[1]

Thus far of one species of this trial by twelve men, which was called *assisa.* It likewise appears, that the oath of twelve jurors was resorted to in other instances than those provided for by this famous law of Henry II., and then this proceeding was said to be *per juratam patriæ,* or *vicineti, per inquisitionem, per juramentum legalium hominum.* This proceeding by jury was no other than that which we before mentioned to have gained ground by usage and custom. This was sometimes used in questions of property; but it should seem more frequently in matters of a criminal nature.

The earliest mention of a trial by jury, that bears a near resemblance to that which this proceeding became in after times, is in the Constitutions of Clarendon, before spoken of. It is there directed, that, should nobody appear to accuse an offender before the archdeacon, then the sheriff, at the request of the bishop, *faciet jurare duodecim legales homines de vicineto, seu de villâ quòd inde veritatem secundum conscientiam suam manifestabunt.*[2] The first notice of any *recognition,* or *assise,* is likewise in these Constitutions; where it is directed, that, should a question arise, whether land was lay or ecclesiastical property, *recognitione duodecim legalium hominum, per capitalis justitiæ considerationem, terminabitur, utrùm,* etc. ;[3] this was A. D. 1164. Again, in the statute of Northampton, A. D. 1176 (which is said to be a republication of some statutes made at Clarendon, perhaps at the same time the before-mentioned provisions were made about ecclesiastical matters), the justices are directed, in case a lord should deny to the

---

[1] Glanv., lib. 13, c. 1; lib. 2, c. 7, 19.   [2] Ch. 6.   [3] Ch. 9.

heir the seisin of his deceased ancestor, *faciant inde fieri recognitionem per duodecim legales homines, qualem seisinam defunctus inde habuit die quâ fuit vivus et mortuus;* and also *faciant fieri recognitionem de disseisinis factis super assisam, tempore quo* the king came into England, after the peace made between him and his son. We see here, very plainly described, three of the assizes of which so much will be said hereafter; the *assisa utrùm fœdum sit laicum an ecclesiasticum;* the *assisa mortis antecessoris;* and the *assisa novæ disseisinæ.* Again, in the statute of Northampton there is mention of a person *rectatus de murdro per sacramentum duodecim militum de hundredo,* and *per sacramentum duodecim liberorum legalium hominum.*

Thus have we endeavored to trace the origin and history of *the trial by twelve men sworn to speak the truth,* down to the time of Glanville: a further account of, it we shall defer, till we come to speak more minutely of the proceedings of courts at this time.

Another novelty introduced by the Normans, was the practice of making deeds with seals of wax and other ceremonies.[1] The variety of deeds which soon after the Conquest were brought into use, and the divers ways in which they were applied for the purpose of transferring, modifying, or confirming rights, deserve a very particular notice.

Of deeds.

Deeds or writings, from the time of the Conquest, were sometimes called *chirographa,* but more generally *chartæ;* the latter became a term of more common use, and so continued for many years; the former rather denoted a species of the *chartæ,* as will be seen presently. Charters were executed with various circumstances of solemnity, which it will be necessary to consider: these were the seal, indenting, date, attestation, and direction, or compellation.

Charters were sometimes brought into court; either the king's, or the county, hundred, or other court, or into any numerous assembly; and there the act of making, or acknowledging and perfecting the charter was performed. This accounts for the number of witnesses often found to old charters, with the very common addition of *cum multis aliis.* When charters were not executed in this public

---

[1] Wilk., Leg. Sax., 289.

manner, they were usually attested by men of character and consequence: in the country, by gentlemen and clergymen: in cities and towns, by the mayor, bailiff, or some other civil officer.[1]

The Anglo-Saxon practice of affixing the cross still continued; yet was not so frequent as before; but gave way to a method which more commonly obtained after the Conquest, namely, that of affixing a *seal of wax*. Seals of wax were of various colors. They were commonly round or oval, and were fixed to a label of parchment, or to a silk string fastened to the fold at the bottom of the charter, or to a slip of the parchment cut from the bottom of the deed, and made pendulous. Besides the principal seal there was sometimes a counter-seal, being the private seal of the party. If a man had not his own seal, or if his own seal was not well known, he would use that of another; and sometimes, for better security, he would use both his own and that of some other better known.

The original method of *indenting* was this. If a writing consisted of two parts, the whole tenor of it was written twice upon the same piece of parchment; and, between the contents of each part, the word *chirographum* was written in capital letters, and afterwards was cut through in the midst of those letters; so that, when the two parts were separated, one would exhibit one-half of the capital letters, and one the other; and when joined, the word would appear entire. Such a charter was called *chirographum*. About the reigns of *Richard* and *John*, another fashion of cutting the word *chirographum* came into use; it was then sometimes done *indent-wise*, with an acute or sharp incision, *instardentium;*[2] and from thence such deeds were called *indenturæ*.

Charters were sometimes dated, and very commonly they had no date at all; but as they were always executed in the presence of somebody, and often in the presence of many, the names of the witnesses were inserted, and constituted a particular clause, called *his testibus*. The names of the witnesses were written by the clerk who drew the deed, and not by the witnesses themselves, who very often could not write. It seems that wives were sometimes witnesses to deeds made by their husbands; monks and other religious

---

[1] Mad., Form., Diss. 26.   [2] Ibid., 14, 28, 29.

persons to deeds made by their own houses; even the king is found as witness to the charters of private men;[1] and in the time of Richard and John, it came in practice for him to attest his own charters himself in the words *teste meipso*.[2]

Charters were usually conceived in the style of a letter, and, at the beginning, they had a sort of direction, or compellation. These were various. In royal charters, it was sometimes, *omnibus hominibus suis Francis & Anglis*: in private ones, sometimes, *omnibus sanctæ ecclesiæ filiis*; but more commonly, *sciant præsentes et futuri*, or *omnibus ad quos præsentes literæ*, etc.

Thus far of the circumstances and solemnities attending the execution of charters. Let us now consider the different kinds of them; and it will be found, that as they were called *chirographa*, or *indenturæ*, from their particular fashion, so they received other appellations, expressive of their effect and design. A charter was sometimes called *conventio, concordia, finalis concordia*, and *finalis conventio*. There were also *feoffments*, demises for *life* and for *years, exchanges, mortgages, partitions, releases*, and *confirmations*.[3]

Conventio and *concordia* had both the same meaning, and signified some agreement, according to which one of the parties conveyed or confirmed to the other any lands, or other rights.

Of all charters the most considerable was a *feoffment*.

Of feoffment. After the time of the Conquest, whenever land was to be passed in fee, it was generally done by feoffment and delivery or livery of seisin.[4] This might be without deed; but the gift was usually put into writing, and such instrument was called *charta feoffmenti*. A feoffment originally meant the grant of a *feud* or *fee*; that is, a barony or knight's fee, for which certain services were due from the feoffee to the feoffor: this was the proper sense of the word: but by custom it came afterwards to signify also a grant of free *inheritance* to a man and his heirs, referring rather to the perpetuity of estate than to the feudal tenure. The words of donation were generally, *dedisse, concessisse, confirmâsse*, or *donâsse*, some one or other of them. It was very late, and not till the reign of Richard II., that the specific term *feoffavi* was used. These

---
[1] Mad., Form., Diss. 31.   [2] Ibid., 32.   [3] Ibid., 3.
[4] Wilk., Leg. Sax., 289.

feoffments were made *pro homagio et servitio*, to hold of the feoffor and his heirs, or of the chief lord.

At this early period feoffments were very unsettled in point of form; they had not the several parts which, in after times, they were expected regularly to contain. The words of limitation, to convey a fee, whether absolute or conditional, were divers. A limitation of the former was sometimes worded thus: to the feoffee *et suis;* or *suis post ipsum, jure hæreditario perpetuè possidendum ;* or *sibi et hæredibus suis vel assignatis:* of the latter thus: *sibi et hæredibus procedentibus ex prædictâ: Richardo et uxori suæ et hæredibus suis, qui de eâdem veniunt: sibi et hæredibus qui de illo exibunt:* from which divers ways of limiting estates (and numberless other ways might be produced) it must be concluded, that no specific form had been agreed on as necessarily requisite to express a specific estate; but the intention of the granter was collected, as well as could be, from the terms in which he had chosen to convey his meaning.[1]

It appears that a charter of feoffment was sometimes made by a feme covert, though generally with the consent of the husband; and a husband sometimes made a feoffment to his wife. A feoffment was sometimes expressed to be made with the assent of the feoffor's wife;[2] or of such a one, heir[3] of the feoffor; or of more than one, heirs of the feoffor;[4] though in such cases, the charter appears to be sealed only by the feoffor. By the assent of the wife, probably, her claim of dower was in those days held to be barred; and indeed, when such feoffment was made publicly in court, it had the notoriety of a fine; and might consistently enough with modern notions, be allowed the efficacy since attributed to fines in the like cases. The assent of the heirs was, probably, where the land had descended from the ancestors of the feoffor; or where by usage it retained the property of *bocland*, not to be aliened *extra cognationem*, without the consent of the heir, where such restriction had been imposed by the original *landboc*.

A clause of *warranty* was always inserted; which sometimes, too, had the additional sanction of an oath. The import of this warranty was, that should the feoffee be

---

[1] Wilk., Leg. Sax., 5.   [2] Mad., Form., 148.   [3] Ibid., 316.
[4] Ibid., 319.

evicted of the lands given, the feoffor should recompense him with others of equal value.¹

A charter of feoffment was not a complete transfer of the inheritance, unless followed by *livery of seisin*. This was done in various ways; as *per fustem, per baculum, per haspam, per annulum*, and by other symbols, either peculiarly significant in themselves, or accommodated by use, or designation of the parties, to denote a transmutation of possession from the feoffor to the feoffee.

This was the nature of a feoffment with livery of seisin, as practised in these early times. It was the usual and most solemn way of passing inheritances in land; but yet was not of so great authority as a *fine*, which had the additional sanction of a record to preserve the memory of it.

A fine. The antiquity of *fines* has been spoken of by many writers (*a*). Some have gone so far as to assert their existence and use in the time of the Saxons.² But upon a strict inquiry, it is said, there were no *fines*, properly so called, before the Conquest,

---

(*a*) Of this there can be no doubt. Mr. Hargreave's opinion also, that fines were originally real concords of existing suits, is clearly well founded. There is a chapter in the *Mirror* about final concords of suits. At what period they became used for the purpose of transfer or conveyance, irrespective of any real concord of a suit, is uncertain; but there is every reason to believe that it would occur very readily to the minds of people in that early age, when the tendency was to have everything recorded. A law of Canute says, "He who has defended land with the witness of the shire (*i. e.*, the county court), let him have it undisputed," which might suggest recovery; and in the laws of Henry I. it is said, speaking of the county court, "Recordationem curiæ regis nulli negare licet" (c. xxxi.), which might easily suggest the idea of fines or recoveries. In the Saxon law mention is more than once made of transactions being attested in the county court. There was a particular reason why fines or recoveries should be of very early origin in our law, that the great body of the people held their land then without deeds or charter of conveyance. This is fully explained in the *Mirror*, in a passage, the antiquity of which is evident. It is said there that the first conquerors enfeoffed persons in knight-service, or villenage (no mention is made of freehold feoffments), and that many held their lands by villein customs — as to plough, etc., the lord's land. The lords might give them estates of inheritance, or if the lord received their homage for such estates, it would be the same thing. Thus the people, it is said, had no charters, deeds, nor muniments of their lands; but it is said many fines were levied of such services, which make mention of the doing of these services (*Mirror*, c. ii., s. 25). It would be natural in such a state of society to resort rather to public transactions in the county courts than to formal conveyances.

¹ Mad., Form., 7.   ² Plowd., 360.

though they are frequently met with[1] soon after that period.[2]

We shall now consider the manner in which fines have been treated, or, as it is now called, *levied*. The account of fines given by Glanville does not enable us to fix any precise idea of the method of transacting them. It only appears from him, that this proceeding was a final concord made by license of the king, or his justices,[3] in the king's court. But the nature of a fine may be better collected from the more simple manner in which it was originally conducted.

The parties having come to an agreement concerning the matters in dispute, and having thereupon mutually sealed a *chirographum*, containing the terms of their agreement, used to come into the king's court in person, or by attorney, and there acknowledge the concord before the justices: it was thereupon, after payment of a fine, enrolled immediately, and a counterpart delivered to each of the parties.[4] This was the most ancient way of passing a fine. In course of time, fines came to be passed with a *chirographum*, upon a *placitum* commenced by original writ, as in a writ of covenant, *warrantia chartæ*, or other writ. When the mutual sealing of a *chirographum* was entirely disused, there still remained a footstep of this ancient practice; for there continues to this day in every fine a chirograph, as it is called, which is reputed as essentially necessary to evidence that a fine has been levied.

The design of *final concords* seems to have been anciently as various as the matters of litigation or agreement among men. By fines were made grants of land in fee, releases, exchanges, partitions, or any convention relating to land, or other rights: in a word, everything might be transacted by fine which might be done by *chirographum*.[5]

Thus far of the two great conveyances in practice for transferring estates of inheritance, namely, *feoffments* and *fines*. The manner in which estates for life or for years (since called demises) were made, was in the way of convention or covenant.[6]

---

[1] Mad., Form., Diss. 7.
[2] The origin of fines is very fully considered by Mr. Cruise, in his valuable Essay on Fines, who thinks, and with great show of reason, that fines were contrived in imitation of a similar judicial transaction in the civil law.—Cruise's *Fines*, p. 5.
[3] Lib. viii., c. 1. [4] Mad., Form., Diss. 14. [5] Ibid., 16, 17. [6] Ibid., 22.

Two other species of conveyance then used were *confirmations* and *releases*. In those unsettled times, when feoffees were frequently disseized upon some suggestion of dormant claims, charters of confirmation were in great request. Many confirmations used to be made by the feoffor to the feoffee, or to his heirs or successors. Tenants in those times hardly thought themselves safe against great lords who were their feoffors, unless they had repeated confirmations from them or their heirs. Releases were as necessary from hostile claimants as confirmations from feoffors. The words of *confirmation* were *dedi, concessi,* or *confirmavi;* and such deeds are distinguishable from original feoffments, only by some expressions referring to a former feoffment. *Releases* are known by the words *quietum clamavi, remisi, relaxavi,* and the like.

During the time which had elapsed since the Conquest, the Norman law had sufficient opportunity to mix with all parts of our Saxon customs. This change was not confined to the article of tenures, duel, juries, and conveyances. The manner in which justice was administered makes a distinguished part of the new jurisprudence. In the Saxon times all suits were commenced by the simple act of the plaintiff lodging his complaint with the officer of the court where the cause was to be heard; and this still continued in the county and other inferior courts of the old constitution. But when it had become usual to remove suits out of these inferior courts, or of beginning them more frequently in the king's court, it became necessary to agree upon some settled forms of precepts applicable to the purpose of compelling defendants to answer the charge alleged by plaintiffs (a). Such a precept was called *breve;* probably, be-

Of writs.

(a) King's writs indicate the jurisdiction of king's courts, for in the county courts men could sue without writs, which were only required to commence actions in the king's superior courts. The usage of such writs, therefore, marks an important era in our legal history. As already shown, the primary jurisdiction, after or before the Conquest, in common suits between party and party, was in the county court, which was called "curia regis" (*Leges Hen. Prim.*). And hence the *Mirror,* in an early chapter, headed, "Of the time of Alfred," gives as the form of remedial writ, a writ to the sheriff to compel him to decide the case and do justice. In a subsequent chapter, however, stating what the law was at the time the book was compiled (Edward I.), it is said, "There are two kinds of jurisdiction, ordinary and assigned; every one hath ordinary jurisdiction," (*i. e.*, in the county,) "but this jurisdiction is now restrained by the power of kings, as none hath power

cause it contained *briefly* an intimation of the cause of complaint. It was directed to the sheriff of the county to hold plea of trespass, or of debt which passeth forty shillings, but the king. Nor hath any one power of conveyance of fees" (*i. e.*, of freehold estates) "without a writ" (c. iv., s. 2), which is also laid down in Bracton and Fleta. Now this change must have taken place after the Conquest, and the origin of it can be traced. Before the Conquest writs went to the sheriff to compel him to hear a case, and it was then contended that writs were necessary to enable him to do so. And the writs were often required to give a better judge. In the case of the Archbishop of Canterbury, already mentioned as having occurred under William I., the case was tried at the county court, but before a foreign prelate, who of course could not have been sheriff, and who could only have sat under the king's writ. And thus the practice having arisen of using the king's writ in important cases, in order to secure a better judge than the sheriff, it by degrees came to be considered that the writ was necessary to give jurisdiction in any but comparatively minor cases. Not a trace of any such doctrine is to be found before the Conquest, nor until long afterwards; and we have seen cases of the greatest character come into the county court. It had, however, evidently become established at the time of the Great Charter, for it is laid down by Bracton; whereas, in the *Mirror*, we find that forty shillings was the limit, not of the county court, but of the court baron (c. i., s. 3). But Bracton, writing just after the time of the Charter, says that the sheriff under the king's writ tried cases he could not try *ex officio*, but tried them as the justice of the king (s. 6). Thus, therefore, the king's writ being required to give jurisdiction, it of course was natural that the suitor should seek to sue in the king's superior court; and hence, just before the Charter, common pleas were brought, as all the records show, in the exchequer; wherefore the Charter said they should not follow the king as that court did, and hence the court of common pleas. Thus, therefore, now the king's writs to the sheriff were required either to give him jurisdiction to try the case, or to give the king's court jurisdiction to try it. In either case the writ went to the sheriff — a curious trace of the old system: for otherwise they would have gone to the party, or to the court. The *Mirror* says that these writs used to contain the names of the parties and the name of the judge, and were directed sometimes to sheriffs, etc., and that they were necessary to give jurisdiction not possessed at common law. At common law, as has been seen, the primary jurisdiction was in the county court in "common pleas" between subject and subject, though they could be removed into the king's court for sufficient cause. But in order to derive a revenue out of the administration of justice, and at the same time promote its improvement, a practice had arisen of requiring the suitor in cases above forty shillings to sue out a writ from the king. And, in like manner, in order to remove a case from the county court into the king's superior court, a writ was required; and to commence an action in the king's court. When the suitor was required to sue out a writ to commence a suit in the county court above a certain value, there was, of course, an inducement to sue in the king's court, as probably the fee was the same. Moreover, there were cases in which the party sued did not reside in the county where the matter arose, and in such cases the suit could not be brought into a county court without a king's writ — as the sheriff of one county had no jurisdiction over men in another, and the men of one county could not try cases arising in another. But the king's writ went into any county, and the case commenced in the king's superior court could still be tried in the county where the matter arose. Hence, for various reasons, the necessity for writs from the king's superior courts. These writs were, it will be seen, of two classes — either

where the defendant lived, commanding that he should summon the party to appear in some particular court of the king, there to answer the plaintiff's demand, or to do some other thing tending to satisfy the ends of justice.

The necessity of such *brevia* was very obvious; for though, while most suits were transacted in the county court, it was sufficient to enter a plaint with the officer of the court; and the process issuing thereupon being to be executed by the sheriff, who was present, or supposed to be present, in court as judge, was not likely to be extremely illegal or irregular, even when warranted perhaps by nothing more authentic than verbal directions; yet, when suits were commenced in the king's court, at a great distance from the habitation of the parties, and process was to issue to him merely as an officer, who knew nothing more of the matter than what the precept explained, it was necessary that something more particular should be exhibited to him; and, therefore, that the precept should be *written*. Hence, perhaps it is, that the *breve* was called also a *writ*.[1]

These *writs* were of different kinds and received different appellations, according to the object or occasion of them. The distinction between writs furnished a source of curious learning, which led to many of the refinements afterwards introduced into the law. The assigning of a writ of a particular frame and scope to each particular

---

to the sheriff to empower him to do justice, and try the case in his county, which was called a writ of justices, or a writ to commence an action in the king's superior court, and therefore "returnable," as the phrase was in that court. In either case, however, so deeply rooted was the county court in our judicial system, the writ went to the sheriff of some county, who was to summon the party sued, to answer in the suit: and to enable him to do so, or inform him what steps to take with a view to the proceeding he might desire to take, the writ briefly stated the cause of complaint. The reason for this was, that the writ commanding appearance in court, and the appearance being personal, and the pleading oral, the parties upon appearance could at once commence their controversy, the plaintiff narrating his cause of complaint more fully; and the defendant, unless he desired time to consider his defence, would at once make his answer; and of course the more clear the writ, the better he would be able thus to answer. The course, upon appearance in the king's court, would, it should seem, as the pleading was oral, be very much the same, at first, as in the county court, until the point in dispute appeared. If it was matter of law, it would at once be decided by the court; if matter of fact, it would be sent into the county to be tried, and that would require a record.

[1] We have before seen that deeds, among the Saxons, were called *Gewrite*. —*Vide ante*, p. 184.

cause of action; the appropriating process of one kind to one action, and of a different kind to another; these and the like distinctions rendered proceedings very nice and complex, and made the conduct of an action a matter of considerable difficulty.

The cultivation of this kind of learning was encouraged by a regulation of the new law, which was designed for the more useful purpose of preserving the judgments and opinions of judges for the instruction of succeeding ages; this was the practice of entering proceedings of courts upon a roll of parchment, which was then called *a record* (a).

Of records.

The practice of registering upon *rotuli*, or rolls of parch-

---

(a) There were other and stronger reasons for records than those here mentioned; and, indeed, records of judicial proceedings will be found necessarily incident to any regular system of judicature and procedure; and, therefore, they are to be traced in the times immediately following the era of the Conquest, when, as we have seen, attempts were made to improve the turbulent popular assemblies of the Saxons, and introduce something like judicial tribunals, and some kind of regular procedure. Lord Coke cites a supposed record of the great suit in the county court soon after the Conquest, of which mention is made by our author at the end of the first chapter, and which has more than once been mentioned in these notes as the first instance of anything like a regular judicial trial (*Preface to the 9th Part of "Coke's Reports"*). Whether or not that particular record is authentic, it is manifest that so soon as regular judges sat, and regular trials took place, in the county court, records of the proceedings would, for various reasons, be required; and it is certain that such judicial records became the practice, for in the *Leges Henrici Primi* mention is more than once made of the records of the "curia regis," which at that time, as the context clearly shows, meant the county court: "Recordationem curiæ regis nulli licet negare." In the reign of Henry I., as we have seen, regular judges sat in the courts of the counties, directed upon matters of law, and directed the juries, who were sworn to determine matters of fact, on whose verdicts judgment was given. These judgments would be of little use if the same matter might be litigated again between the same parties, and, to prevent this, was one great use of records; and this probably was alluded to in the passage from the Laws of Henry I., just quoted, for it has from the most ancient times been the rule of law that a verdict and judgment on the same matter, between the same parties, was final. Again, the great object of law being certainty and uniformity of decisions, this required an appellate jurisdiction, and that necessarily required records; for unless the matter was recorded, the superior court could not exercise its jurisdiction. Hence the appellate jurisdiction of the "curia regis," and the practice of recording judicial proceedings, can be traced together to these ancient times, and have ever since been united. Hence, when it was desired to give an appeal to a court of error from the rulings of the judges upon trials, the statute of Westminster (*temp.* Edward I.) required the matter to be recorded; and hence the ancient writ of "recordare facias," to remove a matter from an inferior court. Thus, therefore, for various reasons, records and regular procedure were necessarily connected together.

ment, was entirely Norman; nor did it obtain to any great extent till long after the Conquest. Among the Saxons the manner of registering was by writing on both sides of the leaf; and this was either in some *evangelisterium*, or other monastic book, belonging to a religious house. It was thus that the memory not only of pleas in courts, but of purchases of land, testaments, and of other public acts was preserved. This practice, like other Saxon usages, continued long after the invasion of William. We find that Domesday, the most important record of the exchequer in those times, consists of two large books. But in the time of Henry I. we find *rotuli annales* in the exchequer for recording articles of charge and discharge, and other matters of account relating to the king's revenue. It is conjectured that the making enrolment of judicial matters in the *curia regis* was posterior in point of time to the same practice in matters of revenue, and was dictated by the experience of its utility in that important department.[1] This innovation gave rise to the distinction between *courts of record* and courts not of record.

A record began with the entry of the original writ; rehearsed the statement of the demand, the answer or *plea*, the judgment of the court, and execution awarded. Thus a record contained a short history of an action through all its stages. When proceedings were entered in this solemn manner, and submitted to the criticism and exception of the adverse party, it became very material to each that his part of the record should be drawn with all accuracy and precision. When this attention was observed in completing a record, it became a very authentic guide in similar cases. Records were in high estimation; and, as they continued the memorials of judicial opinions, tended to fix the rules and doctrines of our law upon the firm basis of precedent and authority.

Such were the more conspicuous parts of the juridical system introduced by the Normans, and such were the changes they underwent during the period that elapsed before the end of the reign of King John.

---

[1] See Ayloffe's Ancient Charters, Introd.

CHAPTER III.
HENRY II. (a.)

OF VILLEINS — DOWER — ALIENATION — "NEMO POTEST ESSE HÆRES ET DOMINUS"— OF DESCENT — OF TESTAMENTS — OF WARDSHIP — MARRIAGE — OF BASTARDY — USURERS — OF ESCHEAT — MARITAGIUM — HOMAGE — RELIEF — AIDS — ADMINISTRATION OF JUSTICE — A WRIT OF RIGHT — ESSOINS — OF SUMMONS — OF ATTACHMENT — COUNTING UPON THE WRIT — THE DUEL — THE ASSIZE — VOUCHING TO WARRANTY — WRIT OF RIGHT OF ADVOWSON — OF PROHIBITION TO THE ECCLESIASTICAL COURT — THE WRIT DE NATIVIS — WRIT OF RIGHT OF DOWER — DOWER UNDE NIHIL.

IN the former chapter it was endeavored to trace the history of the principal changes made in the law from the time of William the Conqueror down to the reign of King John: but the object of this work being to give a correct idea of the origin and progress of our whole judicial polity, something more satisfactory will be expected than the foregoing deduction. It will be required to state fully, and at length, what was the condition of persons and property; how justice, both civil and criminal, was administered; with the process, proceeding, and judgments of courts; in short, to give a kind of treatise of the old jurisprudence, with a precision, and from an authority, that will at once instruct the curious, and have weight with the learned. When this is done, it will be a foundation on which the superstructure of our juridical history may be raised with consistence; every modification and addition being pursued in the order in which it arose, the connection and dependence of the several parts will be viewed in a new light, and the reason and grounds of the law be investigated and explained more naturally, and, it is trusted, with more success than in any discourse or desultory comment upon our ancient statutes, however copious and learned.

In order to lay this foundation of the subsequent history, it seems that some point of time during the period

---
(a) *Vide* note to the heading of c. ii.

between the Conquest and the reign of King John should be chosen, and that the contemporary law of that time, in all its branches, should be stated with precision and minuteness (*a*). The laws of Edward the Confessor, consid-

---

(*a*) It would have been better to have taken the *Mirror of Justice* for this purpose, or at all events to have had some regard to it, since it is more full and complete as regards the scope of its subjects, and because, as it was based upon a work as ancient as the time of the Saxons, and contains cases and ordinances from the time of the Conquest to the time when it was finally completed (Edward I.), it exhibits the course and progression of our legal history far better than any known work; whereas Glanville, to whom our author confines himself, states the law (only upon matters that came within the cognizance of the king's chief court, and upon some subjects not fully, and upon others not at all) as he understood it to be in his day. Elsewhere, in the reign of Edward I., the author notices the *Mirror* cursorily, and merely observes that some part of it was written as late as that reign, and then dismisses it, and makes no more use of it. It is evident that he had read only the first chapter, in which the name of that king was mentioned in this way, "Many ordinances were made by many kings until the time of the king that now is," Edward I. (c. 1, s. 3), from which he hastily inferred that, as it was a work written in that time, it would throw no light upon the history of the law in previous times; whereas, on a little attention to this very passage, he would have seen that it was quite otherwise, and that this work, of all others, is calculated to throw light upon our legal history during its whole course, from the time of the Saxons up to the time of Edward I. And, upon a perusal of it, he would have seen that there is no difficulty at all, with a little attention to the contents, and a knowledge of legal history, in searching out the age or era to which each part belongs. For instance, the large portions which have already been made use of in these notes, as clearly belonging to the Saxon age. In like manner, various portions have been used in the foregoing chapter as belonging to the era of the Conquest, *i. e.*, to the reign of the Conqueror and his immediate successors. So certain portions are clearly marked out as belonging to the period covered by the present chapter, the important era of the reign of Henry II.; as, for example, trial by battle, which was not used at all after John's reign. So as to villenage, which, in its worser or lower sense, probably became obsolete during the same period. It may be convenient in this place to present at once such portions of the *Mirror* as appear plainly to relate to the period covered by this chapter. Sometimes the precise age or time of the law alluded to is marked by the passage itself, as thus, in stating the law as to coroners, "In case a man dieth by a fall, in such a case, according to Ranulph de Glanville, it is ordained that whatever is cause of death is deodand." (B. i., c. 13.) That clearly refers to some decision or judgment of Glanville, who was chief justiciary under Henry II.; and it is observable that the "ordinance" is not to be found in Glanville, whose work, indeed, is confined, as already mentioned, to matters which came under the cognizance of the king's court, and therefore did not include matters which came under the cognizance of sheriffs or coroners, as to which the *Mirror* is very copious. It may be observed upon this passage, as to deodands, that it illustrates the growth and progress of our laws by judicial decisions, sometimes called "ordinances" of the kings under whom they were pronounced, and many of which are to be found scattered through the *Mirror;* and are in these notes collected, under the period to which they appear to belong, as in the instance already adduced. So, again, of misadventures in tournaments, in courts and lists. King Henry II. or-

ered according to the present opinion, as a performance of some writer in the reign of William Rufus, and the laws of Henry I., are the earliest documents that could at all be viewed with any hopes of information of this kind; but these throw so little light on the Norman jurisprudence, that they furnished small assistance, even in the historical sketch contained in the preceding chapter. The new jurisprudence seems not to have been thoroughly established, or at least tolerably explained, till the reign of Henry II., when we meet with the treatise of Glanville. The method, scope, and extent of this venerable book mark the reign of Henry II. as the most favorable period for our purpose. As, therefore, it may be collected with considerable accuracy from that author what the law was towards the end of the reign of Henry II., we shall, with his aid, take a complete view of it; and, having done that, we shall proceed with more confidence to consider the subsequent changes made by parliament and by courts in the reigns of Henry III., Edward I., and his successors, as to an inquiry that may be followed with ease, instruction, and delight.¹ This account of our laws at the close of Henry II.'s reign will be divided into the rights of persons, the rights of things, and the proceedings of courts. We shall begin with the first.

---

dained that "because at such duels happen many mischances, that each of them (the combatants) take an oath that he beareth no deadly hatred against the other, but only that he endeavoreth with him in love to try his strength in those common places of lists and duels, that he might the better learn him to defend himself against his enemies; and therefore such mischances are not supposed to be felony, nor have the coroners to do with such mischances which happen in such common meetings, where there is no intent to commit felony" (*Ibid.*). This is a piece of law applicable at the present day to the case of parties fencing with buttoned foils, etc., and one of them accidentally killing the other; but otherwise of a real duel, where each does intend to strike or to fire, for to strike or fire with a deadly weapon is felony, as the intent to kill or wound is implied from the act. It may here be mentioned that it appears plainly from the *Mirror*, and the manner in which passages speaking of juries in criminal cases are mixed up with passages obviously at least as ancient as this period, that trial by jury in criminal cases was now common. With regard to civil cases, there is a passage fitly inserted here as illustrative of what the law of procedure was previous to the work of Glanville, "An assize in one case is nothing more than a session of the justice; in another case it is an ordinance of certainty, where nothing could be more or less than right. For the great evils which were used to be procured in witnessing, and the great delays which were in the examinations, exceptions, and attestations, Ranulf de Glanville ordained this certain assize (of writ of right) that recognitions should be sworn by twelve jurors of the next neighbors, and so this establishment was called assize" (c. 2, s. 25).

The people, as among the Saxons, were divided into freemen and slaves, though the latter assumed, under the Norman polity, a new appellation, and were called *villani*, or *villeins* (a).

(a) It has been already pointed out that the author was in error in supposing that the villeins ever were slaves. He confounded the "theows" (or thralls), who were slaves, with the "ceorls" (or churls), who were not. It was the latter — the "coloni" of the Roman law, and so called in the Latin version of the Saxon laws — who were the originals of the "villeins" or "villani" under the Normans, though it is certain that in the course of time, and by force of custom, the thralls were raised to the position of villeins, and many of the villeins became in like manner copyholders or tenants in socage, or freeholders; and, on the other hand, the thralls thus raised to the rank of villeins were naturally put to the viler and baser kind of service, as, for instance, the carrying and spreading of dung — the case put by Littleton in his chapter on the subject — and thus by degrees the word villein acquired a lower sense and meaning, as the original villeins became copyholders. It has already been seen that villeins were considered copyholders, and are so called in the *Mirror*, where it is said that the long tenure of copyhold land does not make the freeman a villein (c. iii., s. 2); and it is said elsewhere in that ancient work, "It is an abuse that it is said that villenage is not a freehold, for a villein and a slave are not all one, either in name or signification, as every freeman may hold land in villenage to him and his heirs, performing the services" (c. 5). And again, it is an abuse to hold villeins for slaves, and this abuse causeth great distinction of poor people (*Ibid.*). Yet elsewhere in the same chapter it is said to be an abuse that villeins were deemed freemen, or admitted into frankpledge as freemen (*Ibid.*). It is evident that there were two orders of villeins — the one personally so, from being in the position of feudal serfs, probably from having been slaves, and therefore serfs by birth, and their issue equally so; and tenants in villenage, who might be of this lower class, or might be of a better class, according to the nature of their services. If the services were vile and base, as to spread dung, they were of a lower order, and probably would be serfs, though still not slaves, and not necessarily even serfs, for freemen might be tenants in villenage if they chose to be so. If the services were of a higher nature, as to plough or sow the land, then they were still tenants in villenage, though not serfs or villeins, and by degrees this class became by custom either copyholders or freeholders. The only distinction between those classes, the service of both being to plough and sow, as Littleton shows in his chapter on tenancy in socage, or freehold tenure, was, that in the latter case this sort of service was converted by custom into certainty, and thus gave by customary right or implied grant, if not by actual grant, a freehold; whereas in the other — the copyhold tenure — the service, though not base, was still uncertain in its nature; so that the land was still held by custom according to the will of the lord. As, however, the tenant had a right to his tenement, rendering the service, which by degrees got changed into a money fine or alienation, practically the tenancy, even in the case of copyholds, became legally secure, subject to the liability to such fines; and, as to the socage tenure, that was by degrees converted either into a money rent or a money fine, and thus the tenants who held on plough service became converted into copyholders or freeholders. The villeins, however, whose services were base and vile, still continued for a long time in a state of transition, slowly rising by degrees to the position of husbandry tenants of manors, or continuing in their low and servile condition, and this occa-

Of villeins, those were called *nativi* who were such *à nativitate*, as when one was descended from a father and mother who were both villeins *à nativitate* (a). If a freeman married a woman who was born a villein, and so held an estate in villenage, in her right, as long as he was bound to the villein services due on account of such tenure, he lost, *ipso facto*, his *lex terræ*, as a villein *à nativitate* (b). If children were born

---

sioned the uncertitude as to the real *status* of a villein or a tenant in villenage. The substantial distinction, however, was, that the tenant in villenage might or might not be a villein, and that a villein was so at this period by birth (because there had been no new conquest, and no fresh creation of thralls or villeins since the Norman), and on the same principle their issue also were villeins. In the one class the villenage was personal, though still only predial; in the other, it was merely a character of tenure.

(a) As already shown, at this period there could be no villeins who were not nativi; for villenage was necessarily a personal *status*, whereas *tenure* in villenage was a mere kind of tenure. And thus, in the *Mirror*, it is said that, in an action of villenage the man might say that the services he had rendered, and which were relied on as a proof of villenage, were for the services of villein-land he held, and not by service of blood (c. iii., s. 23). There is not a more interesting branch of the history of the law than that which relates to the gradual emancipation of the slaves and of the villeins. No statutes were passed to effect either; both were the results of judicial decisions. As regards both classes, the courts, it is clear, threw the onus of proof upon the man who claimed another as his slave or serf; and, on the other hand, held any act on the part of the lord which looked like a recognition of freedom, to be evidence of emancipation; the result of which was, that even by the time of the *Mirror*, which was not later than the reign of Edward I., villenage, as a personal estate, was, it is manifest, dying out, though it remained much longer as a character or kind of tenure. The author omitted to notice this indirect means of emancipation, though its effect must have been more powerful than any other. Thus, for instance, the *Mirror* says, that if a man could show a free stock of his ancestors, he would be accounted a freeman, although his father, mother, brother, and cousins, and all his parentage, acknowledged themselves to be the plaintiff's villeins, and testified the defendant to be a villein born: about as powerful an exertion of the principle of presumption in favor of liberty as it is possible to imagine. And it is a most interesting illustration of the efficacy of judicial decisions as a means of modifying the law, and the salutary and certain effect of such judicial means. The *Mirror* states that a villein could be emancipated if his lord suffered him to answer, without him, in a personal action, or to sit as juror among freemen, or by proof of a free ancestor at any period, however remote (for, as Littleton says, a villein could only be by prescription, on the ground that his ancestors had been so time out of mind), also, if the villein departed out of the manor, and was not retaken within a year; or if he were allowed to be a suitor in another court than that of his lord: and so, as it is obvious that the acts or defaults of the lords, which had the effect of emancipating their villeins, were so numerous, that villenage, as a personal state, must have very rapidly disappeared, especially when, in Magna Charta, there was a distinct recognition that a villein was capable of property (*vide post*, c. iv.).

(b) According to Glanville, it was the same where the father was free if

from a father who was *nativus* to one lord, and a mother who was *nativa* to another lord, such children were to be divided proportionately between the two lords[1] (a).

A villein might obtain his freedom in several different ways. The lord might quit-claim him from him and his heirs forever, or might give or sell him to some one, in order to be made free, though it should be observed that a villein could not purchase his freedom with his own money; for he might in such case, notwithstanding the supposed purchase, be claimed as a villein by his lord; for all the goods and chattels of one who was a *nativus* were understood to be in the power of his lord, so as that he could have no money which could be called his own to lay out in a redemption of his villenage (b). However, if some stranger had bought his freedom for him, the

---

the mother was villein-born, or if the father was villein-born though the mother was free. This was contrary to the civil or canon law, under which the maxim was, that the issue followed the mother; and there is a discussion in Fortescue's treatise, *De Laudibus Legum Angliæ*, upon this point, in which the chancellor defends the rule of the common law. That the civil law was right will be seen at once, when it is observed that, from the common law rule (as our author, quoting Glanville, goes on to state), this monstrous result followed, that if the mother was on one manor, and the father was a villein on another, the children were divided between the two lords, as Lord Littleton observed, like cattle. This monstrous consequence did not occur to the chancellor when he was vehemently maintaining the common law, which, wherever it deviated from the civil law, lapsed into barbarism.

(a) The reason of this was, that the woman was a *villein born*, in a personal state of villenage, and he held in her right; and therefore, during her life, lost his *status* of completed freedom; that is, his civil rights, as a freeman, to sit on juries, vote, etc. Lord Littleton, no doubt, intended to convey this when he rendered the meaning thus: "That if a freeman married a woman born in villenage, and *who actually lived in that state*, he thereby lost the legal rights of a freeman, and was considered as a villein by birth, during the lifetime of his wife, on account of her villenage" (and he refers to Bracton, lib. 5). In Britton's time, the wife was enfranchised during the coverture, in such a case (78).

(b) The author has omitted to notice another, and a very efficacious means of emancipation, by a grant of freehold land from the lord. "Villeins become freemen if their lords grant or give unto them any free estate of inheritance to descend to their heirs" (*Mirror*, c. i., s. 28). And be it observed, that mere *possession* and receipt of the profits would be evidence of such a gift; which, it will be remembered, might be by feoffment; and it is also to be remembered, that the rendering of services, of socage or plough service, would be no proof of villenage; for, as Littleton points out, that was the nature of common freehold tenure; nor, at all events, if the socage service rendered was *certain*, would it be any proof of villenage; for it might be tenure in socage, and that would be a *freehold* tenure. The number of villeins who thus obtained their freedom must have been immense.

[1] Glanv., lib. 5, c. 6.

villein might maintain such purchased freedom against his lord; for it was a rule, that where any one quit-claimed a villein *nativus* from him and his heirs, or sold him to some stranger, the party who had so obtained his freedom, if he could establish it by a charter, or some other legal proof, might defend himself against any claims of his lord and his heirs; he might defend his freedom in court by duel, if any one called it in question, and he had a proper witness who heard and saw the manumission. But though a man could make his villein *nativus* free, as far as concerned *his* claim and that of his heirs, he could not put him in a condition to be considered as such by others; for if such a freed man was produced in court against a stranger to deraign a cause (that is, to be the champion to prove the matter in question) or to make his law,[1] or law-wager, as it has since been called, and it was objected to him that he was born in villenage, the objection was held a just cause to disqualify him for those judicial acts; nor could the original stain, says Glanville, be obliterated, though he had since been made a knight. Again, a villein *à nativitate* would become *ipso facto* free, if he had remained a year and a day in any privileged town (a), and was received into their *gylda* (or guild, as it has since been called) as a citizen of the place.[2]

Nothing is said by Glanville (b) concerning the differ-

. (a) This was taken from a law of the Conqueror: "Si servi permanserint sine calumnia per annum et diem in civitatibus nostris vel in burgis in muro vallatis, vel in castris nostris, a die illa liberi efficientur, et liberi a jugo servitutis suæ sint in perpetuum" (*Leg. Will.*, 66). By privileged town, in the text, Lord Littleton thought was meant a town that had franchises by prescription or charter; and this law, he truly observes, "shows the high regard for the law of such corporations, and also a desire to favor enfranchisement as much as the settled rules of property would permit" (*Hist. Hen. II.*, vol. iii., p. 191).

(b) Our author, it will be observed, follows Glanville implicitly, and simply incorporates Glanville's work with his own. It did not fall within the compass of Glanville's work to enter into the distinction of ranks or orders, because he dealt only with the proceedings in the *curia regis;* but there was light to be derived from other sources on the subject, as the *Mirror* and the laws of Henry I., which represent what the body of the law was during the whole of this period, although, no doubt, in a constant course of progression and of development. It is in this, the main element of history, our author is deficient. As regards the question of ranks and grades of the people, the fundamental distinction was between free and servile; and this was most important, and was closely connected with the tenure of land,

[1] *Legem facere.*   [2] Glanv., lib. 5, c. 5.

ent ranks of freemen; we shall therefore proceed to the next object of consideration, which is, the right of property claimed by individuals under various titles and circumstances, as *dos*, or dower, belonging to a widow, *maritagium*, and the like; after which we shall speak more particularly about succession to lands, and the nature of tenures, as the law stood in the reign of Henry II.

Dower.

The term *dos*, or dower, had two senses. In the common and usual sense, it signified that property which a freeman gave to his wife *ad ostium ecclesiæ*, at the time of the espousals (*a*). We shall first speak

---

from which resulted consequences of great importance; for it resulted that, by a change in the tenure of a man's lands, his personal condition might be changed, which would affect his whole *status* and position, and not merely his social position, but his legal rights; for a villein could not sit in the court of the hundred, or the county, nor upon a jury, or a court-leet, nor enjoy any of the legal privileges of freemen. Hence, in the laws of Henry I., it is said that only freeholders could sit in the courts: " Villani vero, vel cotseti, vel qui sunt viles et inopes personæ, non sunt inter regnum judices numerandi, nec in hundreto vel in comitatu" (c. xxix.). So, in the *Mirror* it is said, that villeins cannot be jurors, etc.; and it is put as an abuse that villeins should be in "frankpledges," or pledges of freemen, or that a man should be summoned (*i. e.*, to the courts, or on a jury), who was not a freeholder (c. v., s. 1). In those times, in short, a *liber homo*, or freeman, meant a freeholder; and a man who was not a freeholder was not deemed a freeman, and the two terms were, as in the passage just cited, used as synonymous. But then, on the other hand, it was deemed an abuse to treat villeins as slaves, and an error to think that all who held land in villenage must be villeins. Freemen might hold land in villenage, having freehold land besides; but a man who could *not* hold land for himself was a villein. No villeins, or any who were not freeholders, could be summoned or be summoners (c. ii., s. 29); but, then, villeins became freemen if they became freeholders, and though they could not acquire freehold land from any but their lords, their very incapacity being that they could not, except from their lords, acquire freehold property, yet, if their lords gave them any estate of inheritance, or accepted their homage, they became free. And so, if their lords allowed them to be sworn as jurors, or in the county court, or to remain away from their manors for a year — in these, and many such cases, the villeins became free. The result was, that there was a constant process of change going on in society, men becoming free who were before servile, and thus gaining the position and privileges of freemen.

(*a*) This is all a translation of Glanville. The other sense in which the word is used, he afterwards explains to be that in which it was used by the Romans, as the endowment given to the man with a woman (vol. vii.), which corresponds, he says, with what is called *maritagium*, or marriage-hood, as to which our author proceeds afterwards to translate him. It may be convenient here to recite what is said in the *Mirror* on the subject of dower, in the ancient sense: —" It was ordained that every one might endow his wife, *ad ostium ecclesiæ*, without the consent of his heirs, though widows, if they married without the consent of their lords, would lose their dowries." It is to be observed, that it is further stated in the *Mirror*, that "knights' lands came

of *dos* in this sense of it. When a person endowed his wife, he either named the dower specially, or did not. If he did not name it specially, the dower was understood, by law, to be the third part of the husband's *liberum tenementum;* for the rule was, that a reasonable dower of a woman should be a third part of her husband's freehold which he had at the time of the espousals, and was seized of in demesne. If he named the dower specially, and it amounted to more than the third, such special dower was not allowed, but it was to be admeasured to a fair third; for, though the law permitted a man to give less than a third in dower, it would not suffer him to give more.[1]

If a man had but a small freehold at the time of the espousals when he endowed his wife, he might afterwards augment it to a third part, out of purchases he had made since; but if there had been no provisional mention of new purchases at the time of such assignment of dower, although the husband had then but a small portion of freehold, and had made great acquisitions since, the widow could not claim more than a third part of the land he had at the time of the espousals. In like manner, if a person had no land, and endowed his wife with chattels (*a*), money, or other things, and afterwards made great acquisitions in land, she could not claim any dower in such acquisitions; for it was a general rule, that where dower was specially assigned to a woman *ad ostium ecclesiæ*, she could not demand more than what was then and there assigned.[2]

---

to the eldest son, and that common freehold land was divisible among the right heirs, and that no one might alien more than the fourth part of his inheritance, without the consent of his heirs, and that none might alien his land acquired by purchase away from his heirs, if the power of alienation were not given" (c. i.). It may be doubted whether it was not so unless it were taken away.

(*a*) This is confirmed in Fleta (lib. v., c. 23); but it is added, that the dower, in such case, could only be claimable as far as the *chattels* of the deceased extended (and clear of his debts)—that is, the realty would not be liable to make good the deficiency. Hence, at common law, this kind of dower became obsolete, and in the reign of Henry IV. it was denied to be allowable (*Year-Book*, 7 *Hen. IV.*, f. 13). That is only an illustration of the ignorance of our common law judges, who then had ceased to be students of the civil law, and merely were guided by the fluctuating customs of the time. In later times courts of equity, in this as upon so many other subjects, repaired the deficiency of law; and in our own day jointures have practically superseded dowers.

[1] Glanv., lib. 6, c. 1.   [2] Ibid., c. 2.

A woman could make no disposal of her dower during her husband's life; but as a wife was considered *in potestate viri*, it was thought proper that her dower and the rest of her property should be as completely in his power to dispose of them; and therefore every married man, in his lifetime, might give, or sell, or alien in any way whatsoever, his wife's dower: and the wife was obliged to conform in this, as in all other instances, to his will. It is, however, laid down by Glanville, that this assent might be withheld; and if, notwithstanding this solemn declaration of her dissent[1] and disapprobation, her dower was sold, she might claim it at law after her husband's death; and upon proof of her dissent, she could recover it against the purchaser.[2] Besides, it must be remarked, that the heir in such case was bound to deliver to the widow the specific dower assigned her, if he could; and if he could not procure the identical land, he was to give her a reasonable *excambium*, as it was called, or recompense in value; and if he delivered her the land that was sold, he was in like manner bound to give a recompense to the purchaser.[3] If the assignment at the church-door was in these words, "*Do tibi terram istam cum omnibus pertinentiis;*" and he had no appurtenances in his demesne at the time of the espousals, but he either recovered by judgment, or in some other lawful way acquired such appurtenances; the wife might, after his death, demand them in right of her dower.[4]

If there was no special assignment of dower, the widow was entitled, as we before said, to the third part of all the freehold which her husband had in demesne the day of the espousals, complete and undiminished, with its appurtenances, lands, tenements, and advowsons; so that, should there be only one church, and that should become vacant in the widow's lifetime, the heir could not present a parson without her consent. The capital messuage was always exempt from the claim of dower, and was to remain whole and undivided; nor were such lands to be brought into the division for dower, which other women held in dower upon a prior endowment. Again, if there

---

[1] The word used by Glanville is *contradicere*, which, in this and other places, he seems to use in a sense implying something more formal and solemn than a common dissent and disapprobation.
[2] Glanv., lib. 6, c. 3.   [3] Ibid., c. 13.   [4] Ibid., c. 12.

were two or more manors, the capital manor, like the capital messuage, was to be exempted, and the widow was to be satisfied with other lands. It was a rule, that the assignment of dower should not be delayed on account of the heir being within age.

If land was specially assigned for dower *ad ostium ecclesiæ*, and a church was afterwards built within the fee, the widow was to have the free presentation thereof, so as, upon a vacancy, to give it to a clerk, but not to a college, because that would be depriving the heir of his right forever; however, should the husband in his lifetime have presented a clerk, the presentee was to enjoy it during his life, though the presentation was made after the wife had been endowed of the land, and it might look like an anticipation and infringement of the profits and advantage to which she was entitled by her special assignment of dower. Yet, should the husband himself have given it to a religious house, as this would be an injury to the wife similar to that above stated respecting the heir, the church after his death was to be delivered back to the widow, that she might have free presentation to it; but after her death, and that of her clerk, the church would return back to the religious house to be possessed forever.

If a woman had been separated from her husband *ob aliquam sui corporis turpitudinem*, or on account of blood and consanguinity, she could not claim her dower; and yet, in both these cases the children of the marriage were considered as legitimate and inheritable to their father (a). Sometimes a son and heir married a woman *ex consensu patris*, and gave her in dower some part of his father's land, by the assignment of the father himself. Glanville states a doubt upon this, whether in this case, any more than in that of an assignment by the husband himself, the widow could demand more than the particular land assigned; and whether, upon the death of the husband

---

(a) It is stated in the *Mirror* that it was ordained that knights' fees should come to the eldest son by succession, and that socage lands should be divisible among the right heirs, and that none might alien but the fourth part of his inheritance, without the consent of his heirs, nor his lands acquired by grant, if the power of alienation were not given; though this seems a mistake, for the law had always been that it was alienable, unless there was a restriction upon alienation. But after the time of John, the socage lands went to the eldest son, unless there was a *custom* to divide the land; therefore the above passage must have been written prior to that reign.

before the father, she could recover the land, and the father be bound to warrant her in the possession of it.¹

Thus far of one sense of the word *dos*. It was understood differently in the Roman law, where it properly signified the portion which was given with the woman to her husband, which corresponds with what was commonly called in our law *maritagium*; but we shall defer saying anything of *maritagium* till we have considered the nature of alienation and descent with some other properties of land.

Respecting the alienation of land, the first consideration that presents itself is the indulgence allowed in favor of gifts in *maritagium* (a). Every freeman, says Glanville, might give part of his land with his daughter, or with any other woman, in *maritagium*, whether he had an heir or not, and whether his heir agree to it or not; nay, though he made that solemn declaration of his dissent, which we have just seen had the effect of rendering an alienation of dower ineffectual and void.² A person might give part of his freehold *in remunerationem servi sui* (b), or to a religious place in free alms, so that, should such donation be followed by seisin, the land would remain to the donee and his heirs forever, if an estate of that extent had been expressed by the donor; but if the gift was not followed by seisin, nothing could be recovered against the heir without his consent; for such an incomplete gift was considered by the law rather as a *nuda promissio* than a real donation. Thus, then, on the above occasions, any one might, in his lifetime, give a reasonable part of his land to whomsoever he pleased;

_{Alienation.}

(a) This *marriagehood* or *maritagium*, is what Littleton calls tenure, or frank-marriage, which, he avers, was by the common law, and by which a man, on the marriage of his daughter, gave to her husband land in fee simple (lib. iii., c. 2).

(b) This was the tenure of bishoprics and benefices:—"Potent etiam donatio in liberam eleemosinam; sicut ecclesiis, cathedralibus, conventualibus, parochialibus, viri, religiosi" (*Bracton*, lib. xxvii.). The reason, apparently, why Glanville, whom our author only translates and follows, mixed up the two subjects of gifts on marriage of a daughter with leases by last will, is apparently because, as had been the policy which allowed of gifts to children, *inter viros*, did not apply to bequests to strangers at the close of life, and especially *in articulo mortis*. Apparently there is not any connection between the subjects, because to the extent to which land was allowed to be given to children, *inter viros*, there would be less to bequeath to any one. And as gifts in frank-marriage would be, as Littleton says, for the advancement of the daughters, there could be no objection to them on any ground.

¹ Glanv., lib. 6, c. 17. ² Ibid., lib. 7, c. 1.

but the same permission was not granted to any one *in extremis*, lest men, wrought upon by a sudden impulse, at a time when they could not be supposed to have full possession of their reason, should make distributions of their inheritances highly detrimental to the interest and welfare of tenures. The presumption, therefore, of law in case of such gifts was that the party was insane, and that the act was the result of such insanity, and not of cool deliberation. However, according to Glanville, even a *gift* made *in ultima voluntate* was good, if assented to and confirmed by the heir.[1]

In the alienation of land some distinctions were made between *hæreditas* and *quæstus*, land descended as an *inheritance* and land acquired by *purchase*. If it was an inheritance he might, as was said, give it to any of the beforementioned purposes. But, on the other hand, if he had more sons than one who were *mulieratos*, that is, born in wedlock, he could not give any part of the inheritance to a younger son against the consent of the heir, for it might then happen, from the partiality often felt by parents towards their younger children, that, to enrich them, the eldest would be stripped of the inheritance. It was a question whether a person, having a lawful heir, might give part of the inheritance to a bastard son; for, if he could, a bastard would be in better condition than a younger son born in wedlock; and yet it should seem that the law allowed such donation to a bastard son.

* If the person who wanted to make a donation was possessed only of land by *purchase*, he might make a gift, but not of all his purchased land, for he was not, even in this case, allowed entirely to disinherit his son and heir; though if he had no heir, male or female, of his own body, he might give all his purchased lands forever; and if he gave seisin thereof in his lifetime, no remote heir could invalidate the gift. Thus a man, in some cases, might give away, in his lifetime, all the land which he had himself purchased, but not, as in the civil law, make such donee his heir, for, says Glanville, *solus Deus hæredem facere potest, non homo.*

If a man had lands both by inheritance and by purchase, then he might give all his purchased land to whomsoever

---

[1] Glanv., lib. 7, c. 1.

he pleased, and afterwards might dispose of his lands by inheritance, in a reasonable way, as before stated. If a person had lands in free socage, and had more sons than one, who by law should inherit by equal portions, the father could not give to one of them, either out of lands purchased or inherited, more than that reasonable part which would belong to him by descent of his father's inheritance: but the father might give him his share.

We may here observe, that many questions of law arose, owing to certain consequences which sometimes resulted from this liberality of fathers towards their children. First, suppose a knight, or freeman, having four or more sons, all born of one mother, gave to his second son, to him and his heirs, a certain reasonable part of his inheritance, with the consent of the eldest son and heir (to avoid all objections to the gift), and seisin was had thereof by the son, who received the profits during his life, and died in such seisin, leaving behind him his father and all his brothers alive; there was a great doubt among lawyers, in Glanville's time, who was the person by law entitled to succeed. The father contended, he was to retain to himself the seisin of his deceased son, thinking nothing more reasonable than that the land which was disposed of by his donation, should revert again to him. To this it might be answered by the eldest son, that the father's claim could not be supported; for it was a rule of law, *quòd nemo ejusdem tenementi simul potest esse hæres et dominus*,[1] that no one could be both heir and lord of the same land: and by the force of the same rule, the third son would deny that the land could revert to the eldest; for as he was heir to the whole inheritance, he could not, as before said, be at once heir and lord; for he would become lord of the whole inheritance upon the death of his father, and therefore stood very nearly in the predicament in which we just stated the father himself to be. Thus, as by law the land could not remain with him, there was no reason, says

Nemo potest esse hæres et dominus.

---

[1] In the times of Glanville and Bracton, the reservation of services might be made either to the feoffor, or to the lord of whom the feoffor held; they seem more commonly to have been made in the former manner: thus every such new feoffment in fee made a new tenure, and of course created a new manor; and so the law continued till stat. *quia emptores*, 18 *Edw. I.*, required feoffments in fee to be made with reservation of the services to the chief lord.

Glanville, why he should recover it; and therefore, by the same reasoning it appeared to Glanville that the third son was to exclude all the other claimants.

A like doubt arose, when a brother gave to his younger brother and his heirs a part of his land, and the younger brother died without heirs of his body; upon which the elder took the land into his hands, as being vacant and within his fee, against whom his own two sons prayed an assize of the death of their uncle; in which plea the eldest son might plead against the father, and the younger son against his elder brother, as before mentioned. And here the law is stated by Glanville to be this: that the father could not by any means retain the land, because he could not *simul hæres esse dominus;* nor could it revert to the donor, with the homage necessarily incident to it, if the donee had any heir, either of his body or more remote. Again, land thus given, like other inheritances, naturally descended to the heir, but never ascended: from all of which it followed, that the plea as between the father and eldest son was at an end, as having no question in it; but that between the eldest and younger son went on, as before stated. And in this last case the king's court had taken it upon it to determine *ex æquitate*, that the land so given should remain to the eldest son (particularly if he had no other fee) to hold till the paternal inheritance descended upon him; for while he was not yet lord of his paternal inheritance, the rule *quòd nemo ejusdem tenementi simul potest hæres esse et dominus*, could not be said to stand in the way. But then it might be asked, whether, when he became by succession *lord* of that part of the inheritance, he was not *heir* also of it, as well as of the rest of the inheritance, and then fell within the meaning of that rule? To this Glanville answers, that it was a thing not at first certain, whether the eldest son would be the heir, or not; for should the father die first, he most undoubtedly would be so; and then he would cease to be lawful owner of the land he had acquired by succession from the uncle, and it would revert to the younger son as right heir; yet if, on the other hand, the eldest son die first, then it was plain he was to be the heir of the father; and therefore these two requisites of this rule. namely, the *jus hæreditarium* and *dominium*, did not concur in the same person. Such is the reasoning of Glanville upon this curious point, in the law of descent, as understood in his time.[1]

There are two observations to be made respecting gifts of land, and then we shall proceed to consider the law of descent more fully. One is, that bishops and abbots, whose baronies were held by the eleemosynary gift of the king and his ancestors, could not make gifts of any part of their demesnes without the assent and confirmation of the king:[2] the other is, that the heirs of a donor were bound to warrant to the donee and his heirs the donation, and the thing thereby given.[3]

Having incidentally alluded to some rules which governed the descent of lands, it will now be proper to treat of the law of succession more at large. They divided heirs into those they called *proximi*, and those they considered as *remotiores*. *Proximi* were those begotten from the body, as sons and daughters: upon the failure of these, the *remotiores* were called in, as the *nepos* or *neptis*, the grandson or granddaughter, and so on, descending in a right line *in infinitum;* then the brother and sister, and their descendants; then the *avunculus*,[4] or uncle, as well on the part of the father as of the mother; and in like manner the *matertera*, or aunt; and their descendants. When therefore a person died leaving an inheritance, and having one son, it was a settled thing that the son succeeded to the whole. If he left more sons than one, then there was a difference between the case of *a knight;* that is, a tenant by *fœdum militare*, or knight's service; and a *liber sokemannus*, or *free sokeman.* If he was a knight or tenant by military service, then, according to the law of England, the eldest son succeeded to the father *in totum;* and none of his brothers had any claim whatsoever. But if he was a free sokeman, and possessed of socage-land that had been anciently divisible, then the inheritance was divided among all the sons by equal parts; saving always to the eldest son, as a mark of distinction, the capital messuage ; so, however, as he made a proportionate satisfaction to the other brothers on

Of descent.

---

[1] Glanv., lib. 7, c. 1.   [2] Ibid.   [3] Ibid., c. 2.
[4] This is the expression used by Glanville; which is not strictly correct; *avunculus* and *matertera* being the uncle and aunt on the mother's side; as the uncle on the father's side was *patruus*. Indeed our author, after all, passes over this in a loose way.

that account. But if the land was not anciently divisible, then it was the custom, in some places, for the eldest son to take the whole inheritance; in some, the youngest son.

If a person left only a daughter, then what we have said of a son held good with regard to her. And it was a general rule, whether the father was a knight or a sokeman, that where there were more daughters than one, the inheritance should be divided among them; saving, however (as in the case of the son), the capital messuage to the eldest daughter. Where the inheritance was thus divisible between brothers or sisters, if one of them died without heirs of the body, the share of the party deceased was divided amongst the survivors. It was a rule, in these divisible inheritances, that the husband of the eldest daughter should do homage to the chief lord for the whole fee; the other daughters or their husbands being bound to do their services to the chief lord by the hand of the eldest, or her husband; and not to do homage or fealty to the husband of the eldest: nor were their heirs in the first or second descent; but those in the third descent from the younger daughters were bound by the law of the realm to do homage and pay a reasonable relief to the heir of the eldest daughter for their tenement. It was a rule, that no husbands should give away their wives' inheritance, or any part thereof, without the assent of their heirs: nor could they release any right that might belong to their heirs.

We have said before, that if a person had a son and daughter, or daughters, the son succeeded *in totum;* and therefore, if a man had more wives than one, and had daughters from two, and at length a son from a third, this son would alone take the whole inheritance of his father; for it was a general rule, that a woman could never take part of an inheritance with a man,[1] unless, perhaps, by the particular and ancient customs of some cities or towns: yet if a man had more wives than one, and had daughters from each, they all succeeded alike to the inheritance, the same as if they had been born of the same mother.

Suppose a man died without leaving a son or a daughter,

---

[1] Glanville's words are, *mulier nunquam cum masculo partem capit in hæreditate aliqud.*

but had grandchildren, they succeeded in like manner as children; those in the right line being always preferred to those in the transverse. However, we have before seen,[1] that when a man left a younger son, and a grandson of his eldest son, who was dead, there was great difficulty in determining the succession in such case between the son and grandson. Some thought the younger son was more properly the right heir than the grandson; for the eldest son not having lived till he became heir, the younger son, by outliving both his brother and father, ought properly to be the father's successor. It seemed to others that the grandson should be preferred to the uncle; for as he was heir of the body of the eldest son, and, if he had lived, would have had all his father's rights, he, it was said, should more properly succeed in the place of his father: and so Glanville thought, provided the eldest son had not been *foris-familiated* by the grandfather. A son was said to be foris-familiated, if his father assigned him part of his land, and gave him seisin thereof, and did this at the request, or with the free consent of the son himself, who expressed himself satisfied with such portion; and it was clear law, that in such case the heirs of the son could not demand as against their uncle, or any one else, any more of the inheritance of the grandfather than what was so assigned to their father; though the father himself, had he survived the grandfather, might notwithstanding have claimed more. Where it happened, however, that the eldest son had in his father's lifetime done homage to the chief lord of the fee for his father's inheritance, as was not unfrequently the case, and died before his father, there it was held beyond question, that the son of such eldest son should be preferred to the uncle, although there had been a foris-familiation.

Such was the law of descent in Glanville's time; and this will very properly be followed by a short view of some of the duties incumbent on heirs; with the incidents of inheritance and succession; such as testaments, wardship, bastardy, and escheat.

Heirs, says Glanville, were bound to observe the testaments made by their fathers, or their other ancestors to whom they were heirs, and to pay

Of testaments.

---

[1] *Vide ante,* 361.

all their debts (a). For every freeman, not encumbered with debts beyond the amount of his effects, might, on his death-bed, make a reasonable division of his property, by will; so as he complied with the customs of the place where he lived; one of which commonly was, first, to remember his lord by his best and principal chattel; then the church; and after these, he might dispose of the remainder as he pleased. However the customs of particular places might lay this restriction upon wills, no person was bound, by the general law of the kingdom, to leave anything by will to any particular person, but was at liberty to act as he pleased; it being a rule of law that *ultima voluntas esset libera*. A woman who was *sui juris* might make a will; but if she was married, she could do nothing of this sort without her husband's authority, as it would be making a will of his goods. But Glanville thought it would be a proper testimony of affection and tenderness, for a husband to give to his wife *rationabilem divisam*, that is, a third part of his effects; this being what she would be entitled to, if she had survived him; and it seems that it was not unfrequent for husbands to give a sort of property to their wives in this third part, even during the coverture.

The passage in Glanville from which this and the following account of testaments is taken, throws great obscurity upon the subject, and lays a foundation for the doubt that long divided lawyers, and is not yet settled, respecting the power of making wills of chattels, at common law. After having expressly laid down, that by the general law of the kingdom no person was bound to leave anything by will to any particular person, and that the third part left to the wife was dictated rather by a moral than legal obligation, he goes on in the following remarkable words: "When a person," says he, "is about to make his will, if he has more than enough to pay his debts, then all his movables shall be divided into three equal parts; of which one shall go to the heir, another to the wife; the third be reserved to himself, over which he

---

(a) The author, it is to be again observed, merely follows and translates Glanville (lib. vii., c. 5). It is to be observed, also here, that the author has omitted to explain that the *heirs* inherited chattels as well as lands as late as the time of Hen. II., and that the law was altered some time afterwards (Selden's *Title of Honor*, p. 2, c. 5, s. 21).

has the power of disposal as he pleases; if he dies without leaving a wife, a half is to be reserved to the testator" (a).[1] Thus far respecting the law of testaments for the disposition of movables; to which he adds, conformably with what we have before shown, that an inheritance could not be given by last will.[2]

A testament ought to be made in the presence of two or more lawful men, either clergy or lay, being such persons as might afterwards become proper witnesses thereto. The executors of a testament were such persons as the testator chose to appoint to undertake the charge of it. If the testator appointed none, the *propinqui et consanguinei*, by which were meant, as may be supposed, the nearest of kin to the deceased, might interpose; and if there was any one, whether the heir or a stranger, who detained any effects of the deceased, such executors or next of kin might have the following writ directed to the sheriff, to cause a reasonable division of the effects to be made: *Rex vicecomiti salutem ; præcipi tibi quòd justè et sine dilatione facias stare rationabilem divisam N. sicut rationabiliter monstrari poterit quòd eam fecerit, et quòd ipsa stare debeat*, etc.[3] If the person, summoned by authority of this writ, said anything against the validity of the testament; that it was not properly made, or that the thing demanded was not bequeathed by it; such inquiry was to be heard and determined in the court Christian; for all pleas of testaments, says Glanville, belong to the ecclesiastical judge, and are there decided upon by the testimony of those who were present at the making of the will (b).[4]

(a) This is in accordance with the custom of gavelkind, which is a relic of the old common law or custom of the Britons and Saxons. "Let the goods of gavelkind persons," says the Custumal of Kent, "be divided into three parts, after the funeral and the debts paid, if there be lawful issue in life, so that the dead have one part, and the lawful sons and daughters another, and the wife the third; and if there be no lawful issue in life, let the dead have one half and the wife the other half" (*Robinson on Gavelkind*, p. 287). Hale also recognizes the doctrine in the text, which, it will be seen, is in accordance with the laws of the Saxons (*vide ante*). It is true that Bracton speaks of the custom of London as leaving a freeman at liberty to bequeath his property as he pleased, and Lord Coke misunderstood this as applying generally; but in that he was in error (*Bracton*, book i.).

(b) We learn from this that the maxim had already become established which we find afterwards in Bracton, that pleas of freeholds could not be en-

[1] The progress of this doctrine, and the discussions upon it, will be related in the proper place.
[2] Glan., lib. 7, c. 5.   [3] Ibid., c. 6, 7.   [4] Ibid., c. 8.

If a person was incumbered with debts, he could not make any disposition of his effects (except it was for payment of his debts) without the consent of the heir; but if there was anything remaining over and above the payment of his debts, that residue was to be divided into three parts, as above mentioned; and he might, says Glanville, make his will of the third part. Should the effects of the deceased not be sufficient to pay his debts, the heir was bound to make up the deficiency out of the inheritance which came to him; so that we see the reason why, under such circumstances, the heir's consent was necessary towards a will. It seems, however, that the heir was not bound to make up this deficiency, unless he was of age.[1]

Heirs were considered in different lights, according as they were of full age or not. An heir of full age might hold himself in possession of the inheritance immediately upon the death of the ancestor; and the lord, though he might take the fee together with the heir into his hands, was to do it with such moderation as not to cause any disseisin to the heir, for the heir might resist any violence, provided he was ready to pay his relief and do the other services. Where the heir to a tenant holding by military service was under age, he was to be in custody of his lord till he attained his full age, which, in such tenure, was when he had completed the twenty-first year. The son and heir of a sokeman was considered as of age when he had completed his fifteenth year; the son of a burgess, or one holding in burgage-tenure was esteemed of age, says Glanville, when he could count money and measure cloth, and do all his father's business with skill and readiness. The lord, when he had custody of the son and heir, and of his fee, had thereby, to a certain degree, the full disposal thereof;

Of wardship.

---

tertained without the king's writ. It was thus that the Conqueror sent down justiciaries by his writ to try cases as to freeholds in the county court, as in the case of the Archbishop of Canterbury. This was certainly an innovation, for the county court was originally the only jurisdiction for all cases. It is manifest that by the time of Glanville the above-mentioned maxim had become established. And so in Bracton it is stated that the sheriff exercised jurisdiction in many cases which did not belong to him *ex officio;* but that in such cases he acted, not as sheriff, but as *justiciarius Regis* (154). The importance of this principle can be easily understood; carried out, it effected a complete revolution in our judicature.

[1] Glanv., lib. 7, c. 8.

that is, he might, during the custody, present to churches, have the marriage of women, and take all other profits and incidents which belonged to the minor and his estate, the same as he might in his own, only he could make no alienation which would affect the inheritance. The heir was, in the meantime, to be maintained with a provision suitable to his estate; the debts of the deceased were to be paid in proportion to the estate and time it was in custody of the lord (a), who was not by such liens to be entirely deprived of his benefit by the custody; with that qualification, however, lords were bound *de jure* to answer for debts of the ancestor.

The lord also, as he had all emoluments belonging to the heir, was to act in all his concerns and prosecute all suits for recovery of his rights, where such suits were not delayed by the usual exception to the infancy of the party. But the lord was not bound to answer for the heir, neither upon a question of right or of seisin, except only in one case; and that was, where there had fallen to the heir, since his father's death, the custody of some minor; for then, if the minor came of age, and the inheritance was not delivered to him, he was entitled to have an assize and recognition *de morte antecessoris;* and in this case, as the recognition was not by law *to remain*, on account of the infancy of the heir, his lord was to answer for him. If a minor was appealed of felony he was to be attached by safe and sure pledges; but yet he was not bound to answer to the appeal till he was of age.[1] It was the duty of those who had the custody of heirs and their fees, to restore the inheritance to the heir in good condition, and also free from debts, in proportion, as was before said, to the size of the inheritance and to the time it was in custody.[2] If there was any doubt whether an heir was of age or not, yet still the lord had the custody of the heir

---

(a) What Glanville says is, that the lord is to discharge the debts, so far as the estate and the length of the custody will admit — that is, as far as the proceeds of the estate, deducting the expenses of maintenance, would admit of. The qualification here added by our author is without authority. The general doctrine of Glanville is confirmed by the *Mirror*. "Every guardian is answerable for three things — 1. That he maintain the infant sufficiently; 2. That he maintain his rights and inheritance without waste; 3. That he answer and give satisfaction of the trespasses done by the infant" (*Mirror*, c. 5, s. 1; *Bracton*, 87, a; *Reg. Mag.*, l. 2, c. 62; and *Le Grand Cust. Nor.*, 333).

[1] Glanv., lib. 7, c. 9. [2] Ibid.

and his estate until he was proved to be of age by lawful men of the vicinage, upon their oaths.

If an heir within age had more lords than one, the chief lord, that is, he to whom he owed allegiance for his first fee, was to have the preference of the custody; an heir, however, so circumstanced, was still to pay to the lords of his other fees their reliefs and other services. In the case of a holding of the king *in capite*, the custody belonged to the king completely and fully, whether the heir held of other lords or not, for the maxim was *dominus rex nulum habere potest parem, multò minùs superiorem.* But in burgage-tenure the king had not this preference to other lords. The king might commit to any one such custodies as belonged to him (*a*), and they were committed sometimes *pleno jure*, and sometimes not. In the latter case the committee was to render an account thereof at the exchequer; in the former case he might present to churches and do other acts, as he might in his own estate.[1]

This was the law concerning the custody of heirs in military tenure. The heirs of *sokemen*, upon the death of their ancestors, were, according to Glanville, to be in the custody of their *consanguinei propinqui*, which must mean, as in a former passage, the next of kin; with this qualification, that if the inheritance descended *ex parte patris*, the custody belonged to the descendants *ex parte matris;* and so *vice versâ*. For the opinion was, that the custody of a person should not, by law, belong to one who, standing near the succession, might be suspected of having views upon the inheritance.[2]

We shall next speak of the custody of *female heirs*. If a woman was a minor, she was to be in the custody of her lord till she became of full age

Marriage.

---

[a] (*a*) This is not said by Glanville, who only suggests it was done. "If the king should commit the custody to another, then the distinction will arise which is next adverted to. It appears, as Lord Littleton states, that the wardships of the crown were sold by Henry II., and mention is made, he says, of the practice, without any blame, in the charters of Henry III. and John" (*Hist. Hen. II. and III.*, f. 109). He, however, explains that, by his statement that the other lords did the same, and they were the promoters of the charters. There can be no doubt that it was a vicious and pernicious practice, entirely contrary to legal principle, for the office of guardian is essentially a matter of personal trust and confidence.

[1] Glanv., lib. 7, c. 10. —   [2] Ibid., c. 11.

(*a*), and then the lord was bound to find her a proper marriage. If there were more than one, he was to deliver to each her reasonable portion of the inheritance. If a woman was of full age, then also she was to be in the custody of her lord till she was married by his advice and disposal, for it was the law and custom of the realm that no woman who was heir to land should be married but by the disposal and assent of her lord (*b*); and this rule operated so far that if any one married his daughter, who was to be his heiress, without the assent of his lord, he was by strictness of law to be forever deprived of his inheritance; nor could he retain it but by the mercy and pleasure of the lord. Nevertheless, when such a person applied to the lord for license to marry his daughter, the lord was bound to give his consent or show some reasonable cause to the contrary; if not, the father might even proceed to marry her according to his own wish and inclination, without the lord's concurrence.

Upon this subject of marrying women, Glanville puts a case: Whether a woman possessed of land in dower might marry as she pleased, without the assent of her *warrantor*, that is, the heir of her husband; and whether by so doing she would lose her whole dower? Some thought she ought not to lose her dower, because such second husband was not by the law and custom of the land bound to do *homage* to the warrantor, but only a simple *fealty;* which was merely, in case the wife should die before the husband, to preserve the homage from being entirely lost, for want of some outward mark of tenure. But notwithstanding that, Glanville thought she was bound to obtain the assent of her warrantor, or lose her dower, unless she had other lands, either by *maritagium* or by inheritance; for then it was sufficient if she had the assent of the chief

---

(*a*) This was fourteen (*Bracton*, 86, b; *Year-Book*, 8 *Edw. IV.*, 7).

(*b*) This was, Glanville says, only lest he should be compelled to receive an enemy or improper person as tenant, *i. e.*, military tenant, for all this applied only to military tenures. Lord Littleton indeed thought the reason applied to all fiefs for which homage was done, as well as to those held by knight-service (*Hist. Hen. II. and III.*, 104); but it is conceived that it is not so. Henry I. in his charter promised that he would take nothing for his consent, nor withhold it, unless it were proposed to unite the ward to his enemy (*Leges Henrici Primi*, c. 2, s. 3). It appears plainly that this usage applied only to female heirs, though it was afterwards, abusively, extended to male wards; and even after Magna Charta, on a forced construction of the words, "Heredes mantentur sine disparagatione."

lord; and this was on account of the simple fealty only which the husband was bound to do to the lord. If the inheritance was held of more than one lord, it was sufficient to obtain the assent of the chief lord.[1]

If women, while in custody of their lords, did anything which was a cause of forfeiture (a), and this was made out against them in a lawful way, the offender lost her right to the inheritance, and her share accrued to the rest; but if they had all incurred a forfeiture, then the whole inheritance fell to the lord, as an *escheat*.

Widows were not to be again in custody of their warrantors, though, as has been already related, they were to have their assent before they married. Women were not to forfeit their inheritance on account of any incontinence; not that the maxim, *putagium hæreditatem non adimit*, meant this indemnity of women in case of incontinence, for that was to be understood of the consideration the law had of a son begotten under such circumstances, and born after lawful wedlock; who was thereby entitled to succeed to the inheritance as a lawful heir; according to another rule, *filius hæres legitimus est, quem nuptiæ demonstrant.*[2]

This brings us to consider the law of legitimacy. It was held, that no *bastardus*,[3] or bastard was a legitimate or lawful heir, nor any one not born in lawful wedlock. If any one claimed an inheritance as heir, and it was objected that he was not heir, because he was not born in lawful wedlock; then the plea ceased in

Of bastardy.

(a) "De corporibus suis forisfecerent;" that is, forfeited through incontinence. Lord Littleton observes "that this was a severe punishment for the frailty of a single woman, and without example in other laws; but it undoubtedly arose not so much from a rigorous sense of the heinousness of the fault, as from the notion of an advantage due to the lord from the marriage of his ward, which he probably might be deprived of by her being dishonored" (3 *Hist. Hen. II.*, 119). But a little consideration of the character of the Norman sovereigns may suggest the suspicion that this, which was obviously an indecent encroachment, and an oppressive and abusive exaction, was rather continued with the view of their profiting by the seduction of their wards, to rob them of their lands. Instances of conduct like this in their histories are not infrequent, and Mackintosh hints at it in the reign of John.

[1] Glanv., lib. 7, c. 12. [2] Ibid.
[3] In German *bastart;* from *bas*, says Spelman, which signifies *infimus*, and metaphorically *spurius, impurus;* and *start*, which signifies *ortus*, or *editus*. So we say in English *upstart;* as it were, *subito exortus. Vide* Splem. *voce* Bastardus.

the king's court, and it was commanded to the archbishop or bishop, whichsoever it might be, to make inquiry of the marriage, and signify to the king, or his justices, his judgment thereon; for which purpose there issued a writ to the following effect: *Rex episcopo salutem: Veniens coram me W. in curiâ meâ petit versus R. fratrem suum quartam partem fœdi unius militis in villâ, etc., sicut jus suum; et in quo idem R. jus non habet, ut W. dicit, eò quòd ipse bastardus sit, natus ante matrimonium matris ipsorum. Et quoniam ad curiam meam non spectat agnoscere de bastardiâ, eos ad vos mitto, mandans ut in curiâ christianitatis inde factatis quod ad vos speciat. Et cùm loquela illa debitum coram vobis finem sortita fuerit, mihi literis vestris significetis, quid inde coram vobis actum fuerit, etc.*[1]

Upon the subject of legitimacy, there was this curious question: If a person was born before his father married his mother, whether, after the marriage such child was to be considered as a lawful heir? And Glanville says, that though by the canons and Roman law (meaning a law of Justinian adopted in a constitution made in the time of Pope Alexander III. about thirty years before) such a child was a lawful heir; yet by the law and custom of this realm he was not to be received as an heir, to hold or claim any inheritance (a). The question, whether born before

---

(a) Lord Littleton observes upon this that it shows the entire independence of the law of England on the canon and civil law at this time (3 *Hist. Hen. II.*, p. 125). No one ever supposed that the Roman law, *proprio vigore*, bound this country; but, as Selden put it, Valet pro ratione non pro inducto jure. And the question is, whether the Roman law was not in this, as in every other instance in which ours departed from it, right. There can be no doubt that in this country, in which the law had been mainly customary, and the spirit of insular independence, or perhaps prejudice, arising from ignorance, was so strong; it was this spirit, rather than reason, which dictated an adherence to the national customs, often senseless, and vicious, and pernicious, and probably of very recent introduction. Thus it was that Henry II. talked of his "customs," which had simply risen up under the Conqueror and his sons, and were so bad that even one of them himself declared them bad (*Leges Henri Primi*, 1). And so it was with the custom that only those born in matrimony should inherit; as the Roman law was otherwise, and had been recognized here for centuries, there can be no doubt that our law had been in accordance with it, especially as it was so in the Grand Custumary of Normandy (c. 27). When, therefore, in the reign of Henry III. it was proposed to assimilate our law to that of Europe, the reply of the barons, "Nolumus quod noluit leges Angliæ mutari, quæ hucusque usitatæ sunt et approbatæ," a reply so much vaunted as a proof of patriotism; it was simply an evidence of pride, the result of prejudice, and prejudice, the result of

[1] Glanv., lib. 7, c. 13, 14.

or after marriage, we have seen, was examined before the ecclesiastical judge, whose judgment was to be reported to the king or his justices; but when the spiritual judge had certified the answer to that question, the king's court made use of it as it pleased, and denied or adjudged the inheritance in dispute to either party, according to its own rule of determination; so that the ecclesiastical court only answered whether the party was born before or after marriage; the king's court determined *who* was heir.[1]

As a bastard could have no heir but of his body, this gave occasion to a very particular question of inheritance and succession. If a person made a gift of land to a bastard, reserving a service or anything else, and received homage, and the bastard died in seisin of the land, without leaving any heir of his body, it was a doubt in Glanville's time, who was to succeed to the land; it being clearly held that the lord could not; though it was determined, that if a bastard died without a will, his goods went to his lord; and if he held of more than one, each was to take that which was found within his fee.[2]

It may be remarked here, that all the effects of an usurer, whether he made a will or not, belonged to the king: this was meant as a penalty upon usury, after the death of the party; for in his lifetime he could not be proceeded against criminally. Among other inquisitions which used to be made for the king, one used to be made of a person dying in this offence (or so it was called) by twelve lawful men of the vicinage, upon their oaths: and if it was proved, all the movables and chattels of the deceased usurer were taken for the king's use; his heir was disinherited; and the land reverted to the lord. If a person had been notoriously guilty of usury, but had desisted from the practice, and died a penitent, his property was not to be treated as the property of an usurer. The point therefore was, whether a man *died* an usurer; and only in such case could his effects be confiscated.[3]

Usurers.

To finish the subject of descent to heirs; it must be re-

---

ignorance. For that beyond all doubt the Roman law is the sounder is shown by modern law, as well as by ancient usage. The French code allows, under certain restrictions, the subsequent legitimation of children (*Code Nap.*, s. 331, 332).

[1] Glanv., lib. 7, c. 15.   [2] Ibid., c. 16.   [3] Ibid., c. 17.

marked that next after those we have mentioned, the *ultimus hæres*, if he could be so called, of every man was his lord: for when a person died without a certain heir,[1] the lord of the fee might, of right, take into his hands and retain the fee, whether such lord was the king or any other person. Nevertheless, should any one afterwards come and say he was the right heir, he might, either by the grace of the lord, or at least by the king's writ, be let in to sue for the inheritance, and make his claim out in court; yet in the meantime, the land remained in the lord's hands; it being a rule, that when a lord had any doubt about the true heir to his tenant, he might hold the land till that was made out in due form of law. This was like what we have seen was done, when there was a doubt whether an heir was of age or not; with this difference, that in this case the land, in the meantime, was considered as an escheat, which was to all intents and purposes the absolute property of the lord; in the other, it was not looked upon as his own, but only as *de custodiâ*.

{Of escheat.}

Lands reverted to the lord by escheat, not only on failure of heirs, but by various causes of *forfeiture*. If any one was convicted of felony, or confessed it in court, he lost his inheritance by the law of the land, and it went to his lord as an escheat. Where a person held of the king *in capite*, in such case, as well his land as his movables and chattels, wherever they were found, were taken for the king's use. Again, if an outlaw, or one convicted of felony, held of any one but the king, then also all his movables belonged to the king, and his land was to remain in the king's hands for a year; but at the expiration of that time, it was to revert to the lord of the fee; this, however, was *cum domorum subversione et arborum*

---

[1] This law of *ultimus hæres*, laid down so generally by Glanville, is said by himself, just before, not to take place where a bastard died without heirs of his body. The reason of this exception to the analogy of tenures does not appear. In cases of forfeiture where the goods even went to the king, yet the land escheated to the lord. We shall see, that in the time of Bracton, the land, in this case of bastardy, escheated to the lord, and so it does at this day.

It is worthy of remark, that in Scotland, where feudal rights were in general more regarded than in England, the lord has long been deprived of this casualty, and the king is considered as the *ultimus hæres* not only of the bastard, but in all cases of failure of heirs; upon the principle, *quod nullius est, cedit domino regi*. 2 Blackst., 249; Ersk. Prin., b. iii., tit. 10.

exterpatione, that is, according to the barbarous and unwise policy of those days, not till the king had first subverted all the houses, and extirpated all the trees thereon.

In short, when a judgment passed in court, that a man should be *exhæredatus*, his inheritance reverted to the lord of the fee, as an escheat. If any one was condemned for theft his movables and chattels went to the sheriff of the county; but the lord of the fee took the land without waiting the year, as in the former case, because theft was not an offence against the king's crown, as robbery and homicide were. When any one was regularly and legally outlawed, he forfeited his lands; and though he was afterwards restored by the king's pardon, neither he nor his heirs could, by reason of such pardon, recover the land once forfeited, against the lord; for notwithstanding the king remitted the pains of forfeiture and outlawry as far as regarded himself, he could not thereby infringe the rights of others.[1]

It was to illustrate the title of *maritagium* that we were at first led into this long digression about the law of descent, legitimacy, and escheat: to that we now return; and shall conclude what is to be said upon it, by speaking of the tenure by which a tenant *in maritagio* held his estate.

Maritagium was of two kinds: one was called *liberum* or free; the other *servitio obnoxium*, liable to the usual services. *Liberum maritagium* was when a freeman gave part of his land with a woman in marriage, quit and freed from him and his heirs of all service towards the chief lord. Land so given enjoyed this immunity as low down as to the third heir; and during that time no homage was to be done: but after the third heir was dead, the land became subject to its old services, and homage was again to be done for it. If land was given *in maritagium servitio obnoxium*, that is, with a reservation of the legal services; in that case, the husband of the woman and his heirs, down to the third, were to perform that service, but yet without doing any homage; but the third heir, says Glanville, was to do homage for the first time, and so were all his heirs for ever after; though, in case of *liberum maritagium*, we have

Maritagium.

---

[1] Glanv., lib. 7, c. 17.

seen that homage was not to be done till after the third heir was dead. In all these cases, however, where no homage was done, yet a fealty was to be performed by the woman and her heirs, either by solemn promise or by oath, almost in the same form and words in which homage was done.

When a man having land given him *in maritagium* with a woman, had by that woman an heir born, whether male or female, who was heard to cry within four walls, *clamantem et auditum infra quatuor parietes* (*a*), as they expressed it, and survived his wife; then, whether the heir lived or not, the *maritagium* remained to the husband during his life, and after his death reverted to the donor or his heirs: but if he had no heir of his wife, then the *maritagium* reverted to the donor or his heirs, immediately upon her death (*b*). And this was a sort of reason why homage was not usually received for these *maritagia*. For when land was given in any way, and homage was received for it, the effect of homage was such that the land could not, by law, return to the donor or his heirs; which would be contrary to the intention of these gifts *in maritagium*. If the woman who had land thus given *in maritagium* had survived her husband, and married a second, the law was the same as to his retaining the land in case he survived, whether the first husband left an heir or not.[1]

If land was to be claimed either by the wife or her

(*a*) The *Mirror* states that Henry I. ordained that if the husband survived the wife in such cases, and had issue, he should enjoy the land for life. This was what was called the "courtesy of England." It has long since been limited to life; and, on the other hand, the condition here mentioned of the child being heard to cry has long since been done away with, as it was only evidence of the child being born (*Littleton*, 29, f. 1). But settlements usually provide for such contingencies.

(*b*) Here we see the nature of trial by jury, originally as a trial by witnesses, and, therefore, by persons brought from the vicinage, in order that they might have knowledge of the matter. "Vicinetum" is derived from vicinus, and signifieth neighborhood, or place near at hand, or neighboring place. And the reason wherefore the jury must be of the neighborhood, is for that vicinus (facta vicina præ sumitur scire), (*Littleton*, 158). The writ to summon the jurors, therefore, on the same principle directed the sheriff to summon, "homines de vicineto qui melius veritatem sciunt," *vide post*. Therefore it was necessary that there should be a *venue* laid for every triable material fact, and the venue should be the vill; and it was necessary that there should be some hundredors on the jury, and the panel could be set aside for want of hundredors, until the act 4 Anne, c. 16, for amendment of the law. So tenacious is legal usage.

[1] Glanv., lib. 7, c. 18.

heir, as having been given *in maritagium*, there was a difference between such a claim when against the donor and his heirs, and when against a stranger. If it was against the donor and his heirs, then it might be in the election of the demandant to sue in the court Christian, or in the secular court. For questions of *maritagium* were considered as belonging to the ecclesiastical judge, if the demandant pleased to resort to him, on account of the mutual promises made by the man and woman at the time of the espousals. But if the suit was against a stranger, then it was to be determined in the lay court, in the same way as other suits about lay-fees. It must be observed, that such a suit, like a plea of dower, was not to be conducted without the presence of the warrantor; and as far as concerned the warrantor, everything was to be ordered as in an action for dower; all which will be made plain when we come to speak of that proceeding: only this must be remembered, that the third heir, after he had performed his homage, might go on with the suit without the authority of his warrantor.[1]

The subject of homage and relief deserves further consideration, and will properly enough follow what has just been said (*a*). Upon the death of the father or other ancestor, the lord of the fee was to receive the homage of the right heir whether he was of age or not, so as the heir was a male; for women could, by law, do no homage (*b*), though they sometimes used to

Homage.

(*a*) The reason of homage, says Spelman, was to preserve the memory of the tenure and of the duty of the tenant, by making every new tenant at his entry to recognize the interest of his lord, lest that the feud, being now hereditary, and new heirs succeeding to it, they might by little and little forget their duty, and subtracting these services, at last deny the tenure itself (Spelman, *Reliq.*, 34). Skene considers that homage especially concerned service in war (de verb signi ad voc homagium). For this reason he observes that consecrated bishops did no homage. This view is also adopted by Cowell, and applied to explain the absence of homage by women. The form of homage, "I become your man in life, and limb, and earthly worship," rather supports this view. It was, moreover, feudal; and feudality must have been military. And homage was only done for estates in fee-simple, for which reason it ceased when the feudal system became obsolete, and freehold lands became allodial. The only approach to it in leasehold lands is the fealty to the lessor's title.

(*b*) So Glanville says, but either it is a mistake, or the law had been altered, for in the reign of Edward III. women did do homage, whether single or married, for lands belonging to her, although the form was different. Littleton says, "If a woman sole shall make homage unto her lord, she

[1] Glanv., lib. 7, c. 18.

32*

do fealty; yet, when they are married, their husbands were to do homage for them, in cases where it was due for the fee they held. If a male heir was a minor, the lord could not have custody of the fee nor of the heir till he had received homage; it being a general rule, that a lord could demand no service, relief, or anything else from the heir, whether he was of age or not, till he had received homage for the fee in respect of which he claimed such relief or service; and this was on account of the protection the heir could claim of his lord after homage, but not before. A person might do homage to different lords for different fees; but one of these was to be the chief homage, and distinguished above the rest by being accompanied, says Glanville, with allegiance;[1] which was to be performed to that lord of whom the homager held his chief freehold.

Homage was to be done in this way: the person was to profess that " he became HOMO *domini sui*, the man of his lord, to bear him faith for the tenement in respect of which he did homage, to preserve his terrene honor in all things, saving only the faith he owed to the king and his heirs." From this it is clear that it would be a breach of faith and of homage for a vassal to do anything to the damage of the lord,[2] unless in his own defence or at the command of the king, when his lord had taken up arms against his sovereign lord the king; and, in general, it would be a breach of faith and of homage to do anything *ad exhæredationem domini sui, vel dedecus corporis sui*. If then several lords, to each of whom a tenant had done homage, should make war on each other, it was the tenant's duty to obey the commands of his chief lord and to go with him in person, if he required it, against any of

---

shall not say, 'I become your woman,' for that is not convenient for a woman to say, that she shall become the woman to any one, but only her husband when she is wedded. But she shall say, I make to you homage, to you shall be true and faithful, 'for the tenements I hold of you.'" And he also cites a case, in the reign of Edward III., in which a man and his wife did homage and fealty for lands of the wife's. "We do you homage, and faith to you shall bear, for the tenements which we hold of you," etc., the lord holding their hands jointly between his, and they afterwards kissing him, and, afterwards, the book (*Ibid.* ii., c. 1). Lord Littleton thinks that Glanville was right, and that the usage was afterwards altered (3 *Hist. Henry II.*, 339), observing that bishops did no homage, the reason for which was, that they owed no feudal service.

[1] *Cum ligeancid factum.*   [2] *Dominum suum infestare.*

the rest, notwithstanding which, in all other respects, the services owing to such other lords were still to be duly rendered by the tenant. The penalty of doing anything to the disherison of a lord was for the tenant and his heirs to lose forever the fee held of him; the same if the tenant put violent hands upon him, to hurt or do him any atrocious injury.[1]

Glanville makes it a question, whether a tenant could be put to answer in his lord's court for default in any of the above particulars, and whether the lord could *distrain* him, by judgment of his court, without the command of the king or his justices, or without the king's writ or that of his chief justice. And he thought that the law allowed a lord, by the judgment of his court, to call upon and distrain his homager to come to his court; and if the homager could not purge himself against the charge of his lord *tertiâ manu*, by three persons, or as many more as the court might require, he should be *in misericordiâ domini* to the amount of the whole fee he held of him. Glanville puts another question: whether a lord could distrain his homager to appear in his court to answer for the service of which the lord complained he deforced him, or made default in payment, and he thought that the lord might, without the command of the king or his justices; and that in such a proceeding the lord and his homager might come to the duel, or the great assize, by means of any one of the *pares* who chose to make himself a witness that he had seen the tenant or his ancestors do to the lord and his ancestors the service in dispute, which he was ready to *deraign* or prove; and that if the tenant was in this manner convicted judgment should be for him to lose the whole fee which he held of the lord. Where a lord found he could not in this manner *justitiare*, or compel his tenant to appear in his court, he was obliged to resort to the process of the *curia regis*;[2] that is, to the command or writ of the king or his justices.

Homage might be done by every freeman, as well those within age as those who were of full age, whether clergy or lay. Yet bishops consecrated could not do homage to the king, though they held their bishoprics as baronies (a),

---
[1] Glanv., lib. 9, c. 1.   [2] Ibid.
(a) This is a departure from Glanville. What he says is, that consecrated bishops are not in the habit of doing homage to the king, *even for their baro-*

but only fealty; and this they performed with an oath. It was usual for bishops elect to do homage before their consecration.[1]

It is to be understood that homage was not a mere personal thing. It was done in respect of some benefit derived from property of possession. It was due in respect of lands, tenements, services, rents in certain, whether in money or other things; but without some of these causes no homage was due to a lord, though it might be due to the king. Again, homage was not due in respect of all lands; for it was not due on account of dower, nor free

---

nies, "but merely fealty." And as they were not compelled to do homage before consecration, they were not bound to more than fealty. This would be so, the feudal system being military, and the reason of homage being to preserve the service, they could not be bound to it, because they were not bound to render any earthly service. Glanville says elsewhere, they held in frankalmoigne (lib. iii., c. 1), and Littleton says that tenants in frankalmoigne owed no earthly service (c. vi.). Therefore they could, it is obvious, owe no homage. Lord Littleton says, "Pope Paschal II. allowed bishops elect to do homage and take the oath of fealty before they were consecrated. This was confirmed by the constitutions of Clarendon, and from the words of Glanville it appears that about the end of Henry II.'s reign, homage was done by bishops elect. But he tells us that after they were consecrated, they took the oath of fealty. This was a material difference from what was settled by the constitutions of Clarendon; and it is surprising that we have no account of it in the history of the times" (3 *Hist. Henry II.*, 113). What Glanville says is, not that bishops were accustomed to do fealty after consecration, but that they were not in the habit of doing *more* than that after consecration. The statement which Glanville adds, that it was "usual for the bishops elect to do homage," is to be taken with some suspicion, as the statement of the king's chief justiciary, not long after a protracted controversy with the archbishop on the subject. Sir J. Mackintosh, alluding to the contest on the subject of investitures between Henry I. and Anselm, a former archbishop, says, the controversy was adjusted as it had been in Germany, by settling that the monarch should invest the bishop elect with his temporalities, by touching him with the sceptre (*Hist. of England*, vol. i.); and says that the article in the constitutions of Clarendon which related to the subject, followed the spirit of that compromise, although he allows that it might be historically untrue to allege the customs set up by those constitutions to be ancient (*Ibid.*). The text of the arrangement may be seen in Labbe's Councils, vol. x., p. 90. Ducange defines investiture as the conferring or giving possession of a fief or property by a suzerain lord to his vassal (*Gloss. verb. Investiture*). This definition shows that it could not apply to bishops who were *not* feudal vassals. Homage properly *preceded* investiture (*Ducange, Gloss. verb. Hominum*). Homage, therefore, was incident to investiture, and the main contest was about *investiture*, to which homage was only an incident. But for this one reason it was a part of the great question of investiture, and the chief justiciary of Henry II. would, of course, put the case as strongly as he could for the royal cause. The popes never objected to investiture by the sceptre; what they objected to was investiture by the cross and ring, the symbols of the *spiritualty*.

[1] Glanv., lib. 9, c. 1.

marriage, nor from the eldest sister on account of the fees of younger sisters, till after the third descent ; nor of a fee given in free alms.¹

Homage might be received by any free man or woman, whether of age or not, as well clergy as lay. If homage had been done to a woman, and she married, it was to be done over again to the husband; yet, in a case somewhat similar, namely, when a person, by a final concord made in court recovered land for which a relief had been paid to the chief lord, it was a question, whether the person recovering was bound to pay a relief, upon his coming into possession thereof.²

In consequence of homage being performed, there arose a mutual relation between the parties; according to the rule, *quantum homo debet domino ex homagio, tantum illi debet dominus ex dominio; præter solam reverentiam.* Therefore, when land was given for the service and homage of the tenant, and any one afterwards instituted a suit for that land, the lord was bound to warrant it to him, or to give him in lieu thereof *competens excambium*, an equivalent in value.

When an heir who had been in custody came of age, the inheritance was restored to him without paying a relief; that being remitted in consideration of the profit the lord had derived from the custody. A female heir, whether of age or not, was continued in custody till she was married by the advice of her lord. If she had been within age when she first came into the lord's custody, then upon her marriage the inheritance was quit of all relief; but if she was of age when she first came into the lord's custody, though she continued some time in custody before marriage, yet her husband was to pay relief upon the marriage; and a relief once paid by the husband, was an acquittal both to husband and wife, during their several lives, for any relief on account of the inheritance: so that neither the wife nor her second husband, if she had one, nor the first husband, should he survive her, could be called upon to pay any relief.³

Relief.

If the male heir was of age when his ancestor died, and was well known to be the heir, he might hold himself in

---

¹ Glanv., lib. 9, c. 2.   ² Ibid., c. 3.   ³ Ibid., c. 3.

the inheritance even against the will of the lord, as we before said; provided he made a tender of his homage, and a reasonable relief, in the presence of credible persons.

The relief of one knight's fee, according to the custom of the realm, was said to be reasonable at a hundred shillings. The relief in socage-tenure was one year's value of the land. As to baronies, nothing certain was fixed concerning their relief; but the relief they were to pay was measured by the pleasure and mercy of the king alone, to whom it was due (*a*). The law was the same in serjeanties.[1]

Aids. When the lord and the heir had come to an agreement respecting what was to be paid for relief, the heir might exact reasonable aids from *his* homagers; always proportioning this demand to their circumstances, and the size of their fees; that it might not become such a grievous imposition as would entirely destroy their *contenement*, or, to use an English term which has been formed from it, their *countenance*, and appearance in the world: and no other measure was settled for ascertaining these aids but this regard to facts and circumstances. With the above precautions, a lord, in other cases, might exact similar aids of his tenants; as when he made his son and heir a knight, or when he married his eldest daughter. Glanville made a question, whether lords could demand these aids of their tenants to enable them to carry on their wars? The practice, at least, was for them never to attempt to distrain for aids on this occasion, but to leave them to the voluntary generosity of their tenants. For the other aids, so long as they were reasonable, lords might, by judgment of their courts, without the *precept* or command of the king or his chief justice, distrain their tenants by the chattels that were to be found on their fees, or, if need

---

(*a*) So far from this being the law, though it is so laid down by Glanville, that Henry I. in his charter describes it as one of the *malas consuetudines*, by which, under the Conqueror and his successors, the country had been oppressed, "*quibus regnum opprimebantur*" "*Si quis baronum meorum comitium sive aliorum qui de 'me tenent,' mortuus fuerit, hæres suus non redimet terram suam sicut faciebat tempore patris mei sed legitime et justa relevacione relevabit eum,*" (*Leg. Hen. Pri.*, II.) The law, therefore, was, that the relief must be *reasonable*, and the chief justiciary goes on to say so, in a passage omitted by the author, to the effect that if the lord would not accept reasonable relief, he had a remedy by a certain proceeding he describes. The law was reasserted in Magna Charta, c. ii.

[1] Glanv., lib. 9, c. 4.

were, by the fees themselves; so, however, that the proceeding was had regularly by the judgment of the court, and consistent with the reasonable custom thereof. If a lord could distrain his tenants for payment of these reasonable aids, much more, says Glanville, might he make distress for payment of his relief, and for such service as was due to him on account of the fee.[1] Thus we see the remedy by distress had, in Glanville's time, become a process first against the chattels; and only *si opus fuerit*, was there recourse to the fee itself; though it is probable, that in the origin of this summary method of compelling tenants to do their services, it was usual to take the whole fee into the lord's hands as a forfeiture, to enable him to do that justice to himself which his tenant refused; but this rigorous proceeding was by degrees softened down to one against the movables; and only in default of them, against the land.

Having taken this view of the nature of tenures and estates, it seems necessary to consider the order of administering justice, with the process and modes of proceeding in obtaining redress for any injury to property or to the person; an inquiry not less interesting than the former, as it contains in it the first outline of that course of judicature which prevails, with considerable alterations indeed, at this day. In pursuing this, there will be occasion to notice such parts of the law concerning private rights as have not already been mentioned.

<small>Administration of justice.</small>

Pleas were divided into *civil* and *criminal*. Criminal pleas were again divided into such as belonged *ad coronam domini regis*, and such as were within the jurisdiction of the sheriff (a). The pleas belonging to the king's crown were, the *crimen læsæ majestatis*, as the death of the king, or any sedition touching his person or the realm; pleas concerning the fraudulent concealment of treasure trove; pleas *de pace domini regis infractâ;* pleas of homicide, burning, robbery, rape, and the *crimen falsi;* all which offences were punished with death, or the loss of limbs. Only the

---

(a) This is a mistake. Those within the jurisdiction of the sheriff were equally pleas of the crown, and originally all were within his jurisdiction. The *Leges Henrici Primi* define some as in *misericordia Regis*. The laws of Canute had specified some which were not to be confounded for those above enunciated. But theft remained a plea of the crown, and is so called by Glanville.

[1] Glanv., lib. 9, c. 8.

crime of theft was excepted, which was within the cognizance of sheriff, and determinable in the county court. The sheriff, in like manner, in cases where the lord of a franchise neglected to do justice, had cognizance of *medletæ*, as they were then called, *verbera*, and *plagæ;* unless the party complaining added, as he might if he pleased, an allegation, *de pace domini regis infractâ*, namely, that it was against the king's peace.[1]

(*) Civil pleas were divided in the same way; some being entertained in the king's court, and others in that of the sheriff. In the king's court were determined pleas concerning baronies; that is, manors held of the king *in capite;* pleas concerning advowsons, villenage, dower *unde nihil;* complaints for breach of final concords made in the king's court; questions of homage, reliefs, and purprestures; pleas of debt owing by lay persons, or, as they were called, *placita de debitis laicorum*.[2]

The following civil pleas belonged to the sheriff's court: pleas of right to freehold, when the court of the lord of whom the land was held, had made default in determining the right; and questions upon villenage; and these pleas were always commenced by the king's writ.

Besides these, which were all *de proprietate*, there were other pleas *super possessione*, which were decided by recognition of jurors. Of all these we shall speak in their order.

First, of pleas in the king's court, or *curia regis*, as it was then called. When any one, says Glanville, complained to the king or his justices concerning his fee or freehold, if "the matter was such as was proper for that tribunal, or such as the king pleased should be examined there, the party had a writ of summons to the sheriff, directing him to command the wrong-doer to restore the land of which he had deforced the complainant; and unless he did, to summon him by good summoners to appear

---

[1] In this distinction between the sheriff's jurisdiction and that of the king, we see the reason of the allegation in modern indictments and writs, *vi et armis* of "the king's crown and dignity," "the king's peace," and "the peace;" this last expression being sufficient, after "the peace *of the sheriff*" had ceased to be distinguished as a separate jurisdiction. Glanville, lib. 1, c. 1, 2. [This is a mistake. The criminal pleas before the sheriff were equally pleas of the crown, and Glanville so treats them. The sheriff, in criminal cases, was the king's justice.]

[2] Glanv., lib. 1, c. 3.

before the king or his justices, at such a day, to show wherefore he refused so to do."

The following was the form of the writ: *Rex vicecomiti salutem : Præcipe A. quòd sine dilatione reddat B. unam hidam terræ in villâ* (naming it) *unde idem B. queritur, quòd prædictus A. ei deforceat : et nisi fecerit, summone eum per bonos summonitores, quòd sit ibi coram me vel justitiariis meis in crastino post octabas clausi Paschæ apud* (naming the place where the court sat) *ostensurus quare non fecerit, et habeas ibi summonitores, et hoc breve. Teste Ranulpho de Glanvilla apud Clarendon.*[1] A writ of right.

At the appointed day the party summoned either came or not, or sent a messenger to *essoin*[2] him, that is, to make an *excuse* for his not coming. If he neither came, nor sent an essoin, the demandant was to appear in court, and wait his adversary for three days. If he did not appear at the fourth day, and the summoners offered to prove they had duly summoned him, another writ of summons issued, appointing his appearance in fifteen days at least; and this writ required him, as well to answer upon the merits of the complaint, as for his contempt in disobeying the first summons. When three writs in this form had issued, and he neither appeared nor sent any one to essoin him, his land was taken into the king's hands, and so it remained for fifteen days; and if he did not appear within that time, the seisin of it was adjudged to the complainant, nor could the owner have any remedy to recover it, but by writ of right: yet if he appeared within those fifteen days, and was willing to *replevy* the land, he was commanded to come again on the fourth day, and right should be done; when, if he appeared, the seisin was restored. Indeed, if he had appeared at the third summons, and acknowledged all the former summonses, he would lose the seisin of his land, unless he could produce a writ from the king to the justices, declaring that he had been in the king's service at the time appointed by the court, and commanding that he should not be held as a defaulter, nor suffer as such.[3]

---

[1] Glanv., lib. 1, c. 6.
[2] *Essonium,* or *Exonium,* says Spelman: *ex* privativum, et *soing*, cura; ab angustiâ, curâ, vel labore liberare; which is a more probable derivation than ἐξωνεῖσθαι; though it should signify to excuse by means of an oath; which, to be sure, is the precise nature of an Essoin. *Vide* Spelm., voce Essoniare.
[3] Glanv., lib. 1, c. 7, 8.

If the party denied that he was summoned he was to swear it *duodecimâ manu;* and at the appointed day, should any of the jurors who were to swear it fail, or any be lawfully excepted to, and no other put in his place, that very instant the defendant lost the seisin of his land as a defaulter. If he disproved the summons in the above way he was the same day to answer to the action.

Thus far of appearance and non-appearance; next as to *essoins.* If the party did not appear at the first summons, but sent a reasonable essoin, it would be received, and he might, in like manner, essoin himself three times successively. The causes of excuse, called essoins, allowed in the king's court, were many. The principal essoin was that *de infirmitate.* This was of two kinds: one was *de infirmitate veniendi;* the other *de infirmitate reseantisæ,* of which the first was called afterwards *de malo veniendi;* the latter *de malo lecti.*

<small>Essoins.</small>

If at the first summons the essoin *de infirmitate veniendi* was cast, it was in the election of the complainant, upon his appearing in court to demand from the *essoniator,* or person who made it a lawful proof of the essoin, on the very day; or that he should find pledges,[1] or make a solemn engagement to bring a warrant or proof of the essoin, that is, the principal summoned at a day appointed. And in this manner might the tenant be essoined three times successively. If he did not come at the third day, nor send an essoin, the court awarded that he should appear on another day in person, or by a sufficient attorney (or *responsalis,* as he was then called), who would be received *ad lucrandum vel perdendum* in his place. If the party summoned appeared on the fourth day, after three essoins, and avowed them all, he was required to prove the truth of them by his own oath and that of another, and on the same day was to answer to the action; and if he did not appear at the fourth day, nor send his attorney, his land was taken into the king's hands, as before mentioned. There issued also an attachment against the essoniators *tanquam falsarios* for not performing the engagement they had made for their principal; and in the meantime the principal was summoned to show cause why he did not avow and make good what his essoniator had engaged for

---

[1] Glanville's words are: *vel plegium inveniet, vel fidem dabit.*

in his name; a summons went also against the pledge put in, as above mentioned, by the essoniator, to show cause why he did not produce the principal to make good the essoin.[1]

If the principal appeared within fifteen days, and was willing to replevy the land, a day was given him; and if he then gave his sureties, he recovered his seisin. If he denied all the summonses, and disproved them *duodecimâ manu;* or, if he admitted the first, avowed his three essoins, and on the fourth day produced the above-mentioned writ, testifying that he was in the king's service; he could in that case recover seisin of the land, but if he did not appear within the fifteen days, the seisin was adjudged to the complainant, as before mentioned. The direction in the writ to the sheriff for taking the land in the case of the king was *capias in manum meam;* and of that for giving possession of it to the complainant was *seisias M. de tantâ terrâ,* etc.

In the same manner a man might essoin himself three times *de infirmitate reseantisæ,* or *de malo lecti;* and if the party appeared not at the third summons the judgment of the court was that it be seen whether the infirmity be a *languor* or not. For this purpose a writ issued, commanding the sheriff to send four lawful men of his county to view the party, and if they saw that it was *languor* they were to appoint him to appear, or send his attorney, in a year and a day; but if they thought it not to be a *languor* they were to appoint a certain day of appearance for him or his attorney, at which time the four viewers were likewise to appear and testify their view. Two essoniators were necessary to make this essoin.[2]

Perhaps the first two essoins might be *veniendi* and the third *de reseantisâ;* in which case persons were to be sent to view whether *languor* or not; but if the first two were *de reseantisâ,* and the third *veniendi,* they were adjudged as if all were *veniendi,* for it was a rule always to judge according to the nature of the last essoin.[3]

We have seen that the land of a person who did not appear was taken into the king's hands. It was also the practice, if a person had appeared and answered, and a future day was given, and at that day he neither came

---

[1] Glanv., lib. 1, c. 12–15. [2] Ibid., c. 18, 19. [3] Ibid., c. 20.

nor sent his attorney, that his land should be taken into the king's hands; but Glanville states this material difference, that he could not in this case replevy it; he was also summoned to hear the judgment of the court upon his default; however, whether he appeared or not, he lost his seisin, for the first default, unless he could avoid the summons by the before-mentioned writ *de servitio regis*. A person who had answered in court and departed in a lawful way might recur to the three essoins, unless there was any agreement to waive them.

If a person had essoined himself once, and at the second day he neither came nor essoined himself, we have seen that a writ issued to the sheriff to attach the essoniator *tanquam falsarium*, as before mentioned.[1] That the essoniator might be treated with a reasonable fairness, he also was allowed to essoin himself. Thus, if any obstacle happened to retard him in going to essoin his principal, so that he could not get to the court at the appointed day, he had till the fourth day, as his principal had; and if any one came within that time to essoin him, he was received in like manner as the essoniator of the principal.[2] The principal might also, if he pleased, send a second essoniator, who was to state to the court the excuse of the principal, that he sent that excuse by an essoniator who was detained by accidents on the road, and that he would prove this as the court should award.[3] In all cases of essoins, if the adverse party had departed, upon a day having been given by the essoniator, the appearance of the principal within the fourth day signified nothing: for the day given by the essoniator must still be observed.[4]

Thus far of the essoins *de infirmitate veniendi*, and *de infirmitate reseantisæ*; or, as they have since been called, *de malo veniendi*, and *de malo lecti*. Glanville mentions several others; as that *de ultra mare*; upon which the party had at least forty days. Another was, *subita aquarum inundatio*, or the like unexpected accident, which was allowed to save the four days.[5] Another was called *per servitium regis*; and in that case the plea was put without a day, till the party returned from the service he was on: wherefore this was never allowed to those who were

---

[1] Glanv., lib. 1, c. 20, 21. [3] Ibid., c. 23. [5] Ibid., c. 25, 26.
[2] Ibid., c. 21, 22. [4] Ibid., c. 24.

constantly in the service of the king, such persons being left to the ordinary course of the court. This essoin *de servitio regis* lay only for persons in the king's service before the plea was commenced. If any went into the king's service after the plea commenced, and essoined himself, there was this difference, whether he was there *per mandatum regis ex necessitate*, or *ex voluntate*, without any mandate. In the former case, the above-mentioned order was observed, and the plea was put *sine die:* in the latter, it was not. Another distinction was made, whether the service was *ultra mare*, or *citra mare;* if the former, he had the usual forty days, and was expected at the expiration of them to appear and show the king's writ, as we have before seen: in the latter, it was at the discretion of the justices to give a less or a greater time, as they thought it best suited the king's service.[1]

There was an essoin *per infirmitatem*, which infirmity must be such as had happened since the party arrived in the town where the court was. In this case the court ordered that he should appear the next day, and so on for three days successively; and if he made the same excuse the third day, then four knights were directed by the court to attend and see whether he was able to make his appearance or not: if not, and they testified the same in court, he had a respite for, at least, fifteen days.[2]

Another essoin was *de esse in peregrinatione*. There was a distinction in this case, as in that of the king's service, whether the party had commenced his journey before the suit, or since. If he had been summoned first, the proceeding took its course, as before stated: if not, then there was a difference, whether his journey was towards Jerusalem or otherways. In the former case, he had a respite of a year and a day, at least; in other cases, the respite lay in the discretion of the justices.[3]

Having considered the circumstances relating to the tenant's appearance in court, let us pause a while, and look back to the nature of the writ which was to compel this appearance, and the method taken for its execution. The writ of summons had in it this clause addressed to the sheriff, "*et habeas ibi summonitores, et hoc breve:*" in consequence of which the first inquiry,

Of summons.

---

[1] Glanv., lib. 1, c. 27.   [2] Ibid., c. 28.   [3] Ibid., c. 29.

when the demandant offered himself at the appointed day in court, was whether the sheriff had there the writ and the summoners. If he had, and the summons was proved, they proceeded as before mentioned; but if the sheriff did not appear within the fourth day (which was allowed also to the tenant), then there issued a writ *de secundâ summonitione*, directing him to summon the tenant, and to appear himself and show cause why he did not summon him upon the first writ. This contained the first writ of summons, with the addition of this clause: *et tu ipse sisibi ostensurus quare illam summonitionem ei non feceris, sicut tibi præceptum fuit per aliud breve meum, et habeas ibi hoc breve, et illud aliud breve.* If the sheriff came at the day, and confessed that he had not executed the writ, he was then, as they termed it, *in misericordiâ regis*, that is, he was amerced; the demandant lost a day without effect, and the tenant was to be summoned again: but if the sheriff averred that he commanded lawful summoners to make the first summons, and they, being present, admitted it, they as well as the sheriff were amerced, if they had not obeyed it. But if they denied that the sheriff gave them charge of the summons, then there was a distinction, whether the sheriff gave it in the county court or not. Such matters ought, properly, to be transacted in that court; and if the plea was commenced some time before the county court, Glanville says, *attachiabitur usque ad comitatum*, and then a complete summons was to be made. If, then, the summoners had been enjoined in the county, and it was so proved, the summoners were amerced; for this was a solemn act, which they would not be allowed to deny: if out of the county, and they denied the command, then the sheriff alone was amerced, for executing the writ in a private and improper manner: for all public acts, such as enjoining summons to be made, taking pledges of prosecuting, and pledges *de stando ad rectum*, ought to be transacted in a public manner, that there might be no debate concerning such prefatory process; a circumstance which would lead to great impediments in suits. If the summoners were not present at the appointed day, but sent their essoniators, who essoined them; and added, that they had properly summoned the party; in that case, the first day was considered as not lost to the demandant, and the summoners were amerced for not appearing and proving the summons, as was enjoined them, unless they could excuse themselves by the king's writ *de servitio*. It should be remembered, that one or other of the summoners might excuse himself at the first day; and in that case the first day was not considered as lost to the demandant.[1]

Such was the proceeding where the tenant was simply summoned, without any pledges being given. It may be proper to mention in this place, what the process would be, when an *attachment* was necessary. If the suit was of a kind to make it necessary for the tenant to find pledges *de stando ad rectum* for his appearance (as was the case in pleas for breach of a final concord made before the king or his justices, and for novel disseisin), and these pledges had been recorded in the county court, or before the justices; then if the tenant did not appear, nor essoin himself, the pledges were adjudged to be amerced, and further pledges were required, to engage for his answering to the suit. This was to be done three times; and if he did not come at the third summons, his land was taken into the king's hands, in like manner as before mentioned; and the pledges likewise were amerced, and summoned to appear in court at a certain day, in order to hear the judgment. This was the course of *attachment* in civil causes: but in criminal ones, as in those *de pace domini regis infractâ*, if the party did not appear at the third summons, there issued a *capias* to take the body, the pledges being amerced as in the former cases.[2]

Of attachment.

Thus far of the default of the tenant. If the demandant did not appear at the first day, he might essoin himself in like manner as the tenant. If he neglected both, the tenant was dismissed *sine die;* so, however, as that the demandant might institute another suit for the same cause of action. But as to this, and the consequence of the tenant's default, there was a diversity of opinions in Glanville's time. Some held, that he only lost his first writ, with his costs and expenses, but not his action; so that he was at liberty to commence another: others thought he lost his action totally, without any right of recovery; and that he should be amerced for his contempt of court. Others were of opinion, that he lay at the

---

[1] Glanv., lib. 1, c. 30, 31.   [2] Ibid., c. 31.

king's mercy, whether he should be admitted to bring his action again. In either case, if the demandant had found pledges *de clamors suo prosequendo*, as was the case in some suits, his pledges were likewise to be amerced. Glanville further adds, that in criminal matters and those relating to the peace, where the king had an interest, as he was bound to prosecute, his body was to be taken and kept in custody until he prosecuted his appeal: besides, which, his pledges were still to be amerced.[1] If both demandant and tenant were absent at the day, it was in the discretion of the king or his justices to proceed against both; against the tenant for contempt of court, and the demandant for false claim.[2]

When obedience had been paid to the writs of summons, and both parties were in court, the demandant made his demand of the land in question: and then the tenant might, if he pleased, pray a view of the land. If the tenant had no other land in the same vill, the view was made without delay; but if he had, the tenant was respited, and another day given in court. When he departed in this manner from court, he might claim three essoins; and a writ was directed to the sheriff to send *liberos et legales homines* (not specifying any number) of the vicinage of the vill to view the land in question, and to have four of them to certify their view to the court.[3]

After the three essoins accompanying the view, and after both parties had appeared in court, then the demandant was to set forth his claim in the following manner; *Peto*, etc., "I demand against *B*. one hide of land in such a vill (naming it) as my right and inheritance, of which my father (or grandfather, as it might be) was seized in his demesne as of fee, in the time of Henry I. (or after the first coronation of the king, as it might be), and from which he received produce to the value of fifty shillings at least (as in corn, hay, and other produce); and this I am ready to prove by this my free man John: and if anything should happen to him; by him, or him" (for he could name several, though only one could wage battle) "who saw and heard this." Or he might conclude in this form: "and this I am ready to prove by this my free man John, whom his father, on

<small>Counting upon the writ</small>

---

[1] Glanv., lib. 1, c. 32.   [2] Ibid., c. 33.   [3] Ibid., lib. 2, c. 1, 2.

his death-bed, enjoined, by the faith a son owes a father, that if he ever heard of any plea being moved concerning this land, he would *deraign* (or prove) this,[1] as what his father had seen and heard."[2] This was the manner in which the demandant spread out the substance of his writ; and his reliance was always upon the testimony *de visu et auditu.*

After the demandant had thus made his claim, it was in the election of the tenant, whether he would defend by *duel*, or avail himself of the privilege granted by the king's late statute, and demand that a *recognition* should be made, which of the two had the greatest right to the land. If he chose the duel, he was to defend his right *de verbo in v rbum*, as the demandant had set it forth; either in person, or by some fit champion. It was a rule, that when the duel was once waged, the tenant could not claim the benefit of the new law.

The duel.

After the duel was waged, the tenant might essoin himself three times, as for himself; and in addition to these, three times in respect of his champion. When all these essoins were elapsed, the demandant was to bring his champion into court, ready for the engagement; the champion was to be the same person upon whom he put the proof in his claim: nor could he put any one in his place after the duel was once waged. If he who waged the duel happened to die, and that was declared by the voice of the vicinage, he might recur to one of the others named in the claim; or even a stranger, if that stranger was qualified to be a proper witness; for that qualification was always required in the champion of the demandant. But this was only where the champion died by a natural death; for if it happened by any fault or neglect of his own, no other could be substituted in his place, and the demandant lost his suit. Glanville states it as a question, whether the demandant's champion himself could nominate any one in his place; and he thought, that by the old and established custom of the realm, he could not appoint any one, except his son born in lawful wedlock.

As we before said, the champion of the demandant must be a person who could be a proper witness of the matter

---

[1] Glanville's words are: *Hoc dirationaret, sicut id quod pater suus vidit, et audirit.*
[2] Glanv., lib. 2, c. 3.

in question *per visum et auditum;* the demandant of consequence could not be his own champion; but the tenant might defend himself either *in person,* or by another fit champion. If the champion of the tenant died, it was a question what was to be done; whether the tenant might defend himself by some other, or was to lose his suit, or only seisin of the land. Glanville thought it was to be ordered exactly as in case of the demandant's champion dying.

It sometimes happened, that the champion was a person hired for a reward. This was a good cause of exception; and if the adverse party offered to prove it by one who saw the reward given, he was to be heard to this point; and the duel in the meantime was deferred. If the champion of the demandant was convicted of this charge, or was vanquished in the duel upon the point of right, the demandant lost his suit, and the champion lost his *legem terræ;* that is, he was never after to be received as a witness to wage duel for any one; though he might in a cause of his own, either as defendant or appellant, in matters of the peace and of personal injury; he might also defend by duel his own right to a fee and inheritance. In addition to the loss of his law, he was to be fined in the penalty of sixty shillings, *nomine recreantisæ,* on account of his cowardice. If the champion of the tenant was conquered, his principal lost the land in question, with all the fruits and produce found on it at the time of the seisin, and was never to be heard in a court of justice concerning the same; for it was a rule, that whatever was once determined in court by duel, remained ever after fixed and unalterable. There, accordingly, issued a writ to the sheriff, *quòd sine dilatione seisias M. de unâ hidâ terræ, etc.—quia ea hida terræ adjudicata est ei in curiâ meâ per finem duelli.* When the champion of the demandant was conquered, as before mentioned, the tenant was quit-claimed[1] from any right of the demandant to recover against him.

This was the course of proceeding, when the tenant, in a writ of right, chose to defend his right by duel.[2] But the tenant might avail himself of the provision lately made by Henry II., and put himself upon the assize; to which the demandant might consent, and put himself also upon the assize.

---

[1] *Quietus clamabatur de ejus clameo.*   [2] Glanv., lib. 2, c. 4, 5.

If the demandant had expressed before the justices in open court[1] his consent to put himself on the assize, he was not allowed to retract, but must stand or fall by the assize, unless he could show some good cause why the assize should not pass between them. One cause which might be shown, was, that they were of the same blood, and descended from the same stock whence the inheritance came. If this was admitted by the other party, the assize was waived, and the question was argued and determined by the court; it being a point of law, which was the nearest to the first stock, and the heir with the better title. In this manner the nearest heir obtained the land, unless it could be shown that he or his ancestor had any way lost it, sold it, made a gift of it, changed it, or by any other means had parted with it; and if the cause was rested upon any of these points of fact, it might be determined, says Glanville, by the duel.

Of the assize.

Suppose the person who had put himself on the assize, had denied this impediment of relationship; such a question was tried by calling into court the common relations of both parties. If these agreed unanimously that they were related, it was usual to abide by this declaration; but if one of the litigants still continued to deny it to be so, the last resort was to the vicinage; and if they agreed with the relations, this complete testimony was acquiesced in. Should the relations differ in their testimony, the vicinage was in like manner called in, and their verdict was decisive. If, upon this inquisition being made, it appeared to the court and justices that the parties were not descended from the same stock, the person who made the exception was to lose his suit. If there was no exception taken, then the assize proceeded, and its determination was as final as that by duel.[2]

Before we enter on the proceeding of the assize, let us reflect with Glanville upon the nature and design of this innovation upon the old method of trial. "The assize," says that author,[3] "is a royal benefit conferred on the

---

[1] So I construe *coram justitius in banco sedentibus*, though this phrase has been quoted by some persons to show that, in the time of Glanville, there were justices *de banco*, in the modern sense of those words; a construction which this passage will certainly not warrant.

[2] Glanv., lib. 2, c. 6.

[3] The words of Glanville are: *Est autem assisa regale quoddam beneficium clementiâ principis, de concilio procerum populis indultum.* I quote this from

nation by the prince in his clemency, by the advice of his
nobles, as an expedient (*a*) whereby the lives and interests
of his subjects might be preserved, and their property and
rights enjoyed, without being any longer obliged to submit

(*a*) Nevertheless (whatever may be the true reading, as to which the *Mirror*,
Bracton, and Fleta, all contemporary authorities, *support* the reading contested by the author), it can be clearly shown from history that the constitution was not established either by Henry II. or Glanville; nor does Glanville say so, nor say (as the author evidently supposes him to mean) that
there was any formal ordinance or constitution establishing it, in this reign
or in any other. What he says is merely that it was "a constitution which
the subject owes to the administration of justice, under the royal authority,
with the advice of his council," that is, the chancellors and chief justiciaries
for the time being. There is nothing to denote or indicate that Henry II.
was particularly referred to, and Glanville himself was chief justiciary, and
would well know if there was any new ordinance or constitution establishing
the trial, and would state it if there had been; but he does not state anything
of the kind. And he speaks of the assize, all through his work, as a trial
by twelve jurors, who are called "recognitors," because they found their
verdict upon their own knowledge; and the trial is called an assize merely
because it decided the right to real property, whereas trial by jury was a
general term applicable to all matters. The assize, then, was simply trial
by jury, regulated and adapted to the trial of real actions in the *king's court.*
At the Conquest the jurisdiction in real actions was in the county courts, and
then, as we have seen, the great case of the Archbishop of Canterbury, a
writ of right was tried in the county court of Kent, and tried *by a jury.*
And in the laws of Henry I., the county court is described as the "curia
regis," and no allusion is made to any other, unless it be the exchequer, as a
fiscal tribunal. And in the earlier and older part of the *Mirror*, in like
manner, the only kind of court described directs the *sheriff* to try the case.
It had, however, by slow degrees, been contrived to bring the jurisdiction
into the king's court, which, be it observed, at this time followed the king's
household, wherever he was. And a new procedure was required to provide
for trial by jury in the king's court of assizes of land in another country.
That this was all, is clear from the fact that in the reign of the Conqueror
cases of writs of right were tried by juries in the county court. Lord Coke gives
the record in the Kent case, and it appears that it was a writ of right. That,
therefore, in reality was just the same proceeding as under the assize, and
except that the assize was in the king's court, and *not* in the county, for
which reason Magna Charta provided that the assizes *should* be taken in the
counties.

the last edition of Glanville, adhering to the reading which is warranted by
the consent of the Harleian, Cottonian, and Bodleian manuscripts, in opposition to the old printed text, which reads *magna assisa*, etc., an epithet which,
I am clear, has been interpolated in this and other passages of Glanville by
a later hand, at a period when the distinction between the *great assize* and
other assizes had grown familiar among lawyers. This corruption of the
text in so remarkable a passage as the present, has had the effect of establishing a vulgar opinion, that the alteration made by Henry II. related only to
the trial in the writ of right; an opinion which is not warranted by the history of this revolution, and which is left without any support, as it should
seem, when the concurring testimony of these three MSS. is against the in-
sertion of this epithet in most of the places where it is used.

to the doubtful chance of the duel. After this" (continues he) " the calamity of a violent death, which sometimes happened to champions, might be avoided, as well as that perpetual infamy and disgrace attendant upon the vanquished, when he had once pronounced the *infestum et inverecundum verbum.*" The horrible word here alluded to was *craven;* by which the champion signified that he yielded, and submitted himself to all the consequences attending such a defeat. "This legal institution," says Glanville, "is founded in the greatest equity, and the fullest desire of doing justice. For a question of right, which, after many and long delays, can hardly ever be made out by duel, is investigated with despatch and ease by the benefit of this constitution. The assize itself is not clogged with so many essoins as the duel. By this the expenses of the poor are spared, and the labor of all is shortened. In fine, as the credit of many fit witnesses has a greater influence in judicial inquiries than that of one only; so this constitution contains in it more justice than the duel. The duel proceeds upon the testimony of one witness only (*a*); this constitution requires the oaths of at least twelve lawful men."[1] Such is the manner in which Glanville speaks of the institution of the assize.

The proceeding by assize was thus: The party who had put himself upon the assize, sued out a writ *de pace habendâ*. This was to prohibit the lord (if the suit was in the lord's court) from entertaining any suit, in which the duel had not been already waged, between the same parties for the same land, because one of the parties had put himself upon the king's assize and had prayed a recognition to be made, who had the most right.[2] Upon this, the demandant came

---

(*a*) Here the author has misunderstood Glanville, who says that the trial by duel proceeds upon the oath of *one juror only,* each of the parties being sworn to the truth of his case, and hence the very title of the mode of trial in the *Mirror* is "*Juramentum Duelli*" (c. iii., s. 24). And, as our author elsewhere says, though he constantly forgets, the jurors were witnesses. Hence, when Glanville goes on to say that in the assize there must be the *oaths* of twelve men, he means that they are jurors, for what were jurors but men sworn? And hence in other passages, wherever he speaks of the assize, he speaks of it as tried by twelve jurors (*vide* lib. xiii., c. vii., lib. c. 11). Therefore the assize was simply trial by jury instead of trial by battle. The trial was called the recognition, for the very reason that as jurors found their verdict at that time upon their own knowledge, they were said to recognize; and so were recognitors; but they were for that very reason jurors.

[1] Glanv., lib. 2, c. 7.   [2] Ibid., c. 8, 9.

to the court, and prayed another writ, whereby four lawful knights of the county might be directed to choose twelve lawful knights of the vicinage, who should say upon their oaths, which party had most right to the land in question. As this is the first process for the return of jurors of which we have any mention, it may be proper to insert it at length. It ran in these words: *Rex vicecomiti salutem. Summone per bonos summonitores quatuor legales milites de vicineto de Stoke, quòd sint ad clausum Paschæ coram me vel justitiis meis apud Westmonasterium ad eligendum super sacramentum suum duodecim legales militesde eodem vicineto, qui meliùs veritatem sciant, ad recognoscendum super sacramentum suum utrùm M. aut R. majus jus habeat in unâ hidâ terræ in Stoke quam M. clamat versus R. per breve meum, et unde R. qui tenens est, posuit se in assisam meam, et petit recognitionem fieri, quis eorum majus jus habeat in terrâ illâ, et nomina eorum inbreviari facias. Et summone per bonos summonitores R. qui terram illam tenet, quòd tunc sit ibi auditurus illam electionem, et habeas ibi summonitores,* etc.

At the day appointed the tenant might essoin himself three times; for it was a rule, that as often as either party appeared in court, and did what he was commanded by the law to do, he might again recur to his three essoins. But if this was allowed, the consequence would be, that as many or more essoins would intervene in the proceeding by the assize than by duel, which would ill agree with what we have just said about the conciseness of this new method. For suppose the tenant essoined himself three times, on the election of the twelve knights by the four; afterwards when he appeared in court, some or other of the four knights might essoin himself; and then, after these essoins, the tenant might again essoin himself afresh; so that the assize would hardly ever be brought to any effect; it was therefore necessary to defeat the operation of the above rule, in this instance. A constitution was accordingly passed, enabling the court to make order for removing these obstacles, and expediting the proceeding; in pursuance of which, when the four knights appeared at the appointed day in court, ready to choose the twelve knights, they were authorized, whether the tenant appeared or not, to proceed to the election. If he had been present, he might make a lawful exception to any of the twelve; and therefore the court would, in his absence, direct more than twelve to be elected, that when he appeared, he might have a greater chance to find twelve unexceptionable jurors. Jurors, says Glanville, might be excepted against in the same manner as witnesses were rejected in the court Christian; jurors being in fact only witnesses, and the testimony of witnesses being always considered as a matter of canonical regulation.

So desirous were they of avoiding delay, that upon the tenant appearing, if all the four knights did not appear, yet by the advice of the court, and assent of parties, one of the knights, taking two or three others of the county then in court, though not summoned, might proceed to elect the twelve; though, to avoid all cavil, and in order to have enough to make the election, they usually had the caution to call six or more knights to court. In all such points, the discretion of the court was suffered to govern the established course of proceeding; which, says Glanville, the king or his justices might temper and accommodate to the equity of the case then before them.[1]

When the twelve knights were elected, they were summoned by the following writ: *Rex vicecomiti salutem. Summone per bonos summonitores illos duodecim milites, scilicet, A. B. etc., quòd sint die, etc., coram me vel justitiis meis ad, etc., parati sacramento recognoscere utrùm R. vel N. majus jus habeat in unâ hidâ terræ, quam prædictus R. qui clamat versus prædictum N. et unde prædictus N. qui rem illam tenet, posuit se in assisam nostram, et petiit inde recognitionem, quis eorum majus jus habeat in re petitâ; et interim terram illam, unde exigitur servitium, videant; et summone per bonos summonitores N. qui rem ipsam tenet, quòd tunc sit ibi auditurus illam recognitionem.* At the day appointed for the knights to make their recognition, no essoin could be cast by the tenant, nor was his presence necessary; as he had once put himself upon the assize, he had now nothing to say why the recognition should not proceed. It was different with regard to the demandant; for if he essoined himself, which he might do, the assize remained for that day, and another day was given; for it was a rule, that though any one might lose by his default of appearance, yet no one should gain anything if not present in court. *Perdere potest quis propter defaltum, lucrari verò nemo potest omninò absens.*[2]

---

[1] Glanv., lib. 2, c. 12.   [2] Ibid., c. 15, 16.

The assize being about to make their recognition, it is next to be considered how they were enabled to do it. Now, some, or all, might know the truth of the matter, or all might be ignorant of it. If none of them knew anything of the matter, and they testified the same in court, upon their oaths, the court resorted to others, till they found those who did know the truth. If some were acquainted with the fact, and some not, the latter were rejected, and others called in, till twelve at least were found who could agree. Again, if some were for one of the parties, and some for the other, fresh jurors were to be added till twelve were found who agreed in opinion for one of the parties. It is to be observed, that all who were called in, were to swear that they would not speak what was false, nor knowingly be silent as to what was true; and the knowledge they were expected to have of the matter must have been from what they themselves had seen or heard, or from declarations of their fathers, and such evidence as claimed equal credit with that of their own ears or eyes. *Per proprium visum suum, et auditum, vel per verba patrum suorum, et per talia quibus fidem teneantur habere ut propriis.*[1]

When the twelve knights were agreed in the truth, they then proceeded formally to recognize, whether the demandant had most right in the thing in question. If they said the tenant had most right, or said that which satisfied the king or his justices that he had most right, then the judgment of the court was, that he should go quit of the demandant forever, so as the demandant should never be heard again in court with effect; for a suit once lawfully determined by the king's great assize, could never be stirred again on any occasion whatever. If the assize were of opinion for the demandant, and the court gave judgment accordingly, then the adversary lost the land in question, with all its fruits and profits found there at the time of the seisin.[2]

Upon this there issued a writ of execution, *quòd seisias N. de unâ hidâ, etc., quia idem N. dirationavit terram illam in curiâ meâ per recognitionem, etc.*,[3] reciting the mode of trial, as the before-mentioned writ of seisin did the duel. We may here notice, that the duel and assize had become so

---

[1] Glanv., lib. 2, c. 17.   [2] Ibid., c. 18.   [3] Ibid., c. 20.

coextensive in their consequences, as for it to grow into a rule, that the duel should not be where the assize was not allowed, nor the assize where there was no duel.¹ Assizes lay concerning services, land, demands of service, rights of advowson, and that not only against a stranger, but even against a lord.²

The regal constitution by which the assize was appointed (*a*), had also ordained a punishment for jurors *temerè jurantum*, or who swore falsely. If any were proved, or confessed themselves, guilty of perjury, they were to be spoiled of all their chattels and movables, which were forfeited to the crown; but they were permitted by the clemency of the king to retain their freeholds; they were to be thrown into prison, and be there detained for a year at least; they were to lose the *legem terræ*, or, in other words, incur the brand of perpetual infamy.³

It was a question in Glanville's time, what was to be done, if no knights could be found, of the vicinage or of the county, who knew the truth of the matter, whether the tenant was therefore to prevail, as the person in possession; or the demandant to lose his right, if he had any. Suppose, says he, two or three lawful men, or any other number less than twelve, who were witnesses of the fact, offered themselves in court *ad dirationandum*, and said and did everything in court proper for the occasion, could they or could they not be heard.⁴

This was the order of proceeding, when the presence of the tenant only was necessary, and no one else was brought in to answer. There were many cases where it was requisite to call in a third person; as

Vouching to warranty.

(*a*) There was no such constitution; it is a complete mistake of the author's. What Glanville alludes to is the common law punishment of false jurors, which is mentioned in the *Mirror*. All this he calls the twelve triers jurors, or recognitors, because *being* jurors, they recognized the truth of their own knowledge. What Glanville says is, that a punishment is ordained for those who falsely swear in such a proceeding (*i. e.*, a trial by jury), and is, therefore, introduced into this institution. And then he simply states the common law as to attaint. Hence Lord Coke refers to this chapter, to prove that an attaint lay at common law (2 Just., 236). And the *Mirror* states it as applicable to trial by jury (c. 5). Glanville, being chief justiciary, simply made some regulations for the conduct of the proceeding, and then for the sake of flattery calls it a royal institution. In the *Mirror* are several instances of ordinances, by chief justiciaries, relating to the administration of justice, and more than one of them by Glanville himself, *vide ante*.

¹ Glanv., lib. 2, c. 19. ² Ibid., c. 13. ³ Ibid., c. 19. ⁴ Ibid., c. 21.

when the tenant declared in court that the thing in question was not his own, but that he held it *ex commodato*, or *ex locato*, or *in vadium*, that is, in *gage* or pledge, or committed to his custody, or in some other way entrusted to him by the real owner; or if he should declare the thing was his own, but that he had some one *to warrant* it, as the person who made a gift of it, or sold it, or gave it in exchange: or should he declare in court, that the thing was not his, but belonging to another person, that person was to be summoned by some other similar writ; and so the suit was to be carried on afresh against *him*. When he appeared in court, he, in like manner, might admit the thing to be his, or not. If he said it was not his, the tenant who had said it was, *ipso facto* lost the land without recovery, and was summoned in order to hear the judgment of the court to that effect; and whether he came or not, the adversary recovered seisin.

When the tenant called a person for any of the above reasons *to warrant* the land, a day was given him to have in court his warrantor; and upon this he was entitled to three essoins respecting himself, and three others respecting the person of his warrantor. At length the warrantor appearing in court, he either warranted the land or not. If he would enter into the warranty, the suit was from thence carried on with him, and everything went under his name, in lieu of the tenant; not but that the tenant, if he had essoined himself, would be considered as a defaulter, if absent. If the warrantor, being present in court, declined entering into the warrant, the suit was to be carried on between the tenant and him; and after allegations on both sides, they might come to the duel, although, perhaps, the tenant might not be able to show a charter of warranty, but could only produce a fit witness to deraign it. The object of all this was, to prove the warrantor to be bound to the warranty, which would make the tenant entirely safe; for should the land be recovered from him, the warrantor, if able, was bound by law to give him an *excambium*, as they called it, or an equivalent in recompense.

As this was the effect of a warranty when proved, it often happened that a person called to warranty was shy of coming to court: at the prayer of the tenant, therefore, the court would think it advisable to compel him, by a writ of summons *ad warrantizandum*.[1]

---

[1] Glanv., lib. 3, c. 1–3.

At the day appointed, this person, like all others who were summoned to appear in court, might essoin himself three times. At the third essoin the court would award, that at the fourth appointed day he, or some attorney for him, should appear; but if he did not, there seems to have been a doubt what should be done to punish the contempt: for if the land in question was taken into the king's hands, this would seem unjust to the tenant, who had not been adjudged in default; and yet if it was not done, there seemed to be a want of justice to the demandant, whose suit was delayed. Indeed Glanville thought that, notwithstanding these reasons, the law and custom of the realm required the land to be taken; for no hardship would fall on the tenant, it being a rule, that wheresoever a person lost his land through the default of his warrantor, the warrantor should make him a recompense in value.[1]

It sometimes happened that a tenant neglected to call in the person on whom he had a claim of warranty, and defended the right himself. In this case, if he lost it, he could have no recovery against his warrantor. It was by some made a question whether, upon the same principle as the tenant might defend his right by duel without the assent and presence of his warrantor, he might put himself upon the king's great assize without his assent and presence, but Glanville thought that the same reason should prevail in both cases.[2]

A suit was sometimes impeded by the absence of lords, as when the demandant claimed the land as belonging to the fee of one and the tenant as belonging to the fee of another lord. In this case each lord used to be summoned to appear in court, that the plea might be heard and determined in their presence, lest any injury might otherwise be done to their rights. The lords, when summoned, might essoin themselves three times, as was usual in other cases. If the lord of the tenant had had his three essoins, and the court had directed him to appear or send his attorney, and he made default, the judgment then was for the tenant to answer and take upon him the defence; and if he prevailed he retained the land, and for the future did his suit and service to the king, the lord having lost it by his default till he appeared and did as

---

[1] Glanv., lib. 3, c. 4.   [2] Ibid., c. 5.

the law required. In the same manner the lord of the demandant might essoin himself three times; and if, after that he absented himself, it was Glanville's opinion that his essoniators and the person of the demandant should be attached for contempt of court, and in that manner be compelled to appear.[1]

When the two lords had appeared, and the lord of the tenant said that the land was in his fee, he might take upon him the defence of the suit, or intrust it to the tenant; and in either case, should they prevail, their several rights were secured; but if they lost the suit the lord lost his service, as well as the tenant his land, without any recovery. If the tenant's lord, being present in court, failed of the warranty, and the tenant maintained that he was bound to the warranty because he or his ancestors had done such and such service to him or his ancestors as lords of that fee, and he could produce those who had heard and seen this, or a proper witness to deraign it, or other fit and sufficient proof, as the court should award; if the tenant could say this, then he and the lord might interplead with each other.[2] If the demandant's lord entered into the warranty, and they failed in the suit, the lord in like manner lost his service. But the fate of the demandant was different from that of the tenant if his lord would not enter into the warranty, for he was amerced for his false claim.[3]

Thus has the reader been conducted through the proceeding in a writ of right, with all its incidents and appendages, when prosecuted for the recovery of land. This relation has been somewhat long and minute, but as it contains in it, with some small alteration, the scheme of process and proceeding in most other actions, it was indispensably necessary to trace it with some exactness. After this the remainder of our inquiry into the course of judicial remedies will be more easy, and the matter will be more various and entertaining. We shall now proceed to speak of other methods of recovering property; and first of advowsons.

An action for the advowson of a church might be brought either while the church was full, or when it was vacant. If the church was va-

Writ of right of advowson.

---

[1] Glanv., lib. 3, c. 6.   [2] Ibid., c. 7.   [3] Ibid., c. 8.

cant, and any one obstructed the person who thought himself the patron, in presenting a clerk, and claimed the presentation to himself, there was a difference to be made, whether the contest was for the advowson; that is, upon the *right* of presenting, or upon the *last presentation*—that is, the *seisin* of the right of presenting. If it was upon the last presentation, and the person claiming it said that he or some ancestor of his made the last donation or presentation, then, says Glanville, the plea is to be conducted according to the late ordinance[1] about the advowsons of churches, and an assize was summoned to make recognition *what patron, in time of peace, presented the last deceased person to the church,* of which assize more will be said when we come to speak of other recognitions. For the present it will be enough to remark that he who recovered by such an assize recovered seisin of the presentation so as to present a proper person, with a saving of the demandant's claim as to the right of the advowson.

If the right of advowson only was demanded, the demandant must add something as to the last presentation, either that "he or one of his ancestors had it," or that the tenant or one of his ancestors had it, or that some stranger had it, or that he was ignorant who had it. Whichsoever of these allegations it might be, if the other party claimed the last presentation as his own or his ancestor's, the recognition was, notwithstanding, to proceed upon the right of presenting, except only in one of the above-mentioned cases; that was, where the demandant admitted that the tenant, or one of his ancestors, had the last presentation, for then, without going to the recognition, he was to present at least one person. When, however, the last presentation had been decided[2] by the assize, as before mentioned, or in any other lawful way, and a person was presented accordingly by the successful party, then the party who was resolved to try the right of advowson might go on with the suit and have the following writ:[3] *Rex vicecomiti salutem. Præcipe N. quòd justè*

---

[1] Perhaps Glanville here alludes to the famous statute about assizes; or, from the expression, it seems more probable, a statute had been ordained since that, which directed recognitions to be made in case of last presentations. It is not unlikely that the many assizes which grew into use in the time of Henry II. were introduced at different times, according as this mode of proceeding was recommended by experience of its benefits.

[2] *Dirationata.*   [3] Glanv., lib. 4, c. 1.

et sine dilatione dimittat R. advocationem ecclesiæ in villâ, etc., quam clamat ad se pertinere, et unde queritur quòd ipse injustè ei deforceat: et nisi fecerit, summone per bonos summonitores eum quòd sit die, etc., ibi coram nobis vel justitiis nostris, ostensurus quare non fecerit, etc.[1]

The person summoned had the same essoins as were before mentioned in the plea of land; and if, after these, he did not appear at the fourth appointed day in person, or by attorney, Glanville thought the next process was for taking into the king's hands seisin of the presentation. The sheriff was to execute his writ of *capias in manu* in the following way: he was to go to the church, and there declare publicly, in the presence of some honest men, that he seized the presentation into the king's hands: the seisin remained in the king's hands fifteen days, with a liberty to the tenant to replevy it within the fifteen days, as was before stated.[2] In short, after all the essoins were run out, if one or both the parties absented themselves, the course was ordered as in a plea of land.

When both parties appeared in court, the demandant propounded his right in these words: — *Peto*, etc. "I demand the advowson of this church as my right, and appertaining to my inheritance, of which I (or one of my ancestors) was seized (in the time of Henry I. or) since the coronation of the king; and being so seized, I presented a person to that church (at one of the before-mentioned times); and so presented him, that he was instituted parson according to my presentation: and if any one will deny this, I have here some honest men[3] who saw and heard it, and are ready to prove it,[4] as the court shall award; and particularly this *A.* and this *B.*"[5]

When the claim of the demandant was thus set forth, the tenant might defend himself by the duel, or put himself upon the assize; and in both cases it would be ordered as before-mentioned.[6]

This was the manner of contesting a right of advowson when the church was vacant. It might also be contested when the church was full; as if the *parson*, or he who called himself parson, in the church, claimed his title by one patron, and another claimed the advowson, the latter

---

[1] Glanv., lib. 4, c. 2.
[2] Ibid., c. 3, 4, 5.
[3] *Probos homines.*
[4] *Dirationare.*
[5] Glanv., lib. 4, c. 6.
[6] Ibid., c. 7.

might then have the following writ against the parson: *Rex vicecomiti salutem. Summone per bonos summonitores clericum illum M. personam ecclesiæ. etc., quòd sit coram me vel justiis meis apud Westmonasterium ad diem, etc., ostensurus quo advocato se tenet in ecclesiâ illâ, cujus advocationem miles ille M. ad se clamat pertinere. Summone etiam per bonos summonitores ipsum N. qui advocationem illi deforceat, quòd tunc sit ibi, ostensurus quare advocationem ipsam ei deforceat, etc.*[1]

If the clerk did not appear according to the summons, nor send any to essoin him, or if, after the three essoins, he did not come, or send his attorney, Glanville thought, that having no lay fee by which he might be distrained, the bishop (or his official, in case the see was vacant) should be commanded to distrain him, or punish his default by taking the church into his hands, or using some other lawful means of compulsion.[2]

When the clerk appeared in court, he would, perhaps, admit the demandant to be the patron, and would say, that he was instituted upon his presentation, or that of some of his ancestors; if so, the plea went on no further in the king's court; for if the demandant denied the presentation, he was to maintain his controversy with the clerk before the ecclesiastical judge. Perhaps the clerk said the advowson belonged to the party summoned: now such party was dealt with in this manner: If he came at none of the three summonses, nor sent any essoin; or having essoined himself, neither came nor sent his attorney at the fourth day; the advowson of the church in question was seized into the king's hand, and so it remained for fifteen days; and if he did not appear in those fifteen days, then seisin thereof was given to the demandant. In the meantime, it was a question, what was to be done with the clerk, whether he was *ipso facto* to lose his church or not. But supposing the party summoned appeared, and disclaimed all right in the church, the suit in the king's court ceased, and the patron and clerk contested their claims in the court Christian. Should the church happen to become vacant *pendente lite*, Glanville thought, if there was no question but that, the person against whom the right of advowson was demanded had the last presentation, either in himself or

---

[1] Glanv., lib. 4, c. 8.   [2] Ibid., c. 9.

his ancestors, that he should be allowed to present a
clerk, at least till he had lost the seisin: consistently
with which he thought, that should a vacancy happen
while the advowson was in the king's hands for fifteen
days, the patron did not lose that presentation. If the
party summoned should say the right of advowson was
his, it was tried, as we before said of land. If he prevailed, he and his clerk were freed from the claim of the
demandant; if he failed, he and his heirs lost the advowson forever.[1]

When the right of advowson was in this manner determined, it became a question what was to be done with
the clerk, who admitted in court that he had the incumbency of the church by presentation of the unsuccessful
party. As the king's court could proceed no further
than the right of advowson between the two patrons,
the party who had now recovered the advowson was to
proceed against the clerk before the bishop, or his official:
yet after all, if at the time of the presentation the person
presenting was believed to have been the patron, he was
left in possession of the church during his life; for in the
reign of this king, at the council at Clarendon, a statute
had been made concerning clerks who had enjoyed
churches by the presentation of patrons *pro tempore*,
which ordained that clerks who had violently intruded
themselves into churches during time of war, should not
lose such livings during their lives.[2] This provision
salved the titles of many beneficed clerks at that time.
Nevertheless, in such case, after the incumbent's death,
the presentation returned to the lawful patron.[3]

The following points might arise upon what has been
said concerning the right of advowson and the last presentation. When a patron had recovered an advowson
by deraignment in court, and afterwards, in process of
time, the parson died, it might be asked, whether the
patron against whom the advowson had been recovered,
could maintain an assize *de ultimâ præsentatione;* and what
answer could, in that case, be given to it by the adverse
party. For suppose the person bringing the assize had
not, but some of his ancestors had had the last presentation; and it was objected to him, that he ought not to

---

[1] Glanv., lib. 4, c. 9. [2] *Vide ante*, pp. 325, 326. [3] Glanv., lib. 4, c. 10.

have a recognition, because he had lost the advowson to the tenant in the assize, by a solemn judgment of the court, whether this would be a bar to the assize. It should seem, says Glanville, that it would; because, as he had not the last presentation, he never had seisin of the advowson; but, it should seem, says he, that he might well go upon the seisin of his father, notwithstanding what had been determined respecting the right of advowson. And yet if a question could be thus started upon the last presentation, it looks like invalidating the judgment of the king's court, before given, upon the right of advowson; for when that had been solemnly adjudged, it should hardly seem that he ought by law to recover any seisin, particularly as against him who had before recovered the advowson, unless some new cause had arisen which would entitle him to be heard again. Indeed, if an assize was summoned for that purpose, it would be barred by this answer to it: that the complainant or his ancestors had, it was true, the last presentation; but if he or his ancestors had any right, they lost it by a solemn judgment in court: and this being proved by the record of the court, the suit would be lost, and the complainant amerced.[1]

We have just seen that questions about presentations belonged to the bishop's court, though the right of advowson was cognizable only in the king's court. It sometimes happened, that when one clerk sued another clerk in the court Christian they claimed a church by two different patrons. One of these patrons, not choosing to have a question upon his right agitated before that tribunal, might pray a writ *to prohibit* the court from proceeding, till the right of advowson was decided in the king's court. As this is the first mention we have of a prohibition to the ecclesiastical court, it may be proper to give this writ at length. It was as follows: *Rex judicibus, etc., ecclesiasticis salutem.* INDICAVIT *nobis R. quòd cùm J. clericus suus teneat ecclesiam, etc., in villâ, etc., per suam præsentationem, quæ de suâ advocatione est, ut dicit, N. clericus eandem petens ex advocatione M. milites, ipsum J. coram vobis in curiâ christianitatis inde trahit in placitum. Si verò præfatus N. ecclesiam illam*

Of prohibition to the ecclesiastical court.

---
[1] Glanv., lib. 4, c. 11.

dirationaret ex advocatione prædicti M. palàm est quòd jam dictus R. jacturam inde incurreret de advocatione suâ. Et quoniam lites de advocationibus ecclesiarum ad coronam et dignitatem meam pertinent, vobis prohibeo, ne in causâ illâ procedatis, donec dirationatum fuerit in curiâ meâ, ad quem illorum advocatio illius ecclesiæ pertineat, etc. If they proceeded in the cause after this prohibition, then the judges were summoned to appear in the king's court by the following writ:[1] *Rex vicecomiti salutem. Prohibe judicibus, etc., ne teneant placitum in curiâ christianitatis de advocatione ecclesiæ, etc., unde R. advocatus illius ecclesiæ queritur quòd N. inde eum traxerit in placitum in curiâ christianitatis; quia placita de advocationibus ecclesiarum ad coronam et dignitatem meam pertinent. Et summone per bonos summonitores ipsos judices, quòd sint coram me vel justiis meis die, etc., ostensuri quare placitum illud tenuerunt contra dignitatem meam in curiâ christianitatis. Summone etiam per bonos summonitores præfatum N. quòd tunc sit ibi ostensurus quare præfutum R. inde traxerit in placitum in curiâ christianitatis, etc.*

The next action that demands our attention is that in which questions concerning a man's condition or state were agitated; as when one claimed a person to be his villein; or when one in a state of villenage claimed to be a free man. When one claimed a man who was before in villenage, as his villein *nativus*, he had a writ *de nativis* directed to the sheriff; and so contested before the sheriff the matter with the other who was then in possession of the villein. If the question of villenage or not villenage was not moved before the sheriff, then the plea *de nativis* went on, as will be more fully shown presently. But if the villein said he was a free man, and he gave pledges to the sheriff that he would demonstrate it, then the suit in the county court ceased, because the sheriff was not allowed to determine that point; and if the sheriff persisted in going on to hear the cause, the villein was to make his claim to the justices, and would then obtain the king's writ, as follows: *Rex vic., etc. Questus est mihi R. quòd N. trahit eum ad villenagium de sicùt ipse est liber homo, ut dicet. Et ideo præcipio tibi, quòd si idem R. fecerit de securum de clamore suo prosequendo, tunc* PONAS *loquelam illam coram me vel justitiis*

The writ *de nativis*.

---

[1] Glanv., lib. 2, c. 13.

meis die, etc., et interem eum pacem inde habere facias : et summone per bonos summonitores prædictum N. quòd tunc sit ibi ostensurus quare trahit eum ad villenagium injustè, etc. It may be remarked, that this is the first writ of *pone* we have yet met with.[1]

The person who claimed the party as his villein, was also summoned by the same writ, and a day was fixed for him to prosecute his claim. At the day appointed, if the villein did not come nor send a messenger or essoin, they then proceeded, as we before mentioned, in pleas[2] where attachment lay. If he who claimed the party to be his villein neither came nor sent, the other was dismissed the court *sine die*. In the meanwhile, he who was claimed by both parties as his villein, was put, as Glanville expresses it, into *seisin of his freedom* ;[3] that is, as in pleas of land, a seisin of the land in question was given as a process of contempt : so in this instance, an inchoate temporary possession of his freedom was given to the villein, till the parties could appear in court, and the question of right was fairly heard and determined.

If both parties appeared in court, the freedom was to be made out in the following way : The person who claimed to be free, was to bring into court his nearest relations, descended from the same stock with himself ; and if their freedom was recognized and proved in court, this was construed in his favor, so as to free him from the yoke of servitude. But if the free state of those who were produced was denied, or there was any doubt concerning it, recourse was had to the vicinage, and according to their verdict it was adjudged by the court. In short, if there arose any doubt concerning the declarations of the relations, every doubt or difficulty of this kind was to be solved by the vicinage.[4]

When the freedom of the party was, by one or other of these ways, fairly made out, he was immediately released from the claim, and was adjudged free forever. But if he failed in his proof, or if he was proved by the adversary to be a villein *nativus*, he was accordingly adjudged to belong to his lord, together with all his goods and chattels. There was the same form and course of proceeding in case of a supposed villein claiming his free-

---

[1] Glanv., lib. 5, c. 1, 2.
[2] *Per plegios attachiatis.*
[3] Glanv., lib. 5, c. 3.
[4] Ibid., c. 4.

dom, and a freeman being claimed as a villein. The person whose freedom was in question applied for a writ, to bring the suit into the king's court, and then it went on as has just been stated. It must be remarked, that the duel was not allowed in a suit to prove a man free *à nativitate*.[1]

The next action that comes under our consideration is the remedy a woman had to recover her dower. On the death of the husband, the dower, if it was a parcel of land named and specified, was either vacant or not. If it was vacant, the widow, with the assent of the heir, might take possession thereof, and hold herself in seisin. If part of it only was vacant, she might take possession of that, and for the remainder she might have her writ of right directed to her warrantor — that is, the heir of the husband. The writ was as follows: *Rex M. salutem. Præcipio tibi quòd sine dilatione plenum rectum teneas A. quæ fuit uxor E. de unâ hidâ terræ in villâ, etc., quam clamat pertinere ad rationabilem dotem suam, quam tenet de te in eâdem villâ per liberum servitium decem solidorum perannum pro omni servitio, quam N. ei deforceat. Et nisi feceris, vicecomes faciat, ne oporteat eam ampliùs inde conqueri pro defectu recti, etc.*[2]

Writ of right of dower.

In pursuance of this writ, the plea went on in the lord's court, till proof was made of that court's failure in doing justice; upon which it was removed to the county court, and so to the king's court, if it seemed proper to him or his chief justice. The writ to remove it into the king's court was a *pone*, and was as follows: *Rex vicecomiti salutem. Pone coram me vel justitiis meis die, etc., loquelam quæ est in comitatu tuo inter A. et N. de unâ hidâ terræ in villâ, etc., quam ipsa A. clamat versus prædictum N. ad rationabilem dotem suam. Et summone per bonos summonitores prædictum N. qui terram illam tenet, quòd tunc sit ibi cum loquelâ, etc.*[3]

This plea, as well as some others, might be removed from the county court to the *curia regis*, for many causes; as well on account of doubts which might have arisen in the county, and which they did not know how to decide upon (and on such cause of removal both parties were to be summoned) as at the prayer of one of the parties; and then it was sufficient, if only the party not removing it

---

[1] Glanv., lib. 5, c. 4.   [2] Glanv., lib. 6, c. 4, 5.   [3] Ibid., c. 6, 7.

CHAP. III.] WRIT OF RIGHT OF DOWER. 413

was summoned. If the suit was removed by the assent and prayer of both parties, being present in court, then there needed no summons, for both of them must know the day appointed.

If either or both parties were absent at the day appointed, they proceeded as before mentioned. When both parties appeared, the widow set forth her claim in the following words: *Peto*, etc. " I demand that land, as appertaining to such land which was named for me in dower, of which my husband endowed me *ad ostium ecclesiæ*, on the day he espoused me, as that of which he was invested and seized at the time when he endowed me." To this claim the adverse party might make various answers: he might deny or admit that she was endowed of the land. But whatever was the answer given, the suit ought not to proceed without the widow's warrantor, that is, the heir of the husband; he was therefore summoned by the following writ: *Rex vicecomiti salutem. Summone per bonos summonitores N. filium et hæredem E. quòd sit coram me vel justitiis meis eâ die, etc., ad warrantizandum A. quæ fuit uxor ipsius E. patris sui unam hidam terræ in villâ, etc., quam clamat pertinere ad rationabilem dotem suam de dono ipsius E. viti sui versus N. et unde placitum est inter eos in curiâ meâ si terram illam ei warrantizare voluerit, vel ad ostendendum ei quare id facere non debet, etc.* If the heir did not appear nor essoin himself, and was in contempt, there was a doubt what was the precise way for compelling him. Some thought he was to be distrained by his fee; others thought he was to be attached by pledges.[1]

If the heir, when he appeared, admitted what the widow alleged, he was bound to recover the land against the tenant in possession, and deliver it to the widow; and for this purpose the suit was continued between him and the tenant. If he declined prosecuting the suit, he was bound to give her an equivalent in recompense; for in all events the widow was to be no loser. If he denied what was alleged by the widow, the suit went on between him and her; and if she could produce those who heard and saw the endowment at the church-door, and was ready to deraign it against the heir, the matter might be decided by the duel: and if she prevailed, he must in that case also

---

[1] Glanv., lib. 6, c. 8–10.

deliver to her the land in question, or a sufficient equivalent. It was a rule, that no woman could maintain any suit concerning her dower without her warrantor.[1]

This was the course for a widow to take, when she was obliged to sue for part of her dower: but when she could get possession of no part of it, and was put to sue for the whole, the suit was commenced originally in the *curia regis*, and the person who withheld her dower was summoned by the following writ, called a writ of dower *unde nihil habet: Rex vicecomiti salutem. Præcipe N. quòd justè et sine dilatione faciat habere A. quæ fuit uxor E. rationabilem dotem suam in villa, etc., quam clamat habere de dono ipsius E. viri sui,* UNDE NIHIL HABET, *ut dicit; et unde queritur quòd ipse ei injustè deforceat: et nisi fecerit, summone eum per bonos summonitores quòd sit die, etc., coram nobis vel justitiis nostris, ostensurus quare non fecerit, etc.* Whoever was in possession of the land, whether the heir, or any other person, the presence of the heir, as was above laid down, was always necessary. If a stranger was in possession, he was summoned by this writ, and the heir by the above writ of summons *ad warrantizandum*.[2] The suit between the heir and widow might be varied, according as the heir pleased. If she claimed a certain assigned dower, he might deny any assignment, or deny that to be the land assigned. In both cases the proceeding was as above described. If only a reasonable dower was demanded, a third part was to be allotted her by the heir.[3] If more was assigned to her than a third part, a writ might be had directed to the sheriff, commanding him to admeasure it.[4]

Dower unde nihil.

---

[1] Glanv., lib. 6, c. 11.   [2] Ibid., c. 14–16.   [3] Ibid., c. 17.
[4] Ibid., c. 17, 18.

CHAPTER IV.

HENRY II. TO JOHN. (a)

OF FINES—OF RECORDS—WRIT DE HOMAGIO RECIPIENDO—PURPRESTURE—DE DEBITIS LAICORUM—OF SURETIES—MORTGAGES—DEBTS EX EMPTO ET VENDITO—OF ATTORNEYS—WRIT OF RIGHT IN THE LORD'S COURT—OF WRITS OF JUSTICES—WRITS OF REPLEVIN—AND OF PROHIBITION—OF RECOGNITIONS—ASSISA MORTIS ANTECESSORIS—EXCEPTIONS TO THE ASSIZE—ASSISA ULTIMÆ PRÆSENTATIONIS—ASSISA NOVÆ DISSEISINÆ—OF TERMS AND VACATIONS—THE CRIMINAL LAW—OF ABJURATION—MODE OF PROSECUTION—FORFEITURE—HOMICIDE— —PROCEEDING BEFORE JUSTICES ITINERANT—THE KING AND GOVERNMENT—THE CHARTERS—THE CHARACTERS OF THESE KINGS AS LEGISLATORS—LAWS OF WILLIAM THE CONQUEROR—OF THE STATUTES—DOMESDAY-BOOK—GLANVILLE—MISCELLANEOUS FACTS.

WE have hitherto been speaking of compulsory methods of recovering and confirming rights; but it often happened, as Glanville expresses it, that pleas moved in the king's court were determined by an amicable composition and final concord: this was always by the consent and license of the king or his justices; and was done as well in pleas of land as other pleas. Such a concord used sometimes, by the assent of parties, to be reduced into a writing of several parts; from one of these was the agreement rehearsed before the justices in open court; and, in the presence of the justices, there was given to each party his part, exactly agreeing with the other's (*b*). The following is a specimen of such an instrument, literally translated from one in the reign of Henry II. "This is a final concord made in the court of our lord the king, at Westminster, on the vigil of the

Of fines.

(*a*) *Vide ante*, p. 347.
(*b*) As to fines or final concords, *vide ante*, p. 340. They were originally, no doubt, as Mr. Hargreaves says, real concords of existing suits, and in that sense they are alluded to in the *Mirror*, c. iii., s. 167, "Of final accord"—"No law prohibits pleas nor accords, wherefore it is lawful for every one to release and quit-claim his right and his action." At what period fines or recoveries were fictitious, and used only as modes of assurance, is uncertain: but no doubt soon after the use of *records*, as to which *vide* p. 345.

415

blessed Peter the apostle, in the thirty-third year of the reign of Henry II. before Ranulph de Glanvillâ, justiciary of our lord the king, and before H. R. W. and T. and other faithful and trusty persons of our lord the king, then there present; between the prior and brethren of the hospital of St. Jerusalem, and W. T. the son of Norman, and Alan his son, whom he appointed as attorney in his stead in the court of our lord the king, *ad lucrandum et perdendum* respecting all the land which the said W. held, with its appurtenances, except one oxland and three tofts. Of all which land (except the said oxland and three tofts), there was a plea between them in the court of our lord the king; to wit, that the said W. and Alan concede and attest and quit-claim all that land from them and their heirs to the hospital and aforesaid prior and brethren for ever, except the said oxland and three tofts, which remain to the said W. and Alan, and their heirs, to be held of the said hospital, and the aforesaid prior and brethren, forever, by the free service of fourpence *per ann.* for all service; and for this concession and attestation and quit-claim, the aforesaid prior, and brethren of the hospital have given to the said W. and Alan an hundred shillings sterling."[1]

A concord or agreement of this kind was called *final*,[2] because *finem imponit negotio;* so that neither of the parties could recede from it. If one of the parties did not perform what he was thereby bound to do, and the other party complained of it; the sheriff would be commanded to put him by safe pledges, so as that he appeared before the king's justices, to answer why he did not keep the fine; that is, if the complainant had previously given security to the sheriff for prosecuting his claim. The writ was as follows: *Præcipe N. quòd justè et sine dilatione teneat finem factum in curiâ meâ inter ipsum et R. de unâ hidâ terræ in villâ, etc., unde placitum fuit inter illos in curiâ meâ: et nisi fecerit, et prædictus R. fecerit te securum de clamore suo presequendo, tunc pone cum per vadium et salvos plegios, quòd sit coram me vel justitiis meis, ostensurus die, etc., quare non fecerit, etc.*[3]

If he did not appear, nor essoin himself; or after the three essoins, if he did not appear, nor send his attorney,

---

[1] Glanv., lib. 8, c. 1, 2.   [2] *Vide ante*, 341.   [3] Glanv., lib. 8, c. 3, 4.

they were to proceed as was before shown in case of suits prosecuted by attachments. When they both appeared in court, if both parties acknowledged the writing containing the concord; or if the concord was stated to be such by the justices before whom it was taken, and this was testified by their record; then the party who had broke it was to be in the king's mercy, and to be safely attached till he gave good security to perform the concord in future; that is, either the specific thing agreed on, if it was possible; or otherwise, in some instances, what was equivalent: for it was invariably expected of every one who had acknowledged or undertaken anything in the king's court, in presence of him or his justices, ever after to observe such acknowledgment and undertaking. Moreover, had the final concord been made in a plea of land, then he who was convicted of breach of the fine, if tenant of the land, was *ipso facto* to lose the land. If one or both the parties denied the chirographum, then the justices were to be summoned to appear and *record*, says Glanville, in court the reasons why such a plea, between such parties of such land, ceased; and, if the parties came to a concord and agreement by their assent, what the form of that concord was. As to the method of making this record, there was this difference observed between a concord made in the king's chief court and that before the justices itinerant: if in the latter, then the justices were summoned, that they, with certain discreet knights of the county where the concord was made, who were present at making the concord, and knew the truth of the matter, should appear in court, there to make a record of the plea. Accordingly a writ to that effect was directed to the sheriff to summon the justices and knights.[1] Besides this, the sheriff of the county where the plea had been, was commanded to have the record of the plea then before the king or his justices by four discreet knights of the county. This is the first mention we have of the writ of *recordari*, so named from the words of it: *Præcipio tibi quòd facias* RECORDARI *in comitatu tuo loquelam, etc.*[2] When the justices appeared, and had agreed upon the record, that record was to be abided by, neither party being allowed to make any exception to it; only,

---

[1] Glanv., lib. 8, c. 5, 6.   [2] Ibid., c. 6, 7.

if such doubts should arise, which there was no possibility of removing, then the plea might be recommenced, and proceeded in afresh.¹

Having said thus much of records of courts, it may be proper on this occasion to inquire a little further concerning these muniments of judicial proceedings (a). No court had, generally and regularly, such remembrances of its proceedings as were called and esteemed records, except the king's court, that is, as it should seem, the court where the king's justices sat; though, by what we have just related, it should seem that the justices itinerant had not *regularly* a court of record. In other courts, if any one had said that which he would not willingly own, he might be permitted to deny it, in opposition to the whole court, by the oaths of three persons, affirming that he never said it; or by more or less, according to the custom of different courts.

Of records.

In some special instances, however, county and other inferior courts had records; and that, as we are informed by our great authority, Glanville, by virtue of a law made by the council of the realm.² Thus, if in any inferior court duel was waged, and afterwards the plea was removed into the king's court, then the claim of the demandant, the defense of the tenant, the form of words in which the duel was awarded and waged; of all these the court had a record, which was acknowledged as such by the king's court. But it had a record of nothing else, except only of the change of a champion: for if, after the removal of the plea into the king's court, another champion than he who had waged duel in the inferior court was produced, and a question arose upon it; in this case also it was de-

---

(a) *Vide ante*, p. 346. "Qui placetat in curia cujuscunque curia sit, excepto ubi persona regis est, et quis eum sistat super eo quod dixerit, rem quam nolit empteri si non potest disrationari per intelligentes homines qui interfuerunt placito, et videntes quod non dixerit, recuperet juxta verbum suum" (*Leges Will.* i., c. 28). "Et omnem recordationem domini regis curiæ non potest homo contradicere" (*Leges Hen. Primi*, c. xlix., s. 4). "Si plures alicujus homines simul implacitentur secundum quod causæ fuerint vel pactum inter eos, de omnibus cura die simul vel de singulis sigillatum, rectum faciat: pactum eum legem vincit et amor judicium" (*Ibid.*, i., 5). "Recordationem curiæ regis nulli negare licet: alias licebit per intelligibiles homines placeti" (*Ibid.*, cxxxi., s. 4).

¹ Glanv., lib. 8, c. 8.
² When this law was made, we do not know; nor is it mentioned anywhere, that I know of, but in this passage of Glanville.

cided by the record of the inferior court, according to the direction of the statute before alluded to. Besides, any one might object to the record of an inferior court, declaring that he had said more than was now to be found in the record; and that what he had so said he would prove against the whole court by the oaths of two or more lawful men, according as the usage of the court required; for no court was bound either to maintain or defend its record by duel; this, therefore, was the only proof that could be had. We are informed by Glanville, that a particular law[1] had been made, ordaining that no one should except to a record *in part*, and admit the remainder; though he might deny *the whole* by oath, as just stated.[2]

The king might occasionally confer on any court the privilege to have a *record*. Thus, upon some reasonable cause being shown, he might, as has just been observed, direct a court to be summoned *to make a record* of a matter for the inspection of his own court; so that, if the king pleased, there could be no contradiction admitted to such record. It often happened that a court was summoned to have the record of some plea before the king or his justices, although it had, in truth, no such record. In this case, the parties, by admission and consent, might settle a record of the matter between them. The writ on this occasion used to be of the following kind: *Rex vicecomiti salutem. Præcipio tibi quòd* FACIAS RECORDARI *in comitatu tuo loquelam quæ est inter A. et B. de terrâ, etc., in villâ, etc., et habeas recordum illius loquelæ coram me vel justitiis meis ad terminum, etc., per quatuor legales milites, qui interfuerunt, ad recordum id faciendum. Et summone per bonos summonitores A. qui terram illam clamat, quòd tunc sit ibi cum loquelâ suâ, et B. qui terram illam tenet, quòd tunc sit ibi ad audiendum illud, etc.*[3]

Again, inferior courts had occasionally records of what was done there, which were transmitted to the king's court; as when a lord had a plea in his court of some doubt and difficulty, which could not be well determined there, then he might *curiam suam ponere in curiam domini regis*, as they called it, or adjourn the matter into the king's court, to have the advice of that tribunal what was proper to be done — an assistance which the king owed to all his

---

[1] Of this law also, and the time when it was made, there is no remembrance but this slight intimation.
[2] Glanv., lib. 8, c. 9. [3] Ibid., c. 9, 10.

barons. When a lord was in this manner certified what was advisable to be done, he returned with the plea, and proceeded to determine upon it in his own court. County courts had a record of pledges, or sureties taken there, and of some few other matters.[1]

We before said that courts were not bound to defend their records by duel; but they were obliged to defend their *judgments* in that manner: as if any one should declare against a court for passing *a false judgment* against him, and should state it to be *therefore* false, because when one party said thus, and the other answered thus, the court gave a false judgment thereon in such and such words, and passed that judgment by the mouth of N., and should conclude, that if it was denied, he was ready to prove it by a lawful witness there ready to deraign it; in this case, the question might be decided by the duel. But there were some doubts whether the court was to defend its judgment by one of its own members, or by some stranger. Glanville seems to have been of the former opinion; for he says, the defence was to be by the person who passed the judgment. If the court was convicted in this manner, the lord of the court was in the king's mercy, and lost his court forever; and besides this, the whole court was in the king's mercy.[2]

We shall now speak of the remedy the law allowed to compel a lord to receive the homage of this tenant, and so enable him to claim the protection consequent thereon.[3] If a lord would not receive the homage of the heir, nor a reasonable relief, then the relief was to be kept ready, and to be repeatedly tendered to the lord by good men: and if he would not at any rate accept it, the heir might complain of him to the king or his justices, upon which he would have this writ: *Præcipe N. quòd justè et sine dilatione recipiat homagium et rationabile relevium K. de libero tenemento quod tenet in villâ, etc., et quòd de eo tenere clamat. Et nisi fecerit, summone, etc.*

Writ de homagio recipiendo.

The process against the defendant was the same as has often been mentioned before in cases of summons. If he appeared and acknowledged the complainant to be the heir, and confessed he had tendered his homage and relief,

---

[1] Glanv., lib. 8, c. 11.   [2] Ibid., c. 9.
[3] We have before seen how important it was for the heir that the lord should receive his homage. *Vide ante*, 381.

he was to receive it instantly, or appoint a day for doing it. The same was to be done, if he denied the tender, but admitted the complainant to be the heir; but if he denied he was the heir, then the heir, if he was out of seisin, might have an assize against the lord *de morte antecessoris;* if he was in seisin, he might hold himself in, till it pleased the lord to accept his homage; for the lord was not to have the relief till he had accepted homage. But if the lord doubted whether he was the lawful heir or not, and it had appeared to the vicinage that he was not, the lord might then take the land into his own hands, till it was made appear whether he was the heir. And this was the way in which the king always dealt with his barons: for the king, upon the death of a baron holding of him in chief, immediately retained the barony in his own hands, till the heir gave security for the relief; and this, notwithstanding the heir was of full age.[1]

Lords might defer receiving homage and relief, upon reasonable cause shown; as suppose some other person than the heir pretended a right to the inheritance, or any part of it; for while that suit depended, he could not receive homage or relief. Another cause was, when the lord thought he had a right to hold the inheritance in demesne. In such case, if he commenced a suit by the king's writ, or that of his justices, against the person in seisin of the land, the tenant might put himself upon the king's great assize, which proceeded much in the way we before stated, as will appear by the following writ: *Rex vicecomiti salutem. Summone per bonos summonitores quatuor legales milites de vicineto villæ, etc., quòd sint coram me vel justitiis meis die, etc., ibi, ad eligendum super sacramentum suum duodecim, etc., qui meliùs rei veritatem sciant, et dicere velint, ad faciendam recognitionem, utrùm N. majus jus habet tenendi unam hidam terræ in villâ, etc., de I. vel ipse R. tenendi eam in dominico suo, quam ipse R. petit per breve meum versus prædictum N. et unde N. qui terram illam tenet, posuit se in assisam meam, et petit recognitionem fieri, utrùm ille majus jus habeat tenendi terram illam in dominico, vel prædictus N. tenendi de eo. Et summone per bonos summonitores prædictum N. qui terram illam tenet, quòd tunc ibi sit auditurus illam electionem, etc.*[2]

---

[1] Glanv., lib. 9, c. 4–6. [2] Ibid., c. 6, 7.

If a lord could not, by distress or otherwise, compel his tenant to render his services and customs legally due, recourse was then had to the king or his chief justice, from whom he might obtain the following writ to the sheriff, directing that he himself should see justice done to the complainant; which is the first instance we have yet mentioned of the form of a writ of *justicies: Præcipio tibi quòd* JUSTICIES *N. quòd justè et sine dilatione faciat R. consuetudines et recta servitia quæ ei facere debet de tenemento suo quod de eo tenet in villâ, etc., sicut rationabiliter monstrare poterit cum sibi deberi, ne oporteat cum amplius inde conqueri pro defectu recti, etc.* In pursuance of this writ, the sheriff, in his county court, held a plea of the matter in question, and the party complaining might therein recover his services and dues, according to the custom of the county. If he made out his right, the other party, besides rendering what was due, was in the mercy of the sheriff; for the *misericordia* or *amercement* which arose out of any suit in the county court always went to the sheriff. The *quantum* of this was ascertained by no general law, but depended on the custom of different counties, and the opinion of the persons who assessed it (*a*).[1]

Next, as to the remedy to be pursued in case of purprestures. *Purpresture*, or, according to Glanville, *porpresture*, was when any unlawful encroachment was made upon the king, as intruding on his demesnes, obstructing the public ways, turning public waters from their course, or building upon the king's highway;[2] in short, whenever a nuisance was committed upon the king's freehold, or the king's highway, a suit

Purpresture.

(*a*) But it ought to be reasonable. Thus, Henry I., in his charter, admitted that amercements had been grievous, and promised that they should be henceforth reasonable: "Si quis baronum vel hominum meorum forisfecerit, non dabit vadium in misericordia totius pecuniæ suæ, sicut faciebat tempore patris mei et fratris mei, sed secundum modum forisfacti, ita emendabit sicut emendasset retro a tempore patris mei et fratris mei, in tempore aliorum antecessorum meorum" (*Leges Hen. Pri.*, c. 1; *A.-S. L.*, v. i., p. 500). How utterly, therefore, Henry II. violated all law in the case of Archbishop A'Becket, when, upon a supposed contempt in non-appearance in court — though he sent four knights to represent him and excuse his absence — he was declared to have forfeited the whole of his goods and chattels, may easily be judged (*Hume's Hist. Eng.*, vol. i., c. 8). And so outrageous were the exactions of the Norman sovereigns under the pretence of amercements, that a special clause was introduced into Magna Charta to repress them (*Vide post, et vide* 2 *Inst.*, 27).

[1] Glanv., lib. 9, c. 8-10.   [2] *Regiam plateam.*

concerning such nuisance belonged to the king's crown and dignity (a). These purprestures were inquired of either in the chief court of the king or before the king's justices, who were sent into different parts of the kingdom for the purpose of making such inquisitions by a jury of the country or of the vicinage.[1] Whosoever was convicted by a jury of having committed such purprestures was in the king's mercy for the whole fee he held of the king, and was obliged to restore what he had encroached upon. If the purpresture consisted in building in some city upon the king's street, the edifice, says Glanville, so built, was forfeited to the king, and the party remained in the king's mercy. The *misericordia domini regis*, which has been so often mentioned, is explained in this passage by Glanville to be, when any one is to be amerced by the oaths of twelve lawful men of the vicinage; so, however, *ne aliquid de suo honorabili contenemento amitat*, as not to lose his *countenance* or appearance in the world. When any purpresture was committed against a private person, it was considered in a different way. If it was against the lord of the fee, and not within the provisions of the statute about assizes, then the transgressor was made to appear in the lord's court, provided he held any tenement of him. This was by the following writ: *Rex vicecomiti salutem. Præcipio tibi quòd justicies N. quòd sine dilatione veniat in curiâ I. domini sui, et ibi stet ei ad rectum de libero tenemento suo quod super eum occuparit, ut dicit, ne oporteat, etc.*[2] If, upon this writ, he was convicted of the purpresture in the lord's court, he lost, without recovery, the freehold he held of the lord.

If he held no freehold of the lord, then the lord might implead him by a writ of right in the court of the chief lord. In like manner, if any one committed a purpresture upon a person not his lord, and the fact did not come

---

(a) "It is properly when there is a house built or an enclosure made of any part of the king's demesnes, or of a highway, or a common street, or public water, or such like public thing. It is derived of the French *pourpris*, which signifieth an enclosure" (*Co. Litt.*, 277 b.). It might be committed, as understood by our legal authorities, (1) against the king by a subject, (2) by a tenant against his lord, (3) by one subject against another (*Splem. Gloss.*, and in *Cowell's Interpret. Manwood's Forest Laws*, p. 119). The word used by Glanville is "occupation," and Lord Coke says "occupationes" are taken for usurpations upon the king, and, in a large sense, includes purprestures as well as intrusions and usurpations (2 *Inst.*, 272).

[1] *Per juratam patriæ sive vicineti.*   [2] Glanv., lib. 9, c. 11, 12.

within the provision about assizes, he might be impleaded in a writ of right. But if it was within that law, then there should be a recognition upon the novel disseisin to recover seisin; of which proceeding we shall have occasion to speak more hereafter. In these purprestures it usually happened that the boundaries of lands were broke in upon and confounded; upon which, at the prayer of any of the neighbors, the following writ might be issued: *Rex vicecomiti salutem. Præcipio tibi quòd justè et sine dilatione facias esse rationabiles divisas inter terram R. in villâ, etc., et terram Ade de Byri sicut esse debent, et esse solent, et sicut fuerunt tempore regis Henrici avi mei, unde R. queritur quòd Adam injustè, et sine judicio, occupavit plus inde quàm pertinet ad liberum tenementum suum de Byri; ne ampliùs inde clamorem audiam pro defectu justitiæ, etc.*[1]

We have hitherto treated of the remedies in use for vindicating a right to land, and its appendant services and profits. We shall now take leave of this subject for awhile, and consider the nature of personal contracts, such as buying, selling, giving, lending, and the like, upon which there arose *debts* and obligations to pay. This sub-

De debitis laicorum. ject is entitled, in the language of this period, *de debitis laicorum*, to distinguish it from those debts and dues that were recoverable in the ecclesiastical courts, as being things of a supposed spiritual nature, such as money due by legacy, or upon promise of marriage.[2]

Pleas, therefore, *de debitis laicorum* belonged to the king's crown and dignity. If any one complained to the *curia regis* of a debt owing to him, which he was desirous should be inquired of in that court, he had the following writ of summons: *Rex vicecomiti salutem. Præcipe N. quòd justè et sine dilatione reddat R. centum marcas quas ei debet, ut dicit, et unde queritur quòd ei deforceat. Et nisi fecerit, summone eum per bonos summonitores, quòd sit corum me vel justitiis meis apud Westmonasterium, à clauso Paschæ in quindecim dies, ostensurus quare non fecerit, etc.* This was the form of the writ of debt.

The manner of enforcing an appearance to this writ was as in other cases of summons. It should be observed here, that it was not usual for the *curia regis* in any case to compel obedience to a writ by distraining the chattels;

---

[1] Glanv., lib. 9, c. 13, 14. [2] For this *vide* Fleta, p. 131.

therefore, even in a plea like this, the defendant might be distrained by his fee and freehold, or, as in some other suits, by attachment of pledges.[1]

When they were both in court, then it was to be considered how the demand arose. This might be of various kinds, as *ex causâ mutui*, upon a borrowing; *ex causâ venditionis*, upon a sale; *ex commodato*, upon a lending; *ex locato*, upon a hiring; *ex deposito*,[2] upon a deposit; or by some other cause by which a *debt* arose; for, at this time, all matters of personal contract were considered as binding only in the light of *debts;* and the only means of recovery, in a court, was by this action of debt.

A debt arose *ex mutuo*, when one lent another anything which consisted in number, weight or measure. If a person upon such a lending, received back again more than he lent, it was usury; and if he died under the reputation of an usurer, we have seen the infamy with which his memory was stained. A thing was sometimes lent *sub plegiorum datione;* that is, some one was surety for the restoration of it; sometimes, *sub vadii positione,* that is, a pledge was given; sometimes, *sub fidei interpositione,* when a bare promise was made for the return; sometimes, *sub chartæ expositione,* when a charter was made acknowledging such lending; and sometimes with all these securities together.

When anything was owing *sub plegiorum datione* only, if the principal debtor had not wherewithal to pay, recourse was had to the sureties by the following writ: *Rex vicecomiti salutem. Præcipe N. quòd justè et sine dilatione acquietet R. de centum marcis versus N. unde eum applegiavit, ut dicit, et unde queritur quòd eum non acquietavit inde. Et nisi fecerit, summone eum per bonos summonitores, etc.*[3] If the sureties appeared in court, and con-

Of sureties. ✓

---

[1] Glanv., lib. 10, c. 1-3.
[2] It is almost unnecessary to remark, that these expressions are all borrowed from the civil law; the same may be said of the definitions hereafter given of these different obligations; but, notwithstanding this, the matter of Glanville's discourse upon the subject of debts and obligations bears no resemblance to the imperial jurisprudence. This is one strong and very remarkable circumstance to show, that the use made of the Roman law by our old writers was not to *corrupt*, but to adorn and elucidate our municipal customs. *Vide* Inst., lib. iii., tit. 15.
[3] This writ was, in after times, called *de plegiis acquietandis*, and used to be brought by the sureties against the principal debtor; though in the time of Glanville we find it lay for the creditor against the surety, F. N. B. It must

fessed the suretyship, they were then obliged to pay the debt at certain times affixed in court, unless they could show that they were released from their engagement, or had in some way satisfied the demand. Sureties, if more than one, were held to be severally bound for the whole (unless there had been some special agreement to the contrary), and they were both to be proceeded against for satisfaction; therefore, should any of them be insufficient, the remainder were to be answerable for the deficiency. If the sureties, however, had specially engaged for particular parts of the payment, it was otherwise. There might arise a dispute between the creditor and the sureties, or between the sureties, upon this point. In like manner, if some of the sureties engaged for the whole, and some for parts only, then the former would have a question to debate with the latter. In what manner all these points were to be proved, will be seen presently. When the sureties had paid what was due, they might resort to the principal by a new action of debt, as will be shown hereafter. However, it should be remarked, if any one had become surety for a person's appearance in a suit, and he had fallen into the king's mercy for the default of the principal, he could not recover by action of debt against the principal what he had so paid; for it was a rule, that should any one become surety for a person's answering in the king's court, in any suit belonging to the king's crown and dignity, as for breach of the peace, or the like, he fell into the king's mercy, if he did not produce the principal; but he was thereby, notwithstanding, released from the engagement as a surety, and therefore there could be no further proceeding instituted thereon.[1]

If some of the sureties denied they were sureties, and some confessed it, then the question would be as well between the creditor and the sureties as between the sureties themselves. There was a doubt what should, in this case, be the mode of proof; whether by duel, or whether the sureties were to deny their engagement by the oaths of such number of persons as the court should require. Some thought that the creditor himself, by his own oath, and that of lawful witnesses, might make proof of it against

be confessed, the wording of it in Glanville seems more adapted to the modern than the ancient application of the writ.

[1] Glanv., lib. 10, c. 3-5.

the sureties, unless the sureties could avoid his oath by any lawful objection; and if so, says Glanville, they must resort to the duel.¹

Things were lent sometimes *sub vadii positione;* and then either movables, as chattels, or immovables, as land, tenements, and rents, were given in pledge. A pledge was either given at the time of lending, or not. It was given sometimes for a certain term, sometimes without any fixed term; sometimes in *mortuo vadio,* sometimes not. *Mortuum vadium,* or *mortgage,* was when the fruits, or rent arising therefrom, did not go towards paying off the demand for which it was pledged (*a*). When movables were pledged, and seisin thereof, as it is called, given to the creditor for a certain term, the law required that he should safely keep it, without using it so as to cause any detriment thereto; and if any detriment happened to it within the term appointed, it was to be set off against the debt, according to the damage sustained. If the thing pledged was such as necessarily required some expense and cost, as to be fed or repaired, perhaps there would be some agreement between the parties about it, and that agreement was to be the rule of such contingent expenses. It was sometimes agreed, that if the pledge was not redeemed at the term fixed, it

---

(*a*) The *Mirror* affords a much better explanation by analogy to distresses, which are a kind of pledge, and which it divides into *dead* distresses, as armor, or robes, or jewels, and *live* distresses, as cattle or sheep (c. 2, s. 26). It is singular that so easy an explanation has not occurred to any writer since the time of the *Mirror*. A mortgage is always a *dead* pledge; that is literally the meaning of the phrase, for "gage" or "vadium" is synonymous with pledge, and a distress is only a pledge compulsorily taken, and so it is said in the chapter of the *Mirror* that a man unlawfully takes away a live distress against gages and pledges, as a live distress is not to be taken away, etc. It is not easy to understand the explanation above given, which is copied from Glanville, and of which the author offers no explanation. In our day, rents received, of course, do, *pro tanto,* go in satisfaction of the debt. Littleton's explanation is, "If a feoffment be made upon condition, that if the feoffor pay to the feoffee at a certain day a certain sum, then the feoffor may enter: in this case, the feoffee is called tenant in mortgage, *i. e.*, it is *mortuum vadium,* because it is doubtful whether the feoffor will pay at the day limited or not, and if he doth not pay, then the land which is put in pledge is taken from him forever, and so dead to him, and if he doth pay, then the pledge is dead to the tenant" (*Litt.,* b. 2, c. 5; *Co. Litt.,* 205, *a*). The explanation probably is this — that in ancient times the mortgages were actually forfeited at the day, and the intermediate rents and profits were looked upon in the light of a fine or penalty, or as interest for the delay, which was not very long. This appears by a subsequent passage to be the explanation.

¹ Glanv., lib. 10, c. 6.

should remain to the creditor, and become his property. If there was no such agreement, the creditor might quicken the redemption by the following writ: *Rex vicecomiti salutem. Præcipe N. quòd justè et sine dilatione acquietet, etc., quam invadiavit R. pro centum marcis usque ad terminum qui præteriit, ut dicit, et unde queritur quòd eam nondum acquietavit: et nisi fecerit, etc.*[1]

It was doubted by Glanville in what manner the defendant was to be compelled to appear to this writ; whether he was to be distrained by the pledge itself, or in what other way. This, it seems, was left to the discretion of the court, and might be effected either by that or some other method. He ought, however, to be present in court before the pledge was quit-claimed to the creditor; for he might be able, perhaps, to show some reason why it should not. If he then confessed his having pledged the thing, as he thereby in effect confessed the debt, he was commanded to redeem it in some reasonable time; and if he did not, the creditor had license to treat the pledge as his own property. If he denied the pledging, he must either say the thing was his own, and account for its being transferred out of his possession, as lent or entrusted to him, or deny it to be his; and then the creditor had license to consider it as his own property. If he acknowledged it was his, but denied the pledge and debt both, then the creditor was bound to prove both; and the manner of proof, where pledges denied their suretyship, we have before mentioned. But the debt could not be demanded before the expiration of the term agreed upon.[2]

If the pledge was made without mention of any particular term, the creditor might demand his debt at any time. When the debt was paid, the creditor was bound to restore the pledge in the condition he received it, or make satisfaction for any injury that it had received; for it was a rule that a creditor was to restore the pledge, or make satisfaction for it; if not, he was to lose his debt.[3]

When it happened that a debtor did not made delivery of the pledge at the time of receiving the thing lent, Glanville doubts what remedy there was for the creditor, as the same thing might be pledged, both before and after, to several persons; for it must be observed, says our author,

---

[1] Glanv., lib. 10, c. 8.   [2] Ibid.   [3] Ibid.

that it was not usual for the *court of our lord the king* to give protection to, or warrant private agreements about giving or receiving things in pledge, or about other matters, if made out of court, or if made in other courts than *that of our lord the king:* and therefore, when such conventions were not observed, the *curia regis* would not entertain any suit for the establishment of them. The debtor, therefore, could not be put to answer about the priority of pledging, and [1] the person who was the loser by it must content himself with the consequence of his own negligence.

When a thing immovable was put in pledge, and seisin thereof given to the creditor for a certain term, (*a*) it was generally agreed between them whether the rents and profits should, in the meantime, go towards the discharge of the debt, or not. An agreement of the first kind was considered as just and binding, the latter as unjust and dishonest, and was the *mortuum vadium*, or *mortgage* before mentioned. Though this was not wholly prohibited by the king's court, yet it was reputed as a species of usury, and punishable in the way before mentioned. In other respects, the rules of law respecting this pledge were the same as those before stated in the case of a movable, when pledged. It must be added, that should the debtor pay the debt, and the creditor still detain the pledge, the debtor might have the following writ to the sheriff: *Præcipe N. quòd justè et sine dilatione reddat R. totam terram illam in villâ, etc., quam ei invadiavit pro centum marcis ad terminum qui præteriit, ut dicit, et denarios suos inde recipiat;* OR, *quam ei acquietavit, ut dicit: et nisi fecerit, summone eum per bonos, etc.*[2] The creditor, upon his appearance in court, would either acknowledge the land to be given in pledge, or would claim to hold it in fee. In the first instance, he ought to restore it, or show a reasonable cause why he should not. In the second, it was put either at

Mortgages.

(*a*) It is to be observed, that in Glanville's time (says Sir W. Blackstone), when the universal method of conveyance was by livery of seisin or corporal tradition of the lands, no gage or a pledge of lands was good unless possession was also delivered to the creditor, and having referred to this passage, which is copied from Glanville, he adds, "And the frauds which have arisen since the exchange of these public and notorious conveyances for more private and secret bargains have well evinced the wisdom of our ancient laws" (2 *Black. Comm.*, 159). Quia sine traditione non transferentur rerum dominia (*Bracton*, 61, *b*).

[1] Glanv., lib. 10, c. 8.   [2] Ibid., c. 8, 9.

the prayer of the creditor or debtor, upon the recognition of the country, whether the creditor had the land in fee or in pledge, or whether his father or any of his ancestors was seized thereof, as in fee or in pledge, on the day he died; and so the recognition might be varied many ways, according as the demandant claimed, or the tenant answered to that claim. But if a recognition was prayed by neither party, the plea went on upon the right only.[1]

If the creditor by any means lost his seisin, whether through the debtor or through any one else, he could not recover seisin by any judgment of the court, nor by a recognition of novel disseisin; but if he was disseized of his pledge unlawfully, and without judgment of any court, the debtor himself might have an assize of novel disseisin; and should he have been disseized by the debtor himself, he had no way of getting possession again but through the debtor; for he must resort to the principal plea of debt, to compel the debtor to make him satisfaction.[2]

Thus far of proving a debt by sureties and by pledge; but where the creditor had neither of these to prove his demand, nor any other proof, but only the faith or promise of the debtor, this was held no sufficient proof in the king's court; but he was left, says Glanville, to his suit in the court Christian *de fidei læsione vel transgressione*, for breach of promise. Though the ecclesiastical judge might take cognizance of this as a criminal matter, and inflict a penance upon the party, or enjoin him to make satisfaction; yet we have seen that he was prohibited by one of the constitutions of Clarendon, to draw into that jurisdiction, and determine questions concerning lay-debts or tenements, upon pretence of any *promise* having been made respecting them.[3]

If then the creditor had neither sureties nor pledge, he was driven to find some other proof. He might make out the matter either *per testem idoneum, per duellum*, or *per cartam, i. e.* by a fit witness, or by the duel, or by a charter. If the debtor's charter or that of his ancestor was produced, and he did not acknowledge it, he might controvert it several ways. Perhaps he might admit it to be his seal, but deny that the charter was made by him or with his assent; or he might deny the charter and seal both.

---

[1] Glanv., lib. 10, c. 10.   [2] Ibid., c. 11.   [3] Ibid., c. 12. *Vide ante.*

In the first case, if he acknowledged publicly in court the seal to be his, so great regard was had to a seal, that he was thereby considered as having acknowledged the charter itself, and was bound to observe the covenants therein contained; it being his own fault, if he suffered any injury for want of taking care of his own seal. In the latter case, the charter might be proved in the duel by a fit witness, particularly by one whose name was inserted as a witness in the charter. There were other ways of establishing the credit of a charter; as by showing other charters signed with the same seal, which were known to be the deeds of the person who denied this; and if the seals, upon comparison, appeared exactly the same, it was held as a clear proof; and the party against whom it was to operate lost his suit, whether it related to debts, land, or any other matter: and he was moreover to be *in misericordiâ* to the king; for it was a general rule, that when a person had said anything in court or in a plea which he again denied, or which he could not warrant, or bring proof of, or which he was compelled to gainsay by contrary proof, he always remained *in misericordiâ*. If a person had given more securities than one for a debt, they might all be resorted to at once; otherwise many securities would not be of more benefit than one.[1]

We have hitherto been speaking of lending and borrowing; we come now to a debt arising *ex commodato:* as if one lent another a thing *without any gratuity*, to use and derive a benefit from it; when that use and benefit was attained, the thing was to be restored without detriment; but if the thing perished, or was damaged in his keeping, a recompense was to be made for the damage sustained: but how this damage was to be valued, and if the thing was lent for a certain term, or to be used in a certain place, how a recompense was to be made, should he exceed that term and deviate from that place; or how that excess was to be proved, or whose property the thing was to be considered, Glanville signifies his doubts; only as to the property, he thought that retaining the thing beyond the stated time and place could not well be called *furtum*, or stealing; because he had possession of it originally through the right owner. Glanville also doubted whether the

---

[1] Glanv., lib. 10, c. 12.

owner, if he had any use for it himself, might demand his thing so lent before the time was expired, or before any breach of the agreement as to the place.¹

Next as to debts arising *ex empto et vendito*. A sale was considered as effectually completed when the price was agreed upon, so as there was a delivery of the thing sold, or the price paid, in part or in the whole, or that at least earnest was given and received (*a*). In the first two cases, neither of the contracting parties could recede from the bargain, unless on a just and reasonable cause; as if there had been an agreement at first that either might declare off within a certain time; for in this case, the rule of law operated, that *conventio vincit legem*. Again, if the thing was sold as sound and without fault, and afterwards the buyer could prove the contrary, the seller was bound to take it back; however, it would be sufficient if it was sound at the time of the contract, whatever might afterwards happen: but Glanville had a doubt within what time complaint was to be made of this, particularly where there was no special agreement about it. Where earnest was given, the purchaser might be off his bargain, upon forfeiting his earnest; but if the seller, in this case, wanted to be off, Glanville doubted whether he might, without paying some penalty, for otherwise he would be in a better condition than the purchaser, though it was not easy to say what penalty he was to pay. In general, all hazard respecting the thing sold was to rest with him who was in possession of it at the time, unless there was some special agreement to the contrary.²

In all sales of immovables, the seller and his heirs were bound to warrant the thing sold to the purchaser and his heirs, and upon that warranty he or his heirs were to be impleaded, in manner as we before stated. And if any movable was demanded by action against the purchaser,

---

(*a*) When there is neither writing, earnests, nor delivery, says Bracton, the parties may retract property, not having passed quia sine traditione non transferentur rerum dominia (*Bracton*, 61, *b*). The earnest was given by the civil law as symbol of the contract or part of the price, as Vinnius says. In the former case, the purchaser could not avoid the rule by forfeiture; in the latter, he could (*Deg.*, 18, 1-35, 19, 1-11, 1). It is curious that, after the lapse of centuries, during which the common law as it had thus existed had become obsolete, it was virtually restored by the statute of Frauds in the reign of Charles II., by which either delivery, writing, or part payment is required to bind a contract of sale of goods above the value of £10.

¹ Glanv., lib. 10, c. 13.   ² Ibid., c. 14.

as being before sold or given, or by some other mode of transfer conveyed to another (so as no felony was charged to have been committed of it), the same course was observed, says Glanville, as in case of immovables; but if it was demanded of the purchaser *ex causâ furtivâ*, he was obliged to clear himself of all charge of felony, or call a person to warrant the thing bought. If he vouched a *certain* warrantor to appear within a reasonable time, a day was to be fixed in court. If the warrantor appeared, but denied his warranty, then the plea went on between him and the purchaser, and they might come to the decision of the duel. Glanville made a question whether such a warrantor might call another warrantor; and if so, what limit was to be set to this vouching to warranty. In this case of calling a *certain* warrantor, when a thing was demanded *ex causâ furtivâ*, the warrantor used not to be summoned, as in other cases of warranty; but on account of the particular nature of this charge, he was attached by the following writ to the sheriff: *Præcipio tibi, quòd sine dilatione attachiari facias per salvos et securos plegios N. quòd sit coram me vel justitiis meis die, etc., ad warrantizandum R. illam rem quam H. clamat adversus R. ut furtivam, et unde prædictus R. eum traxit ad warrantum in curiâ meâ, vel ad ostendendum quare ei warrantizare non debeat, etc.*[1]

This was the proceeding if he called a *certain* warrantor whom he could name. But if, in the phrase of that time, he called an *uncertain* warrantor — that is, if he merely declared that he bought the thing *de legitimo mercatu suo*, fairly and honestly, and could produce sufficient proof thereof, he was cleared of the charge of felony, as far as he might be affected criminally; not so, however, but that he might lose the thing in question, if it was really stolen, though not by the defendant. This was the method of proceeding, if any of these special circumstances arose; but if it rested upon the mere debt, that is, whether *ex empto* or *ex commodato*, it was made out by the general mode of proof used in court, namely, says Glanville, that by writing or by duel.[2]

A debt *ex locato* and *ex conducto* accrued, when one let out a thing to another for a certain time, at a certain reward; here the person letting was bound to impart the

---

[1] Glanv., lib. 10, c. 15, 16.   [2] Ibid., c. 17.

use of the thing letten, and the hirer to pay the price. In this case, the former might, at the expiration of the time, take possession of the thing letten by his own authority solely; but Glanville made it a question whether, if the price was not paid according to the agreement, he might deprive the hirer of possession by his own authority. But all these being what were then called private contracts, lying in the knowledge of the parties only, without any evidence to testify their existence, were such, as was before observed,[1] of which the king's court did not usually take cognizance; others, which were *quasi privatæ*, hardly met with more consideration from the king's court.[2] This seems to have been a remarkable part of the jurisprudence of these times; and to have stood in need of the improvement afterwards, though very slowly, adopted in actions upon promises.

Thus have we gone through those actions which were commenced originally in the *curia regis*, all which were called actions *de proprietate*. As these might be attended by the parties themselves, or by their attorneys, it seems proper in this place to say something upon the law respecting attorneys (a). These pleas, as

Of attorneys.

(a) The word used by Glanville, from whom all this is copied, is *responsalis*, and from some expressions in Bracton and Fleta, it has been conjectured that an attorney, an essoiner, and a responsalis differed in some respects (*Bracton*, 212, *b*; *Fleta*, lib. vi., c. 11, *b*. 7). And of this opinion was Lord Coke (*Co. Litt.*, 128, *a*). But these changes of expression, or even of meaning, may merely mark the gradual course of a usage. The terms used in the civil law for attorney would probably be *procurator*, but that is a mere general phrase, and the term "*responsalis*" is used in *Justinian's Novellæ* in the sense of an officer sent with a special commission, and Glanville is speaking of the special function of representation in a court, and in a particular suit. Appearance used to be personal, and it is curious that among the "abuses" specified in the *Mirror*, it is that appearance by attorney was allowed (*Mirror*, c. 5, s. i.). "It is an abuse to answer or appear by attorney" (*Ibid.*, art. 138), but it is also said, "It is an abuse to receive an attorney where the plea is not to be judged in the presence of the parties" (art. 103); and again, "It is an abuse that no one can make an attorney in personal actions, where corporal punishment is to be awarded" (art. 104); and again, "It is an abuse to receive an attorney where no power to do so is given by writ out of the Chancery" (art. 102). It is not easy to understand the precise meaning and force of these objections, but it is manifest that attorneys did appear in court, and it is plain, from other passages, that they were quite different from essoiners. "It is an abuse that an essoiner is admitted in a personal action" (art. 100). There is a distinct chapter, however, upon "attorneys," following that upon essoiners, which shows that they were closely connected. "Before a plea put into court by essoins, attachment, or by appearance — essoins being

[1] *Vide ante.*   [2] Glanv., lib. 10, c. 13.

well as some other civil pleas, might be prosecuted by an attorney; or, as he was called in those times, *responsalis ad lucrandum vel perdendum*. A person, when he appointed such *responsalis*, or attorney, ought to be present, and make the appointment in open court before the justices sitting there upon the bench; and no attorney ought to be received otherwise than from the principal then in court, though it was not necessary that the adverse party should be present at the time, nor even the attorney, provided he was known to the court. One person might be appointed attorney, or two, jointly or severally; so as, if one was not present to act, another might; and by such an attorney a plea might be commenced and determined, whether by judgment or by final concord, as effectually as by the principal himself. It was not enough that any one was appointed bailiff or steward for the management of another's estate and affairs, to entitle him to be received as his attorney in court; but he must have a special authority for that particular purpose, to act in that particular cause, *ad lucrandum vel perdendum*, for him in his stead. It was the practice to appoint in the *curia regis* an attorney to act in a cause depending in some other court; and there then issued a writ of the following kind, commanding the person appointed to be received as such: *Rex vicecomiti* (or whoever presided in the court) *salutem: Scias quòd N. posuit corum me* (or, *justitiis meis*) *R. loco suo ad lucrandum vel perdendum pro eo in placito, etc., quod est inter eum et R. de unâ carucatâ terræ in villâ, etc.; et ideò tibi præcipio quòd prædictum R. loco ipsius N. in placito illo recipias ad lucrandum vel perdendum pro eo, etc.*[1]

When a person was appointed attorney, he might cast essoins for the principal (and for him only, not for him-

---

excuses for non-appearance — none is to be received by attorney, nor is any to be received by attorney in a suit not pending, but only in a suit pending in the county court or elsewhere. All may be attorneys which the law will permit: women may not be, nor infants, nor villeins. Plaintiffs, notwithstanding they have attorneys in personal actions, are not to appear or answer in judgment by attorney (*Ibid.*, c. ii., s. 31). Elsewhere, it is said that attorneys who yield up the inheritance or freehold of their clients in judgment fall into the offence of wrongful disseisin, for it behoveth not attorneys to lose their clients' rights, but to defend them, until a rightful judgment is given (*Ibid.*, c. ii., s. 26). It appears that accountants in the exchequer were usually obliged to come in person (*Mador's Exch.*, c. xxvii., s. 5).

[1] Glanv., lib. 11, c. 1, 2.

self) till his appointment was vacated. When an attorney was appointed, and had acted in a cause, Glanville puts a question, whether his principal could remove him at his pleasure and appoint another, particularly if there had arisen any great disagreement between them. And he thought that the principal had that power; an attorney being put in the place of another only in his absence; and the practice was to remove an attorney at any part of a cause, and appoint another in court, in the form above mentioned.[1]

A father might appoint his son his attorney, an instance of which we saw in the fine above stated, and so *vice versâ*; and a wife might appoint a husband. When a husband acted as attorney to his wife, and lost anything in a plea of *maritagium* or dower, or gave up any right of the wife's, whether by judgment or final concord, it was made a question by Glanville, whether the wife could afterwards institute any suit for it, or was bound, after her husband's death, to abide by what he had done. And it should seem, says he, that she ought not in such case to lose anything by the act of her husband; because, while she was *in potestate viri*, she could not *contradict* him, or contravene his acts; and therefore could not, unless he pleased, attend to her own property and concerns; and yet, adds our author, it might be said on the other side, that whatever is transacted in the king's court ought to be held firm and inviolable.[2] Abbots and priors of canons regular used to be received as attorneys for their societies, of course, without letters from their convent; other priors, whether of canons or monks, if they were cloistered, even though they were aliens, were never received in court without letters from their abbot or chief prior. The master of the Temple, and the chief prior of the hospital of St. John of Jerusalem were received of themselves, but no inferior persons of their order. When one or more were appointed attorneys in the above manner, it was made a question by Glanville, whether one might appoint his colleague to act for him, or some third person, *ad lucrandum vel perdendum*.[3]

The principal might be compelled to fulfil everything that was done by his attorney, whether by judgment or

---

[1] Glanv., lib. 11, c. 3.   [2] Ibid.   [3] Ibid., c. 5.

final concord: though it was settled beyond a question or doubt, that upon the default or inability of the principal, the attorney was not liable.[1] When it is said that the principal must be present in court to appoint his attorney, it must be remembered what was before laid down — namely, that if a tenant did not appear after the third essoin, but sent an attorney, such attorney should be received; but this was allowed for the necessity of the thing, as he was compelled by the judgment of the court, or by process of distress, to put some one in his place, *ad lucrandum vel perdendum.*

The foregoing writs of right were commenced directly and originally in the *curia regis,* and were there determined. There were some writs of right which were not brought there originally, but were removed thither, when it had been proved that the court of the lord where they were brought had *de recto defecisse,* as it was called, or failed in doing justice between the parties; and, in that case, such causes might be removed into the county court, and from thence into the *curia regis,* for the above reason.[2]

When, therefore, any one claimed freehold land, or service, held of some other person than the king, he had a writ of right directed to his lord, of whom he claimed to hold the land, to the following effect: *Rex comiti W. salutem. Præcipio tibi, quòd sine dilatione teneas plenum rectum N. de decem hidis terræ in Middleton, quam clamat tenere de te per liberam servitium fœdi unius militis pro omni servitio. Et nisi feceris, vicecomes de Northamptone faciat, ne ampliùs inde clamorem audiam pro defectu justitiæ, etc.* The form of these writs was capable of infinite variety, according to the subject and circumstances of the demand.[3] Glanville says nothing upon the order and course of conducting these pleas in the lord's court, except intimating that they depended on the custom of the particular court[4] where they were brought.

The way of proving a court *de recto defecisse,* to have failed in doing justice was this: The demandant made his complaint to the sheriff in his county court, and there showed the king's writ; upon this, the sheriff sent some officer of his to the lord's court, on the day appointed by the lord for the parties to appear, that he, in the presence

---

[1] Glanv., lib. 11, c. 4. [2] Ibid., lib. 12, c. 1. [3] Ibid., c. 3–5.
[4] Ibid., c. 6.

of four or more lawful knights, who were to be present by the sheriff's command, might hear and see the demandant make proof that the court *de recto defecisse;* this proof was to be by his own oath, and the oaths of two others swearing with him to the fact. By this solemnity were causes removed out of many courts into the county court, and were there heard over again, and finally determined, without the lord or his heirs being allowed to make any claim for recovery of their judicature, as far as concerned that cause. Should a cause be removed before it had been proved in the above manner that there was a failure of justice, the lord might, on the day appointed for hearing the cause, make claim of cognizance, and for restoration of his court; but this was never done in the *curia regis,* unless he had claimed it three days before, in the presence of lawful men, it not being suitable to the dignity of that court to be ousted, upon slight grounds, of the cognizance of a cause once entertained there. If no day was appointed in the lord's court, and therefore proof of failure of justice could not be made in the above way, the complainant might *falsare curiam,* falsify the court, or deprive it of its cognizance, by making that proof anywhere within the lord's fee, if the lord did not reside usually there; for though a lord could not hold his court without his fee, he might by law have it anywhere within it; if he did reside there, it was probably to be made at his mansion-house.[1]

The writ of right, of which we have just spoken, was to be directed to the lord, of whom the demandant claimed to hold immediately, not to the chief lord. But it might sometimes happen that the demandant claimed to hold the thing in question of one lord, and the tenant claim to hold of another; in this case, because one lord should not be enabled to dispossess another of his court and franchise, the suit of necessity belonged to the county court; and from thence it might be removed to the *curia regis,* where both lords might be summoned, and their several rights discussed in their presence, as we before mentioned in cases of warranty.[2]

We have said that the above-mentioned writs of right
Of writs of justices. belonged to the sheriff, upon failure of the lord's court. To the sheriff also belonged

---

[1] Glanv., lib. 12, c. 7.   [2] Ibid., c. 8.

several other suits, one of which, namely, that *de nativis*,[1] we have already mentioned. In short, all causes where the writ of the king or his justices directed him to do right between the parties (called since writs of *justicies*), and such as contained the provisional clause *quòd si non rectum fecerit, tunc ipse facias*, etc., all these gave the sheriff a judicial authority to hear and determine.[2] These writs were very numerous; some of them are mentioned by Glanville, from whom may be extracted a short account, that will give an idea of this provincial judicature. There was a writ directed to a lord, commanding him, *ne injustè vexes*, by demanding more services than were due; and unless he desisted, the sheriff was commanded to see right done.[3] This is the only provisional writ; the rest are all peremptory, directed to the sheriff solely. One was to give possession of a fugitive villein and his chattels;[4] for admeasurement of pasture which was superonerated;[5] *quòd permittat habere* certain easements;[6] to make *rationabiles divisas*;[7] to observe a *rationabilem divisam* of chattels that had before been made;[8] to respite a recognition directed to be taken by the justices;[9] a *facias habere rationabilem dotem*; to take care of a deceased man's chattels for payment of his debts;[10] and to give possession of chattels that had been taken at a disseisin of the land, after the land had been recovered in an assize of novel disseisin.[11] To these we must add writs of *replevin*, and two of *prohibition* to the ecclesiastical court, which deserve to be mentioned more at length.

In the former part of this inquiry into judicial proceedings, we have seen that when land was seized into the king's hand for default or contempt of the tenant, he might within a certain time replevy his land, upon performing what was required of him by the court. The power of distraining, which lords exercised over their tenants, required a similar qualification — either that the tenant should perform what was due, or at least till it was ascertained by judgment whether anything or what was due, he should replevy; that is, have a return of his goods *upon pledges* given as a security to stand to the award of justice in the matter. In order to effect this, several writs of *re-*

---

[1] *Vide ante*, 410.
[2] Glanv., lib. 12, c. 9.
[3] Ibid., c. 10.
[4] Ibid., c. 11.
[5] Ibid., c. 13.
[6] Ibid., c. 14.
[7] Ibid., c. 16.
[8] Ibid., c. 17.
[9] Ibid., c. 19.
[10] Ibid., c. 20.
[11] Ibid., c. 18.

plegiare or *replevin* were devised. One was in this form, and seems to approach nearest to the modern writ of replevin: *Rex vicecomiti salutem. Præcipio tibi, quòd justè et sine dilatione* FACIAS HABERE G. AVERIA SUA PER VADIUM ET PLEGIUM; *unde queritur, quòd R.* EA CEPIT ET DETINET INJUSTE *pro consuetudinibus quas ab eo exigit, quas ipse non cognoscit se debere; et ipsum præterea inde justè deduci facias, ne oporteat eum, etc.*[1] The next is in the nature of a prohibition, as well as a writ of replevin, though it is not properly a prohibition, which was always to prohibit a judicial proceeding. It is as follows: *Rex vicecomiti salutem. Prohibeo tibi ne permittas quòd R. injustè exigat ab S. de libero tenemento suo quod tenet de N. de fœdo ipsius R. in villâ, etc., plus servitii quàm pertinet ad illud liberum tenementum quod tenet; et* AVERIA SUA QUAE CAPTA SUNT *pro illa demandâ, quam ille non cognoscit ad liberum tenementum suum, quod tenet, pertinere, ei* REPLEGIARI FACIAS *donec loquela illa coram nobis audiatur, et sciatur utrùm illud servitium debeat vel non, etc.*[2]

To these may be added the two writs of prohibition to the ecclesiastical court just alluded to: *Rex, etc., judicibus ecclesiasticis salutem. Prohibeo vobis ne teneatis placitum in curiâ christianitatis quod est inter N. et R. de laico fœdo prædicti R. unde ipse queritur quòd N. eum trahit in placitum in curiâ christianitatis coram vobis, quia placitum illud spectat ad coronam et dignitatem meam, etc.*[3] Besides this writ to the judges there went also an attachment against the party suing in the court Christian, to the following effect: *Rex vicecomiti salutem.* PROHIBE *R. ne sequatur placitum in curiâ christianitatis quod est inter N. et ipsum de laico fœdo ipsius prædicti N. in villâ, etc., unde ipse queritur quòd præfatus R. inde eum traxit in placitum in curiâ christianitatis coram judicibus illis. Et si præfatus N. fecerit te securum de clamore suo prosequendo, tunc* PONE PER VADIUM ET SALVOS PLEGIOS *prædictum R. quòd sit coram me vel justitiis meis die, etc., ostensurus quare traxit eum in placitum in curiâ christianitatis de laico fœdo suo, in villâ, etc., de sicut illud placitum spectat ad coronam et dignitatem meam, etc.*[4] The manner of ordering the before-mentioned suits in the county court, depended on the customs of different counties; for which reasons, as well as because it was not strictly within the design of his work, there is no notice in Glanville.[5]

---
[1] Glanv., lib. 12, c. 12. [2] Ibid., c. 15. [3] Ibid., c. 21. [4] Ibid., c. 22.
[5] Ibid., c. 23.

Before we leave the subject of writs of right, it will be proper to add some observation respecting the form of writs and of the proceedings thereon. The form of words in which a title to land was stated by the demandant, was called his *petition*,[1] or demand, from the word *peto*, with which it begun. It sometimes happened that the writ contained more or less in it than the *petitio* stated to the court, as to the appurtenances of the land, or particular circumstances of the case. Sometimes there was an error in the writ as to the name of the party, or the *quantum* of service, or the like. When the writ contained less than the petition, no more could be recovered than was stated in the writ; but when the writ contained more than the petition went for, the surplus might be remitted, and the remainder might well be recovered by the authority of that writ. If, however, there was any error in the name, then by the strictness of law another writ should be prayed: again, when there was an error in stating the *quantum* of service, the writ was lost. Suppose a writ of right, directed to the lord, stated the land to be held by less services than were really due, Glanville thought that, in such case, the lord could not refuse to receive the writ, and proceed upon it, under pretence of his being concluded thereby, and suffering a detriment to his service; but he was left to make good his claim of service against the demandant, should he recover against the tenant.[2] This is all that is to be collected from Glanville on the formal part of *Pleading;* a branch of our law which grew, in after times, to such a size, and was considered with so much nicety and refinement.

It had become the law and custom of the realm, says Glanville, that no one should be bound to answer in his lord's court concerning his freehold, without the precept or writ of our lord the king, or his chief justice, if the question was about a lay fee; but if there was a suit between two clerks concerning a freehold held in frankalmoigne, or if a clerk should be tenant of ecclesiastical land held in frankalmoigne, whoever might chance to be demandant against him, the plea concerning the right, ought, in such case, to be *in foro ecclesiastico;* unless it should be prayed to have a recognition *utrum fœdum eccle-*

---

[1] This term is borrowed from the civil and canon law, where it is used in a similar sense. The *petitio* is called *count* in our law French.
[2] Glanv., lib. 12, c. 22.

siasticum sit vel laicum, whether it was an ecclesiastical or lay fee, of which we shall say more hereafter; for then that recognition, as well as all others, was had in the king's court.[1]

We have now dismissed the proceedings for the recovery of *rights*, with all their incidents and appendages, as far as any intimation upon this subject has come down to us. The next thing that presents itself to our consideration, is the method of recovering *seisin*, or mere possession The remedies for recovery of seisin seem to be founded on the policy of preserving peace and quiet in matters of property. As seisin was the *primâ facie* evidence of right, the law would not allow it to be violated on pretence of any better right: and had provided many ways of proceeding to vindicate the seisin, sometimes in opposition to the mere right. As questions concerning seisin came within the benefit of the late statute of Henry II., to which we have so often before alluded, and were accordingly in general decided by *recognition*, we shall therefore speak of the different kinds of recognitions.[2]

<small>Of recognitions.</small>

One of those recognitions was called *de morte antecessoris;* another, *de ultimâ præsentatione;* another, *utrùm tenementum sit fœdum ecclesiasticum vel laicum;* another, whether a person was seized at the day of his death *ut de fœdo*, or *ut de vadio;* another, whether a person was within, or of full age; another, whether a person died seized *ut de fœdo*, or *ut de wardâ;* another, whether a person made the last presentation to a church by reason of being seized in fee or in ward; and the like questions, which often arose in court between parties; and which, as well by the consent of parties as by the advice of the court, were directed to be inquired of in this way, to decide the fact in dispute. There was one recognition which stood distinguished among the rest, and was called *de novâ desseisinâ*, of novel disseisin.[3] We shall speak of all these in their order.

First of the recognition *de morte antecessoris*, which seems to be a proceeding particularly calculated for the protection of heirs against the intrusion made by their lords, upon the death of the ancestor last seized (*a*). If any one died seized of land, and was seized

<small>Assisa mortis antecessoris.</small>

(*a*) Before Magna Charta, says Lord Coke, the writs of assize, of novel disseisin, or mort d'ancestor, were returnable either *coram rege*, or into the

[1] Glanv., lib. 12, c. 25.   [2] Ibid., lib. 13, c. 1.   [3] Ibid., c. 2.

CHAP. IV.]   ASSIZE MORT D'ANCESTOR.   443

in dominico suo sicut de fœdo suo; that is, had the inheritance and enjoyment thereof to him and his heirs; the heir might demand the seisin of his ancestor by the following writ: *Rex vicecomiti salutem. Si G. filius T. fecerit te securum de clamore suo prosequendo, tunc summone per bonos summonitores duodecim liberos et legales homines de vicineto de villâ, etc., quòd sint coram me vel justitiis meis die, etc., parati sacramento recognoscere, si T. pater prædicti G. fuit seisitus in dominico suo sicut de fœdo suo, de unâ virgâto terræ in villâ, etc., die qua obiit; si obiit post primam coronationem meam, et si ille G. propinquior hæres ejus est. Et interim terram illam videant, et nomina eorum imbreviari facias. Et summone per bonos summonitores R. qui terram illam tenet, quòd tunc sit ibi auditurus illam recognitionem. Et habeas ibi summonitores, etc.* This writ was varied in some parts of it, according to the circumstances under which the person died seized; as, whether he was seized the day he undertook a peregrination to Jerusalem, or St. Jago, in which journey he died; or the day he took upon him the habit of religion, the latter being a civil death, which entitled the heir to succeed immediately.[1] If the heir was within age, the clause "*si G. filius T. fecerit te securum de clamore suo prosequendo*" was left out, the infant not being able, by law, to bind himself in any security; as was also the clause, "*si T. pater prædicti G. obiit post primam coronationem meam.*"[2]

When the sheriff had received this writ, and the demandant had given security in the county court for prosecuting his claim,[3] they proceeded to make an assize in this way: Twelve free and lawful men of the vicinage were chosen, according to the direction of the writ. This was in the presence, perhaps, of the parties; though it might be in the absence of the tenant, provided he had been properly summoned to attend: for he should always be once summoned, to hear who were chosen to make the recognition; and if he pleased, he might except to some upon any reasonable cause. If he did not come at the

---

court of common pleas, and this appeareth by Glanville, "coram me vel coram justitiariis meis." But after Magna Charta, the writs were returnable, "coram justitiariis nostris ad assissas cum in partes illas venerint" (2 *Inst.*, 24). The "ancestor" meant not merely a parent, but brother, sister, uncle, aunt, nephew, or niece of the claimant (*Bracton*, 254, 261; 3 *Inst.*, 399).

[1] Glanv., lib. 13, c. 2, 3, 4, 6.   [2] Ibid., c. 5.
[3] *De clamore suo prosequendo.*

first summons, they did not wait for him; but the twelve jurors were elected in his absence, and sent by the sheriff to view the land or tenement whose seisin was in dispute: and Glanville says, that the tenant was to have one summons more. The sheriff caused the names of the twelve to be inserted in a writ;[1] then summoned the tenant to be present at the day appointed by the writ, before the king or his justices, to hear the recognition. The tenant might essoin himself at the first and second day (provided the demandant was not an infant), but there was no essoin allowed him at the third day; for then the recognition was taken, whether he came or not; it being a rule, that no more than two essoins should be allowed in any recognition upon a seisin only; and in a recognition upon a novel disseisin, there was no essoin at all. At the third day, then, the assize was taken, whether the tenant came or not. If the jurors declared for the demandant, the seisin was adjudged to him, and a writ of the following kind went to the sheriff to give execution thereof: *Scias quòd N. dirationavit in curiâ meâ seisinam tantæ terræ in villâ, etc., per recognitionem de morte antecessoris sui versus R. et ideo tibi præcipio quòd* SEISINAM *illam ei sine dilatione* HABERE FACIAS, *etc.*[2]

By force of this writ he recovered not only seisin of the land, but seisin of all the chattels and everything else which was found upon the fee at the time of seisin being made by the sheriff. When the seisin was in this manner recovered, the person who lost might afterwards, notwithstanding, contest the right, in a writ of right; but Glanville doubted how long after the seisin so delivered, he might pursue his remedy for the right.[3] If the oath of the jurors was in favor of the tenant, and he was absent, the seisin remained to him, without the adverse party having any power to recover it: though this did not take away his cause of action for the right, as in the former case; nor, on the other hand, did a suit depending upon the right to a tenement, extinguish a recognition upon the seisin of one's ancestor, unless the duel was waged upon the right; though the pursuing such a recognition was a sort of contempt of court; the punishment, however, of which Glanville seems to think was not ascertained.[4]

---

[1] *Imbreviari.*   [2] Glanv., lib. 13, c. 7, 8.   [3] Ibid., c. 9.   [4] Ibid., c. 7.

When both parties appeared in court, it used to be asked of the tenant if he could say anything why the assize should *remanere*, as they called it; that is, should be barred, or not proceed. Many good causes might be shown why the assize should *remain*. If the tenant confessed in court that his ancestor, whose seisin was in question, was seized in his demesne as of fee, the day he died, with all the circumstances expressed in the writ, there was no need to proceed in the assize; but if he confessed the seisin only, and denied all, or some circumstances, the assize proceeded upon those circumstances which were not admitted.

<small>Exceptions to the assize.</small>

There were many other causes upon which the assize *mortis antecessoris* used to remain. The tenant might admit, that the demandant was seized after the death of his father, or some other ancestor (whether such ancestor was seized the day of his death or not); and that being in such seisin, he did such or such an act which deprived him of the benefit of the assize; as, for instance, that he sold the land to him, or made a gift of it, or quit-claimed it, or made some other lawful alienation thereof: and upon these points, says Glanville, they might go to the trial by duel, or any other kind of proof which was usually allowed by the court in questions of right. In like manner, the tenant might say, that the demandant had heretofore commenced a suit against him concerning the same land, and that there was then a fine made between them in the king's court; or that the land fell to him upon a final decision by duel, whether the duel was in the king's court or any other; or that it was his by the judgment of some court, or by quit-claim solemnly made. Villenage might be objected against the demandant; and, if proved, it took away the assize; as also did the exception of bastardy, and the king's charter confirming to the tenant the land in question; the conjunction of more heirs than one, as of women in a military fee, and of men and women together in free socage. Again, if it were admitted, that the ancestor whose seisin was in question had a seisin of some sort or other, namely, that he had it from the tenant or his ancestor, either in pledge, or *ex commodato*, or by any similar means, in these cases the assize was to remain, and the plea to proceed in some other way. Consanguinity was an exception which took away the assize.

Where it happened, as we before mentioned in speaking of frank-marriage, that the eldest brother gave part of his land to his younger brother, who died without heirs of his body; in such case, the assize would remain, on account of the rule before stated, that *nemo potest hæres simul esse ejusdem tenementi et dominus*. In like manner, if the demandant either confessed, or was proved to have been in arms against the king, any assize which he might bring against another would, *ipso facto*, remain. We are told also by Glanville, that by force of a particular law,[1] burgage-tenure was a good exception to cause the assize to remain. When none of these, nor any other cause was stated why the assize should remain, the recognition proceeded in form, and both parties being there present, the seisin was tried by the oaths of the twelve jurors, and, according to their verdict, was adjudged to one party or the other.[2]

When the demandant in this assize was an infant, and the tenant was of full age, the tenant was not allowed an essoin, and the recognition proceeded the first day, whether the tenant appeared or not. It was so ordered for this never-failing reason, that wheresoever the tenant, if present in court, could say nothing why the assize should remain, the recognition ought, by law, to proceed, without waiting for the appearance of the adverse party. Now, in this case, if the tenant were present, the allegation of the demandant's infancy would be no cause for the assize to remain, and therefore the recognition was to proceed of course; but if restitution was made to the infant by the recognition, the minor's coming of age was to be expected, before he could be made to answer upon the question of right, should any be moved against him. The course was the same where both parties were minors.[3]

But where the demandant was of full age, and the tenant a minor, it was different, for there the minor might essoin himself in the usual way: and when he appeared, he might pray that the recognition might not be taken till he was of full age; and thus the recognition *de morte antecessoris* often remained, on account of the age of one of the parties. To procure, however, this delay, the minor

---

[1] This is another law alluded to by Glanville, of which we find no other mention.
[2] Glanv., lib. 13, c. 11. [3] Ibid., c. 12.

CHAP. IV.] ASSIZE MORT D'ANCESTOR: EXCEPTIONS. 447

must say that he was in seisin of the tenement in question, and also, that his father or some other ancestor died seized: for neither a recognition, nor a suit upon the right, would remain as against a minor, if he himself had acquired seisin of the tenement, and he held it by no other right than what he had so made to himself. But should it be replied to what the minor had said, that true it was his ancestor died seized of the tenement in question, yet it was not *ut de fœdo*, but only *ut de wardâ;* then, though the principal recognition would remain on account of the age of the minor, yet a recognition would proceed on that point, and a writ of summons would accordingly issue for twelve jurors to the following effect: *Rex vicecomiti, etc., Summone per bonos summonitores duodecim liberos et legales homines de vicineto de villâ, etc., quòd sint coram me vel justitiis meis ad terminum, etc., parati sacramento recognoscere si R. pater N. qui infra ætatem est, seisitus fuit in dominico suo de unâ carucatâ terræ in villâ, etc., unde M. filius et hæres T. petit recognitionem de morte ipsius T. patris sui versus ipsum N. ut de fœdo suo die quâ obiit, vel ut de wardâ. Et interim terram illam videant, et nomina eorum imbreviari facias. Et summone per bonos summonitores prædictum N. qui terram illam tenet, quòd sit ibi auditurus illam recognitionem, etc.*[1]

In this case the proceeding somewhat differed from other instances of recognitions, for if a day had been given to both parties, there was then no summons to the tenant to hear the recognition; but it proceeded without delay, and according to the verdict of those twelve jurors, delivered upon their oaths, it was declared what sort of seisin the ancestor had; and if it was only *ut de wardâ*, the demandant recovered against the minor. But Glanville doubts whether this was enough to entitle the demandant to recover; for, as yet, it did not appear that his ancestor died seized in his demesne as of fee, nor that he was the next heir; and he puts it as a question whether recourse was to be had to the principal recognition upon that point. However that might be, yet in case it had been proved by the oaths of the twelve jurors, that the ancestor of the minor died seized as of fee, then the seisin was to remain to the minor till he attained his full age; but after he was come of age, the other party might bring

---

[1] Glanv., lib. 13, c. 13, 14.

in question *the right*, either against him or his heirs. It should be remembered that it was only in the above case that a recognition was allowed to proceed against a minor, for it was a general rule that a minor was not bound to answer in any suit by which he might be disinherited, or lose his life or member, except that he was obliged to answer to suits for his debts and also for a novel disseisin. If, in the above case, the seisin had been adjudged to the demandant, restitution was to be made in the form before mentioned; and he, in like manner, could not be compelled to answer the minor upon *the right* till he was of full age. Such mutual permission to stir questions, after a determination, was grounded upon this prevailing reason, that whatever was transacted with persons under age, in pleas of this sort, ought not to remain fixed and unalterable.[1]

If a person claimed the privilege of a minor, and it was objected to him that he was of full age, this was to be decided by the oaths, not of twelve, but of eight free and lawful men, who were summoned by a similar writ with those we have so often mentioned for summoning jurors: *Octo liberos, et legales homines de vicineto de villâ, etc., etc., recognoscere, utrùm N. qui clamat unam hidam, etc., sit talis œtatis, quòd inde placitare possit et debeat. Et interim terram illam videant, et nomina eorum, etc., etc.*[2] If he was proved by this recognition to be of full age, they proceeded to the principal recognition, as in other cases. Here Glanville makes a question, whether he was thenceforward to be esteemed of full age, so as to lose his privilege of age as against all other persons; and again, suppose he had been found a minor, whether that was sufficient, without more, to entitle him to the privilege in all other suits.[3]

The next recognition is that *de ultimâ præsentatione*. *Assisa ultimæ præsentationis.* When a church was void, and a dispute arose about the presentation, the controversy might be determined by this recognition at the prayer of either party. The writ in such case was of the following kind: *Summone, etc., duodecim liberos et legales homines de vicineto, etc., etc., parati sacramento recognoscere, quis advocatus præsentavit ultimam personam, quæ obiit ad ecclesiam de villâ, etc., quæ vacans est, ut dicitur, et unde N. clamat advocationem.*

---

[1] Glanv., lib. 13, c. 15.   [2] Ibid., c. 15, 16.   [3] Ibid., c. 17.

CHAP. IV.] ASSIZE DE ULTIMA PRÆSENTATIONE. 449

Et nomina eorum imbreviari facias. Et summone per bonos summonitores R. qui præsentationem ipsam deforceat, quòd tunc sit ibi auditurus illam recognitionem, etc.[1] What the essoins were in this recognition may be collected from what has gone before. The person to whom or to whose ancestors the last presentation was adjudged by the recognition, was considered as having thereby obtained seisin of the advowson, so that he was to present to the first vacancy, and his parson was to hold the presentation during his life, whatever was the fact about *the right* of advowson, for the person who lost the last presentation by a recognition might yet move a question upon the right of advowson.[2]

The tenant might, in this as well as the foregoing writ, state some reason why the assize should not proceed. He might say that he admitted the ancestor of the demandant made the last presentation, as the real lord and heir, but that afterwards he transferred the fee, to which the advowson was appendant, to the tenant or his ancestors, by a good and lawful title; upon which allegation the assize would remain, and either party might pray a recognition upon the truth of this exception. Again, either party might admit that he or his ancestors made the last presentation, but that it was *ut de wardâ*, not *ut de fœdo;* upon which a recognition might be prayed, which would be summoned by a writ similar to the many we have mentioned: *Duodecim liberos, etc., recognoscere, si R. qui præsentavit, etc., fecerit illam præsentationem ut de fœdo, vel ut de wardâ, etc.* And if the recognition declared the last presentation was made *ut de wardâ*, the advowson of the presentation was at an end, and henceforth belonged to the other party; if *ut de fœdo*, the presentation remained to him.[3]

We come now to the recognition concerning a tenement, *utrùm sit laicum vel ecclesiasticum*, which might be had upon the prayer of either party. For summoning such a recognition, there issued a writ like the former: *Recognoscere, utrùm una hida terræ, quam N. persona ecclesiæ de villâ, etc., clamat ad liberam eleemosinam ipsius ecclesiæ suæ versus R. in villâ, etc., sit laicum fœdum ipsius R. an fœdum ecclesiasticum. Et interim terram videant, etc.*[4] It was a rule in

---

[1] Glanv., lib. 13, c. 18, 19. [2] Ibid., c. 20. [3] Ibid., c. 20-22.
[4] Ibid., c. 23, 24.

this, and indeed in all others, except the great assize, that no more than two essoins should be had, for the third was never admitted; but where the court could be certified of the party's illness, whether he was *languidus* or not; and as this, says Glanville, was not usually done in recognitions, they always were without a third essoin. This recognition proceeded in the same way as the former, and if it was proved by the recognition that the tenement was ecclesiastical, it could not afterwards be considered as a lay fee, though it might be claimed as holden by the church for a certain service.[1]

The next was the recognition, whether a person died seized *ut de fœdo, vel ut de vadio*. If a person claimed a tenement as having been pledged by him or his ancestors, and the other party claimed it not as a pledge, but in fee, then a recognition was resorted to, and was summoned, as in other cases: *Recognoscere, utrùm N. teneat unum carucatum, etc., in fœdo, an in vadio, etc.*, or, it might be, *utrùm illa carucata, etc., sit fœdum vel hœreditas ipsius N. an invadiata ei ab ipso R. vel ab ipso H. antecessore ejus. Et interim terram videant, etc.*[2] Sometimes, when a person seized *ut de vadio*, the heir, upon such seisin, would bring a writ *de morte antecessoris* against the true heir, who had by some means got seisin of the land; and then, if the tenant admitted the seisin of the demandant's ancestor, but said it was *ut de vadio*, and not *ut de fœdo*, a recognition was summoned in the following form: *Recognoscere, utrùm N. pater R. fuerit seisitus in dominico suo ut de fœdo, an ut de vadio, de unâ carucatâ, etc., die quâ obiit, etc.*[3]

If it was proved by the recognition to be a pledge only, and not an inheritance, then the tenant who claimed it as his inheritance lost the tenement, so that he could not even make use of it in the manner we mentioned concerning actions of debt, for the recovery of the debt for which it was a pledge. If, on the other hand, it was recognized to be an inheritance in the tenant, the demandant could recover it no other way (if at all) than by a writ of right. Glanville makes a question, whether in this or any other recognition the warrantor was to be waited for, particularly if he was vouched after two essoins had been had.[4]

The nature of the recognitions which remain to be men-

[1] Glanv., lib. 13, c. 25. [2] Ibid., 26, 27. [3] Ibid., c. 28, 29.
[4] Ibid., c. 30.

CHAP. IV.] ASSIZE DE ULTIMA PRÆSENTATIONE. 451

tioned, may partly be collected from those of which we have already treated, and partly from the terms of the award made in court for their being taken, and the allegations of both parties, which were to be tried. Indeed, some of them have been already noticed; as that for trying whether a person was of age;[1] that for trying whether a person died seized *ut de fœdo*, or *ut de wardâ*;[2] that for trying whether a presentation was made in right of the inheritance, or only in right of a wardship:[3] all these recognitions were conducted as the others, in respect of essoins, and they proceeded or remained for the same reasons as prevailed in the rest.[4]

It must be observed of these *assizes* (for so they are sometimes called by Glanville, but more commonly *recognitions*), that they are not all of the same kind; that *de morte antecessoris* being evidently an original proceeding, independent of any other; the rest (not excepting that *de ultimâ præsentatione*,[5] and that *utrùm laicum fœdum vel ecclesiasticum*) being merely for the decision of facts which arose in some original action or proceeding. Thus, the writs for summoning recognitions of the latter kind were simple writs of summons: they mentioned that a plea was depending in court by the king's writ; and they were granted at the prayer of either party; so that they seemed to be resorted to, by the assent of parties, for settling an incidental question, on which they put the dispute between them. On the other hand, the writ *de morte antecessoris* has all the appearance of an original commencement of a suit. It issued only upon condition that the demandant gave security to prosecute it — SI *G. filius T. fecerit te securum de clamore suo prosequendo* TUNC *summone*—and made no mention of a plea depending. Of the same kind was the writ *de novâ disseisinâ*, which will be mentioned presently. Thus, then, of all the assizes in use in Glanville's time, it was only that *de morte antecessoris*, and that *de novâ disseisinâ*, that were original writs. Whether there were any recognitions for trying collateral facts, besides those mentioned in Glanville, it is difficult

---

[1] Glanv., lib. 13, c. 15–17.   [2] Ibid., c. 20–22.
[3] Ibid., c. 13–15.   [4] Ibid., c. 31.
[5] That the assize *de ultima præsentatione* was such, see what we have before said, p. 408, in the plea upon a right of advowson, where this writ is awarded to try a collateral matter, arising in a writ of right of advowson.

to determine; this being one of the many circumstances of which we must remain ignorant, for want of knowing the terms of the famous law made by Henry II. about assizes.

We shall, lastly, speak of that which was called the *re-*
Assisa de nova *cognitio de nova disseisinâ* (a). When any one
disseisina. disseized another of his freehold unjustly, and without any judgment of law to authorize him, and the fact was within the king's assize; that is, if it was since the last voyage of the king to Normandy,[1] which was, it seems, the time limited for this purpose in the famous law so often alluded to; he might then avail himself of the benefit of that law, and have the following writ to the sheriff: QUESTUS EST *mihi N. quòd R. injustè et sine ju-*

(a) As to the word *novel*, it applied when the action was brought since the last eyre or circuit. The term disseisin is very ancient in our law, and is used in the sense of wrongful seizure by force. Thus the terms are expounded in a chapter in the *Mirror* upon the subject (c. ii., 125): Disseisin, it is said, is a personal trespass in a wrongful putting out of possession, "and if I take from you forcibly anything of which you have had the peaceable possession, I do disseize you; and I do wrong to the king when I use force where I ought to use judgment." The wrong is here taken as well for deforcement or disturbance as for ejection. "Deforcement, as if one entereth into another's tenement when the rightful owner is elsewhere, and at his return cannot enter therein, but is kept out, and hindered so to do. Disturbance is if one disturb me wrongfully to use my seisin which I have peaceably had, and the same may be in three ways — 1. As where one driveth away a distress, so that I cannot distrain in the tenement liable to my distress; 2. Another is where one doth replevy his distress wrongfully; 3. As if one distrain me so outrageously that I cannot manure, plough, or use my land duly." It is further said, "All right is of two kinds — either a right of possession or of property; and therefore the right of property is not determinable by this assize, as is the *known possession*, or that which savoreth of a possessory right. The remedy of disseisin holds not of movables, nor of anything which falleth not into inheritance, as land, tenement, rent, advowson of a church, whether holden in fee or for term of life, or year, or mortgage, until so much be paid. *Ejection of a term of years falleth to the assize*, which sometimes cometh by lease, etc. Into this offence fall farmers (lessees) who lease their land for a longer time than their term endureth in prejudice of the lord or the reversioner" (*Ibid.*).

[1] This was A. D. 1184, in the 30th year of Henry II.; so that the time of limitation, during that reign, was never more than about four years.

In the printed text of Glanville, there are these words between brackets: *Quod quandoque majus quandoque minus censetur;* which passage has been thought to import, that the time of limitation was often varied in this king's reign. Another meaning of this passage may be, that the period (the *terminus a quo*) being fixed, it must necessarily, by the lapse of time, be lengthening every day. After all, the passage lies under some suspicion of interpolation, and was, perhaps, for that reason put between brackets by the editor. This voyage into Normandy is referred to by later writers, as the limitation before the statute of Merton altered it.

dicio disseisivit eum de libero tenemento suo in villâ, etc., post ultimam transfretationem meam in Normanniam: et ideo tibi præcipio quòd SI PRÆFATUS N. FECERIT TE SECURUM DE CLA-MORE SUO PROSEQUENDO, *tunc facias tenementum illud rescisiri de catallis quæ in eo capta fuerunt, et ipsum cum catallis esse facias in pace usque ad clausum Paschæ. Et interim facias duodecim liberos et legales homines de vicineto videre terram illam; et nomina eorum imbreviari facias. Et summone illos per bonos summonitores, quòd tunc sint coram me vel justitiis meis, parati inde facere recognitionem.* ET PONE PER VADIUM ET SALVOS PLEGIOS PRÆDICTUM R. VEL BALLIVUM SUUM, SI IPSE NON FUERIT INVENTUS, *quòd tunc sit ibi auditurus illam recognitionem, etc.*[1]

These writs of novel disseisin were of different forms, according to the nature of the freehold in whose prejudice the disseisin was made. There is one in Glanville for razing or prostrating a dyke *ad nocumentum liberi tenementi;* another for razing a mill-pool *ad nocumentum liberi tenementi;* another for a common of pasture appertaining *ad liberum tenementum*.[2] These are all the writs of novel disseisin mentioned in Glanville.

In this recognition no essoin was allowed, but the recognition proceeded at the first day, whether the disseizor appeared or not—for here no delay was suffered either on account of minority, or a vouching to warranty; unless a person would in court first acknowledge the disseisin, and then he might vouch a warrantor, and the recognition would remain; the disseizor would be in the king's mercy—the warrantor was summoned, and the proceeding went on between him and the disseizor who vouched him. It must be observed that in this recognition whoever lost his suit, whether the demandant or tenant, or, as Glanville terms them (with a view perhaps to there being a sort of criminality[3] in a disseisin), the appellor and the appealed, he was in the king's mercy. If the appellor did not prosecute, by keeping the day appointed, his pledges also were in the king's mercy; and the like happened to the other party if he made default. The penalty ordained by the constitution which established this proceeding was only the *misericordiâ regis,* so often mentioned. It often

---

[1] Glanv., lib. 13, c. 32, 33. [2] Ibid., c. 34–37.
[3] In the canon law, a forcible intrusion into an ecclesiastical benefice is construed *rapina*. Corv. Jus. Can., lib. 4, tit. 24.

happened in this recognition that the demandant, after he had proved the disseisin, wanted a writ to the sheriff to be put in possession of the produce and chattels upon the land, the form of which writ we have before shown.[1] It should be remarked that this writ to recover the chattels pursued the original writ of novel disseisin, which directed the party to be reseized of the chattels; in no other recognition was there any mention in the judgment *de fructibus et catallis*.[2]

Having taken this view of the divers manners in which justice was obtained, it seems to follow that something should be said of the times which were allotted, at this early period, for the regular administration of it. The division of the year into term and vacation has been the joint work of the *church* and *necessity*. The cultivation of the earth, and the collection of its fruits, necessarily require a time of leisure from all attendance on civil affairs; and the laws of the church had, at various times, assigned certain seasons of the year to an observance of religious peace, during which all legal strife was strictly interdicted. What remained of the year not disposed of in this manner was allowed for the administration of justice. The Anglo-Saxons had been governed by these two reasons in distinguishing the periods of vacation and term; the latter they called *dies pacis regis*, the former, *dies pacis Dei et sanctæ ecclesiæ*.[3] The particular portions of time which the Saxons had allowed to these two seasons were adhered to by the Normans, together with other Saxon usages, and their term and vacation were as follows:

Of terms and vacations.

It seems that *Hilary* term began *Octabis Epiphaniæ*—that is, the 13th of January, and ended on Saturday next before Septuagesima; which, being movable, made this term longer in some years than others. *Easter* term began *Octabis Paschæ* (nine days sooner than it now does), and ended before the vigil of Ascension (that is, six days sooner than it now does). *Trinity* term began *Octabis Pentecostes;* to which there does not seem to have been any precise conclusion fixed by the canon which governed all the rest; it was therefore called *terminus sine termino;* it seems to have been determined by nothing but the pressing calls

---

[1] Glanv., lib. 13, c. 38, 39. [2] Ibid., c. 38. [3] Leg. Confes., c. 9.

of haytime and harvest, and the declension of business very natural at that season. But the conclusion of it was fixed afterwards by parliament; by stat. 51 Hen. III. it was to end within two or three days after *quindena sancti Johannis*—that is, about the 12th of July. In later times, by stat. 32 Hen. VIII., Trinity term was to begin *Crastino sanctæ Trinitatis*. *Michaelmas* term began on Tuesday next after St. Michael, and was closed by Advent; but as Advent Sunday is movable, and may fall upon any day between the 26th of November and 4th of December, therefore the 28th of November, as a middle period, by reason of the feast and eve of St. Andrew, was appointed for it. Thus were the terms in the latter part of the Saxon times, and during this period, almost in the same state we have them now; and by them the return of writs and appearances were governed.[1]

Having gone through the law of private rights, and the several remedies furnished for the recovery and protection of property, it remains to say something of the criminal law as it stood at the latter end of the reign of Henry II.; but, previous to this it may be proper to take a view of some few regulations that had been made on the subject of crimes and punishments antecedent to the time of which we are now writing. We have seen that a law was made by William the Conqueror, which took away all capital punishments, and, instead thereof, directed various kinds of mutilation. This law was repealed in one instance, A. D. 1108, in the 9th year of Henry I., when it was enacted, that any one taken *in furto vel latrocinio* should be hanged, without allowing any pecuniary *were* to be paid as a redemption[2] (*a*). The law of William, however, still operated in other cases; the punishment of crimes consisted in mutilations of various kinds; and it will presently be seen that this law of Henry I. was dispensed with or repealed.

The criminal law.

Some provisions respecting the administration of criminal justice had been made by the statutes of Clarendon that

---

(*a*) This is a mistake. The law was, that among the offences which put a man in *misericordiâ regis* was theft, if worthy of death, "Furtum probatum et morte dignum" (~~Leges Henrici Primi~~ c. xiii.). But, in the same chapter, even homicide is allowed its compensation. - - - -

[1] Spelman, Orig. of Terms. [2] Wilk., Leg. Ang.-Sax., p. 304.

were published at Northampton. It was thereby directed, that any one charged before the king's justices with the crime of murder, theft, robbery, or receipt of such offenders, of forgery, or of malicious burning, by the oaths of twelve knights of the hundred; if there were no knights, by the oaths of twelve free and lawful men, and by the oaths of four out of every vill in the hundred; that any one so charged should submit to the water ordeal, and if he failed in the experiment he should lose one foot; and afterwards at Northampton it was added, in order to make the punishment more severe, that he should lose his right hand as well as one of his feet; and also that he should *Of abjuration.* abjure the realm, and leave it within forty days; and even if he was acquitted by the water ordeal, that he should find pledges to answer for him, and then he might remain in the realm unless he was charged with a murder or some other heinous felony by the commonalty and lawful knights of the country. If he was charged with any of those crimes, notwithstanding his acquittal by the ordeal, he was to leave the kingdom within forty days, and carry all his goods with him (with a saving of all claims his lord might have on them), and so abjure the realm and be at the king's mercy as to any permission to return. This regulation was to be in force *so long as the king pleased*, in all cases of murder, treason, and malicious burning; and in all the before-mentioned crimes, except in *small* thefts and robberies committed during the war (which was just concluded), in taking horses, oxen, and the like.

Thus an offender was subjected to a trial, by which, if convicted, he was to lose a limb and be banished; if acquitted, he was likewise to be banished. Such a method of proceeding can be imputed to nothing but some doubt entertained of the justness of this trial by ordeal. It is related that, before this, William Rufus having caused fifty Englishmen of good quality and fortune to be tried by the hot iron, they escaped unhurt, and were of course acquitted; upon which that monarch declared he would try them again by the judgment of his court, and would not abide by this pretended judgment of God, *which was made favorable or unfavorable at any man's pleasure.* The king looked upon this trial to be fraudulently managed, as no doubt it was; and Henry II., convinced of the fraud, would not allow such an acquittal to have its full effect;[1] though it is a strong mark of the barbarism and prejudices of these times, that a practice liable to such suspicions was still suffered to continue, as a judicial proceeding, and that they would rather punish those who were lawfully acquitted by it than altogether abandon such an abominable proceeding.

Another provision made by the statute of Northampton related to the old law concerning decennaries. It declared that no one in a borough or vill should entertain any strange guest in his house more than one night unless he would engage to answer for his appearance; or such guest had some reasonable excuse for staying, which his host was to make known to the vicinage; and when he went away, it was to be by day and in the presence of the vicinage. Another ordinance was to secure the punishment of criminals who had been prosecuted and appealed before the inferior magistrates in order to a final trial before the king's justices; it declares, that any one taken for murder, theft, robbery, or forgery, and confessing himself guilty before the chief officer of the hundred or borough, or before certain lawful men, should not be permitted to deny the fact when brought before the justices.[2]

Such is the substance of certain statutes made for the improvement of criminal proceedings, in this and the preceding reigns. We shall now speak of the penal law in general, and the way of prosecuting offenders, as practised towards the end of the reign of Henry II. But in this we shall confine our inquiries to such objects as relate to the *curia regis* only; contenting ourselves with subjoining a short account of the proceedings before justices itinerant.

When a person was *infamatus*, as Glanville terms it, or accused of the death of a man, or of any sedition moved in the realm or army, it was either upon the charge of a certain accuser or not. If no certain accuser appeared, but he was accused only by the voice of public fame, or, as Glanville says, *fama tantummodo publica accusat* (which signified probably nothing more than what the statute of Northampton calls *per sacra-*

_{Mode of prosecution.}

---

[1] Litt. Hen. II., vol. iv., 279.   [2] Wilk. Leg. Ang.-Sax., 330.

mentum legalium hominum), he was immediately to be safely attached, either by proper pledges, or by a much safer security, that is, *per carceris inclusionem*. Then the truth of the matter was inquired before the justices, by many and various inquisitions and interrogations; every probability was to be weighed, and every conjecture to be attempted, from facts and circumstances, which could be thought to make either on one side or the other. In conclusion, the criminal was either to be entirely acquitted, upon such inquiry, or was to be put to purge himself *per legem apparentem;* that is, by a number of compurgators. If upon this trial *per legem* he was convicted, his life and members depended upon the judgment of the court, and the grace of the king, as in cases of *felony;* for so Glanville calls this offence of *seditio regni vel exercitûs*.[1]

If a certain accuser, or, as he is sometimes called by Glanville, and was afterwards more commonly called, an *appellor*, appeared at first, he was to be attached by pledges, if he could find any, for prosecuting the suit; if he could not find pledges, he was trusted upon his solemn promise and engagement to prosecute; and this was the more common security for prosecuting felonies; lest binding by too severe an obligation might deter persons from assisting in bringing offenders to justice.

When the accuser had given security for prosecuting, then the person accused, as in the former case, used to be attached by safe pledges; and if he had none, was committed to prison: and it was a rule, that in all pleas of felony, except homicide, the accused person was to be discharged upon giving pledges.

Then a day was appointed, upon which the parties might have their lawful essoins. At length the accuser would propose what charge he had to make. He might perhaps say, that he saw, or would by some other means prove, the accused to have attempted or done something against the king's life, or towards moving sedition in the realm or army; or to have consented, or given aid, or counsel, or lent his authority towards such an attempt; and add that he was ready *dirationare*, to deraign or prove it, as the court should award: and if to this the person accused opposed a flat denial, then the whole was de-

---

[1] Glanv., lib. 14, c. 1.

cided by the duel. When the duel was once waged in suits of this sort, neither party could decline or go back, under pain of being esteemed *pro victo*, and suffering all the consequences attending such a defeat; nor could they be reconciled, or the question between them be compromised, any otherwise than by the license of the king or his justices.

If the parties at length engaged in the duel, and the appellor was vanquished, he was to be *in misericordiâ regis;* in addition to which he incurred perpetual infamy, and certain disabilities which always attended the being vanquished in a judicial duel. If the party accused was vanquished, he suffered the judgment of life and limb above mentioned; and besides that, all his property and chattels were confiscated, and his heirs were disinherited forever. A remarkable difference is here to be observed between a conviction *per legem apparentem*, and by duel: on the former, which was a remnant of the old Saxon jurisprudence, a felon suffered only the pains of death; but if convicted on the latter, which was a mode of trial introduced by the Normans, he suffered the additional penalty of forfeiture.

Forfeiture.

Every freeman, being of full age, might be admitted to this sort of accusation, or appeal; yet should a person within age appeal any one, he was nevertheless to be attached in the manner just mentioned. A rustic (by which it may be supposed that Glanville means a person not free) might bring such an appeal; but a woman was not admitted to prosecute an appeal of felony, except in some particular cases, which will be hereafter mentioned. The party accused might decline the duel, in suits of this sort, on account of his age; or some mayhem received; that is, if he was sixty years of age, or if he had broke a bone, or had suffered in his head, either *per incisionem*, or *per abrasionem;* for such only were considered as mayhems. And in these cases, the party accused was to purge himself *per Dei judicium;* that is, by the hot iron, or by water according to his condition; if he was *homo liber*, a free man, by the former; if a rustic, or not free, by the latter.[1]

A suit for the fraudulent concealment of treasure-trove was carried on as above stated, where there appeared a

---

[1] Glanv., lib. 14, c. 1.

certain accuser. But, upon a charge of this crime, like that above called *publica fama*, the law did not permit that any one should be put to purge himself *per legem apparentem*, unless he had been before convicted, or had confessed in court that he had found and taken some sort of metal in the place in question; and if he had been convicted thereof, the presumption then was so much against him, that he was obliged to purge himself *per legem apparentem*, and show that he had not found or taken any more. It should seem, from Glanville, that a particular law had been made to authorize the court to compel such a purgation, even where there was not the presumption before mentioned.[1]

When any one was accused of homicide, it might be in the two ways stated, and the proceeding in either was as has been just seen. Only it should be observed, that the accused was never discharged upon giving pledges unless, says Glanville, by the interposition of the king's particular prerogative and pleasure; by which it has been generally thought,[2] that Glanville alludes to the writ *de odio et atia;* of which writ, however, we forbear to speak particularly, till we arrive at a period when we are certain that it was in use.

There were two kinds of homicide: one that was called *murdrum;* which in the words of Glanville, was *quod nullo vidente, nullo sciente, clam perpetratur, præter solum interfectorem, et ejus complices; ita quòd mox non assequatur clamor popularis, juxta assisam super hoc proditam;* such a secret killing, without the knowledge of any but the offenders, as prevented a hue and cry, ordained by statute to be made after malefactors. In an accusation or appeal for this crime of murder, none was admitted to prosecute except one who was of the blood of the deceased; and a nearer relation might exclude a remoter from deranging the appeal. The other kind was that which was called *simple homicide.* In this crime also no one was admitted to become appellor, and make proof, unless he was allied to the deceased by blood, or by homage, or by dominion, and could speak of the death upon the testimony of his own eyes. Thus we see the qualification of the person to become appellor in simple homicide, extended

Homicide.

---

[1] Glanv., lib. 14, c. 2.   [2] 2 Inst., 42.

further than in cases of murder; though it was required of him in this case that he should have been an eye-witness, which could not be in the former, from the very description of the crime, *nullo vidente;* and therefore the zeal and piety of the relation who charged a man with crime, seems to have been taken instead of proof. Again, in this suit a woman might be heard as accuser, if it was for the death of her husband, and she could speak of what she herself saw. It will be shown presently, that a woman might bring an appeal of an injury done to her own person, and, according to Glanville, it was only upon the consideration of man and wife being *one* flesh, that she was allowed this appeal of the death of her husband. In these cases, the person accused might choose either to let it rest upon the proof made by the woman, or purge himself from the imputed crime *per Dei judicium.* Sometimes a person charged [1] with simple homicide, if he had been taken in flight, with a crowd pursuing him, and this was legally proved in court by a jury of the country, was obliged to undergo the legal purgation, without any other evidence being brought against him.[2]

The *crimen incendii,* or burning, was prosecuted and tried in the same way, as was also the *crimen roberiæ,* or robbery.[3]

The *crimen raptûs,* says Glanville, was, when a woman declared herself to have suffered violence from a man in the king's peace, by which latter circumstance nothing more was meant than that the offence was such as was cognizable in the king's court only. The law directed that when a woman had sustained an injury of this kind she should go, while the fact was recent, to the next village, and there *injuriam sibi illatam probis hominibus ostendere, et sanguinem, si quis fuerit effusus, et vestium scissiones;* she was to do the same to the chief officer of the hundred, and, lastly, was to make a public declaration of it in the first county court, after which she was to institute her plaint, which was proceeded in as in other cases, a woman being suffered to prosecute her appeal in this, as in all other instances of an injury done to her person. It should be remembered, as we before said, that it was in the election of the person accused, either to sub-

Rape.

---
[1] The expression of Glanville which is here construed *charged* is *restatus.*
[2] Glanv., lib. 14, c. 3.   [3] Ibid., c. 4, 5.

mit to the burthen of making purgation, or leave it upon the evidence of the woman herself. The judgment, in this crime, was the same as in those before mentioned. It was not enough for the offender, after judgment passed, to offer marriage, for in that manner, says Glanville, men of a servile or inferior condition would be enabled to bring disgrace upon women of rank, not for once, but forever; and, on the other hand, men of rank might bring scandal on their parents and relations by unworthy marriages. We are informed, however, by the same authority, that it was customary, before judgment passed, for the woman and the man to compromise the appeal and marry, provided they had the countenance of the king's license, or that of his justices, and the assent of parents.[1]

The *crimen falsi*, in a general and large sense, contained in it many species of that crime — the making of false charters, false measures, false money, and other falsifications, the manner of prosecuting which appeals was the same as those we have just mentioned. A distinction, however, was observed between forging royal and private charters; if the former, the party was sentenced as in case of læse majesty; if the latter, the offender was dealt more tenderly with, as in other cases of smaller forgeries, which were punished only by the loss of limbs.[2]

Of the *crimen furti*, or theft, and other pleas which belonged to the sheriff's jurisdiction, Glanville gives no account, as they did not come within the design of his work, which was confined to the *curia regis* (a). The prosecution of them was ordered differently, according to the usage and practice of different counties.[3]

Thus stood the laws of crimes, and the method of proceeding, as far as related to the superior court.

Proceedings before justices itinerant. What was the office of the justices itinerant

---

(a) Yet he regards it as a plea of the crown, for he brings it under that head, and it clearly was so, being so declared in the laws of Henry I. (c. xiii.), "Quæ placita mittunt homines in misericordia regis;" among which is "furtum probatum et morte dignum," etc., c. xlvii.: "De causes criminalibus," which begins, "de furto." Our author imagined that because triable by the sheriff, it was not a plea of the crown; but that was a mistake, for the sheriff was the king's judge, whilst by Magna Charta it was declared that pleas of the crown should not be tried before him, which of itself implied that theft was so, as it was the only felony he tried.

[1] Glanv., lib. 14, c. 6.   [2] Ibid., c. 8.   [3] Ibid.

in the reign of Henry II., we have before stated from the statute of Northampton, when this establishment was revived. The jurisdiction of these justices was considerably increased soon after, as may be collected from certain *capitula*, or articles of inquiry, which were delivered to the justices itinerant in the year 1194, which was the fifth year of Richard I. According to those directions, they were to begin by causing four knights to be chosen out of the whole county, who, upon their oaths, were to elect two lawful knights of every hundred or wapentake; and those two were to choose, upon their oaths, ten knights in every hundred or wapentake; and if there were not knights enough, then free and lawful men. These twelve together were to answer to all the *capitula* which concerned that hundred or wapentake.

When that was done, the justices were to inquire of and determine both *new* and *old* pleas of the crown, and all such as were not determined before the king's justices; also all *recognitions*, and all pleas which were summoned before the justices by the king's writ, or that of his chief justice, or such as were sent to them from the king's chief court. They were to inquire of escheats, presentations to churches, wardships, and marriages, belonging to the king. They were to inquire of malefactors, and their receivers and encouragers; of forgers of charters and writings; of the goods of usurers; of great assizes concerning land worth 100 shillings a year, and under; and of defaults of appearance in court.

They were to choose, or cause to be chosen, three knights and one clerk in every county, who were to be *custodes placitorum coronæ;* the same, probably, who were afterwards called *coronatores*, but they are not mentioned by that name in this reign. They were to see that all cities, boroughs, and the king's demesnes, were taxed. They were to inquire of certain rents in every manor of the king's demesnes, and the value of everything on those manors, and how many carucates or ploughlands they contained. They were also to swear good and lawful men, who were to choose others in different parts of the county, to be sworn to see the king's escheats and wardlands, as they fell in, well stocked with all necessaries. Besides these, there were several articles relating to the Jews, which were occasioned by the outrages that had lately been committed by the populace against that people; as also concerning the lands and goods of John, Earl of Morton, who had incurred great forfeitures to the king.[1]

In the year 1198, being the tenth year of this king, the justices itinerant had certain *capitula* delivered in charge to them, somewhat different from the preceding. As a view of such articles is the only means of gaining a true idea of the commission and office of these justices, it will be proper just to mention its contents. They were directed to hear and determine all pleas of the crown, both new and old, which had not been determined before the king's justices; and all assizes *de morte antecessoris de novâ disseisinâ*, and *de magnis assisis* concerning lands of £10 by the year and under; and of advowsons of churches. They were to inquire of vacant churches, wards, escheats, and marriages, as in the former *capitula;* of usury; of those *in misericordiâ regis;* of purprestures; of treasure-trove; of malefactors and their receivers; of fugitives; of weights and measures, according to the late assize made thereon the preceding year; of customs received by officers of seaports; lastly, of those who ought to appear at the *iter*, but neglected their duty.[2]

This same year, and before the *itinera* of the justices were over, the king appointed his justices of the forest to hold an *iter*, which was as solemn a proceeding as the other, but carried with it more terror, and a degree of oppression, on account of the grievous nature of the institution of forests in all its parts. These justices were commanded to summon, in every county through which they went, all archbishops, bishops, earls, barons, and all free tenants, with the chief officer and four men of every town, to appear before them *ad placita forestæ*, and hear the king's commands.[3]

The king and government. It does not come within the scope of this history to enter minutely into a detail of the constitution and political events in the government of this and the succeeding times. A history, however, of our jurisprudence would be imperfect without giving some

---

[1] Wilk., Leg. Ang.-Sax., p. 46, *et seq.* [2] Ibid., p. 350.
[3] Ibid. For the assize of the forest, and the articles of inquiry before the justices, see Wilk., Leg. Ang.-Sax., p. 351.

small consideration to this subject, so far, at least, as it is connected with the formation and administration of our laws.

In the first ages of civil society, while laws are few, and the execution of them feeble, much must be left to the authority of the sovereign power. As the experience of later times points out the deficiencies of former laws, and particular remedies are applied, the exercise of this sovereign power seems so far to be abridged. The prerogative of the prince, and the dominion of the laws, in this manner occasionally take the place of each other; upon the increase of the latter, the former gives way and retires, collecting all its powers for the sole purpose of aiding and enforcing a due observance of the established law.

The just and requisite prerogative of the crown was perhaps very extensive in the Saxon times; but after the Conquest there concurred a number of circumstances, all tending to increase the power of the sovereign beyond the mere exigencies of orderly government.

The revolution effected by William did, in its consequences, render that prince powerful beyond all the sovereigns of his time, and all that have reigned since in this kingdom; for it threw the greatest part of the nation into a state of dependence on him for their lives and estates. The novelty of his reign, and the peculiar situation in which the prince stood, drove him upon every exertion of which his authority was capable; and, notwithstanding he confirmed to the nation the enjoyment of all their customs and laws, he made those laws themselves occasionally submit to the control of his power, whenever the necessities of his government demanded it. So much was the whole kingdom awed by his greatness, that no infringement of their laws was resented by the people during his reign.

What had been by force acquired to the Conqueror, continued in his successor through the same force, or the prevalence of an established government; and though some concessions were reluctantly made by subsequent monarchs, as will be seen hereafter, and the high claims of the crown were, in some degree, relaxed in favor of the people, they had no lasting effect: the exercise of an extensive prerogative continued in the crown through all these reigns, and rendered the condition of the subject extremely precarious and miserable.

The crown was assisted in the exercise of this prerogative by the manner in which the Norman law was introduced. The English, who had seen the laws of their Anglo-Saxon ancestors confirmed, had the fullest confidence that they should be governed by them in all questions concerning their persons and property. In the meantime, the Normans, who had taken sole possession of the king's court, had the debate and determination of all questions there agitated; and, continually recurring to the notions and principles of law in which they had been bred, determined conformably with that law most points of doubt and difficulty. Thus the English, while they possessed the letter of their law inviolate, saw all their old customs explained away, or so cramped and modified as to amount almost to an abrogation of them.

In this conflict between the Norman and English laws, the prerogative of the king must necessarily have found occasions of enlarging its pretensions. While the rules of property and methods of proceeding were yet fluctuating and unsettled, every chasm was supplied, and every impediment removed, by the great power of the crown; the only subsisting authority which could reconcile the two contending politics. While the rights of persons and of property were not precisely defined, and it was not unanimously agreed by what set of rules and principles they were to be judged, the crown took every advantage, and interfered and dictated absolutely in most judicial inquiries.

It was during this precarious state of our laws that the people were constrained to purchase the favor of the crown, in order to obtain justice in the king's courts.[1] Fines were paid for the express purpose of having justice and right. Presents of a considerable value were made by suitors to obtain the opinion of the king's justices in a cause depending; for writs, pleas, trials, judgments. Sometimes part of the debt in contest was proffered to the crown for a favorable decision. Thus was the common course of justice made liable to the interference and control of royal authority.

---

[1] Madox, Exchequer, 293.

This is only one instance, among many others, of the scope given to the exercise of supreme authority, while the state of our law was so unsettled, and its efforts so feeble. Besides the uncertain condition of our legal polity, other causes, rooted in the constitution of the government, contributed to arm the king with extraordinary powers. The strict feudal submission of a vassal to his liege lord encouraged the notion of an entire obedience in all things to the king, who, being supreme over all the lords in his kingdom, was, of course, to surpass them in the petty prerogatives which they themselves claimed within their own demesnes. These various causes concurring with the immense authority possessed by the first Norman king, enabled this race of monarchs to assume prerogatives, and exercise acts of sovereignty, to the last degree oppressive and tyrannical.

Besides the exertions of prerogative, the law itself, which had been framed under so baneful an influence, was arbitrary and cruel. *Tenures* and the *forest laws* were the source of endless jealousies and discontents, and occasioned most of the public disorders, which broke out with such violence in these times. The forest laws were first introduced by the Conqueror, to protect his favorite diversion of hunting. It was not sufficient that this mighty hunter assigned certain tracts of land, the property of his subjects, to be converted into forests; that he dispeopled and made desolate whole districts of cultivated country; but, to secure the full enjoyment of it, he caused regulations to be framed, calculated to restrain and punish with severity every minute invasion of this new institution. The economy of the forest occasioned a number of grievous penalties; offences respecting vert and venison were punished with barbarous mutilations; and other delinquencies with fine and imprisonment. A regular series of courts was erected to be held at stated periods, in one of which the judges obtained the distinguished style of *Justices in Eyre*.

The fruits and consequences of the feudal constitution made another, and no small part of the grievances then complained of, and were borne with great impatience by both peoples. The English, who had voluntarily consented to the introduction of tenures, principally as a fiction affording a basis for a national militia, ill endured the oppressive conclusions drawn from that establishment; conclusions which, with respect to them, had no foundation in reason or truth. Possessed of their land long before William entered the country, they revolted with indignation at the obligations by which they were now said to be bound to their lords. Feeling the burthens of this new state, they sighed after that freedom which they had enjoyed under their Saxon kings; and, in their discourses with the Normans, instilled into them a persuasion, that other conditions of society, and other institutions than those which they labored under, would consist with a well-ordered government. Nor were the Normans themselves satisfied with the increasing burthens of their own polity, which had accumulated much beyond their original design in establishing it. It was little recompense to a great lord, that he could exercise the like sovereignty over his tenants which he himself suffered from the king; while the rear vassals, who were mostly English, without any power to compensate themselves, were in a state of society truly deplorable. These considerations united the nation in a common cause. The cry was for a restoration of the laws of Edward the Confessor, as a concise way of repealing all the late innovations.

But the abolition of a system to which the kingdom had conformed for some years could hardly be obtained; to procure some alterations that would temper and abate the extreme evils complained of was as much as could be expected. This was done by *charters* granted by several of our kings.

The charters.

Henry I. being possessed of the throne by a precarious title, endeavored to conciliate the people by concessions of this kind. A formal charter was signed by the king. In this he abrogated, in general words, all abuses that had lately crept in; and declared that no reliefs should be taken but such as were just and lawful. He disclaimed any right to exact money from his barons for license to marry their daughters, or other females; and engaged to give all female wards in marriage by the advice of his barons. The dower of widows was secured; and the king engaged not to give them in marriage without their consent. The widow or some other relation was to have the custody of the lands and persons of their children. All barons were enjoined to act in the like manner towards their vassals.

Having made these, with other ordinances relating to crimes and punishments, he expressly confirmed the laws of Edward the Confessor, *cum illis emendationibus quibus pater meus eas emendavit concilio baronum suorum.*[1] Thus were some branches of the feudal law, in a degree, checked in their growth, while the body remained firmly rooted and flourishing.

This charter was confirmed by Stephen,[2] who granted another, merely to secure the liberties of churchmen; to which order he had been mostly indebted for the possession of the crown.[3] The charter of Henry I. was also confirmed by Henry II.[4]

This charter, however, did not reach all the mischiefs that prevailed in the kingdom; nor were the provisions which it did contain faithfully observed (*a*). They, with all the rights of the people, were trampled on by succeeding monarchs. The unstable nature of government in these times made the condition of the people depend very much on the character of their kings: a circumstance which was happily experienced in the reign of John. With all that violence which hurried him on to sport with the liberties of a people, this prince wanted the firmness necessary to command respect and obedience; and while he excited their resentment by a wantonness of tyranny, he encouraged their resistance by his pusillanimity. Exasperated at repeated insults, his barons assembled, and with arms in their hands demanded of him a charter which might secure their property and persons from future invasions of power. A convention was soon held between the king and his people in an open field, called Runnymede, near Staines, in all the terrors of mar-

---

(*a*) The language of the charter of Henry I. was general, and that of Henry II., confirming it, was still more so. And contemporary history amply attests what the statement of Sir J. Mackintosh hints, that John so abused the facilities of oppression which belonged to his paramount seignory, with reference especially to the female wards. It is stated by a contemporary chronicler, and there is no reason to doubt it, that the primate discovered a copy of the Charter of Henry I., and made it the basis of the new one extorted from John. The chief object of the barons, no doubt, was their own protection; and Dr. Henry says, in his *History of Great Britain*, "though the great barons were very desirous to prevent the tyrannical exercise of the feudal authority towards themselves, many of them were much inclined to exercise it in the same manner towards their vassals, and continued to do so after the charter" (B. 3, c. 3). See Sir W. Blackstone's work on the Charters.

[1] Blac. Tracts, vol. ii., p. 8. [2] Ibid., p. 9. [3] Ibid., p. 10. [4] Ibid., p. 11.

tial preparation. The king encamped, with some few adherents, on one side; the barons on the other. After some days of debate and consideration, the barons drew up a set of *capitula*, containing the heads of grievances, grounded upon the charter of Henry I. These, with some small qualifications to which they acceded, were there thrown into the form of a charter; to which the king affixed his seal.

This charter of King John, usually called *Magna Charta*, and the *Charter of Liberties*, is more full and explicit than that of Henry I. (a) In this, reliefs were fixed at a cer-

---

(a) This charter forms an important step or stage in our legal history, and some account of it here will be convenient. As already mentioned, the feudal system had been grossly abused by the king, as it had been by his predecessors. The charter of Henry I. had chiefly been directed against these abuses, and the first articles drawn up for the present charter were founded upon it, and had reference to these abuses. Thus came an article that the king nor his bailiffs shall not seize upon any land for debt, while there are sufficient goods of his debtors; nor shall the securities of a debtor be distressed so long as the principal debtor is solvent; but, if the principal debtor fail in payment, the securities, if they are willing, shall have the lands of the debtor until they shall be repaid, unless the principal debtor shall show himself to be acquitted thereof from the sureties. Then came the article that common pleas shall not follow the court of our lord the king, but shall be assigned to any certain place, and that recognition be taken in the several counties in this manner; that the king shall send two justiciaries four times in the year, who, with four knights of the same county, elected by the people thereof, shall hold assizes of novel disseisin, mort d'ancestor, and last presentation, nor shall any be summoned for this unless they be jurors, or of the two parties (9). That a freeman shall be amerced for a small fault, according to the degree of the fault, and for a greater crime, according to its magnitude, saving to him his contentment. A villein also shall be amerced in the same manner, saving his wainage, and a merchant in the same manner, saving his merchandise, by the oath of faithful men of the neighborhood (10). That a clerk shall be fined according to his lay fee in the manner aforesaid, and not according to his ecclesiastical benefice (11). That no town shall be amerced for the making of bridges for rivers' banks, unless they shall of right have been anciently accustomed to do so (13). That the assizes of novel disseisin and mort d'ancestor be shortened, and made like to other assizes (14). That no sheriff shall of himself enter into pleas belonging to the crown without the crown's authority; and that counties and hundreds shall be at the ancient farm, without increase, unless they be of the manors of our lord the king (15). If any who hold of the king shall die, although a sheriff or other officer of the king shall seize and register his goods by the view of lawful men, yet nothing shall be removed until it be fully known if he owe anything, and his debts to our lord the king shall be paid; then, when the whole of the king's debts are paid, the remainder shall be given up to the executors, to do according to the will of the deceased, and, if he should not owe anything to the king, all the goods of the deceased shall be restored. If any freeman die intestate, his goods shall be distributed by his nearest of kindred and his friends, and by the view of the church. No constable or other officer shall take corn or other goods, unless he shall

tain sum; many regulations were made concerning wardship and marriage, the rights of persons, and the adminis-presently render payment, or unless he shall have respite by the will of the seller. No constable shall distrain any knight to give money for castle guard, if he be willing to keep it in his own person, or by any other true man, if he shall not be able to do so by any reasonable cause. No sheriff or bailiff of the king, nor any other, shall take horses or carts of any freeman for coinage, unless it be by his own free will. Neither the king nor his bailiffs shall take another man's timber for castles or for any other uses, unless it be by the will of him to whom the timber was belonging. That all wears for the time to come shall be destroyed in the rivers of Thames and Medway, and throughout all England. Nothing shall be given for a writ of inquisition of life or limb, but it shall be granted freely without force and not denied. No freeman's body shall be taken or imprisoned, nor disseisined, nor outlawed, nor banished, nor in any ways be damaged; nor shall the king send him to prison by force, except by the judgment of his peers, and by the law of the land. Right shall not be sold, delayed, nor denied. Merchants shall have safety to come and go, buy and sell, without any evil tolls, but by ancient and honest customs. No scutage or aid shall be imposed on the kingdom, except by the common council of the kingdom, unless it be to redeem the king's body, to make his eldest son a knight, or to marry his eldest daughter, and that it be a reasonable aid; and in like manner shall it be concerning the talliage and aids of the city of London and of other cities, which from this time shall have their liberties. That it shall be lawful for any one to go out of the kingdom and return again, saving his allegiance. That the king shall make justiciaries, sheriffs, and bailiffs, of such as know the law of the land, and are disposed duly to observe it. Such were the principal articles proposed, from which may be gathered what were the principal grievances by which the country was oppressed. It may be observed, that as they were all as undoubtedly contrary to the law as it stood — but then it is to be added that much of it had not been declared. There was, however, another and a greater object to be attained even than the declaration of the law, and that was its sanction, protection, or execution. Charters had already been granted, which guaranteed many of the articles; but the guarantees had been found nugatory. And here was the main difficulty. Hence there was a concluding article, providing that by way of security, a certain number of the barons should be appointed, who should see to the observance of the charter by the king, and, if he violated it, and he or his justiciary did not amend it, that they might make war upon him. It is manifest that as the barons were to judge of the breach of the charter, the effect of this article would be nothing less than to transfer the supreme power to them. It would be a complete political revolution. As Guizot observes, it simply authorized civil war. And this was the only result: the king was compelled, indeed, to accede to it, but then he took the first opportunity to protect himself against the transfer of his power to the barons; and a civil war ensued, which lasted the rest of his reign, and broke out again in the next, causing a vast amount of misery. When the charter was drawn up, there were, however, some important variances and departures from the articles. The stipulation as to talliage was omitted, and it was provided that for a common council of the realm for the assessment of scutages and aids, the peers and prelates should be summoned together with all the chief tenants of the crown. The clause as to taking assizes in the counties was altered, and so drawn as to show, in a remarkable manner, the close connection between the "assize," or judicial circuits of the king's judges, and the county courts which they superseded. After providing that

tration of justice; all which will be considered in the succeeding reign, when *Magna Charta* was confirmed, with some alterations, by Henry III.; this of Henry III. being the Great Charter, which is always referred to as the basis of our law and constitution; while the charter of John is only remembered as a monument of antiquity (*a*).

---

justices should be sent into each county, to take the assizes, "if the assizes cannot be taken on the day of the county court, let as many knights and freeholders of those who were present at the county court remain behind as shall be sufficient to do justice." So the article as to amercement of freemen was added: "and none of the amercement shall be assessed, but by the oaths of lawful men of the vicinage." And an article was added, "earls and barons shall not be amerced but by their peers, and that only according to the degree of their delinquency." To the article that no town shall be obliged to repair bridges, etc., unless by ancient prescription, was added, "nor any person." The article as to the criminal jurisdiction of the sheriff ran simply thus: "No sheriff, coroner, etc., shall hold pleas of our crown," without any qualification. To the article as to wears, was added, "except upon the sea-coast." The important article as to personal liberty was altered so as to read thus: "No freeman shall be seized, etc., nor in any way destroyed, nor will we condemn him, nor commit him to prison, except by the legal judgment of his peers, or by the law of the land." And the next was rendered more full and emphatic: "To none will we sell, to none will we deny, to none will we delay, right or justice." Though the king was forced to sign, it only resulted in civil war; and, on the accession of Henry III., another was granted, which omitted the clauses as to scutages and the assessing of aids, the liberty of entering and leaving the kingdom, and some other articles. In the next year, another charter was granted, which contained some important variations. It was provided that a widow should have dower of the third part of her husband's lands, except she were endowed with less. The assizes were to be taken only once a year, and there was this important provision: "And those things which, at the coming of the justiciaries being sent to take the assizes, cannot be determined, shall be ended in some other place in their circuit; and those things which, for the difficulty of some of the articles, cannot be determined by them, shall be determined by our justiciaries of the bench, and then shall be ended No county court shall from henceforth be holden but from month to month; and where a greater term hath been used it shall be greater. Neither shall any sheriff keep his turn in the hundred but twice in the year. Scutage shall be taken as in the time of Henry I. It shall not from henceforth be lawful for any one to give his lands to any religious house, and to take the same land again to hold of the same house; nor shall it be lawful for any religious house to take the land of any, and to leave the same to him from whom they were received. Therefore, if any do give his land to any religious house, his gift shall be void, and the land shall accrue to the lord." Then there was a general saving to all persons, ecclesiastical or lay, the liberties and free customs they had formerly had.

(*a*) This is not quite so. On the contrary, as the charter of John was the original, it is of the greater importance in an historical point of view, and, at all events, it forms an important step or stage in our legal history; and the comparison of its terms with the articles and with subsequent charters, afford very interesting illustrations of the history of the subject, for which reason some account of them has been given.

CHAP. IV.] KINGS' CHARACTERS AS LEGISLATORS. 473

One very striking provision of John's charter, which is omitted in that of Henry III., deserves our notice. It is there declared that no scutage or aid shall be levied on the subject *nisi per commune concilium regni nostri;* except in the three cases in which a feudal lord was entitled to the assistance of his vassal; namely, on marriage of his daughter; on making his son a knight, and to redeem his person from captivity, a restriction that was declared by the charter to hold good, not only between the king and his tenants, but between every lord and his tenants. In order to assemble the *commune concilium regni* to assess such scutages and aids, the king engaged to summon all archbishops, bishops, abbots, earls, and greater barons, *sigillatim per literas; et præterea,* says he, *faciemus summoneri in generali per vicecomites, et ballivos nostros, omnes illos qui de nobis tenent in capite;* a passage that seems, beyond all controversy, to point out the constituent members of the great council of the kingdom in those days.

Several originals of this charter were executed by the king. It is said that one was deposited in every county or at least in every diocese. In pursuance of one of the provisions in the charter, twenty-five barons were elected as guardians of the liberties of the people, who were to see the contents of it properly executed; but the troubles that soon followed, from the want of faith in the king, prevented this scheme of reformation. The king died in the next year, and left the kingdom in all the horrors of a civil war.

We shall now consider the kings whose reigns fall within this period, in their character as legislators. We have before seen, that William the Conqueror, besides confirming the laws of the Confessor, made some himself, which effected no inconsiderable alteration, by introducing tenures, and the trial by duel in criminal questions. Besides these express ordinances, he contrived all means of ingrafting the laws of Normandy upon the common law; for this purpose, he appointed all his judges from among his Norman subjects, and made that language be taught in schools.[1] By the constitution of his courts of justice, and every act of his

Characters of these kings as legislators.

---

[1] Wilk., Leg. Sax., p. 289.

40*

administration, he did all in his power to change the jurisprudence of the country.

We hear nothing of Rufus as a legislator; nor are there any laws of Henry I. except his charter (a); but there is every reason to believe that the latter of these princes paid great regard to the improvement of the law. He was himself a man of learning, and had a disposition to quiet the minds of his subjects by a good administration; the laws, therefore, which go under his name may be considered as a compilation, at least, made in his reign, and as an instance of his attention to the subject of legislation.

The reign of Stephen was a period of continual war and disturbance, and of course gave little room for improvement in legal establishments. The introduction, however, of the books of canon and civil law, must have contributed to the great advances made in the time of his successor, Henry II.; for, though there was always an extreme jealousy in the practisers of the common law, with respect to those two systems, it went no further than to an exclusion of their authority as governing laws; they were still cultivated by them as branches of the same science, and had a great effect in polishing and improving our municipal customs.

The wise administration of Henry II. operating on the advantageous circumstances concurring in the latter end of his reign, when all things were reduced to peace, contributed more to advance our legal polity than all the preceding times from the Conquest put together. Without recapitulating what has been before related, let any one compare the work of Glanville with the laws (or, as it might more properly be called, *the treatise of law in the time*) of Henry I., the great regularity in the order of proceeding, and the refinement with which notions of property are treated, and he will see the superiority of the later reign in point of knowledge. It is probable, that the additions and amendments made in the law of this kingdom were by this prince transplanted into Normandy, and occasioned a still further improvement in the law of tenures; as

---

(a) This is not so. There are, as already mentioned in the *Leges Henrici Primi*, many which are of his reign, though the whole is a compilation, and some have also been already alluded to as scattered in the *Mirror of Justice*. The *Leges Henrici Primi*, however, is rather a treatise of the laws, than a mere collection of them.

lawyers were, by these communications, engaged in a kind of competition to enlarge and polish the same subject of inquiry. The whole of our municipal law was improved to a high degree during the reign of Henry II. and afforded an ample foundation for the superstructure raised on it in the time of Richard and John, and more particularly in the reign of Henry III.

It does not appear that Richard took any part himself in contributing to further the great designs of his father, in matters of municipal regulation, but left things to the course they had been put in by him. This prince, however, stands very high in the history of maritime jurisprudence. Upon his return from the Holy Land, while he was in the Island of Oleron, on the coast of France, he compiled a body of maritime law. This was designed for the keeping of order, and the determination of controversies abroad; and the wisdom with which it was framed, has been evinced by the general reception it has obtained in other nations.[1] King John did nothing memorable in the way of legislation in this kingdom; though he has the praise of having first introduced the English laws into Ireland,[2] where he instituted sheriffs and other officers to interpret and execute them. He likewise appointed a grand justiciary to preside over the administration of justice in that kingdom.[3]

The monuments which remain of the jurisprudence of these times are not very numerous. They consist of some laws, charters, records, and law treatises.

Of the laws of William the Conqueror, some are in Norman-French, and some in Latin. The first fifty *capitula* in Norman-French are what, Ingulphus says, he brought down to his abbey of Croyland, as those which the king had confirmed, and commanded to be observed throughout England.[4] Though the time when they were enacted is not mentioned, it is tolerably clear, that it was not long after Ingulphus went to London on the affairs of his monastery, in the sixteenth year of William's reign. These therefore were, probably, such alterations and additions as he chose to make in the laws of Edward, which had been allowed in the fourth

Laws of William the Conqueror.

---
[1] Black., vol. iv., p. 423.
[2] *Quare*, if not Henry II., *vide* Harris's *Hibernia*, part ii, p. 215. *et seq.*
[3] Tyrr., vol. ii., p. 809. [4] Ingulph.

year of his reign.[1] There follow some other laws of William in the form of a charter; and as the first mostly concern the criminal code, these latter constitute some alterations in the civil. These are in Latin, and go from the fifty-first chapter to the sixty-seventh inclusive. There are also some others in the form of a charter, which, together with the preceding, make in all eighty-one *capitula* of laws of William the Conqueror.

There are no laws remaining of William Rufus, if any were made; nor of Henry I. except his charter. Those that usually go under the title of laws of this king, and are entered in the Red Book of the exchequer, seem to have been reduced into that form by some person of learning, as containing a sketch of the common law then in use; a manner of entitling treatises not then uncommon: for there is now to be seen, in the Cottonian collection, a manuscript of Glanville which bears the title of *Laws of Henry II.*[2] There is no evidence that these laws were enacted by the great council, or granted by any charter. They contain ninety-four *capitula*, and are to be found in the collection of Lambard and Wilkins.

We have no remains of legislation in the time of Stephen. The laws of Henry II. are the Constitutions made at Clarendon, anno 1164, and the statutes made at Northampton, anno 1176. The first fourteen of the Constitutions of Clarendon made several alterations in the civil and criminal part of our laws; the remaining sixteen concern ecclesiastical affairs, and contain those points which were disputed between Henry and Becket, and between this kingdom and the see of Rome.

Besides laws there remain some public acts of this reign, as *articles of inquiry concerning the extortion and abuses of sheriffs* and *the assize of arms*. During the reigns of Richard and John, there are no laws which can be properly so called, but there are commissions and ordinances of a public nature respecting the administration of justice. In the reign of the former there are some *articles of the crown*, with the *forms of proceeding in those pleas* and *directions for preserving the laws of the forest.*[3]

Besides the laws of these kings which have been mentioned, there are many other provisions made in these

---

[1] Tyrr., vol. ii., p. 69.   [2] Claud., D. 2.   [3] Tyrr., vol. ii., p. 578.

reigns which may be found, arranged in the order of time in which they passed, in the *Codex Legum Veterum*, intended for publication by Spelman, and now annexed to the end of Wilkins' Anglo-Saxon Laws.[1]

The great monuments of this period are the *charters*. Under this title might indeed be reckoned those laws of William the Conqueror which we have just noticed to have passed in that form. But the charters, properly so called, and which have become so famous on account of the object they all had in view, namely, the removal and redress of certain grievances, are the following: The charter of Henry I., containing eighteen chapters; that of Stephen, containing thirteen chapters; that of Henry II., containing only two chapters, and expressed in very general terms; the *Capitula Baronum*, being those heads of grievances which were proposed by the barons to John to be redressed; and the *Magna Charta* of that king, drawn up in pursuance of them; these are all to be found in the late Mr. Justice Blackstone's correct edition of the charters,[2] where that great ornament of English law has given a critical and very curious history of these valuable remains of antiquity.

The laws, or *assisæ*, as they were called, made at this early period, deserve a little further consideration. It has been before observed that our law is composed of the custom of the realm, or *leges non scriptæ*, and the statutes, or *leges scriptæ*. Our lawyers have made a distinction among statutes themselves; they have distinguished between statutes made before the time of memory and those made since. The *time of memory* has been fixed in conformity with a provision made in the time of Edward I. for settling the limitation in a writ of right, which was by stat. 1 West., c. 39, fixed at the beginning of the reign of Richard. Though the limitation in a writ of right has been since altered, this period has been chosen as a distance of very high antiquity, at which has been fixed *the time of memory*, as it is called, so that everything before that period is said to have happened before the time of memory.

Of the civil statutes.

Those statutes which were made before the time of memory, and have not since been repealed nor altered by

---

[1] See the Preface to Wilk., Ang.-Saxon Laws. [2] Black. *Tracts*, vol. ii.

contrary usage, or subsequent acts of parliament, are considered as a part of the *leges non scriptæ;* being, as it were, incorporated into, and become a part of, our common law: and notwithstanding copies of them may be found, their provisions obtain at this day, not as acts of parliament, but by immemorial usage and custom; of which kind is, no doubt, a great part of our common law.[1]

Laws were termed sometimes *assisæ*, sometimes *constitutiones*. Though the most solemn and usual way of ordaining laws was to get the concurrence of the *commune concilium regni*, it should seem that in these times the king took upon himself to do many legislative acts which, when conformable with the established order of things, were readily acquiesced in, and became the law of the land. The very frame, indeed, of such laws as were sanctioned with all possible formalities, carried in them the strongest appearance of regal acts: if a law passed *concilio baronum suorum*, it was still *rex constituit.*[2] Of the laws of William the Conqueror, though in some parts they seem to have the authority of the great council, *statuimus, volumus, præcipimus;* yet in others they speak in the person of the king only, *hoc quoque præcipio, et prohibeo.*[3] The form of a charter, in which the king is considered as a person granting, was a very common way of making laws at this time; and this carries in it the strongest proof of the sentiments entertained in those ages concerning legislation: nevertheless, it is to be remarked, that some of these charters, from the solemnities attending the execution of them, might be regarded as having all the validity of laws; as the charter of King John, to which the barons of the realm were parties. There were, however, several other charters which seem to have no authority but that of the sovereign. Indeed, several laws, or *assisæ*, even so low down as Henry II. and the reigns of Richard and John, vouch no other sanction but *rex constituit* or *rex præcipit*, for everything they command or direct.

There is no way of accounting for this extraordinary appearance of the old statutes, but by supposing the state of our constitution and laws to have been this: That the judicature of the realm being in the hands, and under the guidance of the king and his justices, it remained

---

[1] Hale *Hist.*, 3, 4.
[2] *Vide Schmidt der Deutchen, Geschichte*, vol. i., 582.   [3] Wilk., 217, 218.

with him to supply the defects that occasionally appeared in the course and order of proceeding; which, being founded originally on custom and usage, was, in its nature, more susceptible of modification than any positive institution, that could not be easily tampered with without a manifest discovery of the change. In an unlettered age, it was convenient and beneficial that the king should exercise such a superintendence over the laws as to declare, explain, and direct, what his justices should do in particular cases; such directions were very readily received as positive laws, always to be observed in future; and, no doubt, numbers of such regulations were made of which we have at present no traces. While this supreme authority was exercised only in furtherance of justice, by declaring the law, or even altering it, in instances which did not much intrench upon the interest of the great men of the kingdom, it was suffered to act at freedom. But no alteration in the law which affected the persons or property of the barons could be attempted with safety, without their concurrence in the making of it; as, indeed, it could not always be executed without the assistance of their support. Thus it happened that when any important change was meditated by the king, a *commune concilium* was summoned, where the advice of the *magnates* was taken; and then the law, if passed, was mentioned to be passed with their concurrence. On the other hand, had the nobles any point which they wanted to be authorized by the king's parliamentary concurrence, a *commune concilium* was called, if the king could be prevailed on to call one; and if the matter was put into a law, the king here was mentioned to have commanded it, at the prayer and request of his barons; so that, one way or other, the king is mentioned in all laws as the creative power which gives life and effect to the whole.

As laws made in the solemn form by a *commune concilium* were upon the points of great importance, and often the subjects of violent contest, they were in the nature of concords or compacts between the parties interested, and were sometimes passed and executed with the ceremonies suitable to such a transaction. The Constitutions of Clarendon (which, too, were called the ancient law of the kingdom, and therefore only to be declared and recognized as such) were passed in that way. Becket and all the bishops took an oath to observe those laws; and all, except Becket, signed, and put their seals to them. The laws were drawn in three parts. One counterpart, or authentic copy, was given to Becket, another was delivered to the Archbishop of York, a third was retained by the king himself, to be enrolled among the royal charters.[1] The *Magna Charta* of King John was executed with similar solemnity, and bore a similar appearance of a compact between the king and his nobles. It was not uncommon that the people, as well as the makers, should be sworn to observe laws; the *assisæ statutæ, et juratæ,* are mentioned by Bracton as an article of inquiry before the justices in eyre in the reign of Henry III.

The *rotuli annales,* or *great rolls of the pipe,* in which the accounts of the revenue were stated, are the most ancient rolls now remaining, and the series of them is perfect from the first year of Henry II. Besides this there is still remaining in the same archives, a *great* or *pipe roll,* which has been supposed to belong to the *fifth year of King Stephen,* but has been proved by Mr. Prynne and Mr. Madox[2] to be entitled to an earlier date; indeed, to belong to some year of Henry I.; and, according to Mr. Prynne, to the eighteenth of that king.

The plea rolls of the exchequer, now remaining, do not begin till the reign of Edward I. The oldest rules of the *curia regis* now extant begin with the first year of Richard I., as do the *assize rolls* of the justices itinerant. Those of the *bancum* begin with the first year of King John, which is very near the first establishment of that court. There are *charter rolls* of the chancery, of the first year of King John, and *close rolls, fine rolls, patent rolls, liberate rolls,* and *Norman rolls,* of the second, third, and sixth year of that king. All the before-mentioned rolls, except the *great rolls of the pipe,* are said to be now in the Tower of London, and are the earliest specimens of records that have been spared by the joint destruction of time, wilfulness, and neglect. The cruel havoc made by these enemies has occasionally excited a temporary attention to this important article, and measures have, in consequence, been pursued for preserving such muniments as remained. Such events, in the history of our records, will be mentioned in their proper places.[3]

---

[1] Litt. Hen. II., vol. iv., p. 26.
[2] Mad., Hist. Dis., Epist.
[3] See Ayloffe's *Ancient Charters,* Introd.

Among the records and valuable remains of antiquity we must not forget the famous *Domesday-Book*, which, though not strictly a monument of a legal nature, yet has this connection with the history of our law, that it is said to have been made with a view to the establishment of tenures. This book contains an account of all the lands of England, except the four northern counties; and describes particularly the quantity and value of them, with the names of their possessors. King Alfred is said to have composed a book of this kind about the year 900, of which this was in some measure a copy. This work was begun in 1080, and completed in six years. It has always been esteemed of the highest authority, in questions of tenure; and is considered by antiquarians as the most ancient and most venerable record that now exists in this or any other kingdom. The *Black* and *Red Book of the Exchequer*[1] seem very little more connected with our ancient laws than the foregoing work, except that in both of them was found a transcript of a law treatise which will be mentioned presently.

There are two treatises written in the reign of Henry II. which contribute greatly to illustrate the state and history of our law; the one is the *Dialogus de Scaccario*[2]

---

[1] Domesday-Book is a document belonging to the Receipt of the King's Exchequer, and is in the Chapter House at Westminster. It is in two volumes. For a more satisfactory account of this ancient record we must refer the reader to a small quarto pamphlet, entitled, "*A short Account of some Particulars concerning Domesday-Book, with a View of its being published. By a Member of the Society of Antiquarians.*" This is a performance of Mr. Webb, and was read at the society in the year 1755. In this little essay is brought together in one view all that had been said by former historians and antiquarians on the subject of Domesday.

By the munificence of parliament, *Domesday* has been printed; but we must regret that this laudable regard of the legislature towards our ancient records has not been seconded by the common attention which has been paid to every other publication since the earliest times of printing. The reader will be surprised when he is told that this book has no prefatory discourse, or index, not even a title-page, or the name of the printer; it is a mere *fac-simile*, constituting a very large folio, full of abbreviations and signs, that cannot be understood without a key, and much previous information.

[2] *Liber Ruber* and *Liber Niger Scaccarii* are two miscellaneous collections of charters, treatises, conventions, the number of hides of land in several counties, escuage, and the like; many of which, as well as the *Dialogus de Scaccario*, are to be found in both those books. The *Liber Niger* has been printed by Hearne, together with some other things, in two volumes 8vo; of which the *Liber Niger* fills about 400 pages. He entitles it, "*Exemplar retusti codicis MS. (nigro relamine cooperti) in Scaccario,*" etc. The collector of the contents of the *Liber Ruber* is supposed by Mr. Madox to have been

before alluded to; the other is the *Tractatus de Legibus Angliæ*, by Glanville.

The *Dialogus de Scaccario* has generally passed as the work of Gervase of Tilbury, but Mr. Madox thinks it was written by Richard Fitz-Nigel, bishop of London, who succeeded his father in the office of treasurer in the reign of Richard I., and was therefore well qualified for such an undertaking. This book treats, in the way of dialogue, upon the whole establishment of the exchequer, as a court and an office of revenue, giving an exact and satisfactory account of the officers and their duty, with all matters concerning that court, during its highest grandeur, in the reign of Henry II. This is done in a style somewhat superior to the law latinity of those days.

Glanville's book is of a very different sort; this is written without any of the freedom or elegance discoverable in the other, and has all the formality and air of a professional work. It is entitled *Tractatus de Legibus et Consuetudinibus Regni Angliæ*, but, notwithstanding this general title, it is confined to such matters only as were the objects of jurisdiction in the *curia regis*. Having stated this as the limit of his plan, the author very rarely travels out of it. Glanville's treatise consists of fourteen books; the first two of which treat of a writ of right, when commenced originally in the *curia regis*, and carry the reader through all the stages of it, from the summons to the appearance, counting, duel, or assize, judgment and execution; in the third, he speaks of vouching to warranty, which, being added to the two former books, composes a very clear account of the proceeding in a writ of right for recovery of land. The fourth book is upon rights of advowson, and the legal remedies relating thereto. The fifth is upon actions to vindicate a man's freedom. The sixth, upon dower. The seventh contains very little concerning actions, but

---

Alexander de Swereford, archdeacon of Shrewsbury, and an officer in the Exchequer in the latter end of Henry II.

It seems as if the *Dialogus de Scaccario* had been considered as the whole of the *Liber Niger*, till the publication of Hearne; and since Mr. Madox has pronounced Richard Fitz-Nigel to be the author of the Dialogue, and not Gervase of Tilbury, the whole of the *Liber Niger* has been given to Gervase, though it does not appear for what reason. The *Dialogus de Scaccario* is published by Mr. Madox, at the end of his *History of the Exchequer.* See Nicholson's *Eng. Hist.*, p. 173; Hearne's *Liber Niger*, p. 17.

considers the subjects of alienation, descent, succession, and testaments. The eighth is upon final concords; the ninth, upon homage, relief, and services; the tenth, upon debts and matters of contract; and the eleventh, upon attorneys. Having thus disposed of actions commenced originally in the *curia regis*, in his twelfth book he treats of writs of right brought in the lord's court, and the manner of removing them from thence to the county court and *curia regis*, which leads him to mention some other writs determinable before the sheriff. In his thirteenth book he speaks of assizes and disseisins. The last book is wholly upon pleas of the crown.

The subject of this treatise is all along illustrated with the forms of writs, a species of learning which was then new, was probably brought into order and consistency by Glanville himself, and first exhibited in an intelligible way and with system in this book.

The method and style of this work seem very well adapted to the subject; the former opens the matter of it in a natural and perspicuous order, while the latter delivers it with sufficient simplicity and clearness. The latinity of it, however, may not satisfy every taste; the classic ear revolts at its ruggedness, and the cursory reader is perpetually impeded by a new and harsh phraseology. But the language was not adopted without design; the author's own account of it is this: *Stylo vulgari, et verbis curialibus utens, ex industria, ad notitiam comparandam eis, qui hujusmodi vulgaritate minùs sunt exercitati.*[1] The author seems not to be disappointed in his design even at this distance of time, for a person who reads the book through cannot fail of finding in one place an explanation of some difficulty he may have met with in another; the recurrence of the same words and modes of speaking makes Glanville his own interpreter. When the style of Glanville is mastered in this way, it will appear that many obscure sentences have been rendered such through too great an anxiety to express the author's meaning; and perhaps it will not be an affectation of discernment to say that the plain English which it is thus attempted to convey may be seen through the awkward dress which this latinist has spread over it.

---

[1] Prolog. ad finem.

If Glanville confines himself to a part only of our law, he treats that part with such conciseness, and sometimes in so desultory a way, that his book is to be looked upon rather as a compendium than a finished tract; notwithstanding which it must be considered as a venerable monument of the infant state of our laws, and, as such, will always find reception with the juridical historian when thrown aside by the practising lawyer.

It has been a general persuasion that the writer of this book was *Ranulphus de Glanvillâ*, who was great justiciary to Henry II. This great officer, though at the head of the law, united in himself a political as well as a judicial character, and it seems that Glanville was likewise a military man, for he led the king's armies more than once, and was the commander who took the king of Scots prisoner. It might therefore be doubted whether a person of this description was likely to be the author of a law treatise containing a detail of the practice of courts in conducting suits. There was a *Ranulphus de Granvillâ* who was a justice itinerant,[1] and who, it is said, was a justice in the king's court towards the close of this reign. If the author was really of this name, it may be doubted whether he was not the latter of these two persons. Perhaps, after all, this work might be written by neither, but may be ascribed to the great justiciary for no other reason than because he presided over the law at the time it was written, and might be the promoter of the work and patron to its author. Whatever doubt there may be concerning the author, there is no question but it was written in the reign of Henry II. — there are many internal marks to prove it to be of that period, and from one passage it seems to have been written[2] after the thirty-third year of that king. If Glanville is the earliest writer in our law from whom any clear and coherent account of it is to be gotten, this book is also said to be the first performance that has anything like the appearance of a treatise on the subject of jurisprudence since the dissolution of the Roman empire.[3]

---

[1] *Vide* Leg. Ang.-Sax.   [2] Glanv., lib. 8, c. 2, 3.
[3] Barr. Ant. Stat. This is not true, if the *Decretum* is to be considered as a treatise; for Henry II. came to the crown in 1154, and Glanville, being written after the thirty-third year of his reign, could not appear till 1187. Now the *Decretum* was published by Gratian in 1149.

When this book is considered with a view to the progress of our law, it makes a remarkable event in the history of the new jurisprudence. Notwithstanding the attempts of William the Conqueror to introduce the Norman laws, and the tendency in the superior courts to encourage every innovation of that kind, not much had yet been done of a public and authoritative nature to confirm that law in opposition to the Saxon customs. The laws of William, excepting those concerning tenures and the duel, were in the spirit and style of the Anglo-Saxon laws; the same may be said of those which go under the name of Henry I. It is observed that the Constitutions of Clarendon, made about the eleventh year of Henry II., are in the scope of them, as well as the style and language, more entirely Norman than any laws or public acts from the Conquest down to that time.[1] It was not, then, till the reign of this prince that the Norman law was completely fixed here; and when it was firmly established by the practice of this long reign, and had received the improvements made by Henry, then was this short tract drawn up for public use. It is probable this was done at the king's command, in order to perpetuate the improvement he himself had made, and to effect a more general uniformity of law and practice through the kingdom. The work of Glanville, compared with the Anglo-Saxon laws, is like the code of another nation; there is not the least feature of resemblance between them.

While the Norman law was establishing itself here, that nation gradually received an improvement of their own polity from us. The two nations had so incorporated themselves, that the government of both was carried upon the like principle, and the laws of each were reciprocally communicated; a consequence not at all unnatural while both people were governed by one prince. Much more had been done of late in this country than in Normandy for the promotion of legal science. It was not till after the publication of Glanville, and even of Bracton and Britton, that the Normans had any treatise upon their law. One was at length produced in the *Grand Coustumier of Normandy;*[2] a work so like an English per-

---

[1] Mad., Exch., 123.
[2] The *Coustumier of Normandy*, according to Basnage, could not have been composed till the reign of Philip the Hardy, who came to the throne in 1272,

formance, that should there remain any doubt of its being formed upon our models, there can be none of the great similarity between the laws of the two nations at this time.

There are some ancient treatises and statutes in the law of Scotland which bear a still nearer resemblance to our English law. The close agreement between Glanville and the *Regiam Majestatem* leaves no room to doubt that one is copied from the other; though the merit of originality between them has occasioned some discussion. An essay has been written expressly on this subject, in which it is said to be clearly proved, by the internal evidence of the two books, that Glanville is the original. It is observed by that writer, that Glanville is regular, methodical, and consistent throughout; whereas the *Regiam Majestatem* goes out of Glanville's method for no other assignable reason than to disguise the matter, and is thereby rendered confused, unsystematical, and in many places contradictory.[1] To this observation upon the method of the *Regiam Majestatem* it may be added, that on a comparison of the account given of things in that and in Glanville, it plainly appears that the Scotch author is more clear, explicit, and defined; and that he writes very often with a view to explain the other, in the same manner in which the writer of our Fleta explains his predecessor Bracton. This is remarkable in numberless instances all through the book, and is perhaps as decisive a mark of a copy as can be. The other Scotch laws, which follow the *Regiam Majestatem* in Skene's collection, contribute greatly to confirm the suspicion. These, as they are of a later date than several English statutes which they resemble, must be admitted to be copied from them; and so closely are the originals followed that the very words of them are retained. This is particularly remarkable of the reign of Robert II., in which is the statute *quia emptores*, and others, plainly copied from our laws, without any attempt

---

and reigned fifteen years; and our Edward I. came to the throne in 1272. Upon this statement of dates, it is possible that it might be written after the time of Britton. The language seems to have a more modern form than that of Britton; though this must be attributed to some other cause than such a small space of time as could by any possibility intervene between the writing of these two books — *Œuvres de Henri Basnage, Avertissement.*

[1] The essay here alluded to was written by Mr. Davidson, of Edinburgh. Of this tract I have not been able to get a sight, and am obliged to the preface to the new edition of Glanville for this account of it.

to conceal the imitation. These laws, at least, can impose upon no one; and when viewed with the *Regiam Majestatem* at their head, and compared with Glanville and the English statute-book, they seem to declare very intelligibly to the world that this piece of Scotch jurisprudence is borrowed from ours.[1]

The *Regiam Majestatem* is so called, because the volume opens with those words: the prologue to Glanville begins *Regiam Potestatem*. This whim of imitation is discoverable among our own writers. Fleta begins his Procemium in the same way, and goes on, for several lines, copying word for word from Glanville. Indeed, the leading idea in all is taken from the Procemium to Justinian's *Institutes*.

The law-language of these times was *Latin* or *French*, but more commonly the former. The only laws of this time now subsisting in Norman-French are those which compose the first collection of William the Conqueror. All the other laws from that time to the time of Edward I. are in Latin. There are some few charters of the first three Norman kings which are either in Anglo-Saxon or in Latin, with an English version; of which sort there are several now remaining in the Cottonian and other collections.[2]

Without doubt the Norman laws of William were proclaimed in the county court in Anglo-Saxon, for the information of the English, who still continued to conduct business there in their own language, as they did in all

---

[1] It seems unnecessary to contend for the originality of the *Regiam Majestatem*, while a doubt of much more importance remains unsettled; that is, whether that treatise, as well as the others in the publication of Skene are now, or ever were, any part of the law of Scotland. Upon this point, some of the most eminent Scotch lawyers are divided. We find Craig and Lord Stair very explicit in their declarations against these laws, as a fabrication and palpable imposition; on the other hand, Skene the editor is followed, among others, by Erskine, Lord Kames, and Dalrymple, who continually refer to them, as comprising the genuine law of Scotland in former times. That a large volume of laws and law treatises should be pronounced by persons of professional learning to be part of their law and customs, and should be as positively rejected by others, is a very singular controversy in the juridical history of a country; nor is it less singular that this volume should bear such a close similitude with certain laws of a neighboring state, whose legislature had no power to give it sanction and authority. While a fact of this sort continues unascertained, the history of the law of Scotland must be involved in great obscurity. See Craigii *Inst. Feud.*, lib. 1, tit. 8, sect. 7. Stair's *Inst.*, fo. 3, tit. 4, sect. 27. Skene's Preface to the *Regiam Majestatem*. Erskine's *Prin*. Kames' *Historical Law Tracts;* and Dalrymple's *Feudal Property, passim.*   [2] Tyrrell, ii., 101.

inferior courts; but in the *curia regis* and *ad scaccarium* William obliged them to plead in the Norman tongue, as most consistent with the law there dispensed, and that which was best understood by the justices. However, notwithstanding this language was used in pleading and argument, all proceedings there, when thrown into a record, were enrolled in a more durable language, the Latin. This was the language in which all writs, laws, and charters, whether public or private, were drawn, so that the Norman tongue was of no extensive use here; nor was it till the time of Edward I. that French became of common use in the laws, parliamentary records, and law-books; and this was not the provincial dialect of Normandy, but the language of Paris.

It is believed that few were learned in the laws before the Conquest, except the clergy. The warlike condition in which that people lived, and the extreme ignorance which universally prevailed among the laity, left very little ability for the management of civil affairs to any but the clergy, who possessed the only learning of the times; in the reign therefore of the Conqueror, in the great cause between Lanfranc and Odo, bishop of Bayeux, it was Agelric, bishop of Chichester, to whom they looked for direction. He was brought, says an ancient writer,[1] in a chariot, to instruct them in the ancient laws of the kingdom, *ut legum terræ sapientissimus*. It was the same long after the Normans settled here.

Miscellaneous facts.

In the time of Rufus, one Alfwin, rector of Sutton, and several monks of Abingdon, were persons so famous for their knowledge in the laws, that they were universally consulted, and their judgment frequently submitted to by persons resorting thither from all parts.[2] Another clergyman, named Ranulph, in the same reign, obtained the character of *invictus causidicus*. So generally had the clergy taken to the practice of the law at that time, that a contemporary writer (a) says, *nullus clericus nisi causidicus*. The

---

(a) William of Malmesbury. The clergy supplying the lawyers, they would naturally have recourse to the law with which they were best acquainted, the civil law, and the canon law, which as our author elsewhere observes, was founded thereupon. In other words, they would have recourse to the Roman law, modified, in matters ecclesiastical, by the canon law, the Roman church and its law being established and recognized by the state. Hence the recognition of that law in the *Laws of the Conqueror*, and in the

[1] Textus Roff.   [2] Dug. Orig., p. 21.

clergy seem to have been the principal practisers of the law, and were the persons who mostly filled the bench of justice.

Leges Henrici Primi, which formed the basis of the great treatises of Glanville and of Bracton, the foundations of our common law. Thus, therefore, probability, documentary evidence, and the positive facts of history, combine to show that the origin of our law is to be traced back to the Roman law, partly through the traditions and institutions established in this country during the period of the Roman occupation, and partly by reason of the restitution or revival of Roman law, through the medium of the earliest professors of law, the clergy.

END OF VOL. I.

www.ingramcontent.com/pod-product-compliance
Lightning Source LLC
Chambersburg PA
CBHW021425300426
44114CB00010B/648